THE JEWISH EXPRESSION

THE JEWISH EXPRESSION

edited by Judah Goldin

New Haven and London   Yale University Press

1976

Library of Congress catalog card number: 75–27866

International standard book number: 0–300–01948–3 (cloth)

0–300–01975–0 (paper)

Set in Times Roman type.

Printed in the United States of America by
The Colonial Press, Inc., Clinton, Massachusetts.

Published in Great Britain, Europe, and Africa by
Yale University Press, Ltd., London.

Distributed in Latin America by Kaiman & Polon,
Inc., New York City; in Australasia by Book & Film
Services, Artarmon, N.S.W., Australia; in Japan by
John Weatherhill, Inc., Tokyo.

ACKNOWLEDGMENTS

"The Biblical Idea of History in Its Common Near Eastern Setting,"
by E. A. Speiser. From ISRAEL EXPLORATION JOURNAL, Vol. VII, No. 4.
Copyright © 1957 by The Israel Exploration Society of Jerusalem and
reprinted with their permission.

"Some Postulates of Biblical Criminal Law," by Moshe Greenberg.
From YEHEZKEL KAUFMANN JUBILEE VOLUME, edited by Menahem
Haran. Copyright © 1960 by Magnes Press and reprinted with their
permission and that of Moshe Greenberg.

"Amos versus Amaziah," by Shalom Spiegel. Reprinted by permission of The Jewish Theological Seminary of America.

"The Maccabean Uprising: An Interpretation," by Elias Bickerman.
Translated from the German by Krishna Winston. Reprinted with permission by Elias Bickerman.

"The Philonic God of Revelation and His Latter-Day Deniers," by
Harry Austryn Wolfson. From HARVARD THEOLOGICAL REVIEW, 53,
(1960). Copyright 1960 by the President and Fellows of Harvard College. Reprinted by permission of Harvard University Press.

"New Light on Tannaitic Jewry and on the State of Israel of the
Years 132-135 C.E.," by H. L. Ginsberg. From RABBINICAL ASSEMBLY
PROCEEDINGS, Vol. XXV. Copyright 1961 by The Rabbinical Assembly
of America and reprinted with their permission.

"Response," by Saul Lieberman. From RABBINICAL ASSEMBLY PRO-
CEEDINGS, Vol. XII. Copyright 1949 by The Rabbinical Assembly of
America and reprinted with their permission.

FOR
ALFRED AND MILLICENT AARONSON
WITH LOVE

CONTENTS

Introduction

i

The nineteen essays which come after these introductory comments were written by fifteen leading modern scholars in the field of Jewish history and literature, each of them eminent —and quite a number of them universally acknowledged as preeminent—in the specific area of that field to which he has, or had, devoted himself. The learning embodied in these essays, the learning behind the essays even more, is itself extraordinary; but these particular essays are more than examples of erudition. From the outset, many of them were addressed to an audience meant to include more than professional scholars and apprentices in scholarship, though not one of them was composed with an indifference to the strictest demands of scholarship, or without real exertion to bring to light what for many specialists too was still only faintly visible. Some of these essays are accompanied by many footnotes and all the characteristic luggage of the scholar, some have few notes, some appear without documentation of any kind. Most are formal compositions, a few are informal discourses. But all of them are products of years of research or reflection *cum* study, by masters, plus their attempt to reach out to the enduring significance of the phenomenon or event or the literary texts or institutions or period or personality or speculative system which they were discussing at the moment. And all of them were written in the twentieth century.

There is nothing in the pages that follow to imply that the authors of these essays would approve of being assembled in this way, or that they would endorse the views of those in whose close company they are here placed. It is safe to say, however, that even if they disagreed, and even when they refused to accept one another's deductions, they would respect each other's competence and the seriousness which accompanied the conclusions arrived at.

It is not true that scholars ought to have the last word on the subject, any subject, except perhaps purely technical ones where what counts is excellence of craftsmanship and accuracy; and it is a fact, though often a heartbreaking one, that ignorance and misinformation can be and are very dynamic, can set in motion conceptions and activities with an overpowering momentum. Who should appreciate this better than twentieth-century man? Nor—to look at the matter without complete discouragement—are misinterpretations necessarily unfruitful, or, more accurately, disastrous; more than once it has happened, and probably inside every cultural tradition, that a misunderstanding or a misinterpretation has paradoxically filled the inherited teachings and ideals with renewed vitality; so that, strange as it may sound, we may be forced in the end to concede that had it not been for the *mis*conception, there might almost have been a standstill, even the original forces within that culture might have died.

Misunderstanding and misinterpretation are well-nigh inescapable, for we must use our own minds to think the thoughts of other and earlier minds, and only the most fragile, most imperfect devices are available to protect us from anachronism, from seeing what *we* want to see, from confusing our favorite dogmas and self-evident truths with the dogmas and self-evident truths of others and of previous generations. But whatever else it may be, misinterpretation cannot be an ideal, and if consciously pursued, deliberately cultivated, is a lie; if it is a by-product of our unwillingness to explore conscientiously, it is not far from a lie. As for misinformation when the information is available, or ignorance when it need not be present, that seems to me hopeless.

Perhaps, then, I may put it this way: These essays have been selected and assembled (a) because they are the work of men whose learning is trustworthy (and even when they should not have the last word, their word is indispensable for informed and critical appreciation of our subject); (b) because in these particular essays of theirs, there is articulated a quest for meaning relevant beyond the interior of the seminar session or the library cubicle; (c) because these essays are products of men of our own century, and presumably they ought to be intelligible to us.

ii

A word of explanation. In the title of the volume and these introductory remarks I have used the word "expression" as a kind of shorthand. It is intended to serve the purposes of what is generally called literature—in that event, we are discussing literary expression. However, at times it is also intended to apply to decisive actions and institutions that a people (in this instance, the Jewish people) adopts, through which the people expresses itself no less than it does by means of its gifted intellectual or artistic spokesmen. For the most part, it is true, the essays deal with aspects of literature (hence the direction taken also by the introductory comments); but not entirely, as the reader will rapidly discover. I do not mean to confuse the two types of expression, and if in my comments I had decided to investigate all forms of expression, I would almost certainly divide the present analysis altogether differently and also elaborate. But then, these comments would take up more space than they should. Few things are more offensive than introductions that wear one out before the main address. That is the reason for the decision to use the word in the double sense, and the impatience to get done with these remarks quickly, so that the main studies can be attended to promptly.

iii

Upon entering a synagogue it is customary to recite, "How fair are thy tents, O Jacob, thy dwellings, O Israel!" The sentence is a biblical verse (Numbers 24:5, not to mention that its idiom is reminiscent of a Ugaritic parallelism), in fact, a verse originally proclaimed by a non-Israelite visionary, long before there was anything like a synagogue in existence. The Jewish Prayer Book contains much more than biblical selections, and the classic, traditional Prayer Book includes even a poetic composition, recited regularly in the Sabbath eve service, from as late as the sixteenth century: "Come, beloved, to meet the Bride,/ The Sabbath queen, at eventide." Nor need that century be regarded as the terminus. Individual communities have on sundry occasions recited prayers and petitions composed in their own times and circumstances, and sometimes even these ad hoc compositions have enjoyed a longevity and dissemination far beyond their time being. No reader of the Prayer Book, however, will fail to recognize immediately that a substantial amount of the Prayer Book is made up of biblical passages, whole chapters, strings of chapters, individual verses rearranged and put together in novel combinations. And the post-biblical selections too re-echo biblical sounds and speech.

This is not accidental. At the root, and up through the branches and fruits, of all Jewish expression, is the persistent hum of the Hebrew Scriptures, what is generally called the Old Testament. As we shall see shortly, it is an utterly grotesque attempt to reduce Jewish expression to Bible lessons pure and simple (which no one really, to my knowledge, is tempted to do) or to invocations of so-called biblical sentences and doctrine or saga as the sole authority. Even the Karaites did not succeed in that, and twentieth-century Canaanites are strikingly less persuasive. One may take one step further and dare to say, that if it had not been for the long and continuous post-biblical traditions and exercises, no Bible would have survived. Where is the Book of Yashar, where is the Book of the Wars of YHWH, where are the Chronicles of the Kings of Israel? They apparently contained material worthy of quotation, and it would be the sterilest sort of literary criticism that would propose that obviously no more in these ancient sources than has been quoted by biblical authors deserved to survive. Apparently also, however, no one cared long enough to study hard and to explore and to derive by implication from them. There being no post-Book of Yashar, no Book of Yashar survived. The result of all "Nothing but the Bible" slogans is, Nothing.

Having said this, however, we must return to the facts of life: from the pages of the Hebrew Scriptures, all classical Jewish expression took constant nourishment, and I am tempted to add that even revolt against classical Jewish forms, values, and commitments can often be understood best only in terms that derive ultimately and immediately (yes, immediately too) from the biblical heritage. Biblical stories quickly became paradigms for conduct and self-understanding, biblical laws became the fundamentals for subsequent jurisprudence and legislation, prophetic emphases set the basic vocabulary for ethics and eschatology; biblical history furnished the outline of a past, remembrance of which was to teach a permanent lesson, and biblical poetry was the mint from which prayer would be coined; biblical speculation and protest would shock but would also provide the courage to ask a few daring questions of one's own. Even for mystical flights, the Book had adequate springboards.

That exegesis, therefore, should prove to be the most prominent and recurrent form of Jewish expression is hardly surprising. Until practically the last century, even when there was original composition (where an author elects to organize his thoughts in an order independent of the order of the biblical material), the bulk of Jewish literature was essentially commentary; and commentary—in the countless polychromes it is capable of assuming—is far from a vanishing form of expression even in our own days.

In such sustained preoccupation with the biblical material— its words, images, commands, stories, exhortations, promises— the Bible has received its afterlife, as two of our authors put it aptly. Every age poured *its* emotions and its notions into the biblical content and then discovered that the word of God was contemporary: it's as though the Jew felt that to express himself he had nothing better than God's vocabulary. Homilist and moralist, philosopher and mystic, jurist and poet (you'd be amazed how frequently the two extremes united in the same person), all find their prooftexts in that one Book.

Perhaps it is true that, given a gifted commentator, even a genealogical list or telephone book will release profound mysteries, and voices unheard by those not attuned will suddenly become audible. The fact is, however, that the Hebrew Bible, which also has its roll calls, because it is preponderantly a statement of laws, a transcript of prophetic, unremitting insistence on moral behavior, a promise of the ultimate Redemption, and a narrative of the very human nature of its principal personalities—that is, because this collection of inspired books never loses sight of the human factor in the divine design, even its cosmological and eschatological interests turn in an ethical direction, as one of our authors once wrote. You might say that all the principal creations of Jewish literature—Bible, Midrash, Talmud, Responsa, Codes, Piyyut (Synagogue Poetry), Philosophy, Kabbala, Exegesis of the Bible and of the post-biblical classics, Moralizing Chronicles and Treatises —all the principal creations of this literature (and remove these, what is left in the last analysis?), join in one exclamation: "Here is the design; it will be carried out; Man, what do *you* plan to do about it?" Since the principal Book is addressed to man, the enormous literature that grows out of this Book continues this address; and since the Jew is under obligation to study this address so that his conduct will be determined by it—"that ye may learn them, and keep, and do them" (Deuteronomy 5:1)—the endless, intimate, ever recurring associations with that Book and its entourage have reinforced in the Jewish mind a conviction that, regardless of baffling circumstances, often in defiance even of the contradictory evidence of the senses and the statisticians (but not *because* it is contradictory!), life which is God's creation, the course of events, and the redeeming future which was promised, are not meaningless or illusion, but meaningful, certain. At a historic moment the Jew received that message and he is not free to repudiate it on second thought because of its unpopularity or exacting demands, or fail to perpetuate it. See Isaiah 59:21: a verse, incidentally, also taken over by the Prayer Book for daily use.

iv

There are two grave dangers in summary statements like the one just attempted, and they had best be made explicit. First, from beginning to end the statement is abstract, almost unearthly, and from it you would hardly guess that there is such a thing as day-to-day life with all its anfractuosities, non-reflecting habitual conduct, protest, resentment, fatigue, bafflement, amusement, or what else have you. You might legitimately conclude that the Jews were rabbis, "theologians," mystics, docile pietists, and boasted even an occasional Job who had the audacity to ask out loud, "But *is* all this true?" Nowhere in the summary would you detect that in the course of three thousand years there were heresies that shook Jewish society to its foundations; that even when there was assent to what had come to be accepted as the legitimate and normative, there would be lacerating exchanges in the conflict over authority; that there was such a thing as an actual folk, *hoi polloi*, some of whom accepted this accumulated and continually mounting expression without really giving it further thought; others who squirmed because they were burdened with it; and still others who hated it to the point of revulsion and revolt. That there were artisans and bankers, solid citizens and blackguards, deaf-mutes, crackpots, and minors among the Jews seems to be forgotten. Consider, for example, the radical abnormality inherent in an experience like life in exile (the Hebrew word for it is Galut): no more than a casual survey of Jewish history is needed to reveal that even acute consciousness of such a state of existence did not preclude all kinds of self-accommodation to it, and one went on living if they let him live: for long periods not just resignedly but with exciting literary productivity. Focus on what the intellectual passion of Jewry has spent on the meaning of biblical imperatives, and you might almost never discover that Zealots fought a last-ditch stand against Roman legions with enviable, albeit unsuccessful, strategy; or that the year Columbus discovered America one of the most creative centers of Jewish cultural and social activity was completely brought to an end; or that large segments of Jewry, affected by the consequences of European thinking—since the eighteenth century especially (but there were signs in the seventeenth too)—would tire of all this florid (perhaps W. H. Auden, God bless him, would say flosculent) speech about a biblical heritage, and strive to put their conceptions of Jewishness in exclusively secular terms; or that there was a catastrophe, not just a geographical place name, called Auschwitz; or that the re-establishment of the State of Israel has thrust a fresh self-awareness on the Jew, so that if he thinks at all of the Jewish expression he is likely to think in ways he had not contemplated before and with a confidence in the sense of continuity which is palpable and not only theologically predicated.

To repeat, the danger in abstract formulation is that it distracts from the intensely and essentially human factor in the complex experience from which expression grows, and admits only grudgingly, if at all, that much still remains incomprehensible. What relationship is there, for example, between Jewish assertions about reality and the individual who will have nothing of them and yet is a Jew because the fate that overtakes those committed to these assertions overtakes him too? To what extent did the traditional messianic fever inflame those Jews who insisted that their ideal vision demanded a rupture with Jewish identity and the Jewish past? And are not dilemmas like these legitimate subjects for Jewish literature? Can the inherited literature say something instructive about these and related questions? The essays which follow do not, I believe, provide an answer to these questions and others like them, or, at least, a satisfactory answer. But they can make us think more knowledgeably, possibly less facilely, about such questions. Perhaps they may even intimate that, pro tem at least, there aren't anywhere the resources to answer all such questions. At best there are guesses, "only hints and guesses,/ Hints followed by guesses." Perhaps they will suggest what new questions we ought to direct to the old sources and what continuing Jewish expression might do well to turn to for a while.

v

The second danger: Even the best of summary statements tends to censor from the record much of the tension and the unevenness of movement back and forth that led to the inherited formulations. The result, even when not entirely misleading, is to drain all vitality out of the reality. Some of this mischief, I hope, the essays that follow *will* remove. For there was hardly any period when the Jew reflected on what seemed the design (or at times, the seeming designlessness) governing life without adopting an attitude or response to a multiplicity of surrounding influences. To understand the biblical content more fully, we know today that we must refer to the rich legacy from ancient Near Eastern civilizations. While he lived in the Hellenistic-Roman world, the Jew acquired manners of speaking and ideas and premonitions, sometimes by direct borrowing, more often by osmosis, often too in the very act of opposition and self-protection—which to begin with were novelties to him. Without the traditions of Greek philosophy, how could we begin to understand Jewish philosophizing (or Christian or Muslim)? There are cherished forms of Jewish piety that appear only after contact with practices in non-Jewish surroundings: pagan, Christian, Muslim (is there anywhere at any time anything *un*syncretistic or *un*derivative?). Monotheism brings all its antiseptic resources against the pervasiveness of myth, and after almost each victory finds that it still has myth to contend with—and undertakes once again to make it innocuous. Influences were various, and the submission to them every bit as various: the influences weren't always welcome, they weren't always rejected; even when there was acceptance, it was not of a uniform kind, and the reverse, when there was rejection, is also true; often there was awareness of the influence, perhaps more often there was unawareness, but the influence would be operative willy-nilly. Truth to say, it is easy enough to assert this in general terms, but it is the very difficult task of scholarship in each specific instance to establish the clear presence or effect of outside influence, and the clear or likely absence of it. In this sphere, naivete or glibness can only lead to misrepresentation.

But whatever the degree—and to the extent that it can be demonstrated—there is some interaction, and we owe it to the learning and rare discrimination of these scholars that the specific Jewish component or the particular Jewish aspect becomes recognizable and intelligible to us. Thus it is instructive to learn, as one of our authors teaches us, that although Mesopotamian legal systems and biblical law share a number of formulae and refer to a number of similar contingencies, the biblical postulates lead to a fundamental difference in regard to the law of persons. Or again, another author teaches us that though like mystics everywhere the Jewish ones have their problems finding the vocabulary to express what they too declare is ineffable, for the Jewish ones, the Kabbalists, language (the Hebrew language), the faculty of speech, is not a handicap but "a key to the deepest secrets of the Creator and His creation." Greek philosophy had already taught that the human mind cannot comprehend God, but it was Philo, a third author informs us, who introduced the "distinction between the knowability of God's existence and the unknowability of His essence." Or, a fourth example from still one more author, "The Jews were the only people of antiquity who succeeded in divorcing prayer from sacrifice, and so were the first to evolve the modes and manners of public worship as the world knows them now."

However, even when the specific Jewish component in the interaction cannot be so distinctly identified and formulated, there is Jewish expression whenever the Jew strives to understand or explain life in terms which he appropriates from his own tradition. For Jewish experience is the outcome not only of interaction with what is encountered on the outskirts of Jewish teaching. There is what I would like to call a constant internal interplay within the Jewish expression: in the search for principles which will allow inherited laws to be bent or stretched so that all cohesion will not vanish from a scattered community, or one that is brought face to face with unprecedented conditions; in the endowment of traditional practices, sometimes with rational defense and sometimes with mystical reinterpretations and potencies; and in exploration of ancient texts for signs of the later times. Midrash is woven into poetry and amalgamates itself with divine service; local custom discovers prooftexts and imposes itself as the norm for conduct; codifiers juxtapose authorities and hammer out a consensus; exegetes respond to "the Holy Spirit which inspires" them or their academies, by original interpretations of the classical texts; by old speculations and exhortations, new or renewed enthusiasms are stirred up which in turn create a lore that reanimates the life of legend. At times it seems, for example, that the huge compendia—like the *Yalkut Shimeoni* or the Yemenite *Midrash ha-Gadol* or the *Menorat ha-Maor* of Israel ibn Al-Nakawa—were created not merely by the curatorial instinct to save what is dear, but by the impulse to bring into immediate and jostling association all that had been said on biblical verses or on selected themes, so that the interplay of generations of teachers could be enacted right before our eyes: so that from this spectacle the attentive student would learn how wide was the horizon of a brief text or a single law. Or another form of interplay: In the union but simultaneous differentiation of the literal, the traditional, and the haggadic interpretations that Rashi adopts in his biblical commentaries, particularly his commentary on the Pentateuch, he not only exhibits the number of meanings a text may embrace, but in a sense compels these different meanings to fructify each other. Or, again: Exegesis grows and grows until it finally ascends up to the compression and systematization of codifiers, only to produce in turn a suspicion of, discomfort with summary, apodictic generalization; which in its turn becomes the starting point for renewed commentary, for recapitulation of the search for the meaning of the primary sources.

All such expression affects not only the inherited speech habits of the people, but their fresh attempts to understand the realities they must contend with, or their fresh attempts to define their own identity. To the extent that the vocabulary of the past expression is *put to the service* of the experiments with the new, and the latter in turn listen carefully to the voices which once upon a time also resounded with anguish and joy, success or failure, Jewish expression escapes abstraction or becoming some bloodless epithet. As for what lies ahead, *"Pour aboutir au futur, il faut d'abord passer par le présent."*

vi

As one of the very distinguished authors warns us, in an essay which cannot be included in the present collection, after the experiences of the past century, particularly those of the last three to four decades, it is impossible to say that the Jewish people were perpetually dominated by this or that single idea from the beginnings to now. The complexity of Jewish reaction is itself one of the most noteworthy lessons to be learned from a reading of Jewish literature or from a study of the different chapters of Jewish history; the essays in the present volume are themselves reports—analyses and descriptions—of that complexity. But that very complexity, as I have tried to suggest, is itself the outcome of oscillating and nervous and bewildering but constant relationships between primary biblical categories to which the Jew was made heir, and the variety of patterns he seeks to create or creates in order to function in the world and to understand his role in it—or whether he has in it any particular role at all. It is futile if not ridiculous to try to understand the Jew as though there had been no Judaism. This is no less true today than it ever was; in our own day possibly the relationship between Judaism and the Jews is even more agitating, more keenly felt (even resentment is a feeling of relationship, perhaps even an intenser, though pathological [?], feeling of relationship!) than it was either in times when Jewish teachings were everywhere assessed as serious statements, or in times when they were dismissed as meaningless rhetoric from an ancient history, a bygone that would not return. Nothing in the present century suggests that the Jewish experience is of parochial interest or that the expression of that experience is close to exhaustion. And I have assembled these essays for rereading—for rereading together, not as independent units, though that is what they were in composition—because they display brilliantly the range of the historical Jewish responses to experience, and at the same time do two more things: they explain expressions that might otherwise be hard for a modern man to understand, and they disclose many of the currents in that sea on which creative Jewish life can still draw profitably, meaningfully.

Why I have selected just these essays, I said at the outset; but a word or two more may be in order. I decided on *these* essays because I found myself *rereading* them several times, in some cases I think as many as six or seven times. One does that, of course, with many scholarly papers, because of the new information they supply, or because of their particular interpretations which one is eager to master. But in addition to the new facts I learned from these essays, and in addition to their striking interpretations, there was that additional element of tone, this searching for more than the temporary or transitory meaning, which brought me back to them. I was told that the volume had to be of a certain size (I've already exceeded the bounds originally agreed upon); therefore my final test was simply this: which essays affected *me* most deeply? Large and important chapters of Jewish expression are inevitably not represented.

And except for some typographical corrections or some trivial modifications in a few footnotes, with one exception, and even that hardly a major interference, I have not touched these essays in any way. I have not even desired to reduce their different forms of transliteration to a uniform system. My original intention was to take nothing from full-scale volumes, to limit myself to what was from the outset an essay or brief monograph and no more than that. The three selections from "books" finally meant too much to me to adhere faithfully to my first decision. And I have not edited anything on the following pages, because I wanted to retain the full flavor of the scholar's statement. Begin snipping here and there, cut out, modify, interject explanatory paraphrases—assuming even that occasionally some improvement is made—and the original spontaneity is destroyed, the original angle of vision is curved and altogether lost, or the accent is changed. I felt this especially in connection with the less formal papers.

The final selection in this volume speaks for itself. It was included not because the author is today internationally famous, but because in addition to being a great artist, he is a very learned man (as I said, this was to be a collection of statements by scholars), and by his magic he has given incandescent immediacy to a classical Jewish value in the classical Hebrew idiom.*

Agreed-upon limits or not agreed upon, there is one study I would have loved to include (assuming that permission to publish an English translation of it had been granted), and that is Yerushalayim ba-Halakah, Jerusalem as reflected in Jewish Law, by S. Bialoblocki, published in *Alei Ayin*, Jeru-

---

* He died on 17 February 1970.

salem, 5708–5712 (1948–1952). It is not only an extraordinary scholarly accomplishment in comprehensiveness, but a hymn to the eternal city of God. But I was utterly unable to translate it adequately, and could find no one who would persist after his first attempts. Perhaps this statement of mine will encourage some reader to undertake the assignment for the benefit of those who read only what is in English.

Two essays I wanted very much to include we could not get the permission to publish (in translation), as I partly intimated above, for the publication rights had already been given to other presses. Still another essay which I feel is very beautiful and instructive, the author asked that I not republish because, since his undergraduate days when he wrote it, he had come to modify his "way of dealing with" the subject and some of his interpretations of passages he quoted. I must respect his wishes; a genuine scholar deserves no less.

I want to thank the authors and their publishers for the permission to reprint these selections; I also want to thank the members of my Davenport seminar for bothering me for additional readings. I am happy to record my gratitude to my editor, Marc Jaffe, for his patience and uncommon good sense which he allows me to exploit all the time. I have also received generous editorial help from Mrs. Julie Thiele and I am very grateful to her.

I hope that as a result of reading these essays and selections, the reader will be overcome by a curiosity which compels him to locate and read the books and other studies these scholars and their colleagues have produced: and thus acquire a systematic, or orderly, conception of the varieties of Jewish expression. And having advanced that far, why not continue on to the primary sources themselves?

Judah Goldin
Davenport College
Yale University

A Postscript to the Introduction

It is almost a decade since the essays in this volume were assembled as supplementary readings for ten members of an undergraduate seminar in the study of selected Jewish primary texts, from the biblical book of Ruth to Agnon's *In the Heart of the Seas*. The texts had to be read in translation for the students knew no Hebrew. Since discussion under such conditions can easily get out of hand, and it did more than once—for translation hides difficulties and problems from sight rather than highlights them—it was essential to supply "discussions" by leading craftsmen, as demonstration of responsible interpretation. For elementary background information, encyclopedia articles or available textbooks were sufficient. What we needed was not more of these, but expression of the larger discourse to which the individual primary sources belonged.

Scholars themselves become secondary sources but their business above all is with primary ones. The essays chosen were meant to be an example of thought growing out of a profound respect for original data.

Nothing "canonical" was ever intended by this selection, and doubtless on some future occasion some of these essays will be replaced by others. In the present edition, in fact, one essay had to be omitted because its author wanted it for a book of his own and another has been reproduced in its expanded form. But what was said in the original introduction still represents the aim of the present collection.

It was for ten students of Davenport College (Yale) that these essays were first assembled, a purely private and at first tentative affair. When they became a book, it was speedily adopted in many universities as a textbook for courses in Jewish history and literature and philosophy. The present edition is the result of renewed requests for it. I hope this brings pleasure to my former students. If not for them . . . . But the present edition also owes much to the sound counsel and help of Jane Isay and Neal Kozodoy.

March 1976   J. G.
                               Oriental Studies
                               University of Pennsylvania

1.

The Biblical Idea of History in Its Common Near Eastern Setting *

by E. A. Speiser

Among the many celebrated documents from Mari, there is a letter containing this invaluable observation: "No king is powerful on his own. Ten or fifteen kings follow Hammurabi of Babylon. A like number may follow Rim-Sin of Larsa, Ibalpiel of Eshnunna, or Amutpiel of Qaṭanum. There are perhaps twenty who follow Yarimlin of Yamḥad." [1] This incidental comment, addressed by Itur-Asdu, governor of Nahor, to King Zimrilim of Mari, is a sage bit of historical wisdom. It shows a keen awareness of the composite sources of authority and is fully alive to the checks and balances of international relations. We have here, furthermore, an unexpected attempt to reach out beyond the specific detail to broader general principles. To our surprise we find that people of that period were not always just so many unreflecting pawns caught in the web of history. Some of them, at any rate, could stand back and appraise impersonally the historical process. But it is the date of the message that makes it so remarkable. The link with the city of Nahor in the region of Harran and the direct reference to Hammurabi of Babylon point unmistakably to the Patriarchal Age. In short, the generation of Abraham, even the very district where his family was settled, could not have been strangers to the concept of history.

The Bible is first and foremost a unique distillation of history. Now no process of this kind and magnitude can unfold in a vacuum. The people of the Bible, who were to make his-

* This paper was read at the Second World Congress of Jewish Studies, held in Jerusalem in 1957. From *Israel Exploration Journal*, Vol. VII No. 4 (1957), published by The Israel Exploration Society.

tory in more ways than one, were neither politically nor culturally isolated from other societies. Like the kings mentioned by the governor of Nahor, they did not stand alone. They were an integral part of a larger pattern. Hence the ultimate achievement that is the Bible cannot be properly understood, still less appreciated, except in terms of the setting in which this work originated, and of the initial values which it went on to transfigure and transcend.

As a work that bears on history, the Bible embodies a variety of incidental detail. Its central issues, however, are the larger questions of life and destiny. In other words, the Bible is not so much a chronicle of events worth recording, or thought to be worth recording, as an interpretation of significant happenings. Thus it is essentially a philosophy of history. Now any historiosophy, by definition, presupposes an advanced intellectual and spiritual background. It requires the backdrop of a major civilization. The ancient Near East was the home of two independent historic civilizations, one of which flourished in Mesopotamia and the other in Egypt. Accordingly, the biblical idea of history has to be viewed in the context of the native historiosophies of Egypt and Mesopotamia. But before this can be done, it will be necessary to restate for purposes of ready reference the salient characteristics of these two dominant civilizations of the region.

All advanced societies must come to grips with two issues above all. One is the relation of the individual to society. The other is the alignment of both individual and society to nature and the universe. The former is reflected in law and government. The latter finds expression in religion. The essence of a given civilization will be determined in the main by its distinctive answer to these two basic questions. The most pressing political and economic problems of the day are secondary and ephemeral in comparison.[2]

The two issues just mentioned are, in turn, interdependent. Yet they are seldom in true equilibrium. It is this that makes for the immemorial rivalry between church and state. As we go back in time, moreover, our scientific horizons shrink progressively. There may still be a measure of truth in the saying that just as mythology is the science of the past, science is the mythology of the future. The fact remains, nevertheless, that mythology—or what we would today call mythology— had a vastly greater effect on ancient society than theology has on modern life. Hence religion in general was the overriding factor in the older civilizations and a powerful influence on law and government. And because the religious solution of Mesopotamia differed radically from that of Egypt, the two respective societies were sharply at variance with each other, far more than is commonly realized.

The outstanding single feature of the cosmos of the ancient Mesopotamians was the tenet that no single god is the ultimate source of power and authority; none is truly omnipotent. All the leading figures of the Mesopotamian pantheon had themselves been created. Final authority resided in the community of the gods as a body. Only the assembly of the gods had the power to choose the head of the pantheon, as in the case of Marduk, or to bestow immortality on a human being, as was the case with Utnapishtim. This restriction served as an important buffer against absolutism, but it also made for uncertainty and insecurity, in heaven no less than on earth. The destiny of the universe had to be decided afresh each year. Nothing was settled for all time, nothing could be taken for granted.

Another fundamental tenet of the world-view of the Mesopotamians was that human society was an exact replica of the society of the gods, with the temple tower, or *ziggurat,* constituting a tangible link between heaven and earth. No mortal ruler, therefore, could lay claim to absolute authority, inasmuch as that privilege was withheld even from the highest god. The authority of the ruler was thus doubly restricted. On the one hand, his mandate stemmed from the gods, to whom he was accountable for his every action. And on the other hand, the king was subject to the will of the assembly of his elders, just as the head of the pantheon was bound by the wishes of his celestial assembly.

These twin checks on the power of the mortal ruler—one cosmic and the other societal—had a direct effect on the Mesopotamian concept of state. In these circumstances, the state could evolve into nothing but a kind of democracy.[3] For government by assembly and the circumscribed authority of the king could scarcely add up to anything else. The main beneficiary was the individual, whose rights were protected by the law—more specifically the cosmic, unalterable, and impersonal law called *kittum,*[4] an approximate synonym of Hebrew *'emeth.* The ruler was ever the humble servant of the *kittum,* never its master. The presence of writing was a further safeguard against abuses or distortions on the part of the king.

Written compilations of laws are now known to go back to the third millennium. The deeply entrenched legal tradition of the land is reflected, moreover, in the hundreds of thousands of documents about the practice of law which have been dug up in Mesopotamia proper. The law becomes a powerful magnet that draws other areas into the orbit of the expanding Mesopotamian civilization—Elam and Anatolia, the Hurrians and the Hittites, Alalakh and Ugarit. In all these instances the Akkadian language remains the internationally accepted legal medium and goes on to serve as a vehicle for cultural fertilization in other fields. This dynamic legal tradition was to be reflected in part long after the parent civilization had been supplanted, notably in the very name of the Babylonian Talmud and in the several legal schools of Islam which flourished on Mesopotamian soil.

In the light of all this, there is no need to refute the all too common assumption that Mesopotamia subscribed to the concept of a divine king. This view is based on superficial evidence lifted out of its proper context. Deification of rulers in Mesopotamia was never a consistent, widespread, or thoroughgoing practice; it was rather a sporadic and surface manifestation devoid of any lasting influence. Hammurabi was never guilty of this practice, nor was any of the long line of Assyrian kings, even at a time when their authority extended over Egypt. The very idea of a divine ruler was incompatible with the fundamental tenets and spirit of Mesopotamian civilization.[5]

All in all, Mesopotamia's solution of the ubiquitous societal problem proved to be enormously successful and productive. The same cannot be said of her concurrent religious solution. Since nothing in the cosmos was permanent and secure, there could be no values that were truly enduring. The celestial regime was unpredictable and capricious. The gods had to be forever propitiated if a favourable decision was to be obtained from them at all. This called for constant watchfulness and increasingly elaborate ritual. The cosmos, in short, lacked a true basis for an ethical approach to life. Form rather than content promised the best protection against the whims of heaven. In terms of a philosophy of history, the past was desperately important to be sure, but only as a check against the recurrence of previous disasters. It was not a positive factor in the understanding of the present or a more confident facing of the future. In the end, this emphasis on outward forms became a barrier to inward progress. The collapse of Nineveh and of Babylon was due not so much to the superiority of out-side powers as to the crushing weight of the internal structure.[6] By that time, however, the civilization of Mesopotamia had long outgrown its earlier ethnic, linguistic, and political bound-aries.

The Egyptian way was in its essential religious aspects the direct opposite of the Mesopotamian. The cosmos of the Egyptians was the outcome of a single creative process. The demiurge continued his absolute rule on earth through a king in whom the creator was perpetually incarnate. The king was thus himself a god whose world was as stable as the rhythm of the Nile. Because the land was ruled by a divine mediator, the alignment of society with nature was perfect and complete. In this static cosmos, unveiled once and for all in serene splen-dour, there could be no question about the wishes of heaven. Neither was there any room for the kind of impersonal law that the Mesopotamian had in his *kittum*. The pharaoh could never be the servant of any law; he could be only its source and master. In the words of John A. Wilson,

"He, as a god, *was* the state . . . To be sure, it was neces-sary for a new state to have rules and regulations for adminis-trative procedures and precedent, but our negative evidence suggests that there was no codification of law, impersonally conceived and referable by magistrates without consideration of the crown. Rather, the customary law of the land was con-ceived to be the word of the pharaoh . . . The authority of codified law would have competed with the personal authority of the pharaoh." [7]

How does this particular blend of religion and government influence the Egyptian idea of history? On this point one can-not do better than quote a statement from the pen of H. Frank-fort:

". . . the Egyptians had very little sense of history or of past and future. For they conceived their world as essentially static and unchanging. It had gone forth complete from the hands of the Creator. Historical incidents were, consequently, no more than superficial disturbances of the established order, or recurring events of never-changing significance. The past and the future—far from being a matter of concern—were wholly implicit in the present . . . the divinity of animals and kings, the pyramids, mummifications—as well as several other and seemingly unrelated features of Egyptian civilization—its moral maxims, the forms peculiar to poetry and prose—can all be understood as a result of a basic conviction that only the changeless is truly significant." [8]

The deep, indeed the unbridgeable, chasm between the civilizations of Egypt and Mesopotamia—the one with its static and the other with its dynamic world-view—should now be fully apparent. The two existed side by side over a longer period than the whole of the present era. In fact, their interrelations go back to prehistoric times. Material interchanges between them were unavoidable, and important intellectual achievements could not escape diffusion. Nevertheless, the widely-held view of the essential similarity of these two great centres of civilization proves to be a modern myth. Socially and spiritually they differed fundamentally. And their disparity was decisive, since it outweighed their similarities.

It would thus seem that our current practice of classifying civilizations according to their material forms fails to stand the test of subsurface probing. For that matter, even our methods of evaluating material remains may need refining where such products are but the symptoms of underlying spiritual conditions. The mere listing of outward differences may not be sufficient to reflect adequately the inner contrasts. Thus the architectural singularity of the Mesopotamian *ziggurat* as compared with the Egyptian pyramid does not begin to suggest the depth of the conceptual break between the two. The *ziggurat* embodied the aspiration of the Mesopotamians to forge a living bond between heaven and earth, between the abode of immortals and the world of mortals. The pyramid, on the other hand, was a monumental tribute—impressive but jejune —to a dead king. The one tells of hope; the other of resignation. Small wonder, then, that the Mesopotamian way was to survive, in countless transpositions, long after the physical collapse of the parent states. The Egyptian way lacked any comparable means of survival. Consequently, Mesopotamia has left firmer links with the modern West, in spite of the intervening distance of space and time, than she ever shared with contemporary Egypt, her partner in the limelight of history over a period of several millennia. And the dominant factor in these relations was the underlying concept of society and the place of the individual in it. Egypt and Mesopotamia were as mutually incompatible as totalitarianism and democracy—and for precisely the same reasons.

The biblical idea of history must be similarly viewed against a background of ideas of the universe and society—of God, man, and the state. These ideas, in turn, have to be judged in terms of their general Near Eastern setting, since the world of the Bible was an integral part of the ancient Near East. The question, then, narrows down at the outset to this: How does the biblical ideal compare with the mutually contrasted ways of Egypt and Mesopotamia? For the setting is automatically circumscribed by the two dominant civilizations of the region. And when it comes to substance, the Bible is both a primary and a unique source on the subject of the idea of history, for the book as a unit is essentially a work of history. All the other aspects of the Scriptures are subordinated to this central theme.

The truth of this last statement must surely be self-evident. The Pentateuch deals with primeval history, the times of the patriarchs, and the gradual incubation of national consciousness among a people unused to independence. There follow accounts of the conquest, the settlement, and the monarchies. Several of the later books concentrate on post-Exilic history. But the prophetic books, too, are by no means oblivious of the historical process: they are invaluable commentaries on current political and military events. Thus the only portions of the Bible that do not address themselves to history in one way or another are the Psalms, the three wisdom books— Proverbs, Job, Ecclesiastes—and the Song of Solomon. Yet the very fact that these books were included in the canon, and the further fact that certain non-historical matter was introduced into the other books, should help to remind us that the Bible as a whole, although conceived as history, was meant to be history of a very special kind.

For the Scriptures were never intended to be a mere chronicle of events, a story of certain states, or even the biography of a nation. The reader who is interested in such things is told time and again where he can find them: in the book of the wars of the Lord,[9] the book of Jasher,[10] the Chronicles of the kings of Israel,[11] the Chronicles of the Kings of Judah.[12] The aim of the biblical authors was of a wholly different order. Their purpose was not so much to tell the story of a nation or of nations, as to give the history of a society embarked on a particular quest, the quest for an enduring way of life, a way of life that had universal validity.

This inspired objective is implicit both in the tone and in the content of the biblical narratives; and it was honoured and implemented by the successive compilers—perceptive, faithful, and anonymous—to whom we owe the composition of most of the individual works, and by the later sages to whom we are indebted for the final canon. The story of such a society cannot be told in terms of action and events alone. It has to be woven into an intricate fabric and enriched with a variety of pertinent detail: the laws which provide the framework that holds the community together; the religious beliefs and practices; the hymns and the secular poems, the songs gay and sad, the homely maxims, the affirmations and the doubts. This is how the non-historical sections and books came to be included. But at no time did the compilers lose sight of the basic truth that what was thus being put together was the composite record of a profound experience of mankind, perhaps the most profound of all if we are to judge from the influence of the Bible on subsequent generations. The Bible, in short, is basically a work of history, and more especially a work of historiosophy. And while the history with which it deals is necessarily limited in time and space and action, its ultimate significance is ageless and universal.

Now at what point in the course of the growth of the Scriptures did the conviction gain hold that this was a subject matter of extraordinary importance, inspired and sacred? The final canon affirms this conviction for the Bible as a whole. The emergence of the pentateuchal canon carries back the same belief, as applied to a portion of the Bible, several centuries earlier. The reception accorded the book of *torah* that was recovered under Josiah is proof that the concept of canonicity was already known in pre-Exilic days. And the references to the *book of the wars of the Lord* and the *book of Jasher* suggest by their implied distinction between special and routine writings that works of the non-secular kind were earlier still and were immediately recognized as being out of the ordinary.

What is, then, the earliest feasible date for the emergence of a canon—no doubt in oral form at first—which was eventually to develop into the Scriptures? As yet we have no sure means of arriving at a definite and absolute answer to that question. But this much can be asserted even now: the date must be earlier than is commonly supposed. It has to be put ahead of the earliest narrative portions of the Pentateuch, quite probably before the time of Moses, indeed close to the age of the patriarchs. I realize that such an assertion is certain to provoke objections from many quarters. It is my duty, therefore, to develop the theme, and to justify and defend my position. Before this is done, however, we must turn once again to the subject of the biblical idea of history as seen in its general Near Eastern setting.

It is abundantly clear today that, of the two major centres of civilization in the area, it was distant Mesopotamia and not neighbouring Egypt that left the deeper cultural impress upon Israel. This was to be expected. For in the first place, the patriarchs had their roots in the land across the Euphrates and they continued to maintain ties with their original home. And in the second place, the Egyptian way was static and isolationist, whereas the Mesopotamian way was dynamic and expansive—naturally suited to reach out to other lands, Israel included.

These theoretical premises are borne out by concrete evidence. The biblical concept of state can be described as "democratic" with at least as much justice as the Mesopotamian form of government. It is the "people" (i.e. *demos*) of Israel who have a decisive say as to how and by whom they are to be ruled; it is they who set up their kings time and again. The leaders of Israel are invariably presented as mortal and fallible. Even a Moses could be guilty of faults all too human, faults that were to keep him from setting foot in the Promised Land. All this is a very far cry from the Egyptian image of a divine king. To be sure, an analogous belief in divine rulers is still occasionally ascribed to the Bible.[13] However, in our present state of considerably increased knowledge of these matters, such allegations amount to little more than an academic anachronism, utterly irreconcilable with attested biblical theory and practice.

The independent evidence of the law, moreover, serves to emphasize the fact that in the wide area of cultural correspondence between Mesopotamia and Israel, we are likely to be confronted with cases of actual kinship as opposed to mere coincidence. In both societies the law was impersonal and supreme; the king was its servant and not its source and master. Furthermore, the respective legal disciplines are closely linked in spirit and in content, notwithstanding numerous differences in detail. And because many of the features that are common to both lands can now be traced back to the very beginnings of Mesopotamian civilization, Israel has to be regarded in this respect as the cultural descendant of Mesopotamia. Israel and Mesopotamia were jointly separated from Egypt by a con-

ceptual curtain that could and did prove to be more difficult
to penetrate than the most formidable physical barriers.

Such then is the general cultural background against which
the biblical narrative depicts the dawn of Israel's history by
recounting the story of the patriarchs. It is a story told in terms
of its leading characters. As such it is an undisputed literary
masterpiece. But is it history? Certainly not in the conventional
sense of the term. Yet it cannot be set down as fancy. The
author [14] retells events in his own inimitable way: he does not
invent them. What is thus committed to writing is tradition, in
the reverent care of a literary genius. Where that tradition can
be independently checked, it proves to be authentic. This much
has been evident for some time in respect of a number of incidental details. It now turns out that the main framework of the
patriarchal account has also been accurately presented.

The very opening of that account records God's command
to Abraham to leave his birthplace in Mesopotamia and journey to another land on a spiritual mission which will be gradually disclosed. There have been those who would dismiss this
episode as a pious invention by the author, or as a decorative
literary form. We now know, however, that wilful devices were
not within the writer's scope—a point that will be presently
developed more fully. To the narrator, at least, this particular
command was a genuine experience on the part of Abraham.
As such, it was to be honoured by a long line of later writers,
all of whom saw in God's covenant with Abraham the very
cornerstone of the spiritual history of Israel. Small wonder,
therefore, that this covenant is made into one of the two
dominant notes which the Bilbe uses as a recurrent refrain.

Now the country that Abraham was thus bidden to leave
had achieved, as we indicated earlier, enormous social gains
alongside an ever-growing spiritual deficit. The societal system
of Mesopotamia was to spread in course of time to other
lands, Israel included. But the concurrent spiritual solution
lacked the same broad appeal. Israel, for one, would have
none of it. Can it, then, be pure coincidence that Abraham's
departure from his homeland is attributed by tradition to a
need for a healthier religious climate? The stated reasons for
this departure correspond so closely with the facts of the local
religious life as to make fortuitous agreement in this instance
highly improbable. Were Abraham, or tradition, or the literary
executor of the patriarchal traditions to have improvised an
excuse for the fateful journey to the Promised Land, none of

them could have dreamed up a motive more closely in consonance with the actual state of affairs.

Arrival in Canaan brings the patriarchs within the orbit of Egypt and into contact with the Egyptian world-view. But if the Mesopotamian way, in spite of its congenial societal features, was to Israel's forefathers sufficient grounds for departure, the Egyptian way could be little short of abomination. Exposure to Egypt was bound to lead to oppression, spiritually as much as socially. The exodus from Egypt was accordingly much more than just a physical undertaking. It was more truly and profoundly an act of liberation from intolerable spiritual bondage. Indeed, the Hebrew verb employed in this connection (יצא) means both "to leave" and "to go free." The term "exodus" stresses unduly the less significant aspect of that event. The real emphasis belongs instead to "liberation," and more particularly to spiritual liberation; for we are told again and again that it was God who freed the Israelites from the bondage of Egypt for the express purpose of making them His own people.[15] This then is the aspect with which the Bible is principally concerned. Hence the remembrance of the Egyptian experience becomes the other dominant note in all biblical history, a note that is echoed through all the portions of the Scriptures and made into a recurrent refrain together with the covenant between God and Abraham. Only an indelible spiritual experience could sink so deep into the national consciousness.

Thus covenant and liberation, the two focal points of the biblical idea of history, link up unerringly with the two respective centres of civilization which for more than half of all recorded history set the tone for the Near East as a whole. The covenant adverts to Mesopotamia, the liberation to Egypt. Each reflects unalterable opposition to the spiritual values at which one or the other of the dominant civilizations had arrived. All the other aspects of biblical historiosophy—its evolution and its pioneering insights, its literary expression and the characteristics of the various writers who left us these accounts —are secondary questions by comparison. The migration from Mesopotamia and the rejection of Egypt are basic to all that is to follow; they add up jointly to mankind's first declaration of spiritual independence, the resolute proclamation of a new and different faith.

We come, lastly, to what is perhaps the keynote of this essay: to what period should we trace back the idea that Abraham's migration did not entail a change in the physical environment alone but that it meant also, and far more so, a decisive turn in the spiritual orientation of mankind? It was suggested earlier in this discussion that the emergence of this idea may have to be dated to the age of the patriarchs themselves—that is to a time close to the covenant with Abraham as recorded in the biblical narrative. One could reason, of course, that since the tradition about the covenant agrees so intimately with the pertinent internal conditions in Mesopotamia, its accepted dating should likewise be given credence. But this would be begging the question. Independent support is desirable. Can such support be adduced?

We need not look far for an answer. Vast stretches of the second millennium in the ancient Near East, hitherto hidden from view, have been brilliantly illumined in recent years by the finds from Mari, Nuzi, Alalakh, Boghazköi, Ugarit, and elsewhere; these have shed much incidental light on the dawn of biblical history. The separate episodes in the patriarchal account have thus acquired a new status in terms of antiquity and authenticity of background. The work and purpose of the biblical narrator consequently stand out in bolder relief.

Among the patriarchal narratives which have won, or deserve to win, a new respect as a result of the recent discoveries, there are several of exceptional significance in that they had come to be used for centuries as criteria of Israel's moral and ethical principles. These include the repeated motif of passing off one's wife as a sister (Genesis 12:10—13:1; 20:1–8; 26:1–11); the transfer of the blessing from Esau to Jacob (Genesis 27); and the removal by Rachel of her father's household gods (Genesis 21:19, 30, 32). Each of these passages lends itself to a moralizing interpretation; each has been handled apologetically by followers and friends, and with indignation or malicious delight by assorted ill-wishers. Yet all such moral judgments, if indeed they were in order in the past, now prove to be entirely out of place. For the incidents in question turn out to reflect with startling accuracy the customs and usages appropriate to the patriarchal period; they were peculiar to the societies with which the patriarchs maintained relations, and they are—above all—wholly devoid of any ethical implications whatsoever.

The present context will permit only brief comments on the episodes just mentioned as they can now be restored to their proper social setting. The sister-wife motif emerges as a prominent feature of the laws of the Hurrians,[16] a people with whom western Semites are known to have lived in close symbiosis. Similar practices have also been traced to the Hittites.[17] A wife who had at the same time the status, though not necessarily the blood ties, of a sister happened to command greater protection and prestige than an ordinary wife. In the matter of birthright, the direct legal consequence was the title to a double and preferential share in the paternal estate. Yet the birthright—again in Hurrian society—did not always go with the eldest son. In given circumstances the incumbent could be designated by the father from among the younger sons. The primacy of such a position was thus a matter of the father's discretion rather than of chronological priority.[18] And finally, the Nuzi texts revealed some thirty years ago that transfer of the father's household gods was a prerequisite in certain cases where property was to pass to a daughter's husband.[19]

In the light of these discoveries, all three biblical stories assume a new and unsuspected significance. The wife-sister act was based on recognized northern practices. The bypassing of an older son in favour of a younger was in harmony with the Hurrian habit which left such matters to the discretion of the father. And Rachel's removal of the household gods has ample basis in Nuzi law: it was to all intents and purposes the act of a resolute young woman who literally took the law into her own hands as a precautionary measure against a greedy father.

Why is it, then, that the examples just cited, each capable of a simple and straightforward explanation, puzzled and misled so many generations of Bible translators and exegetes? With the help of hindsight, the answer becomes clear enough. The full meaning of these episodes was hidden from Bible interpreters because it had already been lost to the narrator himself; otherwise he would surely have taken the trouble to enlighten his readers just as he did so often elsewhere. Instead, the traditional narrative reflects puzzlement, as in the case of Rachel, or introduces speculation, as in the other instances. That this should be so is not at all surprising. The full significance of each episode depends on specific practices of a particular society remote in time and space from the immediate background of the narrator. Much of the motivation had been lost in transit. Only the bare details had come down intact.

In these circumstances, why were the narratives in question

included at all? The manifest fact that the narrator no longer knew the explanation, yet set down the details—details which prove to be authentic reflections of a forgotten civilization— can mean but one thing: his aim was not to question or to reason why, but only to record faithfully what tradition had handed down to him. His task was to retell, not to originate. He might lavish his genius on the form, but not on the substance. To put it differently, the lives of the patriarchs had already become part of an oral canon some time between the period that was being depicted and the date of their earliest written presentation.

Now canon implies sanctity, and sanctity presupposes that extraordinary importance is thus being attached to the object or objects so venerated. The patriarchal narratives must have acquired such a status well before the date of the literary work in which they were incorporated; otherwise the writer would have felt free to recast them in terms of his own time and environment. In other words, the author approached this particular material as part of the living *torah*. In that context *torah* was not "law"—which never is the primary sense of this term anyway—nor yet teaching and instruction in general. In its canonical sense *torah* stands for the body of teachings which collectively comprise a design for a divinely ordained way of life. Law enters into it only indirectly, in so far as the inner content requires a shell of formal regulations.

It is altogether appropriate, therefore, that the narrative portions which eventually came to be included in the Pentateuch should early have been viewed as integral components of the *torah,* and that they should have been so treated by their writer. By approaching the patriarchal episodes as inviolable, by faithfully reproducing details whose meaning had grown obscure, the narrator bears testimony to the prior canonical, or quasi-canonical standing of such material. Patriarchal traditions had to be viewed with awe because they reflected and illuminated the divine plan for an enduring way of life, an ideal not envisioned by other societies. The seeds of this concept had been planted far away and long ago. Their subsequent growth is but another way of describing the entire course of biblical history.

That the basic concept had a capacity for growth is abundantly demonstrated as we move from milestone to milestone, from the patriarchs to the prophets, from the prophets to the scribes. The record in which the whole experience has been distilled is the product of a thousand years and of many, many hands. Its insights are composite and cumulative. It reflects many variables. But through it all there runs a single central theme, the theme of a quest for a life worth living and, if need be, worth dying for. And basic to this theme is a single constant which embodies Israel's own solution of the problem of the relation of society to the cosmos. This solution proceeds from the affirmation that a sole and omnipotent master is responsible for all creation. But his ways are just and purposeful. Man's destiny is not foredoomed or preordained, for it is affected largely by man's own conduct and by his readiness to embrace the eternally valid teachings of God's *torah*. By thus being granted a share in influencing its own destiny, by being liberated from the whims of capricious and unpredictable cosmic powers, and by being freed from the authority of mortal rulers with divine pretensions, mankind was launched on a new course of responsibility, dignity and hope.

Once glimpsed and embraced, this ideal could prove to be enormously productive and capable of infinite enrichment. It was so in the historic career of Israel. In its simplest form it was certainly not beyond the reach of the sophisticated society of which the patriarchs were a part. Yet the available records would seem to suggest that Abraham alone had the vision and the determination to make this ideal his goal. Such at least is the meaning of God's covenant with Abraham in the light of the cultural history of his age.[20] As an earlier generation used to say of Moses—if Abraham did not exist in reality he would have to be reconstructed in theory. This might appear to oversimplify the whole issue. Yet the most intricate problems can often be reduced to deceptively simple fundamentals.

Thus the covenant with Abraham is the biblical answer to the religious solution evolved by the civilization of Mesopotamia, a civilization with which the biblical way was otherwise in essential harmony. But as a new design for living, a new faith of limitless scope, the ideal that the patriarchs had embraced was destined to be put to its severest test in the other major centre of Near Eastern and ancient-world civilization. The Bible proclaims and the results confirm the fact that the patriarchs' original ideal proved sturdy enough to withstand the temptation of the fleshpots of Egypt and the Pharaoh's political and military might. The Egyptian way was rejected as a horror and an abomination. Abraham and Moses became the spiritual fathers of the biblical experience, and the covenant and the liberation emerged as its enduring historic cornerstones.

The pursuit of such an ideal, however, demands unflagging devotion and dedication. Such a spirit of sacrifice and self-denial cannot long be sustained unless it has become deeply ingrained in the sponsoring society. We thus come back to our earlier assertion that the canonical tradition among the people of the Book must be older than the age of the pentateuchal writers, older indeed than the time of Moses himself. The foregoing discussion has advanced the argument that certain significant elements in that tradition have to be traced back to the period of the patriarchs. If this were not so, the patriarchal narratives could not have been recorded with such startling accuracy, although the writers lacked full knowledge of their social implications. If this were not so, the tradition of God's covenant with Abraham would not have been one of the two principal refrains in all the Scriptures. And if this were not so, the historic experience of Israel could not have become a decisive experience of mankind. Indeed, if it were otherwise, there could never have been the unique phenomenon of Israel.

Notes

1. See G. Dossin: Les archives épistolaires du palais de Mari, *Syria*, 19, 1938, p. 117.

2. Cf. my remarks in *Mid-East: World Center* (Science of Culture Series, ed. Ruth Nanda Anshen, 7). New York, 1956, p. 35. The following remarks on Mesopotamia contain a summary of various themes which I have had occasion to develop in the following publications: (a) Some Sources of Intellectual and Social Progress in the Ancient Near East, *Studies in the History of Culture* (W. G. Leland Volume). Menasha, Wisconsin, 1942, pp. 51–62; (b) The Ancient Near East and Modern Philosophies of History, *Proceedings of the American Philosophical Society*, 95, 1951, pp. 583–588; (c) Early Law and Civilization, *The Canadian Bar Review*, 31, 1953, pp. 863–877; (d) Authority and Law in Mesopotamia, *Journ. American Oriental Society*, Suppl. No. 17, 1954, pp. 8–15; and especially (e) Ancient Mesopotamia, in R. C. Dentan, ed.: *The Idea of History in the Ancient Near East* (American Oriental Series, 38). New Haven, 1955, pp. 35–76, and the literature cited in all these publications. The present summary was thought desirable for purposes of minimal background.

3. Cf. Th. Jacobsen: Primitive Democracy in Ancient Mesopotamia, *JNES*, 2, 1943, pp. 159–172.

4. Speiser, *op. cit.* (supra, n. 2d), pp. 12–13.

5. For the subject in general, cf. R. Labat: *Le caractère religieux de la*

royauté assyro-babylonienne. Paris, 1939; H. Frankfort: *Kingship and the Gods*. Chicago, 1948; C. J. Gadd: *Ideas of Divine Rule in the Ancient East* London, 1948; Speiser, *op. cit.* (supra, n. 2e), pp. 63–64.

6. *Ibid.*, pp. 72–73.

7. *The Burden of Egypt*. Chicago, 1951, pp. 49–50.

8. *The Birth of Civilization in the Near East*. London, 1951, pp. 20–21.

9. Numbers 21:14.

10. Joshua 10:13.

11. I Kings 14:19.

12. II Kings 23:28.

13. See M. Noth: Gott, König, Volk im Alten Testament, *Zeitschrift für Theologie und Kirche*, 47, 1950, pp. 157–191 (= *Gesammelte Studien zum Alten Testament*, München, 1957, pp. 188–229).

14. I use here such terms as "author" or "narrator" in the singular throughout, without implying thereby that there was but one narrative source in the Pentateuch. For purposes of the present discussion it is entirely immaterial to what document a given passage may be assigned. The basic attitude to the subject matter is the same in each instance. The nicer distinctions in regard to numerous details do not affect the major theme under discussion.

15. Exodus 6:7; Jeremiah 11:4; 30:22; etc.

16. Cf. P. Koschaker: Fratriarchat, *Zeitschrift für Assyriologie*, 41, 1933, p. 14.

17. *Ibid.*, pp. 1–13.

18. E. A. Speiser: "I Know not the Day of my Death," *JBL*, 74, 1955, pp. 252–256; cf. also: The Hurrian Participation in the Civilizations of Mesopotamia, Syria and Palestine, *Journ. of World Hist.*, 1, 1953, pp. 323–324.

19. S. Smith, apud C. J. Gadd: Tablets from Kirkuk, *Revue d'Assyriologie*, 23, 1926, p. 127.

20. The machinery of covenant is already in full swing in Mari, especially among the west-Semitic tribes; and west-Semitic terms are used to describe it. On the other hand, the Hebrew word for "covenant" (ברית) may ultimately be Akkadian; cf. M. Noth, Das alttestamentliche Bundschliessen im Lichte eines Mari-Textes, *Annuaire de l'Institut de Philologie et d'Histoire Orientales et Slaves*, 13 (Mélanges Isidore Lévy), 1955, pp. 433–444 (= *Ges. Studien*, supra, n. 13, pp. 142–154).

2.

Some Postulates of Biblical Criminal Law *

by Moshe Greenberg

Among the chief merits of Professor Kaufmann's work must be counted the tremendous impetus it has given to the study of the postulates of biblical thought. The debt that the present paper owes to this stimulus and to the lines of investigation laid down by Professor Kaufmann is patent; it is a privilege to have the occasion to offer it to him in grateful tribute.

i

The study of biblical law has been a stepchild of the historical-critical approach to the Bible. While the law had been a major preoccupation of ancient and medieval scholars, in modern times it has largely been replaced by, or made to serve, other interests. No longer studied for itself, it is now investigated for the reflexes it harbors of stages in Israel's social development, or it is analyzed by literary-historical criticism into strata, each synchronized with a given stage in the evolution of Hebrew religion and culture. The main interest is no longer in the law as an autonomous discipline, but in what the laws can yield the social or religious historian. It is a remarkable fact that the last comprehensive juristic treatment of biblical law was made over a century ago.[1]

The sociological and literary-historical approaches have, of course, yielded permanent insights, yet it cannot be said that

* From *Yehezkel Kaufmann Jubilee Volume,* Jerusalem, Magnes Press, The Hebrew University, 1960.

they have exhausted all the laws have to tell about the life and thought of Israel. Too often they have been characterized by theorizing which ignores the realities of early law and society as we know them at first hand from the written records of the ancient Near East. Severities in biblical law are alleged to reflect archaic notions that have no echo in either ancient civilized, or modern Bedouin law. Humane features are declared the product of urbanization, though they have no parallels in the urban codes of Mesopotamia. Inconsistencies have been discovered and arranged in patterns of historic evolution where a proper discrimination would have revealed that the laws in question dealt with altogether separate realms.

The corrective to these errors lies ready to hand. It is that considerable body of cuneiform law—especially the law collections [2]—which lends itself admirably to elucidate the meaning and background of the biblical law corpora. The detailed studies of these cuneiform collections, made chiefly by European scholars, furnish the student of the Bible with models of legal analysis, conducted without the prejudgments which frequently mar discussions of biblical law.

No clearer demonstration of the limits of literary-historical criticism can be found, for example, than that afforded by the studies made upon the laws of Hammurapi. Inconsistencies no less glaring than those which serve as the basis of analyzing strata in the Bible are found in this greatest corpus of Mesopotamian law. In this case, however, we know when, where, and by whom the laws were promulgated. We know, as we do not in the case of the Bible, that the code as we now have it was published as a whole, and intended—at the very least—as a statement of guiding legal principles for the realm of the king. When like discrepancies were pointed out in biblical laws it had been possible to defend stopping short with a literary-historical analysis by arguing that the discrepancies and inconsistencies of the present text were not found in the original documents that went into it. Attempts to interpret the biblical laws as a coherent whole were regarded as naïve and unscholarly. It was not possible to argue this way in the case of Hammurapi's laws. The discrepancies were there from the beginning, and though, to be sure, they may well have originated in earlier collections, the fact remained that there they were, incorporated side by side in one law.

Two attitudes have been taken toward this problem in the code of Hammurapi. One, represented best by Paul Koschaker, is historical-critical. It aims at reconstructing the original laws which have gone into the present text and have caused the discrepancy; having attained this aim, its work is done. The other, represented by Sir John Miles, is that of the commentator, whose purpose is to attempt "to imagine how this section as it stands can have been interpreted by a Babylonian court." [3] The commentator is compelled in the interest of coherence to look for distinctions of a finer degree than those made by the literary historian. Such distinctions are not merely the recourse of a modern harmonist to escape the contradictions of the text; they are, it would seem, necessary for understanding how an ancient jurist, how the draftsman himself, understood the law.[4] It must be assumed that the laws of Hammurapi were intended as a consistent guide to judges, and had to be interpreted as they stand in as consistent a manner as possible.

The realization that careful discrimination between apparently contradictory laws is needed for this most carefully drafted ancient law corpus is highly pertinent for an understanding of biblical law. The literary-historical aim leads all too readily to a disregard of distinctions in favor of establishing a pattern of development. Only by endeavoring to interpret the laws as they now stand does one guard himself against excessive zeal in finding discrepancies which involve totally different subjects rather than a historical development. Adopting the method of the commentator, then, we are thrown back much more directly upon the laws themselves. Recourse to literary-critical surgery is resisted until all efforts at making distinctions have failed.

Another virtue of the commentator is his insistence on understanding a given body of law in its own terms before leaping into comparisons with other law systems. To do so, however, means to go beyond the individual rules; for it is not possible to comprehend the law of any culture without an awareness of its key concepts, its value judgments.[5] Yet much of the comparative work done in Israelite-Near Eastern law has been content with comparing individual laws rather than law systems or law ideologies. But until the values that the law embodies are understood, it is a question whether any individual law can be properly appreciated, let alone profitably compared with another in a foreign system.

In the sequence I shall attempt to indicate some instances of the gain accruing to the study of biblical law from the application of these two considerations: the insistence, first, upon proper discriminations, and second, upon viewing the law as an expression of underlying postulates or values of culture. The limitations of the sociological and literary-historical approaches will emerge from the discussion. My remarks are confined to the criminal law, an area which lends itself well to comparative treatment, and in which the values of a civilization come into expression with unmatched clarity.

ii

Underlying the differing conceptions of certain crimes in biblical and cuneiform law is a divergence, subtle though crucial, in the ideas concerning the origin and sanction of the law.

In Mesopotamia the law was conceived of as the embodiment of cosmic truths (*kīnātum*, sing. *kittum*). Not the originator, but the divine CUSTODIAN of justice was Shamash, "the magistrate of gods and men, whose lot is justice and to whom truths have been granted for dispensation." [6] The Mesopotamian king was called by the gods to establish justice in his realm; to enable him to do so Shamash inspired him with "truths." [7] In theory, then, the final source of the law, the ideal with which the law had to conform was above the gods as well as men; in this sense "the Mesopotamian king . . . was not the source of the law but only its agent." [8]

However, the actual authorship of the laws, the embodying of the cosmic ideal in statutes of the realm, is claimed by the king. Hammurapi repeatedly refers to his laws as "my words which I have inscribed on my monument"; they are his "precious" or "choice" words, "the judgment . . . that I have judged (and) the decisions . . . which I have decided." [9] This claim is established by the name inscribed on the stele, and Hammurapi invokes curses upon the man who should presume to erase his name.[10] Similarly in the case of the laws of Lipit-Ishtar: Lipit-Ishtar has been called by the gods to establish justice in the land. The laws are his, the stele on which they are inscribed is called by his name. The epilogue curses him "who will damage my handiwork . . . who will erase its inscription, who will write his own name upon it." [11] While the ideal is cosmic and impersonal, and the gods manifest great concern for the establishment and enforcement of justice, the immediate sanction of the laws is by the authority of the king. Their formulation is his, and his too, as we shall presently see, is the final decision as to their applicability.

In accord with the royal origin of these laws is their purpose: "to establish justice," "that the strong might not oppress the weak," "to give good government," "stable government," "to prosper the people," "abolish enmity and rebellion" [12]—in sum, those political benefits which the constitution of the United States epitomizes in the phrases, "to establish justice, ensure domestic tranquility, promote the general welfare."

In the biblical theory the idea of the transcendence of the law receives a more thoroughgoing expression. Here God is not merely the custodian of justice or the dispenser of "truth" to man, he is the fountainhead of the law, the law is a statement of his will. The very formulation is God's; frequently laws are couched in the first person, and they are always referred to as "words of God," never of man. Not only is Moses denied any part in the formulation of the Pentateuchal laws, no Israelite king is said to have authored A LAW CODE, nor is any king censured for so doing.[13] The only legislator the Bible knows of is God; the only legislation is that mediated by a prophet (Moses and Ezekiel). This conception accounts for the commingling in the law corpora of religious and civil law, and—even more distinctively biblical—of legal enactments and moral exhortations. The entire normative realm, whether in law or morality, pertains to God alone. So far as the law corpora are concerned there is no source of norm-fixing outside of Him. Conformably, the purpose of the laws is stated in somewhat different terms in the Bible than in Babylonia. To be sure, observance is a guarantee of well-being and prosperity (Exodus 23:20ff.; Leviticus 26; Deuteronomy 11:13ff., etc.), but it is more: it sanctifies (Exodus 19:5f.; Leviticus 19) and is accounted as righteousness (Deuteronomy 6:25). There is a distinctively religious tone here, fundamentally different in quality from the political benefits guaranteed in the cuneiform law collections.

In the sphere of the criminal law, the effect of this divine authorship of all law is to make crimes sins, a violation of the will of God. "He who acts wilfully (against the law) whether he belongs to the native-born or the aliens, is reviling the Lord" (Numbers 15:30). God is directly involved as legislator and sovereign; the offense does not flout a humanly authored safeguard of cosmic truth but an explicit utterance of the divine will. The way is thus prepared to regard offenses as absolute wrongs, transcending the power of men to pardon or expunge. This would seem to underlie the refusal of biblical law to admit of pardon or mitigation of punishment in certain cases where cuneiform law allows it. The laws of adultery and murder are cases in point. Among the Babylonians, Assyrians, and Hittites the procedure in the case of adultery is basically the same. It is left to the discretion of the husband to punish his wife or pardon her. If he punishes his wife, her paramour also is punished; if he pardons her, the paramour goes free too. The purpose of the law is to defend the right of the husband and provide him with redress for the wrong done to him. If the husband, however, is willing to forego his right, and chooses to overlook the wrong done to him, there is no need for redress. The pardon of the husband wipes out the crime.[14]

In biblical law it is otherwise: "If a man commits adultery with the wife of another man, both the adulterer and the adulteress must be put to death" (Leviticus 20:10; cf. Deuteronomy 22:22, 23)—in all events. There is no question of permitting the husband to mitigate or cancel the punishment. For adultery is not merely a wrong against the husband, it is a sin against God, an absolute wrong. To what extent this view prevailed may be seen in a few extra-legal passages: Abimelech is providentially kept from violating Abraham's wife, Sarah, and thereby "sinning against God"—not a word is said about wronging Abraham (Genesis 20:6). Joseph repels the advances of Potiphar's wife with the argument that such a breach of faith with his master would be a "sin against God" (39:8f.). The author of the ascription of Psalm 51—"A psalm of David, when Nathan the prophet came to him after he had gone in to Bath-sheba"—finds it no difficulty that verse 4 says, "Against thee only have I sinned." To be sure the law also recognizes that adultery is a breach of faith with the husband (Numbers 5:12), yet the offense as such is absolute, against God. Punishment is not designed to redress an injured husband for violation of his rights; the offended party is God, whose injury no man can pardon or mitigate.

The right of pardon in capital cases which Near Eastern law gives to the king [15] is unknown to biblical law (the right of the king to grant asylum to homicides in extraordinary cases [cf. II Samuel 14] is not the same). Here would seem to be another indication of the literalness with which the doctrine of the divine authorship of the law was held in Israel. Only the

author of the law has the power to waive it; in Mesopotamia
he is the king, in Israel, no man.

iii

Divergent underlying principles alone can account for the
differences between Israelite and Near Eastern laws of homicide. The unexampled severity of biblical law on the subject
has been considered primitive, archaic, or a reflex of Bedouin
vendetta customs. But precisely the law of homicide cannot be
accounted for on any such grounds.

In the earliest law collection, the Covenant Code of Exodus,
it is laid down that murder is punishable by death (Exodus
21:12ff.). If homicide is committed by a beast—a goring ox
is spoken of—the beast must be stoned, and its flesh may not
be eaten. If it was known to be vicious and its owner was
criminally negligent in failing to keep it in, the owner is subject to death as well as the ox, though here the law allows the
owner to ransom himself with a sum fixed by the slain person's
family (vss. 28ff.). This is the sole degree of culpability in
which the early law allows a ransom. It is thus fully in accord
with a later law of Numbers (35:31) which states, "You
shall not take a ransom for the life of a murderer who is guilty
of death, but he shall be surely put to death." A ransom may
be accepted only for a homicide not committed personally and
with intent to harm. For murder, however, there is only the
death penalty.

These provisions contrast sharply with the other Near Eastern laws on homicide. Outside of the Bible, there is no parallel
to the absolute ban on composition between the murderer and
the next of kin. All Near Eastern law recognizes the right of
the slain person's family to agree to accept a settlement in lieu
of the death of the slayer, Hittite law going so far as to regu-
late this settlement minutely in terms of the number of souls
that must be surrendered as compensation.[16] Bedouin law is
no different: among the Bedouin of Sinai murder is compen-
sated for by a tariff reckoned in camels for any life destroyed.[17]
The Qur'an is equally tolerant of composition: "Believers," it
reads (2:178), "retaliation is decreed for you in bloodshed:
a free man for a free man, a slave for a slave, and a female for
a female. He who is pardoned by his aggrieved brother shall

be prosecuted according to usage and shall pay him a liberal fine."

In the Babylonian law of the goring ox, otherwise closely paralleling that of the Bible, no punishment is prescribed for the ox.[18]

On both of these counts biblical law has been regarded as exhibiting archaic features.[19] To speak in terms of legal lag and progress, however, is to assume that the biblical and non-biblical laws are stages in a single line of historical development, a line in which acceptance of composition is the stage after strict talion. This is not only incapable of being demonstrated, the actual history of the biblical law of homicide shows that it followed an altogether different principle of development from that governing Near Eastern law.

A precise and adequate formulation of the jural postulate underlying the biblical law of homicide is found in Genesis 9:5f.: "For your lifeblood I shall require a reckoning; of every beast shall I require it. . . . Whoever sheds the blood of a man, by man shall his blood be shed; for in the image of God was man made." To be sure, this passage belongs to a stratum assigned to late times by current critical opinion; however that may be, the operation of the postulate is visible in the very earliest laws, as will be seen immediately. The meaning of the passage is clear enough: that man was made in the image of God—the exact significance of the words is not necessary to decide here—is expressive of the peculiar and supreme worth of man. Of all creatures, Genesis 1 relates, he alone possesses this attribute, bringing him into closer relation to God than all the rest and conferring upon him highest value. The first practical consequence of this supremacy is set forth in Genesis 9:3f.: man may eat beasts. The establishment of a value hierarchy of man over beast means that man may kill them—for food and sacrifice only (cf. Leviticus 17:4)—but they may not kill him. A beast that kills a man destroys the image of God and must give a reckoning for it. Now this is the law of the goring ox in Exodus: it must be stoned to death. The religious evaluation inherent in this law is further evidenced by the prohibition of eating the flesh of the stoned ox. The beast is laden with guilt and is therefore an object of horror.[20]

Babylonian law on the subject reflects no such theory as to the guilt the peculiar value of human life imposes on all who take it. Babylonian law is concerned with safeguardng rights

in property and making losses good. It therefore deals only
with the liability of the owner of the ox to pay for damages
caused by his ox. The ox is of no concern to the law since no
liabilities attach to it. Indeed, one could reasonably argue that
from the viewpoint of property rights the biblical law is unjust:
is it not unduly hard on the ox owner to destroy his ox for its
first offense? Ought he to suffer for an accident he could in no
way have foreseen and for which he therefore cannot be held
responsible?

This view of the uniqueness and supremacy of human life
has yet another consequence. It places life beyond the reach
of other values. The idea that life may be measured in terms
of money or other property, and *a fortiori* the idea that persons
may be evaluated as equivalences of other persons, is excluded.
Compensation of any kind is ruled out. The guilt of the murderer is infinite because the murdered life is invaluable; the
kinsmen of the slain man are not competent to say when he
has been paid for. An absolute wrong has been committed, a
sin against God which is not subject to human discussion. The
effect of this view is, to be sure, paradoxical: because human
life is invaluable, to take it entails the death penalty.[21] Yet the
paradox must not blind us to the judgment of value that the
law sought to embody.

The sense of the invaluableness of human life underlies the
divergence of the biblical treatment of the homicide from that
of the other law systems of the Near East. There the law allows
and at times fixes a value on lives, and leaves it to the kinsmen
of the slain to decide whether they will have revenge or receive compensation for their loss in money or property. Perhaps the baldest expression of the economic valuation of life
occurs in those cases where punishment of a murderer takes
the form of the surrender of other persons—a slave, a son, a
wife, a brother—"instead of blood," or, "to wash out the
blood," or to "make good" the dead person, as the Assyrian
phrases put it.[22] Equally expressive are the Hittite laws which
prescribe that the killer has to "make amends" for the dead
persons by "giving" persons in accord with the status of the
slain and the degree of the homicide. The underlying motive
in such forms of composition is the desire to make good the
deficiency in the fighting or working strength of the community which has lost one of its members.[23] This seems to be the
meaning of Hittite Law 43: "If a man customarily fords a river
with his ox, another man pushes him aside, seizes the tail of

the ox and crosses the river, but the river carries the owner of the ox away, they (i.e. the authorities of the respective village or town) shall receive that very man." The view of life as a replaceable economic value here reaches its ultimate expression. The moral guilt of the homicide is so far subordinated to the need of restoring the strength of the community that the culprit is not punished but incorporated; [24] this is the polar opposite of the biblical law which requires that not even the flesh of the stoned homicidal ox may be eaten.

That the divergence in law reflects a basic difference in judgments of value, rather than stages in a single line of evolution, would seem to be borne out by examining the reverse of the coin: the treatment of offenses against property. Both Assyrian and Babylonian law know of offenses against property that entail the death penalty. In Babylonia, breaking and entering, looting at a fire, night trespass—presumably for theft—and theft from another's possession are punished by death; Assyrian law punishes theft committed by a wife against her husband with death.[25] In view of this, the leniency of biblical law in dealing with all types of property offenses is astonishing. No property offense is punishable with death. Breaking and entering, for which Babylonian law prescribes summary execution and hanging of the culprit at the breach, is punished in biblical law with double damages. If the housebreaking occurred at night the householder is privileged to slay the culprit caught in the act, though this is not prescribed as a punishment (Exodus 22:1f.).[26]

This unparalleled leniency of biblical law in dealing with property offenses must be combined with its severity in the case of homicide, just as the leniency of non-biblical law in dealing with homicide must be taken in conjunction with its severity in dealing with property offenses. The significance of the laws then emerges with full clarity: in biblical law life and property are incommensurable; taking of life cannot be made up for by any amount of property, nor can any property offense be considered as amounting to the value of a life. Elsewhere the two are commensurable: a given amount of property can make up for life, and a grave enough offense against property can necessitate forfeiting life. Not the archaicness of the biblical law of homicide relative to that of the cuneiform codes, nor the progressiveness of the biblical law of theft relative to that of Assyria and Babylonia, but a basic difference in the evaluation of life and property separates the one from the others. In the biblical law a religious evaluation; in non-biblical, an economic and political evaluation, predominates.

Now it is true that in terms of each viewpoint one can speak of a more or a less thoroughgoing application of principle, and, in that sense, of advanced or archaic conceptions. Thus the Hittite laws would appear to represent a more consistent adherence to the economic-political yardstick than the law of Babylonia and Assyria. Here the principle of maintaining the political-economic equilibrium is applied in such a way that even homicides (not to speak of property offenses) are punished exclusively in terms of replacement. It is of interest, therefore, to note that within the Hittite system there are traces of an evolution from earlier to later conceptions. The Old Kingdom edict of Telepinus still permits the kinsman of a slain man to choose between retaliation or composition, while the later law of the code seems to recognize only replacement or composition.[27] And a law of theft in the code (par. 23) records that an earlier capital punishment has been replaced by a pecuniary one.

In the same way it is legitimate to speak of the law of the Bible as archaic in comparison with post-biblical Jewish law. Here again the jural postulate of the biblical law of homicide reached its fullest expression only later: the invaluableness of life led to the virtual abolition of the death penalty. But what distinguishes this abolition from that just described in the Hittite laws, what shows it to be truly in accord with the peculiar inner reason of biblical law, is the fact that it was not accompanied by the institution of any sort of pecuniary compensation. The conditions that had to be met before the death penalty could be inflicted were made so numerous, that is to say, the concern for the life of the accused became so exaggerated, that in effect it was impossible to inflict capital punishment.[28] Nowhere in the account of this process, however, is there a hint that it was ever contemplated to substitute a pecuniary for capital punishment. The same reverence for human life that led to the virtual abolition of the death penalty also forbade setting a value on the life of the slain man. (This reluctance either to execute the culprit or to commute his penalty created a dilemma which Jewish law cannot be said to have coped with successfully.) [29]

Thus the divergences between the biblical and Near Eastern laws of homicide appear not as varying stages of progress or lag along a single line of evolution, but as reflections of differing underlying principles. Nor does the social-political explanation of the divergence seem to be adequate in view of the persistence of the peculiarities of biblical law throughout the monarchial, urbanized age of Israel on the one hand, and the survival of the ancient non-biblical viewpoint in later Bedouin and Arab law on the other.

iv

Another divergence in principle between biblical law and the non-biblical law of the ancient Near East is in the matter of vicarious punishment—the infliction of a penalty on the person of one other than the actual culprit. The principle of talion is carried out in cuneiform law to a degree which at times involves vicarious punishment. A creditor who has so maltreated the distrained son of his debtor that he dies, must lose his own son.[30] If a man struck the pregnant daughter of another so that she miscarried and died, his own daughter must be put to death.[31] If through faulty construction a house collapses killing the householder's son, the son of the builder who built the house must be put to death.[32] A seducer must deliver his wife to the seduced girl's father for prostitution.[33] In another class are penalties which involve the substitution of a dependent for the offender—the Hittite laws compelling a slayer to deliver so many persons to the kinsmen of the slain, or prescribing that a man who has pushed another into a fire must give over his son; the Assyrian penalties substituting a son, brother, wife, or slave of the murderer "instead of blood." [34] Crime and punishment are here defined from the standpoint of the pater-familias: causing the death of a child is punished by the death of a child. At the same time the members of the family have no separate individuality vis-à-vis the head of the family. They are extensions of him and may be disposed of at his discretion. The person of the dependent has no independent footing.

As is well known, the biblical law of Deuteronomy 24:16 explicitly excludes this sort of vicarious punishment: "Parents shall not be put to death for children, nor children for parents; each shall be put to death for his own crime." The proper understanding of this requires, first, that it be recognized as a judicial provision, not a theological dictum. It deals with an entirely different realm than Deuteronomy 5:9 and Exodus 20:5, which depict God as "holding children to account to the third and fourth generations for the sins of their parents." [85] This is clear from the verb יומת, "shall be put to death," referring always to judicial execution and not to death at the hand of God.[36] To be sure, Jeremiah and Ezekiel transfer this judicial provision to the theological realm, the first promising that in the future, the second insisting that in the present, each man die for his own sin—but both change יומת to ימות (Jeremiah 31:29; Ezekiel 18:4 and passim).

This law is almost universally considered late. On the one hand, it is supposed to reflect in law the theological dictum of Ezekiel; on the other, the dissolution of the family and the "weakening of the old patriarchal position of the house father" that attended the urbanization of Israel during the monarchy.[37] This latter reasoning, at any rate, receives no support from the law of the other highly urbanized cultures of the ancient Near East. Babylonian, Assyrian, and Hittite civilization was surely no less urbanized than that of monarchial Israel, yet the notion of family cohesiveness and the subjection of dependents to the family head was not abated by this fact.

A late dating of the Deuteronomic provision is shown to be altogether unnecessary from the simple fact that the principle of individual culpability in precisely the form taken in Deuteronomy 24:16 is operative in the earliest law collection of the Bible. What appears as a general principle in Deuteronomy is applied to a case in the Covenant Code law of the goring ox: after detailing the law of an ox who has slain a man or a woman the last clause of the law goes on to say that if the victims are a son or a daughter the same law applies (Exodus 21:31). This clause, a long-standing puzzle for exegetes, has only recently been understood for what it is: a specific repudiation of vicarious punishment in the manner familiar from cuneiform law. There a builder who, through negligence, caused the death of a householder's son must deliver up his own son; here the negligent owner of a vicious ox who has caused the death of another's son or daughter must be dealt with in the same way as when he caused the death of a man or woman, to wit: the owner is to be punished, not his son or daughter.[38] This principle of individual culpability in fact governs all of biblical law. Nowhere does the criminal law of the Bible, in contrast to that of the rest of the Near East, punish secular offenses collectively or vicariously. Murder, negligent homicide, seduction, and so forth, are punished solely on the person of the actual culprit.

What heightens the significance of this departure is the fact that the Bible is not at all ignorant of collective or vicarious punishment. The narratives tell of the case of Achan who appropriated objects devoted to God from the booty of Jericho and buried them under his tent. The anger of God manifested itself in a defeat of Israel's army before Ai. When Achan was discovered, he and his entire household were put to death Joshua 7). Again, the case of Saul's sons, who were put to death for their father's massacre of the Gibeonites in violation of an oath by YHWH (II Samuel 21). Now these instances are not a matter of ordinary criminal law but touch the realm of the deity directly.[38a] The misappropriation of a devoted object—חרם—infects the culprit and all who come into contact with him with the taboo status of the חרם (Deuteronomy 7:26; 13:16; cf. Joshua 6:18). This is wholly analogous to the contagiousness of the state of impurity, and a provision of the law of the impurity of a corpse is really the best commentary on the story of Achan's crime: "This is the law: when a man dies in a tent every one that comes into that tent, and every thing that is in the tent, shall be unclean" (Numbers 19:14). Achan's misappropriated objects—the story tells us four times in three verses (Joshua 7:21, 22, 23)—were hidden in the ground under his tent. Therefore he, his family, his domestic animals, and his tent, had to be destroyed, since all incurred the חרם status. This is not a case, then, of vicarious or collective punishment pure and simple, but a case of collective contagion of a taboo status. Each of the inhabitants of Achan's tent incurred the חרם status for which he was put to death, though, to be sure, the actual guilt of the misappropriation was Achan's alone.

The execution of Saul's sons is a genuine case of vicarious punishment, though it too is altogether extraordinary. A national oath made in the name of God has been violated by a king. A drought interpreted as the wrath of God has struck at the whole nation. The injured party, the Gibeonites, demand life for life and expressly refuse to hear of composition. Since the offending king is dead, his children are delivered up.

These two cases—with Judges 21:10f. the only ones in which legitimate collective and vicarious punishments are recorded in the Bible [39]—show clearly in what area notions of family solidarity and collective guilt are still operative: the area of direct affronts to the majesty of God. Crimes committed against the property, the exclusive rights, or the name of God may be held against the whole family, indeed the whole community of the offender. A principle which is rejected in the case of judicial punishment is yet recognized as operative in the divine realm. The same book of Deuteronomy that clears parents and children of each other's guilt still incorporates the dictum that God holds children to account for their parents' apostasy to the third and fourth generation (5:9). Moreover it is Deuteronomy 13:16 that relates the law of the חרם of the apostate city, ordaining that every inhabitant be destroyed, including the cattle. For the final evidence of the concurrent validity of these divergent standards of judgment the law of the Molech worshiper may be adduced (Leviticus 20: 1–5): a man who worships Molech is to be stoned by the people—he alone; but if the people overlook his sin, "Then I," says God, "will set my face against that man, and against his family . . ." (See postscript.)

The belief in a dual standard of judgment persisted into latest times. Not only Deuteronomy itself, but the literature composed after it continues to exhibit belief in God's dooming children and children's children for the sins of the parents. The prophetess Huldah, who confirms the warnings of Deuteronomy, promises that punishment for the sins of Judah will be deferred until after the time of the righteous king Josiah (II Kings 22:19f.). Jeremiah, who is imbued with the ideology of Deuteronomy, and who is himself acutely aware of the imperfection of the standard of divine justice (31:28f.), yet announces to his personal enemies a doom that involves them and their children (Jeremiah 11:22; 29:32). And both Jeremiah and the Deuteronomistic compiler of the Book of Kings ascribe the fall of Judah to the sin of Manasseh's age (Jeremiah 15:4; II Kings 23:26f.; 34:3f.). Even Job complains that God lets the children of the wicked live happy (21:7ff.). Thus there can be no question of an evolution during the biblical age from early to late concepts, from "holding children to account for the sins of parents" to "parents shall not be put to death for children, etc." There is rather a remarkable divergence between the way God may judge men and the way men must judge each other. The divergence goes back to the earliest legal and narrative texts and persists through the latest.

How anomalous the biblical position is can be appreciated

when set against its Near Eastern background. A telling expression of the parallel between human and divine conduct toward wrongdoing is the following Hittite soliloquy:

> Is the disposition of men and of the gods at all different? No! Even in this matter somewhat different? No! But their disposition is quite the same. When a servant stands before his master . . . [and serves him] . . . his master . . . is relaxed in spirit and is favorably inclined (?) to him. If, however, he (the servant) is ever dilatory (?) or is not observant (?), there is a different disposition towards him. And if ever a servant vexes his master, either they kill him, or [mutilate him]; or he (the master) calls him to account (and also) his wife, his sons, his brothers, his sisters, his relatives by marriage, and his family . . . And if ever he dies, he does not die alone, but his family is included with him. If then anyone vexes the feeling of a god, does the god punish him alone for it? Does he not punish his wife, his children, his descendents, his family, his slaves male and female, his cattle, his sheep, and his harvest for it, and remove him utterly? [40]

To this striking statement it need only be added that not alone between master and servant was the principle of vicarious punishment applied in Hittite and Near Eastern law, but, as we have seen, between parents and children and husbands and wives as well.

In contrast, the biblical view asserts a difference between the power of God, and that of man, over man. Biblical criminal law foregoes entirely the right to punish any but the actual culprit in all civil cases; so far as man is concerned all persons are individual, morally autonomous entities. In this too there is doubtless to be seen the effect of the heightened stress on the unique worth of each life that the religious-legal postulate of man's being the image of God brought about. "All persons are mine, says the Lord, the person of the father as well as that of the son; the person that sins, he shall die" (Ezekiel 18:4). By this assertion Ezekiel wished to make valid in the theological realm the individual autonomy that the law had acknowledged in the criminal realm centuries before. That God may impute responsibility and guilt to the whole circle of a man's family and descendants was a notion that biblical Israel shared with its neighbors. What was unique to Israel was its belief that this was exclusively the way of God; it was unlawful arrogation for man to exercise this divine prerogative.

The study of biblical law, then, with careful attention to its own inner postulates has as much to reveal about the values of Israelite culture as the study of Psalms and Prophets. For the appreciation of this vital aspect of the biblical world, the riches of cuneiform law offer a key that was unavailable to the two millennia of exegesis that preceded our time. The key is now available and the treasury yields a bountiful reward to those who use it.

POSTSCRIPT. To note 38: Professor I. L. Seeligmann calls my attention to the fact that this interpretation was earlier advanced by D. H. Müller, *Die Gesetze Hammurabis* (Wien, 1903), pp. 166ff. A. B. Ehrlich's interpretation (in his *Rand-glossen*, ad loc.) taking בן and בת to mean "free man" and "free woman" in contrast with אמה, עבד of vs. 32 may now be set aside, ingenious as it is (though forced as well: the suggested parallels John 8:35 and Proverbs 17:2 [Seeligmann] deal with matters of inheritance and ownership where son [not "free man"!] and slave are apt contrasts; not so here. Note also the particle אֹו in Exodus 21:31, indicating the vs. to be an appendix to the foregoing, rather than connecting it with the new clause, vs. 32, beginning with אִם).

To p. 32. This interpretation of Leviticus 20:5, understanding the guilt of the family before God as due merely to their association with the Molech-worshiper, is open to question. The intent of the text may rather be to ascribe the people's failure to prosecute the culprit to his family's covering up for him; see Rashi and Ibn Ezra. In that case "his family" of 5a is taken up again in "all who go astray after him" of 5b, and the family is guilty on its own.

Notes

1. J. L. Saalschütz, *Das Mosaiche Recht, mit Berücksichtigung des spätern Jüdischen,* 2 vols. (Berlin, 1848).

2. The following law collections are pertinent to the discussion of the criminal law of the Bible: the laws of Eshnunna (LE), from the first half of the 19th century B.C.; the code of Hammurapi (CH), from the beginning of the 18th century; the Middle Assyrian laws (MAL), 14th–11th centuries; and the Hittite laws (HL), latter half of the 2nd millennium. All are translated in J. B. Pritchard, ed., *Ancient Near Eastern*

Texts Relating to the Old Testament (Princeton, 1955), pp. 159ff. Henceforth this work will be referred to as *ANET*.

3. G. R. Driver and J. C. Miles, *The Babylonian Laws,* 2 vols. (Oxford, 1952, 1955), henceforth cited as BL. The citation is from I, p. 99; cf. also p. 275, where Koschaker's approach is characterized and Miles' approach contrasted.

4. Contrast, e.g., the historical explanation of the discrepancies in the laws of theft given by Meek in *ANET*, p. 166, note 45 with Miles' suggestions in BL I, pp. 80ff. The historical explanation does not help us understand how the draftsman of the law of Hammurapi conceived of the law of theft.

5. The point is made and expertly illustrated in E. A. Hoebel, *The Law of Primitive Man* (Harvard, 1954); cf. especially chap. 1.

6. Inscription of Yahdun-lim of Mari, *Syria* 32 (1955), p. 4, lines 1ff. I owe this reference and its interpretation to Professor E. A. Speiser, whose critique of this part of my discussion has done much to clarify the matter in my mind; cf. his contribution to *Authority and Law in the Ancient Orient* (*Supplement to the Journal of the American Oriental Society,* No. 17 [1954]), especially pp. 11ff.

7. Cf. CH xxvb 95ff.: "I am Hammurapi, the just king, to whom Shamash has granted truths." We are to understand *the laws of Hammurapi as an attempt to embody this cosmic ideal in laws and statutes.* (After writing the above I received a communication from Professor J. J. Finkelstein interpreting this passage as follows: *"What the god 'gives' the king is not 'laws' but the gift of the perception of* kittum, by virtue of which the king, in distinction from any other individual, becomes capable of promulgating laws that are in accord or harmony with the cosmic principle of *kittum.")*

8. Speiser, *op. cit.,* p. 12; this Mesopotamian conception of cosmic truth is a noteworthy illustration of Professor Kaufmann's thesis that "Paganism conceives of morality not as an expression of the supreme, free will of the deity, but as one of the forces of the transcendent, primordial realm which governs the deity as well" (תולדות האמונה הישראלית, I/2, p. 345).

9. CH xxivb 76f., 81; xxvb 12f., 64ff., 78ff., 99; xxvib 3f., 19ff.

10. Ibid. xxvib 33f. It is not clear, in the face of this plain evidence, how it can still be maintained that the relief at the top of the law stele depicts Shamash dictating or giving the code to Hammurapi (E. Dhorme, *Les religions de Babylon et d'Assyrie* [Paris, 1949], p. 62; S. H. Hooke, *Babylonian and Assyrian Religion* [London, 1953], p. 29). The picture is nothing more than a traditional presentation scene in which a worshiper in an attitude of adoration stands before, or is led by another deity into, the presence of a god; it may be inferred from the context (i.e. the position of the picture above the code) that the figures of this highly conventionalized scene represent Hammurapi and Shamash. See the discussion in H. Frankfort, *The Art and Architecture of the Ancient Orient* (1954), p. 59 (note that Frankfort does not even go so far as Meek who sees in the scene "Hammurabi in the act of receiving the commission to write the law-book from . . . Shamash" [*ANET*, p. 163]). For this and similar representations see J. B. Pritchard, *The Ancient Near East in Pictures* (Princeton, 1954), nos. 514, 515, 529, 533, 535, 707. Miles aptly sums up the matter of the authorship of the laws thus (BL, 39): "Although [Shamash and Marduk] . . . are mentioned a number of times, they are not said to be the authors of the Laws; Hammurabi himself

claims to have written them. Their general character, too, is completely secular, and in this respect they are strongly to be contrasted with the Hebrew laws; they are not a divine pronouncement nor in any sense a religious document."

11. Epilogue to the laws of Lipit-Ishtar, *ANET*, p. 161.

12. See the prologue and epilogue of the laws of Lipit-Ishtar and Hammurapi.

13. The point is made in Kaufmann, *op. cit.*, I/1, p. 67.

14. CH 129; MAL 14–16; HL 198; cf. W. Kornfeld, "L'adultère dans l'orient antique," *Revue biblique* 57 (1950), pp. 92ff.; E. Neufeld, *Ancient Hebrew Marriage Laws* (London, 1944), pp. 172ff.

15. HL 187, 188, 198, 199; cf. LE 48.

16. HL 1–4.

17. A. Kennett, *Bedouin Justice* (Cambridge, 1925), pp. 49ff.

18. LE 54; CH 250, 251.

19. Strict retaliation of life for life is "primitive," a "desert principle"; cf. Th. J. Meek, *Hebrew Origins* (New York, 1936), pp. 66, 68; Alt, *Die Ursprünge des israelitischen Rechts*, in *Kleine Schriften zur Geschichte des Volkes Israel* (München, 1953), pp. 305ff.; A. Kennett, *op. cit.*, p. 49; on the goring ox, cf. BL I, 444; M. Weber, *Ancient Judaism* (Glencoe, 1952), p. 62. For the widely held theory of the development of punishment which underlies this view see BL I, 500.

20. The peculiarities that distinguish this biblical law from the Babylonian are set forth fully by A. van Selms, "The Goring Ox in Babylonian and Biblical Law," *Archiv Orientální* 18 (1950), pp. 321ff., though he has strangely missed the true motive for stoning the ox and tabooing its flesh.

21. From the comment of Sifre to Deuteronomy 19:13a it is clear that this paradox was already felt in antiquity.

22. Driver-Miles, *The Assyrian Laws* (Oxford, 1935), p. 35.

23. Ibid., p. 36; Kennett, *op. cit.*, pp. 26f., 54f.

24. This interpretation follows Goetze's translation (*ANET*, p. 191, cf. especially note 9). Since no specific punishment is mentioned, and in view of the recognition by Hittite law of the principle of replacing life by life (cf. HL 44) there does not seem to be any ground for assuming that any further punishment beyond forced incorporation into the injured community was contemplated (E. Neufeld, *The Hittite Laws* [London, 1951], p. 158).

25. CH 21, 25; LE 13 (cf. A. Goetze, *The Laws of Eshnunna, Annual of the American Schools of Oriental Research* 31 [New Haven, 1956], p. 53); CH 6–10; MAL 3. Inasmuch as our present interest is in the theoretical postulates of the law systems under consideration, the widely held opinion that these penalties were not enforced in practice, while interesting in itself, is not relevant to our discussion.

26. The action of vs. 1 occurs at night; cf. vs. 2 and Job 24:16. Vs. 2 is to be rendered: "If it occurred after dawn, there is bloodguilt for (killing) him; he must make payment only (and is not subject to death); if he can not, then he is to be sold for his theft" (but he is still not subject to death—contrast CH 8). For the correct interpretation see Rashi and U. Cassuto, *Commentary on Exodus* (Jerusalem, 1951), ad loc. (Hebrew); Cassuto points out (ibid., p. 196) that this law is an amendment to the custom reflected in CH's laws of theft—a fact which is entirely obscured by the transposition of verses in the Chicago Bible and the Revised Standard Version. Later jurists doubtless correctly inter-

preted the householder's privilege as the result of a presumption against the burglar that he would not shrink from murder; the privilege, then, is subsumed under the right of self-defense (Mechilta, ad loc.).

27. O. Gurney, *The Hittites* (London, 1952), p. 98.

28. Mishnah Sanhedrin 5.1ff., Gemara, ibid. 40b bottom; cf. Mishnah Makkoth 1.10.

29. To deal with practical exigencies it became necessary to invest the court with extraordinary powers which permitted suspension of all the elaborate safeguards that the law provided the accused; cf. J. Ginzberg, *Mishpatim Le-israel, A study in Jewish Criminal Law* (Jerusalem, 1956), part I, chap. 2; part II, chap. 4.

30. CH 116.

31. CH 209–210; cf. MAL 50.

32. CH 230.

33. MAL 55.

34. HL 1–4, 44; see also note 22 above.

35. Ibn Ezra in his commentary to Deuteronomy 24:16 already inveighs against the erroneous combination of the two dicta; the error has persisted through the centuries (cf. e.g. B. D. Eerdmans, *The Religion of Israel* [Leiden, 1947], p. 94).

36. Later jurists differed with regard to but one case יומת הקרב והזר (Numbers 1:51; 3:10; 18:7) according to Gemara Sanhedrin 84a (cf. Mishnah Sanhedrin 9.6); but the scholar to whom the Gemara ascribes the opinion that יומת here means by an act of God (R. Ishmael) is quoted in the Sifre to Numbers 18:7 as of the opinion that a judicial execution is intended (so Ibn Ezra at Numbers 1:51). The unanimous opinion of the rabbis that Exodus 21:29 refers to death by an act of God (Mechilta) is a liberalizing exegesis; see the ground given in Gemara Sanhedrin 15b.

37. J. M. Powis Smith, *The Origin and History of Hebrew Law* (Chicago, 1931), p. 66; Weber, *op. cit.*, p. 66.

38. Cassuto, commentary ad loc.; P. J. Verdam, "On ne fera point mourir les enfants pour les pères en droit biblique," *Revue internationale des droits de l'antiquité* 2/3 (1949), p. 393ff. (See postscript.)

38a. Recognized by Verdam, *op. cit.*, p. 408, and already by S. R. Driver in his commentary to Deuteronomy (*ICC*, 1909), p. 277.

39. The massacre of the priestly clan at Nob (I Samuel 22:19) and the execution of Naboth's sons (II Kings 9:26) are not represented as lawful. Both cases involve treason, for which it appears to have been customary to execute the whole family of the offender. This custom, by no means confined to ancient Israel (Cf. Jos. Antiq. 13.14.2), is not to be assumed to have had legal sanction, though it was so common that Amaziah's departure from it deserved to be singled out for praise (II Kings 14:6).

40. Gurney, *op. cit.*, pp. 70f.

3.

Amos vs. Amaziah

by Shalom Spiegel

Foreword

[On September 13, 1957, there gathered at The Jewish Theological Seminary of America in New York, a distinguished group of scholars and theologians, laymen, rabbis and students. They assembled to take part in a weekend convocation on the theme, "Law as a Moral Force." Among the members of this gathering were The Honorable Earl Warren, Chief Justice of the United States, and former President Harry S. Truman.

The purpose of the assembly was to study the insights into law as a moral force found in ancient Hebrew texts, and to evaluate the importance of these insights to the problems of modern life. The success of the undertaking was attested by the response of many of the participants who discovered in the ancient materials presented new avenues to analyses of modern moral problems. Chief Justice Warren remarked on the sense of humility which comes with the knowledge that "most of the good things that we find in our law and in our own institutions come from the wisdom of men of other ages."

The analysis of the case of *Amos versus Amaziah,* presented here, was one of the principal addresses of the convocation weekend. Professor Spiegel graciously agreed to prepare his notes for publication in response to the urgent request of members of the audience, who wished to have copies of the speech.]

Amos vs. Amaziah *

The sun and soil of California yield many delights and blessings for all of us to enjoy, among them native sons who (like the sturdy stock of Missouri) are the pride of the nation. In that good soil and sun of the west there thrive gigantic trees, often attaining a height of over three hundred feet, probably the oldest living things on the earth. In the Sequoia National Park I saw a huge trunk of such a redwood used as a visual aid for a history lesson. The mighty stem, cut across, shows annual rings marking spring and summer growth, and so can be used to measure time. It was a happy thought to have major facts of human history indented in the wood. It is sobering to discover how paltry human affairs may seem, how puny all the sweat and swagger of man when set against the lifetime of a tree. Remote and distinctive events in modern history (the discovery of America, for example) are reduced to size by the gnarly rings of the redwood. Still, there are other, older memories of the race which cut an impressive distance in time or space, even when measured by the rings of a giant tree.

Such is the incident I would like to recall from the pages of Scripture, reaching back about 2700 years, or roughly half the life span of the venerable evergreen, *Sequoia sempervirens.*

A. The Trial of Amos

The scene is Bethel in northern Israel, in the second half of the eighth pre-Christian century, a generation or so before the ten tribes of that kingdom were trampled in the dust or scattered to the winds by the fierce onslaught of Assyria. Amos, a shepherd from Tekoa, across the border in Judah, stirred up a commotion when, in a crowded assembly, perhaps in the temple of the realm, he told of dire visions his Lord had shown him:

> Thus He showed me: Behold, the Lord was standing beside a wall built by a plumbline, with a plumbline in His hand.

* New York, Herbert H. Lehman Institute of Ethics, The Jewish Theological Seminary of America, 1957.

And the Lord said unto me: "Amos, what do you see?" And I said, "A plumbline." Then the Lord said: "Behold, I am setting a plumbline in the midst of My people Israel, and I will never again pass by them. The high places of Isaac shall be desolate, and the sanctuaries of Israel shall be laid waste, and I shall rise against the house of Jeroboam with the sword."

Then Amaziah, the priest of Bethel, sent to Jeroboam, king of Israel, saying: "Amos has conspired against you in the midst of the house of Israel; the land is not able to bear all his words. For thus Amos has said: 'Jeroboam shall die by the sword, and Israel must go into exile away from his land.' "

And Amaziah said to Amos: "O seer, go, flee away to the land of Judah, and eat bread there, and prophesy there; but never again prophesy at Bethel, for it is the king's sanctuary, and it is a temple of the kingdom."

Then Amos answered Amaziah: "I am no prophet, nor a prophet's son; but I am a herdsman, and a dresser of sycamore trees, and the Lord took me from following the flock, and the Lord said to me: 'Go, prophesy to My people Israel.' " (Amos 7:7–15)

Amaziah at once instituted legal proceedings for the deportation of an undesirable alien. The Judean prophet promptly challenged his authority to deprive him of the right of free domicile and free speech in a sister state of the union. Fervently Amos declared that he had been summoned by the Lord to prophesy to His people Israel, a people one and indivisible whose union and covenant could not be lawfully dissolved by action of separate tribes or states, or even by their secession.

It stands to reason that the case *Amos vs. Amaziah* attracted wide attention in its own time and remained a *cause célèbre* to be discussed in law classes and debated in moot courts for generations. Unfortunately, Amaziah left no records of his own, or at least they have not survived. But the indictment of the prophet by the people and priests of Bethel, and the brief of argument prepared by the council of experts, were probably widely studied and excerpted in the textbooks and schools of antiquity. Maybe some day a fortunate discovery by the spade of an archeologist, in the warm sand dunes in the Judean desert or in a cave of the Dead Sea region, will turn up a tattered scroll with information now lost. Until such day or find, we must try to reconstruct the case of Amaziah solely on the basis of the scriptural account, the book of Amos. Still, we must remember that this book is but the deposition of the aggrieved party, a victim of expulsion, and that we owe his opponent, the priest of Bethel, a fair and full opportunity to state his version of the encounter with the seer of Tekoa. *Audiatur et altera pars.*

It seems best to start with one initial assumption: that throughout the trial Amaziah never chose to challenge the accuracy of the transcript of public addresses as left by Amos himself or submitted on his behalf by his disciples, in short, essentially the record as preserved in Scripture. Only such a premise would make re-enactment of the trial at all possible in our day, in the absence of any other documentation. But even in his own day, Amaziah could reap thereby two advantages. He could considerably speed up all legal procedures, and if successful, could have the prophet condemned by his own mouth, as it were—a legal master stroke. Astutely, therefore, Amaziah would begin by reading from the speeches admittedly delivered by Amos, for example, the passage spoken in the sanctuary while the priests were offering sacrifices and the people beseeching Heaven to accept their alms and chants with favor:

> I hate, I despise your feasts, and I take no delight in your solemn assemblies.
> Even though you offer me burnt offerings and meal offerings, I will not accept them, nor will I look upon the peace offerings of your fatted beasts.
> Take away from Me the noise of your songs, and let Me not hear the melody of your harps.
> But let justice roll down like waters, and righteousness as a mighty stream.
> Did you bring to me sacrifices and offerings the forty years in the wilderness, O house of Israel?
>
> (Amos 5:21–25)

The words, as rehearsed on the lips of the priest, did seem unmistakably a disturbance of public peace and interference with the rights of free worship. Such unwarranted provocation could not but throw any assembly, however orderly or decorous, into panic and pandemonium, in grave disregard of the fire laws, a clear and present danger to the life and limb of a throng of worshippers. Indeed no better case could be made, anywhere at any time, for immediate action by the police.

It was now up to the court to consider the measures taken by the temple police, and to review the validity of the prophet's banishment from Bethel. Naturally, Amaziah saw to it that his cause was buttressed by a formidable array of experts and leading representatives of public opinion.

The acknowledged head of religion in the realm, Amaziah spoke first, as was expected of him. In measured language, he voiced grave concern over the theological implications in the teachings of Amos, fraught, as he saw them, with hazard and heresy. This was the more dangerous precisely because some of Amos' tenets seemed plausible or even laudable, as, for example, his zeal for justice, and his commiseration with the needy and the poor. These were virtues which the just king Jeroboam and his priests at Bethel enjoined on all citizens, invariably urging pilgrims to the shrines to remember the destitute and help the disinherited. For they were indeed basic requirements of the covenant, primary duties of man to fellowman.

However, beyond and above these, extend the obligations of man to God, among them foremost regular ritual and worship in the sanctuary, which brought as a sweet savor to the Lord the gifts of His children, and implored for all of them the bounty of heaven: rain in season from above and springs in abundance from below, rich fields and teeming flocks, the fruit of the body and the fruit of the earth.

To be sure, in normal times, there need never arise a conflict between the claims of men upon each other and the claims of God upon men. However, should such collision of duties ever occur, there cannot be the slightest doubt which of the two demands must take precedence. Certainly what we owe to creature can never compare to what we owe to the Creator. If neglect of man be sin, neglect of God is sacrilege. This Judean seer, however, would have us turn the tables perversely. So long as men clamor for justice, he would forbid all acts of devotion in the sanctuary. Unless the needs of the poor be supplied, he would have us shut up all the establishments of the cult. But "the poor will never cease out of the land" (Deuteronomy 15:11), which means that all the venerable rites in the temple as practiced by our ancestors from time immemorial, will have to be suspended, and the sacrifices stopped, and religion as known to us abolished from the face of the earth. It is a reckless doctrine, ruinous to worship and to the welfare of the commonwealth. For what are the solemn performances of ritual if not exercises in piety and patriotism? Indeed, what is sacrifice if not learning to give up for the common good? It is through such acts of renunciation—of food, of valuable possessions, of the inordinate part of our wills—that men are led to conform with the will of God and the requirements of religion. The rich and the rapacious are weaned of their selfishness and taught to share with the poor at least a part of their crop or wealth. Greed is thus subdued and charity towards the poor secured precisely through the observances and ordinances of organized religion.

Abolish altars and discontinue sacrifices, would not the lost and miserable be the first to suffer? It is the discipline of temple worship which thrusts fear of the Lord even into the hearts of the mighty, enjoining them to divide their goods with their less fortunate brethren. Without such restraints and donations of piety, would not despair overtake the weak, the widow, and the orphan?

Amos threatens us with an earthquake for our alleged iniquities and abominations. Should *his* view ever prevail, and the land be bare of its altars and shrines and—God forbid—the affronted heavens refuse to yield rain, and the soil be blighted with drought, and man and cattle suffer famine and death, as happens anyhow from time to time; should his view prevail, would not the wretched and the hungry be first to seize the unblest prophet and drive him out in scorn, or in rage fling his mangled body beyond the gates of Bethel, to lie there unburied like the carcass of an ass?

A hushed dread hung over the court and crowd, as the priest spoke of perils to a country bereft of the protection of its divine rites. Now, sure of his impression on the audience, Amaziah turned in conclusion to Amos, speaking forgivingly and almost entreatingly: "O seer, go! Starry-eyed dreamer, impractical idealist, for your own safety, for the peace of your own soul, to keep your virtue untainted and your illusions undamaged, go away of your own accord, flee to the solitude of your flocks and forests of Tekoa!"

If, however, the shepherd should prove obstinate and refuse to leave, Amaziah felt duty-bound to submit to the court an official request and recommendation for deportation, signed without dissent by all the members of the College of Priests at Bethel.

The next speaker was chosen to represent the Association of the Bar of the City of Bethel. Skilled in the arts of rhetoric, and following the custom of the ancients, he would begin with a deft compliment to the wisdom and honesty of the court whose true administration of justice was the firmest pillar of good government. He would then proceed to win the favor of the crowd by a play for laughter. He would ridicule the simplistic jurisprudence of the shepherd of Tekoa with his appeal to the old, good days and ways of the desert: "Did you bring to me sacrifices and offerings the forty years in the wilderness, O house of Israel?" Such return to primitivism would wipe out all the advances of civilization won by a proud and prosperous people in half a millennium since it left the wasteland.

After such preliminaries, the speaker would proceed to the heart of his argument. Examined closely, the new doctrines of Amos amount to arbitrary abrogation of an undisputed part of legal theory and practice regulating the procedure in the gate and the rites of ancestral worship. They break with the tradition of secular and sacred law as heretofore known in Israel. How irresponsible, at bottom, his invocation of justice, always a sign of the ignorant layman unschooled to think in legal terms.[1]

By easy, hazy appeals to righteousness and the whole cluster of virtues, he would have us disestablish the uncontested basis of all common law, whose working rule must be *stare decisis:* to adhere to and abide by decided cases. Without regard, indeed, without reverence for legal precedent, the scales of justice can not be kept even and steady; there would be no stability, no predictability, no certainty in the law. The courts would be thrown open to chance and whim and arbitrariness. There would be no desire for knowledge of law or legal precedent, hence also no need for the practice of law as a profession, and no demand for lawyers. This is no selfish or narrow professional appeal on behalf of the Bar. Without the safeguards of statutory law, and the standards of common law, and the canons of holy law, who would be the first victims of unscrupulous and bribable judges? Certainly not the rich and the haughty who can buy or bully justice in the gate, but the helpless, the fatherless, the friendless would be abandoned to greed and the guile of the moneyed, and to magistrates unrestrained by legal principle or precedent. Would not the very poor in desperation band together against their would-be tribune and cast his maimed body to the dunghill? To forestall mob outburst and lynch law which would sully the good reputation of the country, the lawyers of Bethel in duly convoked plenary session unanimously voted to ask for an injunction restraining the stranger of Tekoa from harassing the public peace, returning him to his native land, in protective custody if necessary, until he had safely reached the borders of Judea.

The third to speak in court was a lady, appearing on behalf of the Daughters of the Confederacy—that is, the Confederacy of the Tribes of Israel. She found the message of the Judean herdsman very disturbing: "Are you not like the Ethiopians to Me, O children of Israel? says the Lord. Did I not bring up Israel from the land of Egypt, and the Philistines from Caphtor, and Aram from Kir?" (Amos 9:7). This seemed ill-bred, ill-tempered, and altogether illogical. Are we not Israel, and thus, unlike the heathen, in a very special and intimate and incomparable relation to the God of Israel? Of course, of course, since there is but one God, He must be the God of the whole world. But does this necessarily imply that God cares no more for the people of the covenant which He freed from bondage than He cares for their inveterate enemies, the uncircumcised Philistines? Naturally lines of communication must be maintained between the one God of the universe and all the peoples of the earth. We, the Daughters of the Confederacy, neither question nor deny any race equal access to the Lord, but cannot such access to the Lord be made *equal but separate?* The doctrine of equal but separate for white Israel and for dark-skinned Ethiopians would secure facilities of religious uplift to all, keeping them universal yet not uniform. Provisions permitting or even requiring the separation of the races do not necessarily imply inferiority of either race to the other. It is a fallacy that such a doctrine would stamp the colored race with the badge of inferiority.[2] If this be so, it is not by reason of anything in Israel's religion or law, but solely because the colored Ethiopians choose to put that construction upon it.

In any event, the lady speaker concluded, there is no reason in the world why this unmannered, unneighborly agitator should be suffered to abuse the traditional freedom and amity of the fair peoples of the North.

Similar disapproval was voiced in the name of the Hebrew Legion, on behalf of the Veterans of the Israelitish Wars of Independence. The spokesman, in a neat army uniform, called attention to the slur on patriotism and danger to good citizenship, if the ideas of Amos were freely to be advocated: "You only have I known of all the families of the earth; therefore I will punish you for all your iniquities" (Amos 3:2). Such notions are plainly subversive of all soldierly and civic virtue, a threat to the security of the nation which had just emerged victorious from a long struggle with Aram. Consider also statements worded with deliberate slipperiness: "Behold, the eyes of the Lord God are upon the sinful kingdom, and I will destroy it from off the face of the earth, except that I will not utterly destroy the house of Jacob, said the Lord" (Amos 9:8). The ambiguity seems designed, permitting two interpretations. Either it is sheer bias in favor of Judah, called here "the house of Jacob," which will escape destruction, while the "sinful kingdom" or our northern realm is threatened with death by this partisan propagandist of the South. Or, still worse, the last clause with its negative particle placed conspicuously out of its customary word order in Hebrew,[3] would seem to suggest that like any other guilty people, sinful Israel, too, will be destroyed: why should the house of Jacob alone claim exception from divine justice? This insults the valiant heroes of the nation and her slain on the field of battle who defended to the very last what all deemed their honor and their duty "right or wrong—my country."

Amaziah received many messages of support which he wisely kept unheralded. An expert in public relations, he shrewdly avoided even the faintest suspicion of being swayed by the pressure of lobbyists for private or collective interests. This is why no mention was made of the protest of the Chamber of Commerce in Bethel and Gilgal, alarmed at what a stoppage of pilgrimages to their shrines might do to the tourist trade of those holy cities. Nor would Amaziah release for publication vehement attacks on the prophet because of his denunciation of sacrifices and rejection of all offerings in the temples, which roused the ire of the *Meat and Poultry Purveyors,* the *Dairymen's League,* and the *Consolidated Wholesale Florists of Northern Israel.* Similarly, he ignored frantic appeals made by powerful temple unions such as the *Congress of Liturgical Organizations* which warned of disastrous unemployment, if the sanctuaries be closed.

Amaziah made only one exception, and disclosed a communication received from the *Israelitish Society of Composers, Authors, and Publishers,* known popularly as *ISCAP.* It minced no words about the boorishness of the Judean shepherd as shown in an utterance incredible in this day and age if it were not well attested: "Take away from Me the noise of your songs, and let Me not hear the melody of your harps." Such hostility to music and psalmody, such hatred of art and culture, shows up the man for what he is, an uncouth rustic and fanatic who should promptly be returned where he belongs, to his sheep and sycamores in Tekoa.

One could go on; with the benefit of hindsight it is easy to laugh at lost causes and caricature the past. That so much wit can be implied in the Writ, shows not only the pertinacity of human traits, but also the pertinence and recurring appeal of Scripture.

In justice to the ancients, however, we must not lose sight of the amazing freedom of speech in the northern kingdom of Israel. After all, Amos was not burned at the stake, nor liquidated in a political witch-craft trial, nor even condemned to drink the cup of hemlock by an enraged citizenry. He was permitted peaceably to repair to his native Tekoa where he wrote his book, which after two years—because of an earthquake he was believed to have foretold—made him nationally famous, and ultimately a part of the most widely read book in civilization.

In short, the banishment of Amos from Bethel proved an act of folly very soon. The prophet was vindicated within his lifetime by his own generation and upheld by every subsequent generation, no one dissenting. The decision of the clergy or court at Bethel was repudiated by the people, and one can say in a very real sense that it was *repealed* by the inclusion of the book of Amos in the biblical canon. It is this unanimous verdict of history, not the blunder at Bethel, which we have in mind when speaking of the case of *Amos vs. Amaziah*. This is the verdict which haunts the memory, and will forever merit the attention of students of religion and students of law.

B. A Parallel in American History: Marbury vs. Madison

And it is in this sense that one may speak of *Amos vs. Amaziah* as a landmark in Jewish history. For a period of three hundred years (from 750–430 B. C.), the age of classical prophecy hammered deeply into the conscience of the people the implications of all Amos thought and taught. In ceaseless, passionate denunciation, his successors and disciples exhorted and upbraided the nation, which hallowed their words, and set them alongside their ancient legacy, the Torah of Moses, as part of Sacred Scripture.

It is difficult to compare the impact of *Amos vs. Amaziah* with anything in secular history. One naturally hesitates to apply modern categories to times when men still walked and talked with God. But there is a good point to what George Eliot said in one of her poems, the gist of which is that God himself might conceivably make better fiddles than Stradivari's, but by no means certainly, since as a matter of fact, God orders his best fiddles of Stradivari. The rabbis may have had something similar in mind when they declared that "Scripture speaks a human tongue," [4] which at once would validate the whole science of comparative law, literature and linguistics, indeed any study of history which sheds light on man. In this spirit, one may suggest a parallel to *Amos vs. Amaziah* from recent history: *Marbury vs. Madison* (1803), a landmark in American constitutional law.

This famous decision of John Marshall laid down the principle of judicial review of the constitutionality of legislation— a peculiarly American doctrine, one which is America's contribution to the science of law. It vests with the Supreme Court exclusive power to pass upon the validity of acts of legislature, and to declare void any statute repugnant to the constitution. No word or hint in the constitution gave the judiciary this power to annul legislation, nor was there any precedent for it in the British system of government where parliament is supreme, free and unrestrained by courts. It is altogether the achievement of a man of courage and vision who lent effectual enforcement to the limitations on power written into the constitution, and thus made possible the American experiment of liberty under law.

John Marshall was a backwoodsman, not a bookman. He was bred by the frontier, and his formal training in the law consisted in attending, for perhaps six weeks in all,[5] lectures at William and Mary College given by George Wythe, afterwards chancellor of Virginia. But Marshall was endowed with a bold mind, extraordinary power of logic, robust common sense, and a love of fun and laughter.

Many a tale preserves the flavor of the man. Rumor had it that he was partial to good wine, that his fondness for a special variety imported from Madeira was so well known, one of the most popular brands of that wine was called "Supreme Court." Now occasionally the judges in Washington had spasms of reform and would decide to get along without wine at dinner, except on rainy days. It was not long before Marshall would turn to his friend and associate at the Court, saying: "Brother Story, step to the window and see if it does not look like rain." Joseph Story (whose learning was the perfect complement to Marshall's gift of logic) would dolefully report that the sun was shining brightly. Whereupon the Chief Justice ruled: "Our jurisdiction extends over so large a territory that the law of chance makes it certain that it must be raining somewhere," and ordered his Madeira.[6]

Obviously, a man of such ready resourcefulness, who could not playfully deny himself, could not in earnest deny the whole nation, about to conquer a continent, the stable government it needed. He was convinced the new republic had passed that stage of its growth when it could advantageously employ either the *appeal to heaven* or the *appeal to the people*. The first, as John Locke taught [7] and as the generation of the war of independence well remembered, meant the people's resort to arms in defense of their threatened liberties. Appeal to heaven was the right to revolution, a dangerous principle of statecraft in a post-revolutionary period of history, when the survival of the new nation demanded a durable social order above all. The ghosts of Daniel Shay's infamous rebellion still lingered in people's memory. Marshall also maintained a healthy scepticism of those who, like Thomas Jefferson, wanted to refer final decision in *every* constitutional controversy to the consent of the governed or the people as a whole, the sovereign fountainhead of legitimacy. Marshall believed the people's exercise of their right to establish a constitution was a very great exertion,[8] a rare historic exaltation which by its nature cannot and ought not commonly and continually be repeated. Furthermore, frequent appeal to the people was no way to ensure or enforce constitutional rights, for it would needlessly disturb the nation's tranquility, and make the passions and not the reason of the public sit in judgment. *Appeal to the courts*, rather than appeal to heaven or appeal to the people, would give the very fabric of government a steadying force. It would moreover render the constitution capable of enduring for ages by interpretative adaptation to the changing needs of the future. In *Marbury vs. Madison* judicial supremacy was recognized and the judiciary declared the protector of basic liberties of the people, and the ultimate arbiter of what is and what is not law under the constitution.

The full implications of this epochal decision John Marshall may have never contemplated, nor may the short span of the century and a half since his time fully exhaust these implications. What Marshall received was scarcely more than a parchment, what he transmitted was a viable instrument for the reign of law on a new and vast mainland. The practice of judicial review of legislation raised the constitution beyond the reach of statute and state, elevating and enthroning it as the paramount law in the land. Marshall made a community of language a community in law as well. He thus became one of the chief architects not only of the supremacy of the constitution, but also of the indivisible oneness of the nation. It has been rightly said [9] that his was the theory of America for which Webster spoke, and Grant fought, and Lincoln died, a theory now a cornerstone of the republic.

To be sure, the theory had its predecessors, and was neither novel nor original. What accounts for its extraordinary effect is its ready acceptance by the people. An old story from the days of the American revolution tells of an excited lady in Philadelphia asking Benjamin Franklin if it were true that we had a republic. "Yes, madam, if you can keep it," was his sage reply. John Marshall succeeded in establishing judicial supremacy because the people have been willing to keep it. The nation took to it, and their common consent and constant cooperation made it work. The sheer existence of judicial review, even without its being exercised, shields the Bill of Rights by restraining Congress and State from passing laws restrictive of liberty. Trust in the law as the mainstay of freedom has become a mark of the national character. As an educational and moral force *Marbury vs. Madison* has shaped the American mind. To all this must be added its legal import, of which it was possible to say without extravagance: "Upon this rock the nation has been built." [10]

Amos vs. Amaziah can be said to have had a similar influence in the history of Israel. The decision has been woven into the very fiber of Jewish institutions, and has molded the character of the Jewish people. Down to this day, its insights color the common outlook of the Jew, inform his folkways, enter his every day speech. The subsequent career of Judaism bears the indelible imprint of that verdict.

C. Semantics of Justice

What made *Amos vs. Amaziah* weigh so heavily in the annals of history? I can only attempt a hint or an inkling of an answer.

I do so best by returning to the vision of Amos, as he saw the Lord standing beside a wall with a plumbline in His hand. It is a homely lesson any mason could understand and impart: a wall to stand and to endure must be straight and strong, without fault of construction. If it be out of plumb, the taller the wall, the surer its fall. The imagery seems to suggest that what the law of gravitation is to nature, justice is to society. Or in the language of Isaiah (30:13–14) who embellished the thought of Amos: iniquity in a commonwealth is like a crack in a high wall; barely visible, it can bring the entire structure tumbling down, the crash coming suddenly, in an instant, like that of a potter's vessel smashed so ruthlessly not one sherd is left with which to scoop up fire from a hearth or to dip water out of a cistern.

Such images and ideas were prompted no doubt by the very meaning of the Hebrew words for "just" and "righteous," and by their synonyms: "straight" (*yashar*), "steady" (*ken*), "firm" (*nakhon*), "sound" (*tam*) or "whole" (*shalem*). "He leadeth me in paths of righteousness" (Psalms 23:3) actually means "in a straight path." "Perfect and just weight you shall have" (Deuteronomy 25:15) refers to whole and intact weight. Even the Hebrew root for "faith" or "truth" can be used of a house: "I shall build you a faithful (or a true) house" (1 Kings 11:38), that is to say, a sure and firm house, able to last. Of the aging Moses who kept his arms in uplifted position until the sun set, it is said in the Hebrew Bible: His hands were "faith," or "truth"; that is, his hands were steady. A sanctuary is "justified" (Daniel 8:14), when it is rebuilt or restored. Righteous and strong can be synonyms in Hebrew (Isaiah 49:24). Therefore when prophet and psalmist stress God's "righteousness and strength" (Isaiah 45:24, see Psalms 71:16–19), they really want to say that His is infinite strength. The examples could be easily multiplied,[11] but enough is indicated to show the underlying notion that *justice is strength,* by which a social structure is able to maintain itself. It is as if the very roots of the Hebrew words would whisper that what soundness is to construction, or health to the body, justice is to society.

These are edifying thoughts worthy of the holy tongue, the language of the Holy Writ. But they are nothing new, they are inherent in Hebrew, inherited and hardened as it were by household habits of the vernacular long before Amos met Amaziah. Amos and Amaziah shared alike the living legacy of the language in which both were bred, and imbibed such figures and metaphors from infancy. These are common speech patterns, natural and native to Hebrew, deriving their persuasiveness from the semantic subsoil of the root words themselves. But is not that precisely their limitation? Their very involvement with the Hebrew language would make them parochial.

D. Rite and Right

There is hardly a people or culture which from the earliest times did not seek a larger validation for its peculiar way of life. All peoples sense a connection between what they hold to be right and mysterious forces operating in nature. "Even the stork in heavens knows her seasons, and the turtle dove, the swallow and thrush keep the time of their coming, but my people know not the ordinance of the Lord" (Jeremiah 8:7). Not only the philosophers assume and assert kinship between the moral law within and the starry universe without. Every society would like to convince itself that what it cares for most is approved of by the gods, and has its source and support in the ground of reality itself. The pity of it is that men only too often succeed in giving their local ardors and tribal zeals cosmic sanction.

To take a concrete example: The more we know of Chinese art, poetry, and philosophy of life, the more we admire the heights that civilization attained. The ideal of the serene sage as exemplified by Confucius, and his vision of a tranquil society, have had a deep hold and long influence on the soul of China, and explain the unique veneration, even state-cult, he enjoyed throughout the ages. Now it is characteristic of Confucianism that it assumes a universal natural order in the heart of man as well as in the physical universe. It knows of five basic relations between men: of prince to subject, father to son, husband to wife, elder brother to younger, and friend to friend. These correspond to five geographic points (center, south, north, east and west), five planets, five metals, five cereals, five colors and five sounds. There is constant interaction between these pentads in the larger order of nature and in the world of man. By living in conformity with the moral law, man helps to sustain the harmony of the universe.

Human society is founded on duties flowing from the five principal relationships, taught by the example of the wise and just ruler, and divined by everybody through the observance of rites which, in association with music, will suffice to secure peace throughout the realm. Scholars, too, perform a useful and necessary function in society by giving things their exact definition and designation. Known as the "doctrine of rectification of names," this praise of learning and of the proper use of logic and language springs from the assumption that if words are misused, language will not conform to reality and affairs will not prosper, rites and music will languish and chaos will ensue both among men and in the nature of things.[12]

Knowledge of the nature of things and compliance with the natural laws are the way (tao) of wisdom and virtue, and concord between heaven and earth is their result and reward. It is natural in winter to dress warmly and in summer to wear lighter clothes. Were one to reverse the procedure and wear heavy clothes in summer, the logic of the argument requires, and so the ancients actually believed, that the very sequence of the seasons would be thrown in confusion, for man's mistakes upset the order and harmony of the universe.

The conviction that moral values are grounded in the ultimate nature of things, the Chinese share with the great religious and philosophical systems of the world. But such insights in Confucianism seem impoverished, because too much is asserted: conventions of dress and decorum, local habits and ceremonials, are treated on a par with general and fundamental law. Failing to distinguish rite (li) from right (fa), Confucianism would seem to attach the same relevance to manners and morals, to picturesque folkways and principal ethical commandments. Such a system remains trapped in primitive magic, unable to transcend its own parochialism.

E.   The Conclusions of Amos vs. Amaziah

What makes Amos vs. Amaziah significant is that here religion compelled a break with pre-scientific thought. It is precisely religion which prompted and induced the advance toward universal standards, valid and applicable everywhere. It is the genius of monotheism which drove the herdsman of Tekoa to pry deeper into the difference between usage and law, between contingent custom and genuine general commandment. In a horizon meant to embrace all the peoples of the earth, as is the case in biblical religion, sooner or later one was bound to make the distinction between mores which fluctuated with the latitude and varied with the meridian, and conduct considered commonly and inherently right.

Some modes of behavior were arbitrary, simply idiosyncrasies of locality. Others were held and shared by all men, were recognized within the borders of Israel and acknowledged beyond them by Israel's foes, the Arameans; they were approved by the people of the covenant and by the uncircumcised Philistines, by fair-skinned Hebrews and dark-skinned Ethiopians, white and black alike. All these peoples and races had a variety of observances and practices which differed with the landscape. But all these peoples and races also were held by the biblical faith to be the children of one God, the father of all men. It would seem inconceivable, if underneath their variety a trace or token of their common origin did not remain. Whatever their differences, the fingerprint of the Creator should be discernible in all His creatures, stamping all as fellow-bearers of the divine image.

Amos found the divine signature in all men in their *sense of justice*. All men have an innate desire for the right, an inborn fear of arbitrary force, an instinctive response to wrong: It is not right! However failing or blundering, legal systems everywhere are but the attempt to articulate this desire for justice and to incarnate it in institutions capable of lifting from the brow of man the fright and curse of brutal force.

Now Amos was not a mandarin, intent upon "rectification of names," nor a professor, immersed in the varieties of anthropology or comparative law. Amos was a seer who beheld God the Lord setting a plumbline to the walls of Israel, and that vision gave him a measure for things human and divine.

Justice has always appeared binding upon men. Therein Amaziah did not differ from Amos. Only, to Amaziah, justice was an obligation like other obligations, a commandment among many commandments of the law. Injustice was improper, of course, but neither more nor less offensive than any other infringement of the rules.

Amos vs. Amaziah makes justice the *supreme command*, overriding every other consideration or obligation, however important to the life of the community. Justice becomes the categorical imperative, transcending all the other requirements of the law. Other ills of society are remediable, but injustice is a stab at the vital center of the communal whole. It instantaneously stops the heartbeat of the social organism. It cuts off the life-giving supply of health and strength that flow through the soul of the community, enabling its members to uphold the harmony, confidence and security of the covenant. The sheer threat and dread of arbitrary force terrorize and brutalize man. They throw him back into the state of nature and its savage standards: *Homo homini lupus.* Arbitrary force shatters the image of God in man.

Justice is the soil in which all the other virtues can prosper. It is the pre-condition of all social virtue, indeed of all community life. It makes civilized existence, it makes human existence possible. In every society justice must be the paramount concern, for it is the very foundation of all society:

"Let justice roll down like waters,
And righteousness as a mighty stream."

By making justice the supreme end and the culminating claim, *Amos vs. Amaziah* at once established a clear distinction between duties of worship and duties of righteousness.

Worship in biblical religion could never be an end in itself, for God is not in need of ritual, as in magic religions of antiquity where the performance of the cult replenished the waning energies or dying fires of the divine. In Israel, worship is God's favor to man, an act of His grace intended for the good of man,—not God. These implications of the biblical faith *Amos vs. Amaziah* clearly recognized by making ritual subserve the ends of righteousness.

Ritual is propaedeutic to religion, exercise and training for spiritual life, discipline in the restraints of holiness. Worship is meant to inspirit man with passion for justice, to purify and prepare him for the encounter with God.

Where ritual becomes estranged from its aim and is pursued for its own sake, instead of facilitating an approach, it may clog and clutter it with impediments and importunities of its own; it may even make the very encounter, if possible, impossible. As an end in itself, ritual may become a stumbling block in religion.

Amos vs. Amaziah has served as an impassioned reminder of the ever present danger and disposition to confuse means with ends. Worship and ritual are means, while justice and righteousness are ends. More, even, righteousness and justice are the encounter. God is justice, and His holiness is exalted in righteousness.

Whenever and wherever such claims will be made in the course of history, and they will be numberless, the decision of *Amos vs. Amaziah* will be invariably invoked or inferred. The heirs to prophecy will rehearse and reaffirm this verdict in varied circumstances with varied stress and ever new choice of words, but the soul and substance of the message will remain unchanged. God requires devotion, not devotions. Sacrifice and prayer cannot serve as substitutes for justice. Fasts and penances may be indulged even by the wicked, while the righteous may delight in the merriments of life without detriment to virtue:

> "Did not your father eat and drink
> And do justice and righteousness?
> Then it was well with him.
> He judged the cause of the poor and needy . . .
> Is not this to know Me?"
>
> (Jeremiah 22:15f.)

In letter and in spirit it is the lesson and legacy of *Amos vs. Amaziah*.

Religion has never been the same since, for that historic decision made plain and clear what does please God most: not skill in worship but will to justice. That decision, however, reaches beyond the realm of religion and has influenced, also, all subsequent notions of biblical law.

All law is innately conservative. *Stare super antiquas vias* is a stubborn tendency of law everywhere. Rules of law commonly grow from what is inherited from the past and handed down by tradition, by ancestral habit and established usage. Observance of customs attaches man to other men, and thus detaches him from himself: it enhances social solidarity and increases the group's sense of security. Usages grow stabilized as laws, and what is laid down by custom becomes accepted as right.

Amos vs. Amaziah insists that a clear distinction be made not only between *rite* and *right,* but also between *custom* and *law.* However ancient or venerable, however conducive to social cohesion or to public safety, a legal practice must recommend and validate itself ever anew by one test and one test only: that it serves the ends of justice. That was the meaning of the vision shown to Amos: the plumbline set to the wall knows no other measure but straight or crooked. It is only natural that such views brought Amos into clashes with the law as exercised in his day and founded on legal usage or the *custom in the gate*.

> "Oh you who turn justice to wormwood
> And cast down righteousness to the earth!
> They hate him who reproves *in the gate*,
> And abhor him who speaks uprightly.
> Seek good, and not evil, that you may live . . .
> Hate evil, and love good
> And establish justice *in the gate*."
> (Amos 5:7, 5:10, 5:14f.)

This new and exclusive measure for the law, that it serve only justice and nothing else, must have precipitated much discord, "hate" and "abhorrence" of the "reprover" who spoke his mind "uprightly." Of course, Amos lashed the abusers and miscarriers of justice with fierce candor. Therein he was joined in his day by the honest and well meaning disciples of the law. But Amos must have driven such good people to distraction no less by his single-minded concentration on justice and justice only. One can well imagine him shocking the scholars of the law by saying that justice can be defeated not only by venality and corruption of judges, but by the intricate craft of the law itself. The mischievous subtlety of the law can frustrate the very ends of the law. The sheer inertia of outlived tradition, the dead weight of the knowledge of the past, may stifle the living flame of justice.

The idiom, of course, is modern, but the issues are as old as the law. *Quieta non movere* is as ingrained in law as in religion. In all ages a predilection for the archaic and ceremonious will often blunt and warp judgment, and predispose it in favor of the bygone rather than the unborn, of the obsolete instead of the untried. Again, the inveterate human bent to confuse means and ends may smother justice in legal technicalities, making the very virtues of the law its worst enemies, turning impartiality into inflexibility, standards of precision into pedantry, the sense of responsibility into either irresolution or a resigned deference to prior rulings. In short, as in religion, law's own preliminaries can conspire to make its purpose, justice, impossible.

In law, as in matters of faith, *Amos vs. Amaziah* rendered a clear-cut decision: what ritual is to religion, *custom in the gate*—or legal precedent—is to justice. The value of precedent is that it secures for posterity the gains of history, the fund of legal experience, won by centuries of painful growth and uphill advance toward civilization. Precedent furnishes a floor beneath which legal practice will not sink, but above which it is free to rise, vouchsafing a minimum of justice and standards of rights achieved by many generations. What ritual is to religion, legal precedent is to justice—beginning and not end, floor and not ceiling, invitation and incentive to ever new ascent toward the right, and ever growng approximation of justice.

Ritual like precedent is a footprint left by the encounter of just and holy men with God who is holiness and justice. Footprints like these deserve to be followed, as they may lead again to the source of holiness and justice. The destination to which they point, to which they summon, makes these footprints priceless. But it would be idolatry to adore them for their own sake, as if they were the ultimate terminal.

F.   Hesiod vs. Perses

Only one other people, one other culture of antiquity was able to disengage *custom* from *right*. This was another of the glories of ancient Greece. One can trace the event also to approximately the eighth century B. C., to the lawsuit of *Hesiod vs. Perses,* the counterpart and contemporaries of *Amos vs. Amaziah.*[13]

Hesiod, the peasant-poet of Ascra near Mount Helicon in Boeotia, left a vivid account of a quarrel with his brother Perses. Idler and spendthrift, Perses dissipated his inheritance, and by bribing the judges sought to gain the hard-won earnings of his brother, the poet and farmer of Ascra. Incensed by his wastrel brother and the greed of the "gift-eating" judges, Hesiod devotes the first half of his *Works and Days* to the theme of justice, the word recurring some twenty-two times, always with grave emphasis. Justice or *Dike* appears here as the daughter of Zeus who sits beside her father in heaven and tells him of men's wicked deeds and the evil of judges "who pervert judgment and give sentences crookedly."

"Beware of this and make straight your judgments
O bribe-devourers!"[14]

"For it is an ill thing to be just,
If the unjust shall have the greater justice." [15]
"O Perses, lay up all this in your heart:
Give ear to justice and wholly forget violence.
This is the way [16] that Zeus has ordained for mankind:
Fish and wild beasts and winged birds shall devour one another,
For there is no justice among them.
But to man He has given justice,
The highest good of all." [17]

The older Greek society, mirrored in the Homeric poems, knew of *Themis,* the protectress of what is established by *custom,* and in this sense is *right.* The concept of *Dike,* the goddess of justice, blazed a new trail and started Greek thought toward heights ultimately attained by Plato and Aristotle.

One might be tempted to trace even beyond the borders of Greece the line of reasoning that began by distinguishing *Themis* from *Dike,* for it led by various stages to profitable principles of ancient and modern jurisprudence, such as, for example, the concept of *natural law.* According to Aristotle, what each thing is at its best, that we call *nature;* hence, natural law is the body of principles based upon man's nature as a rational being.[18] In short, laws of nature are general notions of right and wrong universal to all men, and approved by the common reason of mankind.[19] The idea of natural law, borrowed from the Stoics,[20] was developed in Roman law. Growing first out of trials between natives and foreigners (*peregrini*), it later widened with the Roman expansion, both by discarding legal and national peculiarities and by infiltration of ideas from the law of other nations. It left as a precious legacy to modern man the aspiration toward *ius gentium,* a law common to all peoples. The idea has been especially fruitful in new international law in which it may perform an even more significant function in the future.

It would be rewarding to pursue the different paths traversed by these two peoples of antiquity, the Hellenes and the Hebrews, who by separating custom from right lifted human thought to a new level, and bequeathed a heritage of insight and instruction basic to Western society, perhaps to civilization itself. By divergent roads, the one proceeding from the notion of the common God of mankind, the other arriving at the notion of the common reason of mankind, in their search, and at their summit, the two peoples reached amazing agreement. A famous poetic utterance of the sixth century B. C.

(attributed both to Phocylides [21] and Theognis [22]) is often quoted by later thinkers: "Righteousness contains the sum of all virtue." Plato shares this conviction,[23] and Aristotle expressly quotes the verse [24] and endorses the view, with added emphasis and evidence to the effect that in justice every virtue is embraced and comprehended, and that thus justice is not a part but the whole of virtue. It is also the burden of Hebrew prophecy, and sums up the meaning of *Amos vs. Amaziah.*

Still there remains a difference between the philosophical and the biblical approach to justice. It is the difference between concept and commandment. To the prophets justice is not the expression of an ideal merely conceived, without any effort being made, or even expected, to translate it into practice. It is not something to be respected, or admired, or propounded with a wistful regret at its being too good to be true or practicable. It is never a utopia designed for escape from reality or release from responsibility. It is a line of reasoning, of course, but not devised to halt forever in the zone of pure speculation; like the plumbline in the hand of the mason, it is meant to guide the hand that acts, not only the mind that thinks. To prophecy, justice invariably requires the response of action, not meditation alone. To philosophy, as Plotinus significantly reveals, action is a weakening of contemplation.[25] To prophecy, however, justice is the will of God which must be done, not contemplated. Unlike the philosopher, the prophet can never rest at ease until the interval between contemplation and action is bridged. An irresistible impulse hurls him ever again into attempting the seemingly impossible, making life conform with his vision. He cannot help it, for it is not his to refuse the bidding: "The lion has roared, who will not tremble? The Lord God has spoken, who can but prophesy?" (Amos 3:8)

This is perhaps the reason why philosophic dicta about justice remained theory, divorced from actual life. The long-standing inequalities of class, and the system of slavery within the city gates, not only limited justice to free men, but made it relative and proportionate, depending upon the social status of the individual to whom it was to be applied. The premise of the philosophers, of course, transcended prejudices of class and country and implied fundamental rights common to all men. But no conclusion was drawn from the premise; contemplation was not weakened or disturbed by action.

In *Amos vs. Amaziah* absolute justice could soar above the

limited or relative justice of ancient society, because the biblical idea of man could suffer no qualification or exception, but, on the contrary, did start with an assertion of the incommensurable and absolute sanctity of the human personality. The dignity of the human being as partaker of the divine image makes the rights of all men alike inviolable. *Amos vs. Amaziah* only drew out the latent conclusions of the biblical faith.

G. The Legacy of <u>Amos vs. Amaziah</u>

Judaism has never forgotten how true to the soul of the biblical faith the conclusions of *Amos vs. Amaziah* were. Their epoch-making impact is readily recognizable in the institutions of Jewish law and religion, and even in the character traits of its people.

The legacy of *Amos vs. Amaziah* survives in the Talmudic decision: "The commandment of righteousness outweighs all the commandments put together." [26] It is enshrined in the language of post-biblical Judaism, in which the word "commandment" (*miṣwah*) in itself came to mean the foremost or sum total of all the commandments, namely righteousness.[27] The very word Amos himself used, *ṣedaqah,* came to connote in the passage of time justice made clairvoyant by love, i.e., *charity.*[28]

If ever there was any hesitation lest the majesty of God be slighted by subordination of His worship to the duties of justice, the rabbis of the Talmud make sure to dispel such apprehension. Paraphrasing a prophetic utterance (Jeremiah 16:11), they quote God saying of his children, in the spirit of *Amos vs. Amaziah*: "Would that they had left Me, and kept My law!" [29]

Sticklers for externals in laws and religion were reminded by one of the most representative voices in medieval Judaism, Rabbi Moses ben Nahman, that one can remain "a scoundrel within the letter of the law" [30]—a glorious resonance and résumé of *Amos vs. Amaziah.*

Above all, rabbinic Judaism approved of *Amos vs. Amaziah* because of its choice of justice as the constitutive element of all law. Justice, mind you, not morality. In law proper, morals may become improper. Law may cease to function from over-idealization as well, when it is confused with the whole cycle of virtues, or strained to embrace the entire content of morality. Morals, unlike the law, are unenforceable, which alone would make moral force somewhat of a contradiction in terms. Moral ideals are inherently unrealizable, that is why immoderation is the very heart of saintliness. Essentially irrational and subjective, as the life of the individuals they inform, moral ideas spring from spontaneous intuition and refuse or even resent encroachment from without. It is, however, a valid and lasting insight that justice is the indispensable element of all law. For justice, unlike morality, is impregnated with intellectual discipline, and presents a compound of judgment and action. Justice cools the fierce glow of moral passion by making it pass through reflection. Justice is midway between morality and reason, virtue and intelligence, love and logic. We speak rightly of scales of justice, the image suggesting a precision instrument of intact and incorruptible weights, pondering carefully contending claims. For justice presupposes conflict and competition of claims, as it also implies confidence in the open and mature mind to acknowledge and to reconcile rival claims. Justice requires earnest and ceaseless study, but being the virtue it is or even the sum of all virtue, it also issues forth in action. That is why law became the pursuit of "the disciples of the wise" who have always distrusted untutored piety: "The boor is no fearer of sin." [31] Charity is not enough, it needs the wisdom of justice.

H. Molders of Law—Builders of Peace

Recently Mr. Chief Justice Warren paid a visit to England, leading some 3000 members of the American Bar Association to Runnymede meadow, where the *Magna Charta* was signed in 1215. In a notable address, he recalled the pilgrims who came from England aboard the *Mayflower,* bringing with them, as he said, "that precious cargo, the common law and principles of justice."

"That precious cargo" and the product thereof, the new body of constitutional law born on this continent, are now in the custody of the Supreme Court of the United States, one of the most powerful courts in civilization. The seven virtues of good judges which, following old tradition, Maimonides enumerated,[32] are as praiseworthy and pertinent today as ever before. But modern law adds new requirements of its own.

To be sound legal doctrine, a decision must be grounded in the inner logic of the law. Of course. But logic is not enough. The Dred Scott decision was buttressed by powerful logic, and Roger Brooke Taney heaped mordant scorn upon all who, by holding slavery to be unconstitutional, would make the principles in the Declaration of Independence flagrantly inconsistent with the practice of the men who drafted it. But the nation spoke through Father Abraham and elected Lincoln to save the Union, and the verdict of posterity has been unanimous that *Scott vs. Sanford* in 1857 was one of the Court's self-inflicted wounds. To be sound, a legal doctrine must be kept in consonance with the enlightened common sense of the nation and the civilized conscience of the world.

To be sound, a decision must sustain and strengthen the confidence of the people in the regenerative faculties of the law and the constitution, and in the interpretive resources of the judges to cope successfully with the shift and flux of an expanding future, and to seek stability through progressive adaptation.

To be sound legal doctrine, a decision must endeavor to be ever faithful to the twin aims of the law, seemingly irreconcilable, but in truth interdependent: security of the nation and unabridged liberties of the individual. To be sound, a decision must, if necessary, override passions of the populace, and not shrink from affirming the vitality of principle, confident that the country and the people as a whole will have the moral stamina and strength to live up to the dictates of justice and reason.

Today in this land a free and grateful people sense that their cherished rights are in competent and trusted hands. That is why our highest tribunal commands such widespread respect everywhere. This is also why all of us here so heartily welcome you, Mr. Chief Justice, on this your gracious visit to a seat of Jewish studies, an offshoot of biblical Tekoa and of the other legacies of that sacred soil and sacred book. A house of learning, planted in American soil, nurtured in an ancient people's faith that seekers of truth and guardians of the right increase peace in the world.[33]

Out of your own tradition and independent conviction, you

share the belief that molders of the law in all nations are the builders of peace on this earth. Or as expressed by a seer in Israel, a brother spirit and no doubt a disciple of Amos, in words I know you love to quote,[34] and to which we all know you are witnessing by your dedicated stewardship of the Court: "the work of righteousness shall be peace." (Isaiah 32:17)

Notes

1. Justice Oliver Wendell Holmes: "I have said to my brethren many times that I hate justice, which means that I know if a man begins to talk about that, for one reason or another he is shirking thinking in legal terms" (Letter to Dr. John C. H. Wu, July 1, 1929, in: *Justice Holmes to Doctor Wu, An Intimate Correspondence 1921–1932*, New York 1947, p. 53).

2. See *Plessy vs. Ferguson, U. S. Reports*, vol. 163 (1896) p. 551.

3. Amos 9:8 reads: "*lo* hashmed ashmid," instead of the usual: "hashmed *lo* ashmid."

4. *Berakhoth* 31b.

5. Albert J. Beveridge, *The Life of John Marshall*, vol. 1 (Boston 1916) p. 154.

6. Josiah Quincy, *Figures of the Past*, Boston 1883, p. 189 (New ed. Boston 1926, p. 159).

7. John Locke, *The Second Treatise of Civil Government* (1690) ch. XIX §222. The idea is biblical, and Locke refers to the biblical judge, Jephthah, appealing to the Supreme Judge (Judges 11:27). See ib. §241. Compare also Exodus 22:23, 26.

8. *Marbury vs. Madison*, Wm. Cranch, *Reports of Cases argued and adjudged in The Supreme Court of the U. S.*, vol. I, p. 176. See the introductory essay by Edmond Cahn, in the volume he edited, *Supreme Court and Supreme Law* (Indiana Univ. Press), Bloomington, 1954, p. 19.

9. Justice Oliver Wendell Holmes, "Speech on John Marshall," Febr. 4, 1901 (in: *Speeches*, Boston 1913, p. 87).

10. Justice Harold H. Burton, "The Cornerstone of Constitutional Law: The Extraordinary case of *Marbury vs. Madison,*" in: *Amer. Bar Assoc. Journal*, vol. 36, 1950, p. 882.

11. Emil Kautzsch, *Ueber die Derivate des Stammes ṣdḳ im alttestamentlichen Sprachgebrauch*, Tuebingen 1881, p. 24ff., 58; Johs. Pedersen, *Israel*, London 1926, vol. I, p. 336ff.

12. *Lun Yü* XIII, 3. Comp. Otto Franke, *Ueber die chinesische Lehre von den Bezeichnungen*, Leyden 1906. See Arthur Waley, *The Analects of Confucius*, London 1938, p. 22 about the date of the disquisition on "correcting names."

13. On the age of Hesiod cf. T. W. Allen, *Journal of Hellenic Studies* 35 (1915) p. 85ff., and *idem. Homer: The Origins and the Tranmission*, Oxford 1924, p. 75ff.

14. Hesiod, *Works and Days* 264 (ed. H. G. Evelyn-White, p. 22).

15. Ib. 271f.

16. *"nomos,"* not yet in the late sense of *law*. See U. von Wilamowitz, *Hesiodos Erga* (1928) p. 73, and Werner Jaeger, *Paideia* (Engl. ed.) vol. I, p. 434, n. 44.

17. *Works and Days* 274–280.

18. Aristotle, *Nicomachean Ethics*, Book X, Chap. 7 (1178a): "Reason more than anything *is* man." Law based on reason is, therefore, proper to the nature of man.

19. Aristotle, *Rhetoric*, Book I, ch. 13 (1373b).

20. Cicero, *De Legibus* II 5, 13.

21. Phocylides of Miletus, frg. 16 (*Elegy and Iambus,* ed. J. M. Edmonds, London 1931, vol. I, p. 181).

22. Theognis of Megara 147 (ed. Edmonds, *l.c.* p. 244).

23. *Republic* 433b.

24. *Nicomachean Ethics*, Book V, ch. 1 (1120b).

25. *Enneads* III 8.4 (346b–d), ed. E. Bréhier (1926) p. 158: "Doing is an attenuation of vision." The enfeebled spirit is hurried into action, just as duller children, inept at study, take to crafts and manual labor.

26. *Baba Batra* 9a.

27. See Saul Lieberman, *Midrash Debarim Rabbah,* Jerusalem 1940, p. 36 n.10, also *Journal of Biblical Literature* 65, 1945, p. 69ff.

28. See Max Kadushin, *Organic Thinking,* New York 1938, p. 132ff., and *The Rabbinic Mind,* New York 1958, p. 297; Franz Rosenthal, "Ṣedaka, Charity," in: *Hebrew Union College Annual,* vol. 23 (1950) I, p. 411ff.

29. *Yer. Hagigah* I, 7, fol. 76c.

30. in his commentary on Leviticus 19:2.

31. *Abot* II, 5. See Judah Goldin, *The Wisdom of the Fathers,* New York 1957, p. 90.

32. *Hilkoth Sanhedrin* II 7.

33. *Berakhoth* 64a.

34. Earl Warren, *The Law and the Future* (repr. from *Fortune,* Nov. 1955) p. 3: "Isaiah said that peace is the work of justice."

4.

The Maccabean Uprising: An Interpretation

by Elias Bickerman *

A. Religious Persecution

In the midst of the religious turmoils of the Counter Reformation, the father of modern political science, Jean Bodin, writes in connection with Antiochus Epiphanes: "Although tyrants always practiced the most terrible cruelty toward their subjects, no tyrant before Antiochus ever considered it permissible to issue commands to the human soul." [1] This statement offers a clear formulation of what was unique about the religious compulsion exercised by Epiphanes, a uniqueness which modern scholars tend to overlook when they maintain that the king's goal was to Hellenize the Jews.

We have mentioned earlier that the king had no intention of abolishing religious diversity,[2] and that neither he nor any other ruler suppressed traditional religious practices when Hellenizing a city or a sect.[3] The Hellenic gods were introduced as early as 173 B.C. when the congregation of "Antiochenes" was founded in Jerusalem; its members were exempted from observing the Jewish law. The primacy of "Zeus Olympius" after 167 on Zion implied that the "exclusiveness" of the One God had been abolished, but previously observed rites were not necessarily affected. It is especially important to note that there was no ban on circumcision, keeping the Sabbath or similar customs. To be sure, the Hellenization of a cult or the introduction of Greek gods into the Pantheon of an Orien-

---

* Translated from the German by Krishna Winston, who notes: "The biblical passages quoted by Elias Bickerman in his *Der Gott der Makkabäer* (The God of the Maccabees), Schocken Books (Berlin, 1937), are here given in the wording of the *Jerusalem Bible*. All other passages are translated from Bickerman's German."

tal people naturally involved considerable changes. The Arabs were acquainted neither with wine sacrifices in the cult of Dusares nor with pictorial or plastic representations of the gods. In accordance with their own practices, the Greeks gradually installed both of these elements in the religion of the Hellenized Arabs. Dusares was even represented to look like Dionysus, the god of wine. But these modifications by no means implied impairment or suppression of the Orientals' folk ways. As in the Jerusalem of Epiphanes, the chief god in the Transjordanian city of Gerasa—called "Antiochia" since the rule of Antiochus IV—was "Zeus Olympius." Here, too, he had supplanted the local Oriental gods. Yet even under the Caesars, the citizens of Antioch-Gerasa consecrated their sons and daughters as "holy slaves," just as their ancestors and predecessors had done from time immemorial.[4] Why, then, did Zeus Olympius in Jerusalem refuse to tolerate the customs which for centuries had been sacred to the worshippers of the Lord of Zion? Why was circumcision forbidden to a Hellenized Jew but not to a Hellenized Arab? Why did Epiphanes deem it a crime for a resident of Jerusalem to combine abstention from pork with his worship of Zeus, when the pig was considered unclean by all Syrians and continued to be so?[5]

To understand the significance of the persecutions under Epiphanes, one must perceive that they were double-pronged, including both a prohibition and the imposition of a new mode of existence.

We know of other cases in which "barbarian" customs are proscribed: the Greeks relate that Dionysus of Sicily forced the Carthaginians to give up human sacrifice. The Romans also prohibited the practice, as the British banned the sacrifice of widows (suttee) in India. Hadrian imposed the death penalty for circumcision, which was judged a barbarian rite. During the subsequent uprising in Palestine, observance of other precepts of the Torah was also punished mercilessly. The teachers are known to have suspended all the requirements of the law in order to protect the believers' lives. Only idol worship, murder and unchastity remained prohibited under all circumstances. But Epiphanes compelled the Jews to worship idols. The martyrs at the hands of Hadrian died at the stake; they were wrapped in the scrolls of the Torah as a sign that they had defied the edict and continued to study and teach the law. The Maccabee martyrs, on the other hand, were subjected to the most inhuman tortures, intended to force them

to partake of the heathen sacrificial banquets. The Jews under
Hadrian revolted in protest against the ban on circumcision
and the construction of a temple to Jupiter on Zion. The
Maccabee uprising was caused neither by the introduction of
pagan gods into Jerusalem nor by the bans on circumcision
and keeping the Sabbath. No, Mattathias, a priest from the
tribe of the Jehoiarib, took up arms because roving envoys
of the king came to his village to compel the inhabitants to
perform the pagan sacrifices. In short, every Jew was to come
under the jurisdiction of the new faith. The clearest indication
of this fact is the statement that sacrifices to the idols were
performed not only in the public squares of Jerusalem but
also "at the doors of houses" (I Maccabees 1:55). For it was
then the custom to set up a temporary altar in front of every
house to guarantee that no one could avoid participating in the
festivals of the new cult.[6]

Persecution thus implied not only abolition of the old order
but also introduction of a new one. This fact militates against
all attempts to explain Epiphanes' actions as the result of his
personal idiosyncrasies or historical circumstances. For the
introduction of a new fealty presupposes a missionary zeal
matched only by one instance in the ancient world: Pharaoh
Ikhnaton's forcible imposition of the sun cult. But Ikhnaton
believed in his god. Epiphanes, on the other hand, listened
eagerly to the teachings of the Epicureans and proclaimed himself a member of their school; and while that school maintained that the gods should not be implicated in earthly affairs,
it condoned observance of the traditional rites.

Tacitus assumed that Epiphanes was attempting to introduce
"Greek practices" among the Jews. But attentive study of the
authentic accounts has shown that the new cult on Zion was
in fact not a Greek cult but one unfamiliar to the king.[7] The
Greeks conceived of the deity as manlike. Yet when the Maccabees purified the temple, the "impure stones" which they
removed were not pieces of marble statues but fragments of
an altar that had been erected to an idol on the site of the
old altar for fire sacrifices.

What led Epiphanes to introduce "a god unknown to his
ancestors" (Daniel 11:38), to impose upon the Jews a religion
that was neither theirs nor his own? The unique character of
this persecution presents us with a riddle. The solution should
be sought not in later writers' explanations but in the facts of
the persecution. Our first step should be to establish the legal
basis of Epiphanes' undertaking.

B.   The Edict of Persecution

A royal decree went out ordering the Jews to "abandon their ancestral customs and live no longer by the laws of God." The persecutions were terminated by another royal decree, the content of which has come down to us: "the Jews may make use of their own kind of food and their own laws as formerly." [8] This order was directed at the "gerousia of the Jews and the other Jews," that is to say, at the Jews of Jerusalem and the surrounding region. We can conclude that the conversion effort was restricted to the territory subject to the Sanhedrin at Jerusalem. The site of the persecution was "Jerusalem and the towns of Judah"; those persecuted were the "inhabitants of Judaea and Jerusalem"; the religious persecution was thus a clearly local oppression of "Judaea and Jerusalem." [9]

This conclusion, based on the unanimous accounts of the books of the Maccabees, allows us to draw another conclusion: no persecution took place in the Diaspora, which was also subject to Epiphanes. There are no reports of pressures on the Jews of Antioch or Tyre; [10] in fact, the books of the Maccabees indicate that even the Jews in the Greek cities of Palestine remained unmolested during the years of religious oppression in Judaea (167–164 B.C.). Only after the restoration of the Temple in late 164, when the persecutions in Jerusalem were already ended, did the heathens in nearby areas begin to fall upon "the Israelites living on their territory." [11] In 163 Judas Maccabaeus rushed to the aid of his fellow believers in Transjordan, Galilee and the valley of the Jordan.[12] It was a full year after the decree of persecution was revoked before the people of Joppa (Jaffa) and Jamnia (Jabne) first attacked their Jewish fellow citizens, while Skythopolis spared its Jews entirely. These are ordinary skirmishes between neighbors, unconnected with Epiphanes' persecutions.[13] We read, to be sure, that "a decree was issued at the instance of the people of Ptolemais for the neighboring Greek cities, enforcing the same conduct on the Jews there, obliging them to share in the sacrificial meals . . ." [14] But such accounts merely imply that persecution of the Jewish religion outside of Jerusalem depended upon local initiative and not upon rulings issued for the whole kingdom.[15]

These findings are in no way startling. We recall that the

statutes for the Jews in the cities, whether Jerusalem, Ptolemais or any other, were established according to various special privileges, which were legally binding only in their respective territories.[16] From the legal point of view, Epiphanes' project in Judaea represented modification of the charter granted Jerusalem by Antiochus III. The statutes of other localities were not affected. Thus the Jewish communities of Babylonia and Persia, likewise ruled by Epiphanes, were untouched by the persecution edict in Jerusalem. The best illustration for this point is the fact that Titus, the Roman who had destroyed Jerusalem, upheld the rights of the Antiochian Jews. Epiphanes had desecrated the Temple of Zion. Yet the sacred objects stolen in Jerusalem were donated by the Seleucids to the synagogue at Antioch.[17]

The Mosaic law had prevailed in Jerusalem thanks to a special dispensation granted by Antiochus III. Neither Menelaus nor any other insurgent had the legal power to abolish the law; the king alone could terminate the privilege and introduce a different regulatory system. But once this occurred, the Anti-Torah became as binding on the citizens of Jerusalem as had been the Torah previously. For example, the privilege granted by Antiochus III prohibited all sacrifices forbidden by the Torah. Similarly, a fine of three thousand silver drachmas was levied for importing into the city meats proscribed by the law.[18] Following these precedents, Antiochus now decreed that the pig should be sacrificed and circumcision banned. We consider the implementation of these royal orders and prohibitions "persecution." But for the Seleucid government it did not constitute planned persecution of the Jews; rather it was punishment of disobedient subjects who had opposed the orders of the monarch and his appointed high priest.

This reinterpretation suggests that the "renegades" of Jerusalem were actually "the believers."[19] "We were content," they explained to Antiochus V, the son of Epiphanes, "to serve your father, to comply with his orders and to obey his edicts." The Maccabees, on the other hand, were those who were contemptuous of the king's orders.

An important document, the only one we have that dates precisely from the period of the persecutions, illustrates the position of the Seleucid government: it is a petition submitted in 166 B.C. by the Samaritans to Epiphanes; his reply is included.[20]

At this time the Samaritans, i.e., the inhabitants of that area which had its cult center in the temple on Mount Gerizim and its capital in the village of Shechem, were administratively linked with Jerusalem; we know neither the history of this connection nor its precise form.[21] As a result of the link, Epiphanes appointed his prefects for Jerusalem and Gerizim simultaneously and sent "pagans" and Samaritans as the first troop deployments against Judas' revolt. In addition, the Samaritan territory included Jewish districts which "offer sacrifice in Jerusalem."[22] The administrative situation of the Samaritans occasioned the royal officials to "bring the same charges" against the Shechemites as against the Jews. The central issue was observance of the Sabbath, now outlawed in Jerusalem. In their petition the Samaritans ask not to be confused with the Jews or implicated in "the crimes of the Jews." Antiochus accepts their petition on the grounds that the Samaritans "have no part in the things of which the Jews are accused."

From this document we can conclude that the crime of the inhabitants of Jerusalem was neither observance of the Sabbath nor circumcision as such, but continuance of the practices after they had been forbidden. In fact, this document of 166 B.C. and the Seleucid documents of 164 and 163 preserved in II Maccabees contain no reference to the Jews being barbarians or to any belief on the part of Epiphanes that he had a mission to civilize them. The Samaritans ask the king to leave them in peace "so that we may increase your revenues." In 163 the temple is restored to the Jews "in order that this people, too, may refrain from rebellion." In 164 religious freedom is restored by Epiphanes so that the Jews who had fled to escape persecution "may devote themselves to their usual pursuits." At this time the Jews are pardoned: "no Jew shall be molested on grounds of past offences." This is the standard formula for Hellenic amnesties after civil disorders. The criminal acts attributed to the Jews by the Samaritan petition are disobedience and rebellion. In his letter of 164 the governor Lysias promises the Jews who desire peace that he will intercede for them with the king "if you will remain loyal."

According to these documents, then, the persecution emerges as punishment meted out to an obstinate people for defiance of the royal edict. But why was such an edict, designed as it was to transform the Jews' whole style of life, issued in the first place?

The documents suggest an answer. Antiochus V restores the Temple to the Jews because they do not accept Epiphanes' order to convert "to Greek ways." "Greek ways" here simply means the organization of the *polis*.[23] But Epiphanes replies to the Samaritans that they will be spared because they "have no part in the things of which the Jews are accused and prefer on the contrary to live according to the Greek customs." This document, issued at the height of the persecutions, gives the impression that the goal of the royal measures is to Hellenize the Jews. The Samaritans are accordingly praised for requesting that their sanctuary be dedicated to Zeus.

Yet the statement that the king intended to Hellenize the Jews represents only an apparent explanation for the persecution. For Hellenization could be achieved in several ways and, as we have seen, it never involved forcible abolishment of existing cults and imposition of the new faith.[24] Why, then, was the Hellenization of Jerusalem accompanied by desecration of Zion?

Later apologists for King Epiphanes offered a seemingly reasonable answer: Moses had imposed "strange, inhuman customs on the Jews as laws." The king, who "despised a misanthropic attitude in any people," thus attempted to abolish the Mosaic law. The Samaritan document reveals the falsity of this biased interpretation.[25] It reveals that Epiphanes neither persecuted the Mosaic faith as such nor tried to impose the Greek, or any other, cult on his subjects; the inhabitants of Jerusalem were the only exception. In Shechem the Torah was held just as sacred as in Jerusalem. The "misanthropic" prescriptions of Moses which separated the believers from the pagans were as sacred for the Samaritans as for the Jews. The Samaritan bard Theodotus extolled in Homeric cadences the practice of circumcision. "Thus it is, for God has commanded it," he says, and explains in hexameters that the Hebrews are forbidden to "fetch from foreign parts sons-in-law to marry their daughters." On Mount Gerizim sacrifice was made to the same sole and jealous God as on Zion. The Sabbath was the symbol of the covenant for the rest of Israel as it was for Judah. But only in Judaea was its observance punishable by death, while in Samaria Epiphanes himself recognized the feast of the seventh day, and the Torah remained binding. The king considered it sufficient that the "chief" god of Mount Gerizim should thenceforth be referred to as "Zeus." The chief god on Zion was also announced to be Zeus. But at the same time his sanctuary was desecrated, his rites and prescriptions were abolished, and his faithful were persecuted. Why was there one standard for Gerizim and a different one for Zion? Why does Epiphanes, who tolerated the Torah in Shechem and

Samaria, ordain that in Jerusalem everyone should abandon the "ancestral customs" and conform to the decrees of the king?

C. The Apostates

The fact has been established that the order issued by Epiphanes at the end of 167 B.C. abolishing the authority of the Torah and imposing new customs on the Jews applied only to the *ethnos* of the Jews, to Jerusalem and Judah, in other words, to the territory under the high priest of Zion.

Since the persecution was territorially limited, it would seem probable that it was instigated by local authorities. And in point of fact, sources available to us mention twice that the high priest Menelaus and his followers were responsible for the oppression. Daniel says of Epiphanes that after the second Egyptian campaign, in 168, the king "will retire [to Antioch] and take furious action against the holy covenant and, as before, will favor those who forsake that holy covenant. Forces of his will come and profane the sanctuary citadel . . ." The ancient commentator explains the passage as follows: the king was "impelled to this action by those who had deserted the sacred law and adopted the rites of the pagans." [26]

The prophet's suggestion is corroborated by the Greek historians. They report that in 163, when the reconciliation took place between the Seleucid government and the Jews, Menelaus was executed upon the advice of the grand vizier Lysias, for this man "was the cause of all the troubles, since he had persuaded the father of the king [i.e., Epiphanes] to force the Jews to abandon their inherited cult." [27] The Greek, that is, Seleucid, tradition thus agrees with Daniel's testimony from the time of the persecutions, and confirms his information on who was responsible for the religious oppression. This information in turn serves to explain the legal situation during the persecutions.

But we must also explain the paradoxical phenomenon of a high priest who wishes his own congregation to desert its faith, for neither the Seleucid nor the Jewish historians allow the despised and defeated party of Menelaus to present its case. Two sentences are all we can find in the first Book of Maccabees to indicate the priest's possible motives.

"Then the king issued a proclamation to his whole kingdom that all were to become a single people, each renouncing his particular customs. All the pagans conformed to the king's decree . . ." In three other passages the author specifically states that Epiphanes decreed that one cult only should be observed in his kingdom and was determined to abolish the native rituals of the different peoples.[28] This interpretation, formulated by a Jew writing sixty years after the death of the king, does not survive scrutiny. Antiochus neither ordered nor enforced a unification of religious observances. In Susa, Nanaia continued to be worshipped; in Byblos the god with six wings was retained; and in Babylon sacrifice was made to Marduk.[29] The Jewish historian's mistake becomes understandable if one assumes that the official pretext for the persecutions in Jerusalem was the abolishment of religious particularism.[30] That was the ostensible goal of those who instigated the king's strict measures. This, in fact, was the aim attributed to the "renegades" by the first Book of Maccabees. "It was then that there emerged from Israel a set of renegades who led many people astray. 'Come,' they said, 'let us reach an understanding with the pagans surrounding us, for since we have separated ourselves from them many misfortunes have overtaken us.' " [31]

This statement still expresses the biblical conception of history, which sees every national misfortune as the result of apostasy.[32] Here the sin is not assimilation but separatism. A return is urged to the happy days when the peoples formed one community. Thus, too, after the destruction of Jerusalem, Jeremiah heard people proclaim that they would offer incense " 'to the Queen of Heaven . . . as we used to do, we and our fathers. . . . We had food in plenty then. . . . But since we gave up offering incense to the Queen of Heaven . . . we have been destitute and have perished either by sword or by famine.' " (Jeremiah 44:17)

However, three centuries of adherence to the law separated Jason and Menelaus from the days of Jeremiah. When, under Epiphanes, the apostates asserted that isolation had been Israel's undoing and that in an earlier age separation had been unknown, they were not repeating the lament of Jerusalem's women in exile; rather they were applying the tenets of the Greek enlightenment to their own people. The observant Jew considered his isolation a natural, necessary defense against the folly of idol worship.[33] "Therefore God surrounded us on all sides with laws for purity in eating, drinking, touching and seeing."

But to the Greek, this isolation was merely another evidence that the Jews were barbarians.[34] A generation before Jason and Menelaus, the great geographer Eratosthenes formulated the proposition that "it is a common custom of all barbarians to expel foreigners." [35] In these early days of Hellenism when for instance in Egypt everyone who participated in Greek culture was considered a Hellene, whatever his origins, the Greek-oriented Jew had eventually to relinquish his isolation. "He who created us," the doctrine of those days proclaimed, "created us for life in community with all others." [36] It was in this spirit that the Jewish Hellenists attributed the misfortunes of their people to its habit of isolation. Perhaps the most grievous gap in our knowledge of the Maccabean period is that we do not know the nature of the "many evils" from which the reformers hoped to rescue the Jews: misfortune? the hatred they incurred? spiritual impoverishment? In any case, they wanted to be like other peoples. They even eliminated the traces of circumcision in order to "appear as Greeks even naked." Thus they "abandoned the holy covenant." [37]

In those days the life of the peoples was always bound up with religious cult practices. There was no meeting, no official or private act in which the gods did not participate, which was not accompanied by sacrifices or prayers. If a man slaughtered a kid or drank to a friend, he never forgot to invoke the deity and offer up a few drops. Even nonbelievers maintained the traditional observances. Assimilation for the Jews thus necessarily implied participation in idol worship. The pagans claimed that the only proof of true friendship was worship of their gods, who, in contrast to the god of the Jews, were common to all men. The Jews had to conform in this respect or else "seek another region in which they could live apart and observe their particular law." [38]

The Torah was made somewhat easier for the Hellenized Jews to relinquish by the fact that it was the law of Moses. The Greeks' comparative studies in religion had already established that many lawgivers, from Zarathustra to Lykurgos, had alleged divine inspiration in the same way as Moses.[39] Joining the pagans was thus a transgression not of divine commandment but only of human regulations.[40] Related to this notion is the reformers' claim that in early times there had been no separation. Greek concepts of cultural history placed the blame for distasteful phenomena in the life of a noble people on degeneration.[41] Favorably disposed Hellenes accordingly designated Jewish exclusiveness as a sign of decay. Upon being driven out of Egypt, they explained, Moses had in embitterment ordered his people to hold itself aloof. "Originating in this emotion, aloofness gradually developed into a hallowed way of life." Others saw Jewish separatism as a post-Mosaic development. According to them, Moses had done no more than to prescribe worship without images—for which the Greek philosophers greatly respected him; he had established the Sabbath as a day of rest more or less by accident. Separatism with regard to diet, living conditions and traffic with women had not come until later, when the Jewish sect had become a nation by taking in proselytes. "For since they consisted of the scum of all peoples, they banded together (like criminals) in mutual assistance and in hatred of all other men." A third Greek historian, the famous Posidonius, declared that Moses had won Jerusalem without a fight. For he had promised a form of religious service and sacrifice which would not burden its participants with pomp or meaningless ceremonies. "In this manner he achieved respect and founded a considerable domain, since all the neighboring peoples flocked to him because of his teachings and his promise." It was his successors whose superstition led them to introduce circumcision, dietary prescriptions and so on.[42]

A Hellenized Jew could no more disregard these conclusions of Greek scholarship than an enlightened Jew of today can disregard the results of modern biblical scholarship. Philo, who was at once a devout Jew and an educated Hellene, could accept the spiritual authority of the Torah only if he reasoned that its instructions and descriptions were to be interpreted symbolically. In similar fashion the Greeks rescued Homer's canonical significance by taking his immoral tales as allegories. We know through Philo that many of his predecessors had concluded after observing the symbolic interpretations of the Mosaic law that adherence to its letter was not necessary. Others sought in the Bible the Greek (Cynic) doctrine that in ancient times, when the laws of nature prevailed, life had been perfect. They condemned positive systems of laws, the Jewish one included, as particularistic and thus a lapse from the original world order. Still others "did conceal their vexation with their fathers' ways and constantly criticized the laws." For them the story of the Tower of Babel was a fairy tale similar to the Greek myths.[43]

An examination of these Jewish Hellenists' main trends of thought reveals how similar they were to those of Jason and Menelaus in Palestine. They intended to reform Judaism by discarding the comparatively recent barbarian "separatism" and returning to the original, undistorted form of worship. The reformers under Epiphanes have much in common with such Jewish reformers of the 1840's as G. Riesser, A. Geiger and I. Einhorn, who proposed reform of the Sabbath and abolition of the dietary prescriptions, also declaring that circumcision was not compulsory. They, too, were subject to the pressures of a non-Jewish environment, in this case the Protestant scholars' theories about the origin of the Pentateuch.

The religious service instituted on Zion by Epiphanes did in fact correspond to the Greek concept of a rational natural religion. Posidonius recounts that Moses considered both the Egyptians and the Greeks wrong to attribute the form of an animal or of man to the deity. God was the all-encompassing nature of all things.[44] A sacred spot should be established where God could be worshipped without images. According to the philosophers, the god-fearing king of ancient Rome, Numa Pompilius, had, like Moses, worshipped the gods at unadorned altars and had known neither temples nor statues.[45]

Most of the inhabitants of the *polis* of Akra were colonists; certainly the majority were Syrians and Arabs, not Greeks. They worshipped the gods according to their time-honored Semitic customs. But their cult also accorded with the religion of the philosophers, who liked to link their lofty interpretation to a traditional rite. To the Arab immigrants in Jerusalem the altar stone symbolized the deity. This same stone—being imageless—naturally appeared to the philosophers as a token of the deity.[46] Similarly, the obelisk representing Aphrodite on the island of Paphos was considered "a symbol of the deity." And later on we find a Church father stating that the column of fire and smoke which went before the chosen people in the desert "expressed the fact that its god had no images." [47]

Like the unspoiled children of nature postulated in the Greek theory,[48] the "sons of Akra," Menelaus and his adherents, worshipped the god of their forefathers without temples or statues; at the open air altar on Mt. Zion they worshipped unfettered by the law and united with the pagans in mutual tolerance. What could be more human and natural than their desire to impose this tolerance on their unenlightened co-religionists? This was the intent behind Epiphanes' persecutions.

D. Ideological Foundations of the Persecutions

Although the Church has extolled the Maccabee saints, many Christians reject these martyrs "because of the pork." [49] The Book of Maccabees does indeed stress the fact that the persecutors tried to impose this food on the Jews.[50] This is a curious piece of information. The Greeks actually used the pig only for nonedible sacrifices or for the cult of Demeter or Dionysus.[51] In Erythrae a catalogue of sacrifices indicates that all the gods, including "King Antiochus," receive a sheep and a lamb; only Demeter receives a young pig.[52] The new god of Jerusalem was "Olympian Zeus," who merited a bull.[53] The pig on the other hand was considered unclean not only by the Jews, but also by the Syrians, the Phoenicians, the Arabs and others.[54] The Greeks had never attempted to change the attitude of these peoples. Under Epiphanes not a single Syrian was forced to eat pork; this was required only of the Jews in Jerusalem.

The contradiction is resolved when we realize that the ban on pork was considered characteristic of Israel—a symptom of its foolish superstition.[55] "Why do you refuse to eat pork?" Caligula asks the Jewish delegation. A cultural reform designed to abolish the exceptional position of Jewry might well, with the consistency peculiar to every rationalistic ideology, establish the pig as the prime sacrifice to the Olympian Zeus of Jerusalem, although the pig was despised by the Syrians and was not the usual sacrifice offered by the Greeks to Zeus.

This sort of thinking also underlies the other prescriptions and prohibitions established for the new cult. The obligatory sacrifices consisted of precisely those animals designated as unclean by Jewish law.[56] Since most of the animals used in Syrian and Greek sacrifices corresponded to those used by the Jews,[57] the new order pertained not only to selecting certain species but also to abolishing Jewish ritual slaughter, whereby the animal had to be drained of all its blood.[58] The Jews were ordered to eat animals which had not been slaughtered according to their sacred ritual. A pagan king with the simple goal of of Hellenizing the Jews would have had no need to enforce such a prohibition. But it had great importance for a Jewish reformer anxious to eradicate every particularized custom.[59]

For the same reason the scrolls of the Torah were burned,

and observance of the Sabbath was forbidden; enlightened Greeks saw these things as characteristic of the Jews and typical of the Jews' pointless idiosyncrasies. Indeed there was probably no rite of the ceremonial law which was not somehow considered a sign of superstition and a symptom of particularism. "We deplore," one of the philosophers writes,[60] "the lighting of Sabbath lights, for the gods need no illumination, and not even men can take pleasure in all the smoke." To the Jews of the old faith, circumcision was a sign of the covenant, but to the pagans it was a sign of Jewish exclusiveness. "The Jews instituted the peculiar custom of circumcision as a means of making themselves recognizable to each other." [61] Circumcision was thus particularly despised. Two women who had had their newborn sons circumcised were executed. But first their babies were hung around their necks, and they were led all around the city before being pushed from the top of the ramparts.[62]

A man like Epiphanes, who attended the lectures of the Epicureans, must have been indifferent as to whether people in Jerusalem, as in Hieropolis, abstained from pork or prized it in accordance with Greek taste. But to the reformers, themselves products of Judaism, every iota of the law was as significant as to the orthodox, and like all religious reformers, they surpassed the adherents of the old faith in intolerance, bloodily persecuting those who were "backward." [63]

E. The Significance of the Maccabees' Struggles

Broad sectors of the population joined the reform party out of opportunism or fear. "Those who forsake that holy covenant" (Daniel 11:30) were to be found both in the fortified cities, in Akra, and throughout the countryside.[64] Reports that have come down to us declare repeatedly that "many" (Daniel 9:27) joined the pagans, sacrificed to their idols and abandoned the law.[65]

The Maccabees were fighting primarily against these apostates. The unrest began when Mattathias killed a Jew as he was about to become the first in Modein to sacrifice to the idols. Next Mattathias and his sons struck in nightly raids on cities and villages against "the sinners in their anger and the renegades in their fury." By marching through Judaea to search out the godless, to burn and kill, they turned "wrath away from Israel." [66] Even after the recovery of the Temple the war against the apostates, and particularly against the "Israelites," continued. For their part, the "godless men" joined forces with the Seleucid punitive expeditions and again and again summoned the might of the king against the Maccabees.[67]

The Maccabean movement was primarily a civil war, a religious battle between the orthodox and the reformers. But posterity remembers it as a war against the Seleucids, just as the internal struggles in seventeenth-century Holland are remembered in historical accounts as a revolt against foreign domination. In the Maccabean struggle, one of the parties also relied on the power and strength of a foreign ruler. If Ezra had once introduced the law in the name of Artaxerxes, the abolishment of the law was now ordered by a decree of Antiochus IV. In the edict of Artaxerxes disobedience to the Jewish law, considered synonymous with the royal will, was punishable by death. Similarly, Menelaus and his party did not hesitate to use execution and torture to convert the Jews to a new form of worship, this one also imposed by the ruler.

The basic antinomy of Jerusalem's position is here bloodily illustrated: the paradox that the existence of this theocracy depended on the will of the godless foreign monarch. For if Artaxerxes could institute the law, Epiphanes could abolish it. If Darius II could dictate to the Jews through his satraps how to celebrate the festival of the unleavened bread in the month of Nisan and could decree that "leavened foods shall not be consumed," [68] then Antiochus IV could also feel entitled to command the Jews through his "superintendents" (*epistates*) to eat pork. For Ezra and Artaxerxes were substituted Antiochus and Menelaus. Menelaus was a negative Ezra. Ezra and Nehemiah had isolated the Jews in order to preserve monotheism. Jason and Menelaus abolished monotheism in order to rescue Jewry from isolation. The original reform placed the people under the direct jurisdiction of its God. The counter reform deposed that God to protect the people's welfare. The Maccabees were fighting the Seleucid troops but not the Seleucid rule; they took arms not to oppose any cultural or political system, but to preserve "our lives and institutions." [69] This was not a national struggle but rather a conflict within their own camp, i.e., a religious war between two groups within the Jewish people: between the polytheists, who performed sacrifices in the hope that assimilation would prove their salvation, and the monotheists, who were prepared to give their lives and the life of the entire people in order to preserve the law of Moses. The former relied on the earthly power of the Seleucids, but the Maccabees had God on their side.

If they had been defeated, the light of monotheism would have been extinguished. External pressure would not have brought about its destruction, for remnants of the scattered people would always have preserved the true faith. But it would have been a different case if the entire people had accepted polytheism, if the pilgrims to Zion had found in the Temple enclosure hierodules leading the strangers to an altar dedicated to Allat or Dusares. The blood of the martyrs and the swords of the warriors of God preserved the Jewish promise: "Hear ye, Israel, the Lord is our God, the Lord alone."

A higher meaning thus resides in the historical injustice committed by the monotheistic religions when they commemorated the days of the Maccabees but ignored the family of the Hasmoneans. The figures of Mattathias and his sons are remembered only in history books, but to this day Jewry celebrates Hanukkah in honor of the reconsecration of the Temple and of the miracle of the inexhaustible oil. On August 1 Christianity honors the memory of the "sainted Maccabees," that is, of the martyrs whose death is glorified in the second book of Maccabees. For the deeds of the Maccabees draw their significance simply from the fact that they saved monotheism. In the blood-testimony of the martyrs and in the services held in the newly consecrated Temple, the one truth was preserved for humanity which in the course of thousands of years of erring, of being deceived and disappointed by innumerable alleged truths, has been found unchanging and eternal: the oneness of God. Those who gave their lives during Epiphanes' persecutions to remain true to the Eternal One are thus models of true heroism for all times and all peoples. As Augustine says, "Let men learn from them how to die for the truth." [70]

Notes

1. J. Bodin, *De republica*, IV, ch. 5.
2. See *Der Gott der Makkabäer* (Berlin, 1937), p. 47.
3. *Ibid.*, p. 90.
4. Cf. the inscription of A.D. 69/70 (*Bulletin of the American*

School of Oriental Research, No. 49 [1933], 7): Theon, the son of Demetrius, donates 7100 drachmas of Tyrian silver for the construction of a temple to Olympian Zeus, οὗ ἐστὶν ἱκέτης, ὑπέρ τε ἑαυτοῦ καὶ τῶν τοῦ Διὸς ἱεροδούλων, αὐτοῦ δὲ τοῦ Θεῶνος τέκνων, Σκύμνου καὶ Ἀρτεμιδώρου καὶ Ἀρτεμισίας.

5. The Syrians' and Arabs' practice of circumcision and their aversion to pork are well documented. The Greeks naturally brought the pig along to Syria (see Mark 5:13 on the swine of Gadara). It is noteworthy, however, and as yet unexplained, that traces of pig sacrifices are quite frequently found in Canaanite temples. See Vincent in *Revue Biblique* (1928), 533, 1; J. D. Duncan, *Digging up Biblical History*, II (N.Y./London, 1931), 39. It is also interesting that on Delos pig sacrifices were expressly prohibited for the cult of the gods of Askalon (A. Plassart in *Délos*, XI, 287; cf. also II, 58), but not for the cult of the deities of Jamnia (*Délos*, XI, 279).

6. See for example W. Dittenberger, *Sylloge inscriptionum graecarum* (3rd ed., Leipzig, 1915), p. 695.

7. See *Gott der Makkabäer*, p. 116.

8. II Maccabees 6:1: μετ' οὐ πολὺν δὲ χρόνον ἐξαπέστειλεν ὁ βασιλεὺς γέροντα Ἀθηναῖον ἀναγκάζειν τοὺς Ἰουδαίους μεταβαίνειν ἐκ τῶν πατρῴων νόμων καὶ τοῖς τοῦ θεοῦ νόμοις μὴ πολιτεύεσθαι. II Maccabees 11:27: πρὸς δὲ τὸ ἔθνος ἡ τοῦ βασιλέως ἐπιστολὴ τοιαύτη ἦν· βασιλεὺς Ἀντίοχος τῇ γερουσίᾳ τῶν Ἰουδαίων καὶ τοῖς ἄλλοις Ἰουδαίοις χαίρειν.

9. I Maccabees 1:44; 51; 3:35; 2:6. The statement in 1:51 that the king wrote "to every part of his kingdom" in this spirit is explained below.

10. On the Jews in Antioch see: II Maccabees 4:36; Josephus, *Antiquitatum judaicarum*, 12, 119; *De bello judaico*, 7, 43 and 106; not until the fourth century A.D. was Antioch decided to be the site of the martyrdom of the seven brothers described in II Maccabees 7.

11. I Maccabees 5:11.

12. I Maccabees 5:9; 5:25; 5:15; 5:23.

13. II Maccabees 12:1ff.; 12:30. Accordingly there are no reports of military assistance from the Diaspora for Judas, whereas the royal troops were supported by pagan militia (I Maccabees 3:41).

14. II Maccabees 6:8: ψήφισμα δὲ ἐξέπεσεν εἰς τὰς ἀστυγείτονας πόλεις Ἑλληνίδας Πτολεμαίων ὑποτιθεμένων τὴν αὐτὴν ἀγωγὴν κατὰ τῶν Ἰουδαίων ἄγειν καὶ σπλαγχίζειν. (Alex. Πτολεμαίου ὑποθεμένου.) Lat.: "decretum autem exiit in proximas Graecorum civitates, suggerentibus Ptolemaeis ['Ptolomei' artibus]." The passage has come down to us in corrupt form. Πτολεμαίων should certainly read Πτολεμαέων (Calmet, *Commentaire littéral sur tous les livres de l'Ancien et du Nouveau Testament*, III [Paris, 1724–26]; cf. de Bruyne in *Revue bénédictine*, 1931, 74, who points out the same substitution in manuscripts of the Pseudo-Aristea). On the suggestion, then, either of the city of Ptolemaïs or of Ptolemy, the governor of "Coelesyria and Phoenicia" (II Maccabees 8:8), a royal decision was issued (that is what ψήφισμα means here; cf. Josephus, *Antiquitatum*, 18, 69; 13, 262; W. Dittenberger, *Orientis graecae inscriptiones selectae* [1903]), that the privileges of the Jews in several of Palestine's neighboring states should be abolished. ἐξέπεσεν expresses the impact

of this unexpected order, which "falls" like a lot during a drawing of lots.

15. I Maccabees 1:41 contains the (false) assertion that Epiphanes planned to eradicate *all* established religions in his kingdom (see *Gott der Makkabäer*, p. 30), but nowhere is it mentioned that the Jewish Diaspora was affected. This omission has aroused attention (e.g., G. F. Moore, *Judaism in the First Centuries of the Christian Era, the Age of the Tannaim*, I [Cambridge, Mass., 1927], 52), and Wellhausen could explain it only by assuming the Diaspora did not as yet exist within the Seleucid kingdom (*Israelitische und jüdische Geschichte* [Berlin, 1894], p. 241). But with the exception of the Greek cities, a large Jewish population lived in Babylon, which was at that time under Seleucid domination. The statement in Sulpicius Severus 2, 20, 3—"per Graecas quoque urbes quae in illo imperios erant . . . Iudaeos sacrificare cogebat"—is a conclusion based on II Maccabees 6:8.

16. Cf. for example I Maccabees 10:34 and 37; Josephus, *Antiquitatum*, 11, 338; 12, 119; 125; 150; *De bello judaico*, 7, 44, 110.

17. Josephus, *De bello judaico*, 7, 44.

18. Josephus, *Antiquitatum*, 12, 145.

19. I Maccabees 6:23; 3:14.

20. *Gott der Makkabäer*, Appendix IV, p. 177.

21. II Maccabees 5:23; I Maccabees 3:10. Cf. U. Kahrstedt, *"Syrische Territorien," Abhandlungen der Gesellschaft der Wissenschaften zu Göttingen* (1926), 66; H. Lewy, in *Zeitschrift für die neueste Wissenschaft* (1932), 120.

22. I Maccabees 11:34.

23. *Gott der Makkabäer*, p. 55.

24. *Ibid.*, p. 90.

25. *Ibid.*, p. 23.

26. Daniel 11:30. Porphyry in Jerome to Daniel 11:30: "ab his invitatus sit qui derelinquerant legem Dei et se caermoniis miscuerant ethnicorum."

27. II Maccabees 13:4: Λυσίου ὑποδειξάντος τοῦτον (sc. Menelaus) αἴτιον εἶναι πάντων τῶν κακῶν, προσέταξεν (sc. Antiochus V) . . . προσαπολέσαι. Josephus, *Antiquitatum*, 12, 382 (cf. 20, 235): Λυσίας γὰρ συνεβούλευσεν τῷ βασιλεῖ τὸν Μενέλαον ἀνελεῖν, εἰ βούλεται τοὺς Ἰουδαίους ἠρεμεῖν καὶ μηδὲν ἐνοχλεῖν αὐτῷ· τοῦτον γὰρ ἄρξαι τῶν κακῶν πείσαντ' αὐτοῦ τὸν πατέρα τοὺς Ἰουδαίους ἀναγκάσαι τὴν πάτριον θρησκείαν καταλιπεῖν.

28. I Maccabees 1:41: καὶ ἔγραψεν ὁ βασιλεὺς Ἀντίοχος πάσῃ τῇ βασιλείᾳ αὐτοῦ εἶναι πάντας λαὸν ἕνα, καὶ ἐγκαταλιπεῖν ἕκαστον τὰ νόμιμα αὐτοῦ. The fabulous accounts in Sulpicius Severus, 2, 21, 4 are based on this passage.

29. Cf. Grimm, *Das erste Buch der Maccabäer* (Leipzig, 1853), on this passage. Nanaia: Cumont in *Comptes rendus* of the *Académie des inscriptions et belles lettres* (1932), pp. 271–286. Byblos: E. Babelon, *Les rois de Syrie* (1890), Plates 14, 18. Babylon: E: Unger, *Babylon: die heilige Stadt nach der Beschreibung der Babylonier* (Berlin/Leipzig, 1931), p. 168.

30. Cf. Ed. Meyer, *Ursprung und Anfänge des Christentums* II (Berlin, 1923), p. 144.

31. I Maccabees 1:11: ἐν ταῖς ἡμέραις ἐκείναις ἐξῆλθον ἐξ Ἰσραὴλ υἱοὶ παράνομοι καὶ ἀνέπεισαν πολλοὺς λέγοντες· Πορευθῶμεν καὶ

διαθώμεθα διαθήκην μετὰ τῶν ἐθνῶν τῶν κύκλῳ ἡμῶν, ὅτι ἀφ' ἧς ἐχωρίσθημεν ἀπ' αὐτῶν, εὗρεν ἡμᾶς κακὰ πολλά.

32. Grimm first remarked upon this significance in *Das erste Buch der Maccabäer* (Leipzig, 1853).

33. Pseudo-Aristeas, 142. Cf. L. Couard, *Die religiösen und sittlichen Anschauungen der alttestamentlichen Apokryphen und Pseudoepigraphen* (Gütersloh, 1907), p. 178.

34. Cf. M. Mühl, *Die antike Menschheitsidee in ihrer geschichtlichen Entwicklung* (Leipzig, 1928).

35. Strabo, 802: κοινὸν μὲν εἶναι τοῖς βαρβάροις πᾶσιν ἔθος τῆς ξενηλασίας.

36. *Stoicorum veterum fragmenta* III, ed. Arnim (Leipzig, 1903–24), 346.

37. I Maccabees 1:15: καὶ ἐποίησαν ἑαυτοῖς ἀκροβουστίας καὶ ἀπέστησαν ἀπὸ διαθήκης ἁγίας καὶ ἐξεύγίσθησαν τοῖς ἔθνεσι.

38. Josephus, *Antiquitatum*, 4, 138: δεῖν οὖν αὐτοῖς ἔλεγον ἢ ταῦτα πᾶσιν ἡγητέον ἢ ζητεῖν ἄλλην οἰκουμένην, ἐν ᾗ βιώσονται μόνοι κατὰ τοὺς ἰδίους νόμους. (Speech of the Midianite women [Numbers 31:15] to the Hebrews.)

39. Diodorus Siculus, *Bibliotheca historica*, I, 94. Cf. E. Norden in *Festgabe von Fachgenossen und Freunden, A. von Harnack zum siebzigsten Geburtstag dargebracht* (Tübingen, 1921), p. 296; K. Reinhardt, *Poseidonios über Ursprung und Entartung* (Heidelberg, 1928), p. 16.

40. The statement in Sirach 41:8 probably refers to these renegades: "Woe unto you, you godless ones who have deserted the law of the Most High. When you multiply yourselves, it is a cause of misfortune, and when you beget children, it is a cause of affliction. When you meet your downfall, it is an eternal joy, and when you die, it is a curse." [Based on the German version by R. Smend.—Tr.] Cf. Enoch 92ff. on the mighty who abandon the law and worship idols and on similar cases in the "Testaments of the Patriarchs" etc. (Cf. Ed. Meyer, *Ursprung und Anfänge des Christentums*, II, 167.)

41. Cf. R. Hirzel, "Agraphos Nomos," *Abhandlungen der Leipziger Akademie*, XX (1900); I. Heinemann, *Poseidonios metaphysische Schriften*, I (Breslau, 1920), 88 and 128; K. Reinhardt, *Poseidonios über Ursprung und Entartung*.

42. Hekataios in Diodorus, 40, 3. Tacitus, *Historiae*, 5, 5. Posidonius of Apamea, *Reliquae doctrinae*, 87, Fragment 79 in Jacoby, *Fragmente der griechischen Historiker* (Berlin, 1923). See I. Heinemann, *Poseidonios metaphysische Schriften*, II, 72. Posidonius states similarly (Strabo, 301) that Scythian morals were corrupted by contact with the Greeks.

43. I. Heinemann, *Philons griechische und jüdische Bildung* (Breslau, 1932), p. 455. Philo of Alexandria, *De confusione linguarum*, 2, and the commentary by E. Stein in *Collecteana Theologica* XVI (Lvov, 1935), 6. It is well known that "The Wisdom of Solomon" and Philo (cf. F. Focke, *Die Entstehung der Weisheit Salomons* [Göttingen, 1913], 190, 6) explain the development of pagan idolatry in accordance with the Greek theory of degeneration: paganism begins with a relatively comprehensible worship of the stars and deteriorates into worship of human beings. This idea can be found in Plato (*Cratylus*, 397) and Aristotle (*Metaphysics*, 1074b, 1). Cf. Chaeremon, frag. 2, 5 (E. Schwyzer, *Chairemon* [Leipzig, 1932]); Porphyry, *De abstinentia ab animalibus necandis*, 2, 5; Eusebius, *Evangelica praeparatio*, 3, 4. Cf. H. Doergens, *Eusebius von Cäsarea als Darsteller der griechischen Religion* (Paderborn, 1922).

44. Strabo, 761 (cf. I. Heinemann in *Realencyclopädie für Altertumswissenschaft*, c.l. P. Wissowa, W. Kroll *et al.* [1894ff.], 364): ἀλλ᾽ ἐὰν δεῖν πᾶσαν ξοανοποφιαν, τέμενος δεῖ ἀφορίσαντας καὶ σηκὸν ἀξιόλογον τιμᾶν ἔδους χωρίς. Σηκός is the site of the cult (cf. K. Reinhardt, *Poseidonios über Ursprung und Entartung*, 8, 2). Cf. Strabo, 640: after the burning of the temple of Artemis, the "sekos" was in the open air for a time. The "didymeion" in Miletus, which remained unsheltered, is called "sekos" by Strabo (634). See also Strabo, 395. For this reason the hall of images in the Capitoline temple and the Holy of Holies in the Temple of Jerusalem are also called "sekoi" (Dionysius of Halicarnassus, *Roman Antiquities*, 4, 61; Posidonius, *Reliquae doctrinae*, 87, Fragment 109 in F. Jacoby, *Die Fragmente der griechischen Historiker* [Berlin, 1923], 3).

45. On Numa see: Plutarch, *Lives*, "Lycurgus and Numa," 8; Tertullian, *Apologeticus*, 25; Augustine, *De civitate dei*, 4, 31. The idea that the unspoiled peoples worshipped their god without images was a commonplace of Greek ethnography: A. Schroeder, "De ethnographiae locis communibus" (diss. Halle, 1921), p. 2ff. Zeus Olympius was honored on his Thessalian mountain site only by an altar: Cook, *Zeus: A Study in Ancient Religion* I (Cambridge, England, 1914), 102.

46. The colonists always transported their ancestral cults to their new countries. Cf. for example Jamblichus of Chalcis, *De vita Pythagorica*, 2, 4.

47. Philostratus, *Vita Apollonii*, 3, 58. Apollonios states that the visitor to the sanctuary should be allowed to imagine the form of the deity as he wishes (*ibid.*, 6, 19). Clement of Alexandria, *Stromata*, 1, 24, 163: σημαίνει δὲ ὁ στῦλος τὸ ἀνεικονιστὸν τοῦ θεοῦ.

48. Eusebius, *Evangelica praeparatio*, 1, 9, 29d: ἀλλ᾽ ὅτι μὲν οἱ πρῶτοι καὶ παλαίτατοι τῶν ἀνθρώπων οὔτε ναῶν οἰκοδομίᾳ προσεῖχον οὔτε ζοάνων ἀφιδρύμασιν... παντὶ τῷ οἴμαι συλλογιζομένῳ δῆλον εἶναι. On Greek ideas about the proper worship, without images or temples, see: J. Bernays, *Die heraklitischen Briefe: ein Beitrag zur philosophischen und religionsgeschichtlichen Litteratur* (Berlin/London, 1869), p. 32; C. Clerc, *Les théories relatives au culte des images chez les auteurs grecs du IIme siècle après Jésus-Christ* (Paris, 1915); J. Geffcken in *Archiv für Religionswissenschaft*, 19, 286; I. Heinemann, *Philons griechische und jüdische Bildung*, p. 49. Dio Cocceianus (Chrysostomus of Prusa), 12, 53 and 61 (ed. Arnim) seemingly polemicizes against the idea that the barbarians' cult of natural signs (δενδρὰ ἀργὰ καὶ ἀσήμους λίθους) should be more correct than the worship of idols. The former are no closer to the true form of the gods than the latter (οὐδαμῶς οἰκειότερα τῆς μορφῆς).

49. Augustine, *Sermon 300* (*Patrologia latina*, 38, 1379).

50. I Maccabees 1:47; 6:21; 7:1.

51. The pig is "according to a well-founded belief a particularly welcome offering to the gods of the underworld" (Julian the Apostate, *Orations*, V, 177c). Cf. O. Gruppe, *Griechische Mythologie und Religionsgeschichte* (Munich, 1906), 1178, 2.

52. U. v. Wilamowitz, "Nordionische Steine," *Abhandlungen der Berliner Akademie* (1909), 58. See also R. Herzog, "Heilige Gesetze," *Abhandlungen der Berliner Akademie* (1928): pig offerings for Dionysus (Nr. 1, 45) or for purification (1, 32; 5A, 14 and 19; 6A, 2); a bull is sacrificed to Zeus (Nr. 2; 5A, 23). Cf. also the temple records of Delos (F. Dürrbach, *Les comptes de Délos*, I–III [1926–1934]).

53. A. Cook, *Zeus: a Study in Ancient Religion*, I, 716. L. Farnell, *The Cults of the Greek States*, I (Oxford, 1896), 96 and 413. The pig is sacrificed only to a chthonic Zeus, not the Olympian (Cook, II, 1205).

54. S. Borchart, *Hierozoicon*, II, ch. 57; W. Baudissin, *Adonis und Esmun: eine Untersuchung zur Geschichte des Glaubens an Auferstehungsgötter und an Heilgötter* (Leipzig, 1911), p. 144. On the Arabs, see also Sozomen, *Ecclesiastica historia*, 6, 38.

55. J. Juster, *Les juifs dans l'Empire romain: leur condition juridique, économique et sociale* (Paris, 1914), p. 45; I. Heinemann in *Realencyclopädie für Altertumswissenschaft*, Supplement 5, 21; Philo of Alexandria, *Legatio ad Caium*, 361.

56. I Maccabees 1:47: θυεῖν ὕεια καὶ κτήνη κοινά. 1:63: ἵνα μὴ μιανθῶσι τοῖς βρώμασι. II Maccabees 6:5: τὸ δὲ θυσιαστήριον τοῖς ἀποδιεσταλμένοις ἀπὸ τῶν νόμων ἀθεμίτοις ἐπεπλήρωτο.

57. Cf. R. Dussaud, *Les origines cananéenes du sacrifice israélite* (Paris, 1921), pp. 134ff., p. 154. Cf. Lucian, *De dea syria*, 54; Theophrastus, *De abstinentia*, 25. The variations are slight: milk is forbidden in the Jewish but not in the Syrian (Dussaud, p. 153) and Arab rites (J. Wellhausen, ed., *Reste arabischen Heidentums* [Berlin, 1897], p. 114).

58. This procedure was customary in Greece only for nonedible sacrifices (P. Stengel, *Opferbräuche der Griechen* [Leipzig/Berlin, 1910], p. 103).

59. Cf. Psalms of Solomon 8:13, where the late-Maccabean priesthood is accused of defiling the altar of the Lord with every sort of unclean practice and treating the sacrificial animal at the bloodletting as if it were profane meat.

60. Seneca, *Epistulae ad Lucilium*, 95, 47 (following Posidonius: I. Heinemann, *Poseidonios metaphysische Schriften*, I, 119).

61. Tacitus, *Historiae*, 5, 5: "circumcidere genitalia instituerunt ut diversitate noscantur."

62. II Maccabees 6:10.

63. Cf. I Maccabees Jost, *Geschichte des Judentums und seiner Sekten*, I (Leipzig, 1857), 112: "there was no intention of abolishing the ancestral religion, much less of paving the way for idolatry, but rather of leaving their isolation to become part of the civilized world." A similar argument is given by J. Wellhausen in *Nachrichten der Gesellschaft der Wissenschaften zu Göttingen* (1905), 124.

64. I Maccabees 10:14; 6:21.

65. I Maccabees 1:43, 52; 2:16; 2:23; 6:21.

66. I Maccabees 2:24; II Maccabees 8:6; I Maccabees 2:44; 3:5; 2:48; 7:24.

67. I Maccabees 3:15; 4:2; 7:5; 9:23, 25, 58, 69; 11:21, 25.

68. A. Cowley, ed. and tr., *Aramaic Papyri of the Fifth Century B.C.* (Oxford, 1923), p. 21. Cf. E. Meyer, *Der Papyrusfund von Elephantine* (Leipzig, 1912), p. 91.

69. I Maccabees 2:27, 40, 42, 50, 64; 3:43 etc.

70. Gregory of Constantinople, *Orations*, 15, 31: φιλότιμοι τῆς ἀληθείας ἀγωνισταί. Augustine, *Patrologia latina* 38, 1379: "discant viri mori pro veritate." According to Daniel (8:12), Epiphanes "overthrew the truth." Solomon ben Isaac (RaShI) explains in his commentary on the Pentateuch that this means "the law of the truth," i.e., the Torah.

5.

The Philonic God of Revelation
and His Latter-Day Deniers *

by Harry Austryn Wolfson

Philo, professionally, was not a teacher of philosophy. He was a preacher, a preacher on biblical topics, who dispensed his philosophic thoughts in the form of sermons. And because he was not professionally a teacher of philosophy, some modern students of his works say that he was not a philosopher. For nowadays, as we all know, to be called philosopher one must be ordained and one must be hired to teach philosophy and one must also learn to discuss certain hoary problems as if they were plucked but yesterday out of the air. Some say that Philo was an eclectic. But there is one eminent scholar who would begrudge him even the title of eclectic without further qualification, for, after all, eclecticism is the name of a reputable system in ancient Greek philosophy. The eclecticism of Philo, he says, "is that of the jackdaw rather than the philosopher." [1] Still, while we may deny Philo the honorific title of philosopher, with the privilege of wearing ostentatiously a special garb like that affected by ancient Greek philosophers, we cannot deny him the humbler and more modest title of religious philosopher. As such, Philo was the first who tried to reduce the narratives and laws and exhortations of Scripture to a coherent and closely knit system of thought and thereby produced what may be called scriptural philosophy in contradistinction to pagan Greek philosophy.

* Based upon the Suarez Lecture delivered at Fordham University, 1952, and one of the three Walter Turner Candler Lectures delivered at Emory University, 1959. Published in the *Harvard Theological Review*, 53 (1960): 101–124.

From *Religious Philosophy: A Group of Essays*, New York, Atheneum, 1965. (First published by Harvard University Press, 1947.)

Let us then analyze this scriptural philosophy of Philo into its essential elements, so that we may afterwards see how these essential elements of the Philonic scriptural philosophy were treated in modern philosophy since the seventeenth century.

i

The starting point of Philo's philosophy is an enumeration and assessment of the various views with regard to the ways by which men have arrived, or may arrive, at a knowledge of God. He enumerates three views.

According to some, he says, the way by which men have arrived at a knowledge of God is the way of imagination. The belief in God, according to them, is a fictitious belief, the product of our imagination, like the belief in chimeras and centaurs and hydras. As restated by Philo, the belief in God, according to this view, was invented by some clever legislator in order to tame the rebellious spirit of the people and inspire them with awe and fear and reverence for the law. Philo does not give us the name of the author of this view. But he can be identified as Critias, the leader of the Thirty Tyrants in Athens at the beginning of the fifth century before the Christian era His view, which may be summarized in the maxim that religion is the bugaboo of the people, has been revived in our own time in the maxim, so well familiar to all of us, that religion is the opiate of the people. In principle, if not in purpose, this view, insofar as it makes God a mere concept in our mind, may also be considered as the forerunner of the various forms of modern religious humanism, which identifies God with man's idealized consciousness or with human aspirations for ideal values or with the unity of all ideal ends.

Philo dismisses this view as atheism.[2]

According to others, says Philo, God is the discovery of human reason. God is not a figment of our imagination. He has real existence outside our mind, and we are able to discover Him by the power of our mind. It is the God whom Plato discovered when, starting with a world which he held to have been framed out of an eternal formless matter, he was compelled by reason to assume the existence of a Demiurge or a God who has framed the world. It is also the God whom Aristotle discovered when, starting with an eternal world which is eternally in motion, he was compelled by reason to arrive at the existence of a being who is an immovable mover. It is also the God of the Stoics who, starting with a world in which they saw order and beauty and purpose, found themselves compelled by reason to arrive at the existence of a God, whom they call, among other things, the mind or the soul of the world. In principle, if not in wording, this view is the forerunner of all modern forms of religious rationalism, whether its God is called substance, or central monad, or spirit, or cosmic consciousness, or élan vital, or universal nisus, or principle of concretion, or ground of being.

Philo does not deny that one may arrive by reason at some knowledge of God. In his characterization of Greek philosophers, he distinguishes between those who were believers of God and those who were deniers of God; and Plato, Aristotle, and the Stoics are placed by him among the former. Still he does not believe that reason is the only way of arriving at a knowledge of God; nor does he believe that reason alone can lead us to a true and full knowledge of God. There is to him a third way of arriving at a knowledge of God, the way of revelation.

As conceived by Philo, revelation meant two things.

First, it meant the historical revelation: an event which took place in the past when at Mount Sinai God made himself known to men and gave them the Law. Indeed Philo refers to certain people in his own city who denied the divine and revealed origin of Scripture. He describes them as a sort of amateur students of comparative religions, whose only tool of reasoning was that of analogy and, whenever they observed among various peoples beliefs and customs which were alike in some respects, they inferred that they must be alike in every respect. And so, because they found in Greek mythology stories about appearances of gods to men and the revelation of laws, stories which they themselves considered as false, they argued that the account of the appearance of God at Mount Sinai and the revelation of His Law there is similarly false. Philo does not argue against them; he simply dismisses them as "impious" [3] and asserts his faith in revelation. For revelation to him is a matter of faith and not of reason, though occasionally he tries to confirm his faith in revelation by such arguments as the intrinsic excellency of its teachings and the salutary effect of these teachings upon those who follow them.[4]

Scripture, despite its similarities to other books, is to him a

unique book. All other books are man-made, and their stories
and teachings may be either true or false. Scripture is of
divine origin, and its stories and teachings are all true. As a
philosopher who tried to introduce logical coherence in his
religious beliefs, he tries to remove the apparent inconsistency
between a God who was declared to be invisible and the
story of His having made himself visible to men at Mount
Sinai. In great detail he tells us how the revelation at Mount
Sinai was not a physical appearance of God, how the "words"
in which God "spoke" with His "voice" were not physical
words, uttered, as he says, by means of "mouth and tongue
and windpipe." [5] But still, while all this was a miraculous
event and one unlike ordinary human communication, the
event still had taken place actually as a historical fact, and is
not to be explained away as a fancy or dismissed as a fiction.

Second, revelation meant to him progressive revelation, a
continuous revealment of God to chosen individual human
beings to make known to them the meaning of the revealed
Law. For though he believed that the revelation was final and
perfect, inasmuch as the Law was to be eternal, this belief
did not mean to him that it was a closed revelation. Final and
perfect indeed it was, but as a revelation to men, it had to be
couched in ordinary language, in language intelligible to the
ordinary run of man, and so the perfection of its teaching was
often obscured by the imperfection of human language. Those
to whom the Law was revealed, and who were to believe in it
and to live by it were to search for those inner meanings
hidden behind the uttered words. This search for the inner
meaning of Scripture cannot be successfully pursued without
the aid of God. It is this divine aid in the discovery of the
inner meaning of Scripture, which is called by Philo the Un-
written Law and corresponds to what the rabbis call the Oral
Law, that constitutes a new kind of revelation, a progressive
revelation, and a revelation which comes in response to the
search of human reason. For while Philo, like the rabbis of
Palestinian Judaism, believed in the cessation of prophecy
with the close of the Hebrew Scripture, it is only that special
kind of prophecy which inspired the writings of the prophets
of the Hebrew Scripture that ceased.[6] Divine inspiration and
the work of the Holy Spirit continue to function as a supernatural source of human knowledge, by which man is to discover not new truths but the real meaning of the old truths
which are embedded in the final historical revelation.

Revelation to Philo is not only a new way of coming to a knowledge of God, it also yields a truer conception of God; and hereupon in various places scattered throughout his homilies he explains what the conception of God is as taught by revelation and how that conception of God differs from that taught by reason in the works of the philosophers.

This scriptural conception of God as contrasted with that of Greek philosophers is presented by Philo under three headings, which may be subsumed as a contrast between the conception of God as infinite and the conception of God as finite.

First, God is infinite in the sense that He is incomprehensible, for, that which is infinite, according to a current philosophic maxim, cannot be comprehended by the mind.[7] At the very beginning of his speculation about God Philo declares that in His essence God cannot be known. All that can be known of Him is the fact of His existence. This distinction between the knowability of God's existence and the unknowability of His essence was something new in Greek philosophy. It was introduced by Philo. Among the Church Fathers, about two centuries after Philo, and already under the influence of Philo's teaching of the incomprehensibility of God, the question arose as to whether Plato conceived of God as incomprehensible in His essence.[8] On independent grounds, however, it can be shown that the God of Plato, who was either one of the ideas or a being other than the ideas, could be known in His essence and could be described, though Plato was not unaware of certain logical difficulties arising from his view. Nor was the God of Aristotle unknowable in His essence.[9] The terms ineffable (ἄρρητος), unnamable (ἀκατονόμαστος), and incomprehensible (ἀκατάληπτος), by which the unknowability of God is expressed by Philo, do not occur as a description of God in extant Greek philosophic literature before Philo, but once these terms were used by Philo they begin to occur frequently in Greek philosophy. The chief source of Philo's view of the incomprehensibility of God was his rigid philosophical interpretation of the scriptural prohibition of the likening of God to anything that is in heaven above, or on earth beneath, or in the water under the earth. The unlikeness of God became with him the uniqueness of God. Uniqueness meant that God belonged to no class. And since He belonged to no class, no concept of Him could be formed. He was thus incomprehensible.[10]

Second, God is infinite in the sense of infinite goodness.

As used by Philo, the infinite goodness of God means two things: (a) that God acts freely by will and design and purpose; (b) that God exercises His individual providence over human beings. This conception of the infinite goodness of God, with all its implications, is advanced by Philo as a view in opposition to the views held by various Greek philosophers. Indeed he knew that all Greek philosophers described God as good, and some of them, Plato and the Stoics, though not Aristotle, ascribe to God also providence. But the goodness which they apply to God is not used by them in its ordinary sense as a description of an act performed by will and design and for a purpose. It is applied by them to God in a figurative sense and only because the unwavering, uniform action flowing by necessity from the nature of God has the appearance of an action guided by some intelligent will toward a goal. This is the sense in which not only Aristotle and the Stoics apply goodness to God; it is the sense in which also Plato applies it to God. When Plato, in answer to the question "Why God made this world," says that it is because "He was good" and "desired that all things should be as like unto himself as possible," or that "He desired that all things should be good," [11] despite his use of the term desire there was no choice on the part of God in the creation of this form of the world. He could not create any other kind of world. There were "fated laws" (νόμοι εἱμαρμένοι), as he says later,[12] by which the Demiurge was guided in his act of creation.

Similarly the term providence used by them means inexorable, fated laws. As the Church Fathers, a century after Philo and speaking under the influence of Philo, try to show, the providence of the Greek philosophers means universal providence; not individual providence.[13] Against the Stoic saying, which in fact represents the view of the generality of Greek philosophers, that "the gods attend to great matters, but they neglect the small ones," [14] Philo says that· God has "a providential regard not only for those which are of greater importance, but also for those which appear to be of less importance." [15]

Philo was not unaware of the many difficulties that may arise from applying to God the attribute of goodness. He was especially aware of the difficulty arising from the problem of evil, both physical and moral evil. He discusses this problem in great detail, both in terms of Scripture and in terms of philosophy.[16] Every answer given in native Jewish tradition and in philosophy is made use of by him. But despite all the answers, a residuum of the problem still remains, and this residuum of the problem is solved by him by the principle of the incomprehensibility of God. Not only do we not know the essence of God; we do not also know the ways of God and the purpose of God. "God," he says, "judges by standards more accurate than any which the human mind employs," [17] which is only a paraphrase of the words of Zophar the Naamathite in the Book of Job, with regard to the problem of evil, that one is not to try to find out the deep things of God or to try to attain unto the purpose of the Almighty (Job 11:7).

Third, God is infinite in the sense of infinite power or omnipotence.

By omnipotence Philo means four things: (a) God created the world out of nothing and implanted in it certain laws of nature by which it is governed.[18] (b) Before the creation of this world of ours, God, if He willed, could not have created it at all or could have created another kind of world governed by another kind of law.[19] (c) In this present world of ours, God can override the laws which He Himself has implanted in the world and create what is called miracles.[20] (d) God, if He wills, can destroy this world and create in its stead a new heaven and a new earth, though Philo happens to be certain that God will not will to do so.[21]

This conception of the omnipotence of God, in all its four phases, is presented by Philo explicitly in opposition to every school of Greek philosophy. It is in accordance with this conception of the omnipotence of God that he rejects explicitly the Aristotelian conception of the eternity of the world, and this on the ground, as he says, that it "impiously" postulates in God "a vast inactivity." [22] By this he means that the assumption of a world existing eternally by the side of God would be a restriction on the power of God. By the same token, he makes the Platonic pre-existent matter out of which God created the world to have been itself created by God.[23] Here again the assumption of an eternal uncreated matter could be a restriction on the power of God. It is for this reason also that he rejects the Stoic conception of God as fate,[24] for fate means an internal limitation on the power of God to act according to the freedom of His will.

This conception of the omnipotence of God is most strikingly brought out by Philo in statements in which he tries to answer certain questions which must have arisen in his mind.[25] Why this order of nature? Why do stars sparkle in the sky? Why do birds fly in the air? Why do fish swim in water? Why do trees grow in the field? Pagan Greek philosophers had two answers. According to one answer, that order had been fixed, as if by fate, from eternity and it is unchangeable. According to another answer, that order is the result of chance and it may by chance break down. Against both these two views, Philo maintains that it is all the work of an omnipotent Deity. Before the world came into being God, through His omnipotence, could have created another kind of world, governed by another kind of law, a world in which there would have been no succession of day and night and of seasons, and one in which trees would grow in heaven and stars would sparkle on earth. And now that God created this world in its present order, God can upset that order, though He promised not to upset it unless He had to do it for some good purpose—a purpose, by the way, which more often than not He keeps hidden from us.

His opposition to the generally prevailing view among Greek philosophers as to the inevitability of the present order of nature is expressed by Philo in his oft-repeated statement that "all things are possible to God" (πάντα θεῷ δυνατά) 26—a statement which reflects the Septuagint version of Job's address to God: "I know that Thou art able to do all things and that to Thee nothing is impossible" (Job 42:1).

These four principles of scriptural religion as laid down by Philo have been generally accepted in all the philosophies of the three revealed religions, Judaism, Christianity, and Islam. They all accept the fact of a historical and final revelation, though they may differ as to which historical revelation was final. They all accept the view that while there was one historical revelation that was final, that final revelation was not a closed revelation; there was progressive revelation supplementary to the final revelation. They all accept the principle of the incomprehensibility of God, though there may be some difference of opinion among them as to how to interpret the terms predicated of God in Scripture. Finally they all accept the principle of divine goodness and of divine omnipotence in the manner they are conceived by Philo, and, though they are conscious of the many difficulties arising therefrom, especially the difficulty of the problem of evil, they solve all these difficulties by the incomprehensibility of God's ways.

No wonder, then, that in modern philosophy, ever since the seventeenth century, those who undertook to depose scriptural philosophy concentrated their attack upon these four principles. Let us then examine some of the main arguments raised against the four points in scriptural philosophy as defined by Philo and let us also see how a hypothetical scriptural philosopher would try to refute these arguments.

ii

As representative opponents of scriptural philosophy we shall take three philosophers, one from the seventeenth century—Spinoza; another from the eighteenth century—Hume; a third from the nineteenth century—John Stuart Mill; and let each one of us select a representative opponent of scriptural philosophy from the present century.

They all reject revelation. The arguments they use are all variations of the arguments used by those whom Philo described as "impious," arguments based upon analogy and upon the view that things alike in some respects must be alike in all other respects. Instead of the analogy with Greek myths used by the "impious" critic of Philo's time, Spinoza uses the analogy of "the Koran or the dramatic stories of the poets or ordinary chronicles." [27] Hume uses the analogy of "Arabians" in their records of the miracles of "Mahomet or his successors" and of "Grecian, Chinese, and Roman Catholic" authors.[28] John Stuart Mill endorses Hume [29] and adds a long ponderous argument to show how the alleged evidence for revelation will not pass muster in an English court of justice.

To this our hypothetical spokesman for scriptural philosophers would say: the same old argument for which we can only repeat Philo's answer.

Both Spinoza and Hume reject the principle of the infinity of God in the sense of the unknowability of God.

In Spinoza this rejection is expressed in the proposition that "the human mind possesses an adequate knowledge of the eternal and infinite essence of God." [30] The argument by which he has arrived at this conclusion is not directly and explicitly stated. It may, however, be unfolded as follows:

Spinoza begins by asking himself: What do scriptural philosophers mean when they speak of God as unknowable? They mean, of course, that He cannot be the subject of a definition. And what do they mean by definition? They mean, of course, the Aristotelian kind of definition, which consists of a genus and a specific difference and which is conceived of as prior to the *definiendum* and as its cause.[31] Spinoza refers to this kind of definition as that which must "include the proximate cause" [32] and describes it as applying only to created things.[33] Taken in this sense, Spinoza admits that God is indefinable and hence unknowable. It is in this sense that he says "every substance is absolutely infinite," [34] by which, in the context in which he uses this proposition, he means that God is indefinable and unknowable.[35] But God, according to Spinoza, is immediately known by his third kind of knowledge, the intuitive knowledge, for God being an uncreated thing, which is in itself or is the cause of itself, becomes known to us through himself. It is in this sense that he says that "the human mind possesses an adequate knowledge of the eternal and infinite essence of God." [36] Thereby Spinoza challenges scriptural philosophers: You say that the existence of God can be demonstrated only *a posteriori*, and hence you say that, while His existence can be known, His essence is unknown. I say that His existence can be known *a priori*, and so His essence is known no less than His existence.

To this, I imagine, our hypothetical refuter would answer that those for whom he speaks would deny that God is an object of immediate knowledge. He would remind Spinoza of his own reference to St. Thomas' denial that God could be proved *a priori*.[37] Indeed, some scriptural philosophers speak of direct vision of God, but this is not the same as the intuitive knowledge of Spinoza. None of the scriptural philosophers, their hypothetical spokesman would argue, would admit that the human mind can generate its own knowledge. All knowledge, he would say for them, must come from an external source, though not necessarily a sensible source. He would go further and maintain that no Greek philosopher ever believed that the mind generates its own knowledge. What is the so-called immediate knowledge of Plato if not the recollection of pre-existent ideas? And what are the indemonstrable immediately known premises of Aristotle if not something which have ultimately their source in sense perception? And the common notions of the Stoics, are they not based upon experience? Even the innate ideas of Descartes can be shown to have been considered by him as having an external source. Our hypothetical scriptural philosopher would admit, of course, that Spinoza has an explanation for his intuitive knowledge, which is consistent with his general system of philosophy, but he would challenge both the explanation and the system.

In Hume, the argument against the unknowability of God is more direct and more explicit. Referring to all the scriptural philosophers as mystics, he addresses them as follows: "How do you Mystics, who maintain the absolute incomprehensibility of the Deity, differ from Sceptics or Atheists, who assert that the first cause of all is unknown and unintelligible?" [38] He thus argues from a lack of knowledge of the essence of God to a lack of knowledge of His existence.

Let us see how our hypothetical scriptural philosopher would answer this argument.

First, he would say it is an old argument. It is to be found in Thomas Aquinas.[39] It occurs in St. Thomas' refutation of those anti-rationalist theologians who maintain that the existence of God is a matter of faith only and cannot be demonstrated by reason. For in God, they argue, existence is identical with essence and, inasmuch as God's essence cannot be known, His existence cannot be demonstrated. This argument of St. Thomas' anti-rationalist theologians is exactly the same as that of Hume, except that in St. Thomas the argument is put in the mouth of those who, denying that God can be demonstrated by reason, fall back upon faith, whereas in Hume it is quoted in the name of those who, denying that God can be demonstrated by reason, became sceptics or atheists.

The answer given by St. Thomas is that the existence of God which is said to be identical with His essence is not the same kind of existence of God which can be established by demonstration.[40] Our hypothetical scriptural philosopher, I think, could do better than that. He would go about answering Hume as follows. He would say that Hume's contention that a God who is not known is a God that does not exist has in it a touch of Berkeleyan philosophy. It implies that to exist means to be perceived, or to be known, so that if a thing is not known it does not exist. Our hypothetical scriptural philosopher would admit that, if one really believed that only that exists which is known, one cannot consistently affirm both that God exists and that God cannot be known.

But, scriptural philosophers, their hypothetical spokesman would continue, do not admit the main premise. They do not believe that to exist is to be known. They are old-fashioned philosophers, Aristotelians, if you please. With all their quarrels with Aristotle on matters divine, they are inclined to agree with him in matters mundane. And following the old custom of scriptural philosophers of documenting every statement they make, our hypothetical spokesman of scriptural philosophers

would refer to Aristotle's discussion of the distinction between
a relation in which the correlatives are simultaneous in nature
and a relation in which the correlatives are not simultaneous
in nature.[41] By a relation in which the correlatives are simultaneous in nature, Aristotle means a relation in which the
existence of one of the correlatives necessarily implies the
existence of the other, as, for instance, the correlatives "master" and "slave," in which the existence of "master" necessitates the existence of "slave" and *vice versa* the existence of
"slave" necessitates the existence of "master." By a relation in
which the correlatives are not simultaneous in nature, Aristotle
means a relation in which one correlative may exist even when
the other correlative does not exist. And he illustrates it by the
example of the relation of "knowledge" to the "object of
knowledge." This relation, he says, is one in which the correlatives are not simultaneous in nature, because the "object of
knowledge" may have existence even when there is no "knowledge" of it, as, for instance, the squaring of a circle. And so,
our hypothetical scriptural philosopher would conclude, there
is a difference between the assertion that God's essence cannot
be known and the assertion that God's existence, which is
identical with His essence, can be demonstrated, for this is
exactly a case of a relation between "knowledge" and the
"object of knowledge," by which Aristotle illustrates the kind
of relation in which the correlatives are not simultaneous in
nature and of which he consequently says that one of the
correlatives, the "object of knowledge," may exist, even though
the other correlative, "knowledge," does not exist.

Then Spinoza, Hume, and Mill reject the infinity of God
in the sense of infinite goodness by invoking the old problem
of evil. Spinoza introduces the problem by the statement that
"amidst so much in nature that is beneficial, not a few things
must have been observed which are injurious" and he illustrates it by an old-fashioned list of evils: "storms, earthquakes,
diseases." [42] Hume, with the scriptural expressions "cursed is
the ground" (Genesis 3:17) and "the earth also was corrupted"
(Genesis 6:11) and "the land was polluted" (Psalms 106:38)
in the back of his mind, starts out with the general statement
that "the whole earth . . . is cursed and polluted" and then
proceeds to enumerate the various evils in the world in the
form of an elaboration on an allusion to Hobbes' dictum
about the war of every one against every one.[43] And John
Stuart Mill, lugubriously pointing to history, shows how during

all past ages in all countries mankind's lot was not a happy one.[44]

Logically, the problem presents itself to them in the form of a dilemma. Spinoza, dealing in general with the finitude of the world, which includes the evil therein, phrases the dilemma as follows: "If it is finite through its cause, this must be either because it *could* not give more, or because it *would* not give more. That He should not have been able to give more would contradict His omnipotence; that He should not have been willing to give more, when He could well do so, savors of *ill-will*, which is nowise in God, who is all *goodness* and perfection." [45] Hume, dealing directly with the problem of evil, phrases the dilemma in similar terms as follows: "Is He willing to prevent evil, but not able? Then He is impotent. Is He able but not willing? Then He is malevolent." [46] Both of them finally bring up the sovereign traditional solution, that of Zophar the Naamathite, to the effect that one cannot find out the deep things of God or attain unto the purpose of the Almighty. But Spinoza dismisses it contemptuously in his statement: "And so you fly to the will of God, the asylum of ignorance" [47] and Hume ironically remarks that he is willing to rest the argument with the statement "that these subjects exceed all human capacity, and that our common measures of truth and falsehood are not applicable to them." [48] John Stuart Mill somberly argues: "If the motive of the Deity for creating sentient beings was the happiness of the beings He created, his purpose . . . must be pronounced . . . to have been thus far an ignominious failure." [49]

To all this our hypothetical scriptural philosopher would say that all those for whom he speaks are willing to rest their case with a declaration of our ignorance of God's ways and would ask: Does anybody know of a better solution? and is not resignation out of faith better than resignation out of despair?

They all also reject the infinity of God in the sense of infinite power, which, of course, involves infinite goodness with its implication of will and design. They each have a different argument against it.

In Spinoza there is the implication of an argument that scriptural philosophers in their view on God's omnipotence contradict themselves. Evidently drawing upon statements of Maimonides and St. Thomas to the effect that God has no power over impossibilities, such, for instance, as making contraries to be in the same subject at the same time and in the same respect, or changing himself into a body, or producing a square the diagonal of which be equal to its side, or making the past not to have been,[50] he finds this to be contradictory with their expressed belief that "all things are possible with God." This is implied in his argument that to say that God, if He willed, could not have created the world, is like saying that "God could bring about that it should not follow from the nature of a triangle that its two angles should be equal to two right angles." [51] It is also implied in his argument that it is more in accord with the conception of the "omnipotence of God" to say that the world, and this world only, continuously flows from God by the same necessity and in the same way as it follows from the nature of a triangle that its three angles are equal to two right angles than to say that this world was created by a decision of God's absolute will out of many other possible worlds which He could have created.[52] Both these arguments mean that for scriptural philosophers to be consistent in their view of the infinite power of God they would also have to believe that God has power to change what is described by them as impossibilities.

Let us see how our hypothetical scriptural philosopher would deal with this argument.

To begin with, our hypothetical scriptural philosopher would say that not only Maimonides and St. Thomas, whom Spinoza undoubtedly had in mind in his criticism, but also all other scriptural philosophers would admit that God does not change impossibilities. In support of this he would refer offhand to Origen [53] and St. Augustine,[54] among Christian philosophers, to the Mutakallimūn, among Muslim philosophers,[55] to Saadia,[56] among Jewish philosophers. He would also add, in passing, that all these scriptural philosophers had been re-echoing a sentiment expressed in the same words and illustrated by the same examples by such pagan philosophers as Alexander Aphrodisiensis [57] and Plotinus [58] and others.[59]

Then he would try to show that scriptural philosophers themselves were aware of this apparent contradiction in their own belief. Such an awareness of it, he would show, is implied in a passage in Origen. In that passage Origen quotes Celsus as ascribing to Christians the statement "as if it were said by us, that 'God will be able to do all things' " (δυνήσεται πάντα ὁ θεός) .[60] Origen does not disown the view expressed in this statement. His remark "as if it were said by us" merely means that it is not a verbatim quotation from the New Testament. On the contrary, Origen himself in another place in the same work reproduces with approval the same view in his statement that "all is possible to God" (πᾶν δυνατὸν τῷ θεῷ),[61] which is a paraphrase of the New Testament statement that "all things are possible with God" (πάντα δυνατὰ παρὰ τῷ θεῷ).[62] But while he agrees with this view, he admits that Celsus "might with a show of reason have opposed it." [63] How Celsus could have opposed it "with a show of reason" he does not explain here. But from Origen's statement elsewhere that Christians take the term "all" in the statement as not to include things that are "inconceivable" (τῶν ἀδιανοήτων) [64] it may be inferred that Celsus could have opposed the statement on the ground that it is contradictory to the Christians' own belief that God has no power over things that are "inconceivable." By things "inconceivable," incidentally, he means things which are in violation of such logical rules as the Law of Contradiction or the rules of mathematics and geometry. Our hypothetical scriptural philosopher would also show that this objection is explicitly quoted by pseudo-Dionysius in the name of a fictitious "Elymas the Magician" (cf. Acts 13:8), who found a contradiction between the Christian belief that "God is omnipotent" and Paul's statement that God "cannot deny himself" (II Timothy 2:13).[65]

Finally he would try to answer this objection. It is not for lack of power, he would argue, that God does not change impossibilities; it is rather out of wisdom and justice. God could have created another world in which these impossibilities would have been possibilities. He can also destroy this world and create a new world in which the impossibilities would become possibilities. But having by His wisdom created this world and implanted in it these laws, He would not change these laws except when it served a certain purpose. For God does not change the laws of nature in vain, nor does He, like a stage magician, perform miracles to amuse or to impress the spectators. Miracles are performed and laws of nature changed by God only in His exercise of individual providence, for the purpose of preserving those who deserve to be preserved or for the purpose of instructing those who deserve to be instructed. Now, in the wisdom of God, the world is so ordered that to attain that purpose of miracles there is only a need for a change of the physical laws of nature; there is no need for a change of the laws of thought or of the laws of mathematics. All miracles recorded in the scriptures, from the creation of the world to the resurrection of Jesus, are miracles which involved only a transgression of the physical laws of nature, for these miracles had purpose. No conceivable purpose could be served in the world as it is presently constituted for a miraculous change in the laws of thought or in the laws of mathematics. When scriptural philosophers, therefore, say that God does not change, in this world as it is presently constituted, the Law of Contradiction or the geometrical proposition about the three angles of a triangle, it is not an indication of a lack of power; it is an indication of the fact that God uses His power in accordance with His wisdom and His goodness.

This answer is implied in Origen's explanation of the statement that with God all things are possible by saying that "in our judgment God can do everything which it is possible for Him to do without ceasing to be God, and good, and wise" [66] or that "we maintain that God cannot do what is disgraceful, since then He would be capable of ceasing to be God, for if He do anything that is disgraceful (αἰσχρόν), He is not God." [67] In the same way, some Muslim Mu'tazilites explain that the impossibility for God to do evil is not because God has no power to do evil, but rather because He does not want to exercise that power, and this because of "His wisdom and mercy" [68] or because of "its being disgraceful (qabīḥah)." [69] So also Isaac Israeli (or Judaeus) says that "the fact that it was impossible for Moses to appear at the time of Adam is not due to the powerlessness of God, but to the fact that such a thing would not belong to wisdom but to absurdity." [70] Similarly Maimonides, speaking of the impossibility on the part of God to change human nature with regard to its freedom of action, says that this is not because God has not the power to do it but rather because, in His wisdom, "it has never been His will to do it, and it never will be." [71] It is also implied in St. Thomas' explanation of why God cannot do that which implies a contradiction by saying that a contradiction implies the notion of non-being and is therefore not "the proper effect" (*proprius effectus*) of God's power.[72]

In Hume the argument against the infinite power of God begins with the general proposition that "like effects prove like causes" [73] and then proceeds as follows: "For as the cause ought only to be proportioned to the effect; and the effect, so far as it falls under our cognizance, is not infinite; what pretensions have we, upon our suppositions, to ascribe that attribute to the divine Being?" [74]

Here, again, our hypothetical spokesman of scriptural philosophers would begin by pointing out that this is an old argument. And he would go on to sketch briefly the history of that argument. He would show how it appears in Plotinus in the form of the following questions: "How from the One, as we conceive it to be, can any multiplicity or duality or number come into existence?" [75] or, "How could all things come from the One which is simple and which shows in its identity no diversity and no duality?" [76] Substitute Hume's terms "infinite" and "finite" for Plotinus' terms "one" and "multiplicity" and you get exactly the same argument, based upon the same principle that "the cause ought only to be proportioned to the effect."

Then our hypothetical scriptural philosophers would show how Plotinus tried to solve this difficulty by making Nous, the first emanation from the One, a being who was one numerically but in whose nature there was an inner duality.

He would then go on to show how scriptural philosophers, such, for instance, as Maimonides [77] among the Jews and Thomas Aquinas among the Christians,[78] have discussed the problem raised by Plotinus as well as his solution, how they refuted his solution of the problem, and how, while agreeing with the principle that "the cause ought only to be proportioned to the effect," they argued that this principle applies only to a cause which produces an effect by necessity, but does not apply to an agent who acts by intelligence and will and design, such as God's is conceived by all of them. Being an intelligent agent acting by will and design, their God, they all argued, could produce a plurality of things, though He is himself one, and could produce a finite world, though He is himself infinite.

What Hume really did here, our hypothetical scriptural philosopher would conclude, was to rake up an old difficulty raised against the non-scriptural conception of God, to overlook the arguments of scriptural philosophers that this difficulty cannot be raised against their scriptural conception of God, and to flaunt it before an innocent world as a new argument against the scriptural conception of God.

An argument against the infinite power of God is also advanced by John Stuart Mill.[79] But as the argument has not been summarized by him in one quotable passage, we shall try to summarize it ourselves in some brief intelligible form; and, despite Mill's disparagement of the syllogism, we can find no better method of making his argument intelligible than by reducing it to a syllogism. Thus syllogistically stated, his argument runs as follows:

Everyone who employs means in carrying out his purpose is finite;

God employs means in carrying out His purpose;

Therefore, God is finite.

Here, too, the scriptural philosopher would begin his refutation of this argument by pointing out that the implication of powerlessness in the attribution to God of action for a purpose and by the use of means was a difficulty not unknown to scriptural philosophers of the past. It is this very difficulty that had moved a certain class of Muslim theologians to deny that God acts by the use of means. As represented by Averroes, they believed "that the One, that is, God, acts upon all beings without any intermediary" [80] and, as represented by Maimonides, they believed "that God does not do one thing for the sake of another and that there are no causes and effects, but that His actions are all the direct result of His will," [81] and, as represented by Thomas Aquinas, they believed "that God alone is the immediate cause of everything wrought." [82] This view of Muslim orthodoxy, which was repudiated alike by Averroes and Maimonides and St. Thomas, was later accepted, for the very same reason of safeguarding the infinite power of God, by the Christian philosopher Nicolaus of Autrecourt.[83]

Then our hypothetical scriptural philosopher would try to show how this argument could be answered. He would try to show how God's employment of means differs from the employment of means by other beings. All other beings employ those means because, without them, they are powerless to do the things they are resolved to do. Not so is God. He has the power to do everything directly himself without any means. In fact, whenever He wishes, He does things directly himself without any means. And even when, for certain reasons, known or unknown to us, He employs means, those means act in complete obedience to His will and nowise do they limit His power. Supporting this assertion of his, our hypothetical scriptural philosopher would quote such statements of Thomas Aquinas as that "it is erroneous to say that God cannot himself produce all the determinate effects which are produced by any created cause" [84] and that "it is clear that . . . nothing is a cause of being except in so far as it acts by God's power." [85] He would also quote the view of Maimonides, according to whom the creation of the world was a direct act of the divine will without any intermediate causes [86] and that if in the created world God in His wisdom acts through intermediate causes, these intermediate causes are said by him to act as if commanded by God, with the result that "of everything which is produced by any of these causes it can be said that God commanded that it shall be made or said that it shall be so." [87] And all this, he could conclude, ultimately goes back to Philo who divided God's actions into those which were performed by Him directly and into those performed by Him by means of intermediary causes,[88] and those intermediary causes have no power of their own but act only at the bidding of God.[89]

What Mill really did here, our hypothetical scriptural philosopher would conclude, was to rake up an old difficulty, to overlook the answer given to it, and garnish it up as a new argument.

In my brief survey of some of the reactions to the Philonic conception of God in modern philosophy I have tried to deal with the subject as a historian and not as a theologian. Knowing that scriptural philosophers in the past have raised difficulties against their own belief in revelation and in the various meanings of the infinity of God, I wanted to find out how the difficulties raised by themselves compared with the arguments raised against them by their opponents ever since the seventeenth century. We are often told that the intellectual climate in modern philosophy ever since Spinoza is different and therefore the arguments raised against such beliefs as revelation and the incomprehensibility, goodness, and omnipotence of God are also different. But while indeed it is to be granted that the climate is different, the storms and thunderings and lightnings, as we have seen, are the same. They are not the clash of newly discovered facts with old beliefs. They are still the clash of one kind of interpretation of facts with another kind of interpretation of the same facts.

When philosophers since the seventeenth century deny revelation it is not because new facts have been discovered to discredit it, but rather because, as in the time of Philo, the belief in revelation is held to have no greater historical validity than the myths of the Greeks, though in modern times a greater verisimilitude is lent to this argument by the greater knowledge we now possess of similar myths among other peoples. Logically the argument is still, as Philo characterized it, the refusal to distinguish between Scripture and myth, except that nowadays more people are apt to refuse to distinguish between them.

When they deny the belief that God is infinite in the three senses in which He has been described as infinite it is again not because new facts have been discovered to discredit this belief but rather because, like Job of old, they refuse to acknowledge that one cannot find out the deep things of God and to attain unto the purpose of the Almighty. Logically it is still the same old question whether God is like the world or unlike the world, whether He is part of nature or is above nature, leading on the one hand to the assertion that our knowledge of nature is now greater than in the past and on the other hand to the contention that with all our increased knowledge of nature the facts thereof, not only in their raw state but even in their scientific correlations, are still susceptible of the age-old interpretation of rationalized scriptural theology.

The Philonic type of religious philosophy may be described after Matthew 9:17 as a process whereby old wine is put into new bottles. The speculation about God in modern philosophy, ever since the seventeenth century, is still a process of putting old wine into new bottles. There is only the following difference: the wine is no longer of the old vintage of the revelational theology of Scripture; it is of the old vintage of the natural or verbal theology of Greek philosophy. Sometimes, however, even the bottles are not new; it is only the labels that are new —and one begins to wonder how many of the latter-day philosophies of religion would not prove to be only philosophies of labels.

Notes

1. E. R. Dodds, "The Parmenides of Plato and the Origin of the Neoplatonic 'One,' " *Classical Quarterly,* 22 (1928): 132 n. 1.

2. Cf. my *Philo,* rev. ed. (Cambridge, Mass., 1948), I, 165–167.

3. *Conf.* 2, 2.

4. Cf. my *Philosophy of the Church Fathers,* I (Cambridge, Mass., 1956), 19.

5. *Decal.* 9, 32f.

6. Cf. *Philo,* II, 52f.

7. Aristotle, *Physica* I, 4, 187b, 7; *Metaphysica* II, 2, 994b, 27–30.

8. Cf. *Philo,* II, 112–113.

9. Cf. my paper "The Knowability and Describability of God in Plato and Aristotle," *Harvard Studies in Classical Philology,* 56/57 (Cambridge, Mass., 1947): 233–249.

10. Cf. *Philo,* II, 94ff.

11. *Timaeus* 29 D–E.

12. *Ibid.* 41 A.

13. Cf. Justin Martyr, *Dial. cum Tryph.* 1.
14. *Apud* Cicero, *De Natura Deorum* II, 66, 167; cf. III, 35, 86; Plutarch, *De Stoicorum Repugnantiis* 37, 2.
15. *Migr.* 33, 186.
16. Cf. *Philo*, II, 279–303.
17. *Provid.* 2, 54; cf. *Philo*, II, 291 n. 49.
18. Cf. *Philo*, I, 325–347.
19. Cf. *ibid.*, I, 315–316.
20. Cf. *ibid.*, I, 347–356.
21. Cf. *ibid.*, I, 316.
22. Cf. *ibid.*, I, 295ff.
23. Cf. *ibid.*, I, 300–316.
24. Cf. *ibid.*, I, 328–330.
25. Cf. *ibid.*, I, 315–316.
26. *Opif.*, 14, 46; cf. *Jos.* 40, 244; *Mos.* 1, 31, 174; *Qu. in Gen.* IV, 17.
27. *Tractatus Theologico-Politicus* 5 (*Opera,* ed. Gebhardt, Heidelberg, 1925, III, 79, ll. 19–20).
28. *An Inquiry Concerning the Human Understanding* X, 2 (*Philosophical Works,* Boston, 1854, IV, 138).
29. "Theism, Part IV: Revelation," in *Three Essays on Religion* (New York, 1878), p. 217.
30. *Ethics* II, Prop. 47.
31. Aristotle, *De Anima* II, 2, 413a, 15; *Anal. Post.* II, 10, 93b, 38ff.
32. *Short Treatise* I, 7, § 9.
33. *Tractatus de Intellectus Emendatione* §96ff. (*Opera,* II, 35).
34. *Ethics* I, Prop. 8.
35. Cf. my *Philosophy of Spinoza* (Cambridge, Mass., 1934), I, 138.
36. *Ethics* I, Prop. 47.
37. *Short Treatise* I, 1; cf. Thomas Aquinas, *Sum. Theol.* I, 2, 1c; *Cont. Gent.* I, 10–11.
38. *Dialogues Concerning Natural Religion* (*Philosophical Works,* II, 451).
39. *Cont. Gent.* I, 12.
40. *Ibid.*
41. *Categoriae* 7, 7b, 15–35.
42. *Ethics* I, Appendix (*Opera,* II, 79, ll. 18–20).
43. *Dialogues Concerning Natural Religion,* part X (*Philosophical Works,* II, 496f.).
44. "Theism, Part II: Attributes," *Three Essays on Religion,* p. 192.
45. *Short Treatise* I, 2, 5 (*Opera,* I, 20, ll. 18ff.).
46. *Dialogues Concerning Natural Religion* (*Philosophical Works,* II, 501; cf. p. 505).
47. *Ethics* I, Appendix (*Opera,* II, 81, ll. 10–11).
48. *Dialogues Concerning Natural Religion* (*Philosophical Works,* II, 505).
49. *Three Essays on Religion,* p. 192.
50. Maimonides, *Moreh Nebukim* II, 13 (3); *Cont. Gent.* II, 25.
51. *Ethics* I, Prop. 17, Schol. (*Opera,* II, 61, ll. 27–32).
52. *Ibid.* (p. 62, ll. 10–30).
53. *Cont. Cels.* III, 70; V, 23.
54. *Cont. Faust. Manich.* XXVI, 4–5.
55. Ibn Ḥazm, *Fiṣal fi al-Milal* (Cairo, A.H. 1317–1327), IV, 192. ll. 13–14; Ghazālī, *Tahāfut al-Falāsifah,* XVII (ed. Bouyges), §24, p. 292, ll. 2ff.; *Moreh Nebukim* I, 73, Prop. 10.
56. *Emunot ve-De'ot,* II, 13 (ed. Landauer), p. 110, ll. 4–7.

57. *De Fato* 30.

58. *Enneades* VI, 8, 21.

59. Cf. chapter on "Omnipotence" in R. M. Grant, *Miracles and Natural Law in Graeco-Roman and Early Christian Thought* (Amsterdam, 1952), pp. 127–134.

60. *Cont. Cels.* III, 70.

61. *Ibid.,* V, 23.

62. Mark 10:27; cf. Matthew 19:26.

63. *Cont. Cels.* III, 70. Incidentally, Celsus' statement would seem to be a paraphrase of the Septuagint version of Job's address to God (Job 42:1): "I know that Thou art able to do all things (πάντα δύνασαι)."

64. *Ibid.,* V, 23.

65. *De Divinis Nominibus* VIII, 6.

66. *Cont. Cels.* III, 70.

67. *Ibid.,* V. 23. Cf. H. Chadwick's notes in his translation of *Contra Celsum, ad loc.*

68. Al-Ash'arī, *Maqālāt al-Islāmīyīn* (ed. Ritter), p. 555, ll. 6–8.

69. Al-Shahrastānī, *Al-Milal wa'l-Nihal* (ed. Cureton), p. 37, ll. 8–9.

70. The Book of Substances, Fragment II, in A. Altmann and S. M. Stern's *Isaac Israeli* (London, 1958), p. 82.

71. *Moreh Nebukim* III, 32; cf. II, 29.

72. *Cont. Gent.* II, 22, *Item.*

73. *Dialogues Concerning Natural Religion,* part V (*Philosophical Works,* p. 459).

74. *Ibid.* (p. 461).

75. *Enneades* V, 1, 6.

76. *Ibid.,* V, 2, 1.

77. *Moreh Nebukim* II, 22.

78. *Cont. Gent.* II, 21–24.

79. "Theism, Part II: Attributes," *Three Essays on Religion,* pp. 126–167.

80. *In IX Metaph.,* Comm. 7 (Venice, 1574), fol. 231H; XII, Comm. 18, fol. 305F.

81. *Moreh Nebukim* III, 25.

82. *Sum. Theol.* I, 105, 5c.

83. Cf. J. R. Weinberg, *Nicolaus of Autrecourt* (Princeton, 1948), pp. 84ff.

84. *Sum. Theol.* I, 105, 2c.

85. *Cont. Gent.* III, 67.

86. *Moreh Nebukim* II, 18 (2).

87. *Ibid.,* II, 48.

88. Cf. *Philo,* I, 223, 269–270, 282.

89. Cf. *ibid.,* I, 332–347.

6.

New Light on Tannaitic Jewry and on the State of Israel of the Years 132–135 C.E.*

by H. L. Ginsberg

"The State of Israel of the years 132–135 C.E." is the regime set up by the Second Revolt (of Judea against Rome). (The First Revolt was that which resulted in the destruction of Jerusalem in 70 C.E.) My designation of this episode was suggested by the picture that emerges from records that have come to light in recent years of the functioning of an actual independent Jewish state by the name of Israel and, I may add, by the welcome and attractive light that they shed on the head of that state: *Shim'on ben Koseva, Nesi Yisrael,* "Simeon ben Koseba, Prince of Israel." Finally, I have included in the title the words "Tannaitic Jewry," because, while the majority of the documents I am going to speak of date from the years 132–4, others date from various other times in the first two centuries of the Christian Era, and all of these monuments of Jewish Palestine in the Roman Age have something distinctively "tannaitic" about them. When one reads them, one feels translated into the world of the Mishnah.

The modern State of Israel has just celebrated its nineteenth anniversary. It is about coeval with what I call the Scroll Age of Palestinology. For although the first scroll cave was discovered by the Ta'amireh Bedouin in 1947 at the latest, the world at large was informed of the fact only in 1948.

It will be recalled that the site of the first cave is near

---

* This essay was adapted from a lecture delivered by Dr. Ginsberg in 1961, when the Bar Kochba finds were first reported.

An earlier version appeared in *Rabbinical Assembly Proceedings,* vol. XXV (1961), The Rabbinical Assembly, N.Y.

Khirbet Qumran, in what became in 1948 Jordanian territory, and that this was the seat of a monastic order of a peculiar Jewish sect—in all probability the Essenes—to which the discovered manuscripts belonged. To the Bedouin's amazement, the Jordan Government offered a very generous price for any further scrolls or fragments of scrolls that any private persons might have in their possession. The sons of the desert promptly began to explore the environs of Khirbet Qumran intensively, with the result that by 1956 the number of known scroll caves in that region had risen to eleven, and the number of distinct manuscripts to about 700.

But the Bedouin did not confine their archeological activities to the neighborhood of Khirbet Qumran. It was in October 1951 at the latest that they began to ransack some grottoes halfway up the sheer 200 meter wall of a well-nigh inaccessible canyon, known as Wadi Murabba'at, some eleven miles to the southwest of Khirbet Qumran. (Please note now, and recall later that nearly *all* the wadis that empty into the Dead Sea from the west become deep canyons as they approach the sea.) Some of the spoils from these caves were sold between November 1951 and January 1952 to Père Roland de Vaux, O.P., Director of *l'Ecole Biblique et Archéologique Française*, in Jordanian Jerusalem, and in January 1952 de Vaux himself set out on an expedition to the source. Of the four caves he found there, two in particular contained remains of intermittent human occupation from about 3000 B. C. E. to about 1000 C. E. Most abundant were the remains from the first two centuries of the Common Era, including Roman coins and, especially, nine coins of *Shim'on Nesi Yisrael,* "Simeon Prince of Israel," the tragic hero of the Second Jewish Revolt. Since very little rain falls in that section of the country, and since the deep caves are inaccessible to any moisture at all, it is not to be wondered at that the remains of antiquity preserved in them included articles of wood, leather, basketry, and cloth—and *documents of leather and papyrus.* These writings, in contrast to those of the Qumran area, are mostly of a secular character, and de Vaux had been able to tell from the contents of even those of them that were sold to him in Jerusalem that the majority of them dated from the reign of the aforementioned Simeon, Prince of Israel. As early as 1953 he published an actual order by Simeon to one of his officers, Yeshua ben Galgula, and another addressed to the same officer from another source, mentioning incidentally the proximity of "the *Goyim,*" or Romans. At that time he did not publish but only mentioned the existence of contracts dated according to the era of "Israel's Freedom"—meaning the reign of Simeon, Prince of Israel—and of some documents, about whose character he was not clear at the time, dated "in the year *x* of the Liberation of Israel through Simeon *ben Koseba*, Prince of Israel." (Note now the form "Ben Koseba"; I shall discuss it later.) Hints about the contents of other documents were divulged from time to time, and since 1961 we have had a complete publication of all the *Murabba'at* finds. It is a collective work. The purely archeological description is done by de Vaux, with a chapter on the textiles and basketry by G. M. and Elizabeth Crowfoot. The Hebrew and Aramaic documents are described and interpreted by l'Abbé J. T. Milik who, though neither a Frenchman (he is a Pole) nor a Dominican friar (he is a secular priest), has been associated with de Vaux's institution in the work on the scrolls. The Greek and Latin documents are again the province of a Dominican friar of the Ecole, Père P. Benoit. And the few Arabic documents, which are of course the latest of all, are published only from photographs by Professor Ad. Grohmann, a German Arabist at the University of Prague.

This volume (really two volumes of Text and Plates) will be the principal source of our new information on Jewish Palestine in the first two centuries of the Common Era. But there are two other sources. Along with the material from *Wadi Murabba'at*, de Vaux purchased from the Bedouin some documents from "an unknown location," some of which were dated "in the year *x* of Israel's freedom," and all of which were obviously either from the time of Simeon's Revolt or somewhat earlier. From this source, unfortunately, only an interesting recension of the Septuagint of the Minor Prophets and three legal documents have thus far been published. Interestingly enough, one of those legal documents is composed in the Nabatean dialect and script. One of the parties to it is a Jew (Eleazar bar Nikarchos) and one of the witnesses' signatures which happens to be preserved is "Joseph bar Judah" and is executed not in the Nabatean script but in a cursive variety of the Jewish script which is employed in many Jewish documents of this age and region. And it is not the only Nabatean papyrus among the "manuscripts from an unknown locality."

If even de Vaux and his aides were uncertain as to the exact location of the find, and if at least one of the former owners of these writings owned some property in the territory of the Nabateans, which began near the *southern* end of the Dead Sea, how could the archeologists in Israel fail to suspect that the "unknown locality" was somewhere south of the line which divides the Jordanian half of the western shore of the Dead Sea from the Israeli half? I recall reading in the *New York Times* in 1953 an item about an archeological exploration of the Israeli shore of the Dead Sea that was either about to be launched or already in progress. Although all of the positive results that were later announced concerned Masada, the canyons between the Jordan border and Masada were also searched, but no scrolls were found. Meanwhile, however, the secret of the "unknown site" probably traveled in Jordan from the houses of the Ta'amireh Bedouin (for the money they have made by scroll mining has enabled them to substitute stone buildings for their goat hair tents) to the older part of Bethlehem and to Arab Jerusalem, and it may have been a European scholar who had visited Jordan who, late in 1959 or early in 1960, tipped off the Israeli archeologists that the place to look in was *Wadi Seyl* or, in Hebrew, *Nahal Tse'elim,* the canyon immediately north of Masada. A preliminary exploration by Ahroni in *Nahal Tse'elim* did produce some fragments and so, in the spring of 1960, all four of the canyons between Masada and En-gedi were explored in a large-scale operation. The territory between Masada and En-gedi was divided into four sectors, and the most sensational finds were made in the years 1960 and 1961, in the northernmost sector, the north bank of *Nahal Hever,* under the direction of Yigal Yadin. Thus far they have only been published provisionally, in newspapers and periodicals.

What do we learn from the Israeli finds, and what from the Jordanian ones?

First of all, it is now apparent that both the *Wadi Murabba'at* caves in Jordan and the scroll caves in the four canyons in Israel were *hideouts* to which officers and soldiers of Simeon ben Koseba and their families and others fled with their papers and other effects in the last stage of the Revolt, as one town after another fell into the hands of the Romans.

Where the refugees of *Nahal Hever* fled from we know for sure: from nearby *En-gedi,* a beautiful oasis by the Dead Sea just south of the Jordan-Israel border. The documents that Yadin discovered there in 1960 are (apart from a fragment of the Book of Psalms) letters addressed, mostly by Simeon ben Koseba, Prince of Israel, to Jonathan ben Ba'ya and Masabala ben Simeon, two officials of Simeon ben Koseba's

who were stationed at *En-gedi* and charged with the administration of a district extending up to Tekoa, high up in the
hill country. It is because of the fruitfulness of the *En-gedi* area,
and because *En-gedi* also served as a port (Ben Koseba orders
them to unload "a ship in the harbor of *En-gedi*"), to which
supplies could come from any other point on the Dead Sea
(including the south and east shores), that Ben Koseba sends
insistent orders for supplies to these men. In one letter he complains, "You live in ease, eating and drinking Israel's goods,
and have no care for your brethren." This irritation may reflect a late stage in the Revolt, when things were going badly.
As in one of the orders to Yeshua ben Galgula found in *Wadi
Murabba'at* (mentioned above), the commander-in-chief frequently ends with a threat, "If you fail to do this, it is you
who will pay the penalty." We learn in the course of one of
the letters that Ben Koseba is dissatisfied with the people of
Tekoa (between Bethlehem and Hebron) and orders Jonathan and Masabala to get after them, which means that it was
part of their district. It is well known that some non-Jews
helped Ben Koseba. One such may have been the man with
the Greek name Thyrsos son of Thinonos whom Ben Koseba
orders Jonathan and Masabala to receive because "we need
him." Possibly pagans were also the senders of two letters in
the Greek language which were included in the bundle. They
are fragmentary, but one of them preserves the words Simon
Khosiba (Σιμων Χωσιβα) in Greek characters.

Special interest attaches to one letter in this lot which is
addressed not to Jonathan and Masabala but to a certain
Judah bar Manasseh in a place called *Kiriath 'Arbayya*, which
is doubtless identical with the *Birath 'Arba of Bethlehem* of
rabbinic lore and with modern Khirbet Gharib, south of
Bethlehem. Therefore, since Ben Koseba's headquarters were
in the neighborhood of Jerusalem, Judah bar Manasseh was
stationed between Ben Koseba and Jonathan and Masabala.
To him Ben Koseba writes: "I am sending you two donkeys,
which you are to send to Jonathan bar Ba'yan and Masabala,
for them to load with palm branches and citruses and send
back to camp. You for your part send other men (no doubt
to the neighborhood of the modern garden village of Artas,
south of Bethlehem) for myrtle branches and willow branches.
Prepare these and dispatch them to my camp here." The season was evidently close to Sukkoth. By the way, the *ethrog*
and the *lulab* with the two bunches of greens attached are a
motif on some of Ben Koseba's coins.

To complete the religious picture as it emerges from what is known of the Israeli finds, let me state the following: One of the letters adressed to Jonathan and Masabala mentions a Rabbenu Betaniah bar Miyasa. In another letter Ben Koseba orders them to send a certain person to him "at once, before the Sabbath"—no doubt because otherwise he could not be sent until after the Sabbath (though according to the Halakhah he could be, if it was militarily necessary). Finally, from one of the caves in *Nahal Tse'elim* (most of whose treasures were evidently carried off to Jordan by Bedouin infiltrators), the Israeli excavator recovered fragments of *tefillin*. The only thing that the Chief Rabbinate of Israel today might find wrong among the effects left behind by Ben Koseba's subordinates in caves on the Israel side of the border are a hoard of copper libation vessels which were evidently captured from a Roman regiment. Since the mythological reliefs with which they were adorned were defaced, it would seem that their new Jewish owners meant to keep them for their own use; but according to the Halakah the entire vessels, as appurtenances of idolatry, ought to have been ground to powder and cast upon the Dead Sea, unless they were defaced by non-Jews. Perhaps some of Ben Koseba's Gentile allies obliged.

But it is when we turn to the *Wadi Murabba'at* material (which is much richer than the Israeli material but may be equaled when the Israelis have completed all their explorations and published all their material), that we can hardly believe that the picture of living tannaitic Judaism that confronts us is real. We are not surprised to read in an unfortunately fragmentary letter from Ben Koseba to the aforementioned Yeshua ben Galgula instructions to accommodate some products and/or people over the Sabbath. We are, however, very interested to discover that the remnants of Scriptures (their fragmentary character and the wild manner in which some of the strips are torn seem to point to vandalism on the part of Roman soldiers frustrated by the slow and costly task of crushing skillfully directed guerillas) are all—basically—standard texts, down to the spelling and *parashiyot,* and we are more than a little intrigued to discover phylacteries of both the Rabbenu Tam and another type (with all four *parashiyot* in the order in which they occur in the Bible). It is without doubt only an accident that all the complete Ben Koseba phylacteries that have been found seem to have been *shel yad,* inasmuch as the *din* that a *shel rosh* box has to have four compartments was observed even among the pre-Yavneh and frankly heretical Qumranites.

But most excitingly informative, even on religious matters, are the secular documents. First of all, the trilingual character of Jewish Palestine is vividly brought home to us. On the one hand, we have letters addressed to Ben Koseba's officer Yeshua ben Galgula not only by Ben Koseba himself but also by the notables of *En-gedi* and by those of an otherwise unknown town by the name of *Beth Mashko*—all written in Hebrew. We have even quite a number of Hebrew legal documents from the time of Ben Koseba's revolt. But, on the other hand, we have the marriage contract of a lady of the Galgula family, executed in the year 124 C. E. (eight years before the revolt), in Greek; and in one of the two Hebrew deeds of sale from Jerusalem the vendor, a certain Kleopos son of Eutrapelos, signs his name in Greek, though his wife, Shappirah bath Yeshua, co-signs in Hebrew characters. And of course there are even more documents in Aramaic than in Hebrew.

It must not be supposed that the language of the Hebrew documents was artificial. On the contrary, just these documents have elicited from their editor, l'Abbé J. T. Milik, this observation: "The thesis of scholars like Segal, Ben Yehuda, and Klausner, who have maintained that mishnaic Hebrew was a language spoken by the people of Judea in the Persian and Greco-Roman Ages, is no longer a hypothesis; it is an established fact." I can see no evidence for dating the transition from biblical to what is usually called mishnaic Hebrew so far back as the Persian period, but otherwise I agree entirely with Milik; and I believe that you will too, if you will only consider the following two facts. In talmudic literature we frequently find *himmenu* for *mimmenu, himmakh* for *mimmakh,* etc. The Hebrew of our documents employs only forms with *himm—*. What earthy reason could either the Rabbis or the authors of our documents have had for using such forms, other than the fact that they were current in everyday Hebrew? They are neither Aramaic (which would read *minneh, minnakh,* etc.) nor Old Hebrew, but can only have been developed from the Old Hebrew forms, in living speech, by dissimilation (*mimm> himm—*). Perhaps you will object that though mishnaic Hebrew did at one time evolve naturally from biblical Hebrew it had ceased to be spoken by ordinary people long before 130 C. E., and that Ben Koseba and his officers and officials were merely imitating the literary language of the Rabbis. That, however, is untenable. The Rabbis continued to say *et habbayit, et hammakom,* etc. Ben Koseba's scribes and officials, on the other hand, have reduced the particle *et* to a single sound, *t,* analogous to the prepositions *b, k,* and *l* and, as sometimes happens with the latter, the article *ha* is syncopated after this *t,* so that one says *takkevalim* for *et hakkevalim, tammakom* for *et hammakom,* etc. This, again, can only be a natural development which took place in *spoken* Hebrew. (There is nothing like it in Aramaic.) It cannot be doubted but that there were still in Ben Koseba's time villages in Judah which were Hebrew-speaking.

One such town was in all probability *Ir-Nahash.* It is mentioned once in the Bible (I Chronicles 4:12), and in Ben Koseba's time it evidently was included in a toparchy (or county) whose administrative center was the fortress of Herodium, southeast of Bethlehem. The *Murrabba'at* documents include a number of agreements entered into in the year 133, at Herodium with various persons from *Ir-Nahash,* by one Hillel ben Garis, acting in the name of Ben Koseba, by which those persons obtained on lease from Ben Koseba the farms on which they lived. There is reason to believe that the land was not Ben Koseba's private property but crown land which he had taken over from the ousted Roman authorities. The interesting thing is that every one of these deeds stipulated that the lease is to run only until *sof erev hashshemittah* (the end of the year before the Sabbatical year), for of course Ben Koseba would permit neither his private land nor any crown land to be cultivated during the *Shemittah.* Moreover, the grain which the tenant undertakes to pay as rent must be tithed.

It is not, however, only the piety of Ben Koseba and his men that I had in mind when I mentioned the hardly believable picture of living tannaitic Judaism that these documents present, for they also bring home very forcefully the fact that our *Hakhamim,* in prescribing forms of marriage contracts, bills of divorce, and even business contracts, were not creating anything out of whole cloth but were merely regulating customary usage. The resemblance of these documents to those prescribed by the Mishnah is astonishing, if one comes with the preconceived notion that the latter were pure theorizing. But they were not. The *get pashut* and the *get mekushshar* (Mishnah *Baba Batra* 10:1) were living realities, and not only in Palestine, before the rabbis worked out their rules. When the rabbis cite the forms of legal documents in

Aramaic, it is because in the time of the Mishnah the forms in actual use by the majority were Aramaic, though the Mishnah itself testifies that in Judah (southern Palestine) Hebrew marriage contracts were in use. And when they contemplate the possibility that the amount stated in a document in terms of *zuzim* does not tally with the amount stated in terms of *sil'in* (Mishnah *Baba Batra* 10:2), it is because it was a common *practice* in Palestine, whether one wrote in Hebrew, Aramaic or Greek, to state the amount as "X silver denarii, equivalent to ¼ of X tetradrachmas." Only when the study of the oral law was transplanted to other lands (e.g. Babylonia) and other ages did the discussions of such matters become abstract theory. (It is not certain that even the Palestinian Talmud knows just what a *get mekushshar* is.) So, too, the rabbis certainly did not invent the concept of *nikhse melug*, property of a wife, of which the husband has the usufruct. The very word *melug* goes back to Akkadian and is encountered in a Ugaritic poem about marriage. How real the institution was can be seen from the fact that purchasers of real estate in deeds from both *Murabba'at* and the "unknown locality" take care to have the wife of the vendor append a waiver of all claims she may have to the property in question. In one document, the woman implies that she in fact has some claim to the property by stating the consideration she has received from her husband for waiving it.

I may note in passing that one of the two deeds from Jerusalem that I mentioned before shows by its date that Ben Koseba still had control of that city as late as in the autumn (*Tishre*) of the year 134, which perhaps ought not to come as a surprise, seeing that it has always been known that his last stronghold (which fell in 135) was Better, only seven miles to the southwest of Jerusalem. Whether his authority ever extended far north of Jerusalem we cannot say.

I have consistently referred to the leader of the Second Revolt as Ben Koseba, inasmuch as the many contemporary documents now available prove that that was his true surname. Bar Kocheba, the name with which you are all familiar, was only introduced into Jewish usage in the Middle Ages, from Christian sources. It was no doubt current during the Revolt as a nickname of the hero ("the Son of the Star"); for the device on some of his coins is a shrine with a star above it, and we know that the greatest man among his contemporaries, Akiba, believed that this was the Messiah and applied to him the verse (Numbers 24:17) "A star comes forward from Jacob." But the old Jewish sources never call him anything but Ben Kozeba or Bar Kozeba. The z may be due to partial assimilation of the s to the b or to disappointment over his failure (kozeb, disappointing, unreliable). We now know that it was originally s. Let us henceforth call him by his rightful name, since we have nothing to be ashamed of in Shim'on ben Koseba, Nesi Yisrael. He held out three and one-half years against all-powerful Rome, and sold his people's liberty so dearly that Emperor Hadrian omitted from his report of victory to the Senate the customary formula "I and the army are well." He distinguished himself from the leaders of the First Revolt by preferring death in battle to being dragged through the streets of Rome to grace the triumph of a Roman emperor. He was, in addition, a pious Jew, and if Jamnia (Yavneh) had not been situated on the coast, and therefore always remained under Roman control, we may be sure other rabbis would have openly agreed with Akiba's opinion that Simeon was the Messiah. Everybody is familiar with the dispute between Rabbi Akiba and Rabbi Yohanan ben Toretha. I wish to point out what is usually overlooked, namely, that Rabbi Yohanan did not deny Ben Koseba's messiahship because he found anything for which to criticize him; it was only that the Messiah, in Rabbi Yohanan's opinion, had not yet come. Within the territory that Ben Koseba controlled, Rabbenu Betaniah ben Miyasa, whom he refers to in one of his letters (see above), was evidently on good terms with him. As Maimonides explains, only the outcome can prove whether or not a leader is the Messiah. The outcome proved that Ben Koseba was not the Messiah, but the record proves that he is deserving of reverent remembrance as Shim'on ben Koseba, Prince of Israel.

These records of the ephemeral second-century State of Israel—these copies of the Scriptures, these letters which bear witness to the Prince's solicitude for the observance of the Sabbath, and even for the supplying of his soldiers with etrogim and lulabim for Sukkoth—help to explain the rise of the vigorous State of Israel of today. The latter was of course brought into being by the utilization of opportunities, but what explains the existence of somebody to utilize—and in fact largely create—the opportunities? What explains the existence, in the nineteenth and twentieth centuries, of a Jewry with the will to rebuild its national life? Consult the records of the preceding State of Israel for the answer: That which has preserved Jewry through the intervening eighteen centuries of dispersion is Judaism.

7.

Response to the Introduction
by Professor Alexander Marx *

by Saul Lieberman

Mr. Chairman, Professor Marx, Professor Finkelstein,
Ladies and Gentlemen: At the outset, I should like to thank
Professor Marx for the lovely things he said about me. At the
Jewish Theological Seminary, you see, we have no need to
import people from other institutions in order to praise each
other. This at least shows the love and harmony which exist
between the members of the faculty. I suspect that Professor
Marx feared that I was going to talk about him, so he wanted
to neutralize in advance the effect of anything that I should
have to say.

Here, in the intimate circle of rabbis who are former students of yours, Professor Marx, I should like to say a few
words to you. I wish to utilize this occasion to extend to you
our heartiest congratulations and best wishes on the occasion
of your seventieth birthday. May it be granted to you to continue for many years in your work, in your fruitful literary
activities.

I should like to thank the Rabbinical Assembly for granting
me this opportunity to see all of you together, and especially
for this chance to see former students of mine, many of whom
I have not seen for a number of years. You realize what such
an opportunity means to a teacher. It was especially gratifying
to me to see that you associated my address with the Siyyum
Hashas which is so dear to all of us. It was indeed gratifying
to see or rather to hear the Hadran of Rabbi Abrams. I'm convinced that he has studied at least one tractate of the Talmud.

---

* From *Rabbinical Assembly Proceedings*, vol. XII (1948). The Rabbinical Assembly, N.Y.

Since I am a guest, I will not venture to offer you any suggestions. Permit me, however, to make one observation. It
may be worthwhile that at your annual convention of the Rabbinical Assembly, lots be cast as to who should deliver the
Hadran. Then at least one could be sure that all of you will
have studied the assignment.

Gentlemen, I originally intended to talk about Palestine.
However, in view of what has happened in the last few days,
I really do not feel competent or articulate enough to talk
about Palestine, to talk about the martyrs of Palestine. I feel
that whatever I could say would only devaluate the subject,
and I should, therefore, prefer to pass over it in silence. לך
דמיה תהלה: אלהים בציון.

I shall, therefore, employ the easier method, which is the
traditional way, of discussing a few passages which are recorded at the end of the "Shas."

We will not discuss the mother, that is Palestine, or the
father's wife, namely Babylonia, as the Palestinian Talmud
calls these two countries. We will rather discuss a sister of
Jerusalem, Alexandria, and thus pay tribute to the achievements and contributions of one of the ancient Jewish communities, that of Alexandria. We will later also proceed to make
a comparison between the Alexandrian community and the
Jewish community of Rome.

At the end of the Talmud (Nidda 69b), we read: The people
of Alexandria put twelve questions before Rabbi Joshua b.
Hanania. Three questions concerned Halaka, three Aggada,
three דברי בורות (I will return to this term afterwards), and
three questions were problems in practical wisdom.

Let us first of all, dispense with six questions which are
not of immediate interest to us here, namely, the three problems
in practical wisdom, and the three questions in Aggada. These
subjects are discussed in other parts of the Talmud, and different replies are given in advice. Furthermore, they are
merely simple questions—not real problems—and do not
evince any particular mark of learning.

We would, however, like to dwell on the third set of three
questions, so that we may be able to determine the exact meaning of דברי בורות.

R. Joshua was asked: Does Lot's wife impart impurity? He
replied that a dead body imparts impurity, not so a pillar of
salt. Again he was asked: Did the son of the Shunamite whom
Elisha revived impart impurity? He replied: A dead body

imparts impurity, but not a living man. The third question
was: Would the dead, after their resurrection, require purification with the ashes of the red heifer? To this he replied: At
that time, we will consider the question. Another version of
this reply was: At that time, Moses will be with them; let
him decide.

Rashi explains דברי בורות as silly questions. Although I do
not wish to question the interpretation of the highest authority, we know that there are sources which were not available to
Rashi in his time, or which he did not consult or consulted but
rarely. Such a source is the Sifre Zutta where we read (ed.
Horowitz, p. 305): Only the man who touches a dead body
is impure; the dead body itself, however, is not impure. Only
one who touches a dead body becomes unclean, but the son
of the Shunamite himself was not unclean. You see, then, that
serious attention was given to these questions in a Halakic
source, and I would, therefore, hardly dare to call these silly
questions. If one compares these questions with the practical
ones, which were submitted to R. Joshua, one could translate
the term דברי בורות to mean hypothetical, theoretical, or
questions divorced from any real existing situation. Here, then,
lies the whole key to the idiom and passage which we are considering. It was customary at that time to test the wisdom of
learned men with questions, in order to determine the true
extent of their wisdom. The questions addressed to R. Joshua
were arranged according to a definite plan. According to
rabbinic etiquette, one did not ask more than three questions
in any one subject (Tosephta Sanhedrin VII.7). There are
here twelve questions, then, divided equally into four categories.

Now let us proceed to examine the three problems in Halaka. The first two questions are quite simple, and they are to
be found elsewhere in the Talmud where they are not recorded
in the name of the Alexandrian Jews.*

What is of real concern to us is the third question. The problem posed to R. Joshua was this: If the sin offerings of two
lepers became mixed up, so that the sacrifice of neither one
could be identified; and if one of the sacrifices had already
been offered, and then, one of the lepers dies; what was to be

---

*The authenticity of this passage is beyond question. The term משולחת
instead of the usual מחזיר גרושתו is known to me from no other source
and is patently of local usage. It was not employed in the schools of
Palestine or Babylonia.

done? The living leper could not offer the other sacrifice, because the sacrifice that had been offered was possibly his, whereas the remaining sacrifice was that of the dead person. Now, it is forbidden by Law to offer a sin offering belonging to a dead person. On the other hand, there remains the possibility that the sacrifice which had been offered belonged to the dead leper. Hence, the living one remains obligated to bring a sacrifice. (Furthermore, he cannot bring an entirely new sacrifice, for it is quite possible that the one which had been sacrificed was his, and he will be transgressing the prohibition of bringing חולין בעזרה.)

Now, here one sees a real puzzle. I do not believe that this problem stemmed from a real situation which came up in Alexandria.

Nevertheless, this was a clever theoretical problem. R. Joshua himself remarked to the Alexandrians, "Now you have asked a clever question." (Tosephta, Nega'im, end.) Actually, what we have here is a typical riddle. The Alexandrians merely wished to pose puzzles before R. Joshua to see how he would extricate himself. This he did by replying: Let the living leper transfer the ownership of all of his property to someone else, and he will thus become a poor man. Now the poor, instead of offering a kid as a sacrifice, may bring a pigeon, which is acceptable even if the obligation is a doubtful one. This is how the learned rabbi solved this problem.

This is the only example of genuine rabbinic erudition in the Alexandrian schools which has been preserved in Tannaitic literature.

In Amoraic sources, however, we have another Talmudic passage which stems from the Alexandrian schools. This consists of two questions which were sent by R. Zakkai of Alexandria to Palestine. The first question (Yer. Yebamoth VII.5) concerns the daughter of an Egyptian proselyte, a question which in Egypt, of course, may very well have been a practical one, and which we may, therefore, dismiss for the purpose of our discussion.

The other question, however, was more along the same lines as illustrated above. There is a law that the findings of a minor daughter belonged to her father, while the fruits of her field, that is the income of her property, belong to the daughter. Now R. Zakkai of Alexandria asked the following question (Yer. Ketuboth IV.6): What would be the law if something which belongs to nobody happened to come into the field of the minor daughter. Ordinarily, she would acquire ownership over this thing by dint of her ownership of the field. However, is this thing to be considered a finding and consequently belongs to her father; or since she acquired this through the force of her own property, should it rather be considered as income of her property and consequently belongs to her. You see that this too is a difficult question, a problem in the nature of a puzzle, and it was left to the Palestinians to solve it.

These two questions are constructed in the spirit of the Alexandrian schools, of the sophistic schools of Alexandria where all kinds of puzzle-problems were asked.

Now, what do the rabbinic sources record about the Jewry of Alexandria? Very little. We have an occasional remark about them, such as that they brought their dough offerings to Palestine (Mishna Halla IV.10). This was contrary to the law. Again, they wished to behave like Palestinians on the first day of Succoth that fell on a Sabbath. The Palestinian scholars sent them a message, saying: "Please do not depart from the traditions of your ancestors." (Yer. 'Erubin III, end.)

Other questions sent by the Alexandrian school to Palestine were connected with local scandals. As you know, the Alexandrians abducted girls betrothed to other men. The problem which came to Palestine concerned the status of their children (Tosephta, Ketuboth IV.9 and parallels). Similarly, the Alexandrians asked about the status of children of mixed marriages (Yer. Kiddushin III.14). I do not wish to dwell on these practical questions which could have been asked by any laymen.

The only scholarly material which we have explicitly recorded in the name of the Alexandrian Jews is these two puzzles which I have discussed before. We too must differentiate between questions and problems.

This, therefore, is all that we know in rabbinic literature concerning the erudition of the Jews of Alexandria. Alexandria, however, was, according to tradition, a very old Jewish community which was established around the fourth century B. C. E. In the time of Philo, Egypt had a population of about 1,000,000 Jews. A great number of them lived in Alexandria, and we can suppose that there were certainly hundreds of thousands of Jews there. Alexandria was very near Palestine, and yet this is all that has remained of their rabbinic learning.

Even the problems which we have from them, as I said, are very removed from the reasoning of the Palestinian Talmud.

The Alexandrian Jews may have very well been influenced by the secular schools which flourished in Alexandria. The character of the Alexandrian Jews was not much different from that of the Alexandrian Gentiles. The Alexandrians were notorious at that time for their short temper, their boisterousness, their seditious character, their harshness and their sharpness. The occasional remarks found in the Talmud about the Alexandrian Jews bear out this record. It is told of the Alexandrian Jews that they were extremely impatient, and that they used to pull the hair of the man delegated to drive off the scapegoat on the Day of Atonement. What is more, they wished to be forgiven immediately. When they were hungry, they were so impatient that they refused to wait for their meat to be cooked but rather ate it raw. Since there is another version of these traditions, attributing these characteristics, not to the Alexandrians, but to the Babylonian Jews, we may, of course, give them the benefit of the doubt. Nevertheless, we have a remark in the Yerushalmi (Hagiga III.1) about a scholar who gave a sharp reply to his friends; they, in turn, said: He is a real, genuine Alexandrian.

The famous letter of the Roman Emperor, Claudius, written in 40 C. E., confirms the rabbinic tradition. Pleading with the Alexandrian Jews, the Emperor writes: "Please do not intrude into the Gymnasia and Cosmetic games. Do not bring over your brethren from Egypt and Syria to help you, because I may suspect that you are fomenting a sedition, a plague which will become dangerous to the whole world." Usually, when a Jew commits a wrong, his action becomes a source of danger for the entire world. Nevertheless, Claudius' remark about the intrusion of Jews into the Cosmetic games and Gymnasia does properly characterize the Alexandrian Jews. They attempted to force their way into restricted clubs and into other places where they were not wanted.

Now, what do we know of the institutions of the Alexandrian Jews? The Rabbinic sources (Tosephta, Ketuboth III.1 and parallels) mention a regular Jewish court that had formerly existed in Alexandria. From Greek Papyri which have come down to us, we know that the Jews had archives of their own as distinct from the archives of the city, and there can be little doubt that the Jews also had their own courts. Though we do not know to what extent these courts had authority or competence, they certainly existed. To what extent the Jews had recourse to these courts we do not know.

The Jews of the Diaspora had other institutions which may have been constructed on the lines of Jewish Centers. We know that there was an institution in the Diaspora called *Judaikei*, which, to my mind, signifies a Jewish house, a Jewish center where many activities were conducted.* From the context in which this term is employed (Yer. Gittin I.1) it is obvious that the *Judaikei* was *not* a synagogue.

Similarly, we have a dated inscription from Cyprus of the year 390 in which a Jew boasted that he renovated or repaired the whole building of the *Hebraikei*. There is no doubt that the reference is to the same institution, namely, the Jewish Center. Apparently, then, the Jewish Center is not an innovation of American Jews.

Of course, the synagogue remained the main place of Jewish activity. You have all heard of the great Basilica in Alexandria which, according to the exaggeration of the Aggada, could accommodate 1,200,000 Jews. Though we need not take these numbers literally, there was doubtless a great center there.

We know from Philo that there were a number of synagogues in Alexandria where the Jews gathered together to study Torah. At the end of the 4th century C. E., many of the synagogues were destroyed. The Jews in the Diaspora paid special attention to the external appearance of the synagogue, to its embellishment, and to its decorations. On the walls of the remains of these synagogues, we have found pictures illustrating scenes from the Bible and the Aggada. These decorations were meant for the masses, so that the preacher might be able to demonstrate, to illustrate his sermons, and thus to attract the masses to the synagogue. We now understand what it meant to the Jews when the Christian emperors later forbade them to embellish and to decorate their synagogues.

Within the synagogue, of course, the usual petty ambitions of people were not lacking. People wanted to be presidents of synagogues, and some prided themselves on the fact that they were presidents, the sons of presidents, or the grandsons of presidents of synagogues. However, in one inscription we find a president boasting that all his life, he conducted himself in accordance with the tenets of Judaism. This would seem to have been an exceptional case.

The role played by women in the synagogue was then a considerable one. We find women bearing the titles of "The Mother of the Synagogue," and "President of the Synagogue." We need not take these expressions too seriously, for they may

---

*[Correct as in *P'raqim*, 1, 102. S. L.]

have been mere honorary titles. In an inscription of the 6th century, found in Venice, we read: "The Tomb of Callistos, a baby, president of the synagogue, three years and three months old."

Nevertheless, we know that the role of women in the synagogue should not be underestimated. The inscriptions of the synagogue in Apamea from the end of the 4th century C. E. are quite instructive in this respect. In seven out of fourteen inscriptions, only women are mentioned. In the remaining inscriptions, men and women are mentioned together. The men list the contributions of their wives, their children and their mothers-in-law. We may safely assume, therefore, that the role played by women in the Alexandrian community was not inferior to that played by them in the rest of the Diaspora.

Now what is the Jewish legacy of this great community? Outside of the two puzzle problems which I mentioned before, the entire bequest of Alexandrian Jewry mainly consists of translations of sacred texts and of apologetic literature. It is interesting that the translations of the sacred texts and the apologetic literature were not preserved by the Jews but rather by the Christians. The Jews did not preserve the apologetic literature of their Alexandrian brethren. They preserved only the works which had permanent and everlasting value. But they ignored the apologetic literature composed *ad usum gentilium* as well as for assimilated Jews.

Far be it from me to minimize or to underestimate the great value of this legacy. Apologetic literature was written by Jews throughout the ages and throughout the world. The Jews cannot be dissociated from Judaism. There can be no Judaism without Jews, and there can be no Jews without Judaism.

Apologetic literature was intended to preserve the Jew and to counteract the anti-semitic literature of the Gentiles. The Jews lived in abnormal conditions in a strange country, in a hostile environment where they had to defend themselves. Sometimes this defense succeeded in checking the prejudice of the Gentiles. This mere remedy, however, was very much like a medicine. In each case it had to conform to the peculiar constitution of the patient, to the form which his disease assumed and was, consequently, ever changing. Sometimes remedies help, sometimes they are ineffective, and, on rare occasions, they may even cause harm. Still, it would be preposterous to suggest that one ought not to use medication in the event of illness. Indeed, one must properly diagnose the case before him and use the appropriate tools. I think, therefore, that the legacy of Alexandrian Jewry in the way of apologetic literature has its immense merits. This literature was a service to the Jews as well as to Judaism.

If, however, we read the secular literature of that time, we see that the Gentile world was much more impressed by the behavior of Jews than by their teachings, by their actions more than by their words. Josephus did not exaggerate when he said that the Gentiles admired Jewish unanimity, Jewish practices, Jewish love for charity, and Jewish study and zeal for study of the Torah. We have no cause to discredit his statement. Indeed, the heathen writers confirm it. They were especially impressed by the Jewish zeal for the Law. The pagan writers called the Jews a nation of philosophers, a whole nation of philosophers, because they saw them devoting themselves to the study of the Law. Later, in the Middle Ages, the Christians were also impressed by this characteristic, and the same has held true even in modern times.

An illustration of this is afforded to us by a German writer of the 20th century who was interested in biblical studies. While serving in the German intelligence office in Warsaw during the First World War, the members of his office learned that something very mysterious was going on in the Jewish section. It was said that coachmen come one after another without passengers and disappear mysteriously into a certain courtyard. This German officer went to investigate for himself and arriving at the place in question with two detectives, stood and watched. It was true. Coachman after coachman was driving in with no passengers in his carriage. All of them disappeared into a courtyard into which the German officer followed them. He finally came into one of the upper stories of the building. There he opened the door and saw two long tables surrounded by coachmen who were sitting in their high hats, bent over books, and listening attentively to a man who was expounding something. The officer realized at once that there could be no question about a plot being fomented against the government here. Nevertheless, he stood in amazement. He reports that he remained motionless, observing the occupants of the room without being able to comprehend what was going on. Finally, he motioned to one of the listeners, for, before that, no one had even taken notice of the intruders. Speaking with his fragmentary knowledge of Yiddish, the German motioned to one of the coachmen and asked him, "What is this?"

"Why, this is a synagogue," the Jew replied.

The German repeated his question, "What is this?"

"Why, they are sitting and studying the law."

The German asked, "Is today Yom Kippur, a holy day?"

"No," the Jew said, "this is what we do every day."

"You mean to say that every day you come here and listen to a lecture on the law?"

"Why, certainly," the Jew said.

"After a day of labor and hard work?"

"Yes, that is what we do."

The German was convinced, and he concluded his account, saying: "It is amazing. It is unthinkable. It is inconceivable that German drivers, whose intellectual level is higher than that of Jewish coachmen in Warsaw, should come every day to the University of Berlin and listen to lectures in law."

The German officer did not express it, but what doubtless rose in his mind was the statement of a classical writer: "It is really a people of philosophers." In modern times, as in ancient times, it is this traditional Jewish behavior that has evoked the admiration of the Gentile.

We should like now to compare the Jewish community of Alexandria with another great Jewish community, the Jewish community of Rome. This, too, was an old Jewish community, and by the first century B. C. E., we know, it was a very powerful community. The words of Cicero in this regard are by now a commonplace, but they are still very striking and bear repetition. In an address that Cicero delivered in 59 B. C. E., in defense of Flaccus, who had confiscated Jewish gold designated for the temple in Jerusalem, Cicero said: "And now about the Jewish gold," and turning to the accuser, he said: "I know why you chose this place, the neighborhood of the grades of Aurelius. It is on account of the nature of the accusation that you chose this place and this mob. You know how great are its numbers; you know how strong is its concord; how powerful it is in the political assemblies. Therefore, I am delivering my plea in a whisper, so that only the judges may hear me, because I am afraid."

If one eliminates the anti-semitic remarks in this passage, it is possible to see that if so prominent a citizen as Cicero admitted, as it were, that he was afraid, then, indeed, the Jewish community of Rome must have been a strong and powerful one. Thus, as early as the first century, B. C. E., the Jewish community of Rome was already a powerful and influential one.

Did the Jews confine themselves to political activities alone? We have reliable information indicating that the Jews of Rome had many learned men among them, and that at least for a time, Rome was a center of Jewish learning. You are doubtless all familiar with the name of תודום איש רומי whose statement is recorded in the Talmud. You know that he instituted the practice whereby the Jews of Rome ate a roasted kid on the first night of Passover, a practice against which the Palestinian rabbis demurred. We also know of פלטיון איש רומי whose teachings are preserved in the Palestinian Midrashim though he, himself, is not mentioned in the Talmudic literature. The school of R. Mathias b. Heresh in Rome was so famous that the Palestinian rabbis explicitly recommended it to the scholars saying, *"Justice, Justice shalt thou follow* (Deuteronomy 16:20); follow R. Mathias b. Heresh to Rome." This accounts for the fact that in the name of the Jewish scholars of Rome we have, not merely questions, but positive teachings which emanated from their schools.

It is natural to expect that with the Torah in Rome there should also be an observance of Jewish laws. The works of the pagan writers abound in remarks ridiculing the Jewish observances. They ridiculed the observances of the Sabbath and the Jewish dietary laws, showing, at any rate, that the Jews did practice them. As a matter of fact, vases were found in the ruins of Pompeii inscribed with the words *garum castum, muria casta* which, in all likelihood, meant kosher fish brine. The meaning of these words is not certain, since Pliny tells us that there was special brine prepared in Italy for devotees of superstitious observances. This brine, he says, was prepared from fish without (!) scales for the sacred rites of the Jews. Although there existed some heathen groups who observed certain dietary laws, nevertheless, Pliny, in mentioning the special brine, associated it with the Jews. It is, therefore, safe to assume, that a kosher food industry existed in Italy as early as the first century C. E.

Moreover, the observance of the Sabbath by Roman Jews appears to have been quite common. The Roman writers ridiculed the Jewish Sabbath. They affirmed that the Jews were a lazy people who spent the seventh part of their lives in indolence and in refraining from work. Despite their abuse, the Roman writers themselves found in these practices something to envy.

Josephus reports how much the Gentiles admired the lighting of the candles, and he goes on to say that there was not one community among the Greeks as well as among the barbarians where some Gentiles did not practice the lighting of the candles. Indeed the *ritus lucernarum* was practiced far and wide. In this respect, the description of Perseus is particularly interesting. Perseus, who did not like the Jews, has a picture of the Jewish Sabbath in one of his Satires. He portrays a scene of the tail of a fish floating in sauce on a clay dish. White jars are filled with wine. Pale faces are visible through greasy windows and the smoke being poured forth by flickering candles. This picture was undoubtedly drawn from direct observation of the lower rungs of society in the Roman ghetto. It was a poor house. The faces were white; of the fish there was only a tail. The jars were cheap, and the windows were greasy. And yet, through these greasy windows, the flickering of the dim light inflamed the Gentiles. This they began to imitate.

Only in those communities, then, where there was Jewish learning could Jewish observance be seen in the streets. We read in the Yerushalmi (Sanhedrin VII.19) that when three prominent Palestinian rabbis came to Rome, they wandered about in the streets looking for a Jewish neighborhood. Finally, they came to a place where they saw children playing in the sand. The children would heap up piles of sand and then, removing some of the sand, would say: "This is מעשר and this is תרומה. This is how the Jews do in Palestine." These children had no play-toys. They played in the sand, but yet they knew that "this is how the Jews do in Palestine." The influence of the Torah was to be found in the street even among children playing in the sand.

From Alexandria we have questions associated with local scandal. In Rome, the questions dealt with tithes (Yer. Ma'aser Sheni IV.1), with כתמים ומקוואות, with the purity of Jewish family [life] (Tosephta Nidda VII.1; ibid. Mikwaoth IV.7). In Alexandria, the Jews asked Rabbi Joshua puzzle problems, while in Rome, they asked serious questions of a dogmatic character (Sanhedrin 90b). In the name of the Alexandrian scholars, the rabbis record questions only, while in the name of the Roman scholars, we have positive teachings as well.

Of course, much in the different characteristics of the two communities is to be attributed to their surroundings. We mentioned above the character of the Alexandrian Gentiles, and the Jews were bound to take on some of the color of their neighbors. On the other hand, the Romans were more sober, more conservative and more pious than the Alexandrian

Greeks. Consequently, the Jews of Rome also presented a different appearance from their Alexandrian brethren. But this is not all. The part played by Jewish learning in molding the practices of the two communities cannot be overestimated.

Mention must also be made here of the great political wisdom of the Roman community. At a time when Palestine and its Jews underwent utter destruction, the Roman community preserved a loyal attitude towards the Roman government. There is no record of a single measure taken by the Roman government at that time against the Jewish inhabitants of Rome. Afterwards, indeed, they were in a position to help the Jewish refugees who came to Rome. They supplied the first captives whom Titus brought to Rome with food and drink, and they were in a position to redeem many captives. Afterwards, they were also able to help the Jewish delegations which came over from Palestine. We can imagine what went on in the hearts of the Jews of Rome. Nevertheless, they ostensibly remained faithful citizens.

I do not wish to elaborate on this point. One observation, however, I should like to make. It is clear that one can be a very good citizen and at the same time a bad Jew. One cannot, however, be a bad citizen and a good Jew. Judaism enjoins upon its adherents to remain loyal and to maintain allegiance to the country which affords them protection. We believe that this attitude and behavior of the Jewish community of Rome was owing, at least in part, to the influence of the Torah. In Palestine, the peaceful efforts of the rabbis were unsuccessful, but they certainly could achieve their goal without difficulty in the Jewish community of the capital of Italy.

We must not forget the influence of the Palestinian scholars on the life of the Roman Jewish community. The great center of Jewish learning at Rome was established in the second century by a Palestinian scholar, R. Mathias b. Heresh. Palestinian scholars left their native land to establish academies of Torah throughout the Diaspora. The Sifre (II.80, ed. Finkelstein, p. 146) lists the names of these scholars and describes their feelings at the moment that they were about to leave Palestine for the Diaspora. We are told that when they approached the border of Palestine, they turned their eyes back in the direction of their land, and their eyes began to flow with tears. They tore their garments and returned to Palestine. They finally left for the Diaspora, but not before they showed how difficult it was for them to part with Palestine. For a while they returned, but later, they left. In this connection, we should like to quote a lovely Midrash (which has been lost, but partially preserved in פיוטי יניי p. 116). The Midrash says that when Moses was about to cast away the Tables of the Law, he held them in both hands and, passing them from both hands to one hand, threw them away. דחם משתי ידיו לידו אחת כי אין להשליך אוהב בת אחת. "He passed them from his two hands to one of his hands, for one ought not cast away a beloved in a single instant." Similarly, the scholars of Palestine had to leave, but before leaving it permanently, they showed their love for their country by returning to it for a while.

It is this love for Palestine, these ties with Palestine which give us legal claim now for the restoration of our country. The Palestinian Talmud (Kilayyim VI.5; 'Orla I.2) states the following law: אעפ"י שאין קרקע נגזל יש ייאוש לקרקע "Though soil cannot be stolen, a man can forfeit his right to this soil by giving up hope of ever regaining it." Thanks to the teachings of the rabbis, the Jews never for a moment gave up hope of regaining the soil of Palestine. Never did they renounce their right to Palestine and never have they ceased claiming it in their prayers and in their teachings. It is on this foundation that we now claim that Eretz Yisrael belongs to us.

On the other hand, the attitude of the Palestinians to the Diaspora was not one of disparagement but rather an attitude of love, hesitation and expectation. True, the Palestinian rabbis said עבדים ושפחות אלו בתי דינין שבחוץ לארץ "Slaves and handmaids (Koheleth 2:7) refers to the courts of the Diaspora." Or, אחינו שבחוץ לארץ הדיוטות הן והן טועין את ההלכה "Our brethren in the Diaspora are not competent and do not know the Law." They said that the courts of the Diaspora were unfamiliar with the details of the laws of divorce, שאין בקיאין בדקדוקי גיטין. Later, they did admit that the courts of the Diaspora subsequently became competent in the Law, לאחר שלמדו. Nevertheless, they always feared שמא יחזור דבר לקלקולו, that the Jews in the Diaspora might relapse into their ignorance. That is to say, that one can never be sure that Jewish learning will forever thrive outside of Palestine. That is why also, we in the Diaspora have always to be on our guard. In the Diaspora, we ought to be especially careful to establish Jewish learning, to support the existing Yeshivoth and to found new ones. Now, here, really, I have come to the main point in my address.

You, the men who arranged the program, so concisely and pointedly called my address a "Response." My words are concerned with the response of the Diaspora to the call of the

Torah, with the response of the Jews of the Diaspora to Palestine, and with your response to the call of learning, to the call of Torah and Mitzvot, to the call to fight ignorance and its monstrous twin brother, cynicism. It is cynicism which constitutes the greatest danger to Judaism.

I should like to conclude with a personal incident which recently happened at the Jewish Theological Seminary. About ten days ago, on a Saturday night, I was walking to the Seminary. It was a lovely night. People were flocking to the movies and theatres. At the Seminary, I found many sights shining from the dormitory windows. I came to the fifth floor, and there was not a living soul there. You know, there are offices on the fifth floor. I was seated in my study working, and I knew that at that time I would not disturb anybody if I studied in a loud voice. Late, at about midnight, when I stopped to ponder over a passage which I did not understand, I could hear the voice of someone studying in the dormitory. It was such a sweet voice that I immediately realized that it was not that of a student preparing for his examinations. It was something different. It was a real קול תורה. I could not refrain from going down to one of the floors of the dormitory and listen. The voice attracted me, and I must have stood there for a long time, because my cigar had already begun to burn my fingers. I stood there meditating until the voice stopped. I thought that what happened to me happened to him. He probably doesn't understand something, and so he too has stopped. I knocked on the door of the student, and he was startled, as a matter of fact, frightened.

"Professor," he said, "I have probably disturbed you by studying in a loud voice."

"No," I said, "you didn't disturb me. I merely thought that you came across a difficult passage and that I might help you."

"No," he said, "I am simply tired." Finally the student observed, "I am sorry, but from now on you'll know when I am not studying."

I must tell you that this kind of study, this voice of Torah which had the genuine longing of our ancestors for the Torah brought back to me the voice of the Yeshivoth of the old country. It was gratifying to see that this boy was American born, a son of one of our graduates. I could not help but reflect that as long as this goes on at the Seminary, as long as these mysterious ties between the ivory tower of the fifth floor and the floors of the dormitory continue עוֹד לֹא אָבְדָה תִקְוָתֵנוּ.

8.

Introduction
(to Legends of the Bible by Louis Ginzberg)*

by Shalom Spiegel

The word *legend* is derived from the Latin *legenda* meaning *to be read*. The term originally applied to narratives of the Middle Ages, such as lives of the saints, which had *to be read* as a religious duty. However, what the word suggests need not be limited to its ecclesiastical usage. In a broader sense, legend may be taken to imply whatever will come *to be read* by successive ages into an event or record of the past: the ever-new and ever-changing rereading of old sources by new generations of men. Great events and great books have a posthumous story of their own. Each following period pours its inner life into the patient and pliant texts of old. In turn the familiar documents reward and surprise new inquirers with new answers.

Widely and reverently read, the books of the Bible have had an afterlife unique in the annals of history. Devout centuries wove endless fantasies around the characters and occurrences depicted in the Holy Writ. Both folk imagination and scholar's wit coaxed and forced from its pages a multitude of tales and a host of fancies unforeseen and unsuspected by the writers of the Bible. This creative partnership of posterity, freshly and freely embellishing and embroidering the ancient design, has borne a rich crop of legends in which the biblical text has become disengaged from its first intention, revised and enriched by the faith and fantasy of innumerable readers throughout the ages.

The Bible has been the most widely read book of civiliza-

* From *Legends of the Bible* by Louis Ginzberg, New York, Simon & Schuster, 1956.

tion, and its stories, even before they were written down, had moved the minds and hearts of men for centuries. So the legends of the Bible enshrine musings and meditations inspired by the contents or words of Scripture over the course of thousands of years. Behind these legends is the glory of a book as transformed by a hundred generations of men. Behind them is also the glory of generations whose daily thoughts and deeds were shaped and very lives transformed by the book of books.

A. Sources

The biblical history of Israel, as it left its traces in the writings of the Hebrew Scriptures, spans the course of more than one millennium. If the pristine sagas of the patriarchal age are excluded, it opens with the exodus from Egypt and the legislation at Mount Sinai, the historic foundation or the birth of the people of Israel. The latest biblical document, the apocalypse in the book of Daniel, mirrors the attempt by Antiochus of Syria to destroy an ancient faith and remake the Jews into Greeks. His persecutions succeeded only in driving the faithful into a furious revolt which won a new independence for their people. In rough figures, it is the interval between 1250 and 150 B.C.

The selection of books which constitute the canon of Scriptures was decided upon at the close of the first century of the common era, after the fall of Jerusalem and the conquest of the Jewish state by the Romans. It is inaccurate, of course, to speak of a decision, for the canonizers did not make that selection, but only sanctioned and stabilized a body of writings which had long been considered sacred among their people. But what these scholars endeavored to achieve, and their disciples to maintain, was a clear distinction between inspired Scripture, the inheritance of their early ancestors, and the creations of later centuries. Only the former was permitted to be fixed in writing as the *Writ*, or recorded revelation. All the rest was to remain as the *oral* tradition of Israel.

This sharp demarcation between the two types of tradition, the written and the oral, explains why the remains of the post-biblical age were taught and transmitted only by word of mouth for long centuries. As a result the written records of all

oral tradition, including the legends of the Bible, are comparatively late.

The biblical legends suffered from still another handicap.
While attempts were repeatedly made to systematize the *halakah,* or the law, no such efforts were made for the non-legal
parts of oral tradition, all the miscellany of literature known
as *haggadah.* The term cannot be adequately translated, but
suggests a *tale* implied or derived from Scripture. It is also the
native Hebrew word for the legends of the Bible.

The legends proper were not cleared and sifted from the
mass of extraneous material in which they are embedded. Nor
were they ever collected in their entirety. They have to be
culled from a vast literature, scattered over many countries
and centuries. They will be found, for example, in both the
Palestinian and Babylonian Talmud, which contain the scholarly achievements of the first five centuries of our era. Here
the legends are interspersed with legal discussions which constitute the heart and bulk of the Talmud.

Even when the legends were assembled in special books, the
principle of their arrangement was purely mechanical: they
were strung to the passages of Scripture which they employed
or elaborated. This method gave them the false appearance of
being a running commentary on sections or selections of the
Writ. A further disadvantage of the method was that it broke
up and dispersed many a legend which quoted more than one
passage of the Bible. On the other hand, this link with holy
Scripture secured for the legends station and rank in the curriculum and calendar of the Synagogue.

The form in which the legends were grouped around Scripture usually followed from their function. Collections of
legends which adhered to the order of the biblical text were
the product of instruction and answered the needs of the
school. An early example of such a work is founded on the
book of Genesis and was compiled in the fifth century. Other
collections center around the portions of Scripture assigned for
public reading on sabbaths or on solemn seasons of the synagogal year. They are the outgrowth of preaching and were
designed for *worship.* The oldest of this group is based on
scriptural lessons from the book of Leviticus and was edited
early in the sixth century. In the course of time the two types
of collections were often thrown together, just as in practice
the school often served as a house of prayer.

The work of assembling the ancient legends continued late

into the Middle Ages. Large-scale compendia were made in the fourteenth century, one in the south of France, another in South Arabia. The most popular and comprehensive compilation of legends covering all the books of Scripture stems from the thirteenth century. These late medieval works preserved valuable excerpts from older sources now lost altogether. Sometimes they retrieved from oblivion survivals of authentic lore going back to the golden age of the legends of the Bible, and of the highest flowering of the Palestinian *haggadah*, in the first few centuries of the common era.

While this was their classic age, the legends of the Bible are not limited to antiquity. New legends grew with time and the telling and retelling of old stories. The medieval legends, although rooted in the past, often went their own way, both in original creation and in receptive exchange with the cultures of West and East.

The territorial conquests of Islam brought many races and religions within one political orbit larger than any known to antiquity. From the welter of different traditions there arose centers of learning and literature, art and philosophy. In cities like Bagdad or Cordova representatives of all religions freely commingled, contesting the claims of their respective traditions and submitting all of them to critical inquiry. A fresh approach to the classics of the past became a necessity, if the records of tradition were to survive the challenge of the new ideas. Under the impact of the philosophical critique of religion, the study of the Bible underwent a profound change which also left its traces on the legends of the Bible. The prephilosophic innocence was gone, and the naïve anthropomorphisms of the ancient *haggadah* were attacked or allegorized, refurbished or relinquished. For a time, this age of rational exegesis seemed to spell a death sentence on all creations of folk fancy and of legend.

A reaction set in as if with a vengeance. In the mystic literature of *kabbalah* one can see the resurrection of myth in medieval Judaism. Its great classics—such as the *Zohar*, or the Book of Splendor, a work of thirteenth-century Spain—are replete with old and new legends of the Bible, and with old and new ideas about the presence and power of evil in the good world of God. Ancient tales of the *haggadah* were revived or revised to express dissent from cherished beliefs of the past. The heresies of Gnosis burst forth anew in the heart of ancient monotheism. It took several centuries before the unrest crystallized in the remarkable doctrines of the mystics of Safed, in sixteenth-century Palestine. Eventually the spiritual turmoil spent itself in a new movement of religious revival, called *Hasidism,* which swept East European Jewry in the eighteenth century, yielding still another harvest of folk tales and new legends of the Bible.

B.　Ginzberg's Legends

Louis Ginzberg (1873–1953) grew up in the shadow of legend. An aura of wonder and a mist of fable surrounded the memory of his famous ancestor, Rabbi Elijah of Vilna. At Kovno, Ginzberg's birthplace in Lithuania, and indeed wherever Hebrew books were cherished, the magic of this eighteenth-century saint and scholar continued as a living inspiration. Ginzberg often referred to Rabbi Elijah as both the last classic of Judaism and the pioneer of its modern scholarship. That paradox is characteristic of Ginzberg's own aspiration and achievement. For in him, too, the old and the new were admirably blended. In seats of learning of East European Jewry he early gained thorough knowledge of talmudic and rabbinic lore. At the University of Strassburg, under Theodor Nöldeke, he studied Semitic languages and literatures which, with his own wide reading in ancient and modern classics and his ingrained sense for method, gave him full command of the tools of critical inquiry. The past and the present seemed in him to sustain each other in fruitful concord. Current thought and modern science kept ever fresh and fertile the native soil of ancient tradition in which he was firmly rooted.

Ginzberg began his investigation of the legends of the Bible with a dissertation on the *Haggadah of the Church Fathers,* published in two parts in 1899 and in 1900. Four more installments followed on the same theme, all the overflow of his first effort and the harbingers of his ultimate attainment.

In these monographs Ginzberg set out to search in the writings of the Church Fathers for remains of *haggadah* or legends of the Bible. Such a task would seem comparatively easy whenever the writers themselves mentioned their sources and said expressly: the Hebrews report (*tradunt Hebraei, aiunt Hebraei*). But open acknowledgment was not the medieval practice, and the authors often kept their information undisclosed, or inaccurate, or tantalizingly vague. Furthermore, unless what was said in Greek or Syriac or Latin could be rendered back into the language of the Hebrew Scriptures, and related to kindred records of legendary lore in the Hebrew tradition, the reading of the Fathers would remain fruitless and unrewarding for the exploration of *haggadah*. Because Ginzberg brought to the study of the Church Fathers his unrivaled knowledge of rabbinics, he was often able to follow up a faint hint or trace, and to ferret out from blurred accounts a wealth of legendary material.

The keenness displayed in such restoration can be appreciated only in the idiom of the original documents. But the perspicacity of historical insight may perhaps be illustrated by an example.

Ephraem of Edessa, preacher and poet of the Syriac Church in the fourth century, records a tale reported "by some bookmen." Ginzberg at once recognized here a legend which in this particular form survived only in a work of the thirteenth century. This Hebrew source describes the contest on Mount Carmel between Elijah and the priests of Baal. Not relying only on their prayers, these priests cunningly hid the wicked Bethelite Hiel in the hollow of the altar to light a fire at the first mention of the word *Baal*. But the fraud was foiled, for a serpent crept beneath the altar and killed Hiel. "In vain the false priests cried and called Baal! Baal!—the expected flame did not shoot up."

The Syriac is nine hundred years earlier than the Hebrew: would one not ordinarily assume dependence upon the older document? But Ginzberg argued, on the contrary, that it is the late medieval version which preserved the original legend. For Ephraem knew neither the name of the culprit, Hiel, nor the circumstances of his death. Ephraem had Hiel die in answer to Elijah's prayer. Ginzberg's brilliant guess was confirmed by the recent excavations of a caravan city in the Syrian desert, Dura-Europos, where an ancient synagogue was unearthed with remarkable fresco paintings, among them one depicting Hiel as he is bitten by a serpent inside the altar. The synagogue was destroyed in about 253, or a century before Ephraem.

It is such sound reasoning which assures to the works of Louis Ginzberg their weight in scholarship. On the basis of the first few scraps of the Dead Sea Scrolls (long before the many new documents from the caves came to light) he was able to establish their date with amazing accuracy. His volume on *The Unknown Sectaries* (1922) withstands the most acid of tests, the flood of new information. His contributions to Jewish law are noted for their broad horizons and devotion to detail. His inquiry into the origins of the first post-biblical code, the *Mishnah,* penetrates through the literary sources to their roots in life, in the interplay of social and economic forces in the ancient Near East. To the study and elucidation of the Jerusalem Talmud he devoted several volumes in which he was able to secure new witnesses for its poorly preserved text and to prove and trace the independent growth of the Palestinian institutions. His pioneering exploration of *Geonic,* or post-talmudic, letters lit up an obscure period in the history of rabbinic law.

To his massive and masterly tomes in the domain of *halakah,* or law, in which he saw the mainspring of his people's genius and achievement, he added, as though in passing, the seven volumes of his *Legends* as they were originally published. They represent not only the greatest single contribution to the study of the subject within a century, but also easily rank as the most significant work on Jewish lore ever published in the English language.

The task he set before himself was to reproduce the mainstream and the undercurrents of the biblical *haggadah.* The mainstream he saw mirrored in the records of rabbinic lore, or what is known as the talmudic-midrashic literature. "Covering the period from the second to the fourteenth century, they contain the major part of the Jewish legendary material," he wrote in the preface to his first volume in 1909. The undercurrents he believed reflected in the writings usually called apocryphal-pseudoepigraphic, a polyglot literature stemming directly or indirectly from works of Palestinian or Hellenistic origin.

The sources thus indicated by these two branches of literature cover the period from the last pre-Christian centuries to the fourteenth century of this era, or more than a millennium and a half. But in the execution of his plans, Ginzberg included many later works which seemed to him to embody or to preserve authentic traditions or lost legendary lore.

Take for example the account of Eve as she surrendered to temptation and ate of the forbidden fruit: "She could not bring herself to disobey the command of God utterly. She made a compromise with her conscience. First she ate only the outside skin of the fruit, and then, seeing that death did not befall her, she ate the fruit itself." Such gay insight into the complexities and ambiguities of human behavior seems unexpectedly modern. It does come from a book written after Columbus had sighted the New World. Ginzberg thought that it is "very likely dependent upon a lost *midrash*," or legend. The source is indeed a rich mine of *haggadah*, and Ginzberg used it thoroughly. Called *Bundle of Myrrh*, by Abraham Ibn Sabba, victim and witness of the expulsions from Spain and Portugal, it was written in the very last years of the fifteenth century.

There are even later writings from which Ginzberg uncovered genuine and ancient materials. The fantastic description of the giant animal *reëm*, "of which only one couple, male and female, is in existence," otherwise "the world could hardly have maintained itself against them," is a quotation from a book by the widely traveled Rabbi Haim Joseph Azulai, who died in 1807.

In other words, the sources from which Ginzberg culled his *Legends* reach to the very threshold of modern days, lengthening the span of time to about two thousand years. Or even longer, since occasionally he would draw upon the memories of his youth, and upon the legitimate source of all folklore, the lips of the people themselves.

Ginzberg believed the legends of the Bible to be popular "in the double sense of appealing to the people and being produced in the main by the people." He wanted them restored to the people. He knew, of course, that his was "the first attempt to gather from the original sources all Jewish legends, in so far as they refer to Biblical personages and events, and reproduce them with the greatest attainable completeness and accuracy." He could not fail to realize that his was the most comprehensive corpus of biblical *haggadah* in any language, past or present. He intended it, however, "for the general reader and not for the scholar. It is true, I flatter myself, that the latter too will welcome the opportunity offered him for the first time of reading hundreds of legends in connected form instead of being forced to hunt for them in the vast literature of Jews spreading over a period of two thousand years and in Christian writings of many a century. In the arranging and setting of the material in order, however, my main effort was to offer a readable story and narrate an interesting tale."

Ginzberg possessed a natural gift of storytelling which hides the prodigious array of knowledge crowded into every page of the *Legends*. His simple and smooth narrative is often pieced together from shreds of conflicting and confused accounts, scattered in countless books across the distant ages.

The treasury of biblical legendry as garnered by Louis Ginzberg will appeal by direct charm of story and sheer marvel of learning. He wore his scholarship lightly, with ease and grace and a lively sense of humor. He loved in the Bible and in the legends of the Bible not only the sublimity but also the simplicity and unsqueamishness with which the lowliest is linked with the loftiest, and the divine image dwells within the all too human. He tried to retain the folk flavor of the ancient legends. It is a mark of success that his rendition makes us lose sight of the distant times and half-forgotten tongues from which these narratives were gleaned. For the characters in these tales have little in common with the elongated, solemn figures of holy legend. They are real people, true to life and fond of life, and able to laugh at the things they love. They are convincing and even engrossing because they are so human.

The informed reader can never weary of the feast of scholarship, and the completeness of documentation offered in the notes which fill two volumes in the original edition. One only has to thumb the index of passages cited (in still another volume, a labor of love and learning by a distinguished disciple, Professor Boaz Cohen) to guess or gasp at the wealth of knowledge stored up in these Legends. At home in a vast and many-tongued literature, Ginzberg illuminéd and explored many unknown or little-known bypaths of the Hebraic book-land, adventuring resolutely into the remoter regions of Egypt and Babylon, Persia and India, Hellas and Rome, medieval Europe and Islam, and tracing the footprints of the Jews as "the great disseminators of folklore, who on their long wanderings from the East to the West, and back from the West to the East, brought the products of oriental fancies to the occidental nations, and the creations of occidental imagination to the oriental peoples."

C.   Growth of Legends

With the sacred writings of the Jews there traveled to the nations of East and West who had adopted them traditions and tales current among the Jews. Along with the Bible, legends of the Bible spread far and wide, leaving their imprint in many a celebrated center of art and literature, gaining at times a surprising hold upon popular imagination.

For example: the Sainte-Chapelle in Paris has been rightly called the most wonderful of pictured Bibles. Eleven huge windows (out of a total of fifteen) are devoted to the Hebrew Scriptures, illustrating in countless medallions of stained glass the history and heroes of ancient Israel. The Genesis window (mostly a modern restoration, but following the thirteenth-century pattern) unrolls the stages of creation and the story of the patriarchs in eighty-four medallions. They follow a set sequence of scenes, familiar to any reader of the Bible and easily recognizable, from Adam's disobedience to the death of Abel. But what comes next (in medallion 21) records the story, unknown to the Bible but current as a legend of the Bible, of how the blind Lamech, in an untoward hunting accident, killed his ancestor Cain, unwittingly avenging the slaying of Abel.

One can study the details of the tale in two panels of a stained-glass window at Tours, or in related illustrations such as the Manchester Bible, or the Munich Psalter of Queen Isabella, or in two frescoes by Italian masters, one by Pietro di Puccio in the Camposanto at Pisa, the other in the Green Cloister at Florence, attributed to Paolo Uccello or to Dello Delli. The legend is also vividly carved in many famous cathedrals of France, England, Spain and Italy. It was known to the Eastern Church as well, and survives in Greek Bible miniatures and superb Byzantine mosaics. The printing press and the mystery plays made the tale even more widely known. It was still capable of imaginative retelling in the sixteenth century, both in the East and West. The Greek poem by Georgios Chumnos, a native of Crete, displays no mean power of narration and feeling, and must have warmed many a pious soul by its chaste restatement of medieval faith. On the other hand, the engraving by the Dutch artist Lucas van Leyden, dated 1524, revels in candid corporeality as exhibited in the nude bodies of the huge Lamech and his chubby boy. It bespeaks the spirit and temper of the new age, impatient and wearied with the austerity and otherworldliness of the Middle Ages.

The vitality and popularity of the legend of Cain and Lamech in song and image, glass and mosaic, fresco and relief, across so many lands and centuries, in the traditions of the Orient and Occident alike, would in itself commend the story, as embroidered by scholars of the Synagogue and the Church, to the attention of the student of history. No other rabbinic tale seems to have had such persistent appeal in the literature and art of West and East.

The story further merits attention in being first conveyed to the West by St. Jerome. It bears witness to the early transmission of a considerable body of Jewish legends by the Church Fathers. In the Latin world no other name can rival the influence of Jerome, the champion of *Hebraica veritas,* the Hebrew verities of the biblical text, and, also, of the postbiblical traditions among the Jews. His grateful Church, in her oration on his feast day (September 30) calls St. Jerome her "greatest teacher in setting forth the Sacred Scriptures" (*doctor maximus in exponendis Sacris Scripturis*). This honor has been conferred upon him primarily because of his crowning achievement, the translation of the Hebrew Bible into Latin which became not only the "commonly accepted," or *Vulgate,* Bible in the Western Church, but was proclaimed by the Council of Trent, in 1546, as the "authentic" Bible of the Latin Church which "none should dare or presume to reject under any pretext whatsoever." Since Jerome avowedly sought from his Hebrew teachers the interpretation of Scripture as current in the Synagogue of his day, he willingly admitted rabbinic exegesis into his translation and exposition. Jerome's *Vulgate* and commentaries became a repository of Hebrew traditions, invaluable to the historian who seeks to date them, and the principal channel of transmission to the lands of Western Christendom—both for the Hebrew Bible and for the legends of the Bible.

In addition to its link with the great doctor of the Church, and its fame in the history of art, the tale of Cain and Lamech recommends itself through the very ease with which it can be analyzed. It offers ready insight into the origin and growth of legend.

Just as a pearl results from a stimulus in the shell of a mollusk, so also a legend may arise from an irritant in Scripture. The legend of Cain and Lamech has its foothold in two passages of Scripture. One passage tells of a sign granted by God to Cain as a warning to all who might threaten his life: anyone that slays Cain shall suffer sevenfold vengeance (Genesis 4:15). The other is the address of Lamech to his wives, reckless with swagger or savagery: I kill a man for just wounding me! (Genesis 4:24).

This is a brutal and bad boast in a book such as the Bible,

but in reality it is less bothersome than the earlier statement in Genesis 4:15 which it echoes and exaggerates. After all, the bluster of a braggart or bully need not be believed literally. His fierce or fantastic deeds of daredevilry may have been enjoyed, even in ancient days, with a twinkle in the eye, as tall talk indulged before, and intended for, womenfolk.

Genesis 4:15 cannot be so lightly dismissed. However interpreted, whether as a protective sign of traveling tinkers (the name *Qayin* signifying "smith"), or as a tribal mark of a nomad clan such as the Kenites, the pledge given to Cain presupposes a peculiarly ferocious form of blood-feud: any attack on the bearer of the sign is to be avenged by the slaughter of seven members of the tribe to which the assailant belonged. The archaeologist might conclude, and even rejoice in the fact, that some of the stories in the book of Genesis preserve exceedingly ancient traditions, fossils of archaic ages, often antedating by centuries the birth of biblical religion, or even the dawn of conscience on the planet. But in all times men have turned to the Bible not only for antiquarian curiosities, but for spiritual uplift and guidance. To such readers it must be distressing, or simply incomprehensible, to find the Holy Writ ascribing to the deity itself the acceptance without protest of an institution of primitive law, long outgrown by the advances of civilization. Many will prefer to believe that this cannot be the meaning of the sacred writings.

When facts or texts become unacceptable, fiction or legend weaves the garland of nobler fancy. This is how the story of Cain's slaying was born, and a fitting finale furnished for the unfinished report in the Bible of the murder of Abel.

The tale runs: Lamech was a burly but blind giant who loved to follow the chase under the guidance of his son, Tubalcain. Whenever the horn of a beast came in sight, the boy would tell his father to shoot at it with bow and arrow. One day he saw a horn move between two hills; he turned Lamech's arrow upon it. "The aim was good, and the quarry dropped to the ground. When they came close to the victim, the lad exclaimed: 'Father, thou hast killed something that resembles a human being in all respects, except it carries a horn on its forehead!' " Lamech knew at once what had happened: he had killed his ancestor Cain who had been marked by God with a horn for his own protection, "lest anyone who came upon him should kill him" (Genesis 4:15). In bitter remorse Lamech wept: "I killed a man to my wounding"! (Genesis 4:24).

What accounts for the success of this story and the appeal

it exercised? Could it be the interest in a proper penalty for the first murderer on earth? Indeed the legend was made to serve for many centuries as a solemn warning that crime does not pay, and that the killer, even if he escape the arm of the law, will not elude the vigilance or vengeance of heaven. This may perhaps explain the wide circulation and long tenacity of the tale in the arts and letters of the medieval Church.

However, there were other and older legends about Cain's dire end, none of which attained anything like comparable currency. What else worked in favor of this particular legend? What seemed to be shocking Scripture was made by this legend to yield a moral tale. Genesis 4:24 was turned from a barbarian boast into a cry of contrition: The offensive "I kill a man for just wounding me" was now read "I killed a man to my wounding and sorrow." The Hebrew permits this change by a mere inflection of voice. But above all, the stumbling block in Genesis 4:15 was removed: the assurance of the deity that Cain's vengeance shall be *sevenfold* was made to mean that his punishment will be exacted from him *in the seventh generation*. His sentence was to be carried out by Lamech, the *seventh* in the succession of generations since Adam. The savage reprisal, so repugnant in Scripture, became a deserved but deferred penalty, the merciful Judge, slow to anger, granting the sinner a long reprieve to repent and mend his ways. In brief, two passages of the sacred Writ, disturbing the peace and disquieting the faith of a host of pious readers in every age, were metamorphosed in this legend of Cain and Lamech to yield the edifying lesson: even the arrow of a sightless archer obeys the holy will and word of God.

The symbolism of the sacred number seven has been a staple item of legend and a favorite pastime of devout generations. We can watch such exercises spelling out scriptural intimations in other legends about Cain. The apocryphal *Testament of the Patriarchs,* from the last pre-Christian century, speaks of Cain as the first among men to draw the sword, "the mother of seven evils" which are mustered, such as bloodshed, exile, famine, panic and destruction. "Therefore was Cain also delivered to seven vengeances by God, for in every hundred years the Lord brought one plague upon him." One can read in Jerome a detailed list of the seven sins of Cain, such as gluttony and greed, envy and fraud, murder and brazen denial of any misdeed, and doubt in God's mercy. Similar catalogues of sins, varying in detail, are known also to the Eastern Church. Underlying all such meditation is the premise of divine justice which makes sense of sevenfold requital.

Common to all the schools of interpretation and the entire cycle of legends is the amazing disregard of the plain meaning of the biblical text: In Genesis 4:15 God threatens the *slayer* of Cain with sevenfold vengeance. Rabbinic exegesis and legend make instead *Cain,* and not his killer, suffer dreaded retribution. Apparently it was felt better to outrage grammar than moral sense. Any vestige of reprehensible or primitive practices was read away, and Scripture brought to conform to the advanced conscience of a later state in civilization.

Other hints of the Bible, not only its numerical secrets, are explored or exploited in still other legends of Cain. Poetic and religious justice alike required that divine discipline should fit the offense even in detail. Hence the ardent precision with which legend pursues even the most minute particulars in the biblical story.

For example, how was Abel slain? What instrument did the first murder? Various answers are offered in legend. One fancy has it that it was a stalk or a cane (in Hebrew *qaneh*) and hence its assonance with the name of Cain. The apocryphal *Life of Adam and Eve* supposes that Abel was bitten to death. Since Cain was a tiller of the ground, it was only natural to think of tools such as a hoe or sickle. Or perhaps, as in *Paradise Lost* (XI, 445), it was the preference of heaven shown to the sacrifice of Abel that maddened Cain against his brother:

> Whereat he inly raged and, as they talked,
> Smote him into the midriff with a *stone*
> That beat out life.

Milton echoes the legend in the *Book of Jubilees,* going back to the last pre-Christian century or even earlier. Here the implement of the crime suggested the proper punishment: Cain met his end when "his house fell upon him, and he died in the midst of his house, and he was killed by its stones; for with a stone he had killed Abel, and by a stone was he killed in righteous judgment." This tradition survives also in some variants of the legend about the blind Lamech, who is said to have hurled a stone and thus to have killed Cain.

The scene of the murder is also the subject of early curiosity. Jerome reports as a true tradition of the Hebrews (*He-braeorum vera traditio*) that the spot where Abel was slain was Damascus, which can mean either *blood-soaked* (*dam, shaq*) or the *sack cloth* worn in penance by the murderer for the *blood* shed (*dam, saq*). Perhaps not only etymology but also geography gave rise to the legend. Cain's retreat "east of Eden" (Genesis 4:16) was identified with Beth Eden (Amos 1:5) mentioned together with or in the vicinity of Damascus. The legend was known to Shakespeare, who in *Henry VI* has the bishop of Winchester speak to the Duke of Gloucester:

> This be Damascus; be thou cursed Cain,
> To slay thy brother Abel, if thou wilt.

"*East* of Eden" provided the rabbis with a clue to a legal institution which seemed to them to be endorsed by the entire story of Cain in the Bible. Trained to respect economy of utterance in inspired Scripture, they believed no word to be superfluous, and even the mere mention of a locality to have its purpose in holy Writ. They found therefore in Cain's place of refuge an intended reference to the cities of refuge commanded by the Mosaic law: In the *East, toward the sunrising,* beyond the Jordan, Moses set apart three cities of refuge so that he who kills his neighbor unintentionally might flee there, and save his life (Deuteronomy 4:41). Did Cain deserve such leniency in being adjudged an unwitting slayer and afforded shelter and safety "east of Eden"? The legists, "the disciples of the wise," so plead on his behalf. Cain had none to give him warning or instruction. He never saw a man die and breathe no more. He did not yet know the irreversible finality of death. He was, therefore, sentenced to flee the joys of men and to dwell in exile and banishment, the law of all who kill unawares. Scripture, far from sanctioning indiscriminate bloodshed, condemns the savage customs of antiquity, and recommends instead sparing of the innocent and mercy to the sinner.

Thus students and scholars in many an age read into the scriptural account of Cain a message and meaning worthy of the Scriptures. Resourceful imagination wedded to moral purpose knew how to remake even difficult and disappointing verses after the likeness, and in the image, of the best of the biblical legacy.

The tales of Cain aptly illustrate the growth of legends from creative interplay between a book and posterity, the original intention of a saying and the reflection of future generations. The legend of Cain and Lamech highlights a particularly troublesome passage of Scripture in its pilgrimage through history. It reveals a reciprocal benefit accruing with time and effort: the sacred writings educate generations, elevating their minds with images of grandeur human and divine; in turn, the biblical books themselves are weighted with the compassion and charity of sages and saints in every century. The entire cycle of biblical legends about the punishment and death of Cain has its roots in Genesis 4:15 and in the refusal of the religious conscience to admit as valid any interpretation which would suffer inspired Scripture to trail behind the moral sense of man.

D. Folklore, Fable and Myth

Few legends so clearly and candidly bespeak their origin in the *workshop of scholars* as does the legend of Cain. Nevertheless, even this legend is spun from materials originating and circulating among the common people, from rudiments of genuine *folklore*. Other legends are the outgrowth of folk fancy rather than the product of the school. They spring, not from biblical exegesis, but from play and pleasure of the imagination, out of sheer delight in telling a story. They not only find favor with the people, but often are fathered by the people. The legends of the Bible teem with such elements of popular creation, designed for the people or derived from the people. They also deserve inspection.

When Adam for the first time saw the sun die in the evening and the shadows of the night fall, legend records, he grew frightened: "Woe unto me, because of my sin the world is being plunged back into darkness!" When the new day began to dawn, he rejoiced without end, and built an altar, and brought an offering to God: "a *unicorn* whose horn was created before his hoofs, and he sacrificed it on the spot on which later the altar was to stand in Jerusalem."

Another mysterious animal, the *tahash*, was created for one function only, to furnish skin for the cover of the Tabernacle. Having done so, it disappeared, leaving the scholars baffled as to whether it was a domestic or wild animal. This much is known, however: "it had a *horn on its forehead*, was gaily colored like the turkey-cock, and belonged to the class of clean animals"—how else could it have served so holy a purpose?

A dreaded spirit is *Keteb*, "the destruction that wasteth at noonday" (Psalms 91:6), or the monster of the summer heat. He rolls like a ball, and has the head of a calf, with but one eye midway in his heart and a single *horn on his forehead*.

It is such freakish and spooky company that Cain joins, when legend puts a horn on his forehead, a free loan from the ever-green wonderland of folk fantasy or folk superstition which in all lands and in all ages loves the whimsical and the weird, the odd and the abhorrent. It is an echo of household tales from the infancy of the race, when the earth was young and people still could wonder or worry whether the sun will rise tomorrow. Shadows of that enchanted world linger on to this day in nursery rhymes and stories of all peoples, thrilling the hearts of children with memories of ancient marvels and nightmares.

Such is also the fairy land of the antediluvian age in which Cain lived. Before the flood, people had nothing to worry about. There was plenty of food. "A single sowing bore a harvest sufficient for the needs of forty years." The raising of children was no trouble either. "They were born after a few days' pregnancy, and immediately after birth they could walk and talk; they themselves aided the mother in severing the navel string. Not even demons could do them harm. Once a new-born babe, running to fetch a light whereby his mother might cut the navel string, met the chief of the demons, and a combat ensued between the two. Suddenly the crowing of a cock was heard, and the demon made off, crying out to the child, "Go and report unto they mother, if it had not been for the crowing of the cock, I had killed thee!" Whereupon the child retorted, "Go and report unto thy mother, if it had not been for my uncut navel string, I had killed thee!"

This is also the way Cain was born: leaving his mother's womb, at once "the babe stood upon his feet, ran off, and returned holding in his hands a stalk of straw which he gave to his mother. For this reason he was named Cain, the Hebrew word for stalk of straw."

Such carefree life as before the deluge, with hardly a chore in house or farm, and no baby linen to launder, is the dreamland of womenfolk everywhere and at all times. It still stalks on in some creations of folk fancy such as the plant-man. "His form is exactly that of a human being, but he is fastened to the ground by means of a navel-string, upon which his life depends. This animal keeps himself alive with what is produced by the soil around about him as far as his tether permits him to crawl. No creature may venture to approach within the radius of his cord, for he seizes and demolishes whatever comes in his reach." The cord once snapped, he dies amid groans and moans.

In the cycle of legends about King Solomon, the brood of Cain, or the Cainites, provided a specially difficult problem of jurisprudence. As a rule, these four-eyed monsters lived underground. But Asmodeus brought one of them to earth where he remained, married, and begot seven sons, of whom only one resembled his father. "When the Cainite died, a dispute broke out among his descendants as to how the property was to be divided. The double-headed son claimed two portions." Solomon, in his wisdom, poured hot water on one of his heads, whereupon both mouths cried out in pain: "We are one, not two," a self-confession that settled the dispute.

Legends of the Bible borrow freely not only from folk tale but also from folk belief. The primitive mind ascribes conscious life to all natural objects, to nature in general. The child, and the poet, keep alive this universal and ancient notion that animals, plants and stones are endowed with will or inhabited by spirits or souls kindred and comprehensible to our own. This pre-literate animism, characteristic of archaic mentality, may be designedly employed as a principle of make-believe so pleasing, for example, in the *fable*.

In the realm of legend, also, the inanimate world is endued with human properties. The letters of the Hebrew alphabet vie with one another for a place of distinction in the Holy Writ. The mountains of the Fertile Crescent fight for the honor of being the scene of revelation. Twelve stones on the road to Haran engage in a contest: which of them merits to be put under the head of Jacob as he lies down to sleep. Such eagerness to serve the righteous is rewarded, and a miracle joins the twelve into one stone which at once becomes soft and downy like a pillow, for the greater comfort of the patriarch. Before his duel with Goliath, there came to David, of their own accord, smooth stones out of the brook. One stone said: Take me in the name of Abraham; another said: Take me in the name of Isaac; and the third said: Take me in the name of

Jacob. David took them all, and they became one stone with which he struck the Philistine. Visions of future bliss paint similar wonders. In time to come, if one will try on a Sabbath to pluck a fig, it will exclaim: It is Sabbath. In a Christian apocalypse, when any of the saints will take hold of a grape, another will cry out: I am a better grape, take me, through me bless thou the Lord!

The legends of Cain abound in such elements of folk fable. The earth itself, enmeshed in the sin of man, suffered a radical transformation. Originally, its surface was level and unwrinkled. It became mountainous as a punishment for having received the blood of Abel, as though the ancients had seen in the mountains petrified shrieks of horror. "The ground changed and deteriorated at the very moment of Abel's violent end. The trees and the plants in the part of the earth whereon the victim lived refused to yield their fruits, on account of their grief over him, and only at the birth of Seth those that grew in the portion belonging to Abel began to flourish and bear again. While before, the vine had borne nine hundred twenty-six different varieties of fruit, it now brought forth but one kind. And so it was with all other species. They will regain their pristine powers only in the world to come."

In a like poetic animation of inert or dumb nature, legend makes the earth quake under Cain, refusing rest and repose to the footsore fugitive. The animals, both wild and tame, shudder at his sight, and say to each other: This is his brother's murderer. In fact, it is their condemnation and hostility which unnerved Cain at last, and he broke down in weeping: "everyone that findeth me shall slay me" (Genesis 4:14). Who could threaten him with death? His parents would not kill their only son, however guilty? Besides them, there was no other human being to be feared in the world. Cain lived in constant dread of the birds and the beasts which gathered around him to avenge the innocent blood of Abel. To protect Cain from the onslaught of *the animals* God inscribed one letter of His holy name upon the murderer's forehead, and addressed to the beasts the warning not to attack Cain, lest vengeance be taken on the animals sevenfold!

This is delightful exegesis, offered seriously, no doubt, but with a grain of salt and wit. It exorcises as if with a wand of magic all the ghosts of primitive blood feud from the Bible. We deal with zoology, not ethics; with categories of fable, not law. Humor shatters the rigidity of literal-mindedness.

The animal lore of the rabbis is fraught with kindly contemplation of the incongruities of life, and their good-natured chuckle often enlivens a page of the Talmud. "He teaches us through the beasts of the earth, and makes us wise through the fowls of heaven" (Job 35:11). If the law had not been revealed to us, we might have learned cleanliness from the cat, regard for the property of others from the ant, and the art of wooing from the cock. "When he desires to unite with the hen, he promises to buy her a cloak long enough to reach to the ground. When the hen reminds him of his promise, the cock shakes his comb and says: May I be deprived of my comb, if I do not buy it, when I have the means."

Folk tales float like driftwood from people to people, and animal stories of various cultures show kinship, and suggest common origins. In many a language one will find analogues to the merry adventures in living by one's wits, as exemplified in the fables of the fox and the lion, or the fox and the Leviathan, or the fox outsmarting death itself. Only that our fox knows his Bible. When, grown fat in a vineyard, he must fast and reduce again, in order to get out through the narrow hole in the fence through which he had entered, he contemplates the vanity of all earthly gains, and quotes from the wisdom of Ecclesiastes: "Naked shall he return to go as he came."

The children of the Holy Land must have gaped openeyed and openmouthed at the escapades of Jonah, or at his sight-seeing tour within the belly of the fish. The whale "was so large that the prophet was as comfortable inside of him as in a spacious synagogue. The eyes of the fish served Jonah as windows, and besides, there was a diamond which shone as brilliantly as the sun at midday, so that Jonah could see all things in the sea down to its very bottom."

Another hit of the nursery must have been the story of Joshua, the doughty warrior of the Lord. He was a bit on the heavy side, and no donkey, or mule, or even horse could bear his weight, until a good steer carried him to his victory at Jericho. In gratitude Joshua kissed the steer on his nose. That's why no hair grows now on his nose, although originally all of the steer's face was overgrown with hair.

Such etiological stories, the "that's whys" of folk tales, are a staple item in the repertoire of fairy tales in all lands. Why does the camel have short ears? In punishment for greed, for he looked for horns, and lost his ears, a reflection of the Persian fable in the *Pend-Nameh*. Why does the raven hop clumsily? Why do dogs fight cats? Why the mouse has a seam in her mouth is a story as old as Noah, and it happened indeed in his ark. The cat clawed the mouse and ripped her cheek, and good Noah sewed up the rip with a hair plucked by the mouse from the tail of a sleeping swine: "thence the little seam-like line next to the mouth of every mouse to this very day."

The idyllic serenity of such a tale is appreciated perhaps even more when its counterparts in European or Moslem fable are remembered: there a legend with many variants tells of the devil who finally succeeded in entering the ark of Noah as a mouse and made it leak dangerously, until a miracle and a cat foiled the hell-born wile.

The enmity between cat and mouse is explained by a tale of punished envy, a motif known from Aesop. The mouse should have been forewarned "by the example of the moon who lost a part of her light, because she spoke ill of the sun." Though the mouse had erred in her folly, she accepted God's judgment, and like the whole of creation, she too has her special hymn wherewith to extol her Creator: "Howbeit Thou art just in all that is come upon me; for Thou hast dealt truly, but I have done wickedly." And the cat sings: "Let everything that hath breath praise the Lord. Praise ye the Lord."

The story of the demoted or dimmed moon has several versions, some playful, some somber. "When God punished the envious moon by diminishing her light and splendor, so that she ceased to be the equal of the sun as she had been originally, she fell, and tiny threads were loosed from her body. These are the stars." The *Book of Enoch* retains a trace of graver tales about open disobedience of the host of heaven: "They transgressed the commandment of the Lord in the beginning of their rising, because they did not come forth at their appointed times." The rebel stars were bound like great burning mountains in a deep abyss which serves as their prison, "till the time when their guilt shall be consummated, even for ten thousand years."

These apocryphal traditions, going back to pre-Christian centuries, remember a similar penalty inflicted upon the insurgent angels. In their lust for the comely daughters born to the children of men, the angels betrayed "the eternal secrets which were preserved in heaven." They taught men to make weapons, and "filled the earth with blood and lawless deeds." For their indiscretion the fallen angels must suffer dire chastisement: for seventy generations they will remain, bound with chains of iron, in the dark valleys of the earth, pinned under jagged mountain rocks, to be hurled on the day of great judgment into the fiery pit of hell.

As early as the first century, Josephus, the historian, observed that the deeds ascribed to the rebel angels resemble Greek myths. One is indeed reminded of the giants and the titans, sons of Heaven and Earth, who rose to dethrone the Hellenic gods, until they were overwhelmed in a fierce struggle and buried under the volcanoes in various parts of Greece or Italy where they were believed to be rumbling in impotent wrath under the crust of the earth.

Such myths, stories of the supernatural, survive in biblical legends. Sometimes their obvious disagreement with Scripture is startling. "And God said, Let there be light; and there was light." That's all there is to the story of creation as told in Genesis. The word or will of God is the sovereign and sole source of all reality, and there is no other power or partner to assist or to resist Him in the work of creation. But legend seems to recall that God met with obstruction, or even defiance of His command.

When the Holy One, blessed be He, was about to create His world, He said to the Prince of Darkness: Retreat before Me, for I desire to create the world in light. Whereupon the Prince of Darkness who has the shape of a bull, thought to himself: If I obey Him, and permit darkness to recede before the light, I shall be His slave forever. It is better that I feign as though I did not hear the command, as if I erred rather than rebelled. But the Holy One, blessed be He, rebuked him, and the Prince of Darkness and all his cohorts scattered in hasty retreat.

Allied with the Prince of Darkness were "the dark waters" (Psalms 18:12), conceived as chaotic primeval matter. Unlike the Scriptural account of creation, legend knows of mutiny and rebellion of the waters. The waters above the firmament which are male, desired to mate with the waters under the firmament which are female. They sank down to the valleys and rose to the mountains, and had they commingled, the world would have been plunged back to chaos. But God tore them apart, and kept them within their borders, as it is written (Psalms 104:7): "At Thy rebuke they fled, at the sound of Thy thunder they took to flight."

In other versions of the legend, all the waters moved upward, although half of them were bidden to remain under the firmament. Said the waters: we shall not descend. They bore their head high, and so they were called "the mighty waters" (Isaiah 43:16). God had to thrust them down by force, and drive them under the earth. Or as told by Rab, who died in 247: When the Holy One, blessed be He, desired to create the world, He said to the Prince of the Sea: Open your mouth and swallow all the waters of the world. Said he: Lord of the world, I have enough of my own. The Lord trod upon him and slew him, as it is written (Job 26:12): "By His power He stilled the sea; by His understanding He smote Rahab." Said Rabbi Isaac: We learn from here that the name of the Prince of the Sea was Rahab.

North Canaanitish epics, discovered in our days and older than the Bible, vividly depict the exploits of the weather-god Baal, the Rider of the Clouds. With two clubs he bludgeoned the gods of the sea and river, Prince *Yamm* and Judge *Nahar*, confining them to their proper spheres. Thereupon his father, the bull god, *El*, commanded that the victor be given a mansion worthy of his valor. There must have existed in early biblical antiquity Hebrew epics of struggle and triumph over the primeval monsters, for Scripture retains vestiges of such combat and conquest. "O arm of the Lord, awake as in days of old. Was it not Thou that didst cut Rahab in pieces, that didst pierce the dragon? Was it not Thou that didst dry up the sea, the waters of the great deep?" (Isaiah 51:9ff.) "Thou didst divide the sea by Thy strength; Thou didst shatter the heads of the sea monsters in the waters. Thou didst crush the heads of Leviathan" (Psalms 74:13ff.).

The cycle of legends about Leviathan seems to revert to these ancient heathen myths which the account of creation in Genesis sought to supplant or to suppress. In these legends Leviathan is described as the mightiest wonder of creation. "Originally the Leviathan was created male and female like all the other animals. But when it appeared that a pair of these monsters might annihilate the whole earth with their united strength, God killed the female." The male is to be slain in the end of days for the last feast of the pious and their farewell to the delights of the body, before the pure life of spirit will commence for ever and ever. "When his last hour arrives, God will summon the angels to enter into combat with the monster. But no sooner will Leviathan cast his glance at them than they will flee in fear and dismay from the field of battle." He will finally meet his end in a duel with Behemoth in which both will drop dead. From the skin of Leviathan the Lord will spread a radiant canopy over Jerusalem, "and the light streaming from it will illumine the whole world."

These fantastic details unblushingly echo the Old Babylonian epic of creation, going back to the early second millennium B.C. The Babylonian gods all shrank in dread before Tiamat, the monster of the sea and her fierce crew, until Marduk, the chief god of Babylon, defeated her, and split her like a shellfish into two parts. Half of her he set up and ceiled as a canopy of heaven, assigning stations in the sky to the great gods and their constellations to cheer with light the twelve months of the year.

Such palpable reminiscences or relics of pagan mythology in the legends of the Bible will seem surprising. Reported in the name of renowned scholars flourishing in the third century, they clash patently not only with the whole legacy of the biblical faith, but with the austere monotheism which these founders of rabbinic Judaism consistently maintained and invariably sought to implant and enforce in their people. It is altogether out of the question to consider such cosmogonic fancies as the invention of the period or personalities to which they are ascribed in our sources. Obviously the stories precede their storytellers by long centuries, often by more than a millennium, harking back to the earliest tales of their remote ancestors or heathen neighbors. The imaginative accounts of strife with monsters of the deep, or the Princes of Darkness or of the Sea, with rebellious waters and insurgent stars, would appear most reasonably to be but splinters of ancient myths from pre-biblical or early biblical days. These remnants of dim sagas and residues of faded traditions, frowned upon by the makers of the Bible and discarded by them, survived, as it were, subterraneously for countless generations down to the last centuries of antiquity, or even the early centuries of the Middle Ages—an amazing testimony to the tenacity of folk memories.

Why were these myths not hushed up altogether? Banished from the Bible (save for a few snatches of poetic imagery), how were they readmitted to the legends of the Bible?

These ancient myths had charm and appealed to the imagination. The people, an eternal child, loved them. The stories were replete with stirring action and adventure, fight and suspense. They recalled the distant days, believed to be lost forever, when the world was gay and bold, innocent and savage at once. Moreover, they dealt with matters of immediate concern, the combat of seasons, spring and winter, rain and drought, increase or failure of crops and cattle, blessing or blight of the fruit of the body and the fruit of the ground. With the directness of primitive poetry they spoke to all the senses, and yet seemed to make sense as well, confirming everyday experience of the world in which the word of God goes not unopposed. They appeared to reckon with and account for the stubborn reality of evil which the theologians chose to ignore.

Bootleg myths are dangerous. This much even the theologians agreed. On second thought, were the myths indeed dangerous? The ancient gods were safely dead. The faith of the Bible prevailed everywhere, and its hold upon the people was firm and secure. Could not the enchanted fancies of defeated paganism be made to serve not idols, but God? The vagaries of heathen mythology could perhaps be pruned or trimmed to accord with the spirit or even the letter of Scripture. Since the ingenuity of scholars is never at a loss, imaginative exegesis need not bolt the door, but can hospitably leave it a trifle ajar.

The Synagogue handled the pagan past in a manner not unlike the advice of Jerome to his Church, when the ancient gods of Greece and Rome were dying beyond all doubt. In earlier days, the danger of the classics was still real, and the pagan authors were forsworn. "What has Athens to do with Jerusalem, the Academy with the Church?" asked Tertullian. Jerome too could still echo that question: "What has Horace to do with the Psalter, Virgil with the Gospels?" He reports a famous dream in which he heard himself condemned in heaven: *Mentiris, Ciceronianus es, non Christianus:* Thou liest, thou art a Ciceronian, not a Christian. Toward the close of his life, Jerome still had to defend himself for breaking his vow never again to read the Gentile authors. But to his Church he could bequeath the counsel which became in later centuries one of the most popular quotations of Christian scholarship. The great Hebraist of the Church hit upon a passage in Deuteronomy 21:10f., setting forth the conditions on which an Israelite might take unto himself a captive maid, and Jerome applied it to pagan myth and poetry: "Whatever is in her of love, of wantonness, of idolatry, I shave; and having made of her an Israelite indeed, I beget sons unto the Lord."

Fortunately, much of the native charm in the alien myth (and maid, I suppose) survives the shaving. Here is an example of a captive myth naturalized as a legend of the Bible: "He binds up the streams so that they do not weep" (Job 28:11). Why were the waters overflowing with tears? "The waters had been the first to give praise to God, and when their separation into upper and lower was decreed, the waters above rejoiced, saying, 'Blessed are we who are privileged to abide near our Creator and near His Holy Throne.' Sadness fell upon the waters below. They lamented: 'Woe unto us, we have not been found worthy to dwell in the presence of God.' Therefore they attempted to rise upward, until God repulsed them, and pressed them under the earth. Said the humbled waters: Lord of the universe, Thou knowest that we strove upward but for the sake of Thy glory. Said the Holy One, praised be He: To reward you, whenever the waters above desire to utter their song, they must first seek permission from the waters below, as it is written (Psalms 90:4): 'By consent of the mighty waves of the sea, the Lord on high is praised.' " In brief, what in the pagan myths was mutiny and rebellion of the lords and gods of the deep, the eternal waters, becomes in the legends of the Bible an act of homage and adoration of the created waters to their Creator and Lord, the eternal God of Scripture.

The legends of the Bible love to dwell on the opposition of the angels to man; in fact, the hosts of heaven are said time and again to have objected or even sought to prevent the creation of man. This point is stressed with particular emphasis, perhaps hiding a clue why the myths of the insurgent angels were not rebuffed altogether.

These legends are clustered around a solitary verse, or rather a strange plural, in Genesis 1:26: "And God said, Let us make a man." Audacious heresies are reported in ancient records to have been read out of or read into these biblical words. For example, the gnostics, in the early Christian centuries, saw here scriptural proof for their repudiation of the body, and of matter in general. Only the soul was created by the Most High, but the body with its ills and lusts was the work of the malignant demiurge, or of incompetent angels. These notions crudely echo subtler doctrines of Plato, and Philo, for the differentiation between mind and matter seemed to the Greek philosophers and their disciples to suggest at last an answer to the problem of physical and moral evil in the world.

To Jews and Christians alike such views were anathema.

They implied a streak of malice, or an innate blemish in original creation itself, as though from the outset, or in his very makeup, man were vitiated and cheated of all likelihood of redemption. Hence the different exegesis of Genesis 1:26 in the legends of the Bible.

When God resolved to create man, He asked counsel of all around Him—"an example to man, be he ever so great and distinguished, not to scorn the advice of the humble and lowly. First God called upon heaven and earth, then upon all other things He had created, and last upon the angels." The angel of truth opposed the creation of man, as did the angel of peace: man will be full of lies, and quarrelsome. God wisely kept silence and concealed from the angels that wicked, not only righteous, generations will proceed from man. Even though they knew but half the truth, the angels could not suppress their mistrust and astonishment: "What is man that Thou art mindful of him?" A band of angels under the arch-angel Michael went too far in their scorn and sullenness against the creation of man. "God thereupon stretched forth His little finger, and all were consumed by fire except their chief Michael. And the same fate befell the band under the leadership of archangel Gabriel; he alone of all was saved from destruction." Warned by the dire punishment, and convinced that nothing would deter God, the remaining angels meekly acceded: Do according to Thy will.

Legend does not fail to detail, step by step and hour by hour, all the stages of the divine labors in creating man. God Himself, and no one else, collected the dust of the ground from all four corners of the earth, of various colors, black and white and yellow and red, adding a spoonful from the site of the atoning altar, so that man be forgiven and endure. God Himself again formed with infinite care every part of the body, fashioned all limbs, opened the orifices, and blew into the soulless lump the breath of life. There was none to assist Him, as He would relegate no function to anybody else, but with loving solicitude Himself attended to every item of both the body and the soul of man. And when the ministering angels came down to harm man, the Holy One, blessed be He, took him up and put him under His wings, as it is written (Psalms 139:5): "And Thou hast laid Thy hand upon me."

In the background of this entire cycle of legends lurk religious issues and philosophical passions, agitating the hearts and minds of men for generations. The issues are long forgotten and the passions spent, but what still endures and entertains are the tales. The theme they play and vary is the struggle of light with darkness, good with evil. The strife is older than man, or even prior to creation itself. In fact, the very creation of man was a battle won against the cohorts of heaven and hell which seem forever to oppose and obstruct the will of God and the work of man. Intimately connected with this cluster of tales are the stories of the insurgent and fallen angels, and the conspiracy of Satan against Adam, of which the misdeeds of Satan's brood, Cain and his descendants, are but an episode. All this multitude of tales is preserved in the legends of the Bible, and offers a striking example of how *folklore, fable and myths were reminted in the workshops of schoolmen.*

The alien or pre-biblical memories, and the homeborn elements of folk fancy, were recast and revised by the makers of the legends of the Bible to suit the biblical view of God and man.

As retold and rewritten by the teachers of the Synagogue, the ancient myths themselves became a vivid and dramatic refutation of the pagan creeds and dualist heresies which had given birth to these very myths, and vogue to the beliefs that powers other than God have a stake or share in man. On the lips of the later heirs, these myths are made to unsay their disturbing infidelities or subversions, and to assert with poetic vigor and imagination the verities and sincerities of the biblical religion. To be sure, sometimes the uncouth energy of the past or the myths of dead paganism prove stronger than the intention of the living, and into a pious legend there fall, like shooting stars, glimpses of demonic caprice and spite and nonsense, denying and defying the orderly universe of reason and moral purpose. The pristine power of the original tales prevails over the later censor or editor, and the strange or savage captive maid captures her Israelite conqueror.

Such accidents of derailment or backsliding, annoying perhaps to the humorless theologian, will please the folklorist and instruct the student of history. They bespeak not only a hospitality of the mind, open to all winds of doctrine, but call attention ever again to the basic incompatibility of myth and monotheistic religion.

The legends of the Bible, growing from grass roots of folklore, and groping to be engrafted, or at least entwined in Scripture, attempt the seemingly impossible: to impart vitality, without impairing the purity of the biblical faith. Memorable art and living religion both require the courage of images. But it is the distinctive genius of the biblical conception of God to forbid the human presumption of images, "or any likeness of anything that is in heaven above, or that is in the earth beneath, or that is in the water under the earth." To obey both demands is the miracle of creativity. To have kept the two opposites in fruitful check and tension, vivid vision and phantasy, enriching and reinforcing the austere iconoclasm of Scripture, is not the least of the glories of the legends of the Bible.

9.

Jewish Thought as Reflected in the Halakah *

by Louis Ginzberg

It was not without hesitation that I accepted the kind invitation extended to me to deliver the Zunz Lecture of this year. Greatly as I appreciated the honor conferred upon me, I did not find it an easy task to free myself from a deep-rooted conviction that, to speak in the words of the great Frenchman, Pascal, most of the mischief of this world would never happen if men were content to sit still in their parlors and refrain from talking. As a compromise with this strong conviction, I have chosen as my subject, "Jewish Thought as Reflected in the Halakah." On a subject of this sort one would talk only when one has something to say, or at least thinks so—otherwise one would be prompted to keep silence.

To be candid, keeping silence strongly commends itself to one who has spent the greater part of his life in the study of the Halakah and, believing himself to have a good deal to say about it, is at a loss how to do so within the limited space of a single paper. It would be impossible within the compass of anything less than a substantial volume to present an analysis of the ideas comprised or implied in the term Halakah, or even to set forth the various senses in which the term has been employed. It has often been observed that the more claim an idea has to be considered living, the more various will be its aspects; and the more social and political is its nature, the more complicated and subtle will be its issues and the longer

---

* Second Zunz Lecture of the Menorah Society, delivered at the University of Chicago, December 29, 1920.

From *Students, Scholars and Saints,* Philadelphia, Jewish Publication Society of America, 1928.

and more eventful its course. The attempt to express the "leading idea" of the Halakah I must perforce leave to those whose forte is omniscience and whose foible is knowledge. What I propose to do is something less ambitious than to sketch the nature and scope of the Halakah. It is more closely connected with the problem of the nature of Jewish history.

The Talmud remarks: "He who studies the Halakah daily may rest assured that he shall be a son of the world to come." [1] The study of the Halakah may not commend itself to everyone as a means of salvation. Some may desire an easier road thereto; but we may well say that he who studies the Halakah may be assured that he is a son of the world—the Jewish world—that has been. Not that the Halakah is a matter of the past; but the understanding of the Jewish past, of Jewish life and thought, is impossible without a knowledge of the Halakah. One might as well hope to comprehend the history of Rome without taking notice of its wars and conquests or that of Hellas without giving attention to its philosophy and art. To state such a truism would be superfluous were it not for the fact that the most fundamental laws of nature are often disregarded in dealing with the Jews, and their history has undergone strange treatment at the hands of friend and foe alike.

If we further remember that Jewish historiography in modern times dates from the days when the Hegelian conception of history reigned supreme, the "peculiar" treatment of the history of the "peculiar people" is not in the least surprising. Historians who believed with Hegel that "history is the science of man in his political character," and consequently were of the opinion that there could be no history of a people without a state, could not but ignore the Halakah, a way of life that was rarely sustained by the power of the state but was frequently antagonized by it. What was the result of this conception of history applied to the Jews? The three main subjects dealt with in works on Jewish history in post-biblical times are: religion, literature, martyrology, to which a little philosophy with a sprinkling of cultural history is added; but of actual history in the modern sense of the word we find very little indeed. History as now generally understood is the science establishing the causal nexus in the development of man as a social being. The Jew may well say: *homo sum, nihil humani a me alienum puto*. State or no state, even the Jew of the diaspora lived for almost two thousand years a life of his own and has developed accordingly a character of his own.

Modern students of man teach us that three elements contribute to the formation of his character—heritage, environment, and training. What is true of individual character holds good also of national character. We hear a good deal of the importance of heritage or race, to use the favored phrase of the day, in appraising the character of the Jew and in the interpretation of his history. Dealers in generalities especially are prone to call in the racial features and characteristics to save the trouble of a more careful analysis which would show that these racial qualities themselves are largely due to historical causes, though causes often too far back in the past to admit of full investigation. The explanation of history from the narrow point of view of race is tantamount to affirming, as Hegel did, that the whole wealth of historic development is potential in the beginnings of mind, a view which it would be impossible to justify historically. The lessons of history indicate rather that at certain times men of genius initiate new movements which though related to the past are not explained by it, and that there are various possibilities contained in a given historic situation. Which of the possibilities is to become real would depend solely upon the training of the people confronted with the historic situation. Nothing is easier and nothing more dangerous than definitions. I shall not define what Halakah is; yet one is safe in asserting that its chief feature is education of oneself or training. Accordingly, the Halakah is a true mirror reflecting the work of the Jew in shaping his character.

No man who is badly informed can avoid reasoning badly. We can hardly expect to understand the causal nexus of our history if we disregard the most valuable source of information we seek. Here is a plain example in arithmetic to prove it. The literary output of the eighteen centuries from the beginning of the common era to the year 1795, the date of the emancipation of the Jews in France and Holland when the modern history of the Jew begins, contains seventy-eight per cent of halakic material. We may easily convince ourselves of the exactness of this statement by looking at the classification of the Hebrew books in the British Museum, the largest collection of its kind in the world, prepared by such an eminent and careful bibliographer as Zedner. Yet it is not the quantity of the halakic Literature that makes it so valuable a source of Jewish history; by far more important is its quality.

Historians divide historical sources into two main groups: (a) historical remains and (b) tradition. By the first group we understand all that remains of an historical event. For instance, we find in certain parts of Germany ruins of Roman castles, places with Roman names, burial-grounds containing the bodies of Romans, their armor, pottery and so on. Let us suppose for a moment that the writings of Cæsar, Tacitus and other Roman historians treating of the relations between Rome and Germania had disappeared; these remains of the actual life of the Romans in Germany would suffice to establish beyond any doubt the fact that at a certain time in history the Romans lived in Germany and were its masters. The second group of historical sources, tradition, is much less reliable, since it is only a subjective reflection in the human mind of historical events and can therefore be made use of only after a critical analysis has separated the subjective element of reflection from the objective facts reflected. We often hear of the lamentable dearth of sources of Jewish history. As far as historical tradition is concerned, the correctness of this statement is beyond dispute; but of historical remains we have in the Halakah a veritable treasure of material. The Halakah, as its meaning "conduct" indicates, comprises life in all its manifestations—religion, worship, law, economics, politics, ethics and so forth. It gives us a picture of life in its totality and not of some of its fragments.

You will ask how it could happen that all the historians and scholars who devoted their lives and great abilities to the study of Jewish history ignored its most important source, the Halakah? The answer to this question is not a difficult one. The importance of the Halakah as an historical source is equalled by the difficulty of its utilization. Its faults lie not in its substance but in the form which the conditions of its growth have given to it. It is a system extremely hard to expound and hard to master. So vast is it and so complicated, so much are its leading principles obscured by the way in which they have been stated, scattered here and there through the vast expanse of the "sea of the Talmud," in an order peculiar to the latter, which is the perfection of disorder, that it presents itself to the learner as a most arduous study, a study indeed which only a few carry so far as to make themselves masters of the whole. Hence the favorite phrase that a general impression of the Halakah suffices without the study of its details. Of course this is a cover for incapacity. To understand the whole, the knowledge of the parts is as indispensable in the study of the Halakah as in any other branch of human thought.

I do not wish to be misunderstood. Not everything that happens is history, and, consequently, the first requirement of the historian is to distinguish between essentials and non-essentials, between historical and non-historical happenings. The individual performs countless acts daily which the most conscientious and careful Boswell would pass over in silence as irrelevant. So also in the lives of nations and peoples, many things happen daily that are of no historical value. Not all the minutiae of the Halakah are historical material, but to quote the saying of an old Jewish sage: "If there be no knowledge, how could there be discernment?" [2] To distinguish the essential from the non-essential in the Halakah one must master it entirely if one is not to become a prey to his subjective likes and dislikes—and we all know how Jewish history is marred by bias and prejudice.

The problem of subjectivity in the presentation of Jewish history leads me to remark on another aspect of the Halakah—its authoritative character. Writers on the phase of Judaism that comprises Jewish theology and ethics in post-biblical times, have based their studies exclusively on the Haggadah, which means that they erected their structures upon shifting sand. Whatever else the Haggadah may be, it certainly is either individual, consisting of opinions and views uttered by Jewish sages for the most part on the spur of the moment, or creations of popular fancy. The haggadic sayings of the rabbis belong to the first division; the apocryphal-apocalytpic writings belong to the second.

All work, it is true, is done by individuals. We have nothing beyond the dicta of definite—known or unknown—persons. Yet the great men of a people give the impulses only, and all depends upon what the mass of the people make thereof. It is doubtless as important for the history of Judaism to know what Hillel said, what R. Akiba thought and what R. Meir taught as it is important for Christianity to study the writing of Augustine, Luther and Calvin. But not all Christians are Augustines or Luthers, nor all Jews Hillels and Akibas. The great moulders of Christian thought did indeed succeed in making the masses of Christianity accept their doctrines at solemn councils and representative covenants, but that was not true of the spiritual leaders of the Jews. Even if we admit that whatever is alive in the nation finds expression in the works and words of individuals and that many individual contributions are products of the national spirit, there still remains a vast array of intellectual products that are temporary, accidental and individual, in which the national soul has but a small share. The devil, according to Shakespeare, quotes Scripture. But if he is really as clever as he is reputed to be, he ought to quote the Talmud, as there is hardly any view of life for and against which one could not quote the Talmud.

No less uncritical is the attempt made by many theologians to give us a system of the religious thought of the Jew based upon the apocalyptic literature, the fantastic fabric of popular imagination. As the author of a large work on Jewish legends, I believe myself to be above suspicion of lacking sympathy for the creations of popular fancy. Theology, however, is a rational system of religious values and cannot be built up of material furnished by fancy and imagination. As often as I read books on Jewish theology, and I may say with Faust: *Ich habe leider auch Theologie studiert,* the diametrically opposing views expressed in them remind me of the following story so popular in my native country, Lithuania. A rabbi, trying a case—for the rabbi of olden times was more of a judge than a theologian—after listening to the plaintiff, exclaimed: "You are right, my son"; and then made the same remark to the defendant, after the latter had pleaded in his own behalf. The rabbi's wife, who was present at the trial, could not refrain from remarking to her husband: "How can both litigants be right?" To which the rabbi in genuine meekness, as becoming a husband and a rabbi, replied: "You, too, are right, my dear." I frequently feel like saying to the diametrically opposed theologians: What you say is so profoundly true and so utterly false! You are profoundly right in what you tell us about the beliefs and doctrines of this rabbi or that apocalyptic author, but you are utterly wrong in your attempts to stamp as an expression of the Jewish soul what is only an individual opinion or a transitory fancy.

It is only in the Halakah that we find the mind and character of the Jewish people exactly and adequately expressed. Laws which govern the daily life of man must be such as suit and express his wishes, being in harmony with his feelings and fitted to satisfy his religious ideals and ethical aspirations. A few illustrations will often explain better than long abstract statements, and I shall therefore present a few concrete examples of the Halakah applied to the study of Jewish thought.

At the risk of causing Homeric laughter I shall begin *ab ovo,* not as the poet did, with the egg of Leda, but rather with that no less famous one that, to speak with Heine, was unfortunate enough to be laid on a holiday. He who does not appreciate Heine lacks the ability to appreciate something genuinely Jewish, and I, for one, greatly enjoy his merry remarks on that unfortunate egg. But grave historians, or rather theologians, the majority of whom are not usually distinguished by a sense of humor, do not show deep historical insight in ridiculing the great schools headed by Shammai and Hillel for discussing the question whether an egg laid on a holiday is permitted for use or not.[3] We hear a great deal of Judaism being a view of life for which religion is law. I am at present not interested in showing the fallacy of this dictum nor in inquiring why we hear so little about the second part of this equation, to wit: for the Jew law is religion. But if it be true that religion is law for the Jews, the conception underlying Jewish law must necessarily be expressive of Jewish religious thought. The discussion of the old schools about the egg is tantamount to the question of the extent to which the principle of intent is to be applied. *Actus non est reus nisi mens sit rea*, say the Roman jurists, and similarly the Rabbis: Actions must be judged by their intent. Since, according to biblical law, food for the holy days must be prepared the day before, the progressive school of Hillel maintained that an egg laid on a holy day must not be used because, though prepared by nature, it was without the intent of man and hence can not be considered prepared in the legal sense. As strong men exult in their agility, so tendencies that are strong and full of life will sometimes be betrayed into extravagancies. It may be extravagant to prohibit an egg laid on a holy day on account of not having been intentionally prepared for food. But of what paramount importance must intention have been to the religious conscience of the Jew if it could assume such an exaggerated form as in the case before us! And could there be a better criterion of the development of a religion than the importance it attaches to intent, the outcome of thought and emotion, in opposition to merely physical action?

Now let us examine another Halakah that might throw light on the question as to the relation of thought and emotion to acts and deeds in Jewish theology. Sin, we are told by leading theologians, consists, according to the Jewish conception, in acting wrongly, and hence forgiveness, or, to use the more technical term, atonement, is of a purely mechanical nature. Originally there were different kinds of sacrifices, the sin offerings, the guilt offerings, and so forth, by means of which the sinner could right himself with God. Later the Rabbis substituted prayer, fasting and alms-giving for the sacrifices which, after the destruction of the Temple, could no longer be brought. So far our theologians. And now let us hear what the Halakah has to say about it. In a large collection of laws treating of marriage with conditions attached, which is to be found in the Talmud, we read: If one says to a woman, I marry thee under the condition that I am an entirely righteous man, the marriage is valid, even if it is found that he was a very wicked man, because we apprehend that at the time of the contraction of marriage he repented in his heart. If one says to a woman, I marry thee under the condition that I am a completely wicked man—sin is homely but also attractive!—the marriage is valid.[4] For even if it is found that he was very pious, we apprehend that at the time of the contract he had thoughts of idolatry. Sin as well as forgiveness are thus understood by Jewish law to be entirely independent of acts and deeds; the evil thought in the heart turns the perfectly just into the completely wicked, and vice versa, the change of heart changes the completely wicked into the perfectly just.

The ethical principles and ideals that shaped and formed the Halakah have been made a subject of study by many; however, as we are still in need of a thorough investigation of Jewish ethics, a few remarks on the Halakah as a source of Jewish ethics may prove to be profitable. I shall, however, content myself with touching upon those parts of the Halakah that treat either of ceremonial law or of the forms of civil law; my purpose in doing so being to show to what use the knowledge of these minutiae may be put.

Whether Jewish ethics are of a positive or a negative nature is a question often propounded, and of course answered according to the nature of the quotations one is able to gather from Jewish writings.[5] A favorite argument for the negative character of Jewish ethics is drawn from the number of commandments, which is said to consist of two hundred and forty-eight positive and three hundred and sixty-five negative. I doubt whether the good Rabbi who first computed these numbers was aware of the consequence of his statistics.[6] There can, however, be no doubt in my mind that modern theologians are not aware of the fact that statistics are as fatal to theology as theology to statistics. A prompt and decisive answer to the question concerning Jewish ethics is given by the Halakah in its ruling: that in all conflicts of laws the positive takes precedence of the negative.[7] This legal maxim applies of course to conflicts of ceremonial laws, but it is the outcome of the legal mind or, to use the more adequate term of the Germans, das Rechtsbewusstsein, of a people which conceived ethics as something very positive.

Many of us are undoubtedly acquainted with the favorite diversion of many popular writers who deny to the Jew any claim to creative genius; his religion and his ethics are said by them to be merely different manifestations of his commercial spirit; do ut des being the guiding power of his life. Hence the insistence upon the dogma of reward and punishment in his religion and the utilitarian character of his ethics. We have had enough of theology for the present and I shall not enter upon a discussion of the dogma of reward and punishment. Yet I cannot help quoting to you the very wise words of one of the finest minds among contemporary thinkers. The world, says Mr. Balfour, suffers not because it has too much of it—the belief in reward and punishment—but because it has too little; not because it displaces higher motives, but because it is habitually displaced by lower ones. To those who maintain the utilitarian character of Jewish ethics my advice is: study the part of civil law in Jewish jurisprudence which treats of gifts. While the ancient Roman law, as has been pointed out by the great jurist and legal philosopher Ihering,[8] does not recognize gratuitous transfer of ownership, but only for value, the promise of a gift attained an independence of form in the very earliest stages of the Halakah. For the Roman law gift is a sort of exchange; one makes a gift in order to receive a gift in return, or, in the words of the Roman jurists: ad remunerandum sibi aliquem naturaliter obligaverunt, velut genus quoddam hoc esse permutationis.[9] The Halakah, on the other hand, had overcome the egoism of man, and beneficence and love dictated by altruism had come to their full right in legislation as well as in life.[10] The importance of this phenomenon only he can fail to recognize who sees in the forms of the laws mere forms and not the expression of ideas.

The only point where liberality comes to the surface in the Roman law is in regard to wills, and it is highly interesting for the appraisal of the Jewish character to notice that

Jewish law is rather inclined to limit the power of the testator to the extent that it prohibits the disinheritance of an ungrateful and wicked son in favor of a good and dutiful son.[11] It has been noticed by others that bequests have psychologically not the value of a gift—the gift of the cold hand is compatible with an icy cold heart; it is not a gift of one's own, but from the purse of the legal heir. In the long course of the development of the Jewish people the underlying bond was the family; the ties of blood were of absolute and undisputed strength. Consequently, the Halakah is not in favor of any measure that might disrupt this bond of union. In this connection I may call attention to the fact that the Halakah failed to develop the law of adoption, notwithstanding the fact that the Bible offers some precedents in certain forms of adoption.[12] The idea of blood relationship forming the basis of the family was too strong with the Jew to permit the development of a law that would undermine it.

This leads us to the burning Jewish question of the day: Are the Jews a nation or merely a religious community? Of course I am not going to discuss it from the point of view of the Jew of today, but justice to my subject requires that we discuss this question from the point of view of the Halakah. And the answer to this question is given unmistakably in the following two laws of inheritance. A Jew, converted to paganism, inherits his father's estate; a pagan, who is converted to Judaism, does not inherit his father's estate, whether the father also becomes a convert or not.[13] The idea underlying these Halakot is that the ties of blood binding the Jew to the Jewish people can never be loosened, and that, on the other hand, by becoming a Jew, a pagan severs his national connections with those to whom he previously belonged. There is a logical contradiction in these two laws of inheritance as formulated by the Halakah. But what is life but a conglomerate of logical contradictions? The Halakah would not be a true mirror of Jewish life, if it were free from all logical inconsistencies. The Jew is bound forever to his people, and yet anybody who enters Judaism becomes a true son of Israel.

A little reflection will, however, convince anyone who comes to the question with an open mind that both these theories concerning Judaism, the purely nationalistic as well as the purely religious, are alike incomplete and, being incomplete, are misleading. They err, as all theories are apt to err, not by pointing to a wholly false cause but by extending the efficiency of a true cause far beyond its real scope. Considered from an historical point of view there is no such thing as nationalism in general. History knows only a particular form of nationalism. It is not the military or economic organization of a state which makes it a national body but the spiritual idea represented by its people. When we speak of the Greek nation we primarily think of the form in which the genius of this nation expressed itself. And is not Jewish nationalism an empty phrase if we do not connect with it Jewish religion and Jewish ethics, Jewish culture and the Jewish mode of life which gave it its individuality?

Notes

1. Megillah 28b, bottom.
2. Yerushalmi, Berakot V, 9d.
3. Mishnah Bezah, beginning.
4. Kiddushin 49b.
5. Comp. the very pertinent remarks on this point by Moore, *Judaism* II, 287.
6. R. Simlai, a Palestinian Amora about the middle of the third century is the first to mention these numbers, though it is quite possible that the computation originated with an earlier authority. The attempts of Halper, *Book of Precepts*, 1–5, to find traces of this computation in tannaitic sources are not successful. Midrash Hagadol I, 226 top, has it in a statement by the Tanna, R. Eliezer b. R. Yose—this passage escaped Halper—but there is no telling whether the number תרי"ג is not a later interpolation. Comp. also Guttmann, בחינת המצוות, 24ff.
7. Yebamot 3b, bottom, ff. and in many other passages of both Talmudim. Comp. Guttmann, *Emléköny Bloch Moses* 1–20 (Hebrew section). I wish to call attention to the fact that the term used by the Tannaim is: מצות עשה קודמת ללא תעשה (comp. Mekilta Mishpatim 20) and not מ' ע' דוחה לא תעשה as in the amoraic terminology. Guttmann has no references to tannaitic sources.
8. *Law As a Means to an End*, 209–211.
9. D. 5. 3. 25. 11.
10. A verbal promise to the poor is binding; comp. Baba Kama 36b, bottom; see also Baba Batra 148b.
11. Baba Batra 133b.
12. Jacob adopted two sons of Joseph, comp. Genesis 48:5–6.
13. Kiddushin 17b.

10.

On Medieval Hebrew Poetry *

by Shalom Spiegel

i

To some the mere notion of postbiblical Hebrew poetry will seem a presumption. As if the Bible could have a sequel, or as if at the end of the Psalter one could promise: To be continued. The objection will sometimes be stated in purely aesthetic categories. After the heights ascended by Second Isaiah, or the depths plumbed by Job, can aught be said or sung in the Hebrew language, and not be a poor or pitiable anticlimax? It is true, all great poetry leaves us with a sense of discouragement or defeat, diffident to exercise again the craft of the poet. Awed by extraordinary accomplishment, men are prone to invoke the miraculous and to speak of inspiration. Still, poets in every age and culture will pray and strive for the miracle to happen again.

Could a Hebrew poet in postbiblical times expect a similar grace of Heaven, or did the canonization of Scripture forbid it?

The conception of a canon attests and implies a feeling and a belief that the age of direct communication with God is past, and that with the death of the latter prophets, the holy spirit departed from Israel. This doctrine of the sealing of prophecy would appear to put a ceiling to the aspiration of even the most gifted poet ever to rise in postbiblical Hebrew. To be sure, though God may hide His face, His hand is stretched lovingly over Israel, and hints of His revelation may still be disclosed in dreams.[1] Moreover, there persists in all the ages the hope of the ultimate renewal of prophecy in the end of days.[2] But in the

* From *The Jews: Their History, Culture and Religion,* Louis Finkelstein, ed., vol. I, New York, Harper and Brothers, 1960.

concrete here and now, after the completion of the canon, all one could hope for, at best was *bat kol,* the "daughter of the voice," an echo of the glories of the past.[3]

With the expiration of prophecy, Israel was to incline its ear to the words of the Sages.[4] In fact, some took it to apply already to the entire period of the Second Temple in which the Divine Presence, the source of all prophecy, no longer resided.[5] The reliance in the Torah and its scholars became more urgent and insistent after the loss of state and sanctuary, when the very future of Judaism seemed imperiled. Jerusalem lay in ashes, her gates sunk to the ground. Was one still to believe that "the Lord loveth the gates of Zion more than all the dwellings of Jacob" (Psalms 87:2)? If the Holy Writ was to retain any meaning, and Jewish life any hope, was one not driven to conclude, in the face of the disasters that had overtaken the nation, that the gates of Zion (*ziyyon*) henceforth must mean gates marked (*ziyyun*) or distinguished in the Law? "Ever since the Temple was destroyed, the Holy One, blessed is He, has nothing else in His world but the four cubits of *halaka.*" [6] To these four cubits of the law the people clung desperately as to its only remnant of freedom and insurance of restoration. All that mattered from now on was the preservation of the Torah, little else was permitted to weigh as much in the scales of Israel. "The elders have ceased from the gate, the young men from their music" (Lamentations 5:14): when the elders ceased from the Sanhedrin, the highest seat of Jewish learning and the supreme court of Jewish law, how could the young be allowed to make music or to indulge in song? [7] One was in no mood to encourage the arts or "to rejoice in mirth as other peoples." [8] This, too, like the renewal of prophecy, must wait until God's own good time: Then only will our mouth be filled with laughter, and our tongue with singing, when it will be said among the nations: the Lord hath done great things with Israel! [9] Embattled by a hostile world, often reduced to mere subsistence, the synagogue had to maintain an austere economy of spiritual resources and to huddle all its strength for its prime task of keeping the light of the Torah aflame.

The Jewish Middle Ages build upon this twofold legacy of the Rabbinic age. Divine inspiration is relegated to the remote past or the distant future, and the word of the Lord is sought in the present from the disciples of the wise, the scholars of *halaka.* Certain critical remarks of the Rabbis against prophecy

are retained and elaborated, no doubt, to strengthen the hold
of the Torah upon the people. A poet as devoted to his calling
as Moses ibn Ezra (d. after 1135) writes in his *ars poetica:* [10]

> When our sins increased, and we were scattered among the
> nations because of our evil doings, and God (exalted is He)
> allowed the period of prophecy to come to a standstill, the
> Almighty was gracious unto us and sustained us with His
> servants who transmitted to us His Torah and the words of
> the prophets from generation to generation. It is from them
> that we have inherited our faith and institutions. The prophet
> Zechariah (peace be unto him) whose prophecy was late,
> foresaw this succession of sages (their memory be blessed)
> when he said (Zechariah 9:12): "Return to the stronghold, ye
> prisoners of hope; even today do I declare that I will render
> double unto thee." The words allude to the company of
> illustrious scholars upon whom the holy spirit has rested.
> They are the luminaries of the Torah who lead us to good-
> ness in this world and to bliss in the world to come. In this
> verse the prophet announced to the children of Israel that they
> will return from Babylon to their homeland, and that there
> will rise among them, in place of the prophets who will have
> ceased, men whose wisdom will be double that of the prophets,
> as was said: "A sage is superior to a prophet." [11] For the
> prophet delivers his message as it was given to him, and the
> prophecy as made known to him by God, whereas the Sage
> hands down what he received from the prophets, and draws
> one thing from another in accordance with the powers granted
> to him by the Torah, and contributes from his own mind in
> conformity to the laws of reason. His is therefore the excel-
> lence of originality. This is evident and indicated, I believe, in
> Scripture (Jeremiah 18:18): "Instruction shall not perish from
> the priest, nor counsel from the wise, nor the word from the
> prophet." Thus Scripture, making three distinctions, awards to
> the prophet merely "the word," *i. e.,* the word which he is to
> make known in the name of God. The entire matter was
> summed up in a wonderful adage of the sage (peace be unto
> him): "Where there is no vision, the people perish" (Proverbs
> 29:18). Hence he immediately exhorted the people to hold
> on to the words of the wise, when prophecy and prophets will
> have ended, saying: "But he that keepeth the law, happy is
> he."

A compatriot and contemporary of this Spanish poet, the
great talmudic scholar and head of the academy at Lucena,
Joseph ibn Migas (d. 1141) words it more tersely:

> A sage is superior to a prophet, because the prophet reports
> only what he heard and what was put in his mouth to be said,

while the sage reports what was said to Moses from Mt. Sinai, although he did not hear it.[12]

The gift of inspiration is disparaged for the greater glory of the wisdom in the holy Law. This doctrine adhered to by artist and rabbi alike in the period of the highest flowering of the poetic genius in Spain, is characteristic of the whole of the Jewish Middle Ages. In agreement with talmudic teaching, the Sage is accorded what is denied to the seer, continued possession of the holy spirit. "From the day the Temple was destroyed, although prophecy was withdrawn from the prophet, it has not been withdrawn from the wise," [13] the custodians and interpreters of the law in each age.

Modesty naturally forbade the medieval scholar to boast of or lay claim to inspiration, at least, not openly. But there were exceptions to the rule, and men famed for their learning and piety, dropping all restraint, admit receiving missives from heaven. Rabbi Abraham son of David of Posquières (d. 1198), the keen critic of the code of Maimonides, is audacious or outspoken enough to avow that "the holy spirit appeared in our school." [14] There may be sin of pride in such assertions, but not heresy. "Saintliness leads to the holy spirit" [15] and "God's secret is with them that fear Him" (Psalms 25:14).[16] In reply to some knotty question in the law, a medieval Rabbi will write: "This is what I was shown in heaven," [17] a legal locution not hackneyed, but not improper. A scholar's faith or fidelity is not impugned because of such revelations.

Nothing of the sort is ever permitted to the medieval poet. To be sure, he had often enough to blow his own bugle (in absence of the modern art of the paid advertisement), but however frivolous or extravagant his self-praise, he never dared to include in it the faintest pretension to the holy spirit. It would have had the effect of a bad joke. There are sundry varieties of religious delusion in the Middle Ages, but we never hear of a poet to have come forward unreservedly as a prophet, as did in Arabic letters Mutanabbi, i.e., "the pretender to prophecy" (d. 965), in the estimate of his countrymen the most famous of all the poets born or made in Islam.[18]

Of course, a true poet will always await and witness anew the miracle of inspiration and sing of its ecstasies. Hebrew literature, also, has some magnificent examples of poetry quivering with the excitement of the unaccountable but unmistaken event. Invariably, however, there is a chaste reticence about such visitations of the Divinity. The experience is stated almost impersonally, in the traditional imagery, as if to hide the new rapture of the poet in the ancient and familiar memories of his people. Hence the ease with which the medieval synagogue could turn these intimate revelations of the individual into collective prayers of Israel. Take for example the lovely nocturne of Judah Ha-Levi (d. after 1140):

> My thought awaked me with Thy Name,
>   Upon Thy boundless love to meditate;
>   Whereby I came
> The fullness of the wonder to perceive,
>   That Thou a soul immortal shouldst create
> To be embound in this, my mortal frame.
>   Then did my mind, elate,
> Behold Thee and believe;
>   As though I stood among
>   That hushed and awe-swept throng
> And heard the Voice and gazed on Sinai's flame!
>
>   I seek Thee in my dreams,
>   And lo, Thy glory seems
> To pass before me, as of old, the cloud
>   Descended in his sight, who heard
>   The music of Thy spoken word.
> Then from my couch I spring, and cry aloud,
> "Blest be the glory of Thy Name, O Lord!" [19]

Quite fittingly, the poem is included in the liturgy of Shabuot, the holiday of revelation, commemorating the covenant established at Sinai. Originally, however, it is the record of a very personal encounter. In answer to long probings into the riddle of soul and body, the poet experiences, half awake and half in a dream, how into the clouds of his soul there descends the glory of God as into a tabernacle: "My heart beheld Thee and believed Thee, as though I were standing at Sinai." Purged of vanity by such undeserved favor of heaven, the poet's lips murmur a benediction, not a boast. The individual experience loses itself in the event basic to all Israel, the inspiration of today reaffirms the dawn of the historic faith, and the new seeks humbly to bring home the old revelation.

The same poet, as others before and after him, is also familiar with some of the formal aspects of inspiration: the feeling of being but a passive tool and mouthpiece, of being "carried away and overpowered" (Jeremiah 20:7), of saying not what one pleases, but what one cannot help saying. He knows also the sense of exhilaration, when the halting tongue is quickened of a sudden by the onrush of words, heaven born, pouring in effortlessly, infallible in their felicity, so convincing and compelling as to leave simply no other choice. "The speech of a prophet at the time when he is enwrapped by the holy spirit is in every part directed by the divine influence, the prophet himself being powerless to alter one word." [20] The description has personal accents, as has in the same book the impassioned and insistent inquiry into the state of the prophet and the secret of prophecy, but there is a self-imposed censorship and discipline of silence about any such adventures or aspirations of the poet. The restraint reflects a climate of opinion reared on a doctrine which stressed the pathos of distance separating the present from the ancient days when holy men still walked and talked with God.

In the medieval world one was ready to exercise patience and forbearance even with inordinate claims when made in the name of religion, not poetry. Saadia Gaon (d. 942), perhaps under the influence of certain Moslem ideas, evolved a remarkable doctrine that God never fails to provide His people with a "scholar" in each age whom He enlightens and inspires to guide his generation and make them prosper through him. Significantly, the Gaon adds that such was his own experience, having witnessed "what God in His grace has done for me and for the people." [21] The word used is *talmid*, or disciple (of the wise) or scholar in the law, and thus the claim is advanced on behalf of the Torah and its foremost exponent in every age. But since Saadia was also a prolific poet, and his contemporaries could not help being apprised of the opinions he entertained about himself, we hear the resentment voiced that his poetic compositions were written in verse units and supplied with accents and vowel points. Such resemblance to the Sacred Writ was seized upon by his opponents, who denounced it as a pretense to prophecy.[22] The last such instance, on the threshold of the modern era, is that of Moses Hayyim Luzzatto (d. 1747). Under the spell of inspiration, he believed himself to be receiving revelations from a mentor-angel and to write a second *Zohar*, a sequel to the classic book of Jewish mysticism. But since he was also a gifted poet, he had to contend with the rumor that he had written one hundred and fifty poems to supplant the Psalms of David. In vain did the poet disavow any such claim or comparison, his devout teacher aiding him by testifying that the poems were the product of toil and skill, not inspiration, as could clearly be seen from the many corrections and deletions, in the handwriting of the author, "such as occur in the natural process of composition, when one writes and crosses out and writes again." [23] The suspected manuscript had to be surrendered to a Rabbinic court, a portion was burned and the remainder buried in the ground, and so lost to posterity.[24] It is true, those were days of the Sabbatian heresies when the guardians of the law may have thought it their duty to be especially severe.

Not only in times of crisis or peril to religion, but throughout the Middle Ages one can detect a latent or patent hostility to the craft of the poet. On second and serious thought, it must have appeared to be dangerous folly for a scattered and threatened community to dissipate its meager resources in toying with verse or enjoying poesy. Nor is it strange that the philosophic spirits in medieval Judaism were just as inimical to the poets, and particularly to the religious poets. Unrestrained fancy and loose talk, so the philosophers contended, could not but offend against the true precepts of an enlightened faith and breed crude or corrupt notions about God.[25] Rationalists and traditionalists alike seemed to concur that the cause of religion is best served, and error best eschewed, by banning poetry altogether from the worship of the synagogue. If piety prompts one to add or amplify praises to God, there is always inspired Scripture to draw upon with profit, or one can at all times safely turn to the Psalter.[26]

ii

The advice was heeded. The Psalter served throughout the ages as a primer of prayer and praise, and handbook of devotion. It became the hymnal of the synagogue and the common man's household book of poetry. It would be difficult to overrate the effect of this most widely circulated anthology of Hebrew verse on the language of faith and the habits of piety of countless generations. Multitudes of men at every period of history discovered in the Psalms the stirrings and strivings of their hearts, and clothed in the venerable words of the book their own penitence and hope. This power of the Psalter stems from the belief that it is not merely a collection of priceless poetry, or a formulary of edifying prayers, but that it is part and parcel of the Holy Writ.

> There is nothing more precious than the Book of the Psalms which contains everything. Therein are many praises to His Name, hallowed is He, and many a summons to repentance as well as many supplications for forgiveness and mercy . . . By

reciting the Psalms, we at once offer prayer and study Holy
Scripture, for King David, peace be unto him, long ago be-
seeched heaven that whoever will read the Psalter should receive as much reward as he who delves in the depths of the
Torah.[1]

This, then, was the unique distinction of the Psalter, that it
combined the two fundamental elements of all Jewish worship:
it served as a pattern of *prayer* and as a repository of guidance
and *instruction* in holy living. The two functions are inseparable, of course, and yet it is the latter that carried most weight
in the eyes of the believer. His standards of value are succinctly
stated in a maxim current in the Middle Ages:

> He who prays, speaks to God; but he who reads the Writ,
> God speaks to him, as it is said (Psalms 119:99): "Thy
> statutes are (Thy) converse with me." [2]

It is in this double capacity of the Psalter to furnish both
request and reply, search and solution, the cry of human
want and the answer of Divine bounty, that one must seek
the secret of the unrivaled influence exercised by the book in
all ages.

Being a part of Scripture, the Psalms share the fate of that
widely read Book: they are subject to ever-new and ever-
changing rereading by new generations of men. Each period
pours its own inner life into the patient and pliant texts of old
which engagingly oblige new inquirers with new answers.
Devout centuries extract or extort from the familiar documents
messages undreamt of or unsuspected by the original writers.
Such fresh and fanciful embroidering upon the ancient design
is properly called legend, as the Latin *legenda* literally means:
that *which will be read* by successive ages into the events or
records of the past. The more a book is used, the more it will
be abused, fiction prevailing over fact, or—to vary Aristotle [3]
—poetry outlasting history.

The Bible, too, had such a posthumous adventure in its
passage through the centuries, its text becoming disengaged
from the original intention and enriched by the faith and
fantasy of innumerable readers. We can follow this afterlife
of the Bible in scattered comments or orderly commentaries
which mirror the temper and the trends of the Jewish Middle
Ages. Moreover, the centrality of Scripture in the medieval
scene accounts not only for the natural and unconscious
metamorphosis of the biblical legacy in the course of time,
but also for the frequency with which so much of the original

creation of the Middle Ages was sunk into biblical exegesis. To gain foothold in medieval Israel, every spiritual endeavor had to be related to the chief concern of the people, Torah. Hence medieval expression is so often cast in the form of a commentary on Scripture. Even dissent and revolt are clothed in what is in name or shape but a commentary. The form succeeded in disguising and preserving a great deal of the independent achievement of the Middle Ages. Whatever their usefulness for the study of the Bible itself, the medieval Bible commentaries are invaluable and indispensable for the revelation of the internal life of the Jew in the Middle Ages.

An example from the Psalter will illustrate the vigor and variety of this invisible creativeness passing unchallenged as biblical interpretation.

Psalm 29 is probably a very old hymn, voicing the dread and the wonder of ancient man before the fury of the elements. A storm is gathering out at sea, "upon many waters," and breaks upon the land, tossing the cedars of Lebanon and rocking the snow-capped Hermon to its foundations. The massive mountains seem to shake helplessly like frightened animals. The storm and the winds, the peals of thunder and the "flames of fire" or the lightning flash herald the power of "the God of glory" as He sets out to strike at the insurgent foes. When the tempest dies away in the desert, all rebellion is quelled, and the conqueror can return to His celestial palace, built "upon the flood" or the upper waters above the firmament, there to receive the tribute and honor due to a "king for ever." The heavenly ceremony is pictured after the fashion of earthly courts, or rather in images borrowed from prebiblical myths.[4] We see the lesser divinities, the *bene elim*, or "the sons of the gods," assemble to pay homage to the victorious godhead. With such "praise on high" the Psalm opens, and it ends with a prayer for "peace on earth."

Quite appropriately we find the earliest use of the Psalm in the liturgy of the festival of Sukkot, when prayers for rain were offered.

Already in the age of the *Tannaim,* the meaning of the Psalm was thoroughly overhauled:

> Rabbi Eleazer of Modaim said: When the Holy One, blessed be He, appeared to give the Torah to Israel, the earth shook and the mountains quaked, and all the sons of the mighty (*bene elim*) trembled in their palaces, as it is said: "And in his palace every one says 'Glory' " (Psalms 29:9). Whereupon the kings of the world assembled and came to Balaam,

saying: What is the uproar that we heard? Is a flood to come to destroy the earth? Said he to them: "The Lord sitteth upon the flood" (ibid., 10). The Holy One, blessed be He, swore long ago that He would not bring a flood upon the world for ever. They then said to him: He will not bring a flood of water, but He may bring a flood of fire as it is said: "For by fire will the Lord contend" (Isaiah 66:16). But he said to them: He is going to bring neither a flood of water, nor a flood of fire. However, He possesses in His storehouse a priceless treasure, the Torah which He is to present to His sons, as it is said: "The Lord will give strength unto His people" (Psalms 29:11). As soon as the kings heard that from him, they joined in the benediction: "The Lord will bless His people with peace" (Ibid.).[5]

Rabbi Eleazer of Modaim died during the siege of Bethar (c. 135 C.E.) and taught in days when it became clear that the natural base of the Hebrew polity, the state and the sanctuary, were lost. However impoverished, Israel still possessed a priceless treasure from God's storehouse, the Torah. Hence the new stress on the gift of revelation, and on God's power in history rather than nature. Transposed, as it were, into a new key, the Psalm was employed in the liturgy of the Feast of Weeks, which commemorates the covenant at Sinai, when the Torah was given to Israel.[6] In medieval Spain [7] the custom seems to have originated of reciting the Psalm on the Sabbath, the traditional day of Revelation,[8] as the Torah is being returned to the Ark, or the treasure brought back to His storehouse, a practice still observed in our synagogues.

Echoes of darker centuries survive in the Midrash to the Psalms, a collection of homilies from various times, some perhaps going back to days of Roman or Byzantine rule and oppression: [9]

> Bene elim or "the sons of the gods"—what does that mean? The sons of the dumb (bene ilmim) and of the deaf (i. e., the sons of Israel) who could answer back the Holy One, blessed be He, but they refrain from answering back, and suffer the yoke of the nations for the sanctification of His name. This is what Isaiah said (42:19): "Who is blind, but my servant, or deaf, as my messenger that I sent?"
> Bene elim—what else can that mean? The sons of those who are slain like rams (elim). Abraham said: I slay; Isaac said: I am (ready to be) slain.[10]

Pained and puzzled by the triumph of the wicked, the religious conscience sought solace and support in the examples of patriarchal piety or the songs of the suffering servant. The ways of God were inscrutable. Abraham did not comprehend how a father could be commanded to slay his only son, but he did not refuse or reproach God, he obeyed instead, to be rewarded and relieved in the end. Silently also the servant of the Lord must bear his martyrdom, a spoil and sport of all mankind, and yet it is with his stripes that the world will be healed. It was in the light of such memories or monition that Psalm 29 was reread in the early Middle Ages.

When the swift victories of Islam and the vast realm conquered by the new faith seemed to make the hopes of Jewish repatriation impracticable or illusory, the troubled heart turned again to the Psalter for courage and comfort. Psalm 29 was rendered as summoning the children of Israel to be *bene elim,* sons of might or men of valor, and to persevere in the faith as there was hope in their future. Verse 10 was understood to contain the solemn assurance that just as the Lord guards the universe against the flood, so He remains His people's king forever: "For as I have sworn that the waters of Noah should no more go over the earth, so have I sworn that I would not be wroth with thee, nor rebuke thee. For the mountains shall depart, and the hills be removed, but my kindness shall not depart from thee, neither shall the covenant of my peace be removed, saith the Lord that hath mercy on thee" (Isaiah 54:9f.). The Psalm was so translated by Saadia, and his version is still current among Arabic-speaking Jews.[11]

In the lands of medieval Christendom, the Psalm was construed as a prophecy about the days of Messianic deliverance, when "the cedars of Lebanon," the proud kingdoms of the earth will be humbled. The Lord will thunder "upon many waters"; these are the rich and rapacious that grab the goods of this world as greedily as waters cover the sea. But in the end, justice will be enthroned for ever, and in His temple all will say "Glory," as it is said: "Then will I turn to the peoples a pure language, that they may all call upon the Name of the Lord, to serve Him with one consent" (Zephaniah 3:9).[12]

After the banishment from Spain (1492), which uprooted the most populous and prosperous community of the Middle Ages, mystical tendencies gained the ascendancy. The Psalter was read fervently as an apocalypse in which every word is infused with references to the events of the imminently expected Messianic catstrophe or redemption. In fact, the Psalms themselves were discovered to be a book of war songs, an arsenal of mystic or magic weapons, "a sharp sword in Israel's hand" [13] to strike at the root of evil and thus precipitate the end. When the crack of doom failed to come, and the Messianic fever wore away, there spread from Safed, a town in northern Galilee, audacious new doctrines such as the cabbala of Isaac Luria (d. 1572), which gave a new answer to the basic and baffling facts of the historic experience of the Jew and a new meaning to his acts of worship. [14]

The homelessness of the Jewish people was conceived to be but a detail in the general dislocation of the whole of existence due to a primordial flaw or fracture of all creation which the new cabbala called "the breaking of the vessels." Because of it, all realms of being were unhinged and deranged, thrown out of their proper and purposed station, everything in the order of creation was displaced, all were in exile, including God. Supernal lights fell in the abyss of darkness, and sparks of holiness became imprisoned in shells of evil. The unity of the Divine Name was shattered (the new cabbala speaks of the letters YH being torn away from WH in the name YHWH). It was the mission of man and the purpose of religion to restore the broken name of God and so heal the original blemish of all the visible and invisible worlds. By observing the commandments of the Torah and the ordained discipline of worship, every Jew could become a partner in the work of redemption: he could help to lift the fallen lights of God and set free the holy sparks from the powers of evil.

With ardent precision every detail in form and language of the Psalms was instilled with mystic meaning and function. Concretely, in Psalm 29, three times it was said "Give unto the Lord," seven times "the voice of the Lord," eighteen times the Divine Name is spelled, making seventy-two letters or the numerical value of *hesed,* or mercy. The eleven verses of the Psalm equal WH in the tetragram, while the ninety-one words in the whole Psalm correspond to the sum total of YHWH and Adonai. [15] By means of each of these mysteries of prayer, the worshiper who knew the secrets of the holy letters and was capable of utter inwardness (*kavvanah*) in his devotion, could work miracles of *tikkun* or restitution by which sparks scattered in the lower depths could be reassembled, and "the Holy One, praised be He, reunited with His exiled *Shekinah.*" Acts of religion determine the fate of the world, and it is the essential distinction and dignity of man that without his free choice the breach of creation could not be mended. Feeble as man is, unlike the angels, he alone knows, in every breath of his, about the struggle of good and evil, and can influence it by his freedom of action. Hence only man, and not any of the celestial beings, can lead the banished glory of God back to the Master, and thus literally "give unto the Lord glory and strength," thereby completing His enthronement as "king for ever."

In this new myth, which burst forth in the heart of Judaism at so late a stage of the historic faith, mystic notions verge on magic, or perhaps revert to the origins of all worship in which prayer and spell commingle. As if the wheel had come full circle, and the new cabbala had recovered, on another plane, the prebiblical rudiments of magic, residual in the Psalms and perhaps irreducible from man's vocabulary of prayer.

These few examples of Rabbinic and cabbalistic interpretation of Scripture will suffice to indicate the amazing freedom with which the Middle Ages were able to make the words of an old text yield new meaning. Even though the syllables and sentences of the Bible remained intact, a new sentiment infused them with new significance, and transformed the Psalm, far beyond the purposes of the first author, into an untrammeled expression of a new religious attitude and outlook. Often it is an original conception that asserts itself in, or despite, the ancient and venerable vocables, which suffer no outward change through the centuries. The new creation escapes notice (also by the historians of literature), for it is deposited invisibly in the same old words of the Writ.

Above all, even a hurried glimpse into biblical lore of the Middle Ages will prove how futile was the endeavor to exorcise error and heresy from the synagogue by advising the faithful to turn with a safe conscience only to inspired Scripture, particularly the Psalms. We saw traditionalists and rationalists agreeing that it would be best to praise God with the songs of King David alone.[16] Little did either of them dream what dangerously novel ideas could nest in the innocent and time-honored words. The letter is too feeble to imprison the spirit. It is useless to try to freeze the tides of spiritual life into permanent retrospection. Ancient meanings cannot be perpetuated through the ages. At best, the sounds may be reproduced, or perhaps only the symbols of script, but a new spirit will transfigure them in each age.

Fortunately, the synagogue discovered quite early how hopeless it would be to invite the great poetry of biblical antiquity to keep new expression suppressed in Judaism. It was better insight to make room in the synagogue, along with the classical heritage, also for new creative endeavor, and thus enlist the genius of the poets to lend freshness and vigor to the religious quest of medieval Jewry.

iii

The beginnings of poetry in the synagogue may well go back to the dawn of public prayer, or to the very origin of the synagogue. The Jews were the only people of antiquity who succeeded in divorcing prayer from sacrifice, and so were the first ·to evolve the modes and manners of public worship as the world knows them now. The new institution of the synagogue was to grapple first with the two basal needs of all congregational service: conformity and nonconformity. Untutored or undisciplined prayer may grow haphazard and slipshod, self-seeking or disreputable, anarchical and antisocial. Regulated for public propriety, or legislated for the good of society, it may become a stale and spiritless convention. The synagogue strove to retain and reconcile both the requirement of agreement and informality. The oldest order of services includes, along with instruction in the Writ meant for the whole congregation, private devotions or confessions. These elements of spontaneous or subjective piety (called *debarim,* words, or *tahanunim,* supplications) originally followed the recitation of the *Shema,* or the creed of Judaism, and thus hark back to a time before the eighteen benedictions/ or the principal prayer became an established order of the synagogue.[1] Moreover, even when the eighteen benedictions were finally agreed upon, toward the close of the first century C.E., only their sequence was settled, the wording remaining in flux for centuries. As a matter of fact, there continues for generations the deliberate tendency to keep the prayer fresh and fluid, modified with something new each day, to quote a Rabbi of the fourth century.[2]

Probably there was here at work a rejection of the heathen notion of piety which rigidly forbade any deviation from the hallowed formulary of ancestral ritual. Even the slightest change would only weaken the potency of the prayers, believed by the ancients to be missives from the gods themselves and hence especially efficacious and inviolable.

To prevent the confusion of religion with magic, the Rabbis emphasize that there are no set or sacred spells certain to force down the blessing from heaven. On the contrary, prayer must not be fixed,[3] but free, welling out of the depths of a contrite heart and reaching out entreatingly for the unpredictable grace and goodness of God.

Whatever the motives of the Rabbis, the religious and aesthetic benefit was indisputable. By asking with variety of circumstance also variety of words, the synagogue admitted or even invited into its midst the craftsmen of words, or the poets. As a result the common prayers of Judaism gained increasingly in richness of inspiration and beauty of expression.

The Middle Ages followed the Rabbinic age in the endeavor to preserve both obedience to tradition and individual assertion. The standard prayers, the oldest nucleus of the liturgy, always and everywhere became the center of Jewish worship, a bond of union despite geographic dispersal, and a bridge across the ages linking the present to the past. At the same time, each period and place was left free, if not encouraged, to speak its own mind in new compositions added to, or inserted within, the ancient prayers. These additions, called *piyyut,* or poetry, constitute—in contrast to the stable and stationary standard prayers—an ever-changing and restless element in the Jewish liturgy. They enliven with personal accent or local color the established and universal order of services, and unlike the latter, frankly bespeak the soil and sun, season or situation, which nurtured or ripened them. In fact, it was the vigorous and abundant growth of the *piyyut* that was responsible for the development within medieval Judaism of about half a hundred different rites.[4] Within the larger brotherhood of Israel, and the stock of prayers common to all generations, the medieval synagogue attempts and attains both a contemporary note and regional differentiation. The religious expression varies in the Byzantine age and in the era of Islam; in the same century, Franco-German Judaism differs from Spanish Judaism, as do the rites of Aleppo and Yemen, Prague and Amsterdam. Yet there underlies them all, despite the dissimilar and distinctive body of their poetry, the core of ecumenic prayer invariable in all Jewries.

In fine, before the invention of printing slackened or congealed its growth, medieval Judaism essayed and effected a conciliation and concordance of two contrary but complementary necessities of all spiritual life, arriving at a remarkable synthesis of liberty and order, unity and diversity, permanence and change. The old and the new, the recent and the remote, the casual and the constant, blend to enrich and to reinforce

each other. It is this peculiar and pregnant amalgam of opposites, of pattern and freedom, system and vitality which
imparts to medieval utterance both strength and suppleness,
the discipline of a consistent doctrine and accord with the
tune of the times.

A few examples of religious verse may serve as illustration,
and help to point out some of the forms and functions of
medieval Hebrew poetry.

The heart of the Jewish service is the *Shema*, the Jew's acceptance of the Kingship of Heaven. It begins with a sum-
mons to the worshipers: "Bless ye (*bareku*) the Lord!" It is
here, before the call is sounded, that the medieval poet asks
"leave" (*reshut*) to intersperse the hallowed prayers with his
own effort. Such introductions usually strike the note of
preparation for the actual prayer. For example, the poet medi-
tates upon what is to be affirmed in the *Shema*. The first words,
after the avowal of faith, command to love God "with all thy
heart and all thy might" (Deuteronomy 6:5), that is to love
Him "in truth" (cf. Jeremiah 32:41). For in the holy tongue,
God's name is Truth (Jeremiah 10:10), and in the view of the
Rabbis, His seal is truth.[5] These are, also, the very last words
of the *Shema:* "I am the Lord your God—Truth," in prayer
the immediately following word being joined to the last of recited Scripture (Numbers 15:41). The beginning and the end
of the *Shema* set the theme of one of the magnificent preludes
by Judah Ha-Levi:

> With all my heart, O Truth, with all my might
> I love Thee; in transparency, or night,
> Thy Name is with me; how then walk alone?
> He is my Love; how shall I sit alone?
> He is my Brightness; what can choke my flame?
> While He holds fast my hand, shall I be lame?
> Let folk despise me: they have never known
> My shame for Thy sake is my glorious crown.
> O Source of Life, let my life tell thy praise,
> My song to Thee be sung in all my days! [6]

When promptly thereafter the congregation is summoned to
praise or bless the Lord, the familiar *bareku* of the prayer
book seems now immeasurably widened in its meaning, or
perhaps restored to its real meaning. For what is required
cannot be the mere mouthing of pious words, but the truth
of a whole life given in service to the Truth that is God. Given?
Gained is the better word, for what speaks here is not renunciation, nor even resentment over the world's scorn and hate,

but the glad surrender of the failing self to the "source of life" wherefrom every breath is borrowed and all our strength supplied.

The first of the benedictions preceding the *Shema* voices gratitude for the gift of light. It is probably a very old practice, going back to the ancient mystics of Palestine, the Essenes, who, as Josephus records, would not speak before daybreak about profane matters, but would first greet the dawn with prayers that had come down to them from their forefathers, "as if praying for the sun to rise." [7] Adopted into the synagogue, the morning prayer grew to include the glorious words of Second Isaiah (45:7) about the One God "Who formeth (*yozer*) light and createth darkness." The *piyyut* which is here inserted is called *yozer* and usually hymns the wonders of creation. But sometimes, as in the following example, the poet ponders over the darker might of God which the medieval community had so often to experience. Bewildered by the ways of God with men and His incomprehensible neutrality or apparent assent to evil, the distressed heart seeks in the Holy Writ a clue to the uncanny power and purpose of darkness. Four Scriptural passages on the theme of darkness voice the complaint and the comfort, and form the final line and rhyme of each stanza:

> O silent Dove, pour out thy whispered prayer,
> Stricken amid the tents of Meshekh;
> And lift thy soul unto God—
> Thy banner, thy chariot and thy horseman—
> Who kindleth the light of thy sun:

Is. 45:7   *Who formeth light and createth darkness.*

> To the whole He called with His word,
> And it arose in a moment, at His bidding,
> To show unto all the strength of His glory
> In the world which unto life, not waste, He had formed,
> When from the east, unto His light

Ex. 10:21   *He called and moved the darkness.*

> And the host of His heavens heard
> The word: "Let there be Light"; and learned to know
> That there is a Rock by whom are cleft
> The firmaments, and the earth's foundations laid.
> And they gave thanks to their Maker, now understanding

Eccl. 2:13   *The excellency of light over darkness.*

> So will He yet light up my gloom,
> And help to raise my fallen estate,
> And shed radiance over mine assembly.

Then His people shall yet rejoice:
"Behold the light of the Rock of my praise

Mic. 7:8   *Is mine, though I sit in darkness.*" [8]

One must read in Hebrew the assurance of the ancient seer broken off suddenly, in the middle, as if to indicate the yet unfinished processes of history, to understand the triumph of trust which amidst all the terrors of medieval darkness never despairs of a new dawn: "As for me, I will look unto the Lord; I will wait for the God of my salvation: my God will hear me. Rejoice not against me, O mine enemy: though I am fallen, I shall arise; *though I sit in darkness,* the Lord is a light unto me" (Micah 7:7–8). When the worshiper is returned to the prayer book, the innocent blessing at sunrise of the ancient mystics does not seem innocent at all: it is heavy with the sighs and salted with the tears of yesterday and today.

Toward its close, the benediction of light contains a prayer for the renewal of the light of Zion. On logical grounds, some schoolmen (notably Saadia) objected to having the praise of creation and the prayer for redemption rolled into one.[9] In vain: the homeless people clung in fervent hope precisely to this correlation between the first wonders of light and the last wonders of the new day of the Lord. Here the poets of the synagogue interpose a composition called *meora,* for it precedes the praise of the Creator of the luminaries (*meorot*). Sometimes the grief and faith of the captivity are worded in a poignant dialogue, as in the selection here presented, between the "curtains of Solomon" and a pilgrim. He remembers them in their former glory, the pride of a palace, and barely believes his eyes to find them now, faded and frayed, in a Bedouin tent:

Ye curtains of Solomon, how, amid the tents of Kedar,
Are ye changed? Ye have no form, no beauty!

"The multitudes which dwelt aforetime in our midst,
Have left us a desolation, a broken ruin, unprotected—
The holy vessels have gone into exile and become profane,
And how can ye ask for beauty of a lily among thorns?"

Rejected of their neighbors, but sought of their Lord,
He will call them each by name, not one shall be missing.
Their beauty, as in the beginning, He shall restore in the
    end,
And shall illume as the sevenfold light their lamp which is
    darkened.[10]

The rebuff of the world is forgotten in knowing oneself befriended by God Who, in the language of the great Unknown of the first captivity, forgets none among His hosts, calling each by his first name, the faithful on earth as His stars in heaven. "Why sayest thou, O Israel: my way is hid from the Lord, my right is passed over from my God?" (Isaiah 40:26–31). Again, one comes back to the accustomed prayers with a heart revived through proud memories and new hope.

The second benediction before the *Shema* turns from nature to history, or from creation to revelation. It renders thanks for the gift of the Torah, "the statutes of life," which in His everlasting love God chose to communicate to Israel, and it asks for divine aid properly to understand the commandments and to fulfill them in love. The *piyyut* here ingrafted is called *ahaba* (love), and as its name and place implies, has for its theme the love of God for Israel and of Israel for God. Medieval piety spoke its inmost soul in some of these poems:

> Let my sweet song be pleasing unto Thee—
> The incense of my praise—
> O my Beloved that art flown from me,
> Far from mine errant ways!
> But I have held the garment of His love,
> Seeing the wonder and the might thereof.
> The glory of Thy name is my full store—
> My portion for the toil wherein I strove:
> Increase the sorrow:—I shall love but more!
> Wonderful is Thy love! [11]

Amid all degradation, Israel knows herself borne and sustained by God's boundless love: "Enough for me the glory of Thy Name!" Clinging to the fringe of His love gives bliss and strength enough to endure all the taunt and torment of the world. If the price of mere knowledge be sorrow (Ecclesiastes 1:18), what would not one readily brave for the love of God?

In another *ahaba,* such love is driven to an even bolder extreme:

> Since Thou has been the abode of love,
> My love hath camped wherever Thou hast camped.
> The reproaches of mine enemies have been pleasant to me
> for Thy sake:
> Leave them, let them afflict him whom Thou dost afflict!
> My foes learned Thy wrath, and I loved them,
> For they pursued the victim whom Thou didst smite.
> From the day that Thou didst despise me, I despised
> myself,

For I shall not honor what Thou hast despised.
Until the indignation be overpast, and Thou send
    redemption,
To this, Thine inheritance that Thou didst once redeem.[12]

Divorced from power, unable to retaliate, how was one to
remain free from the corrosions of hate in a dark and cruel
age? The medieval Jew won such internal freedom in external
bondage through his unconditional trust in God: it was His
inscrutable will that redemption should be preceded by penance in exile. The evil forces of the world do unknowingly
the will of God. The Jew's love for God enables him to recognize in the enemy the instrument of Divine Judgment, "the
rod of His anger," and compels the incredible or impossible:
love for one's enemy.

But though love is the willing obedience of all wills to the
Will of God, the poet never confuses the remediable ills of
society with Divine Purpose. He will not acquiesce in injustice,
nor suffer the unworldliness of the saints to benefit tyranny.
He knows that lazy opportunism and religious perfectionism
may alike cripple the attempts at self-liberation.

In an *ahaba* which must have offended the leadership of its
day, our poet warns sternly against the perils of political ex-
pediency. These were the times when the charities and welfare
funds of Jewish Spain were engaged in aiding the refugees
from the Moslem south to establish themselves in the Christian
north. The kings of Christian Spain welcomed the influx of
Jewish commerce and capital for reasons of statecraft and
strategy: such exodus could not but weaken the Moslem
provinces and facilitate their reconquest. Was it safe, the poet
seems to ask, to put confidence in transitory interests of the
crown, and disregard the growing enmity of the populace,
the lawless independence of the nobility, the unrelenting opposition of the Church? Will not the Jewish confidants of the
king see that they build the future of their people upon a
smoldering volcano? Will not the Jewish philanthropists recognize the futility of the endeavors to solve the Jewish question through a policy of new migration in the lands of
dispersion?

The hand of my rescuers is short,
It cannot save.
O that my ways were straight before God,
Maybe He would see how powerless
Are all my would-be-redeemers . . .

> Weary am I to tread
> The old itinerary of woe,
> Find anew the foe cast his greedy eye
> Upon the remnant of my survivors . . .[13]

Piety and political realism prompt this disagreement with the notables of Jewish Spain, and will ultimately influence the poet to leave his home and journey to the Holy Land. But what interests us momentarily is the fact that the current issues and controversies of the times often found their way and vehicle in the *piyyut*.

After the *Shema* there follows in our prayer book the assurance by the congregation that the Divine behest is cherished in the present as it was in the past, and that it will forever endure in the hearts of Israel, for "there is no God *beside* (*zulat*) Thee." Here a poem may be installed, called *zulat* because of its location in this passage of the liturgy. Often it echoes the strife of the environment against the Jew, the subtle or coarse coercion to make him renounce his faith:

> They reproach me
> When I seek to serve Him,
> And revile me
> When I give glory to His Name.
> They seek to set me far,
> O God, from Thy service:
> But my suffering and oppression
> Are better than Thine estrangement;
> My portion and my pleasure,
> The sweet fruit of Thy law.
>
> Let my right hand forget—
> If I stand not before Thee;
> Let my tongue cleave—
> If I desire aught but Thy law.
> My heart and mine eyes
> Will not suffer my feet to slip,
> For He, the Lord, is One,
> There is none beside Him.[14]

The concluding benediction of the *Shema* strikes the third chord of the Jewish faith, redemption, the previous blessings being devoted to creation and revelation, respectively. Here a poem may be embedded named *geulla*, or redemption. Its frequent theme is the pain and plight of the present which seeks relief or redress from the Rock of Israel:

> Let Thy favor flow over me,
> Even as Thy wrath hath overflowed.

> Shall mine failings for ever
> Stand between me and Thee?
> How long shall I search
> For Thee beside me, and find Thee not? . . .
> My Redeemer! to redeem my multitudes
> Rise and look forth from Thine abiding place.[15]

There are yet other poetic additions to the morning prayer, but the above are in the main the typical. Perhaps mention should be made also of the *ofan* (wheel), a poem deriving its name from the passage in the prayer book that describes the heavenly host, winged and wheeled (as in the visions of Isaiah and Ezekiel), chanting the praises of God on high, as Israel does on earth. Here the poet has occasion to delve into the labyrinth of heaven or the music of the spheres, or the mysteries of the Divine Name, or the very secret of prayer. Sometimes stress is laid on the daily experience of God's ubiquity, which is more wondrous than even the celestial chariot:

> O Lord, where shall I find Thee?
> Hid is Thy lofty place;
> And where shall I not find Thee,
> Whose glory fills all space? [16]

The paradoxes of God are then itemized: All-hidden, He is revealed everywhere; transcendent, and enclosed in the breast of lowly man; a God afar off, and yet near at hand (Jeremiah 23:23); exalted above all praise, He inhabits the praises of Israel (Psalms 22:4):

> Oh, how shall mortals praise Thee
> When angels strive in vain—
> Or build for Thee a dwelling,
> Whom worlds cannot contain?
>
> Yet when they bow in worship
> Before Thy throne, most high,
> Closer than flesh or spirit
> They feel Thy Presence nigh.[16]

Such is the miracle of prayer that we forget to think of the very presumption of all prayer. For in the inwardness of the act, the offering of man and the gift of God are indistinguishable. With the Psalmist, one experiences "my prayer" to be "His mercy" (Psalms 66:20). He already answered us, when He prompted our heart to pray. Hence the sense of surprise and gratitude voiced by the medieval poet when he finds that God is invariably ahead of His children in the game of hide and seek:

> I have sought Thy nearness,
> With all my heart have I called Thee,
> And going out to meet Thee
> I found Thee coming toward me.[17]

It is by such disclosure of fresh exploration and adventuring away from the beaten track that the poets of the Middle Ages kept the windows in the house of prayer open to the breezes of the green outdoors. Spontaneous piety continually interrupts the order of established service and quickens it with a breath of fragrant life. New expression adds relevance to the legacy of ages, and the timeless is enhanced by the timely.

The poetic embellishments of the standard prayers were, of course, not restricted to the morning service, or to the benedictions of the *Shema.* The *Amidah,* or the prayer proper of the synagogue, is copiously adorned by the poets, especially on distinguished Sabbaths and holidays. Every event of the Jewish liturgical calendar is enriched by poetic compositions which vary in form and structure and show steady growth and intricate development through the centuries. In the course of time the *piyyut* penetrated into every part of the religious life and every portion of the service. Nor was it confined to public worship in the synagogue.[18] It entered the Jewish home, cheered the family at meals, welcoming the Sabbath and bidding it farewell, partaking in the jollities as well as in the trials of the house from birth to death.

iv

At least 35,000 poems by 2,836 poets are listed by Israel Davidson in his *Thesaurus of Medieval Hebrew Poetry,*[1] an indispensable reference book for all study of the subject. New discoveries have added to our knowledge of medieval letters, however a vast amount of medieval creation still lies buried in unpublished manuscripts.

The discovery of the Genizah in Cairo [2] brought to light the forgotten remains of the ancient *payyetanim,* or poets, of Palestine. Their activity spans the centuries between the compilation of the Palestinian Talmud, toward the end of the fourth century, and the havoc wrought to Jewish Palestine by the Crusades. We have now the evidence of literary endeavor in the Holy Land and its environs that extends for more than twenty generations. Slowly there emerges the outline of rec-

ognizable growth from the artless prayers of the earlier talmudic age to the more stately and studied diction of the first
poet known to us by name, Yose ben Yose (*c.* 400 c.e.?),
down to the more intricate and involved patterns of speech
and poetry characteristic of the Palestinian school of *payyetanim* and their imitators in other lands. The most important
single find in that period of literature is the recovery of the
lost poetic work of Yannai (*c.* 550 c.e.), the first poet consistently to employ rhyme in Hebrew. It is he, also, who loaded
his verses with the lore of the Midrash, so that his *Kerobah,*
or poetic elaboration of the *Amidah,* is in fact a rhymed
homily on the portion of the Writ read that week in the
synagogue.[3] His disciple is said to be Eleazar ben Killir, the
most fertile and influential among the early *payyetanim.* There
is no season of the sacred year which he did not supply with
prolific compositions some of which are still recited on the
major holidays. For long generations, late into the Middle
Ages, he remained the model and legislator of synagogal
poetry. He is remembered especially for his bold or bizarre
word formations some of which were criticized by medieval
or modern biblical purists. However, we know now that his
was not wholly a private idiom, and that many of his forms
and locutions occur in other, both earlier and later, poets of
the Palestinian school, or even in the nonpoetic remains of
Palestinian literature. All of this tends to prove that the Palestinian *piyyut* is also valuable as a surviving witness of the
postbiblical Hebrew vernacular.[4]

There are extant fragments of literary production by a score
of poets living in the Holy Land or its vicinity, all of them
new surprises of the Genizah, *e.g.,* Joseph ben Nisan of
Shaveh-Kiriathaim or Nawe in Trans-Jordan, or Pinehas ben
Jacob of Kefar, a suburb of Tiberias (*c.* 800 c.e.), or Samuel
ben Hoshana whom we encounter in Egypt in 1011, or Solomon ben Amr al-Singari, named so probably from his native
town in Kurdistan, a fecund versifier who wrote *Yozerot* and
Kerobot for all the sabbaths and festivals, his compositions
mirroring the mind and mood of Near Eastern Jewry on the
eve of the Crusades.[5]

Saadia Gaon (882–942), reared in Egypt and head of the
academy in Sura, old seat of Babylonian learning, is a versatile
writer who used Hebrew verse for a variety of purposes. We
have from his pen polemical [6] and didactic,[7] liturgic [8] or even
philosophic [9] compositions, some facile and fluent, others dark
and difficult. An adept student of the Palestinian *piyyut,* he

outdid all *payyetanim* by his audacious innovations and playful artificialities of language. The poems of his elder contemporary, the blind and saintly Nissi Nahrawani [10] win by
their simplicity and sincerity. The poets of the house of al-
Baradani for two or three generations serve as chief *hazzanim*
in Bagdad and as supervisors of all the *hazzanim* in Iraq: it is
through them that the Palestinian *piyyut* as well as their own
creations spread in the East, or even to northern Africa. We
can trace such channels of transmission thanks to a letter in
the Genizah written in 1106 to Kairuan by the Gaon Hai
(d. 1038) who is also a poet of considerable stature. Some of
his *selihot* voice stirringly the sense of homelessness, and
hence the helplessness of the medieval Jew.[11]

Recent yields of scholarship permit us to trace poetic development in both Egypt and Babylonia down to the thirteenth
century. In the first half of that century, Eleazar Hababli,[12]
poet of wealthy patrons in Bagdad, records the conditions of
the closing period of the Abbassid caliphate, while in the
second half of the century, Joseph ben Tanhum Yerushalmi,[13]
house poet of the Nagid in Cairo, sheds light on Jewish ways
and worthies in Egypt under the Mamelukes.

From Palestine *piyyut* spread not only to the east and south,
but also to the west and north, to Byzantium, Italy, and the
German lands. Southern Italy is the first center of Hebrew
culture in Europe and several of its poets, such as Shefatiah
(d. 886) and his son Amittai, contributed fine lyrics to our
prayer book, some recited in the most solemn part of the
service on the Day of Atonement.[14] The ritual for the same
day preserves a *keroba* by the son of Kalonymos of Lucca,
Meshullam. He died in Mayence in the beginning of the
eleventh century. Both the style and the structure betoken
the influence of the Palestinian *piyyut*, like most creations
of the *payyetanim* in Frankish and German territories, from
Simon bar Isaac bar Abun in Mayence in the tenth century,
and his younger contemporary Gershom the Light of the Exile
(d. 1028), to Rabbenu Tam of Rameru (d. 1171) and Ephraim of Regensburg (d. 1175), foremost *payyetan* of medieval
Germany, the last two showing acquaintance with elements
of meter as developed in Spain.[15]

The first to adapt the Arabian quantitive or metrical scansion to Hebrew verse was Dunash ben Labrat,[16] a disciple of
Saadia, active in Cordova in the middle of the tenth century.
The first great poet of Hebrew Spain is Samuel Ha-Nagid
(993–1056), the vizier of the Berber kings of Granada,

equally distinguished as statesman, grammarian, and talmudic scholar. He is the outstanding representative if not the founder of the knightly and courtly taste and tradition in Hebrew secular poesy. For nearly two decades he used to accompany the armies of his state on their yearly campaigns and to write in his bivouac poetic reports to his family, describing in detail his military exploits or political feuds, the intrigues at the court or the designs of the rival city-states of Andalusia, appending prayers before battle or songs of victory which breathe a robust, almost antique faith. In decisive crises on the battlefield, or dire danger to his very life, he never despairs, firmly convinced that even on the brink of disaster a vow or prayer, and the intercession of his ancestors in the cave of Machpelah, will summon help from heaven, and the stars in their courses will fight against the enemy as in the days of Sisera. Intermingled with such martial verse are solicitous inquiries about the health of his sons or the progress of their education, exhortation and counsel how to win favor in heaven and friends on earth, and what or how best to study, and moving lyrical outbursts of love and longing for Zion, where he would rather be a humble Levite in the courts of God than retain rank and rule among the great on earth. In short, his *diwan,* or collected poetry, is a diary in verse of a scholar-father turned warrior-statesman, a rare and revealing human document which bares the private cares and the public career of an altogether remarkable man of affairs and man of letters in eleventh-century Spain.[17]

His younger contemporary is Solomon ibn Gabirol (b. 1021), who died early in his thirties and yet won immortal fame as one of the foremost thinkers and poets of the Middle Ages. Known as Avicebron to the scholastics, his *Fons Vitae* is a landmark in medieval philosophy, and he is equally distinguished as one of the most gifted poets in the Hebrew language. The conflict of the genius with his environment, his being forever nettled and lacerated by "the thorns and thistles of the earth," [18] the mass of the uncreative who set themselves up as "the norm" and dismiss as "abnormal" the endeavor or the behavior of the creative individuality, this perpetual martyr-dom of the spirit is unforgettably uttered in his sorrowful lyrics, or impassioned invective, or his landscape pictures of night and storm, the comrades and symbols of his somber and restless soul. Conscious of his gifts, proud of his calling, as-cetically devoted to the search of truth, he was constitutionally unable to serve men or stoop before the mighty "like the

priest of Edom before his icons." [19] Hence the inevitable misunderstandings and untoward setbacks of his life which must
have sowed the seeds of his early disease and death. Pure and
chaste are his sacred songs, the finest fruit of medieval devotion. Discontent and discord die away, and rid of resentment
and resistance, "humble of spirit, lowly of knee and stature," [20]
he bows before the throne of glory, "like the beggar who
cries at the door for grace." [21] But when he rises from prayer,
the knowledge of being loved by God gives him such peace
and power that nothing can bow him down. Restored to His
favor, the lowly self knows itself restored to lordliness, capable
again to recollect and redeem the innate kingliness of the
soul and her kinship with God:

> Thy life to God's life is akin,
>   Concealed like His beneath a veil,
> Since He is free of flaw or sin,
> Like purity thou too canst win,
>   To reach perfection wherefore fail? [22]

His religious verse, notably *The Royal Crown,* a lofty poem
charting the solar system of medieval science, entered the rites
of many Jewries, bringing to humble houses of worship in
distant lands glimpses of vision and insights of contemplation
which immeasurably enhanced the sense of wonder at the
mystery and vastness of the universe, and in the same breath
increased the spirit of magnanimity for all that share the sight
of the stars and the warmth of the sun:

> Thou art God, and all creatures are Thy witnesses and Thy
>   worshipers.
> Yet is not Thy glory diminished by reason of those that
>   adore aught beside Thee,
> For the intention of them all is to reach Thee . . .[23]

The sun-kissed summit of Hebrew poetry is Judah Ha-Levi
(d. after 1140), the heart and harp of medieval Judaism.
His is the most beloved name among his people who feel that
he voiced and embodied the best in Israel. Wittily but reverently, they apply to him the Scripture (Deuteronomy 12:19):
"Take heed to thyself that thou forsake not Ha-Levi (the Levite)," and heartily endorse the homage of his contemporary,[24]
kol Jaakob mityahadim, "the entire household of Jacob keeps
faith with *Judah.*" Because he is an authentic mouthpiece of
his people and representative of the genius of its faith and
art, all the selections from medieval verse in the foregoing

chapters were drawn from his poetry, and yet they give no
adequate notion of his grandeur. Every translator of his ad-
vises in the end: "Dear reader, study Hebrew, and throw my
version in the fire!" [25] For no rendering can recapture the
music and magic of his Hebrew, abounding in perfect miracles
of sense and sound.

He started as a prodigy in the literary salons of Andalusia.
A lively lad and singer born, he showed uncanny skill in
adapting Hebrew words to the strains and stanzas of the
Arabian love ballads then in vogue. He could match with
amazing ease the lightsome lilt or the licentious lines of any
of the song hits of the day, as a comparison with the *muwassah*
by the popular poet of Seville, al-Abyad, will show:

barrid ġalīl	rakīk belīl
ṣabb al-'alīl	nofeth kelīl
lā yastaḥīl	yōfī we-lyl-
fīhi 'an 'ahdi	-'oth sefath maddi
wa lā yazāl	hatter we-gal
fī kulli ḥāl	shad kam ke-gal
yarġū 'l-wiṣāl	ki-shdē shegal
wa-hwa fī 'ṣ-ṣaddi [26]	hēn we- 'as daddi [27]

Such amatory verses unexpectedly turn panegyrical, including
a toast or tribute to the patron or benefactor whose name and
fame they spread abroad on the wings of a favorite tune.
The praise or dispraise of song writers could thus make or
mar the reputation of their friends or clients. No wonder that
our poet soon became the darling of polite society and the
despair of his fellow minstrels, as he facilely mingled frolic
with flattery to his hosts or backers, and gaily caroled the
delights of the body and the merriments of youth with a se-
ductiveness in the holy language which perhaps a few regretted,
and all the others relished. "Why not fill my *kad* (the Hebrew
for a *jug* of wine), while my years are not full *kad* (*i.e.*,
twenty-four)!" [28] With such inborn gift of mirth and wit
and pun, one wonders what would have become of him in
another environment or tradition. The poet himself later rued
his celebrity as the acknowledged master of the exquisite trifle.
But that was the mood of the changed and harsh realities of
the Spanish scene, when the *reconquista* and the counter-
attacks of Islam plunged the Peninsula into turmoil and strife.

> They fight in their frays,
> And we fall in defeat,
>   As is the custom in Israel.[29]

The poet found a theme for his tongue, touched with the live coals of the ancient altar. At first, the poems that welled out of his new heart were dark and penitential, unsparing in remorse and reproof, austere and ascetic. His friends shook their heads, or began inquiring about his health. A few scholars nodded assent. The spokesmen for religion were delighted. Only the poet felt more and more ashamed, precisely for being a religious poet. Was not that the burden of his message that since men cannot save, the Will of God must be done? Done, not sung. So he decides to put lived life behind his written lines. He turns his back on the Jewish court society, its Arabian meters and melodies, its culture of the senses and its Grecian wisdom, its trust in princes and its worship of men, and in obedient servantship of his Lord, seeks a threefold return to the holy language, the holy law and—hardest of all—the Holy Land. Such resolve is not easy, and the poet does not conceal his lapses, love of life, irresolution. But when he braved all and risked all in utter surrender to his God, he came to his own at last. The wintry mind of the aging poet experienced a belated Indian summer of poetic exultation. Never before had all the wells of inspiration burst in such jubilant and masterly song as on the eve of his departure from Spain, or his voyage on the sea, or in Egypt where he falters and nerves himself anew to go whence there is no return. In these last years of his life, he left some of the finest bits of poetry written by the hand of men.[30]

The days of Judah Ha-Levi are the golden age of Spanish literature. We know about fifty names of contemporary Hebrew poets in Spain,[31] among them writers of renown such as Moses and Abraham ibn Ezra.[32] No Hebrew poet in subsequent generations was able to recapture the glories of this classical epoch. Some excellent verse is still written, and some new patterns of literature are adopted from the Arabic, e.g., the *maqamah* ("assembly," often rendered as "miscellany"), a picaresque genre in rhymed prose intersected by verse, a rather curious blend of mime and satire, tract and tale, farce and homily. Its best known examples in Spain are *The Book of Delight* by Joseph Zabara (written *c.* 1190) and the *Tahkemoni* by Judah al-Harizi (d. before 1235).[33]

Of the poets of the thirteenth century Meshullam de Piera deserves to be singled out for his originality and integrity. Rooted in the mystic faith of the circle of Gerona, center of Spanish cabbalism, he writes with mordant scorn of the pedantries and platitudes of both grammarians and philosophers to whom Writ and Prophecy were but a playground for linguistic or allegorical exercises. A proud and independent spirit, unbribable alike in his blame and praise, he walked his own ways with men or even with the Hebrew language. He sets it free from the pinfold of the biblical vocabulary, resolutely employing all its resources from Midrash and Talmud or even medieval science.[34] His most admired friend and compatriot was the illustrious Moses ben Nahman (1194–c. 1270), one of the master minds of medieval *halaka*. In his poems one finds the first intimations of mystic ideas in Spanish Hebrew sacred poetry, and his hymn on the descent of the soul, its sojourn as a stranger on earth, and its homeward journey to God, entered the liturgy of the New Year.[35] The *diwan* of Todros (son of Jehudah) Abulafia (d. after 1300) is a kind of poetic diary, containing the memoirs and fragments of autobiography in verse by a courtier in thirteenth-century Castile. It mirrors the light and gay mores of the upper stratum of Jewish society, and the inroads of Averroistic enlightenment which the mystic revival and the classic books of the Spanish cabbala sought to counteract.[36] Little is known about the poet Nahum, whose *meorot* and *geullot* have the fragrance and radiance of dew. Ecstatic faith blends with a delicate feeling for nature: a blossoming twig in the garden stirs the hope for the branch out of the stem of Jesse, and the sunrise, or the spring, whispers in the ear prospects of freedom and deliverance.[37]

The political decline and spiritual breakdown of the Jewish society in its last century in Spain, the tragic chapter of Marranism and defection since the pogroms of 1391 and the disputation at Tortosa in 1414, are reflected in the verses of Solomon de Piera (c. 1340–1420), mentor and minstrel of the Jewish aristocrats and apostates in Saragossa.[38] Proud of his historic faith, though contemptuous of its plebeian new leaders, is Solomon Bonafed (d. c. 1450), humanist, polemist, satirist who pleaded with the renegades, heartened the vacillating, rebutted the assailants, and generally voiced the conviction, the consternation, and the confidence of the faithful remnant resolved to persevere in the path of their ancestors.[39]

Provence, a bridge and intermediary between the Arabic culture in Spain and the lands of Christian Europe,[40] saw flowering of Hebrew poetry in the thirteenth century. Preciosity and artificial fanciness seem to be characteristic of this school of poets who delight in toying with language, in ingenious grammar games and all manner of whimsicality to parade their prowess in Hebrew. Abraham Bedershi (*i.e.*, of Béziers) wrote a piece for the Day of Atonement in which only the first half of the letters of the Hebrew alphabet is used, while another of his devotional poems consists of a thousand words each beginning with the same letter.[41] Similar feats of virtuosity are exhibited in the poetic efforts of his son Yedaiah Penini (*c.* 1270–1340) who is best known for his *Behinat Olam* (Scrutiny of the World), one of the most popular and frequently reprinted moral tracts of the Middle Ages.[42] A genuine poet who versed, vagabonded and vilified like a true Provençal troubadour is Isaac Gorni (*i.e.*, of Aire): impecunious and impudent, he never came to good, either in his own time or in the memory of posterity.[43]

A kindred spirit is Immanuel of Rome (*c.* 1270–1330), the greatest poet of medieval Italy.[44] A delightful rogue with an uproarious sense of humor and irrepressible relish for mischief, he can make the holy language utter the naughtiest improprieties, for which he was placed on the list of prohibited authors.[45] Of course, he keeps assuring the reader, as have all poets since Ovid (*crede mihi lasciva est nobis pagina, vita proba est*) that lascivious is only his lay, not life, and that far from being dissolute, he is devout. But there is something to his protestations. Flippant and frivolous, he has his graver moods, and there runs through his poetry a serious strain of religion and asceticism, nourished from native founts of Jewish piety and reinforced by kindred currents in contemporary Christendom.[46] Immanuel introduced into Hebrew the form of the *sonnet* which had just been transferred into Italian from Provençal; otherwise his diction discloses the impact of the Hispano-Arabic patterns of song and scansion. His vision of hell and heaven, the last of his *maqamat*, or miscellanies, is the first attempt at an imitation of Dante in Hebrew letters. It was followed, almost a century later, by the more ambitious effort of Moses da Rieti (1388–d. after 1460), rabbi, physician, and philosopher who in his *Little Shrine* [47] achieved hardly more than a versified survey of the Jewish Sages and the principal philosophers of the past. But his use of the *terza rima* was deft and in his decasyllabic lines (with the *shewa mobile* counted as a vowel) he follows the Italian syllabic-tonic (rather than the Arabian quantitive) meter.[48] No wonder that the Italian Jewish communities were so proud of this Hebrew disciple of Dante that they adopted one of his cantos into the ritual, dividing it into seven parts, one for each day of the week.

Exiles from Spain enrich Hebrew writing in Italy. Judah Abrabanel, known also as *Leone Ebreo,* the celebrated author of the *Dialoghi di Amore,* excelled in Hebrew verse as well. In a moving elegy, written in Naples in 1503, he depicts the vicissitudes of his life and his sorrow of separation from his firstborn son who was snatched away from his parents in Portugal and forcibly baptized: paternal affection and fidelity to his faith are voiced with fiery passion of feeling and almost frosty perfection of form.[49] The most engaging poet of the Italian Renaissance is Joseph Sarphati (d. 1527), known in his professional life as Giuseppe Gallo, a physician and son of an eminent physician to Pope Julius II and the Medici. He wrote satirical, humorous and erotic verse full of salt and sparkle, small pieces as a rule, since he took delight and pride in brevity. He seems to have been the first to introduce into Hebrew poetry the *ottava rima,* as he was the first to translate a play into Hebrew, the famous Spanish tragicomedy *La Celestina,* of which only his own introductory poem survived.[50] The earliest original attempt at Hebrew drama seems to be the comedy by Judah Sommo (1527–1592), playwright and producer at the court of Mantua who wrote in Italian a dozen or so theatrical pieces, and a pioneering treatise on stagecraft. He also engaged in the favorite fashion of the times of interchanging poems in commendation or condemnation of the female sex, of course gallantly chiming a paean of praise to the noble lady of his heart in his *Magen Nashim* (Shield or Defense of Women).[51]

One will look in vain for such uses or examples of Hebrew poetry in the northern lands of Europe. Massacres by the Crusaders,[52] persecutions and expulsions (from England in 1290, from France in 1306, 1322, and 1394, from Austria in 1421, from Bavaria in 1452), successive waves of pogroms in which during the frightful year of the "Black Death" alone, in 1348–1349, some three hundred Jewish communities were drowned in blood and fire, left their traces in the poetry of the synagogue, in *selihot,* or penitential verse, and *kinot,* or dirges. The sacrifice of Isaac, the *akeda,* or the story of the *ten martyrs* of antiquity,[53] a prefiguration of Israel's passion and pilgrimage of pain through the centuries, is the recurrent theme of the poets in these lands who mingle recent with ancient grief, and draw new hope from the timeless tale. Poets they are sometimes not by choice or inclination, but perforce, under the lash of brute facts or fate. Often it is the scholar in Rabbinic law who feels the duty to appeal to heaven and to report to posterity the plight of his people or the cruelties of hatred and superstition in his day. Accusations of ritual murder (such as wiped out the community of Blois in 1171, and found expression by several poets, among them Rabbi Ephraim of Bonn [54] and Rabbi Barukh of Mayence [55]), the burning of the Talmud (*e.g.*, in Paris in 1244, bewailed by Rabbi Meir of Rothenburg [56]), the charges of poisoning the wells or of desecrating the Host by which mobs were incited to slaughter the Jews (*e.g.*, on the Easter Sunday of 1389 in Prague, mourned by Rabbi Abigdor Kara [57]), such are the topics and pursuits of poetry in these dark centuries and countries.

Poland, where the persecuted found shelter, became in the sixteenth century a stronghold of talmudic studies so that its *payyetanim* are as a rule its leading rabbinic authorities as, for instance, Solomon Luria (d. 1573).[58] In the next century, the bloody Cossack revolts in 1648 in which several hundred communities were wiped out, shook East European Jewry to its depth, taking such heavy toll in lives that altogether the Jewish population in the world sank to its smallest number in history.[59] Again it was the foremost talmudists in their time who believed they were called upon to be the tongue and the graving tool which would keep alive in the memory of the after ages the anguished shrieks of the murdered multitudes and the atrocious details of the carnage: hence the lamentations or chronicles by rabbinic scholars such as Rabbi Yomtob Lipman Heller (d. 1654) and Sabbetai Cohen (d. 1663).[60]

The shores of the Mediterranean, in both Africa and the Balkans, as well as in other Jewish centers of the Ottoman Empire, witnessed a revival of Hebrew poetry in the sixteenth century as a result of the influx of Spanish refugees. Much of the classical heritage of the Middle Ages was preserved, and some good new poetry written in the literary circles that sprang up in Constantinople (*e.g.*, the poet Solomon ben Mazaltob), in Salonica (Saadia Longo, and especially the splendid poet David Onkeneyra), on the islands of the Aegean (Judah Zarko at Rhodes), in Oran, Tlemcen, and Algiers (Abraham and Isaac Mandil Abi Zimra and Abraham Gavison).[61] But it was particularly Safed in Galilee, a city of legists and mystics,[62] which decisively determined the spiritual outlook and also the poetic utterance of the closing centuries of the Jewish Middle Ages. The new cabbala which spread from there over all the scattered communities was the last religious movement in Judaism to reach and affect every country of the Diaspora without exception.[63] This mystic revival influenced the rites and usages of the synagogue, pervaded the liturgy and the prayer book,[64] and imbued Hebrew expression with new fervor and urgency. The hymn *Lekha dodi* (Come, my beloved) by Solomon Alkabez, the teacher and brother-in-law of the famous Safed cabbalist Moses Cordovero (d. 1570), entered all rituals and is sung all over the Jewish world, when Queen Sabbath is welcomed to the tents of Jacob.[65] In almost all the prayer books of Eastern Jewry there will be found also the hymns for the Sabbath meals of Isaac Luria (d. 1572), the inspired visionary of the new cabbala.[66] The sweetest of all mystic singers and the most significant poet of his century is Israel Najera (*c.* 1542–1619) who in over a thousand songs gave utterance to the new temper of devotion and to the feverish Messianic urge of his times. Set to various Turkish, Armenian, Spanish, and new Greek airs, which the wandering minstrel picked up in his younger and gayer life of the road, and suffused with erotic-mystic imagery, these hymns and elegies treat—in alternating mood and melody, now tender, now tearful, now triumphant—of the quarrel and conciliation of the lovers, of estrangement, forgiveness, and renewal of the covenant between the heavenly bridegroom and His earthly spouse, the community of Israel. The stark sensuality at places met with censure. To some such love songs to the *Shekinah* seemed to speak "the language of adulterers," [67] especially when suited to strains or reminiscent of sounds known to be flagrantly culpable in a carnal way. But all such misgivings were silenced, when Isaac Luria himself endorsed the *piyyutim,* saying that they were listened to with delight in heaven.[68] The liturgy of the Oriental Jews abounds with his poetry, which spread far and wide not only in the Near East and the Balkan Peninsula, but even to Aden, Calcutta, and Cochin-China. His literary influence was likewise far reaching and pervasive,[69] as attested, among others, by the poetry of Shalom Shebesi (d. after 1677), foremost poet of the remote and remarkable tribe of the Jews of Yemen.[70]

The Messianic ardor of the Lurianic cabbala was bound to erupt in movements such as were precipitated by the appearance of Sabbatai Zevi as the Messiah and Nathan of Gaza as his prophet (1665–1666), and the kindred mystical heresies of that century. One can study the literary reflections of that convulsion best in Italy again. There earlier than anywhere else, within two decades after the death of Luria, a self-styled disciple of his carried on lively propaganda on behalf of the new school.[71] The struggle for or against cabbalism and Sabbatianism is mirrored in the literature and poetry of seventeenth-century Italy which produced such colorful and contradictory personalities as Leon Modena (1617–1648) and the gifted pair of poets and brothers, Jacob (1615–1667) and Immanuel (1618–d. after 1703) Frances, intrepid fighters against all mystic or Messianic delusions.[72] An eager votary of the new cabbala was Moses Zacuto (1625–1697), rabbi in Venice and Mantua, whose secular verse and dramatic works prove that he was sensitive also to other winds of doctrine. His first drama betrays the Spanish background in Amsterdam from where he stems, for its theme—Abraham shattering the idols of his father—carries overtones of the contemporary conflict of the Marranos who sought to return to Judaism.[73] His mystery play on life beyond life [74] is a remarkable artistic attainment. Gifted beyond all others, as well as comprehensive, is Moses Hayyim Luzzatto (1707–1747), poet, dramatist, mystic, and moralist, in all alike distinguished, a self-confessed Messiah in the days of Voltaire, and the reputed father or forerunner of modern Hebrew literature.[75] He still belongs to an age that did not know, nor would have approved, our new compartments and labels: secular and religious. He wrote secular dramas to gladden friends at their wedding which he considered a religious commandment. This was as little ruse on his part as the inclusion of erotic verse as nuptial songs in the prayer books especially of Oriental Jewries. Both are rather the outcome of that all-embracing unity of the Middle Ages in which what is termed the religious included all that was to be found in the nonreligious, and much else besides. Anyhow, the new and the old fuse imperceptibly even in nineteenth-century Italy, as can be seen in the devotional verse of Samuel David Luzzatto (1800–1865), the last of the *payyetanim* to write an *Aboda* or a poetic description of the ritual of the Day of Atonement.[76]

It was also S. D. Luzzatto who toiled most to retrieve for the new age the lost classics of the Middle Ages. For when the poets of the *Haskala* or the era of Enlightenment set about reviving Hebrew, they found for their endeavors, in Berlin or Vienna, in Zolkiew or Vilna, no usable past. The masters of medieval song had long sunk in oblivion, and even their names faded from memory. "Who is Yannai?" asks in 1829 the best informed scholar of the times.[77] The choicest lyrics of

Judah Ha-Levi were clean forgotten until his *diwan* was recovered and parts thereof printed in 1840 and 1864 by S. D.
Luzzatto.[78] The bulk of the poetry of Samuel Ha-Nagid remained unknown until our day, and was published for the
first time in 1934.[79] Other admirable poets of the Middle
Ages are still hidden in the dust of libraries.

Notes

i

1. Hagigah 5b, citing Deuteronomy 31:17f. and Isaiah 51:16.
2. Tanhuma, Behaalotka 6.
3. Tosefta Sotah, 13, 2. Cf. Sotah 48b; Yoma 9b; Sanhedrin 11a.
4. Seder Olam R. c. 6.
5. Yer. Taanit II, 1f. 65a; b. Yoma 21b and parallel passages.
6. Berakot 8a.
7. Cf. Mishna Sotah 9, 11; Sotah 48a; Yer. *ibid.*, IX, 12f. 24b.
8. Hosea 9:1 and Gittin 7a; Yer. Megilla III, 2f. 74a.
9. Psalms 126:2f. and Berakot 31a.
10. Transl. by B. Halper, *Shirat Yisrael* (Leipzig, 1924), pp. 51f.
11. Baba Batra 12a.
12. Shita mekubbezet on Baba Batra 12a. See Abraham J. Heschel, in
Alexander Marx Jubilee Volume (New York, 1949).
13. Baba Batra 12a.
14. Hasagot on Hilkhot Lulab 8, 5.
15. Mishna Sotah 9, 15 end.
16. Sotah 4b.
17. Examples from the age of the Geonim, see Aptowitzer, in *Tarbiz* 1,
4 (1930), pp. 82f. In Spain, see Louis Ginzberg, *Genizah Studies*, II,
273; R. Gershom, "the Light of the Exile," see S. Assaf, in *Ziyyunim*
(Berlin, 1929), p. 119.
18. R. A. Nicholson, *A Literary History of the Arabs* (Cambridge,
1930), pp. 304ff.
19. *Diwan of Jehudah Halevi*, ed. H. Brody, III, 65. Transl. by
Solomon Solis-Cohen, in *United Synagogue Recorder*, I, 1921, No. 3.
20. Judah Ha-Levi, *Kitab al Khazari*, transl. by H. Hischfeld (London,
1931), p. 251 (ch. 5, 20).
21. A. Harkavy, *Zikron la-Rishonim* (St. Petersburg, 1891), pt. 5,
pp. 166f.
22. *Ibid.*, pp. 160f.
23. *The Letters of M. H. Luzzatto and his Contemporaries*, ed. by S.
Ginzburg (Tel-Aviv, 1937), p. 357.
24. *Ibid.*, pp. 381, 397.
25. *e.g.*, Maimonides, *Guide for the Perplexed*, I, ch. 59.
26. Cf. Jonah of Gerona (d. 1263) and Aaron Ha-Levi (*c.* 1300)
quoted by Joseph Caro, *Bet Joseph*, Orah Hayyim 113. See also Shem
Tob Falaquera, *Sefer ha-Mebhakkesh*, Haag, 1779, f. 27b.

ii

1. Isaiah Horovitz, *Shne Luhot ha-Berit* (Wilhelmsdorf, 1686), f. 185b.
2. *Yosippon*, ed. D. Guenzburg (Berditchev, 1913), p. 22; *Iggeret Musar* by Kalonymos b. Kalonymos, ed. Isaiah Sonne, in *Kobez al Yad* 1, 1936, p. 103. See A. M. Habermann, in *Tarbiz*, 13, 1941, p. 55.
3. Poetics, ch. 9 (1451b).
4. H. L. Ginsberg, *The Ugarit Texts* (Jerusalem, 1936), pp. 129ff., and Th. H. Gaster, JQR 37, 1946, 55ff.
5. Mekilta, ed. Lauterbach, II, 162, 198, 233f. Sifre Deut. 343, ed. Friedmann p. 142b. Zebahim 116a.
6. Mas. Soferim, ed. Higger, p. 314.
7. Jacob b. Asher, *Tur Orah Hayyim*, 284 end.
8. Shabbat 86b.
9. Cf. Ch. Albeck in the Hebrew edition of Zunz, *Die gottesdienstlichen Vortraege* (Jerusalem, 1947), pp. 132f.
10. Midrash Tehillim, ed. Buber, p. 231.
11. Saadia's Arabic transl. of the Psalms with Commentary, ed. S. Lehmann (Berlin, 1901), pp. 10 and 32f.
12. See the commentaries of David Kimhi (d. 1232) and Menahem Meiri (d. *c.* 1315), ed. J. Cohn (Jerusalem, 1936), pp. 63f.
13. *Kaf ha-Ketoret* on Psalms 29, quoted from Ms. Paris by Gershom G. Scholem, *Major Trends in Jewish Mysticism* (New York, 1946), p. 408, n. 9, and p. 248.
14. On the Cabbala of Luria and his school see the excellent chapter by Scholem, *loc. cit.*, pp. 253ff.
15. *Siddur Ozar ha-Teffillot* (Vilna, 1923), p. 586. Cf. *Siddur ha-ARI* (Zolkiew, 1781), f. 108bff. and *Shaar ha-Kavvanot* (Jerusalem, 1873), f. 64cff.
16. See above i, n. 26.

iii

1. Tosefta Berakot 3, 6. See Louis Ginzberg, *A Commentary on the Palestinian Talmud* (New York, 1941), I, p. 68–73.
2. R. Aha (*c.* 325 C.E.): Yer. Berakot IV, 3f. 8a; cf. also Berakot 29b: Rabba (d. 331) and R. Joseph (d. 333).
3. Berakot 4, 4, and Abot 2, 13. See Louis Ginzberg, *loc. cit.*, III, 333.
4. See Israel Davidson in *Festskrift* in honor of Dr. Simonsen (Copenhagen, 1923), pp. 89ff.
5. Yer. Sanhedrin I, 1f. 18a.
6. Ed. Brody, II, p. 221. Transl. by Judah Goldin in *Menorah Journal,* 33, 1945, p. 196.
7. Josephus, *Jewish War* II, 8, 5. See S. J. Rapoport, *Toledoth R. Eleazar ha-Killir*, n. 20.
8. *Selected Poems of Jehudah Halevi*, ed. H. Brody, transl. by Nina Salaman (Philadelphia, 1924), p. 130. Here, as elsewhere, I have occasionally revised the translation, to bring it closer to the Hebrew.
9. See *Siddur R. Saadia Gaon,* ed. Davidson-Assaf-Joel (Jerusalem, 1941), p. 37, and Ismar Elbogen. *Der juedische Gottesdienst*, 3 ed. (Frankfurt a.M., 1931), p. 19. See also N. Wieder, in *Saadya Studies* (Manchester, 1943), pp. 254ff.
10. *Selected Poems of Jeh. Halevi*, p. 116.

11. *Ibid.*, 117 and 165.

12. *Diwan*, ed. Brody, IV, 232.

13. *Ibid.*, III, 18f., and I. F. Baer, in *Zion* 1, 1935, p. 23.

14. *Selected Poems*, p. 97f.

15. *Ibid.*, p. 109.

16. *Ibid.*, p. 134, transl. by Solomon Solis-Cohen, *Judaism and Science* (Philadelphia, 1940), pp. 174ff.

17. *Selected Poems*, pp. 134ff.

18. Zunz, *Die synagogale Poesie des Mittelalters* (Berlin, 1855), p. 70.

iv

1. 4 vols. (New York, 1924–1933). See also the *Supplement* in *Hebrew Union College Annual*, 12–13, 1937–38, pp. 715ff.

2. See S. Schechter, *A Hoard of Hebrew Manuscripts* (1897), repr. in his *Studies in Judaism* (Philadelphia, 1908), II, 1–30.

3. Fragments of Yannai were first identified by Israel Davidson and published in his *Mahzor Yannai* (New York, 1919). All extant compositions were edited by Menahem Zulay, *Piyyute Yannai* (Berlin, 1938). Cf. also his valuable monograph in *Studies of the Research Institute for Hebrew Poetry* (SI) (Berlin, 1936), II, 213ff. The Institute, founded by Salmann Schocken, has in Jerusalem an unrivalled collection of photostats of the scattered remains of poetry in the Genizah, and its publications have greatly advanced the study of medieval poetry. New fragments of Yannai were found by P. Vidor (in *Jubilee Volume in Honor of Bernhard Heller* [Budapest, 1941], pp. 32ff.), and Isaiah Sonne, in HUCA, 18, 1944, pp. 199ff. See also Zulay, in *Haaretz* (Tel-Aviv, February 8, 1947), release No. 100 of the Schocken Institute, and in *Semitic Studies in Memory of Immanuel Loew* (Budapest, 1947), pp. 147f. On historic and halakic aspects in the research of Yannai, cf. Saul Lieberman, in *Sinai* (Jerusalem, 1939), II, 221ff.

4. Some historical and critical problems of this *payyetan* are discussed by the writer in SI, 5, 1939, 269ff., also in *Encyclopaedia Judaica*, vol. 9, col. 816–820.

5. See Menahem Zulay, in SI, 3, 1936, pp. 164ff., and 5, 1939, pp. 109ff., and in *Sinai*, 9, 1945, pp. 296ff.

6. I. Davidson, *Saadya's Polemic against Hiwi Albalki* (New York, 1915); *Esa meshali*, ed. B. M. Lewin, in J. L. Fishman's collection *Rav Saadia Gaon* (Jerusalem, 1943), pp. 481ff. Cf. B. Klar, in *Tarbiz*, 14, 1943, pp. 156ff. and 15, 1944, pp. 36ff.

7. *E.g.*, "Saadia's Piyyut on the Alphabet," ed. by S. Stein, in *Saadya Studies*, (Manchester, 1943), pp. 206ff.; cf. Zulay, in *Melilah* (Manchester, 1946), II, 162ff.

8. The sacred poetry is ed. by Israel Davidson, *Siddur Saadia Gaon* (Jerusalem, 1941). See also Zulay, in *Tarbiz*, 16, 1945, pp. 57ff.

9. Parts of a philosophical poem were published anonymously by Joseph Marcus, *Ginze Shirah u-piyyut* (New York, 1933), pp. 81ff., now identified by Zulay, *Haaretz*, March 9, 1945, release No. 78.

10. See Zulay, *Haaretz*, September 25, 1946, release No. 96.

11. On Joseph and Nahum al-Baradani see J. Mann, *Texts and Studies in Jewish History and Literature* (Cincinnati, 1931), I, 122, and Spiegel, in SI, 5, 1939, p. 272. The poems of Hai Gaon were edited by H. Brody, in SI, 3, 1936, pp. 5ff.

12. *Diwan*, ed. H. Brody (Jerusalem, 1935). On his sacred poetry cf. S. Bernstein, in *Sinai* 9, 1945, No. 104, pp. 8ff.

13. See J. Mann, *Texts and Studies*, I, 435ff.; J. Schirmann, in *Kobez al Yad*, 3, 1939, pp. 40ff.; A. M. Habermann, *Inbe-hen* (Tel-Aviv, 1943), pp. 31ff.

14. Ed. by Benjamin Klar, in his *Megillat Ahimaaz* (Jerusalem, 1943), pp. 71ff. Cf. J. Schirmann, in SI, 1, 1933, pp. 96ff.

15. A. M. Habermann edited the *Liturgical Poems* of Simon bar Isaac (Berlin, Jerusalem, 1938), of R. Gershom (Jerusalem, 1944), and of Ephraim of Regensburg in SI, 4, 1938, pp. 119ff.

16. Ed. Nehemiah Allony (Jerusalem, 1947).

17. *Diwan*, ed. D. S. Sassoon (Oxford, 1934); a vocalized ed. by A. M. Habermann (Tel-Aviv, 1945–1947). For a full bibliography see J. Schirmann, *Kirjat Sefer*, 13, 1936, pp. 373ff., and cf. *idem. Ziyyon*, 1, 1936, pp. 261ff. and 357ff., and *Keneset*, 2, 1936, pp. 393ff. See also Joseph Weiss, preliminary announcement of a contemplated study, *Tarbut hasranit veshirah hasranit* (Jerusalem, 1947).

18. *Shire Shelomo b. Jehudah Ibn Gabirol*, ed. Bialik-Ravnitzky (Berlin, 1924), I, 29, 1.42.

19. *Ibid.*, I, 9, 1.33, and correction, III, 3, pp. 115 and 31.

20. *Selected Religious Poems of Solomon Ibn Gabirol*, ed. I. Davidson, transl. into English verse by Israel Zangwill (Philadelphia, 1923), p. 17.

21. *Ibid.*, p. 16.

22. *Ibid.*, p. 69.

23. *Ibid.*, p. 86. A selected bibliography is appended to J. Schirmann, *Shlomo Ibn Gabirol Shirim nivharim* (Tel-Aviv, 1944), pp. 161f., to which his recent study in *Keneset*, 10, 1946, pp. 244ff., and José M. Millás Villacrosa, *S. Ibn Gabirol como poeta y filósofo* (Madrid-Barcelona, 1945), may be added.

24. Jehudah ben Abun of Seville, cf. Brody-Albrecht, *Shaar ha-Shir* (Leipzig, 1905), p. 129, No. 115, line 3.

25. Franz Rosenzweig, *Jehuda Halewi, Zweiundneunzig Hymnen und Gedichte*, p. 153. See also S. Solis-Cohen, "Judah Halevi," in his *Judaism and Science* (Philadelphia, 1940), p. 174.

26. A. R. Nykl, *Hispano-Arabic Poetry* (Baltimore, 1946), p. 246: about the sweet lips of the beloved, "may they refresh the thirsty one, the lover in pain," etc.

27. *Diwan of Jehudah Halevi*, ed. Brody, I, 136: the last lines parody Ezekiel 23:21. Cf. now S. M. Stern, in *Tarbiz*, 18, 1947, pp. 168ff.

28. *Diwan*, ed. Brody, II, 309.

29. *Ibid.*, IV, 131, lines 9f.

30. The best study on the life of Judah Ha-Levi is by J. Schirmann, in *Tarbiz*, 9, 1938, pp. 35ff., 219ff.; 10, 1939, pp. 237ff.; on his age by I. F. Baer, in *Zion*, 1, 1935, pp. 6ff.; cf. also his paper in *Schocken Almanach 5699* (1939), pp. 74ff., and his Hebrew book on the *History of the Jews in Christian Spain* (Tel-Aviv, 1945), p. 49ff. See also Salo W. Baron, in *Jewish Social Studies*, 3, 1941, pp. 243ff.

31. J. Schirmann, in SI, 2, 1936, pp. 119ff.; 3, 1938, pp. 249ff., and 6, 1946, pp. 253ff.

32. *The Diwan of Moses b. Ezra*, ed. H. Brody (Berlin, 1935), and the *Commentary* (Jerusalem, 1941). *Selected Poems*, ed. H. Brody, transl. by S. Solis-Cohen (Philadelphia, 1934). Cf. also Brody, *JQR*, 24, 1934, pp. 309ff. *The Diwan of Abraham b. Ezra*, ed. Jacob Egers (Berlin, 1886); *Reime und Gedichte*, ed. D. Rosin (Breslau, 1885–1894); *Kobez hokmat RABE*, ed. D. Kahana (Warsaw, 1894). See also Simon Bern-

stein, in *Tarbiz*, 5, 1934, pp. 61ff., and 10, 1939, pp. 8ff., and H. Brody, in SI, 6, 1945, pp. 1ff. On his life cf. the various papers by J. L. Fleischer and the recent literature surveyed by Alexander Marx, in *Essays and Studies in Memory of Linda R. Miller*, ed. by I. Davidson (New York, 1938), pp. 135f.

33. Zabara's *Sepher Shaashuim*, ed. Israel Davidson (New York, 1914), rev. Hebrew ed. (Berlin, 1925). An English transl. by Moses Hadas (New York, 1932), Records of Civilization, v. 16. Cf. Hadas, *JQR*, 27, 1936, pp. 151ff. Harizi's work, ed. P. de Lagarde (Goettingen, 1883); ed. A. Kaminka (Warsaw, 1899). See J. Schirmann, *Die hebr. Uebersetzung der Maqamen des Hariri* (Frankfurt a.M., 1930), pp. 113ff. (full bibliography) and in *Moznayim*, 11, 1940, pp. 101ff. Cf. also S. M. Stern, in *Tarbiz*, 17, 1946, pp. 87ff.

34. Ed. Brody, in SI, 4, 1938, pp. 12ff. See Joseph Patai, *Misefune ha-Shirah* (Jerusalem), pp. 44ff. Cf. Schirmann, in *Haaretz*, Jan. 1, 1940, and J. N. Epstein, in *Tarbiz*, 11, 1940, pp. 218f.

35. M. Sachs, *Die religioese Poesie der Juden in Spanien* (Berlin, 1901), Hebrew section p. 50, and the transl. p. 135. See also G. G. Scholem, in *Schocken Almanach 5696* (1935), pp. 86ff. Another example of his religious verse, A. M. Habermann. *Be-ron yahad* (Jerusalem, 1945), p. 79.

36. *Gan ha-meshalim we-ha-hidot*, ed. David Yellin (Jerusalem, 1932–1936); cf. Brody, SI, 1, 1933, pp. 2ff. On the poet and his age see I. F. Baer, in *Zion*, 2, 1937, pp. 19ff.

37. Brody-Weiner, *Anthologia Hebraica* (Leipzig, 1922), pp. 299ff., and Habermann, *Be-ron yahad*, p. 83. Cf. D. H. Mueller-Schlosser, *Die Haggadah von Serajevo* (1896), pp. 59 and 64. See J. Schirmann, *Kirjat Sepher*, 22, 1945, p. 128.

38. *Diwan*, ed. Simon Bernstein (New York, 1942), and sacred verse *HUCA*, 19, 1946, pp. 1–74. Cf. also Brody. *Leket shirim u-piyyutim* (Jerusalem, 1936), pp. 3ff., whose author is de Piera, and not Bonafed. See next note.

39. See J. Schirmann, in *Kobez al-yad*, 14, 1946, p. 11, where the literature is summarized. Cf. also *Haaretz*, Aug. 12, 1938, release No. 13, and July 19, 1946, release No. 93.

40. Zunz, *Zur Geschichte und Literatur*, pp. 439ff.

41. *Bakasha beth-El*, cf. Davidson, *Thesaurus*, III, 37, No. 800, and *Eleph alphin* (Daniel 7:11) in *Kerem Hemed*, 4, pp. 59ff. See I. Davidson, "Eccentric Forms of Hebrew Verse," in *Students Annual*, Jewish Theol. Seminary (New York, 1914), p. 82.

42. The *mem* prayer, Davidson, *Thesaurus*, III, 178, No. 2353, also the *rehuta*, ibid., I, 271, No. 5957. See also *Zunz Jubelschrift* (Berlin, 1884), Hebrew section 1–19.

43. Ed. H. Gross, in *Monat. Ges. Wiss. Judentums (MGWJ)* 31, 1882, 510ff. (cf. *ibid.*, 27, 1878, 476f.); Steinschneider, in G. J. Polak's edition of Bedershi, *Hotem tokhnit* (Amsterdam, 1865), p. 4; Schirmann, in *Haaretz*, April 4, 1944, release No. 69.

44. For editions and literature cf. Schirmann, *Die hebr. Uebersetzungen der Maqamen des Hariri*, pp. 121ff. Cf. also H. S. Lewis, in *Proc. Amer. Academy for Jewish Research*, 6, 1935, pp. 277ff.

45. Joseph Caro, *Shulhan Arukh*, Orah Hayyim 307:16.

46. Cf. Isaiah Sonne, in *Tarbiz*, 5, 1934, pp. 324ff.

47. *Mikdash meat*, ed. J. Goldenthal (Vienna, 1851). Selections in J. Schirmann's *Mivhar ha-Shirah ha-Ivrit beitalia* (Berlin, 1934), pp. 195ff.

48. Rhine, JQR, n. S. 1, 1911, pp. 349ff., and especially M. Hack, in *Tarbiz,* 11, 1939, pp. 91ff.

49. Schirmann, *Mivhar,* pp. 217ff.

50. Schirmann, *ibid.,* pp. 223ff., and in *Haaretz,* Sept. 25, 1942, release No. 57, and Oct. 8, 1944, release No. 75; Umberto Cassuto, in *Jewish Studies in Memory of G. A. Kohut* (New York, 1935), Hebrew section pp. 121ff., and in *Gaster Anniversary Volume* (London, 1936), pp. 58ff. Cf. Cecil Roth, *The History of the Jews in Italy* (Philadelphia, 1946), p. 220.

51. *Zahot bedihuta de-kiddushin,* ed. Schirmann (Jerusalem, 1946); *Magen Nashim, ibid.,* pp. 149ff.; cf. *idem,* MGWJ, 75, 1931, pp. 97ff., and *Keneset,* 1, 1935, pp. 430ff.

52. See A. M. Habermann, *Sefer gezerot Ashkenaz VeZarephat* (Jerusalem, 1946), with an introduction on the age by I. F. Baer.

53. See Louis Finkelstein, in *Essays and Studies in Memory of Linda R. Miller* (New York, 1938), pp. 29ff., and Solomon Zeitlin, JQR, 36, 1945, pp. 1ff. and 209ff.

54. S. Bernfeld, *Sefer ha-Demaot* (Berlin, 1924), I, 225ff., and Habermann, *Sefer gezerot,* pp. 133ff.

55. Ed. Habermann, in SI, 6, 1945, pp. 133ff.

56. Brody-Weiner, *loc. cit.,* pp. 295ff.; Habermann, *Be-ron yahad,* p. 169, and *Sefer gezerot,* pp. 183ff.

57. S. Bernfeld, *loc. cit.,* II, 159ff.

58. Habermann, *Be-ron yahad,* pp. 175ff. Cf. Davidson, *Thesaurus,* IV, 475.

59. Salo W. Baron, *A Social and Religious History of the Jews* (New York, 1937), II, 165, and III, 129f.

60. Bernfeld, *loc. cit.* (Berlin, 1926), III, 173ff. and 169ff. On the chronicles cf. M. Steinschneider, *Die Geschichtsliteratur der Juden* (Frankfurt a.M., 1905), pp. 120ff. Cf. Simon Bernstein, in *Ha-toren,* 10, 1923, pp. 83ff.

61. Sol. b. Mazaltob, in *Shirim u-zemirot* (Constantinople, 1545); cf. I. Zinberg, *Hist. of Jewish Literature* [in Yiddish] (Vilna, 1933), vol. 4, p. 353, n. 7, and p. 492. On the Society of Poets in Salonica cf. J. Patai, pp. 86ff., who also published the poetry of Onkeneyra, in *Kobez al Yad,* 2, 1937, pp. 77ff. On Saadia Longo cf. also H. Brody, in *Minha le-David* [Yellin] (Jerusalem, 1935), pp. 205ff. Jehudah ben Abraham Zarko, *Sefer Lehem Yehudah* (Constantinople, 1560); cf. Schirmann, in *Haaretz,* May 17, 1945, release No. 81. Abraham, and Jacob, and Abraham (Jr.) Gavison, see *Omer ha-Shikhah* (Leghorn, 1748), where also verses by Abraham Abi Zimra (f. 135b, see also 134a, 138a and 106a) and by Mandil (122b, 138bf. and 4b preface) are printed. See also Habermann. *Be-ron yahad,* p. 192. Generally on the state of research in this epoch cf. Schirmann, *Kirjat Sefer,* 12, 1935, pp. 389ff.

62. See S. Schechter, *Studies in Judaism* (Philadelphia, 1908), II, 202ff.

63. G. G. Scholem, Hebrew lecture on the *Idea of Redemption in the Cabbala* (Jerusalem, 1941), p. 13; and *Major Trends,* pp. 285f.

64. Abraham I. Schechter, *Lectures on Jewish Liturgy* (Philadelphia, 1933), pp. 40ff.

65. A. Berliner, *Randbemerkungen zum taegl. Gebetbuch* (Berlin, 1909), I, 43ff. Cf. Simon Bernstein, *Shomere ha-homot* (Tel-Aviv, 1938), pp. 83ff.

66. G. G. Scholem, *Major Trends,* pp. 271f. Cf. Meir Wiener, *Die*

Lyrik der Kabbalah (Vienna, 1920), pp. 75ff. (reviewed by Scholem, in *Der Jude*, 6, 1921, pp. 55ff.)

67. See Menahem Lonzano, *Shte Yadot* (Venice, 1618), f. 142ab.

68. Najera's *Zemirot Yisrael* were recently edited by Judah Fries-Horeb (Tel-Aviv, 1946). See also David Yellin in *Jewish Studies in Memory of G. A. Kohut* (New York, 1935), Hebrew section pp. 59ff.; I. Davidson in *Jubilee Volume* in honor of *Samuel Krauss* (Jerusalem, 1937), pp. 193ff. and in *Sefer ha-Shanah liyhude Amerika* (New York, 1939), pp. 282ff.; Isaac Mendelsohn, in *Horeb*, 9, 1946, pp. 53ff., and A. Mirsky, in *Sefer Ish ha-Torah Vehamaaseh* in honor of Rabbi M. Ostrowski (Jerusalem, 1946), pp. 125ff. On the data of his life cf. S. A. Rosanes (Hebrew), *Hist. of the Jews in Turkey* (Husiatyn, 1914), Pt. III, pp. 173ff. and 309ff., and M. D. Gaon, in *Mizrah u-maarab*, 5, 1930, pp. 145ff.

69. On the influence of Najera on Joseph Ganso in Brusa, see Simon Bernstein, *Shomere ha-homot*, pp. 114ff., on Solomon Molkho II, *ibid.*, pp. 163ff., on the rite of Corfu, see *idem*, in *Horeb*, 5, 1939, pp. 46, 48ff.

70. *Kobez shire kodesh* (Jaffa, 1931). See A. Z. Idelsohn and H. Torczyner, *Diwan of Hebrew and Arabic Poetry of the Yemenite Jews* (Cincinnati, 1930), pp. 88ff. Older literature listed by R. Levy, in *I. Abrahams Mem. Volume* (Vienna, 1927), p. 266, n. 1. See recently on the Yemenite *piyyut* Y. Ratzaby in *Kirjat Sefer*, 19, 1942, pp. 65ff. and the list *ibid.*, 22, 1946, pp. 247ff.

71. G. G. Scholem, in *Ziyyon*, 5, 1940, pp. 215ff., and briefly also in his *Major Trends*, p. 257.

72. Dr. Simon Bernstein edited *The Diwan of Leo de Modena* (Philadelphia, 1932) and *Immanuel Frances* (Tel-Aviv, 1932); cf. *M. Wilensky*, HUCA, 18, 1944; also poems by Jacob Frances in his *Mishire Yisrael beitalia* (Jerusalem, 1939), pp. 73ff.

73. Cf. A. Berliner, in his ed. of Zacuto's *Yesod Olam* (Berlin, 1874), and J. Schirmann, in *Moznayim*, 4, 1936, pp. 625ff.

74. *Tofteh Arukh* (Venice, 1715). See the introduction by D. A. Friedmann to his edition of the play (Berlin, 1922).

75. Cf. my *Hebrew Reborn* (New York, 1930), pp. 29ff. and 441f., where the literature is listed. Add now S. Ginzburg, *The Life and Works of M. H. Luzzatto* (Philadelphia, 1931); Isaiah Sonne, in *Sefer ha-Shanah liyhude Amerika*, 1935, pp. 218ff., and 1938, pp. 154ff., and *Horeb*, 6, 1941, pp. 76ff.; F. Lachower, in *Keneset*, 4, 1939, pp. 365ff., and Benjamin Klar, in his introd. to Luzzatto's *Sefer ha-Shirim* (Jerusalem, 1945).

76. Published in *Bikkure haIttim*, 1825, pp. 29ff. See I. Elbogen, *Studien zur Geschichte des jued. Gottesdienstes* (Berlin, 1907), p. 95.

77. S. J. Rapoport, in his biography of Killiri, n. 19.

78. *Betulat Bat Yehudah* (Prague, 1840), and *Diwan R. Yehudah Halevi* (Lyck, 1864).

79. Ed. D. S. Sassoon (Oxford, 1934).

Bibliography

DELITZSCH, FRANZ, *Zur Geschichte der juedischen Poesie.* Leipzig, 1836.

DUKES, L., *Zur Kenntnis der neuhebraeischen religioesen Poesie.* Frankfurt a.M., 1842.

(Both these works are rather antiquated.)

Still basic and by far the best are the works of

ZUNZ, LEOPOLD, *Die synagogale Poesie des Mittelalters.* Berlin, 1855.

——, *Der Ritus des synagogalen Gottesdienstes.* Berlin, 1859.

——, *Literaturgeschichte der synagogalen Poesie.* Berlin, 1865.

A survey of the major *payyetanim* will be found also in

ELBOGEN, ISMAR, *Der juedische Gottesdienst,* pp. 280–353. Frankfurt, a.M., 1931.

For an introduction to Spanish poetry, see

YELLIN, DAVID, *Ketabim nibharim* II, pp. 165–352. Jerusalem, 1939.

——, *Torat ha-Shirah ha-Sepharadit.* Jerusalem, 1940.

MILLÁS VALLICROSA, JOSÉ M., *La Poesía sagrada hebraicoespañola.* Madrid, 1940.

See also the relevant chapters in

ZINBERG, ISRAEL, *Die Geschichte fun der Literatur bei Yiden.* Vilna, 1929–1937.

WAXMAN, MEYER, *A History of Jewish Literature.* New York, 1930–1941.

11.

General Characteristics of Jewish Mysticism *

by Gershom G. Scholem

i

It is the purpose of these lectures to describe and to analyse some of the major trends of Jewish mysticism. I cannot of course hope to deal comprehensively in a few hours with a subject so vast and at the same time so intricate as the whole sweep and whirl of the mystical stream, as it runs its course through the movements which are known to the history of Jewish religion under the names of Kabbalah and Hasidism. Probably all of you have heard something about these aspects of Jewish religion. Their significance has been a matter of much dispute among Jewish scholars. Opinion has changed several times; it has fluctuated between the extremes of hostile criticism and condemnation on the one hand, and enthusiastic praise and defense on the other. It has not, however, greatly advanced our knowledge of what may be called the real nature of mystical lore nor has it enabled us to form an unbiased judgment as to the part this lore has played and continues to play in Jewish history, or as to its importance for a true understanding of Judaism.

It is only fair to add that the exposition of Jewish mysticism, or that part of it which has so far been publicly discussed, abounds in misunderstandings and consequent misrepresentations of the subject matter under discussion. The great Jewish

---

* From *Major Trends in Jewish Mysticism*, New York, Schocken Books, 1954.

scholars of the past century whose conception of Jewish history is still dominant in our days, men like Graetz, Zunz, Geiger, Luzzatto and Steinschneider, had little sympathy—to put it mildly—for the Kabbalah. At once strange and repellent, it epitomised everything that was opposed to their own ideas and to the outlook which they hoped to make predominant in modern Judaism. Darkly it stood in their path, the ally of forces and tendencies in whose rejection pride was taken by a Jewry which, in Steinschneider's words, regarded it as its chief task to make a decent exit from the world. This fact may account for the negative opinions of these scholars regarding the function of mysticism in Jewish history. We are well aware that their attitude, so far from being that of the pure scholar, was rather that of the combatant actively grappling with a dangerous foe who is still full of strength and vitality; the foe in question being the Hasidic movement. Enmity can do a great deal. We should be thankful to those zealous early critics who, though their judgment and sense of values may have been affected and warped by their prejudices, nevertheless had their eyes open to see certain important factors with great distinctness. Often enough they were in the right, though not for the reasons they themselves gave. Truth to tell, the most astonishing thing in reading the works of these critics is their lack of adequate knowledge of the sources or the subjects on which in many cases they ventured to pass judgment.

It is not to the credit of Jewish scholarship that the works of the few writers who were really informed on the subject were never printed, and in some cases were not even recorded, since there was nobody to take an interest. Nor have we reason to be proud of the fact that the greater part of the ideas and views which show a real insight into the world of Kabbalism, closed as it was to the rationalism prevailing in the Judaism of the nineteenth century, were expressed by Christian scholars of a mystical bent, such as the Englishman Arthur Edward Waite [1] of our days and the German Franz Josef Molitor [2] a century ago. It is a pity that the fine philosophical intuition and natural grasp of such students lost their edge because they lacked all critical sense as to historical and philological data in this field, and therefore failed completely when they had to handle problems bearing on the facts.

The natural and obvious result of the antagonism of the great Jewish scholars was that, since the authorized guardians neglected this field, all manner of charlatans and dreamers came and treated it as their own property. From the brilliant misunderstandings and misrepresentations of Alphonse Louis Constant, who has won fame under the pseudonym of Eliphas Lévi, to the highly coloured humbug of Aleister Crowley and his followers, the most eccentric and fantastic statements have been produced purporting to be legitimate interpretations of Kabbalism.[3] The time has come to reclaim this derelict area and to apply to it the strict standards of historical research. It is this task which I have set myself, and in the following lectures I should like to give some idea of the conclusions to which I have come in trying to light up this dark ground.

I do not have to point out that what I am going to say can in the nature of things be no more than a brief outline of the main structure of mystical thought, as it reveals itself in some of the classics of Jewish mysticism—more often than not in an obscure guise which makes it none too easy for modern minds to penetrate into its meaning. Obviously it is impossible to give a summary of the subject without at the same time attempting to interpret its meaning. It is a dangerous task to summarize in a few chapters a religious movement covering many centuries. In trying to explain so intricate a matter as Kabbalism the historian, too, must heed Byron's query: "Who will then explain the explanation?" For the rest, selection and abbreviation themselves constitute a kind of commentary, and to a certain extent even an appreciation of the subject. In other words, what I am going to present is a critical appreciation involving a certain philosophical outlook, as applied to the life texture of Jewish history, which in its fundamentals I believe to be active and alive to this day.

ii

Since Jewish mysticism is to be the subject of these lectures, the first question bound to come up is this: what is Jewish mysticism? What precisely is meant by this term? Is there such a thing, and if so, what distinguishes it from other kinds of mystical experience? In order to be able to give an answer to this question, if only an incomplete one, it will be necessary to recall what we know about mysticism in general. I do not propose to add anything essentially new to the immense literature which has sprung up around this question during the past half-century. Some of you may have read the brilliant books written on this subject by Evelyn Underhill and Dr. Rufus Jones. I merely propose to rescue what appears to me important for our purpose from the welter of conflicting historical and metaphysical arguments which have been advanced and discussed in the course of the past century.

It is a curious fact that although doubt hardly exists as to what constitutes the phenomena to which history and philosophy have given the name of mysticism, there are almost as many definitions of the term as there are writers on the subject. Some of these definitions, it is true, appear to have served more to obscure the nature of the question than to clarify it. Some idea of the confusion engendered by these definitions can be gauged from the interesting catalogue of "Definitions of Mysticism and Mystical Theology" compiled by Dr. Inge as an appendix to his lectures on "Christian Mysticism."

A good starting-point for our investigation can be obtained by scrutinizing a few of these definitions which have won a certain authority. Dr. Rufus Jones, in his excellent "Studies in Mystical Religion" defines his subject as follows: "I shall use the word to express the type of religion which puts the emphasis on immediate awareness of relation with God, on direct and intimate consciousness of the Divine Presence. It is religion in its most acute, intense and living stage." [4] Thomas Aquinas briefly defines mysticism as *cognitio dei experimentalis*,[5] as the knowledge of God through experience. In using this term he leans heavily, like many mystics before and after him, on the words of the Psalmist (Psalms 34:9): "Oh taste and see that the Lord is good." It is this tasting and seeing, however spiritualized it may become, that the genuine mystic desires. His attitude is determined by the fundamental experience of the inner self which enters into immediate contact with God or the metaphysical Reality. What forms the essence of this experience, and how it is to be adequately described—that is the great riddle which the mystics themselves, no less than the historians, have tried to solve.

For it must be said that this act of personal experience, the systematic investigation and interpretation of which forms the task of all mystical speculation, is of a highly contradictory and even paradoxical nature. Certainly this is true of all attempts to describe it in words and perhaps, where there are no longer words, of the act itself. What kind of direct relation can there be between the Creator and His creature, between the finite and the infinite; and how can words express an experience for which there is no adequate simile in this finite world of man? Yet it would be wrong and superficial to conclude that the contradiction implied by the nature of mystical experience betokens an inherent absurdity. It will be wiser to assume, as we shall often have occasion to do in the course of these lectures, that the religious world of the mystic can be expressed in terms applicable to rational knowledge only with the help of paradox. Among the psychologists G. Stratton, in his "Psychology of Religious Life" (1911), has laid particular stress on this essential conflict in religious life and thought, even in its non-mystical form. It is well known that the descriptions given by the mystics of their peculiar experiences and of the God whose presence they experience are full of paradoxes of every kind. It is not the least baffling of these paradoxes—to take an instance which is common to Jewish and Christian mystics—that God is frequently described as the mystical Nothing. I shall not try now to give an interpretation of this term, to which we shall have to return; I only want to stress the fact that the particular reality which the mystic sees or tastes is of a very unusual kind.

To the general history of religion this fundamental experience is known under the name of *unio mystica,* or mystical union with God. The term, however, has no particular significance. Numerous mystics, Jews as well as non-Jews, have by no means represented the essence of their ecstatic experience, the tremendous uprush and soaring of the soul to its highest plane, as a union with God. To take an instance, the earliest Jewish mystics who formed an organized fraternity in Talmudic times and later, describe their experience in terms derived from the diction characteristic of their age. They speak of the ascent of the soul to the Celestial Throne where it obtains an ecstatic view of the majesty of God and the secrets of His Realm. A great distance separates these old Jewish Gnostics from the Hasidic mystics one of whom said: [6] "There are those who serve God with their human intellect, and others whose gaze is fixed on Nothing. . . . He who is granted this supreme experience loses the reality of his intellect, but when he returns from such contemplation to the intellect, he finds it full of divine and inflowing splendor." And yet it is the same experience which both are trying to express in different ways.

This leads us to a further consideration: it would be a mistake to assume that the whole of what we call mysticism is identical with that personal experience which is realized in the state of ecstasy or ecstatic meditation. Mysticism, as an historical phenomenon, comprises much more than this experience, which lies at its root. There is a danger in relying too much on purely speculative definitions of the term. The point I should like to make is this—that there is no such thing as mysticism in the abstract, that is to say, a phenomenon or experience which has no particular relation to other religious phenomena. There is no mysticism as such, there is only the mysticism of a particular religious system, Christian, Islamic, Jewish mysticism and so on. That there remains a common characteristic it would be absurd to deny, and it is this element which is brought out in the comparative analysis of particular mystical experiences. But only in our days has the belief gained ground that there is such a thing as an abstract mystical religion. One reason for this widespread belief may be found in the pantheistic trend which, for the past century, has exercised a much greater influence on religious thought than ever before. Its influence can be traced in the manifold attempts to abandon the fixed forms of dogmatic and insti-tutional religion in favour of some sort of universal religion. For the same reason the various historical aspects of religious mysticism are often treated as corrupted forms of an, as it were, chemically pure mysticism which is thought of as not bound to any particular religion. As it is our intention to treat of a certain definite kind of mysticism, namely Jewish, we should not dwell too much upon such abstractions. Moreover, as Evelyn Underhill has rightly pointed out, the prevailing conception of the mystic as a religious anarchist who owes no allegiance to his religion finds little support in fact. History rather shows that the great mystics were faithful adherents of the great religions.

Jewish mysticism, no less than its Greek or Christian counter-parts, presents itself as a totality of concrete historical phe-nomena. Let us, therefore, pause to consider for a moment the conditions and circumstances under which mysticism arises in the historical development of religion and particularly in that of the great monotheistic systems. The definitions of the term *mysticism,* of which I have given a few instances, lead only too easily to the conclusion that all religion in the last resort is based on mysticism; a conclusion which, as we have seen, is drawn in so many words by Rufus Jones. For is not religion unthinkable without an "immediate awareness of re-lation with God"? That way lies an interminable dispute about words. The fact is that nobody seriously thinks of applying the term *mysticism* to the classic manifestations of the great religions. It would be absurd to call Moses, the man of God, a mystic, or to apply this term to the Prophets, on the strength of their immediate religious experience. I, for one, do not intend to employ a terminology which obscures the very real differences that are recognized by all, and thereby makes it even more difficult to get at the root of the problem.

iii

The point which I would like to make first of all is this: Mysticism is a definite stage in the historical development of religion and makes its appearance under certain well-defined conditions. It is connected with, and inseparable from, a certain stage of the religious consciousness. It is also incompatible with certain other stages which leave no room for mysticism in the sense in which the term is commonly understood.

The first stage represents the world as being full of gods whom man encounters at every step and whose presence can be experienced without recourse to ecstatic meditation. In other words, there is no room for mysticism as long as the abyss between Man and God has not become a fact of the inner consciousness. That, however, is the case only while the childhood of mankind, its mythical epoch, lasts. The immediate consciousness of the interrelation and interdependence of things, their essential unity which precedes duality and in fact knows nothing of it, the truly monistic universe of man's mythical age, all this is alien to the spirit of mysticism. At the same time it will become clear why certain elements of this monistic consciousness recur on another plane and in different guise in the mystical consciousness. In this first stage, Nature is the scene of man's relation to God.

The second period which knows no real mysticism is the creative epoch in which the emergence, the break-through of religion occurs. Religion's supreme function is to destroy the dream-harmony of Man, Universe and God, to isolate man from the other elements of the dream stage of his mythical and primitive consciousness. For in its classical form, religion signifies the creation of a vast abyss, conceived as absolute, between God, the infinite and transcendental Being, and Man, the finite creature. For this reason alone, the rise of institutional religion, which is also the classical stage in the history of religion, is more widely removed than any other period from mysticism and all it implies. Man becomes aware of a fundamental duality, of a vast gulf which can be crossed by nothing but the *voice;* the voice of God, directing and law-giving in His revelation, and the voice of man in prayer. The great monotheistic religions live and unfold in the ever-present consciousness of this bipolarity, of the existence of an abyss which can never be bridged. To them the scene of religion is no longer Nature, but the moral and religious action of man and the community of men, whose interplay brings about history as, in a sense, the stage on which the drama of man's relation to God unfolds.

And only now that religion has received, in history, its classical expression in a certain communal way of living and believing, only now do we witness the phenomenon called mysticism; its rise coincides with what may be called the romantic period of religion. Mysticism does not deny or overlook the abyss; on the contrary, it begins by realizing its existence, but from there it proceeds to a quest for the secret that will close it in, the hidden path that will span it. It strives to piece together the fragments broken by the religious cataclysm, to bring back the old unity which religion has destroyed, but on a new plane, where the world of mythology and that of revelation meet in the soul of man. Thus the soul becomes its scene and the soul's path through the abysmal multiplicity of things to the experience of the Divine Reality, now conceived as the primordial unity of all things, becomes its main preoccupation. To a certain extent, therefore, mysticism signifies a revival of mythical thought, although the difference must not be overlooked between the unity which is there before there is duality, and the unity that has to be won back in a new upsurge of the religious consciousness.

Historically, this appearance of mystical tendencies is also connected with another factor. The religious consciousness is not exhausted with the emergence of the classic systems of institutional religion. Its creative power endures, although the formative effect of a given religion may be sufficiently great to encompass all genuine religious feeling within its orbit for a long period. During this period the values which such a religious system has set up retain their original meaning and their appeal to the feelings of the believers. However, even so new religious impulses may and do arise which threaten to conflict with the scale of values established by historical religion. Above all, what encourages the emergence of mysticism is a situation in which these new impulses do not break through the shell of the old religious system and create a new one, but tend to remain confined within its borders. If and when such a situation arises, the longing for new religious values corresponding to the new religious experience finds its expression in a new interpretation of the old values which frequently acquire a much more profound and personal significance, although one which often differs entirely from the old and transforms their meaning. In this way Creation, Revelation and Redemption, to mention some of our most important religious conceptions, are given new and different meanings reflecting the characteristic feature of mystical experience, the direct contact between the individual and God.

Revelation, for instance, is to the mystic not only a definite historical occurrence which, at a given moment in history, puts an end to any further direct relation between mankind and God. With no thought of denying Revelation as a fact of history, the mystic still conceives the source of religious knowledge and experience which bursts forth from his own heart as being of equal importance for the conception of religious truth. In other words, instead of the one act of Revelation, there is a constant repetition of this act. This new Revelation, to himself or to his spiritual master, the mystic tries to link up with the sacred texts of the old; hence the new interpretation given to the canonical texts and sacred books of the great religions. To the mystic, the original act of Revelation to the community—the, as it were, public revelation of Mount Sinai, to take one instance—appears as something whose true meaning has yet to unfold itself; the secret revelation is to him the real and decisive one. And thus the substance of the canonical texts, like that of all other religious values, is melted down and given another form as it passes through the fiery stream of the mystical consciousness. It is hardly surprising that, hard as the mystic may try to remain within the confines of his religion, he often consciously or unconsciously approaches, or even transgresses, its limits.

It is not necessary for me to say anything further at this point about the reasons which have often transformed mystics into heretics. Such heresy does not always have to be fought with fire and sword by the religious community: it may even happen that its heretical nature is not understood and recognized. Particularly is this the case where the mystic succeeds in adapting himself to the "orthodox" vocabulary and uses it as a wing or vehicle for his thoughts. As a matter of fact, this is what many Kabbalists have done. While Christianity and Islam, which had at their disposal more extensive means of repression and the apparatus of the State, have frequently and drastically suppressed the more extreme forms of mystical movements, few analogous events are to be found in the history of Judaism. Nevertheless, in the lectures on Sabbatianism and Hasidism, we shall have occasion to note that instances of this kind are not entirely lacking.

iv

We have seen that mystical religion seeks to transform the God whom it encounters in the peculiar religious consciousness of its own social environment from an object of dogmatic knowledge into a novel and living experience and intuition. In addition, it also seeks to interpret this experience in a new way. Its practical side, the realization of God and the doctrine of the Quest for God, are therefore frequently, particularly in the more developed forms of the mystical consciousness, connected with a certain ideology. This ideology, this theory of mysticism, is a theory both of the mystical cognition of God and His revelation, and of the path which leads to Him.

It should now be clear why the outward forms of mystical religion within the orbit of a given religion are to a large extent shaped by the positive content and values recognized and glorified in that religion. We cannot, therefore, expect the physiognomy of Jewish mysticism to be the same as that of Catholic mysticism, Anabaptism or Moslem Sufism. The particular aspects of Christian mysticism, which are connected with the person of the Saviour and mediator between God and man, the mystical interpretation of the Passion of Christ, which is repeated in the personal experience of the individual—all this is foreign to Judaism, and also to its mystics. Their ideas proceed from the concepts and values peculiar to Judaism, that is to say, above all from the belief in the Unity of God and the meaning of His revelation as laid down in the Torah, the sacred law.

Jewish mysticism in its various forms represents an attempt to interpret the religious values of Judaism in terms of mystical values. It concentrates upon the idea of the living God who manifests himself in the acts of Creation, Revelation and Redemption. Pushed to its extreme, the mystical meditation on this idea gives birth to the conception of a sphere, a whole realm of divinity, which underlies the world of our sense-data and which is present and active in all that exists. This is the meaning of what the Kabbalists call the *world of the "Sefiroth."* I should like to explain this a little more fully.

The attributes of the living God are conceived differently and undergo a peculiar transformation when compared with the meaning given to them by the philosophers of Judaism. Among the latter, Maimonides, in his "Guide of the Perplexed," felt bound to ask: How is it possible to say of God that He is living? Does that not imply a limitation of the infinite Being? The Words "God is living," he argues, can only mean that he is not dead, that is to say, that he is the opposite of all that is negative. He is the negation of negation. A quite different reply is given by the Kabbalist, for whom the distinction, nay the conflict, between the known and the unknown God has a significance denied to it by the philosophers of Judaism.

No creature can take aim at the unknown, the hidden God. In the last resort, every cognition of God is based on a form of relation between Him and His creature, i.e. on a manifestation of God in something else, and not on a relation between Him and Himself. It has been argued that the difference between the *deus absconditus,* God in Himself, and God in His appearance is unknown to Kabbalism.[7] This seems to me a wrong interpretation of the facts. On the contrary, the dualism embedded in these two aspects of the one God, both of which are, theologically speaking, possible ways of aiming at the divinity, has deeply preoccupied the Jewish mystics. It has occasionally led them to use formulas whose implied challenge to the religious consciousness of monotheism was fully revealed only in the subsequent development of Kabbalism. As a rule, the Kabbalists were concerned to find a formula which should give as little offense as possible to the philosophers. For this reason the inherent contradiction between the two aspects of God is not always brought out as clearly as in the famous doctrine of an anonymous writer around 1300, according to whom God in Himself, as an absolute Being, and therefore by His very nature incapable of becoming the subject of a revelation to others, is not and cannot be meant in the documents of Revelation, in the canonical writings of the Bible, and in the rabbinical tradition.[8] He is not the subject of these writings and therefore also has no documented name, since every word of the sacred writings refers after all to some aspect of His manifestation on the side of Creation. It follows that while the living God, the God of religion of whom these writings bear witness, has innumerable names—which, according to the Kabbalists, belong to Him by His very nature and not as a result of human convention—the *deus absconditus,* the God who is hidden in His own self, can only be named in a metaphorical sense and with the help of words which, mystically speaking, are not real names at all. The favorite formulae of the early Spanish Kabbalists are speculative paraphrases like "Root of all Roots," "Great Reality," "Indifferent Unity," [9] and, above all, *En-Sof.* The latter designation reveals the impersonal character of this aspect of the hidden God from the standpoint of man as clearly as, and perhaps even more clearly than, the others. It signifies "the infinite" as such; not, as has been frequently suggested, "He who is infinite" but "that which is infinite." Isaac the Blind (one of the first Kabbalists of distinguishable personality) calls the *deus absconditus* "that which is not conceivable by thinking," *not* "He who is not etc." [10] It is clear that with this postulate of an impersonal basic reality in God, which becomes a person—or appears as a person—only in the process of Creation and Revelation, Kabbalism abandons the personalistic basis of the Biblical conception of God. In this sense it is undeniable that the author of the above-mentioned mystical aphorism is right in holding that *En-Sof* (or what is meant by it) is not even mentioned in the Bible and the Talmud. In the following lectures we shall see how the main schools of Kabbalistic thought have dealt with this problem. It will not surprise us to find that speculation has run the whole gamut—from attempts to re-transform the impersonal *En-Sof* into the personal God of the Bible to the downright heretical doctrine of a genuine dualism between the hidden *En-Sof* and the personal Demiurge of Scripture. For the moment, however, we are more concerned with the second aspect of the Godhead which, being of decisive importance for real religion, formed the main subject of theosophical speculation in Kabbalism.

The mystic strives to assure himself of the living presence of God, the God of the Bible, the God who is good, wise, just and merciful and the embodiment of all other positive attributes. But at the same time he is unwilling to renounce the idea of the hidden God who remains eternally unknowable in the depths of His own Self, or, to use the bold expression of the Kabbalists "in the depths of His nothingness." [11] This hidden God may be without special attributes—the living God of whom the Revelation speaks, with whom all religion is concerned, must have attributes, which on another plane represent also the mystic's own scale of moral values: God is good, God is severe, God is merciful and just, etc. As we shall have occasion to see, the mystic does not even recoil before the inference that in a higher sense there is a root of evil even in God. The benevolence of God is to the mystic not simply the negation of evil, but a whole sphere of divine light, in which God manifests Himself under this particular aspect of benevolence to the contemplation of the Kabbalist.

These spheres, which are often described with the aid of mythical metaphors and provide the key for a kind of mystical topography of the Divine realm, are themselves nothing but stages in the revelation of God's creative power. Every attribute represents a given stage, including the attribute of severity and stern judgment, which mystical speculation has connected with the source of evil in God. The mystic who sets out to grasp the meaning of God's absolute unity is thus faced at the outset with an infinite complexity of heavenly spheres and stages which are described in the Kabbalistic texts. From the contemplation of these "Sefiroth" he proceeds to the conception of God as the union and the root of all these contradictions. Generally speaking, the mystics do not seem to conceive of God as the absolute Being or absolute Becoming but as the union of both; much as the hidden God of whom nothing is known to us, and the living God of religious experience and revelation, are one and the same. Kabbalism in other words is not dualistic, although historically there exists a close connection between its way of thinking and that of the Gnostics, to whom the hidden God and the Creator are opposing principles. On the contrary, all the energy of "orthodox" Kabbalistic speculation is bent to the task of escaping from dualistic consequences; otherwise they would not have been able to maintain themselves within the Jewish community.

I think it is possible to say that the mystical interpretation of the attributes and the unity of God, in the so-called doctrine of the "Sefiroth," constituted a problem common to all Kabbalists, while the solutions given to it by and in the various schools often differ from one another. In the same way, all Jewish mystics, from the Therapeutae, whose doctrine was described by Philo of Alexandria,[12] to the latest Hasid, are at one in giving a mystical interpretation to the Torah; the Torah is to them a living organism animated by a secret life which streams and pulsates below the crust of its literal meaning; every one of the innumerable strata of this hidden region corresponds to a new and profound meaning of the Torah. The Torah, in other words, does not consist merely of chapters, phrases and words; rather is it to be regarded as the living incarnation of the divine wisdom which eternally sends out new rays of light. It is not merely the historical law of the Chosen People, although it is that too; it is rather the cosmic law of the Universe, as God's wisdom conceived it. Each configuration of letters in it, whether it makes sense in human speech or not, symbolizes some aspect of God's creative power which is active in the universe. And just as the thoughts of God, in contrast to those of man, are of infinite profundity, so also no single interpretation of the Torah in human language is capable of taking in the whole of its meaning. It cannot be denied that this method of interpretation has proved almost barren for a plain understanding of the Holy Writ, but it is equally undeniable that viewed in this new light, the Sacred Books made a powerful appeal to the individual who discovered in their written words the secret of his life and of his God. It is the usual fate of sacred writings to become more or less divorced from the intentions of their authors. What may be called their after-life, those aspects which are discovered by later generations, frequently becomes of greater importance than their original meaning; and after all—who knows what their original meaning was?

v

Like all their spiritual kin among Christians or Moslems, the Jewish mystics cannot, of course, escape from the fact that the relation between mystical contemplation and the basic facts of human life and thought is highly paradoxical. But in the Kabbalah these paradoxes of the mystical mind frequently assume a peculiar form. Let us take as an instance their relation to the phenomenon of speech, one of the fundamental problems of mystical thought throughout the ages. How is it possible to give lingual expression to mystical knowledge, which by its very nature is related to a sphere where speech and expression are excluded? How is it possible to paraphrase adequately in mere words the most intimate act of all, the contact of the individual with the Divine? And yet the urge of the mystics for self-expression is well known.

They continuously and bitterly complain of the utter inadequacy of words to express their true feelings, but, for all that, they glory in them; they indulge in rhetoric and never weary of trying to express the inexpressible in words. All writers on mysticism have laid stress on this point.[13] Jewish mysticism is no exception, yet it is distinguished by two unusual characteristics which may in some way be interrelated. What I have in mind is, first of all, the striking restraint observed by the Kabbalists in referring to the supreme experience; and secondly, their metaphysically positive attitude towards language as God's own instrument.

If you compare the writings of Jewish mystics with the mystical literature of other religions you will notice a considerable difference, a difference which has, to some extent, made difficult and even prevented the understanding of the deeper meaning of Kabbalism. Nothing could be farther from the truth than the assumption that the religious experience of the Kabbalists is barren of that which, as we have seen, forms the essence of mystical experience, everywhere and at all times. The ecstatic experience, the encounter with the absolute Being in the depths of one's own soul, or whatever description one may prefer to give to the goal of the mystical nostalgia, has been shared by the heirs of rabbinical Judaism. How could it be otherwise with one of the original and fundamental impulses of man? At the same time, such differences as there are, are explained by the existence of an overwhelmingly strong disinclination to treat in express terms of these strictly mystical experiences. Not only is the form different in which these experiences are expressed, but the *will* to express them and to impart the knowledge of them is lacking, or is counteracted by other considerations.

It is well known that the autobiographies of great mystics, who have tried to give an account of their inner experiences in a direct and personal manner, are the glory of mystical literature. These mystical confessions, for all their abounding contradictions, not only provide some of the most important material for the understanding of mysticism, but many of them are also veritable pearls of literature. The Kabbalists, however, are no friends of mystical autobiography. They aim at describing the realm of Divinity and the other objects of the contemplation in an impersonal way, by burning, as it were, their ships behind them. They glory in objective description and are deeply averse to letting their own personalities intrude into the picture. The wealth of expression at their disposal is not inferior to that of their autobiographical confrères. It is as though they were hampered by a sense of shame.

Documents of an intimate and personal nature are not entirely
lacking, but it is characteristic that they are to be found almost
wholly in manuscripts which the Kabbalists themselves would
hardly have allowed to be printed. There has even been a kind
of voluntary censorship which the Kabbalists themselves
exercised by deleting certain passages of a too intimate nature
from the manuscripts, or at least by seeing to it that they were
not printed. I shall return to this point at a later stage, when
I shall give some remarkable instances of this censorship.[14]
On the whole, I am inclined to believe that this dislike of a
too personal indulgence in self-expression may have been
caused by the fact among others that the Jews retained a
particularly vivid sense of the incongruity between mystical
experience and that idea of God which stresses the aspects of
Creator, King and Law-giver. It is obvious that the absence of
the autobiographical element is a serious obstacle to any
psychological understanding of Jewish mysticism as the psychology of mysticism has to rely primarily on the study of
such autobiographical material.

In general, it may be said that in the long history of Kabbalism, the number of Kabbalists whose teachings and writings
bear the imprint of a strong personality is surprisingly small,
one notable exception being the Hasidic movement and its
leaders since 1750. This is partly due to personal reticence,
which as we have seen was characteristic of all Jewish mystics.
Equally important, however, is the fact that our sources leave
us completely in the dark as regards the personalities of many
Kabbalists, including writers whose influence was very great
and whose teachings it would be worth while to study in the
light of biographical material, were any available. Often
enough such contemporary sources as there are do not even
mention their names! Frequently, too, all that these writers
have left us are their mystical tracts and books from which
it is difficult, if not impossible, to form an impression of
their personalities. There are very few exceptions to this rule.
Among hundreds of Kabbalists whose writings are known
to us, hardly ten would provide sufficient material for a
biography containing more than a random collection of facts,
with little or nothing to give us an insight into their personalities. This is true, for example, of Abraham Abulafia (13th
century), of Isaac Luria (16th century) and, at a much later
period, of the great mystic and poet Moses Hayim Luzzatto
of Padua (died 1747), whose case is typical of the situation
I have described. Although his mystical, moralizing and

poetical works fill several volumes and many of them have been published, the true personality of the author remained so completely in the shadow as to be little more than a name until the discovery and publication, by Dr. Simon Ginzburg, of his correspondence with his teacher and his friends threw an abundance of light on this remarkable figure." [15] It is to hoped that the same will gradually be done for other great Jewish mystics of whom today we know very little.

My second point was that Kabbalism is distinguished by an attitude towards language which is quite unusually positive. Kabbalists who differ in almost everything else are at one in regarding language as something more precious than an inadequate instrument for contact between human beings. To them Hebrew, the holy tongue, is not simply a means of expressing certain thoughts, born out of a certain convention and having a purely conventional character, in accordance with the theory of language dominant in the Middle Ages. Language in its purest form, that is, Hebrew, according to the Kabbalists, reflects the fundamental spiritual nature of the world; in other words, it has a mystical value. Speech reaches God because it comes from God. Man's common language, whose prima facie function, indeed, is only of an intellectual nature, reflects the creative language of God. All creation—and this is an important principle of most Kabbalists—is, from the point of view of God, nothing but an expression of His hidden self that begins and ends by giving itself a name, the holy name of God, the perpetual act of creation. All that lives is an expression of God's language—and what is it that Revelation can reveal in the last resort if not the name of God?

I shall have to return to this point at a later stage. What I would like to emphasize is this peculiar interpretation, this enthusiastic appreciation of the faculty of speech which sees in it, and in its mystical analysis, a key to the deepest secrets of the Creator and His creation.

In this connection it may be of interest to ask ourselves what was the common attitude of the mystics toward certain other faculties and phenomena, such as intellectual knowledge, and more particularly rational philosophy; or, to take another instance, the problem of individual existence. For after all, mysticism, while beginning with the religion of the individual, proceeds to merge the self into a higher union. Mysticism postulates self-knowledge, to use a Platonic term, as the surest way to God who reveals Himself in the depths of the self. Mystical tendencies, in spite of their strictly personal character, have therefore frequently led to the formation of new social groupings and communities, a fact which is true also of Jewish mysticism; we shall have to return to this fact and to the problem it involves at the end of these lectures. At any rate, Joseph Bernhart, one of the explorers of the world of mysticism, was justified in saying "Have any done more to create historical movement than those who seek and proclaim the immovable?" [16]

vi

It is precisely this question of history which brings us back to the problem from which we started: What is Jewish mysticism? For now the question is: What is to be regarded as the general characteristic of mysticism within the framework of Jewish tradition? Kabbalah, it must be remembered, is not the name of a certain dogma or system, but rather the general term applied to a whole religious movement. This movement, with some of whose stages and tendencies we shall have to acquaint ourselves, has been going on from Talmudic times to the present day; its development has been uninterrupted, though by no means uniform, and often dramatic. It leads from Rabbi Akiba, of whom the Talmud says that he left the "Paradise" of mystical speculation safe and sane as he had entered it—something which cannot, indeed, be said of every Kabbalist—to the late Rabbi Abraham Isaac Kook, the religious leader of the Jewish community in Palestine and a splendid type of Jewish mystic.[17] I should like to mention here that we are in possession of a vast printed literature of mystical texts which I am inclined to estimate at 3,000.[18] In addition, there exists an even greater array of manuscripts not yet published.

Within this movement there exists a considerable variety of religious experience, to use William James' expression. There have been many different currents of thought, and various systems and forms of speculation. There is little resemblance between the earliest mystical texts in our possession, dating from Talmudic and post-Talmudic days, the writings of the ancient Spanish Kabbalists, those of the school which later flourished in Safed, the holy city of Kabbalism in the sixteenth century, and finally the Hasidic literature of the modern age. Yet the question must be asked whether there is not something more than a purely historical connection uniting these *disjecta membra,* something which also provides us with a hint as to what renders this mystical movement in Judaism different from non-Jewish mysticism. Such a common denominator can, perhaps, be discovered in certain unchanging fundamental ideas concerning God, creation and the part played by man in the universe. Two such ideas I have mentioned above, namely the attributes of God and the symbolic meaning of the Torah. But may it not also be that such a denominator is to be found in the attitude of the Jewish mystic towards those dominant spiritual forces which have conditioned and shaped the intellectual life of Jewry during the past two thousand years: the Halakhah, the Aggadah, the prayers and the philosophy of Judaism, to name the most important? It is this question which I shall now try to answer, though without going into detail.

As I have said before, the relation of mysticism to the world of history can serve as a useful starting-point for our investigation. It is generally believed that the attitude of mysticism toward history is one of aloofness, or even of contempt. The historical aspects of religion have a meaning for the mystic chiefly as symbols of acts which he conceives as being divorced from time, or constantly repeated in the soul of every man. Thus the exodus from Egypt, the fundamental event of our history, cannot, according to the mystic, have come to pass once only and in one place; it must correspond to an event which takes place in ourselves, an exodus from an inner Egypt in which we all are slaves. Only thus conceived does the Exodus cease to be an object of learning and acquire the dignity of immediate religious experience. In the same way, it will be remembered, the doctrine of "Christ in us" acquired so great an importance for the mystics of Christianity that the historical Jesus of Nazareth was quite often relegated to the background. If, however, the Absolute which the mystic seeks is not to be found in the varying occurrences of history, the conclusion suggests itself that it must either precede the course of mundane history or reveal itself at the end of time. In other words, knowledge both of the primary facts of creation and of its end, of eschatological salvation and bliss, can acquire a mystical significance.

"The Mystic," says Charles Bennett in a penetrating essay,[19] "as it were forestalls the processes of history by anticipating in his own life the enjoyment of the last age." This eschatological nature of mystical knowledge becomes of paramount importance in the writings of many Jewish mystics, from the anonymous authors of the early *Hekhaloth* tracts to Rabbi Nahman of Brazlav. And the importance of cosmogony for mystical speculation is equally exemplified by the case of Jewish mysticism. The consensus of Kabbalistic opinion regards the mystical way to God as a reversal of the procession by which we have emanated from God. To know the stages of the creative process is also to know the stages of one's own return to the root of all existence. In this sense, the interpretation of *Maaseh Bereshith,* the esoteric doctrine of creation, has always formed one of the main preoccupations of Kabbalism. It is here that Kabbalism comes nearest to Neoplatonic thought, of which it has been said with truth that "procession and reversion together constitute a single movement, the diastole-systole, which is the life of the universe." [20] Precisely this is also the belief of the Kabbalist.

But the cosmogonic and the eschatological trend of Kabbalistic speculation which we have tried to define, are in the last resort ways of escaping from history rather than instruments of historical understanding; that is to say, they do not help us to gauge the intrinsic meaning of history.

There is, however, a more striking instance of the link between the conceptions of Jewish mysticism and those of the historical world. It is a remarkable fact that the very term *Kabbalah* under which it has become best known, is derived from an historical concept. Kabbalah means literally "tradition," in itself an excellent example of the paradoxical nature of mysticism to which I have referred before. The very doctrine which centres about the immediate personal contact with the Divine, that is to say, a highly personal and intimate form of knowledge, is conceived as traditional wisdom. The fact is, however, that the idea of Jewish mysticism from the start combined the conception of a knowledge which by its very nature is difficult to impart and therefore secret, with that of a knowledge which is the secret tradition of chosen spirits or adepts. Jewish mysticism, therefore, is a secret doctrine in a double sense, a characteristic which cannot be said to apply to all forms of mysticism. It is a secret doctrine because it treats of the most deeply hidden and fundamental matters of human life; but it is secret also because it is confined to a small élite of the chosen who impart the knowledge to their disciples. It is true that this picture never wholly corresponded to life. Against the doctrine of the chosen few who alone may participate in the mystery must be set the fact that, at least during certain periods of history, the Kabbalists themselves have tried to bring under their influence much wider circles, and even the whole nation. There is a certain analogy between this development and that of the mystery religions of the Hellenic period of antiquity, when secret doctrines of an essentially mystical nature were diffused among an ever-growing number of people.

It must be kept in mind that in the sense in which it is understood by the Kabbalist himself, mystical knowledge is not his private affair which has been revealed to him, and to him only, in his personal experience. On the contrary, the purer and more nearly perfect it is, the nearer it is to the original stock of knowledge common to mankind. To use the expression of the Kabbalist, the knowledge of things human and divine that Adam, the father of mankind, possessed is therefore also the property of the mystic. For this reason, the Kabbalah advanced what was at once a claim and an hypothesis, namely, that its function was to hand down to its own disciples the secret of God's revelation to Adam.[21] Little though this claim is grounded in fact—and I am even inclined to believe that many Kabbalists did not regard it seriously—the fact that such a claim was made appears to me highly characteristic of Jewish mysticism. Reverence for the traditional has always been deeply rooted in Judaism, and even the mystics, who in fact broke away from tradition, retained a reverent attitude towards it; it led them directly to their conception of the coincidence of true intuition and true tradition. This theory has made possible such a paradox as the Kabbalah of Isaac Luria, the most influential system of later Kabbalism, though the most difficult. Nearly all the important points and major theses in Luria's system are novel, one might even say excitingly novel—and yet they were accepted throughout as true Kabbalah, i.e. traditional wisdom. There was nobody to see a contradiction in this.

vii

Considerations of a different kind will take us even deeper into the understanding of the problem. I have already said that the mystical sphere is the meeting-place of two worlds or stages in the development of the human consciousness: one primitive and one developed, the world of mythology and that of revelation. This fact cannot be left out of account in dealing with the Kabbalah. Whoever tries to gain a better understanding of its ideas, without attempting anything in the nature of an apology, cannot fail to notice that it contains, side by side with a deep and sensitive understanding of the essence of religious feeling, a certain mode of thought characteristic of primitive mythological thinking. The peculiar affinity of Kabbalist thought to the world of myth cannot well be doubted, and should certainly not be obscured or lightly passed over by those of us to whom the notion of a mythical domain within Judaism seems strange and paradoxical and who are accustomed to think of Jewish Monotheism as the classical example of a religion which has severed all links with the mythical. It is, indeed, surprising that in the very heart of Judaism ideas and notions sprang up which purported to interpret its meaning better than any others, and which yet represent a relapse into, or if you like a revival of, the mythical consciousness. This is particularly true of the Zohar and the Lurianic Kabbalah, that is to say, of those forms of Jewish mysticism which have exerted by far the greatest influence in Jewish history and which for centuries stood out in the popular mind as bearers of the final and deepest truth in Jewish thought.

It is no use getting indignant over these facts, as the great historian Graetz did; they should rather set us thinking. Their importance for the history of the Jewish people, particularly during the past four centuries, has been far too great to permit them to be ridiculed and treated as mere deviations. Perhaps, after all, there is something wrong with the popular conception of Monotheism as being opposed to the mythical; perhaps Monotheism contains room after all, on a deeper plane, for the development of mythical lore. I do not believe that all those devoted and pious spirits, practically the vast majority of Ashkenazic and Sephardic Jewry, ceased, after the exodus from Spain, to be Jews also in the religious sense, only because their forms of belief appear to be in manifest contradiction with certain modern theories of Judaism. I, therefore, ask myself: What is the secret of this tremendous success of the Kabbalah among our people? Why did it succeed in becoming a decisive factor in our history, shaping the life of a large proportion of Jewry over a period of centuries, while its contemporary, rational Jewish philosophy, was incapable of achieving the spiritual hegemony after which it strove? This is a pressing question; I cannot accept the explanation that the facts I have described are solely due to external historical circumstances, that persecution and decline weakened the spirit of the people and made them seek refuge in the darkness of Mysticism because they could not bear the light of Reason. The matter appears to me to be more complicated, and I should like briefly to set out my answer to the question.

The secret of the success of the Kabbalah lies in the nature of its relation to the spiritual heritage of rabbinical Judaism. This relation differs from that of rationalist philosophy, in that it is more deeply and in a more vital sense connected with the main forces active in Judaism.

Undoubtedly both the mystics and the philosophers completely transform the structure of ancient Judaism; both have lost the simple relation to Judaism, that naiveté which speaks to us from the classical documents of Rabbinical literature. Classical Judaism expressed itself: it did not reflect upon itself. By contrast, to the mystics and the philosophers of a later stage of religious development Judaism itself has become problematical. Instead of simply speaking their minds, they tend to produce an ideology of Judaism, an ideology moreover which comes to the rescue of tradition by giving it a new interpretation. It is not as though the rise of Jewish philosophy and of Jewish mysticism took place in widely separated ages, or as though the Kabbalah, as Graetz saw it, was a reaction against a wave of rationalism. Rather the two movements are interrelated and interdependent. Neither were they from the start manifestly opposed to each other, a fact which is often overlooked. On the contrary, the rationalism of some of the philosophical *enlighteners* frequently betrays a mystical tendency; and conversely, the mystic who has not yet learnt to speak in his own language often uses and misuses the vocabulary of philosophy. Only very gradually did the Kabbalists, rather than the philosophers, begin to perceive the implications of their own ideas, the conflict between a purely philosophical interpretation of the world, and an attitude which progresses from rational thought to irrational meditation, and from there to the mystical interpretation of the universe.

What many mystics felt towards philosophy was succinctly expressed by Rabbi Moses of Burgos (end of the 13th century). When he heard the philosophers praised, he used to say angrily: "You ought to know that these philosophers whose wisdom you are praising, end where we begin." [22] Actually this means two things: on the one hand, it means that the Kabbalists are largely concerned with the investigation of a sphere of religious reality which lies quite outside the orbit of mediaeval Jewish philosophy; their purpose is to discover a new stratum of the religious consciousness. On the other hand, though R. Moses may not have intended to say this, they stand on the shoulders of the philosophers and it is easier for them to see a little farther than their rivals.

To repeat, the Kabbalah certainly did not *arise* as a reaction against philosophical "enlightenment," [23] but once it was there it is true that its function was that of an opposition to it. At the same time, an intellectual dispute went on between the Kabbalah and the forces of the philosophical movement which left deep marks upon the former's structure. In my opinion, there is a direct connection between Jehudah Halevi, the most Jewish of Jewish philosophers, and the Kabbalists. For the legitimate trustees of his spiritual heritage have been the mystics, and not the succeeding generations of Jewish philosophers.

The Kabbalists employed the ideas and conceptions of orthodox theology, but the magic hand of mysticism opened up hidden sources of new life in the heart of many scholastic ideas and abstractions. Philosophers may shake their heads at what must appear to them a misunderstanding of the meaning of philosophical ideas. But what from the philosopher's point of view represents a flaw in the conception can constitute its greatness and dignity in the religious sense. After all, a misunderstanding is often nothing but the paradoxical abbreviation of an original line of thought. And it is precisely such misunderstanding which has frequently become productive of new ideas in the mystical sphere.

Let us take, as an example of what I have said, the idea of "creation out of nothing." In the dogmatic disputations of Jewish philosophy, the question whether Judaism implies belief in this concept, and if so, in what precise sense, has played an important part. I shall not go into the difficulties with which the orthodox theologians found themselves faced whenever they tried to preserve the full meaning of this idea of creation out of nothing. Viewed in its simplest sense, it affirms the creation of the world by God out of something which is neither God Himself nor any kind of existence, but simply the non-existent. The mystics, too, speak of creation out of nothing; in fact, it is one of their favorite formulae. But in their case the orthodoxy of the term conceals a meaning which differs considerably from the original one. This *Nothing* from which everything has sprung is by no means a mere negation; only to us does it present no attributes because it is beyond the reach of intellectual knowledge. In truth, however, this Nothing—to quote one of the Kabbalists—is infinitely more real than all other reality.[24] Only when the soul has stripped itself of all limitation and, in mystical language, has descended into the depths of Nothing does it encounter the Divine. For this *Nothing* comprises a wealth of mystical reality although it cannot be defined. "Un Dieu défini serait un Dieu fini." In a word, it signifies the Divine itself, in its most impenetrable guise. And, in fact, *creation out of nothing* means to many mystics just *creation out of God*. Creation out of nothing thus becomes the symbol of emanation, that is to say, of an idea which, in the history of philosophy and theology, stands farthest removed from it.

viii

Let us return to our original problem. As we have seen, the renaissance of Judaism on a new plane is the common concern of both the mystics and the philosophers. For all that, there remains a very considerable difference, a good example of which is afforded by the conception of *Sithre Torah,* or "Secrets of the Law." The philosophers no less than the mystics talk of discovering these secrets, using this esoteric phraseology with a profusion hardly distinguishable from the style of the real esoterics and Kabbalists. But what are these secrets according to the philosopher? They are the truths of philosophy, the truths of the metaphysics or ethics of Aristotle, or Alfarabi or Avicenna; truths, in other words, which were capable of being discovered outside the sphere of religion and which were projected into the old books by way of allegorical or typological interpretation. The documents of religion are therefore not conceived as expressing a separate and distinct world of religious truth and reality, but rather as giving a simplified description of the relations which exist between the ideas of philosophy. The story of Abraham and Sarah, of Lot and his wife, of the Twelve Tribes, etc., are simply descriptions of the relation between matter and form, spirit and matter, or the faculties of the mind. Even where allegorization was not pushed to such absurd extremes, the tendency was to regard the Torah as a mere vehicle of philosophic truth, though indeed one particularly exalted and perfect.

In other words, the philosopher can only proceed with his

proper task after having successfully converted the concrete realities of Judaism into a bundle of abstractions. The individual phenomenon is to him no object of his philosophical speculation. By contrast, the mystic refrains from destroying the living texture of religious narrative by allegorizing it, although allegory plays an important part in the writings of a great many Kabbalists. His essential mode of thinking is what I should like to call symbolical in the strictest sense.

This point requires a little further explanation. Allegory consists of an infinite network of meanings and correlations in which everything can become a representation of everything else, but all within the limits of language and expression. To that extent it is possible to speak of allegorical immanence. That which is expressed by and in the allegorical sign is in the first instance something which has its own meaningful context, but by becoming allegorical this something loses its own meaning and becomes the vehicle of something else. Indeed the allegory arises, as it were, from the gap which at this point opens between the form and its meaning. The two are no longer indissolubly welded together; the meaning is no longer restricted to that particular form, nor the form any longer to that particular meaningful content. What appears in the allegory, in short, is the infinity of meaning which attaches to every representation. The "Mysteries of the Torah" which I just mentioned were for the philosophers the natural subject of an allegorical interpretation which gave expression to a new form of the mediaeval mind as much as it implied a veiled criticism of the old.

Allegorization was also, as I have said, a constant preoccupation of the Kabbalists, and it was not on this ground that they differed from the philosophers; nor was it the main constituent of their faith and their method. We must look for this in the attention they gave to the symbol—a form of expression which radically transcends the sphere of allegory. In the mystical symbol a reality which in itself has, for us, no form or shape becomes transparent and, as it were, visible, through the medium of another reality which clothes its content with visible and expressible meaning, as for example the cross for the Christian. The thing which becomes a symbol retains its original form and its original content. It does not become, so to speak, an empty shell into which another content is poured; in itself, through its own existence, it makes another reality transparent which cannot appear in any other form. If allegory can be defined as the representation of an expressible something by another expressible something, the mystical symbol is an expressible representation of something which lies beyond the sphere of expression and communication, something which comes from a sphere whose face is, as it were, turned inward and away from us. A hidden and inexpressible reality finds its expression in the symbol. If the symbol is thus also a sign or representation it is nevertheless more than that.

For the Kabbalist, too, every existing thing is endlessly correlated with the whole of creation; for him, too, everything mirrors everything else. But beyond that he discovers something else which is not covered by the allegorical network: a reflection of the true transcendence. The symbol "signifies" nothing and communicates nothing, but makes something transparent which is beyond all expression. Where deeper insight into the structure of the allegory uncovers fresh layers of meaning, the symbol is intuitively understood all at once— or not at all. The symbol in which the life of the Creator and that of creation become one, is—to use Creuzer's words [25]— "a beam of light which, from the dark and abysmal depths of existence and cognition, falls into our eye and penetrates our whole being." It is a "momentary totality" which is perceived intuitively in a mystical *now*—the dimension of time proper to the symbol.

Of such symbols the world of Kabbalism is full, nay the whole world is to the Kabbalist such a *corpus symbolicum*. Out of the reality of creation, without the latter's existence being denied or annihilated, the inexpressible mystery of the Godhead becomes visible. In particular the religious acts commanded by the Torah, the *mitswoth*, are to the Kabbalist symbols in which a deeper and hidden sphere of reality becomes transparent. The infinite shines through the finite and makes it more and not less real. This brief summary gives us some idea of the profound difference between the philosophers' allegorical interpretation of religion and its symbolical understanding by the mystics. It may be of interest to note that in the comprehensive commentary on the Torah written by a great mystic of the thirteenth century, Moses Nahmanides, there are many symbolical interpretations as defined here, but not a single instance of allegory.

ix

The difference becomes clear if we consider the attitude of philosophy and Kabbalah respectively to the two outstanding creative manifestations of Rabbinical Jewry: Halakhah and Aggadah, Law and Legend. It is a remarkable fact that the philosophers failed to establish a satisfactory and intimate relation to either. They showed themselves unable to make the spirit of Halakhah and Aggadah, both elements which expressed a fundamental urge of the Jewish soul, productive by transforming them into something new.

Let us begin with the Halakhah, the world of sacred law and, therefore, the most important factor in the actual life of ancient Jewry. Alexander Altmann, in raising the question: What is Jewish Theology? is quite justified in regarding as one of the decisive weaknesses of classical Jewish philosophy the fact that it ignored the problem presented by the Halakhah.[26] The whole world of religious law remained outside the orbit of philosophical inquiry, which means of course, too, that it was not subjected to philosophical criticism. It is not as if the philosopher denied or defied this world. He, too, lived in it and bowed to it, but it never became part and parcel of his work as a philosopher. It furnished no material for his thoughts. This fact, which is indeed undeniable, is particularly glaring in the case of thinkers like Maimonides and Saadia, in whom the converging streams meet. They fail entirely to establish a true synthesis of the two elements, Halakhah and philosophy, a fact which has already been pointed out by Samuel David Luzzatto. Maimonides, for instance, begins the *Mishneh Torah,* his great codification of the Halakhah, with a philosophical chapter which has no relation whatever to the Halakhah itself. The synthesis of the spheres remains sterile, and the genius of the man whose spirit moulded them into a semblance of union cannot obscure their intrinsic disparity.

For a purely historical understanding of religion, Maimonides' analysis of the origin of the *mitswoth,* the religious commandments, is of great importance,[27] but he would be a bold man who would maintain that his theory of the *mitswoth* was likely to increase the enthusiasm of the faithful for their actual practice, likely to augment their immediate appeal to religious feeling. If the prohibition against seething a kid in its mother's milk and many similar irrational commandments are explicable as polemics against long-forgotten pagan rites, if the offering of sacrifice is a concession to the primitive mind, if other *mitswoth* carry with them antiquated moral and philosophical ideas—how can one expect the com-

munity to remain faithful to practices of which the antecedents
have long since disappeared or of which the aims can be
attained directly through philosophical reasoning? To the
philosopher, the Halakhah either had no significance at all,
or one that was calculated to diminish rather than to enhance
its prestige in his eyes.

Entirely different was the attitude of the Kabbalists. For
them the Halakhah never became a province of thought
in which they felt themselves strangers. Right from the beginning and with growing determination, they sought to
master the world of the Halakhah as a whole and in every
detail. From the outset, an ideology of the Halakhah is one
of their aims. But in their interpretation of the religious
commandments these are not represented as allegories of
more or less profound ideas, or as pedagogical measures, but
rather as the performance of a secret rite (or *mystery* in the
sense in which the term was used by the Ancients).[28]

Whether one is appalled or not by this transformation of
the Halakhah into a sacrament, a mystery rite, by this revival
of myth in the very heart of Judaism, the fact remains that
it was this transformation which raised the Halakhah to a
position of incomparable importance for the mystic, and
strengthened its hold over the people. Every *mitswoth* became
an event of cosmic importance, an act which had a bearing
upon the dynamics of the universe. The religious Jew became
a protagonist in the drama of the world; he manipulated the
strings behind the scene. Or, to use a less extravagant simile,
if the whole universe is an enormous complicated machine,
then man is the machinist who keeps the wheels going by
applying a few drops of oil here and there, and at the right
time. The moral substance of man's action supplies this "oil,"
and his existence therefore becomes of extreme significance,
since it unfolds on a background of cosmic infinitude.

The danger of theosophical schematism or, as S. R. Hirsch
put it,[29] of "magical mechanism" is, of course, inherent in
such an interpretation of the Torah, and it has more than
once raised its head in the development of Kabbalism. There
is danger of imagining a magical mechanism to be operative
in every sacramental action, and this imagination is attended
by a decline in the essential spontaneity of religious action.
But then this conflict is inseparable from any and every
fulfilment of a religious command, since every prescribed
duty is also conceived as assumed willingly and spontaneously.

The antinomy is, in fact, inescapable, and can only be over-come by religious feeling so long as it is strong and unbroken. When it begins to flag, the contradiction between command and free-will increases in proportion and eventually gathers sufficient force to become destructive.

By interpreting every religious act as a mystery, even where its meaning was clear for all to see or was expressly men-tioned in the written or oral Law, a strong link was forged between Kabbalah and Halakhah, which appears to me to have been, in large part, responsible for the influence of Kabbalistic thought over the minds and hearts of successive generations.

A good deal of similarity to what I have said about the Halakhah is apparent in the attitude of philosophers and mystics, respectively, to the Aggadah. Here too, their ways part right from the beginning. The Aggadah is a wonderful mirror of spontaneous religious life and feeling during the rabbinical period of Judaism. In particular, it represents a method of giving original and concrete expression to the deepest motive-powers of the religious Jew, a quality which helps to make it an excellent and genuine approach to the essentials of our religion. However, it was just this quality which never ceased to baffle the philosophers of Judaism. Their treatment of the Aggadah, except where it pointed an ethical moral, is embarrassed and fumbling. They almost certainly regarded it as a stumbling-block rather than as a precious heritage, let alone a key to a mystery. And thus it is not surprising that their allegorical interpretation of its meaning reflects an attitude which is not that of the Aggadah. Only too frequently their allegorizations are simply, as I have said, veiled criticism.

Here again the Kabbalists conceive their task differently, although it also involves a transformation of the subject's meaning. It would be too much to say that they leave the meaning of the Aggadah intact. What makes them differ from the philosophers is the fact that for them the Aggadah is not just a dead letter. They live in a world historically con-tinuous with it, and they are able, therefore, to enhance it, though in the spirit of mysticism. Aggadic productivity has been a constant element of Kabbalistic literature, and only when the former disappears will the latter, too, be doomed to extinction. The whole of Aggadah can in a way be regarded as a popular mythology of the Jewish universe. Now, this mythical element which is deeply rooted in the creative forms of Aggadic production, operates on different planes in the old Aggadah and in Kabbalism. The difference between the Aggadic production of the Kabbalah and that of the early Midrash can be easily gauged: in the Aggadah of the Kabbalists the events take place on a considerably wider stage, a stage with a cosmic horizon. Earth and heaven meet already in the ancient Aggadah, but now an even greater stress is laid on the heavenly element which comes more and more to the fore. All events assume gigantic dimensions and a wider significance; the steps of the heroes of the Kabbalistic Aggadah are directed by hidden forces from mysterious regions, while their doings react, at the same time, upon the upper world. Seen that way, there is nothing more instructive than a comparison between the two great and truly comprehensive collections, or *Yalkutim*, each one representing, respectively, one of the two types of Aggadic creation. The compiler of the *Yalkut Shim'oni* collected in the thirteenth century the old Aggadahs which, as preserved by the Midrashic literature, accompanied the Biblical text. In the *Yalkut Reubeni*, on the other hand, we have a collection of the Aggadic output of the Kabbalists during five centuries. The latter highly interesting work which was compiled during the second half of the seventeenth century bears full witness to the growing strength and preponderance of the mythical element and to the great difference between Aggadah and Kabbalah in their interpretation of the stories of Biblical heroes. At the same time it is obvious that in comparison with the older Aggadah the realistic element in the later Aggadah has decreased because the realistic foundations, in which Jewish life was rooted, have grown more and more narrow. In fact, this explanation falls in well with the historical experience of the different generations. The old Aggadah is fed by deep and comprehensive experience; the life which it reflects has not yet become colourless, nor did it lose its impetus. The Kabbalistic Aggadah, in contrast, reflects a narrow and circumscribed life which sought, nay, was compelled to seek, inspiration from hidden worlds, as the real world turned for them into the world of the Ghetto. The Aggadic myth of the *Yalkut Reubeni* expresses the historical experience of the Jewish people after the Crusades, and we may say that it is expressed with rather greater force because it is not directly mentioned at all. The depth of the penetration into the hidden worlds which can be encountered here at every step stands in direct proportion to the shrinking perimeter of their historical experience. There is thus a mighty difference of function between the two types of Aggadic creation but no difference of essence.

There is another point worth mentioning. No Kabbalist was ever embarrassed by or ashamed of an old Aggadah; in particular those Aggadahs, which were anathema to "enlightened" Jews, were enthusiastically hailed by the Kabbalists as symbols of their own interpretation of the Universe. The anthropomorphical and paradoxical Aggadahs belong to this class, as well as certain epigrams, such as R. Abbahu's saying, that before making this world God made many others and destroyed them because he did not like them.[30] The philosophers, who had passed through the school of Aristotle, never felt at home in the world of Midrash. But the more extravagant and paradoxical these Aggadahs appeared to them, the more were the Kabbalists convinced that they were one of the keys to the mystical realm. Their vocabulary and favorite similes show traces of Aggadic influence in proportions equal to those of philosophy and Gnosticism; Scripture being, of course, the strongest element of all.

x

What has been said of the Halakhah and the Aggadah is also true of the liturgy, the world of prayer; the last of the three domains in which the religious spirit of post-Biblical Judaism has found its classical expression. Here too the conclusion is inescapable that the philosophers had little of value to contribute. Of entire prayers written by philosophers only a few have been preserved, and these are often somewhat anaemic and half-hearted in their approach, especially where the authors were not, like Solomon ibn Gabirol and Jehudah Halevi, motivated in the last resort by mystical leanings. There is in many of them a curious lack of true religious feeling. The case is entirely different when we turn to the Kabbalistic attitude towards prayer; there is perhaps no clearer sign that Kabbalism is essentially a religious and not a speculative phenomenon. The novelty of its attitude to prayer can be viewed under two aspects: the vast number of prayers whose authors were mystics themselves, and the mystical interpretation of the old traditional community prayers—the backbone of Jewish liturgy.

To begin with the former, it is hardly surprising that the

new religious revelation, peculiar to the visionaries of the Kabbalah, for which there existed no liturgical equivalent in the older prayers, strove after some form of expression and had already inspired the earliest mystics to write their own prayers. The first prayers of a mystical character, which can be traced back to the Kabbalists of Provence and Catalonia,[31] are carried forward by a long and varied tradition to the prayers in which, about 1820, Nathan of Nemirov, the disciple of Rabbi Nahman of Brazlav, gave valid expression to the world of Hasidic Zaddikism.[32] This mystical prayer, which bears little outward resemblance to the older liturgy, and in particular of course to the classical forms of communal prayer, flows from the new religious experience to which the Kabbalists were entitled to lay claim. Often these prayers bear the mark of directness and simplicity, and give plain expression to the common concern of every form of mysticism. But not infrequently their language is that of the symbol and their style reveals the secret pathos of magical conjuration. This has found a profound expression in the mystical interpretation of the phrase of Psalms 130:1 "Out of the depths I have called unto Thee"; which, according to the Zohar, means not "I have called unto Thee from the depths [where I am]" but "from the depths [in which Thou art] I call Thee up." [33]

But side by side with these original productions of the Kabbalistic spirit we find from the earliest beginnings down to our time another tendency, that of mystical reinterpretation of the traditional community liturgy which transforms it into a symbol of the mystical way and the way of the world itself. This transformation, which has meant a great deal for the true life of the Kabbalist, has become crystallized in the conception of *Kawwanah*, i.e. mystical intention or concentration, which is its instrument.[34] In the words of the liturgy as in the old Aggadahs, the Kabbalists found a way to hidden worlds and the first causes of all existence. They developed a technique of meditation which enabled them to extract, as it were, the mystical prayer from the exoteric prayer of the community the text of which followed a fixed pattern. The fact that this form of prayer was conceived not as a free effusion of the soul but as a mystical act in the strict sense of the term, as an act, that is to say, which is directly linked with the inner cosmic process, invests this conception of *Kawwanah* with a solemnity which not only approaches but also passes the border of the magical. It is significant that of all the various forms of Kabbalistic thought and practice this meditative mysticism of prayer has alone survived and has taken the place of all the others. At the end of a long process of development in which Kabbalism, paradoxical though it may sound, has influenced the course of Jewish history, it has become again what it was in the beginning: the esoteric wisdom of small groups of men out of touch with life and without any influence on it.

xi

As I have already said, mysticism represents, to a certain extent, a revival of mythical lore. This brings us to another and very serious point which I should like at least to mention. The Jewish mystic lives and acts in perpetual rebellion against a world with which he strives with all his zeal to be at peace. Conversely, this fact is responsible for the profound ambiguity of his outlook, and it also explains the apparent self-contradiction inherent in a great many Kabbalist symbols and images. The great symbols of the Kabbalah certainly spring from the depths of a creative and genuinely Jewish religious feeling, but at the same time they are invariably tinged by the world of mythology. In the lectures on the Zohar and on Lurianic Kabbalism I shall give a number of particularly outstanding instances of this fact. Failing this mythical element, the ancient Jewish mystics would have been unable to compress into language the substance of their inner experience. It was Gnosticism, one of the last great manifestations of mythology in religious thought, and definitely conceived in the struggle against Judaism as the conqueror of mythology, which lent figures of speech to the Jewish mystic.

The importance of this paradox can hardly be exaggerated; it must be kept in mind that the whole meaning and purpose of those ancient myths and metaphors whose remainders the editors of the book *Bahir*, and therefore the whole Kabbalah, inherited from the Gnostics,[35] was simply the subversion of a law which had, at one time, disturbed and broken the order of the mythical world. Thus through wide and scattered provinces of Kabbalism, the revenge of myth upon its conqueror is clear for all to see, and together with it we find an abundant display of contradictory symbols. It is characteristic of Kabbalistic theology in its systematical forms that it attempts to construct and to describe a world in which something of the mythical has again come to life, in terms of thought which exclude the mythical element. However, it is this contradiction which more than anything else explains the extraordinary success of Kabbalism in Jewish history.

Mystics and philosophers are, as it were, both aristocrats of thought; yet Kabbalism succeeded in establishing a connection between its own world and certain elemental impulses operative in every human mind. It did not turn its back upon the primitive side of life, that all-important region where mortals are afraid of life and in fear of death, and derive scant wisdom from rational philosophy. Philosophy ignored these fears, out of whose substance man wove myths, and in turning its back upon the primitive side of man's existence, it paid a high price in losing touch with him altogether. For it is cold comfort to those who are plagued by genuine fear and sorrow to be told that their troubles are but the workings of their own imagination.

The fact of the existence of evil in the world is the main touchstone of this difference between the philosophic and the Kabbalistic outlook. On the whole, the philosophers of Judaism treat the existence of evil as something meaningless in itself. Some of them have shown themselves only too proud of this negation of evil as one of the fundamentals of what they call rational Judaism. Hermann Cohen has said with great clarity and much conviction: "Evil is non-existent. It is nothing but a concept derived from the concept of freedom. *A power of evil exists only in myth.*" [36] One may doubt the philosophical truth of this statement, but assuming its truth it is obvious that something can be said for "myth" in its struggle with "philosophy." To most Kabbalists, as true seal-bearers of the world of myth, the existence of evil is, at any rate, one of the most pressing problems, and one which keeps them continuously occupied with attempts to solve it. They have a strong sense of the reality of evil and the dark horror that is about everything living. They do not, like the philosophers, seek to evade its existence with the aid of a convenient formula; rather do they try to penetrate into its depth. And by doing so, they unwittingly establish a connection between their own strivings and the vital interests of popular belief—you may call it superstition—and all of those concrete manifestations of Jewish life in which these fears found their expression. It is a paradoxical fact that none other than the Kabbalists, through their interpretation of various religious acts and customs, have made it clear what they signified to the average believer, if not what they really meant from the beginning. Jewish folklore stands as a living proof of this contention, as has been shown by modern research in respect of some particularly well-known examples.[37]

It would be idle to deny that Kabbalistic thought lost much of its magnificence where it was forced to descend from the pinnacles of theoretical speculation to the plane of ordinary thinking and acting. The dangers which myth and magic present to the religious consciousness, including that of the mystic, are clearly shown in the development of Kabbalism. If one turns to the writings of great Kabbalists one seldom fails to be torn between alternate admiration and disgust. There is need for being quite clear about this in a time like ours, when the fashion of uncritical and superficial condemnation of even the most valuable elements of mysticism threatens to be replaced by an equally uncritical and obscurantist glorification of the Kabbalah. I have said before that Jewish philosophy had to pay a high price for its escape from the pressing questions of real life. But Kabbalism, too, has had to pay for its success. Philosophy came dangerously near to losing the living God; Kabbalism, which set out to preserve Him, to blaze a new and glorious trail to Him, encountered mythology on its way and was tempted to lose itself in its labyrinth.

xii

One final observation should be made on the general character of Kabbalism as distinct from other, non-Jewish, forms of mysticism. Both historically and metaphysically it is a masculine doctrine, made for men and by men. The long history of Jewish mysticism shows no trace of feminine influence. There have been no women Kabbalists; Rabia of early Islamic mysticism, Mechthild of Magdeburg, Juliana of Norwich, Theresa de Jesus, and the many other feminine representatives of Christian mysticism have no counterparts in the history of Kabbalism.[38] The latter, therefore, lacks the element of feminine emotion which has played so large a part in the development of non-Jewish mysticism, but it also remained comparatively free from the dangers entailed by the tendency towards hysterical extravagance which followed in the wake of this influence.

This exclusively masculine character of Kabbalism was by

no means the result of the social position of Jewish women or their exclusion from Talmudic learning. Scholasticism was as much exclusively a domain of men as Talmudism, and yet the social position of women in Islam and in Mediaeval Christianity did not prevent their playing a highly important part among the representatives—though not the theoreticians —of Islamic and Christian mysticism. It is hardly possible to conceive Catholic mysticism without them. This exclusive masculinity for which Kabbalism has paid a high price, appears rather to be connected with an inherent tendency to lay stress on the demonic nature of woman and the feminine element of the cosmos.

It is of the essence of Kabbalistic symbolism that woman represents not, as one might be tempted to expect, the quality of tenderness but that of stern judgment. This symbolism was unknown to the old mystics of the Merkabah period, and even to the Hasidim in Germany, but it dominates Kabbalistic literature from the very beginning and undoubtedly represents a constituent element of Kabbalistic theology. The demonic, according to the Kabbalists, is an off-spring of the feminine sphere. This view does not entail a negation or repudiation of womanhood—after all the Kabbalistic conception of the Shekhinah has room for the, to orthodox Jewish thought, highly paradoxical idea of a feminine element in God Himself —but it does constitute a problem for the psychologist and the historian of religion alike. Mention has already been made of the dislike shown by the Kabbalists for any form of literary publicity in connection with mystical experience, and of their tendency towards the objectivization of mystical vision. These traits, too, would appear to be connected with the masculine character of the movement, for the history of mystical literature shows that women were among the outstanding representatives of the tendency towards mystical autobiography and subjectivism in expressing religious experience.

If, finally, you were to ask me what kind of value I attach to Jewish mysticism, I would say this: Authoritative Jewish theology, both mediaeval and modern, in representatives like Saadia, Maimonides and Hermann Cohen, has taken upon itself the task of formulating an antithesis to pantheism and mythical theology, i.e., to prove them wrong. In this endeavour it has shown itself tireless. What is really required, however, is an understanding of these phenomena which yet does not lead away from monotheism; and once their significance is grasped, that elusive something in them which may be of value must be clearly defined. To have posed this problem is the historic achievement of Kabbalism. The varying answers it supplied to the question may be as inadequate as you like; I shall certainly be the last to deny that its representatives often lost their way and went over the edge of the precipice. But the fact remains that they faced a problem which others were more concerned to ignore and which is of the greatest importance for Jewish theology.

The particular forms of symbolical thought in which the fundamental attitude of the Kabbalah found its expression, may mean little or nothing to us (though even today we cannot escape, at times, from their powerful appeal). But the attempt to discover the hidden life beneath the external shapes of reality and to make visible that abyss in which the symbolic nature of all that exists reveals itself: this attempt is as important for us today as it was for those ancient mystics. For as long as nature and man are conceived as His creations, and that is the indispensable condition of highly developed religious life, the quest for the hidden life of the transcendent element in such creation will always form one of the most important preoccupations of the human mind.

Notes

1. A. E. Waite, The Secret Doctrine in Israel (London 1913). This book is incorporated in the author's later work, The Holy Kabbalah (1930).

2. Philosophie der Geschichte oder ueber die Tradition. 4 vols. (Münster 1827–1855). The book appeared anonymously. On the philosophy of the author cf. Carl Frankenstein, Molitors metaphysische Geschichtsphilosophie (1928).

3. In my Bibliographia Kabbalistica (1927), p. 94, I have listed the writings of Constant pertinent to the subject of Kabbalism. Eliphas Levi is a Judaization of his Christian names Alphonse Louis. No words need be wasted on the subject of Crowley's "Kabbalistic" writings in his books on what he was pleased to term "Magick," and in his journal, The Equinox.

4. Rufus Jones, Studies in Mystical Religion (1909), p. XV of the Introduction.

5. I owe this quotation from Thomas' Summa Theologiae to Engelbert Krebs' little book, Grundfragen der kirchlichen Mystik (1921), p. 37.

6. Levi Isaac, the "Rabbi" of Berditchev, in his work קדושת לוי at the end of section פקודי:

יש אדם שעובד את הבורא בשכלו שכל אנושי ויש אדם שהוא מסתכל אל
האי״ן כביכול וזה אי אפשר בשכל אנושי רק בעזר השם ית׳ . . . (וכשזוכה
האדם להסתכל אל האי״ן) אז השכל האנושי שלו בטל במציאות ואח״ב
כשחוזר אדם על עצמות השכל אז היא מלא שפע.

7. Molitor, Philosophie der Geschichte vol. II (1834), p. 56.

8. מערכת האלהות ascribed sometimes to Perez of Barcelona, Mantua
1558 fol. 82b: דע כי האין סוף אשר זכרנו איננו רמוז לא בתורה ולא
בנביאים ולא בכתובים ולא בדברי רז״ל אך קבלו בו בעלי העבודה קצת
רמז. In the fixed terminology of this author, the mystics are referred to
as בעלי העבודה "the masters of worship."

9. The terms המציאות הגדול, שורש כל השרשים and האחדות השוה
(or השואת האחדות) are to be found in particular in the writings of
those thirteenth-century Kabbalists in Spain who show an outspoken
tendency towards Neoplatonism.

10. Hebrew: מה שאין המחשבה משגת which sounds like a paraphrase
of a Neoplatonic ἀκατάληπτος. It is to be found, in the place of the
term En-Sof, in Isaac's comentry on the "Book of Creation" and in the
writings of his disciples.

11. This term עמקי האין is a favorite metaphor of the thirteenth-
century Kabbalists, cf. my remarks in the Gaster Anniversary Volume
(1936), p. 505.

12. Cf. Philo's De vita contemplativa, ed. Conybeare, p. 119.

13. Cf. Martin Buber's eloquent dissertation on this point in the
introduction to his anthology, Ekstatische Konfessionen (1909).

14. See the first and last sections of the fourth lecture.*

15. Simon Ginzburg, ר׳ משה חיים לוצאטו ובני דורו (Tel Aviv, 1937).

16. J. Bernhart in an essay, Zur Soziologie der Mystik, in Sued-
deutsche Monatshefte vol. XXVI (1928), p. 27.

17. Rabbi Kook's great work entitled אורות הקודש, the first two volumes of which were published in Jerusalem in 1938 from papers left by
the author, is a veritable *theologia mystica* of Judaism equally distinguished by its originality and the richness of its author's mind. It is the
last example of productive Kabbalistic thought of which I know.

18. A bibliography of Jewish mystical literature is still a *pium de-
siderium* of Kabbalistic research. My "Bibliographia Kabbalistica" (1927)
lists only the scholarly literature on the subject of Jewish Mysticism, not
the texts themselves.

19. Charles Bennett, A Philosophical Study of Mysticism (1931),
p. 31.

20. E. R. Dodds, in his commentary on Proclus' Elements of Theology
(1933), p. 219.

21. This thesis is elaborated particularly by Meir ibn Gabbai in
עבודת הקודש part III (written in 1531). The idea that the Kabbalah
represented the lost tradition of the earliest state of mankind was familiar also to the "Christian Kabbalists" of the late fifteenth and sixteenth
centuries, such as Pico della Mirandola and Johannes Reuchlin.

22. הפילוסופים שאתם משבחים חכמתם דעו באמת כי מקום מעמד ראשם
מעמד רגלינו, quoted by Isaac of Acre, cf. *Tarbiz* vol. V (1934), p. 318.

23. I have enlarged on this point in my essay, Zur Frage der Enste-
hung der Kabbala, which appeared in Korrespondenzblatt der Akademie
fuer die Wissenschaft des Judentums 1928 p. 4–26. See also Julius Guttmann, Die philosophie des Judentums (1933), p. 238.

* Not included in this volume. Ed.

24. David ben Abraham Ha-Laban מסורת הברית (written about 1300), published in קובץ ע"י של חברת מקיצי נרדמים new series vol. I (1936), p. 31. Exactly the same imagery is used by Dionysius the pseudo-Areopagite (quoted by Inge, The Philosophy of Plotinus vol. II p. 112) and by John the Scot, called Erigena, in De divisione naturae, liber III, 19–23.

25. Friedrich Creuzer, Symbolik und Mythologie der alten Voelker. Second edition, first part (1816), p. 70.

26. Alex. Altmann, Was ist juedische Theologie? (Frankfurt-on-Main 1933), p. 15.

27. This analysis is to be found in the third part of the "Guide of the Perplexed." On its importance for the history of religion cf. Julius Guttmann. John Spencer's Erklaerung der biblischen Gesetze in ihrer Beziehung zu Maimonides, in Festskrift af Professor David Simonsen (Copenhagen 1923), p. 258–276.

28. Since the days of the Kabbalistic school of Gerona (about 1230), Kabbalistic writings are full of such mystical interpretations of טעמי המצוות. Specifically Ezra ben Solomon and Jacob ben Sheshet (the true author of the ספר האמונה והבטחון which has later been ascribed to Nahmanides) were the first to treat at considerable length on such questions.

29. Samson Raphael Hirsch, Neunzehn Briefe ueber Judentum. Fourth edition (1911), p. 101.

30. Gen. Rabba ed. Theodor, p. 68. This conception of primeval worlds also occurs in the "orthodox Gnosticism" of such Fathers of the Church as Clement of Alexandria and Origen, albeit with a difference, in as much as for them these worlds were not simply corrupt but necessary stages in the great cosmic process.

31. To this category belong the prayers grouped under the title תפלת היחוד which are ascribed to Rabbi Nehuniah ben Hakanah and Rabban Gamaliel but the style of which is the enthusiastic one of the Kabbalistic Neoplatonists. Cf. also the great prayer of Jacob ben Jacob Hacohen of Segovia (Castile, about 1265), published by me in מדעי היהדות vol. II (1927), pp. 220–226.

32. לקוטי תפלות לנורא תהלות printed first at Brazlav, 1822.

33. Zohar II, 63b and III, 69b; cf. also Joseph Gikatila שערי אורה (Offenbach 1715), f. 40bff.

34. Cf. H. G. Enelow, Kawwana, the Struggle for Inwardness in Judaism, in Studies in Jewish Literature issued in honour of Professor K. Kohler (1913), p. 82–107, and my own exposition Der Begriff der Kawwana in der alten Kabbala, in MGWJ vol. 78 (1934), p. 492–518.

35. See my article Buch Bahir, in EJ vol. III col. 969–979.

36. H. Cohen, Ethik des reinen Willens; second edition (1907), p. 452.

37. Cf. Jacob Lauterbach's studies: The Ritual for the Kapparot-Ceremony, in Jewish Studies in Memory of George A. Kohut (1935), p. 413–422; Tashlik, a Study in Jewish Ceremonies, in Hebrew Union College Annual vol. XI (1936), p. 207–340.

38. The single case of a woman, Hannah Rachel "the Maid of Ludomir," who became the spiritual leader, or Zaddik, of a Hasidic community (in the middle of the nineteenth century), constitutes no convincing evidence of the contrary. Cf. about her S. A. Horodezky, Leaders of Hasidism (1928), p. 113ff.

Bibliography

On mysticism in general:

CHARLES A. BENNETT, A Philosophical Study of Mysticism. New Haven 1931.

MARTIN BUBER, Ekstatische Konfessionen. Jena 1909.

HENRI DELACROIX, Etudes d'Histoire et de Psychologie du Mysticisme. Paris 1908.

FRIEDRICH VON HUEGEL, The Mystical Element of Religion, [especially:] Second Volume, Critical Studies. London 1908.

WILLIAM RALPH INGE, Christian Mysticism, Considered in Eight Lectures. Second Edition. London 1912.

RUFUS M. JONES, Studies in Mystical Religion. London 1909.

RUDOLF OTTO, Mysticism East and West. A comparative Analysis of the Nature of Mysticism. New York 1932.

E. RÉCÉJAC, Essay on the Bases of the Mystic Knowledge. London 1899.

EVELYN UNDERHILL, Mysticism, A Study in the Nature and Development of Man's Spiritual Consciousness. London 1926.

On Jewish mysticism in general:

FRANZ JOSEPH MOLITOR, Philosophie der Geschichte oder ueber die Tradition. Vol. I–IV. Muenster 1827–1857.

G. SCHOLEM, Bibliographia Kabbalistica. Leipzig 1927.

——, Kabbala, in Encyclopaedia Judaica vol. IX col. 630–732 (1932).

J. ABELSON, Jewish Mysticism. London 1913.

ARTHUR EDWARD WAITE, The Holy Kabbalah, A Study of the Secret Tradition in Israel. London 1929.

12.

Safed in the Sixteenth Century: A City of Legists and Mystics *

by S. Schechter

Safed is a small city in Upper Galilee situated on a hill in a mountainous country, and forming part of the Holy Land assigned in the Scriptures to the tribe of Naphtali. Of the various cities of Palestine boasting of a large Jewish population it is relatively the most modern. Neither the Bible nor the Talmud has any definite reference to it, whilst the mention of a locality Zephed, by Kalir, is obscure, and can serve little for purposes of identification.[1]

Yet this was the spot of which R. Joseph Caro wrote in the sixteenth century: "After nearly fifteen hundred years of living in the exile and persecution, he (God) remembered unto his people his covenant with their fathers, and brought them back from their captivity, one of a city and two of a family, from the corners of the earth to the land of glory, and they settled in the city of Safed, the desire of all lands."[2]

The *impulse* under which the "one of a city and two of a family" acted when they preferred the "land of glory" to the great commercial centres of Europe was a *religious* one.

Samuel Usque, the famous author of the *"Consolacam as tribulacoes de Ysrael"* ("The Consolation and the Tribulations of Israel"), has the following passage in praise of the country in which most of his fellow-sufferers from the Pyrenean peninsula found an asylum: "Great Turkey, . . . there the gates of freedom and equal opportunity for the unhindered practice of Jewish worship are ever open to Israel; they are never closed against thee. There thou canst renew thy inward

* From *Studies in Judaism*, Second Series, Philadelphia, Jewish Publication Society of America, 1908.

life, change thy condition, strip off thy habits, cast away erroneous teachings, recover thy ancient truths, and abandon the practices which, by the violence of the nations among which thou wast a pilgrim, thou wast forced to imitate. In this land thou receivest boundless grace from the Lord, since therein he granteth thee unlimited freedom to begin thy repentance." [3]

The inducement thus held out to the exiled from Spain and Portugal was not only that they would in the new country be allowed to serve their God, without let or hindrance, but also that an opportunity would be granted them of a total regeneration and renewal of heart.

The sense of sin apparently weighing so heavily on Usque may be detected also in other writers, as, for instance, Joseph Jabez, who depicted the spiritual condition of the Jews in Spain in the darkest colours, and describes the men who witnessed the expulsion as an "evil generation, increasing rebellions and transgressions without number." He declared that it was mainly the Spanish Jewesses who remained faithful, and who themselves suffered, and made their husbands suffer, martyrdom for the Sanctification of the Name.[4] Another instance is found in the chronicler Abraham ben Solomon, of Torrutiel in Spain, who says, "Our iniquities had increased over our heads, and our trespasses had grown up unto the heavens, seeing the evils and the sin and the terrible pride so rampant among the Jews in the kingdom of Spain." Jabez and Abraham ben Solomon belonged to the anti-rationalistic party of the Spanish Jews, and may have exaggerated the evils of the situation in their accusations, but their feelings were very likely shared, to some extent, by all other exiles.[5] Nathan Nata of Hanover, the well-known author of the *Yeven Mezulah*, concludes his account of the terrible suffering of the Jews during the Chmielnicki persecution with the words: "What shall we speak, or how shall we call ourselves? The Lord has found out our sins. Does God execute judgment without justice?"[6] The sufferers of Spain doubtless viewed their misfortunes from the same standpoint. And since these evils must have been in some way proportionate to the greatness of the catastrophe which had overtaken them, those of deeper religious sensitiveness must certainly have felt the need of a new life and a regeneration.

It is to this need that we have to attribute the fact that large numbers of the exiles were impelled to emigrate to the Holy

Land, the country which, from the times of the prophets down to Judah Halevi in the twelfth century, and from the time of Judah Halevi down to the disciples of Elijah Wilna and Israel Baal Shem in the eighteenth and nineteenth centuries, was always considered a country of great "spiritual opportunities." As a Spanish Jew of the thirteenth century who took a vow to emigrate to the Holy Land expressed it, "There (in Jerusalem, or near it) is the place for fulfilling the commandments and receiving upon oneself the Kingdom of Heaven. Our worship there is acceptable, for there is the House of our God and the Gate of Heaven." [7]

Indeed, it may be stated without fear of contradiction, that there never was a time in which the Holy Land was not an object of attraction and deep longing for the pious Jew, even though he was not always able to gratify his longing in this respect. As we know now, there were for centuries after the destruction of the Holy Temple, every year during the Feast of Tabernacles, large meetings on the Mount of Olives constituted of pilgrims from Palestine itself, Babylon, Egypt, and perhaps also from Europe. [8]

These meetings were probably brought to an end in the eleventh century through the troubles of the Crusades; but the second decade of the thirteenth century witnessed the famous pilgrimage of three hundred Rabbis from France, England, and Spain to the Holy Land. [9] In the fourteenth century the well-known traveller Pharchi explored the Holy Land, and reported about different settlements in various localities. [10] Emigration to Palestine assumed, however, larger dimensions in the fifteenth and sixteenth centuries, caused by the general distress of the Jews in almost all parts of Christendom. The majority of the refugees escaped to Turkey, but a considerable minority, composed, as already indicated, of the more spiritual-minded among them, directed their steps to the Holy Land.

As hinted before, Safed has no Biblical nor even Talmudic record. Its first appearance in Jewish history dates from about the beginning of the thirteenth century, when the traveller Samuel ben Shimshon reports the existence of a community there of more than fifty members. Somewhat later it is mentioned in connexion with a document relating to the Maimonides controversy, which bears also the signatures of R. Moses ben Judah and his colleagues, the Rabbis of Safed. [11] R. Hananel Ibn Askara and R. Shem Tob Ibn Gaon, of Spain, migrated to Safed in the same century; [12] whilst R. Isaac ben Joseph Chelo, of Laresa in Spain, and Pharchi, mentioned above, visited Safed in the fourteenth century and speak of a large Jewish community dwelling there.[13] Joseph Mantabia, who visited Safed in 1481, speaks of it as a "fine" community, numbering about three hundred families, including those living in the neighbouring villages.[14]

It is, however, not until the last decade of the fifteenth century that Safed begins to be especially noted for the importance of its Jewish population. The man who was the most significant factor in the development of this Jewish settlement, which excelled Jerusalem not only in the size of its Jewish population but also in the number of great men it harboured, was R. Joseph Saragossi. Saragossi, hailing perhaps originally from Spain, was an exile from Sicily, and, after a residence in Beyrout and Sidon, finally settled in Safed, where he most likely established a school. He was of humble disposition, making peace between man and man, including non-Jews, and he probably did his best to blend the various elements of the new settlement, consisting of natives, of exiles from Spain, and of immigrants from the Barbary States, into one great community.[15]

The preference given to Safed, a non-Scriptural town, over Jerusalem, the historical metropolis of Palestine and the holiest city of the Holy Land, may be accounted for by the unfavourable conditions prevailing in Jerusalem at that time. As evidenced by certain contemporary documents, the administration of the Jewish community in Jerusalem was influenced by a rather ungenerous spirit, imposing heavy taxes on new arrivals, and making residence there a great hardship. The Mohammedan population seems also to have been hostile to the Jews, rapacious, and extortionate.[16] Safed, on the other hand, never having had before this time an important Jewish population, the community there had no occasion to make regulations calculated to exploit the foreigner, whilst the non-Jewish population seems to have been more kindly disposed toward the Jews, sparing them the heavy taxation which was the rule in Jerusalem. R. Obadiah of Bertinoro, who had no opportunity to visit the north, writes, in his famous letter dated 1489, that, according to report, the Jews of Safed and of other places in Galilee lived in peace and in quiet, not being exposed to persecution on the part of the Mohammedans. He writes, "They are mostly poor, spending their time in villages, going about peddling in houses and on farms, asking for food." [17]

Another reason which may have been decisive in favour of attracting immigrants to Safed was the simple life led by the inhabitants of that city. The old saying, "Love work and hate lordship" (in modern parlance, snobbery), was followed by them to the letter. An anonymous traveller who passed through Safed in the year 1496 writes of the learned Rabbi Pharez Colobi, the head of the community, that he kept a shop where articles of food were sold, by which he made a living.[18] Shlomel of Moravia, the author of one of the legendary biographies of Loria, writing from Safed in the year 1607, says of its citizens that there were to be found among them "great scholars, saints, and men of action, full of Divine wisdom, so that they were worthy of the gift of the Holy Spirit," but what he seemed to admire most was the simplicity and the humility of spirit which they possessed. "None among them," he writes, "is ashamed to go to the well and draw water and carry home the pitcher on his shoulders, or go to the market to buy bread, oil, and vegetables. All the work in the house is done by themselves," without servants. Shlomel's statement may be illustrated by the following story: Once, R. Abraham Galanti, the leading disciple of Cordovero and the author of many works, was carrying a sack of flour on his shoulders from the market. But there came the famous scholar R. Solomon Sagis (?) and snatched away the sack from the shoulders of Galanti, and pronounced an oath, that no man should be permitted to carry this sack of flour to its destination except himself, who was so much younger and stronger. On another occasion, Galanti was carrying a cask of water on his shoulders from a village near Safed when the Saint R. Misod met him and said, "Master, give me a drink, as I am very thirsty." Whereupon Galanti offered him the cask. R. Misod then snatched away the burden and carried it to Galanti's home in Safed.[19]

Thus material as well as spiritual considerations combined to make Safed the chosen city for the time being. The rapid growth of Safed may easily be seen by the fact that whilst, according to one account, Safed counted three synagogues in 1522, and could point perhaps to only one Talmudic college established by Saragossi, it could a few years later boast of being the centre of learning in Palestine, and, in 1603, according to Shlomel's letter of that year, it contained not less than eighteen Talmudic colleges and twenty-one synagogues, besides a large school for the children of the poor, with twenty teachers and four hundred pupils, maintained by wealthy Jews in Constantinople, who also provided the latter with clothes. The Jews in Turkey were particularly interested in maintaining the Safed schools, and special messengers were sent from this community to collect moneys. We even find mention of a single bequest for the Yeshiboth of Safed amounting to 100,000 *lebanim*.[20]

The history of the world, some maintain, is but the record of its great men. This is especially true of the history of Safed in the sixteenth century, which is essentially spiritual in its character, made and developed by men living lives purified by suffering, and hallowed by constant struggle after purification and holiness. The two figures standing out most prominently among these are R. Joseph Caro, the leading legist of the time, and his contemporary, R. Isaac Loria, the generally recognised head of the mystical school of Safed. It will, therefore, be advisable to group our remarks around these two heroes. From their eminence we shall be able to obtain a general view of the lives of the other mighty men in Israel engaged in the same general religious activities and pursuing the same spiritual ends, contributing their share to the fame which Safed has achieved in Jewish history.

R. Joseph Caro was born in the Pyrenean peninsula (probably Spain) in the year 1488, whence he emigrated as a boy of four, in the year 1492, with his father Ephraim, who was also his first teacher. After many wanderings and great suffering, they reached Nicopolis, in European Turkey, in which city the son Joseph remained until the year 1522.[21] He was advised there by his Maggid, a kind of Mentor-Angel (of whom more presently), to leave this place, whose inhabitants seem to have been rather close-fisted in their relations to the poor, and lacking in devotion to the Torah, and to move to Adrianople, in European Turkey, one of the various gathering points of the Spanish exiles.[22] There he remained for some years, serving in the capacity of the head of the Yeshibah, or Talmudic College. It was in this town that he began the composition of his work *Beth Joseph*, which occupied him for the next thirty years of his life (1522–1552).

The *Beth Joseph* is a gigantic work comprising four big folio volumes, the first edition of which appeared 1550–1559. It forms a sort of commentary to R. Jacob ben Asher's "Digest of the Law," *Arba Turim*, tracing each law to its original sources for nearly fifteen hundred years, pursuing it through its various stages of different interpreters and codifiers, giving in disputed cases the arguments on both sides, and bringing it down to his own time. It is hardly necessary to point to the tremendous learning and unsurpassed acquaintance with the Law in all its branches and ramifications displayed in the *Beth Joseph*. But what distinguishes it above other work of its kind is not only its comprehensiveness, covering as it does all the contents of the Oral Law which had not become obsolete by the destruction of the Holy Temple, but also the methodical treatment in which he was a master, and which enabled him to bring system and order into this chaos of argument, accumulated in every department of the Law, in its passage through the discussions of the schools for many centuries. Caro was by this work soon recognised as the greatest legist of his time, and was appealed to in matters of law even by his contemporaries, as the first Halachic authority.

Next to this in importance is his work *Shulchan Aruch*, which he finished in the year 1555. It forms only a sort of manual intended by Caro to serve chiefly as a repertory for his great book. The *Shulchan Aruch* soon proved to be the most popular code with students, both on account of its practical qualities and its close correspondence with the greater work of Caro, in which the origin of each law could be easily traced. It passed through several editions, and it is still consulted with profit by Rabbis engaged in giving ritual decisions according to the Law of Moses and the Talmud, even at this day representing the great bulk of the Jews—eleven millions and nine hundred thousand out of twelve millions. The *Shulchan Aruch* is disfigured by a few paragraphs expressing views incompatible with our present notions of tolerance. But there the discretion of the Rabbi comes in. By tacit consent these are considered obsolete by all Jewish students. Every Jewish scholar well knows that the fugitive from the tyranny of the pious royal couple, Ferdinand and Isabella of Spain, was not the person to make an effort to suppress intolerant matter. To meet intolerance with equal intolerance was considered a sort of self-defence. Nay, the student is even convinced that Caro himself would have hesitated to put such laws into practice. He would rather have followed the rule laid down by himself for himself, which was never to be betrayed into anger, even in matters of religion.

The other works of Caro published during his life or after his death add little to the greatness of Caro as a scholar, except, perhaps, certain portions of his *Keseph Mishneh,* forming a commentary to Maimonides' *Mishneh Torah,* and in his *Kelale ha-Talmud,* on the methodology of the Talmud, as well as certain Responsa embodied in various collections, in which Caro's passion for system and order and lucid and logical thinking is displayed even more clearly than in the works before named.

There is still one work to be considered, which brings us closer to Caro's personality, and that is the *Maggid Mesharim,* which appeared some thirty years after the death of its author.[23] The *Maggid Mesharim* is a long dream, lasting for nearly half a century. For, remarkable enough, the great legist and logical thinker was at the same time a dreamer of dreamers. Caro was passionately fond of the Mishnah, to which he is supposed to have written a commentary, lost to us, and its contents became so identified with his own self, that they shaped themselves into a species of Genius taking the form of a living reality personified in the Mentor-Angel above mentioned. This Mentor-Angel addresses him with such expressions as, "I am the Mishnah that speaketh through thy mouth; I am the soul of the Mishnah; I and the Mishnah and thou are united into one soul." [24]

As a rule, this *I-Mishnah* appeared to him in the depths of the night, after Caro had studied for some time one or more chapters of the Mishnah. Then the voice of his beloved, as Caro expressed himself, would begin to sound in his mouth, "singing of itself." [25] The voice was also audible to by-standers, as is clear from the famous letter of Alkabez, of whom I shall speak later, who was once fortunate enough to observe his friend Caro in such a fit of ecstasy, and who has left us a full account of the message delivered by the Mentor-Angel on that occasion.[26] From a description given by Caro himself of his prospects of being worthy one day to hold communion with the prophet Elijah, and the manner in which this communion will take place, we may also conclude that the listeners recognised in the strange sounds of the Mentor-Angel Caro's own voice, though to Caro himself these sounds appeared something alien, *not* himself. His other organs seem to have been at complete rest, which fact produced the impression in Caro that he served only as a sort of musical instrument to the sweet melody of the Mishnah. On the other hand, his mental faculties remained fairly unimpaired, as he retained complete recollection of all the Mentor-Angel revealed to him. This recollection he wrote down in the *Maggid Mesharim,* which thus forms a mystical diary, recording the spiritual experience of a long lifetime. The fact that the book containing these recollections fills only a small volume proves nothing against this theory, as we possess it in a very defective state, whilst we also know that he did not always commit to writing the contents of his visions, for which neglect he is reproved by the Mentor-Angel.[27]

It must, however, not be thought that it is the explanation of obscure passages of the Mishnah that is revealed to Caro in his Mishnah visions. In the whole of the *Maggid Mesharim* there are only a few lines of a legal nature. Caro was sober enough not to allow his mystical proclivities to have a marked influence upon his judgment in matters of law. What occupied his thoughts in these moments of rapture was chiefly the mysteries of the Torah, as well as matters of conduct, falling under the heading of "superior holiness." I say "chiefly," for the "I," or Self, occasionally asserts itself and introduces matter which is rather of a private nature, as, for instance, his matrimonial affairs. From these we learn that he became a widower twice. His third wife, who brought him a large dowry, was the daughter of R. Zechariah Zechsel.[28] Caro also refers in a somewhat unkindly manner to certain great personalities. These reflections, which might have better been left unexpressed, were jotted down probably in moments of depression and resentment, for which we may not judge him too severely.[29] In the great majority of cases, however, Caro's Self was under the strict control of the Mishnah, or his ideal Mentor-Angel.

The Mentor-Angel is very exacting in his demands. "I am the mother that chastises her children," the Mishnah says to him, "be strong and cleave unto me." [30] This chastisement consisted partly in imposing upon Caro a number of regulations of an ascetic nature. He is bidden to fast on various occasions, and even on ordinary days his menu is prescribed for him, reduced to a minimum. He must not fully satisfy his desire for food and drink, not even in the first meal after a day of fasting.[31] Of course, he must not indulge in much wine, but he is at the same time rebuked by his Mentor-Angel for having allowed himself to be filled with water.[32] He is likewise warned against too much sleep, and when he married one of his daughters and, according to custom, spent much time at the banquet, so that he went to bed late and got up just one hour after the breaking of dawn, he was reproved for his slothful behaviour, and the Mentor-Angel tells him that it would only serve him right were he to abandon him, seeing that he separated his heart from the Torah for so long a time.[33] On another occasion, when Caro went to market to buy meat and poultry for Sabbath and failed in his errand, the Mentor-Angel declared himself responsible for this failure, proceeding to say that he wanted to show Caro that meat and wine are the habitation of the Evil One, that the Sabbath can be honoured without such luxuries, and concluding his admonition with the words, "Think about nothing but the Law of the Lord; thou art strictly observed in all thy actions, hence, be careful." [34]

Other instructions worth mentioning here are these: Be exceedingly lowly in spirit.—Never be betrayed into anger, not even in matters relating to Heaven.—Be chaste in thy behaviour.—Have always thy sins before thine eyes, and mourn over them.—Never speak an idle word.—Give a mild answer to every man.—Never indulge in laughter and in scoffing.—When thou readest the *Shema,* let thy thoughts be so single-minded that they become the seat of the Divine Presence.[35]

He is also reminded by the Mentor-Angel of the necessity of reading devotional books; among these the abridged version of Bachye's "Duties of the Heart" is especially recommended.[36] He is further bidden by the Mentor-Angel to devote himself more diligently to the study of the Cabbala, which Caro seems to have neglected for a long time. "If thou wilt have appointed times for the acquisition of the knowledge of the Cabbala, I will open thy heart so that thou shalt receive the most hidden secrets unrevealed to man for many years." [37]

The Mentor-Angel, however, was not always severe. His motherly ways are not limited to chastisement. Thus he once began his address, "Behold, I kiss thee the kiss of love; behold, I embrace thee." [38] Nor does he confine himself to rebukes and strictures. He also holds out hopes and promises. These give us a fair insight into Caro's aspirations as a scholar and a saint. They may, perhaps, be summed up in the following three points.

The first aspiration was that the books with which Caro happened to be occupied, especially the *Beth Joseph,* should be free from error, and after publication accepted as standard works all over the Dispersion, whilst he himself should be recognised as an authority of the first rank.[39] There is a human touch in the fact, that notwithstanding this anxiety Caro regards it as a joyful message when his Mentor-Angel tells him that he will be blessed with a son who, besides being one of the greatest mystics of the time, will also write strictures on his father's works.[40] Caro was especially anxious for the privilege of spreading Torah in Israel, and had the repeated promise from his Mentor-Angel that he would be worthy of presiding over the greatest gathering of disciples in Israel, and that he would also receive sufficient material support for his college to enable his disciples to devote themselves entirely to the study of the Torah.[41]

As a mystic, all things on earth are to Caro only a reflex of some original in heaven, and thus in his capacity as the master of the greatest Torah-school here below, he is brought into communion with its prototype in the regions above. It is from there that his Mentor-Angel often brings him greetings in the typical expression, "Peace from the College of Heaven." [42] Sometimes the greeting begins with the words, "Behold the Holy One, blessed be he, and all the sons of the (heavenly) college, send unto thee peace, and are opening unto thee the gates of light." [43] Occasionally these greetings drift off into a string of solemn promises of the bliss and reward awaiting Caro in the world to come, where he will associate with all the heavenly hosts and the souls of the departed saints and scholars whose interpreter he was in this world.[44] It is interesting to see how the Mentor-Angel, with pedagogical insight, uses these very promises for a moral lesson. For instance, in one place where he gives him a full description of the glorious reception with which he will meet in the circle of the righteous, headed by the Divine Presence, and the fêtes which will be given in his honour, he winds up with the words: "Beloved, the Holy One and all the members of the Heavenly Academy send me to make thee acquainted with this secret, in order that thou mayest see thyself in this high degree, and thus thou wilt never come into the power of sin, not even by an evil thought. Should temptation become overpowering, rebuke it and say, 'Shall a man like me, whose future is meant for such glories, allow himself to sin, be it even only by an evil thought?' " [45] This is indeed one of the Mentor-Angel's pedagogical tactics, to impress Caro with his great importance, and at the same time show what duties such importance involves. By the very breath of his mouth when occupied with the uttering of the Mishnah, Caro creates whole hosts of angels, surrounding him as a suite surrounds a king. Every word of his, every thought, creates worlds; but so does it destroy worlds if it is of an unworthy and idle nature.[46]

The second aspiration of Caro was that he might be worthy to settle in the Holy Land.[47] This is a thought which probably occupied his mind for many years before he settled in Safed. The promise to help him realise that wish turns up again and again in the addresses of the Mentor-Angel. Solomon Alkabez, in the letter referred to above, reports how the Mentor-Angel said, "Lose no moment to go up to the Holy Land, for not all times are favourable. Regard not your stuff (i.e., household things) . . . I will maintain thee." It would seem that material considerations, at least for a time, prevented Caro from accomplishing the wish of his heart, for we find in another place, in which the Angel promises him that within a year he will be in Palestine, he says to him: "There is no need for thee to trouble thy mind; thou hast wanted nothing these last forty years, and thou wilt never know want. Thy income is prepared for thee. Thou hast seen this very moment that the Holy One, blessed be he, gave thee as much profit in two thousand Zuz as in five thousand." [48] When Caro tarries too long on his way, through war and other causes, the Mentor-Angel tells him that he may stay in certain cities, such as Salonica and others, for some time, but he must never settle anywhere until he reaches the Holy Land. Of course, with this aspiration is also connected his hope that he will be worthy of becoming the head of the Yeshibah and an elder of the Holy Land.[49]

His third aspiration was that he should die the death of a martyr at the stake. This is a wish which Caro cherished when he was still in Nicopolis, and which mingled with his dreams throughout his entire life.[50] Caro assures us that in visions without number he received the promise that he would be worthy to be burned for the sanctification of the Holy Name,[51] so that every taint of sin which may have cleaved unto him in his passage through this world would be removed, and his soul cleansed, and thus reach the degree of the holy and pure ones. Here again the Mentor-Angel employs this dearest wish of Caro's heart for his pedagogical purposes, as when he tells him: "Behold, I have singled thee out to be a burnt-offering, to be consumed in fire for the sake of the sanctification of the Name, but thou knowest that in the burnt-offering no blemish may be found, not even in thought. Hence, take care that all thy thoughts are absorbed by the Torah." [52] On the whole, the promises of the Mentor-Angel were fairly kept, except this. Turkey was perhaps at no time the country in which the crown of martyrdom could be easily gained. For this, one had to go to the lands of Christendom, where love was preached and murder acted. Caro showed no particular desire to return to Europe. In this connexion it is rather interesting to note that Caro was not quite free from anxiety, for he found it worth his while to write down the following apparently good message of his Mentor-Angel: During the afternoon prayer, when the reader was chanting the portion from the scroll of the Law, I was told, "Know, my beloved and dear Joseph, that the Sultan will win the battle in which he is now engaged against the King of Edom." [53]

The *Maggid Mesharim* occasionally contains references to different personages mentioned in Caro's other works. But whilst in these latter they are cited with their proper titles, as "Rabbi," "Master," or "the great Rabbi," in the *Maggid Mesharim,* as befitting a production of an angelic being, this official stiffness disappears. Titles are, for the most part, dropped, and they are introduced with such endearing epithets as "my chosen Moses" (Maimonides), "my saintly Asher" (Rosh), "my God-fearing Jonah" (Rabbenu Jonah), "my dear Jacob" (Jacob ben Asher, the author of the *Turim*), "my modest Jeruham" (author of a well-known code of the Rabbinic Law). But the name which occurs most frequently is that of "my chosen Solomon." [54] This name is at most times used for Solomon Molko, but it is not impossible that in one or two places it refers to Solomon Alkabez, two beautiful souls who seem to have been the especial favourites of Caro. [55]

We must digress for a moment from Caro himself to consider the career of these two worthies. Solomon Molko deserves a monograph to himself. He would best form the subject of a great historical novel. If our novelists were somewhat less of realists, and would stop their eternal harping on the problem of mixed marriages, which is certainly no problem to those who begin to consider it in the light of a problem, and if they further possessed something of the sympathetic intuition of a Disraeli and the artistic insight into the past of a Sir Walter Scott or Charles Reade, they would find Molko the hero of one of the greatest historical romances ever written. For our purpose of presenting the friend of Caro a few data must suffice.[56]

Solomon Molko was born in Portugal about the year 1501, as a crypto-Jew, or Marrano, where he received the name Diogo Pires. He was endowed with all the graces of Nature calculated to make his personality both pleasing and impressive. He enjoyed an excellent education, and at an early age he was able to speak and write Latin, the learned language of the time. Like so many other Marranos, he received, in secret, instruction in Hebrew subjects, such as the Bible and the Talmud, and even the Cabbala, in which branches of study he acquired great proficiency. His various accomplishments secured for him rapid advancement in official circles. He was very young when he was appointed secretary at one of the high courts of justice in Lisbon. He was also a great favourite at the Court. But neither the duties of his office nor the diversions of Court life were sufficient to fill the vacuum he felt under the false life he led. His thoughts and his heart were with Judaism, over whose destiny and his part in it he constantly brooded. This brooding soon resulted in all sorts of visions and wild dreams, which visited him day and night. At the first impulse, supposed to have been given him by the famous adventurer David Reubeni, who was then travelling in Europe in the questionable capacity of an ambassador of the lost Ten Tribes, he was initiated into the covenant of Abraham, and became a Jew. This occurred about the year 1523. He then entered upon a course of ascetic practices, fasting for many days without interruption, depriving himself of sleep, and spending his time in prayer and meditation, which was naturally followed by more visions of an apocalyptic nature. The visions were manifested to him, as in the case of Caro, by a Maggid, who communed with him from heaven in dreams. In obedience to the command of this heavenly messenger, he left Portugal for Turkey, which was a safer place for men of Molko's cast of mind. There, as it would seem, he spent the next five or six years. The appearance of this enthusiastic, handsome young mystic made a deep impression upon the Jewish communities visited by him. Molko probably visited also Jerusalem and Safed in Palestine. There is no positive evidence for this fact, but it is hardly possible that he should have failed to explore the places which he saw with his spiritual eye in his mystic moments. Legend reports also that even after his death he would pay visits to his *fiancée* in Safed on every Friday evening, reading in her presence the Sanctification-Benediction over the cup of wine (*Kiddush*) with which the Sabbath is initiated. This would doubtless suggest that he had once been at this place.[57] The end of the year 1529 finds him at Ancona in Italy where he preached on the advent of the Messiah. His sermons seem to have made a great sensation, and were listened to by large crowds, both Jews and Christians, including some high dignitaries of the Church. Some time after this he repaired to Rome, in which city he had again all sorts of visions and dreams. He soon gained access to the Pope, Clement VII, who felt rather attracted toward him, and together with certain cardinals, not less favourable to Molko than the Holy Father himself, protected him against the dangers threatening him from the Roman police as a renegade from the Christian faith. He predicted to the Pope the flood which was soon to come upon Rome, and went to Venice for a time. He returned to Rome and had several more conferences with the Pope and other high personages, all the time preaching publicly repentance as a preparation for the approaching advent of the Messiah, in which he was to play a conspicuous part, either as the forerunner of the Messiah or as the Messiah ben Joseph. But all the patronage he had did not protect him from the intrigues of his deadly enemy, the Jewish physician Jacob Mantino, who is not to be held entirely guiltless of his falling into the hands of the Emperor, Charles V. The latter, in turn, handed him over to the Inquisition. The end was that Molko was burned as a heretic in Mantua, in 1532. When approaching the stake, he was offered pardon in the name of the Emperor, if he would recant. Molko replied that he longed for the death of a martyr, to become "a burnt-offering of sweet savour unto the Lord; if he had anything to repent of, it was that he had been a Christian in his youth."

Caro's acquaintance with Molko must have been formed either in Adrianople or in Salonica, both of which cities were visited by the latter during his travels. The acquaintance grew into a strong attachment, at least on the part of Caro, who thought himself indebted to Molko for certain spiritual influences which he had on his life. Thus said the Mentor-Angel to Caro, "God brought thee together with my chosen Solomon to see whether thou wilt know him, and it was a merit (or rather, good fortune) that thou didst learn to know him and also didst learn from him to fear me."[58] It is, however, an exaggeration to think that it was Molko who converted Caro to his belief in the Cabbala, or that it was the martyr-death of Molko that incited in Caro the desire to end his life in a similar manner. Cabbala was in the air; the greatest men of Israel were committed to it, and it required no special agencies to make Caro one of its adherents. The fact is, that Molko was lovable, and Caro loved him. That the tragic death of Molko made a deep impression upon Caro, and mingled with his dreams and visions, only proves that the legalistic studies which formed the main occupation of Caro's life, do not incapacitate a man for the qualities of admiration and love. As to the longing of Caro for the death of a martyr, we have seen that he had the privilege of calls from the Mentor-Angel while he was still a resident of Nicopolis, and it was there that he received the promise of martyrdom for the first time from his heavenly messenger. This occurred about 1522, long before Caro even knew of the existence of such a person as Molko. It is to be noted that martyrdom in case of necessity is a regular command, forming one of the six hundred and thirteen laws. According to some authorities, the supreme act of martyrdom, like the fulfilment of any other command of the Law, should be preceded by a benediction, namely, "Blessed art thou, O Lord our God, King of the world, who hast sanctified us with thy commandments, and hast bidden us to hallow thy Name among the many." Now, if we consider how anxious a legist of Caro's frame of mind must have been to fulfil a com-mandment—the characteristic of the legalistic saints of every generation—no further explanation is needed for Caro's longing for martyrdom. It was simply his desire to fulfil a commandment of the Torah. As one of the saints expresses it: If the Heavenly Court were to decree hell punishment against him, he would jump into the pit with all his might and without a moment's delay, embracing with joy the op-portunity to fulfil a Divine command.[59]

Much less is known of the life of the second Solomon— Solomon Halevi Alkabez. There are no records enabling us to determine the place where he was born, nor the dates of his birth and death. We know, however, that he flourished about the first half of the sixteenth century, that he was the disciple of Joseph Taytasak, Rabbi of Salonica, and that later he became the master and brother-in-law of the famous Cabbalist Moses Cordovero. His acquaintance with Caro

probably dates from the third decade of that century, he
having met him in Salonica or Adrianople. Alkabez was a
scholar and a poet. Of his books it suffices to mention here
the *Manoth ha-Levi* (Gifts of the Levite), a homiletical
commentary on the Book of Esther, in which he showed his
wide acquaintance with Rabbinic literature, having had, as
it seems, access to manuscripts which he very judiciously
used in the said work. The story is that the title of the book
was suggested by the fact that it formed a present to his
fiancée on the occasion of the Purim festival. His father-in-
law and the girl, the tradition is, were more pleased with
this gift than with costly jewelry, which young men were
then in the habit of sending to their sweethearts on the day
of Purim. But he is best known by his poem, *Lechah Dodi,*
"Come, my Beloved, etc.," with which he and his friends
used to receive Queen Sabbath. The Sabbath was to him a
living reality to be welcomed after a six days' absence with
that expectant joy and impatient love with which the groom
meets his bride. It is perhaps one of the finest pieces of
religious poetry in existence, and has been translated by
Herder and by Heine into German. Catholic Israel, whose
love for Bride Sabbath and whose hope for final redemption
it echoed so well, soon honoured Alkabez' poem with a
prominent place in almost all its rituals; and the *Lechah
Dodi* is now sung all over the world on Sabbath eve, when
Queen Sabbath holds her *levée* in the tents of Jacob.[60]

To return to Caro and Safed: When Caro arrived in
Palestine, which could not well have been earlier than after
the middle of the year 1536, Safed was already grown to
the size of one thousand Jewish families. The additions to
the community were mostly made up of Spanish and
Portuguese exiles, who were soon in a position to build a
second synagogue for the purpose of accommodating their
newly arrived countrymen.[61] Their numbers were so increased that they considered themselves strong enough to
attempt to force their special usages with regard to the
regulating of dowries upon other sections of the community.
The Spanish language, the vernacular of the Sephardim,
became soon the teaching medium in the schools, suppressing
all other languages.[62] They quickly won, both by their numbers and by the distinction of their leaders, such an exceptional position that we find men of importance and standing

among the native Jewish population vain enough to call themselves Sephardim, the name common to Jews hailing from Spain and Portugal.[63] There is reason to believe that at this time also a German Jewish community was established in Safed perhaps presided over by the father-in-law of Caro. We have furthermore references to a Portuguese synagogue, an Italian synagogue, and a Greek synagogue, dating from about the same time.[64] The constitution of these communities seems to have been strictly autonomous, each community having its own synagogue, its own preacher, and its own Yeshibah. They were even, to a certain extent, jealous of every outside interference, and it was expected that each new arrival would join the congregation composed of his own fellow-countrymen.[65] On the other hand, there is evidence that they had a *Beth ha-Wa'ad* (meeting house), forming a sort of general board consisting of the Rabbis of the various synagogues, to which occasionally Rabbis attached to no congregation in particular were invited. This board probably dealt only with matters of grave importance and of general interest.[66]

The means of gaining a livelihood were various. The natives, or, as they were called, the Moriscos, were probably still engaged in peddling, as their ancestors had been.[67] There is also evidence that they cultivated the ground in the neighbouring villages, producing wheat, barley, beans, cotton, oil, wine, and figs. Those, again, who possessed some capital, which was probably the case with many of the Spanish immigrants, were engaged in trading, exporting grain, wine, and oil to Damascus and other places, and importing from there articles for which there was a demand in Safed.[68] There also grew up in Safed a large trade in the weaving of wool and in the manufacturing of clothes; these trades were entirely in the hands of the Jews.[69] Indeed, R. Levi ben Chabib, of whom I shall speak presently, sarcastically asks whether it was because of the large quantity of clothes manufactured there that Safed arrogated to itself the leadership of Judaism.[70] Wealthy Jews in Constantinople and in Damascus would, as it seems, send ships laden with wool to Safed for the purpose of encouraging the wool industry there and giving employment to those engaged in it. About the year 1600, such a ship, containing wool to the value of nearly 100,000 *Keseph* and 10,000 *Keseph* in cash for the desperate poor, was wrecked on its voyage, which caused

distress in Safed.[71] There was also in Safed a great demand
for such artisans as weavers, smiths, tailors, tanners, wood-
workers, and builders. There was probably also some demand
for men connected with the printing trade, which was established in Safed about the year 1653 by two German Jews.
The first book printed there was the commentary of R.
Moses Alsheich to Daniel, and was followed by several
other works. "The print of these books is excellent, and
testifies to the good taste and the prosperity of the Safed
community at that time." [72] The only profession for which
there was not any room in Safed was that of teacher, since
the community was, we are told, sufficiently provided with
schools and instructors. Nor was there any place for servants,
as everybody, as we have seen, attended to his own domestic
work.[73] The prosperity was so great that they were envied
for it by their brethren abroad. Thus a Roman Jew writes
in 1543, "The good message has come from the land of
Desire (Palestine) that the Lord remembered his people
and his land and the Children of Israel, granting to them
wealth and honour in most trades." [74]

However, men did not settle in Palestine for the purpose
of developing the natural resources of the country. What
led them there was, as indicated above, the spiritual wealth
which the Holy Land alone could afford. In such wealth,
Safed, at this period, was particularly rich. I have already
mentioned the letter of Shlomel, with its reference to the
population of Safed and the various Talmudical colleges
maintained there.[75] Though Shlomel writes at the beginning
of the seventeenth century, there is nothing to indicate that
the last decades of the sixteenth century witnessed a particular increase of immigration out of proportion to that of
the preceding decades. Indeed, we shall see later on that
in his time the glory of Safed was already on the wane.
We have the right to assume that the number of Rabbis of
the sixteenth century was at least not smaller than that of the
seventeenth. Shlomel's statistics are, of course, like all statistics, not very reliable; indeed, the number three hundred
occurs too frequently in the letters relating to Safed. It has
also to be pointed out that the term "Rabbi" with Shlomel
does not exactly mean the officiating minister, but simply
a man who, both on account of his learning and his saintly
life—two indispensable qualifications for a Rabbi in olden
times—might easily perform the functions of a Rabbi. Still,
there can be little doubt that no place in Jewish history

since the destruction of the Holy Temple could point to so brilliant a gathering of men, so great in their respective branches, so diversified in the objects of their study, and so united by the dominant thought of religion, as were attracted to Safed during the greater part of the sixteenth century.

The fame of the "saints and men of action" must have spread "outside of the land" early in the sixteenth century, and it was probably the desire for their society which determined Caro in his choice of Safed. For such was the promise given him by the Mentor-Angel: "I will give thee places to walk among these that stand by" (Zechariah 3:7), "making thee worthy to go up to the land of Israel and join there my beloved Solomon and the Associates to learn and to teach." [76]

The most prominent among these was doubtless R. Jacob Berab.[77] Berab, who was an emigrant from Castile, Spain, and held the office of Rabbi in various Jewish communities, settled in Safed about the year 1535, where he soon became the recognised head of the Jewish community, which consisted at that time of at least seven congregations. It seems that he gathered around him some of the best minds of Safed, who acknowledged themselves as his disciples. Caro himself recognised him as an authority, quoting him as a rule with the epithet "our great master." Berab has left us a volume of Responsa, to which are appended commentaries on certain portions of the Talmud, but he is best known to history by his unsuccessful efforts to re-introduce the institution of "Ordination" (*Semichah*) among the Jews. This attempt was made in the year 1538, and bears evidence to the high position held in Jewry by the sages of Safed, both by their numbers and by the weight of their great learning: this fact alone could have emboldened Berab and his friends to embark upon their daring enterprise.[78] Ordination, as they intended it, was not the mere ceremonious laying on of hands in connexion with a candidate for Rabbinical office with some solemn speech attendant thereon. What Berab aimed at, was the re-establishment of the body of the Sanhedrin (that could exist only in Palestine), which would wield supreme authority over the whole of Israel in various ways, thus forming a new Jewish spiritual centre. His great opponent in this matter was R. Levi ben Chabib, a former resident of Safed, living then at Jerusalem.

This is not the place to enter into the arguments of both

sides, which both parties drew from the Talmud. There may have been also some petty personal jealousies; some of the arguments are certainly of a rather petty character, particularly on Berab's side. Berab was something of what we might call a strong man, of strenuous tendencies, and his treatment of Ben Chabib was by no means tender. But there is no doubt that Berab's aspirations were of great national importance, and if realised would have served to strengthen the bonds of union in Israel. The scholars of Safed worked in harmony with Berab, twenty-five of their number signing the epistle sent to the sages of Jerusalem that contained the resolution of the former to re-introduce Ordination. The resolution was soon translated into action, Berab ordaining four elders, representing the flower of Safed's scholarship.[79] Caro, who was one of the four, and apparently figured also among the signatories of the correspondence with Jerusalem, is especially complimented by his Mentor-Angel for the zeal shown by him for the great cause. He must also have entertained the hope that he might succeed one day where Berab had failed; at least, he received the heavenly promise that he would be the instrument through which Ordination should be restored.[80] This is another of the Mentor-Angel's unfulfilled prophecies.

The excitement of the Ordination controversy subsided with the death of Berab, which occurred shortly after 1540. Caro, who devoted his time to lecturing to his disciples, writing his books, and attending to social work, or, as it is usually called in Hebrew literature, the "needs of the congregation," was constantly growing in influence and authority. He apparently felt trouble in his mind about this interference with his studies, for we find that the Mentor-Angel has to comfort him and make it clear that the social work in which he was engaged was also a part of his duties, which he had no right to ignore.[81]

His most formidable rival was R. Moses ben Joseph Trani, who settled in Safed in the year 1518, and became Rabbi of the Spanish congregation Beth Jacob, and the head of the Yeshibah connected with it, in 1521, which offices he retained until his death in 1580.[82] Like Caro, he was ordained by Berab, to whom he stood in the relation of a colleague-disciple, and he showed even more zeal for the honour of his master than Caro. Indeed, he resents in one place the indifference of Caro to the attacks made on Berab in connexion with certain legal decisions.[83] Trani wrote several works, one of which was of a semi-philosophical nature on doctrinal questions, but he is chiefly famous for the collection of his Responsa, which show him to have been a Talmudist of the first order and regarded as such by his contemporaries. Though generally, like all other Rabbis of the place, confined in his jurisdiction to his own congregation, he seems to have been regarded by the whole community as a specialist in real estate questions. "I have," he says, "been one of the first in everything relating to the holiness of the land in the city of Safed since the year 5335. God put it in my heart to build up the desolate places thereof. I have watched over them in most of their building enterprises, that no man should encroach upon the property of his neighbour, and other matters relating to questions of surveying and ancient rights, even with regard to the synagogues which were built all these years, when (the worshippers) coming from Turkey and other places divided according to their languages." [84]

Several cases occurred in which Trani had the opportunity to clash with Caro's opinions; the most important of these seems to have been one in connexion with the observance of the Sabbatical Year, the laws in regard to which were not considered entirely obsolete in the Holy Land. The great majority of scholars, however, were in favour of Caro's opinion, to enforce it as the norm for the practice.[85] This case arose in the year 1574, a year before Caro's death, but his recognition as a master of the Holy Land or, as he expressed it somewhere else, "the great codifier of the Holy Land," came long before. In almost all the Opinions of that generation, Caro's signature appears first, and his Yeshibah had, according to tradition, a seating capacity of seven hundred students.[86] This is probably an exaggeration, but the attendance at his Yeshibah was undoubtedly very large, and included some of the greatest names of the time. As one of the Safed scholars expressed it, "We are all his disciples, drinking his waters, and bound to honour him." [87] Among these, Cordovero and Alsheich deserve special mention, both because of their connexion with the history of Safed and their influence on posterity.

R. Moses Cordovero was born in 1522 and died in 1570. Little is known about his private life except that he married a sister of Solomon Alkabez. In Talmud he was a disciple of Caro, who was apparently very proud of him and applied to him the verse, "My son, if thy heart be wise, my heart shall rejoice, even mine" (Proverbs 23:15). We know also that he acted as one of the Dayanim (Judges) of Safed and had a Yeshibah of his own. A Responsum of his incorporated in the Responsa Collection of Caro, testifies to his ability as a Rabbinical scholar, but his fame rests on his mystical work, in which he by far excelled all his predecessors.[88] At the early age of twenty, the Voice warned him to "heal the altar of the Lord which is broken down," under which he understood his neglect of a proper study of the mysteries of the Torah.[89] The "healing" came from his brother-in-law, Alkabez, in whom he perceived a holy angel come down from heaven, and who apparently figured at that period as the leading Cabbalist of Safed. Even Caro himself did not hesitate to seek instruction from Alkabez about a certain obscure passage in the Zohar.[90] At the age of twenty-six (1548), we find Cordovero in the company of the Associates (*Chaberim*). This was a society consisting of mystically inclined students of Safed, apparently presided over by Alkabez. Very little has come down to us relative to the activity of this society, beyond the fact that its members used occasionally to undertake excursions to visit the graves of the ancient Rabbis supposed to be buried in the neighbourhood of Safed, on which occasions they would discuss mystical subjects.[91] But we possess in manuscript a list of moral precepts drawn up by Cordovero, of which there is good reason to assume that they were not meant exclusively for the guidance of their author, but formed a sort of hand-book for all the Associates. The following extracts will convey some idea of the frame of mind and the tender conscience of these men.

They are bidden not to divert their thoughts from the words of the Torah and things holy, so that their hearts become the abode of the *Shechinah;* not to be betrayed into anger, as anger delivers man into the power of sin; not to speak evil of any creature, including animals; never to curse any being, but to accustom oneself to bless even in moments of anger; never to take an oath, even on the truth; never to speak an untruth under any condition; to be careful not to be included among the four classes excluded from the Divine Presence, namely, the hypocrites, the liars, the scoffers, and the tale-bearers; not to indulge in banquets except on religious occasions. They are enjoined to mingle their minds with the minds of their fellow-men (that is, not to stand aloof from the world, but to share both in its joys and in its sorrows), and to behave in a kindly spirit toward their fellow-men, even though they be transgressors; to meet with one of the Associates for one or two hours every day for the purpose of discussing matters spiritual; to talk over with an Associate every Friday the deeds accomplished during the week, and then set out for the reception of Queen Sabbath; to pronounce Grace in a loud voice, letter by letter and word by word, so that the children at the table can repeat after the reader; to confess their sins before every meal and before going to sleep; to use the sacred language when speaking with the Associates, and to let this be always the language of conversation on Sabbath with other scholars as well. In another set of precepts drawn up by Alkabez, dating from this time and probably also meant for the guidance of these Associates, we have the ordinance that the students should rebuke or admonish each other, but the person admonished or rebuked must not make any reply in his defence before the lapse of three days.[92]

The most prominent among those for whose benefit these regulations were composed was the author himself, Cordovero, whose interviews with Alkabez seem to have been more frequent and of a more intimate nature than those of the other Associates. At a later period the relations of the latter to their master appear to have been almost forgotten, and they are quoted as the Associates of Cordovero. Indeed, it would seem that it was the great popularity achieved by the works of Cordovero that is responsible for the comparative oblivion into which the mystical writings of Alkabez fell, so that the greater part of them remained unpublished.[93]

Cordovero's *magnum opus* is the *Pardes* (the Garden), the clearest and most rational exposition of the Cabbala in existence, distinguished by the same qualities of methodical thought and logical argument which distinguished Caro's works in the department of things legal. The *Pardes* gave rise to a great number of works written by various mystics in Safed, in Italy, and in Germany.[94] The book is still considered a standard authority, even by modern scholars who have ever written anything worth reading about the Cabbala. Cordovero wrote besides this many other works, some of which are extant only in manuscript. The library of the Jewish Theological Seminary of America possesses a fine copy of his famous work *Alimah*, known from quotations by certain mystics. But these by no means fully represent his literary activity. R. Menahem Azariah, of Fano, in Italy, one of the greatest of Cordovero's students, states that the *Pardes*, in itself a big folio volume, forms only a thirtieth part of the works which Cordovero wrote, not counting many additions, appendixes, and a number of larger and smaller treatises which he composed.[95] His master, Caro, who survived him, gave the funeral oration at his death, in which he spoke of him as "the Holy Ark of the Torah, to be hidden away in the grave," whilst Loria is said to have seen two pillars of fire attending the hearse, a compliment shown by Heaven only to one or two men in a generation. Loria is also reported to have applied to him, in allusion to his name (Moses), the well-known phrase, "Moses is true, and his teaching is true." [96]

The second of the disciples of Caro deserving especial mention is R. Moses Alsheich, who survived his master for many years, being still alive in the year 1593. The master of his early youth was probably Joseph Taytasak. We possess from Alsheich a volume of Responsa in which his opinions in matters of the law were solicited by various Rabbis of repute. He also wrote Talmudical discourses and a commentary to the *Midrash Rabbah* lost to us. He lectured in two Yeshiboth in Safed (which Vital attended in the capacity of a pupil), and performed all the other functions of a Rabbi of that time. He is, however, best known by his homiletical Commentary on the Bible, which was studied both by preachers and laymen for centuries afterward, and is still popular with preachers in various countries. This Commentary is usually cited under the title, "the Holy Alsheich." Loria gave the testimony that most of his interpretations "hit the truth," though in spite of the efforts of Vital he did not admit him into his mystical circle.[97]

Besides these and other Rabbis known more or less to posterity, we have in the contemporary literature any number of references to sages and saints of Safed flourishing about this time, in addition to a goodly number of Rabbis and students whose spiritual pedigree cannot be easily determined. The influence of these scholars was not confined to the schools. A religious atmosphere seems to have pervaded all classes of the Jewish population, so that the impression the Safed of the sixteenth century leaves on us is that of a revival camp in permanence, constituted of penitents gathered from all parts of the world. Life practically meant for them an opportunity for worship, to be only occasionally interrupted by such minor considerations as the providing of a livelihood for their families and the procuring of the necessary taxes for the government. Prayer was the main and universal occupation. For this purpose special teachers were appointed to instruct women and children in the liturgy and in the prescribed benedictions. But the regular order of the service, with its fixed hours, morning, afternoon, and evening, did not satisfy their longing for prayer. For them the day began in the middle of the night, when the "learned" and the "men of action" would repair to the synagogues dressed in black, seating themselves upon the floor and reading a special liturgy, the burden of which was mourning over the destruction of the Holy Temple and the downfall of the people of God, and which concluded with a confession of the sins of Israel delaying the redemption. The example set by them seems soon to have infected the general Jewish public. The man who was especially distinguished for his religious activity among the masses was the mystic R. Abraham Halevi Beruchim. His main work was of a missionary nature. He was constantly preaching to the multitudes and exhorting Israel to repentance. In the middle of the night he would rise and walk through the Jewish quarter, exclaiming in tears, "My brethren of the House of Israel! Is it not known to you that our Strength, the very Divine Presence, is in exile because of our sins; that our Holy Temple is laid in ashes; that Israel is subjected to the most bitter persecutions, saintly men and women being daily martyred by sword and by fire. . . .? And ye, my brethren, allow yourselves to enjoy your sleep on your beds in quiet and rest. Come, my brethren; come, my friends! Rise, ye holy children, blessed by the Lord, and let us supplicate the Lord our God, the King who sitteth on the throne of Mercy." Thus he used to walk about, knocking on the doors, giving the inhabitants no rest until they rose and went to their places of worship, so that at one o'clock in the morning the voice of prayer or of the study of the Torah could be heard from all the synagogues. On Friday afternoon, again, he would go about in the market-place, in the high-roads, reminding the people to be prompt in their preparations for the coming day, so that they might not, by being late, become involved in the sin of the desecration of the Sabbath.[98] The eve of the New Moon offered another opportunity for an additional service, when all the people fasted, and "men, women, and students" would spend the day in supplications, confession of sin, and in various ascetic practices. The eve of the seventh day of Passover, of the first day of the Feast of Weeks, of the Day of Atonement, and of the seventh day of the Tabernacle Feast were also distinguished by special readings from the Scriptures and the chanting of hymns, lasting nearly the whole of the night.

R. Abraham Halevi was probably assisted in his missionary work by certain "saints and men of action" of whom it is reported that they used, on certain occasions, to preach on the subjects of meekness, sin, and repentance. Possibly they were members of the society Tent of Peace (*Succath Shalom*), mentioned by R. Eliezer Azkari, for which he wrote his devotional treatise, *Sepher Charedim*. In this he tried to show how "those that tremble at the commandments of our God" (Ezra 10:3) should consecrate the whole of man, in his various functions and different occupations, to the service of the Lord. The thought absorbing the minds of the "tremblers" and forming the object of their discussions at their meetings, was the delay of the advent of the Messiah, and the sins responsible for this delay, but it was also a part of their programme to cause "the many to turn away from sin" by lectures and exhortations. Like the Associates of Cordovero, the members of this society were also pledged to auricular confession, each of them giving at their weekly meetings a full and detailed account of his actions during the preceding week. The necessity of having to lay bare one's life before his fellow-men, and the shame following upon it in the case of an unworthy action would, so they thought, prove a preventive against sin. It should, however, be remarked that Vital, notwithstanding all his other vagaries and ascetic tendencies, protested against this institution, and declined to follow his friends in its practice.[99]

Besides the Tent of Peace, we have also on record the existence of a Society of Penitents, especially distinguished for its ascetic practices, which were of a very severe nature. Some of its members, we are told, refrained from food and drink during the day, performed their afternoon devotions in tears, and put on sackcloth and ashes. Others, again, observed every week a fast extending over two or three days and nights in succession. R. Elijah de Vidas, in his attempt to show how much one can accomplish in the ascetic line, points with evident pride to these Penitents, saying: "I saw many of them rise in the middle of the night, when they would commence to study, which occupied them until the morning, and then fast the whole of the day. All this they were able to accomplish by special Divine aid, for man does not live by bread alone." [100] Of the Associates of Cordovero we read that some among them used to observe a fast extending over three or four days and nights, at the change of the four seasons of the year. It is further recorded that there were many pious scholars who refrained from wine and meat during week-days, whilst others observed on certain days of the year the same laws of levitical purity in respect to their food as the priests in olden times when eating the heave-offering and other sacrificial pieces.

It should, however, be remarked that "doing penance" and chastisement of the flesh were not considered by them as synonymous with repentance. Repentance meant chiefly the absolute determination never to return to sin at the very risk of one's life, which must precede all regeneration of the heart. As Azkari himself expresses it, "Fasts and ascetic practices are vanity and the work of error without this preceding resolution," and he goes on to quote his contemporary, the Saint R. Jacob Gavinezo, who communicated to him the fact that a man committed a most atrocious crime after a continuous fast of three days. Like the sacrifice in the Temple, penance is only of value when preceded by purification of the heart, humility, and meekness.[101]

It is hardly needful to say that charity formed an important item in the Safed scheme of salvation. The injunction of the mystic is to give alms every day according to one's means.[102] This injunction, though originally intended for a small circle, was accepted by the general public, following the example of the saints of old, who used always to make some donation to the poor before beginning their prayers. The custom in Safed was to make a regular collection during the morning prayers in the synagogues. The men, however, with special aspirations to saintliness would tax themselves to the amount of twenty per cent of their income, and it is stated that even among the poor there were persons known to give two tithes. Others, again, would adopt boys and girls early orphaned, educating them in their own families, and bringing them into the holy state of matrimony when they approached the marriageable age.

Yet Safed shows certain characteristics of its own which

greatly redeem it from many an unpleasant feature which we are accustomed to associate with the modern revival camp. It is true that the strain was great, salvation being the absorbing topic of the community, and the terror of sin delaying this salvation ever present. No opportunity was allowed to pass for reminding men that Zion was still in ruins, and that man is a sinful creature and in need of grace, hence the injunction to confess sins before meals and before retiring to sleep, whilst the 137th Psalm, "By the rivers of Babylon we sat, etc.," was added to the Grace after meals.

That this strain should produce certain psychological phenomena more interesting to the pathologist than to the theologian, is hardly necessary to state. The literature of the time, abounding in stories of all sorts of demoniacs, bears ample evidence to this fact.[103] We also have stories of men who through their importunate storming of Heaven for Salvation were, for some relapse from grace, suddenly hurled down to the very depths of hell, and doomed to perdition. The most tragic among these is the story of Joseph de la Reina, who flourished in Safed in the early decades of the sixteenth century. De la Reina is a sort of Jewish Faust, who, in his passion for salvation, did not hesitate to employ certain exorcisms and conjurations of a very daring nature. He succeeded in bringing the Evil One into his power, whose destruction is a preliminary condition to the advent of the Messiah. But in an unfortunate moment he was persuaded to show compassion to this fallen angel, allowing him to smell of the frankincense. The fiend then regained his former strength, and achieved full mastery over his captor, who, after realising his fall, abandoned himself to the most revolting immoralities, and ended his life by suicide.[104]

In spite of this strain, however, with all its hysteria and its dire results in some cases, it must not be thought that the Safed community was constantly on the mourning-bench and spent all its vitality in groaning and lamentations. Cordovero laid down the rule not to indulge in pretentious meals except on religious occasions, but these religious occasions were happily not infrequent, and the people were apparently not slow to avail themselves of the opportunities given to them. The Sabbath was such an opportunity, being held as a day of joy and recreation in every respect, physically and spiritually. Fasting was not only strictly prohibited on the Sabbath, but it was considered a religious work to partake of three meals, which, Caro's Mentor-Angel to the contrary notwithstanding, had to be distinguished by certain delicacies. Wine also was served at these meals, which even the Penitents would drink. The meals were further distinguished by a special set of hymns sung or chanted during the intervals between the various courses. The prescribed ritual, again, in the synagogue was all joy and promise, containing no confession or the slightest reference to anything of a despondent nature. Indeed, the Sabbath should give man a foretaste of the blissful Messianic times when sin and sorrow shall have disappeared from the world.[105] Reluctant to part with these hours of serene peace and unalloyed joy, and anxious to prolong them as much as possible, the Sabbath received an extension both at the beginning and at the end. Thus they would, early Friday afternoon, dress in their best clothes and set out in groups to receive Queen Sabbath, with song and praise, reciting certain Psalms and singing certain hymns composed for the occasion. In like manner, they would refrain from work for several hours after the Sabbath sun had set, and spend them in chanting hymns and in feasting. They had even a special society whose members would meet to spend the end of the Sabbath, reaching way into the night, with song and dance. The New Moon was also observed as a partial holiday, affording an opportunity for relaxation and enjoyment, not to speak of festivals prescribed in the Bible, such as the Passover, the Pentecost, and the Feast of Tabernacles.

All these things must have contributed more or less toward mitigating the evil effects of an exaggerated asceticism. Nor must it be forgotten that joy forms a prominent feature in the programme of the mystic. His maxim was: the Divine light reaching man through the fulfilment of the commandment is only in proportion to the joy expressed by him when performing a religious action.[106]

Moreover, it must be borne in mind that Safed was just as famous for its scholarship as for its piety. Most of the leaders of the ascetic and mystical movements were at the same time distinguished scholars. Ranting in such intellectual society was just as much out of place as idle brooding and unprofitable gloom. The study of the Torah, to which they were so much devoted, was always considered a joy, and the Safed of the sixteenth century must have been a veritable Paradise on earth to any man with a tendency toward intellectual pursuits. If his interests lay in the regions of the visible, he would attend the lectures of Caro, Trani, or Sagis, and various other Rabbis at the head of the great Yeshiboth of the place. If he were mystically inclined, he would attach himself to Alkabez or Cordovero; if he had a taste for homiletics, he would go to listen to the Biblical expositions of Alsheich, whilst he might also spare an hour for the lectures of R. Samuel de Useda on the Chapters of the Fathers (*Pirke Aboth*), whose work on this ethical tractate is still considered a standard commentary. He might besides this pay a visit with profit to the ancient R. David ben Zimra, who, though at the period of his second settlement in Safed, he must already have reached the age of ninety, was still a member of the General Board mentioned above, and interested in public affairs. An occasional walk with Vital might also have possessed its own attractions, for, besides being an adept in the Cabbala, he was, like so many devotees of nature-mysticism, likewise interested in alchemy, astronomy, astrology, magic, and all kinds of occult sciences. In the way of recreation one might attend recitals of the mystical bard, R. Israel Nagara, the author of the hymn book *Zemiroth Israel,* who, though somewhat "vividly erotic" in his metaphors, counted angels among his auditors, and probably came often to Safed on visits to his father, R. Joseph Nagara, a famous scribe of that city.[107]

Safed reached the zenith of its fame with the advent of Loria.[108] R. Isaac Loria was born in Jerusalem in the year 1534. He was a descendant of the famous German family Loria, on account of which fact he was also called Isaac Ashkenazi. It is not impossible that his ancestors came from the Rhine Provinces, from which most of the earlier scions of the Loria family hailed. Elijah Loanz (flourished about the end of the sixteenth century), who claimed some relationship with our Loria, was a native of Frankfort. One branch of this family settled in Poland, whilst the other seems to have emigrated to Palestine. The emigration of German Jews to Mohammedan countries was by no means confined to this case. The impulse to this expatriation from a land in which they had lived for many centuries and in which they had almost the claim of original settlers, came from the Epistle of a certain Joseph Zarphathi, whom fate drove from Germany to Turkey in his early youth. In this Epistle he described "the happy lot of the Jews under the Crescent as compared with their hard fate under the shadow of the Cross," and called upon them to escape from the German house of bondage and emigrate to Turkey. If the German Jews, he said, could realise but a tenth part of the prosperity awaiting them in

Turkey, they would brave rain and snow, and would rest neither by day nor by night before reaching there. Another inducement that he offered them was that there is a route to the Holy Land lying open to them through Turkey. Though distance forbade emigration *en masse* from Germany, there can be no doubt that Zarphathi's Epistle was not quite without effect, for we soon find small congregations, both in Turkey and in Palestine, composed of Jewish emigrants from Germany. The Karaite Elijah Bashiatsi, of Adrianople, even complained of the bad influence of these newly arrived Rabbinical students from Germany, alarming the community with their fringes and phylacteries, and their long gowns and their hoods, making themselves conspicuous and overawing the crowds.[109]

The birth of Loria was, as in the case of so many wondermen, heralded to his father by the prophet Elijah, who said unto him: ". . . Be it known unto thee that the Holy One, blessed be he, sent me to bring thee the good message that thy wife will bear thee a son. Thou shalt name him Isaac; he will deliver Israel from the power of the Husks (that is, the powers of evil and contamination which are at war with the powers of the good and the holy, and obscure them); and he will redeem many souls that are undergoing the agony of transmigration, and through him shall be revealed the teaching of the Cabbala to the world." He was further bidden not to begin the initiation of his son into the covenant of Abraham until aware of the prophet's presence in the synagogue. The father did as he was bidden, and the boy proved indeed a wonder-child. At the tender age of eight he was considered to be a marvel of Rabbinical learning, so that none of the Jerusalem scholars could compete with him in a Talmudic discussion. Unfortunately, the father, Solomon, died about this time, and left his widow in such needy circumstances that she was not able even to procure the necessary books which her son required for his studies. There was nothing left for them to do but emigrate to Cairo, where her brother, the wealthy tax-farmer Mordecai Francis, resided. Mordecai received them kindly, and made generous provision for his sister and those dependent upon her. Her son Loria he adopted as his own, and placed him under the care of R. Bezaleel Ashkenazi, the famous author of the *Shittah Mekubezeth*, under whose guidance he continued his Rabbinical studies until he reached the age of fifteen, when he married the daughter of his benefactor.[110] His introduction to the teaching of the Cabbala followed some two years later. According to legend, it took place in the following way: A stranger, whose business transactions led him to Cairo, came one day to perform his devotions at the synagogue in which Loria was in the habit of worshipping. It so happened that he took his seat opposite Loria and ostensibly began to read his prayers from a written book which he held in his hands. Loria, whose curiosity was evidently aroused by the sight of the manuscript, managed to take a glance at the volume, and was surprised to see that its contents embodied the great mysteries of the faith. Whereupon he approached the owner of the book and questioned him as to his person and his profession, and also demanded from him some information as to the contents of the manuscript. The owner, who felt embarrassed by Loria's importunate questioning, stated finally that he was a mere Marrano, and even ignorant of the Hebrew letters of the Torah, and confessed that he was only simulating the reading of the volume in his hands out of sheer shame before the other worshippers, who were all reading their prayers from the prayer-books open before them. Loria then began to urge him to sell him the manuscript, since it was of no real value to its owner. This request was at first refused, but afterwards our Marrano agreed to part with his treasure on condition that Loria would employ his good offices with his father-in-law, the tax-farmer, to have the duties upon the wares he was about to import to Egypt remitted for him.

The book, as it seems, proved to be the Book of Splendour, or *Sepher ha-Zohar,* ascribed to R. Simon ben Yochai, of the second century, and being, as is well known, the main classic of the Cabbalists. Loria then, for eight years, abandoned himself to the study of the Cabbala with all the energy and "fanatical enthusiasm" of which he was capable. The principal subject of his devotion was the Zohar, but it would seem that during the first six years of his study he did not always succeed in divining the real meaning of its supposed author, Simon ben Yochai. However, he received indications from "heaven" that to reach the desired end it would be necessary for him to submit to a more austere mode of living than had been his habit until then. He thereupon retired to a certain village, in the neighbourhood of Cairo, which belonged to his father-in-law, where he built for himself a cottage on the banks of the Nile. Here he lived during the whole week, returning to his family in the city only for the Sabbath. The other six days were spent in strict solitude, and in fasting, praying, and frequent ablutions, besides other kinds of voluntary self-chastisement. This continued for two years, when Loria, by reason of his holy life and complete absorption in meditation upon the holy mysteries, reached the degree of being worthy of the gift of the Holy Spirit, as well as of having communion with the prophet Elijah. Nothing is known of Loria's occupation during the next eight or ten years, preceding his emigration to Safed. We are told that this exodus was undertaken in obedience to a distinct command from Heaven, which announced to him that his tenure of life would be a short one, and ordered him, among other things, to leave the polluted land (Egypt) and go up to Safed in Upper Galilee.[111]

It will have been observed that no mention has been made of Loria's master in the department in which he was most to excel. Legend, which has served us as the source for the preceding description, is quite silent on this point. Nor was there any real need for a master in human shape. For, according to legend, it was the prophet Elijah himself who performed the functions of teacher in the case of Loria. It is further narrated that every night Loria's soul, released from all earthly ties, would ascend to heaven in the company of the "ministering angels," who watched over him until he reached the abode of the Celestials. Upon his arrival there, he would have his choice of attending any of the supermundane academies, in which the souls of departed saints and great sages continue the occupations which formed their moments of bliss in the course of their earthly careers. But it may be humbly suggested also that Loria had, besides, a very fair library, in which, apart from the Zohar, were contained the works of various mystics who had preceded him. We know that he occasionally referred to them, assigning to each his proper place in the chain of mystical tradition. It is also possible that in the beginning he may have received some aid from R. David ben Zimra, at that time the Chief Rabbi of Cairo, who was also a great Cabbalist; as well as from his master, Bezaleel, who is recorded as having been learned in the mysteries of the Torah.[112]

More important is the indebtedness of Loria to Cordovero. This indebtedness is suggested by a passage in the "Writings" of Loria, in which Cordovero is cited as "our master and teacher." [113] The vagueness of the plural, however, as well as the uncertainty as to the genuineness of these "Writings" make it rather hazardous to base an important biographical fact upon them. But we are fully justified in doing so after the evidence of Sambari, who reports that "Cordovero was the master of Loria for a short time," whilst Conforte describes him as a disciple-colleague of Cordovero.[114] This evidence gathers strength from certain occasional remarks in a version of the life of Loria, in which the personal relations between the two masters are not entirely obliterated. Thus we learn that among the "men of wisdom and understanding whom Loria found in Safed upon his arrival there, were Caro, Cordovero, and R. Joseph Ashkenazi." The fact that these three sages were singled out by name, would suggest that Loria came into close relationship with them. From another place it is clear that it was practically Cordovero himself who designated Loria as his successor. Naturally, legend accounts for it by a miracle. Indeed, we are told that it was only to spare Cordovero's sensitiveness that Loria hesitated so long before revealing his greatness to the world.[115] But we may conclude that while Cordovero lived, Loria occupied the inferior position—that is, that of a disciple in the presence of his master.

I lay no claim to be initiated in the science of the invisible, and am thus unable to determine with any exactness how far this indebtedness of Loria to Cordovero extended. To cite a Biblical expression frequently used in such connexion, I am merely "looking through the lattice." And what one can perceive by means of such dim vision is that all the Cabbalists laboured under an awful alternative—the dread of confusing the creature with his Creator, and the dread not less keenly felt of the *horror vacui,* or a God-less world, in addition to the well-known metaphysical, or rather physical, difficulty of the possibility of evolving a finite world from the Infinite. This dread called into being a whole system of emanations and immanations, of straight rays and reflected lights, of radiations and beams, crossing each other and commingling, and forming endless combinations, creating universes. But these universes are, on the other hand, affected by a whole series of checks and balances, or defects and faults, disabling them from becoming identical with the life permeating them, but (just because of these defects) giving them tangible substance, by which process alone the creation of the world, as we see it, becomes possible. Still, this world, notwithstanding the endless gradations and disguises and husks, is not only reached by a Divine Essence, which created it, but is pervaded by it and is full of it. Cordovero's expression with regard to the first immanations, that they are identical and not identical, may be applied also to all other developments in the scale of the universes.[116] They are just effect enough not to be entirely confused with their cause, but in such close proximity or contiguity to the cause that they cannot be thought separated from the cause. Some mystics were bold enough to declare the world not only united with God, but one with God. Even the lowest worm in this scale becomes to a certain extent identical with all the causes of worlds or emanations preceding it. There is, accordingly, a constant blending of the temporal and the eternal. Indeed, the action of the first emanation, which assumes some room for immanation, became possible only by the process of the Divine Essence concentrating itself into itself, and thus making a place for a world or the possibility of emanations. This self-concentration of the Divine, creating space for the universes, or for ideas or attributes from which a universe might evolve, is counteracted by a process of expansion, or an outflow of the Divine Essence, thus making Creation God-full. The impossibility, however, on the part of the universes, or the "vessels," to become a real receptacle for the light emitted from Divine Grace, inasmuch as the receptacle cannot be identical with the thing received, caused a deterioration in the descending *scala* of universes or worlds, which brought about the condition of chaos, in which the origin of evil is to be sought. The chaos is so thorough and so complete that evil cannot be entirely without good, indeed, it would have no existence; whilst the good, in the lower worlds at least, is not entirely free from evil. This is especially the case with this world of ours, the most substantialised. It is the world of the Husks, of mere appearances or disguises, obscuring the real realities, and but for the "sparks," or beams, of the holy and pure scattered in it, it would disappear into nothingness, and be swallowed up by its own unredeemable darkness. The elimination of evil, and the restoration of the world to Divine goodness, is the great problem under which creation is labouring.

Loria is usually described as the author of this system of Concentration, called in Hebrew *Zimzum*. Now, it is true that Cordovero, as far as I could see, only once uses this term in his *Pardes*.[117] But it should be remarked that R. Sabbatai Horwitz, the author of the *Shepha Tal* (Abundance of Dew), an avowed disciple of Cordovero, and considered the best expounder of his system, is constantly operating with Zimzum, at the same time giving the most lucid expositions of the Concentration theory to be found in any Cabbalistic book; but he never so much as mentions Loria. However, I am prepared to accept in good faith the testimony of R. Menahem Azariah of Fano, mentioned above, who spent a large fortune in procuring the writings of Cordovero and in giving them wide circulation, but who subsequently declared that the system of Loria bears the same relation to that of Cordovero as the latter sustains to the Biblical commentaries of Kimchi, which give only the simple meaning of the Scriptures and never touch on the mysteries of the Torah.[118]

Some light perhaps may be thrown on this point by a remark ascribed by legend to Cordovero himself, to the effect that Cordovero on a certain occasion expressed his opinion that there was no real disagreement between his system and that of his successor (Loria); only whilst he himself dwelt more on the aspect of the *Sephiroth* (Emanations), his successor enlarged more on the *Parzuphim,* as they are to be found in the *Idras* of the Zohar.[119] Parzuphim, a Greek term, signifies, when occurring in the regular Rabbinical literature, faces, visages, forehead, and features. The mystic seemed to use the term in the wider sense of the "full stature," comprising all parts of the human body, allegorised, sublimised, to represent attributes and ideas. Starting from the favoured notion of the mystics, conceiving man as a microcosm (or the world in miniature), virtually connected with and focussing all the different orders of creation, and pressing (rather unduly) the logical consequence involved in the Scriptural statement, "So God created man in his own image" and similar verses, the mystic reverses the process, and if he does not exactly create God in the image of man, he conceives even in the ideal universe "man in enlargement," and looks to his image for the illustration of all Existence and Generation. His language then becomes less abstract and his metaphors much bolder. He imposes on himself, it is true, absolute silence with regard to the Infinite, or the Unknowable, or the Super-Essential, who is transcendentalised beyond language and beyond thought. But more intrepid grows his phraseology when he reaches the first manifestation of the Most Hidden of all Hidden, which he terms the Original Man, or the Ideal Man (*Adam Kadmon*), the archetype of creation, endowed with certain qualities making it possible to establish likeness "between the image and him who fashioned it." The danger of this system, with its bold negations on the one hand, and its hazardous "anthropology" on the other, is evident enough and needs no further explanation. It should, however, be remarked that no one felt this danger more deeply and warned against it more emphatically than the Cabbalists themselves. It is sufficient here to refer to the compiler of the Idras, which, as just indicated, were the main source of Loria's inspiration. The Idras may, perhaps, be characterised as the mystical anatomy of the "Original Man." They dilate, naturally, upon the corporeal expressions of the Bible in connexion with the Deity, but add to them also limbs and organs of the human body not occurring in the Scriptures, describing them minutely and explaining them in a theosophic and mystical manner. But this lengthy discourse (especially the so-called Great Idra, claiming to have been promulgated in the circle of the ancient Rabbis) is prefaced by a solemn warning by R. Simon ben Yochai, the alleged hero of this gathering, not to take these metaphors and terms literally. He enjoins them to rise and lift their hands when he pronounces the anathema over those not heeding his warning, with the Scriptural words, "Cursed be the man that maketh any graven or molten image an abomination unto the Lord, the work of the hands of the craftsman, and putteth it in a secret place. And all the people shall answer, and say Amen (Deuteronomy 27:15).

Loria was apparently more given to this branch of the Cabbala than to any other. This is, at least, the impression one receives on examining the works or the hymns attributed to him. There the anthropomorphistic element is more conspicuous, and the terminology more concrete than in the works of his predecessors, and it is not impossible that it was just this novel feature in his teaching which proved attractive to the more daring spirits. But there must have been, besides, something great and attractive about Loria's personality that gave him this overwhelming influence in a city so abounding in great scholars and great mystics as was Safed. This will be more clearly seen if we follow his career in his new home.

The whole ministry of Loria in Safed lasted at the utmost six years.[120] With the exception of R. David ben Zimra, whom he had known in Cairo, there is nothing on record to show that he had any connexion with the leading spirits of Safed before his settling in this city. But we find him soon, as shown before, in the society of Caro and Cordovero, the recognised heads of the Talmudic and mystical schools respectively. His relation to Cordovero was that, as we have already pointed out, of a disciple or disciple-colleague to his master. As to Caro, we are in possession of a Responsum showing that Loria solicited his advice in the decision of a civil case, which suggests a certain subordination on the part of Loria in purely Rabbinic matters. But this did not prevent Caro from being counted, according to legend, among the greatest admirers of Loria. Their relations must have grown more intimate when Loria's son became engaged to a daughter of Caro. Shlomel, to whom we owe the knowledge of this fact, reports in this connexion, in the name of Caro's widow, that when her husband came home from the banquet given in honour of this betrothal, he said to her, "My wife, I can hardly describe to you how much I profited in my knowledge of the secrets of the Torah coming from the mouth of Loria at this banquet. Not even an angel is in possession of such heavenly lore as he displayed this night, his soul being that of an ancient prophet." It should, however, be noted that Shlomel naïvely proceeds to say that Loria rather discouraged Caro in his efforts to become his disciple in the Cabbala, maintaining that Caro's soul was only fit to receive wisdom on the plane of Cordovero. As a proof of this, Loria is supposed to have given the fact, that as often as he began to reveal some great mystery to Caro, the latter would fall asleep, so that Caro himself became convinced that he was not sufficiently prepared for the revelations of Loria.[121]

The ascendency of Loria probably dated from the year 1570, when he succeeded Cordovero as the head of the mystical school. But whilst Cordovero was admired and revered as a saint and a scholar, Loria was looked upon as one of those superhuman beings who, by a special act of Providence, are permitted to visit us mortals for the especial purpose of our salvation. Their real home is heaven, and they come to us only on leave of absence. According to his biographers, his face was shining like the sun, and his thoughts were chaste and holy. In his knowledge of the Divine there was none like him since the glorious days of R. Simon ben Yochai. He was, moreover, master of all the sciences. He knew physiognomy and chiromancy, and understood the conversation of the trees, and the language of the birds, and the speech of the angels. Looking at the forehead of a man he could tell at a glance from what particular source his soul was derived, and the processes of transmigration through which it had passed, and what its present mission was on earth. He also could discern the souls of the wicked which (as a punishment) had taken up their abode in woods and in stone quarries, in the beasts of the field, in insects and unclean birds. He was able to tell men their past as well as predict their future, and to prescribe for them the rules of conduct calculated to make amends for their shortcomings in a previous existence.[122]

The name under which Loria usually appears in this new hagiology is ARI (Lion), forming the anagram of the Hebrew words signifying "the Divine Rabbi Isaac," whilst his disciples and other enthusiastic followers are termed "the Lion-Whelps." Probably they included among their number several of the old Associates of Cordovero who, indeed, under the leadership of Loria seem to have become more consolidated and to have figured more prominently as a compact body than in former days. It is true that we have indications that some of the disciples of Cordovero hesitated for some time in their recognition of the new master, putting him to the test in various ways. But all opposition seems soon to have ceased, so that Loria maintained the field.[123]

The most important acquisition to the Lion-Whelps was R. Chayim Vital who, it seems, had until then pursued his mystical studies entirely independent of the Cabbalists of Safed. At the time of Loria's appearance on the stage, Vital was living in Damascus, occupied in writing a commentary on the Zohar. He paid little attention to the rumours reaching him from Safed, that a great new master had arisen in Israel. These rumours, however, were strengthened by visions in dreams of the night, which, according to legend, Vital could no longer disregard, so that he determined to go to Safed and meet Loria. They had hardly met before Vital had occasion to learn that at last he had found a master. He soon became the most devoted member of Loria's school and the most active in the propagation of his teaching.[124]

The text-book of the school was the Zohar, which Loria would expound to his disciples after due preparation for it on their part. The Idra, referred to above, seems to have been the object of their particular inquiry and curiosity. But it must be remarked that even in the narrow circle of his trusted pupils, Loria was not very communicative in the revelation of what he considered to be the "mystery of mysteries." The few revelations he did make were made, according to the testimony of his disciples, only under protest, at their urgent solicitation and at the very risk of the life of the master, he having been apparently unwilling to reveal such great secrets to insignificant mortals. But even his disciples could not prevail upon him to give a presentation of his system in a book for the benefit of posterity. Nay, even the permission to take down notes of his lectures was given only grudgingly and, as it seems, was withdrawn subsequently.[125]

Next to the mysteries of the Torah, it was apparently the personality of Loria himself which exercised their minds. Loria, it is true, was vaguely known to the general population of Safed as "the Holy Man" and "the Divine Cabbalist." Occasionally he gave an edifying lecture in some synagogue. There is also a tradition that he was a member of the Board of Censors in Safed, composed of various Rabbis who were responsible for the morals of the city, and that he distinguished himself there by defending the honour of a woman who lay under grave suspicion.[126] According to another account, he came also in contact with the world through his business relations, to which he gave up three days of the week.[127] I do not think that this report is correct. It is more probable that he had some competency granted to him by his rich uncle and father-in-law. Be this as it may, there is no doubt that he was best known to the Associates, numbering ten or twelve, who constituted the inner circle of Loria's acquaintance and converted themselves into as many Boswells. None of his movements escaped them. They watched to see how he rose from his bed and when; how he washed his hands, how he cut his nails, how he read his prayers, how he ate his meals, and more often, how he fasted and when; how he said Grace after meals, how he addressed himself to his fellow-men, and what his relations to them were; how he prepared himself for the Sabbath, and how many garments he wore on that day; what songs he intoned during the meal, and how he cut the bread, and what shape the table had at which these meals were served. This fitted in well with their system, in which man, as already hinted, plays the important part, especially the "superman," surrounded by that Divine halo which makes him, to use a Talmudical expression, a partner of the Holy One, blessed be he, in the creation of the world.[128]

In the Talmud, this distinction of creating worlds is bestowed on the man who administers justice.[129] In the Cabbala, this function of creating worlds, and not less of destroying worlds (in the case of evil-doers), is extended to all the actions of man by reason of his soul being the *plexus* of the whole scale of worlds. This makes a whole universe sensitive to all his motions. In the case of Loria arose a whole literature, dealing with what is called Attentions, or Devotions, including the rules of conduct observed by Loria. The Attentions are for the most part of a mystical nature, bearing upon Loria's interpretation of the contents of the ritual and the mystical meaning which he divined in the performance of every commandment; but there are also Attentions of more general interest.[130]

Loria's first care was naturally for the young "Lions," or the Associates, who were apparently in need of a little taming and discipline, to effect which he erected for them an "enclosure," or rather, square, a block of buildings, providing chambers also for their wives and children. Isolation from the world, though living in the world, forms a part of the programme of every mystic. But the experiment was not successful. After a few months had passed, the women began to quarrel, and imparted their grievances to their husbands, leading to unpleasantness among the Associates. This mortified Loria very deeply.[131]

The Associates were divided into two classes, probably in accordance with their knowledge of mystical lore, but this did not prevent Loria from considering them as one body in the fullest sense of the word, each of the Associates being held only as a member or a joint of the body, so that in loving himself he loved the whole organism. Loria further bade them to pray constantly one for the other, and especially to feel the distress of each other in the case of sickness and misfortune. The love of the organism, however, extended to the whole of Israel, and Loria prescribed, that before beginning prayers man should receive upon himself the affirmative commandment, "And thou shalt love thy neighbour as thyself" (Leviticus 19:17), so that he may pray for Israel, in Israel, and with Israel. And it was this overwhelming sense of his solidarity with Israel which urged him to read the Confession prescribed for Yom Kippur (Day of Atonement) in all its fullest details, explaining that though there may be sins which he himself had not committed, he felt himself to be a member of the great body of Israel whose individual members form only one great unit of souls.[132] Vital, the favourite pupil of Loria, prescribes as one of the conditions for the acquiring of the gift of the Holy Spirit, "Love all creatures, including non-Jews." Loria himself was careful not to kill any living creature, be it even an insect or a worm. This was probably a result of his belief in the teaching of Metempsychosis, so prominent in Loria's system, which peopled for him the animate world with the souls of a fallen humanity, now appearing in the shapes of lower creation.[133]

Prayer, as may be expected, was to Loria one of the main functions of life, there being, according to him, no prayer in which man, by reason of his close communion with God, does not become the receptacle of new Divine light and a new outflow of Divine mercy. Every word of the ritual, every letter in it, had, besides its literal meaning, also its awful mysteries, occupying a most prominent place in the writings attributed to him or to his disciples. He saw in the lack of proper devotion during prayer the great obstacle in the way of the redemption of Israel.[134] It is hardly to be wondered at that such sublime prayer, accompanied by all the "Attentions" as Loria prescribed them, should be preceded by a series of ablutions, forming a part of the mystical programme at all times. It is reported that Loria said that physical purity, obtained by such ablutions, is greatly helpful to man, and he would perform them in the severest cold. On the other hand, it is recorded that when his mother objected to them on account of his delicate health, he would defer to her wishes cheerfully.[135]

This trait of considerateness was an essential feature of his character. He led, as we can imagine, a very simple life, dressing very plainly and spending little on himself, but he would accept the budget of his wife without a protest, and grant all the expense she considered fit.[136] It was also his custom to pay for any object required for religious purposes the amount asked, whatever it might be. Anger he declared to be the source of all evil, considering it as a sort of spiritual suicide, and though he was very tender in the treatment of his disciples, he once rebuked one of the Associates who showed too much resentment against his brother for not being sufficiently attentive to his studies.[137] The man who is betrayed into anger puts up a strange god in his heart, which is a sanctuary, and where the Divine Presence should dwell. Hence, let no man be betrayed into anger, either against a Gentile or a Jew, not even in the case when he has been robbed or insulted, but let always his mind remain calm. "The Lord, his God, is with him, and the shout of the King is in him." It is reported that the Loria Associates made it a rule not to initiate anyone into the mysteries of the Cabbala who was by temperament inclined to anger.[138] There is also a story about Loria that he would, on his walks, usually place himself behind a certain student of Safed. It seems that his disciples rather resented this humility of their master, and expostulated with him. His answer was to the effect that he could see that the student felt especially honoured by walking before him; since this was his desire, Loria thought it his duty to satisfy it; just as we, according to the Rabbinic law, are bound to provide a proper escort for the poor of noble descent, if they have been accustomed to it all their lives.[139]

It is hardly necessary to say that Loria was charitable; he had appointed times every day when he gave a certain amount of alms to the treasurer of his synagogue, but he further considered it as a solemn act, and would, as in the most important prayers, stand on his feet when he gave his *Perutah*. Often he would give all the money in his possession, not looking to see whether anything remained in his pocket.[140] This is certainly against all the rules of scientific charity. I hope that we shall overlook this defect in his character when we remember the remark of a French philosopher of the eighteenth century, who said that "magnanimity owes no account of its motives to prudence."

He was especially strict in the fulfilment of the command bidding us to pay the workman his wages on the very day on which he has performed his labour (Deuteronomy 24:15), and it went so far with him that he would not allow himself to read the afternoon prayer before getting the necessary money to pay off debts of this kind, saying, "How dare I approach my Maker when such a commandment came within my reach and I did not accomplish it?" [141]

In this connexion, the following story may be reproduced: As we have seen, many Jews in Safed were engaged in the clothing trade. Among these was R. Abraham Galanti, referred to above. One day Galanti came to Loria asking him, as the phrase was, to "give an improvement to his soul,"— that is, to tell him whether Loria had not detected that he was backward in the fulfilment of one of the commandments.

Loria at first declined to comply with his wish, as Galanti was one of the scholars and saints of Safed; but after much urging, he fixed his eyes on Galanti's forehead and said to him, "that he was defective in the commandment 'Thou shalt not defraud thy neighbour, neither rob him' " (Leviticus 19:13). The mystical notion is that sin and passion leave their impression on the face of man, and disfigure the image of God. Galanti went home trembling in every limb, and deeply mortified that he should have disgraced himself so far as to be involved in the sin of dishonesty. He put on sackcloth and spread ashes on his head in accordance with the usage of penitents, and called a meeting of all the hands engaged in his factory. When they arrived, he said to them: "Know ye not that I am only flesh and blood, and therefore subject to error? Accordingly, I must ask that you should examine most carefully your accounts with me, to see that I do you no wrong." Their answer was: "We have no account against you. Since we have been in the master's employ we are wanting in nothing, and the Lord has sent us his blessing. There is none among us who would think of making a bill of his demands." Thereupon the Rabbi said: "It is through your negligence in this respect that I have become the victim of sin. I will, therefore, put money before you; take what you desire, and forgive any claims you may have against me." But they would not touch the money, except one woman, who stretched out her hands and took two *Perutoth*. Galanti then went to Loria, who said, as he came out to meet him, "Why did you feel so mortified?" Galanti answered, "Is it a small matter that I should feel that I may possibly have robbed somebody? Now, if I have found grace in your eyes, tell me if the mark of this sin is still upon my forehead?" Loria answered, "No sign of sin is visible any longer," and revealed to him that the mistake consisted in the fact that this woman who had taken two *Perutoth* was one of the best weavers in his factory, and should have been better paid than the other employees. "But they are very particular in heaven about such things," said Loria, "hence the ugly mark which I perceived on you." [142]

Sabbath was the day of days with Loria and the Associates, new heavenly light reaching our sublunar regions on that day. The preparation for the Sabbath began Friday morning, when Loria would read the portion of the week from a scroll of the Pentateuch. Then would come dressing the hair, ablutions, and arraying himself in white garments in honour of the Sabbath. Early in the afternoon, Loria would form a procession, together with the Associates, to the fields to receive there Queen Sabbath with the song, "Come, my Beloved." [143] It was on such occasions that Loria, who was otherwise, as we have seen, rather reserved in revealing the mysteries of the Torah, would become communicative and uncover Divine secrets which no ear had been worthy enough to listen to before. And not only would the living profit by this hour of grace, but also the souls of the departed would benefit, wandering about for eternities, and taking up their abodes in the different kingdoms, the mineral, the vegetable, and the animal. These would on such occasions come to Loria, asking for his prayers to lift them up into the higher regions. "He saw spirits everywhere, and heard their whispers in the rushing of the water, in the movements of the trees and grass, in the song or twittering of the birds, even in the flickering of flames." [144] The neighbourhood of Safed, to which legend, long before this period, had transferred from Judæa the earthly remains of prophets and ancient sages, became to Loria, who saw their souls hovering on the graves, a veritable Valley of Jehoshaphat in the hour of resurrection. He held intercourse with them, and united, in "concentrated prayer," his soul with theirs. [145] But, above all, it was contemporary humanity which harboured these souls, if such an expression be permissible with Loria. Indeed, recognising as Loria did, by the process of metempsychosis, in every person he met old acquaintances from history, with whom he had associated in a former existence, and believing further, as he did, that it was only with the advent of the Messiah that this transmigration of souls would cease, all limits of space and time practically disappeared for him. To him the "generations past and the generations to come formed with those who are alive one single whole." All souls were evolved from the "original soul" of Adam, derived from the different parts of his body, and they suffered by his Fall. All live eternally, and are swayed by almost the same passions and by the same ideals as they were before. A certain neighbour of Loria, of a quarrelsome disposition, was none else to him than Korah of old, whilst Loria himself was a spark of the soul of Moses. [146] R. Abraham Halevi referred to above, was reported by legend to have perceived the Divine Glory during his prayers at the Holy Wall in Jerusalem. Loria thereupon discovered in him a spark of the soul of the prophet Jeremiah, who, according to a Rabbinical legend, had a similar vision on the same consecrated spot.[147] R. Moses Alsheich, again, famous, as noted above, for his homiletical works, was pregnant with the soul of R. Samuel ben Nachmani, the famous Agadist of the fourth century.[148] Loria himself and the Associates, in their present capacity as mystics, represented the reincarnation of the supposed heroes of the Zohar, headed by R. Simon ben Yochai and his son R. Eleazar.[149] Men were not to him what they were, but what they had been once, and it was their former existence which determined his relations to them. Thus it is reported that one morning his disciple R. Samuel de Useda entered the house of Loria, who was lecturing to the Associates. Loria, upon perceiving him, at once arose before him and greeted him with the words, "Blessed be he that cometh," took him by the hand, placed him at his right side, and had a long conversation with him. Vital, who was present, was curious to know why his master showed this young man so much honour, and asked him the reason. He said: It was not before him that I arose, but before the soul of R. Phinehas ben Jair, who lived some eight hundred years ago, and was especially distinguished by his acts of charity and lovingkindness. Of this soul the young man became possessed to-day. Upon inquiry, Useda confessed that that morning, on his way to the synagogue, he had passed by a house from which the voice of lamentation and crying reached his ears. When he went in, he found the tenants all naked, robbers having taken away their clothes. He at once gave them all the raiment he had on, and returned home, where he clad himself in his Sabbath garments.[150]

Such things Loria saw best on the eve of the Sabbath by the aid of the Divine light radiating from the holiness of the day to come. When the prayers and the songs in the fields were over, Loria would return home, where he would be met by his mother, whom he kissed on entering the house. As it would seem, he was accompanied by Vital, who used to spend the Sabbath with him. Then would begin, as we can imagine, the *Kiddush* (Sanctification of the day over the cup of wine), and the meal, at which any number of concentrated "Attentions" were observed. We are also in possession of three mystical songs composed by Loria himself, sung at the three meals by which the Sabbath day was distinguished.[151]

The Sabbath emitted its rays, lighting up the whole week, sanctifying even such moments of human life as those in which material needs and common passions are very little favourable to spirituality. Loria, in common with other mystics, succeeded in spiritualising the whole life of man, just as the legalist finds nothing in human affairs which is either above or below the Torah. De Vidas, referred to before, the favourite pupil of Cordovero, wrote a book, *Reshith Chochmah*, dealing with such topics as the fear of God, the love of God, holiness, humility, sin, reward and punishment, and repentance, but he did not disdain to devote whole pages to such subjects as the intimate relations or intercourse between the sexes, commerce and trade, good manners and social etiquette, all of which form a part of the sacred life. The same thing may be observed of the pupils of Loria. The book, *Ez ha-Chayim* (The Tree of Life), ascribed to Vital and supposed to represent a compilation of the most important of Loria's teachings, is prefaced among others by this motto, "Depart from evil and do good" (Psalms 34:14). It is followed by a number of rules, some of which we have already met with in the preceding remarks. The first of them impresses upon the mystic the necessity of the strict fulfilment of the Law in all its minutiæ, whether Scriptural or traditional.[152] "The Gates of Holiness," by Vital, gives a set of rules for those who are in search of eternal perfection, the absorption in the Divine, and is pervaded by the same spirit of loyalty to the Law, both in its ceremonial and moral parts.

Thus the Safed of the sixteenth century, at least, is free from all antinominian tendencies, which are the supposed inevitable consequences of mysticism. The Safed Jew of that period saw no antagonism of principle between Caro and Loria. Caro was for him the authority, Loria the model. But just as Loria was amenable to the discipline of the Law, so was Caro not unresponsive to the finer impulses of love and admiration.

Loria died in the year 1572 (according to some, in 1574) after a short illness of three days.[153] Vital took over the leadership, and it was under his direction that various writings and works were soon compiled and put into circulation, claiming the authority of Loria. How far Loria would have felt himself responsible for all that was then written and said in his name, is a question not to be easily decided. Probably he would have disowned a great deal of what was afterwards known as the writings of Loria. I have already referred to his hesitation in giving publicity to what he considered to be the secrets of the Torah, but he must also have felt that his highly coloured metaphors and rich imagery might become a stumbling-block to those who had not passed through all the grades of holiness, and were not satisfied with being brought near God on the "religious-fatigue" system, but preferred to have God brought down to them. We have it also on good authority that before his death he said to his disciples, "Know for a truth that you have not a single Proposition (of the mystical lore expounded by Loria) that can be considered complete." When they said to him, "Not even R. Chayim Vital?" he answered: Perhaps he knows a little more than you, but not much.[154]

The Propositions, however, concerned only a few exalted personages among the mystics, who made them the special subject of their studies and further development. What filtered through these Propositions and reached those who laid no claim to this title, "was not metaphysic but moral, not immanence but sin," or rather the fear of sin. The Propositions placed man, as already hinted at, upon a pedestal, the eminence of which caused giddiness to many an exalted personage, who, deeming himself a god or a demi-god, lost his balance and fell beyond hope of redemption. The great majority of Israel remained mindful of the old warning, "Be not rash with thy mouth, and let not thine heart be hasty to utter anything before God: for God is in heaven, and thou upon earth: therefore let thy words be few" (Ecclesiastes 5:2). Haste and rashness became especially discredited after the bursting of that theological bubble known in history as the Pseudo-Messianic claims of Sabbatai Zebi. The Propositions, with the over-emphasis of the God-likeness of man, were only allowed to stand so far as God-likeness demanded superior holiness on the part of man. With a proper instinct the people at large left the *Ez ha-Chayim* by Vital, with its Propositions, to the few, and it lasted nearly two centuries till it first appeared in print; but his book "The Gates of Holiness," with its deeply ethical contents, became at once a popular tract, and passed through many editions. Likewise, the Jewish public took but little notice of R. Moses Chayim Luzzatto's "One Hundred and Thirty-Eight Doors of Wisdom," but it did appreciate at once his noble "Path of the Upright," preaching morality and holiness. The book is constantly going through new editions, and in certain parts of the East there are special "Path of the Upright Societies" devoted to the study of this book. The Safed influence is especially marked on the devotional works of R. Isaiah Horwitz, R. Aaron Kaydanower, and R. Elijah Cohen, which works became the common spiritual good of the people. Their morality is austere, their tone sombre, and their demands on man's religious capabilities exacting. All this is traceable enough in the work of the Safed penitents. They certainly have not erred on the line of self-complacency and self-righteousness. They warn man not to behave "as so many fools do," who are so over-confident of their salvation because they are engaged in their trade the whole day, recite punctually the three prescribed prayers for the day, and neither steal nor rob nor commit any other acts of gross immorality, and harm nobody. These are cheap virtues, according to our moralists, of which even the Gentiles are not devoid, and which one's neighbours from motives of self-preservation would compel one to observe. What justifies man to entertain exalted hopes of the "world to come" is, according to the stern moralists, the minute observance of the Law in all its details "in great love," the constant increasing in the quality of saintliness; the possession of the quality to please God and man, and the readiness to give up his life in perfect joy for the sake of the love of God. On the other hand, they have, as indicated above, retained enough of the Safed emphasis of the God-likeness of man to disregard in the end the dualism of flesh and spirit, a conception un-Jewish in its origin, and now revived only under a mistaken notion of "spirituality." In spite of the ascetic teachings, with their depreciation of the "turbid body," to be threatened by the terrors of hell and cajoled by the joys of paradise, they were thus able to insist upon the holiness of the flesh (*Kedushath ha-Guph*) and upon its purity as much as upon that of the soul, as well as to accord to the flesh a share in the bliss to come, held out to man as a consequence of a holy and religious life, which a supercilious philosophy entirely denied.[155]

Caro passed away in 1575, Trani five years later (1580). The decline of Safed soon set in. Samson Bak, who travelled in Palestine in 1588, was compelled to leave Safed for Jerusalem on account of the distress which had overtaken the former city at that period. R. Isaiah Horwitz, who settled in Palestine soon after the beginning of the seventeenth century, describes the Jerusalem population as richer in numbers than that of Safed.[156]

The men who succeeded Caro and Loria were, for the most part, their disciples. R. Moses Galanti, an ordained disciple of Caro and an adherent of Loria, R. Yomtob Zahalon, described as the head of the city of Safed and of the Yeshibah, and R. Joseph Trani, the son of R. Moses Trani, who obtained in later life even more distinction than his famous father, seem to be the most prominent names of this period. At least this is the impression we receive from their Responsa collections, in which they figure as men of weight and authority. They still meet in the general board; and in a document giving the minutes of such a meeting dating from the first decade of the seventeenth century, we have the signatures of not less than twenty Rabbis, with some of whom we made acquaintance in the former pages. Mention is also made of a rabbi Joshua ben Nun, who is described as the Chief Rabbi and the head of all the heads of the colleges, and who was, besides, the administrator of all the charities of the city. The old devotion to the study of the Torah and the occupation with mystical literature are still continued. After they finished their prayers, the whole congregation formed themselves into groups, listening to lectures on such subjects as Bible, Halachah, Hagadah, or the Zohar, so that none left the Synagogue to go to business before he gave some time to study. The fifth day in the week (Thursday) seems to have been a special day of devotion, when they would all gather in one big synagogue to pray for Israel and to bless those who sent support for the poor of the Holy Land. The service would conclude with a sermon by Galanti and other men distinguished for their humility and saintliness. It is not impossible that this synagogue was the one built by a wealthy man in Constantinople in memory of Loria, and richly endowed by him.[157] None, however, was sufficiently great to make his authority felt in such a way as to give him any real prominence over his contemporaries. Even Vital's authority does not seem to have been quite undisputed. He afterwards left Safed and died in Damascus in 1620, and the sons of Caro and Trani emigrated to Turkey. The Chmielnicki persecutions of the middle of the seventeenth century, which must have taxed the resources of Jewry to its utmost, probably withdrew a good deal of the support which Safed had received till then for its Talmudical Colleges; whilst the excesses of certain Cabbalists about the same period, who joined pseudo-Messiah movements, must have put a damper upon the zeal of the mystics and the study of mysticism which was the special glory of Safed.

Safed thus ceases to be a centre of attraction. It decays slowly, and Jerusalem comes to its rights. It lives on the past, profiting by the glory of Caro, Trani, Loria, and Cordovero. Even to-day the Synagogue of Caro and the Synagogue of Loria form the main sights in Safed. But it is not any longer the Safed of the sixteenth century.

Abbreviations Occurring in Appendix and Notes

AN. JB.   Letter by an anonymous traveller, published in the *Jahrbuch für die Gesch. des Juden.*, vol. 3. Leipzig, 1863.

AZ. or AZULAI.   Chayim Joseph David Azulai.—שם הגדולים.

AZKARI.   Eliezer b. Moses Azkari.—ספר חרדים (ed. Warsaw, 1879).

BERTINORO.   Letters of travel by R. Obadiah, of Bertinoro, published in the *Jahrbuch für die Gesch. des Juden.*, vol. 3. Leipzig, 1863.

CALIMANI.   R. Baruch b. Simchah Calimani.—Introduction to the Commentary of R. Moses Alsheich to the Pentateuch (Venice, 1601).

CARO I.   R. Joseph Caro—Responsa.—אבקת רוכל.

CARO II.   Responsa on דיני נשים (ed. Mantua, 1730).

CHABIB.   R. Levi Aben Chabib.—Responsa (Venice, 1565).

CH. Y.   חמדת ימים, ascribed to Nathan of Gaza; but see also כבוד חכמים by Menahem Mendel Heilperin (ed. Livorno, 1762–4).

CON. or CONFORTE.   David Conforte.—קורא הדורות (ed. Cassel).

FRUMKIN.   Arye Löw Frumkin.—אבן שמואל.

GHIRONDI.   Samuel Mordecai Ghirondi, partial author of תולדות גדולי ישראל.

ג"ל.   ספר הגלגולים (Przemysl, 1875).

KAHANA.   David Kahana.—אבן נגף.

KAYDANOWER.   R. Zebi b. Aaron Samuel Kaydanower.—קב הישר.

MI.   Heimann Joseph Michael.—אור החיים (Frankfurt, 1891).

MM.   מגיד משרים, by Caro (ed. Wilna, 1879).

MN.   ספר הכונות ומעשה נסים (Constantinople, 1720).

PARDES.   Moses b. Jacob Cordovero.—פרדס רמונים.

RABINOWITZ.   Saul Pinchas Rabinowitz.—מוצאי גולה (Warsaw, 1894).

RADBAZ (usually abbreviated רד״בז (ר׳ד׳ב״ז). David b. Solomon Abi Zimra.—Responsa.

SAMB. or SAMBARI. "Mediæval Jewish Chronicles" (ed. Neubauer, Oxford, 1887).—Containing also extracts of the Chronicles of Joseph b. Isaac Sambari, pp. 115–162.

SCHWARZ. תבואות הארץ, by Joseph Schwarz (ed. A. M. Luncz, Jerusalem, 1900).

SG. Moses ben Jacob Cordovero. ספר גרושין, Venice,1600.

SH. J. Baruch (Jacob b. Moses Chayim).—שבחי ירושלים (containing also a traveller's account of Palestine, in 1522, by an anonymous author. Livorno, 1785).

SHLOMEL. R. Solomon b. Chayim Meinsterl, better known as Shlomel.—שבחי הארי, together with the לקוטי ש״ם (Livorno, 1790).

TRANI. R. Moses b. Joseph of Trani.

VITAL. R. Chayim b. Joseph Vital.—שבחי רי חיים וויטאל (Ostrog, 1826).

Appendix

AARON B. ELEAZAR (the Blind). Mi., p. 147.

ABRAHAM ארומטי (ארואיטי). See Manasseh b. Israel's *Nishmath Chayim*, III:10; Caro I, 124.

ABRAHAM DE BOTON. Con. 48a.

ABRAHAM GABRIEL. Con.; Mi.; נ׳ל, 88b.

ABRAHAM GALENTI. Con.; Samb.; Az.

ABRAHAM B. GEDALIAH B. ASHER. Con.; Samb.; Az.; Mi.

ABRAHAM HALEVI ברוכים. Con.; Az.; Mi. (p. 61. See references, but confused there with Abraham Halevi the Elder. Cf. Frumkin, 72).

ABRAHAM B. ISAAC LANIADO. Mi. no. 145.

ABRAHAM B. ISAAC ZAHALON. Mi.

ABRAHAM B. JACOB BERAB. Con.

ABRAHAM LACHMI. See Manasseh b. Israel's *Nishmath Chayim*, III:10.

ABRAHAM SHALOM (the Elder). Con. (see especially 33b); Samb.; Mi.

ABRAHAM SHALOM (the Younger). Con.; Mi. (p. 122).

ABRAHAM B. SOLOMON עלון. See Preface to Zechariah b. Saruk's Commentary on Esther.

BENJAMIN HALEVI. Con. (p. 49b.) (?); Samb.; Mi. (pp. 280–281).

CHAYIM B. ISAAC החבר. Con.; Samb.; Az.; Mi.

CHAYIM VITAL. See text.

CHIYA ROFE (the physician). Con.; Samb.; Az.; Mi.

DAVID AMARILLO. See Solomon Adeni, Introduction to his Commentary מלאכת שלמה.

DAVID DE קאשטריש. Con. 48a. See Notes.

DAVID COHEN. Vital, 14b.

DAVID HABILLO. Con.; Samb.; Az.; Mi.

DAVID NAVARRO. Con.; Samb.

DAVID B. ZECHARIAH ורנק. See Mi., nos. 718 and 813. See also Frumkin, 58.

DAVID ABI ZIMRA. Con.; Samb.; Az.; Mi.

ELIEZER AZKARI. Con.; Samb.; Az.; Mi.

ELIEZER GINZBURG, son-in-law of רמ"א. See David Grünhut, טוב רואי, title page.

ELEAZAR B. ISAAC ארחא. Con.; Az.; Mi.

ELEAZAR B. YOCHAI. Con.; Samb.; Az.; Mi.

ELIJAH FALCON. Con.; Samb.; particularly p. 152; Az., and *s. n.* Moses Alsheich. Ni. See Manasseh b. Israel's *Nishmath Chayim*, III:10.

ELIJAH DE VIDAS. Con.; Samb.; Az.; Mi. See also text.

ELISHA GALLICO. Con.; Samb.; Az.; Mi. See also Zunz, Introduction to De Rossi, *Meor Enayim*.

GEDALIAH ALKABEZ. See Az. Cf. Steinschneider, Catalogue, col. 1002.

GEDALIAH CORDOVERO. Con.; Mi.

GEDALIAH HALEVI. Con. 48a; identical with Vital's brother-in-law; see Vital, 3a, and ג"ל, 87b.

ISAAC ALFANDARI. Con. 46b.

ISAAC ארחא. Con., especially p. 41a.

ISAAC DE BOTON. Con. 48a.

ISAAC COHEN. Vital, 20a, 23b; cf. Con. 41a.

ISAAC GERSON. Con.

ISAAC KRISPIN. Samb. 152 (?).

ISAAC LORIA. See text.

ISAAC B. MENAHEM בסמו. See Neubauer, Cat., no. 411.

ISAAC MISOD. Con. 36a. Perhaps identical with Isaac b. David, called "Misod," mentioned by Trani, I, 32.

ISAAC משען. See Az.; Abraham b. Asher and references; Con. (?).

ISHMAEL HALEVI ASHKENAZI. Vital, 14b.

ISRAEL CORIEL.   Con.; Samb.; Az.

ISRAEL SARUK.   Con. 46b.; Az., and sub Solomon Loria.

ISSACHAR SASSON.   Con.; Samb.

JACOB ABULAFIAH.   Samb.; Az. MN 7b and 12a. See, however, Modena, *Ari Noham,* 19b.

JACOB איש תם, etc.   Samb. 151 (?).

JACOB אלטרף or אלטריץ or אלטרם.   Vital, 14b; Samb.

JACOB BERAB.   See text.

JACOB BERAB (B. ABRAHAM) (the Younger).   Con.; Samb.
162.

JACOB B. CHAYIM.   Pref. to באר שבע.

JACOB FALCON.   Con.

JACOB גוילי.   Perhaps a corruption of גוינינו. See Samb.;
Vital, 25a, 151, and Azkari, 95.

JACOB SASSON.   Con. 48a.

JACOB ZEMACH.   Con.; Az.

JEDIDIAH GALENTI.   Con.; Mi.

JEHIEL GINZBURG.   See תולדות משפחת גינצבורג, p. 187.

JEHUDAH B. URI (of Heidelberg).   See Cairo II, 62c.

JEREMIAH OF CANDIA.   Con. 48b.

JONATHAN GALANTI.   Con. 48a.

JONATHAN SAGIS.   Con. 48a; Vital, 23b; ג"ל, 88a.

JOSEPH ARZIN.   Vital, 23b; ג"ל, 81a. Cf. מאמץ כח, by R.
Moses Almosnino, 18b.

JOSEPH ASHKENAZI.   Con.; Samb.; Az. Cf. Kaufmann, *Monatsschrift,* vol. 42, p. 38 seq., and Bloch, vol. 47, p. 153.

JOSEPH BARZILLAI.   Mi.

JOSEPH קלדירין.   Con. 48a.

JOSEPH OF ליריאה (LIERIA).   Az.; Samb.

JOSEPH SAGIS.   Con.; Samb.; Az. (?).

JOSEPH SAJJAH.   Con.; Az.

JOSEPH SARAGOSSI.   Samb.; Az.

JOSEPH SKANDRANI.   Con.; 30b; Az.; Mi., no. 1042.

JOSEPH B. TABUL.   Con. 40b and 48a; Vital, 23b. Probably
identical with Joseph Maarabi.

JOSEPH TIBBON.   Con. 41a.

JOSEPH VITAL.   Samb.; Az.

JOSHUA B. NUN.   Con.; Az.

JUDAH משען.   Vital, 23b; Con. 40b; ג"ל, 88a.

LAPIDUTH.   Az. See Vital, 1a.

LEVI B. CHABIB.   Con.; Samb.; Az.; Mi. See also Frumkin,
30a.

MENAHEM B. ABRAHAM GALANTI.   Kaydanower, ch. 15.

MENAHEM HA-BABLI. See Caro II, 35b (?).

MENAHEM GALLICO. Ghirondi, 252.

MISOD AZULAI. Con. Perhaps identical with Misod Maarabi. See Shlomel, 34b, and Con. 40b.

MORDECAI HA-COHEN (author of a commentary on the Bible). Con.; Az.

MORDECAI DATO. Con. 42b; Landshut, עמודי העבודה, *s. n.*

MOSES ALKABEZ. Con.; Ghirondi, 242.

MOSES ALSHEICH. See text.

MOSES BARUCH. Con.; Az. See also Caro II, 17a.

MOSES BASULA. Con.; Ghirondi, 250. Cf. also Mortara, p. 7.

MOSES CORDOVERO. See text.

MOSES GALANTI. Con.; Samb.; Az.

MOSES HALEVI מרינקי. Con.; Samb.

MOSES B. ISRAEL NAGARA. Con.; Samb.; Az.

MOSES JONAH. Con. 41a; ג"ל, 89a.

MOSES B. JOSEPH TRANI. See text.

MOSES OF לירייאה (LIERIA). Boton, לחם רב, no. 184.

MOSES B. MACHIR. Con.; Az.

MOSES MINTZ. ג"ל, 88b; *Ez ha-Chayim,* 6a. Cf. Mi., no. 531.

MOSES NIGRIN. Con.; Az.; cf. also Ghirondi, 226.

MOSES ONKENEYRA. Az. See Caro I, 124, spelled somewhat variously.

MOSES OF ROME. See שערי ג"ע.

MOSES SAADYA. Con.; Samb. See also Caro II, 17a. Cf. Vital, 12b, 15b.

PHAREZ COLOBI. See text.

SABBATAI MANASSEH. Samb.; cf. Caro I, 124, and ג"ל, 91a.

SAMUEL BIAGI. See Manasseh b. Israel's *Nishmath Chayim.*

SAMUEL GALLICO. Con.; Az.

SAMUEL B. SHEM TOB ATIYA. Con.; Samb. See Frumkin, 51.

SAMUEL DE USEDA. Con.; Samb.; Az.

SAMUEL VERGA. Con.; Samb.; Az.

SHEM TOB ATIYA. Con.; Az.

SIMON ASHKENAZI. See *Peri Ez Chayim.*

SOLOMON אבסבאן. Con.; Samb.; Az. See also Jewish Quarterly Review, IX, p. 269.

SOLOMON ADENI. See his Introduction to his Commentary מ"ש to the Mishnah (Wilna, 1887). For this reference I am obliged to Dr. L. Ginzberg.

SOLOMON ALKABEZ. See text.

SOLOMON COHEN. Con. 48a.

SOLOMON SAGIS. Con.; Az.

SOLOMON סירילין. Con.; Samb.; Az. Cf. Frumkin, 44.

SOLOMON B. YAKAR. Chabib, Responsa, 322a.

SULAIMAN B. אוחנא. Con.; variously spelled. See especially p. 42a, and Cassel's note; Samb.; Az. ס 1, identical with the writer of the same name known by his notes to the Siphre and the Mechilta. Cf. Pardo's Preface to his commentary to the Siphre.

TOBIAH HALEVI. Con.; Samb.; Az.; Mi.

YOMTOB ZAHALON. Con.; Az.

ZECHARIAH B. SOLOMON זעכשיל (father-in-law of Caro). Differently spelled by various authors. Samb.; Az.; Mi. (p. 364). Cf. also Frumkin, 59.

Notes

1. See Schwarz, p. 476; cf. Baedeker, Index. See also Rapoport, Introduction to קורא הדורות of Shalom Cohen (Warsaw, 1838).
2. See Caro I, 1.
3. See Graetz, *Geschichte d. Juden,* 2d ed., IX:29 seq.; cf. also English Translation, IV:400 seq.
4. אור החיים, ch. V; cf. Kayserling, *Geschichte d. Juden in Portugal,* pp. 42 and 96.
5. See Neubauer's "Mediæval Jewish Chronicles," I:111. Similar sentiments may also be found in R. Isaac Arama's חזות קשה.
6. Ed. Pietrkow (1902), p. 42.
7. See *Responsa* of R. Asher (Rosh), VIII:10.
8. See Epstein, *Revue des Etudes Juives,* XLII, p. 18, and Büchler, XLIV, p. 241 seq.
9. See Graetz, *Geschichte,* VII:13; cf. Schwarz, 443. Of course, this brief outline has to be completed by the accounts of the travels of Benjamin of Tudela, and R. Pethahiah, and similar works.
10. See Pharchi, כפתר ופרח.
11. See Hebrew Appendix *Ozar Tob* to *Magazin,* I:027; see also Graetz, *Geschichte,* VII:182; cf. Hebrew periodical *Jerusalem,* edited by Luncz, II, p. 7.
12. See Graetz, *Geschichte,* VII:308–9, and *Jerusalem,* II, p. 12.
13. See Carmoly, *Itinéraires,* 261, from an unpublished MS. (cod. Paris, 1070); cf. also Pharchi, 284.
14. See *Jerusalem,* VI, p. 337.
15. See Graetz, *Geschichte,* IX:28; cf. the Hebrew translation, VII:26, notes 2 and 4. The name points to a Spanish origin; cf. also Azkari, 24a, and Azulai, *s. n.* The date of Saragossi's settling in Safed cannot be ascertained, but it must have been during the first two decades of the sixteenth century.
16. See Bertinoro, 209 and 222; cf. Graetz, *Geschichte,* VIII:278, and IX:26, and Rabinowitz, 213; but see also Luncz in *Jerusalem,* I, p. 58.

It should, however, be remarked that the travellers are not quite unanimous in their evidence as to the hostility of the Mohammedan population toward the Jews. On the other hand, it seems that matters with regard to taxes deteriorated later in Safed. Cf. Caro I, 1, and *Jerusalem, V*, p. 161.

17. See Bertinoro, 222.

18. See An. Jb., 277.

19. See Shlomel, 42d; see also Kaydanower, ch. 16, and הקודש מהרת, I, 43a.

20. See Sh. J., 16b; Shlomel, 43a; see also Responsa of R. Solomon Cohen, II, 38; Responsa לחם רב, by R. Abraham Boton, 148; מאמץ כח by R. Moses Almosnino, 16a.

21. See in general about Caro, Graetz, *Geschichte*, IX, Index; Rabinowitz, Index; Cassel, *Joseph Karo und das Maggid Mescharim* (Berlin, 1888), and the authorities mentioned in Dr. Louis Ginzberg's article "Caro," J. Encycl. See Neubauer, Catalogue, no. 2578, containing a list of ten eulogies on the death of Joseph Caro, and as to the *untrustworthiness* of the Mentor-Angel, see Rabinowitz, p. 43, note 4.

22. MM 17a.

23. Cassel, ibid., is almost the only writer who doubted the authenticity of this work. His arguments are in every respect weak, whilst there is contemporary evidence to the contrary. See Rabinowitz, 242 seq., Brüll, *Jahrbücher*, IX:150, and Ginzberg, ibid.

24. See MM 4a, 13c, 18c, 23d, 33b, 49a.

25. See MM 3c.

26. See Horwitz, של"ה (ed. Warsaw), 162a seq.

27. See MM 22c.

28. See MM 11c, 12a, 17a, 25c, cf. Graetz, *Geschichte*, IX:340 and 561, but see also Hebrew translation, VII:415, and appendix at the end by Jaffe.

29. See especially MM, pp. 25c and 26a about ?רייוסף (הרי"ש מאיטאצק); cf. Kahana, 77, note 1.

30. See MM 18c and 28a.

31. See MM 4a, 16a, 37a.

32. See MM 6b, 34a, 50a.

33. See MM 28a.

34. See MM 35c.

35. See MM 2b.

36. See MM 30d, 37b.

37. See MM 16a, 18d, 46a.

38. See MM 46d.

39. See MM 3a, 14a, 21c, 24c, 25d, 34d, 44d.

40. See MM 3b.

41. See MM 3d, 21b, c.

42. See MM 52b.

43. See MM 29d.

44. See MM 3b, 41d.

45. See MM 3b.

46. See MM 13a, 18c.

47. See MM 8a, 10b, 19d, 23d, 26b.

48. See MM 8b, c.

49. See MM 50d.

50. See MM 4d, 13d, 14a, 19d, 20d, 21a, 27a, 29b. About Nicopolis in particular, ibid., 17b.

51. See MM 25c.

52. See MM 12d, 13a.

53. See MM 23a.

54. See MM 5a, 6b, 8d, 14c, 25b, and c, 27a, b, c, 28d, 30a and b. 34b, 42c.

55. See MM 3d, 4b and c, 8c, 9c, 16d, 19d, 24d, 30c, 46c, 50a and a. About the possibility of references to Alkabez, see Rabinowitz, 245, note 1. See also below, note 76.

56. The following remarks about Molko are mostly based on Graetz, *Geschichte,* IX, Index. See also English translation IV, Index, and Vogel-stein and Rieger, *Geschichte der Juden in Rom,* II, Index.

57. See Graetz, *Geschichte,* VIII:253 and 562, and references given there, to which Sambari, p. 147, may be added. See, however, Rabino-witz, 152, note 1. His doubts are fully justified, as there is not a single real trace in all the contemporary literature coming from Palestine point-ing to Molko's staying in that country.

58. See references given to MM in note 55, especially the one to MM 50a.

59. See above, note 50. See also Horwitz, שלי"ה, I, 134b and Gutt-man, דרך אמונה ומעשה רב, Warsaw, 1898, 14b.

60. See Azulai *s.n.;* cf. also Ghirondi, p. 380 seq. See also Alkabez, Introduction to his ברית הלוי (Lemberg, 1863); cf. Brüll, *Jahrbücher,* IX, 150, and Rabinowitz, 245. See also Landshut, עמודי העבודה, *s. n.*

61. See MM 50d (headed עמום), which is dated in the MSS. of the MM the second Adar רצו (March, 1536), and it is clear from the con-tents that Caro was still in חוץ לארץ at that period. For the fact that there were about one thousand families in Safed, I have only the au-thority of Graetz, *Geschichte,* VII:302. See Trani, III, 48.

62. See Trani, I, 28; Caro II, 16c. Alsheich, Responsa, no. 27, and cf. Shlomel, 43a.

63. See Frumkin, 7.

64. See Responsa of Berab, no. 22; Bacharach, 109c; Boton, לחם רב, no. 92, and Vital, 13b. There are also in the book תקון יששכר, by R. Issachar b. Mordecai b. Shushan, references to קהלות הספרדים and קהל האשכנזים.

65. See Trani, III, 48.

66. See Trani, I, 106; II, 115 and 131; Responsa by Alsheich, no. 27; Responsa by R. Joseph Trani, I, 82.

67. See Sh. J., 16b, and Bertinoro, 222.

68. See Sh. J., 16b, and Trani, III, 46.

69. See Berab, no. 22; Trani, I, 171; II, 25; Radbaz, II, 638, and Responsa of R. Moses Galanti, no. 11.

70. See Chabib, 292d.

71. See R. Chayim Alsheich's Preface to the Pentateuch Commentary of R. Moses Alsheich, ed. Venice, 1601, p. 6a. Cf. Leo Modena's *Briefe* (ed. by Prof. Dr. L. Blau), Letter 147.

72. See Berliner, periodical *Jerusalem,* II, 68 seq. The Jewish Theo-logical Seminary Library possesses the most important productions of this press.

73. See Sh. J., 16b, and Shlomel, 43a.

74. See Responsa of R. Isaac de Latas, p. 54; cf. Graetz, *Geschichte,* IX, end.

75. See above, p. 262.

76. See MM 19d; cf. ibid. 4d. There can be little doubt that the Solomon mentioned there is Solomon Alkabez.

77. About Berab and the history of the Ordination controversy, see Graetz, *Geschichte,* IX:300 seq.; Rabinowitz, 218 seq.; and the references given there, especially to the אגרת הסמיכה forming an appendix to the Responsa of Chabib. It should never be forgotten that in judging Berab we are entirely dependent on material coming from an opponent, who in the heat of the controversy could with all his meekness not remain impartial to his antagonist, and therefore large deductions should be made from all that is said of the harshness of Berab's character and of the real motives for his action. Cf. also Frumkin, 38 seq.

78. See Chabib, 186d, 198d, 302b, and 305c.

79. See Chabib, 188d. Of the four ordained, we have only the names of Caro and Trani. Graetz, *Geschichte* IX:307, note, and Frumkin, 73, note 1, advance hypotheses as to the names of the other two. Yachya in his שלשלת הקבלה speaks of ten who received the Ordination, but the meaning of the passage is not quite certain.

80. See MM 29a; cf. Graetz, ibid. 311, Caro seems to have given up the matter altogether afterwards, there being not a single reference to the Ordination question, either in his חשן משפט, no. 61, or in his commentary to Maimonides' משנה תורה ה' סנהדרין, IV. Only in his בית יוסף to the חשן משפט, no. 295, there is a faint reference to it. Cf. Azulai's ברכי יוסף to חשן משפט, 64.

81. See MM 16d.

82. About Trani, see Fin, הכרמל (octavo edition), II, 586 seq.

83. See Trani, II, 67; cf. also I, 41 and 47.

84. See Trani, III, 48.

85. See e. g. Trani, I, 156, 189, 274, 336; II, 46 and 180; cf. Caro I, 24.

86. See אהבת ציון, Anon., 26d. Cf. also Caro I, 14, where he speaks of his lack of time, which is given to lecturing to the *Chaberim* both in the morning and in the evening.

87. See Alsheich, Opinion incorporated in Caro I, 73.

88. See Caro I, 92; II, 14 seq. Cf. R. Menahem Azariah of Fano, Preface to the פלח הרמון. Cf. also Azulai; Conforte; Sambari; and Kahana, p. 80 seq.

89. See *Pardes,* Preface.

90. See ברית הלוי, 39b seq.

91. See SG, pp. 1a, 23a and b, 24b; cf. Kahana, p. 80, note 2.

92. With regard to Alkabez see מהרת הקודש, II, 25b.

93. See אור הישר by Popers, 23p. See also reference given above, note 60.

94. See Kahana, p. 145, note 6, to which are to be added R. Menahem Azariah of Fano and R. Sabbatai Horwitz, the author of של שפע.

95. See Preface to the work mentioned in note 88. Cf. *Catalog der hebräischen Handschriften der kgl. Bibliothek in Modena,* S. Jona, p. 10 seq.; cf. also Kaufmann.

96. See the authorities quoted above in note 88; cf. also Bacharach, 7a and 33c.

97. Besides the usual authorities, such as Conforte (Index), Sambari (Index), and Azulai, *s. n.,* see also Calimani, and Alsheich's Preface to his Commentary to Proverbs. Cf. Leo Modena's *Briefe,* Letter 98. Most of the biographers give the relation of Loria as stated in the text. Cf. also Vital, 2b. Rabbi Abraham Chazkuni, however, in his book זאת חוקת התורה, states in the name of Alsheich that he had a direct tradition from Loria regarding a certain mystic point, whilst according to Calimani he was one of the direct recipients of Loria's mystical teachings. See also Steinschneider, *Jerusalem,* III, no. 33c, to a MS. חזות קשה

by Alsheich on the precarious condition of the Jews of Safed. Unfortunately, the MS. was inaccessible to me.

98. See Conforte (Index), and Azulai, *s. n.* Cf. Bacharach 109c; Ch. Y. II, 4a, and IV, 10b; Kaydanower, 93, and Popers, 7b.

99. See Azkari, Preface; cf. Kahana, p. 149.

100. See ראשית חכמה (ed. Cracow), 174a.

101. See Azkari, 95a seq.

102. See *Baba Bathra,* 10a, ש"ע א"ח, no. 92, end.

103. See Shlomel and Vital, where such legends are scattered over the books, parallels to which are to be found in Bacharach's and Kaydanower's works in various places. Sambari, of whose chronicles the Jewish Theological Seminary Library possesses a good copy, is also replete with such stories. Cf. also נשמת חיים, III, 10; see Kahana, pp. 146, 148, and 150. Yachya in his שה"ק has also any number of such stories.

104. The legend about Joseph is incorporated in the book לקוטי ש"ם (Livorno, 1790); Kahana, p. 11, note 5.

105. Cf. *Shabbath,* 12a and b, and the references given there on the margin to the codes of Maimonides and Caro.

106. See אורחות צדיקים incorporated in the Hebrew book mentioned above in note 104, 69b.

107. See Azulai, *s. n.;* Ch. Y., II, 55b.

108. The main sources for Loria's biography are the legendary accounts, of which two versions exist. The one is that first published in the *Sammelwerk* נובלות חכמה (see Zedner, 356), and republished any number of times both as appendix to other works as well as by itself under the name of שבחי האריי. This is the version made use of by almost all writers on the subject. The second version, strongly related to it, but in a somewhat more connected form as well as more precise in its dates, is the ספר הכונות ומעשה ניסים published first in Constantinople in 1720, and then in Safed by R. Samuel Heller in the year 1876. See also אור האמת by Moses Mordecai Lebtob, pp. 214–216, where the first two or three pages of this version are reproduced. Sambari's account of the life of Loria is omitted by Neubauer, but the Jewish Theological Seminary Library possesses a photograph copy of the whole work as preserved in the Paris MS., and a copy of the omissions relating to Safed from the Oxford MS. This account of Sambari is almost identical with the second version. Much material is also to be found in Bacharach, 6a, 7b, 10b to 14a, 33a to 34a, 77a, 109c, 116b and c, 126a and d, 138a, 141c, 142a and b, 143a, 146b, c, and d, 152 to 154. Bacharach's story is, as is well known, based on Shlomel. Kaydanower has also various legends about Loria (see chs. 2, 5, 7, 9, 12, 16, 22, 31, 34, 46, 48, 77, 80, 87, and 93), which agree on the whole with the second version. Ch. Y. also made use of this version. This version, hardly known to any modern writer except Bloch, in his *Die Kabbalah auf ihrem Höhepunkt und ihre Meister* (Pressburg, 1905), is extant in various MSS. It is hardly necessary to say that all these legends are greatly exaggerated, and sometimes even written "with a purpose." Cf. Modena, ארי נהם, ch. 25; but on the whole, the legends fairly represent the estimation in which Loria was held by his contemporaries. Cf. also Calimani, Conforte Index, Sambari Index, and Azulai, *s. n.* See further, Graetz, *Geschichte,* IX, Index, and Kahana. The account in the text is mostly based on the Constantinople edition, to be quoted as MN, the initials of the *Maaseh Nissim* version. Cf. also Dr. Ginzberg's

article "Cabala," Jewish Encyclopedia, and the literature given there
about the various mystical systems, to which has to be added Bloch as
above. The reader who will study the question will find that we are
still in want of a good exposition of Loria's Cabbala, its strange and
bewildering terminology, and how far it is to be considered a development of Cordovero's system. The best essay on this subject is undoubtedly
the just mentioned article by Dr. Ginzberg, and the book of Mieses
mentioned by him; but even in these articles we have more of the system
of Cordovero as expounded by R. Sabbatai Horwitz than that of Loria
as conveyed by his disciple Vital.

109. See Graetz, *Geschichte*, VIII:211–213. See also ibid., p. 292,
note. Cf. Frumkin, pp. 15, 58, 61–68. From the Responsa of R. Samuel
de Modena, 2, it is clear that the German-Jewish settlements in the
Turkish Empire preceded thost of the Spanish Jews. Cf. Solomon Ro-
sanis, דברי ימי ישראל בתוגרמה, p. 163 seq. Graetz's statement in *Geschichte*, IX:24, that the Jewish settlement in Jerusalem counted in the
year 1522 fifteen hundred families rests on 'a mistaken reading of his
authority, where Graetz, by some oversight, added the word מאות,
which is not to be found in the text. The sense in the Sh. J. is plain
enough, that the German community counted fifteen families. Cf.
Schwarz, pp. 453 and 457. See also Epstein, משפחת לוריא, pp. 33 and 35.
It is interesting to see that our Loria's son was named Solomon Loria,
probably after his grandfather.

110. See MN 2a. Cf. Azulai, *s. n.*, and Ch. Y., 13b. According to
Conforte (40b), however, Loria was the pupil of R. David Abi Zimra
and the colleague of R. Bezaleel, 'a view which is supported by Vital,
9a, רדב״ז רבך.

111. See MN 2a–b. The MS. has the following important additional
matter: . . . ויתן לו הספר ההוא וילך ויתבודד בביתו בחצירו ששה שנים
ולפעמים אומרים לו . . . צריך סיגופים אחרים קשים מהראשונים וכראיותו
כן יצא מחצירו והלך כן להתבודד במצרים הישנה סמוך לנהר נילוס ב'
שנים אחרים ובכל ערב שבת הולך לביתו Sambari has the following
words: במצרים הישנה בכפר אחד שני המקייאץ שבצוען מצרים הנקרא
See Shlo- אל״רודא ע״י חמיו שהיה עשיר גדול וזה הכפר היה ברשותו
mel's chronology (p. 33d), which is somewhat different. It is to be
observed that the MS. contains no statement as to the date of Loria's
leaving Egypt, so that it may be fixed with Graetz, *Geschichte*, IX:587,
not later than 1568. This would allow ample time for his making the
acquaintance of Cordovero, who died in 1570, and becoming his
regular disciple. Kahana's arguments against Graetz (p. 150) are not
convincing. We have always to remember that the tendency was to
reduce Loria's residence in Safed to a minimum, so as to make him
entirely independent of Cordovero.

112. See Shlomel, 33b, and Preface to the עץ החיים. About the mystical writings of R. David Abi Zimra, and those of R. Bezaleel, see
Azulai, *s. n.*

113. See Kahana, p. 203, note 1.

114. See Sambari, 151, and Conforte, 40b.

115. See MN 1b. The MS. adds Joseph Ashkenazi.

116. See *Pardes*, 77a.

117. *Pardes*, 26a.

118. Introduction to the פלח הרמון, 3b.

119. See MN 2b and 3a. More fully in the MS. 3a–b. וכובש
ובואהו מפני הרמ״ק . . . וביום שנפטר אמר להם . . . שבימי הוו צינורי

קדושה חתומים כתבתי דברי בסיתום גדול בבחינת ספירות אבל אחרי
מותי יתגלו יותר הצינורות ויפרש האיש ההוא דברי בבחינת פרצופים
אידרות ד״ץ בס״פ כראיתא. See also Preface to עה״ח. Cf. Graetz, *Ge-*
schichte, IX:589. See also Bloch (as above, note 108), p. 35.

120. See above, note 111, and below, note 153, as to the date of
Loria's death.

121. See Shlomel, 44b, and Bacharach, 6c. It is to be noticed that
Vital maintained a sceptical attitude toward the relations of Caro's
Maggid. See Kahana, p. 268, text and notes, and Rabinowitz, 243. It is
not impossible that the distrust was mutual.

122. See Shlomel, 34b seq. See also Preface to עה״ח.

123. See MN 3a and 5b. The author of the קול בוכים was a disciple of Cordovero.

124. See MN 3ab.

125. See MN 4ab. The MS. 5a has that Loria said: לכן עצתי שכל
אחד מכם יכתוב לו מה שישמע ממני . . . אמנם לא ניתן רשות לכתוב
זולת למה רח״י. The question whether Loria wrote anything, and how
far these so-called traditions in his name are to be relied upon is still
a very mooted one. See Kahana, p. 202, text and notes, and references
given there. The general impression one receives from the various
legendary accounts quoted above is that he declined to write anything,
and that he was reluctant to impart any mystical knowledge even by
word of mouth.

126. See Azulai, *s. n.* See MN 3a with regard to Loria's serving on a
board.

127. See Modena, ארי נהם, p. 66.

128. See such works as the ספר הכונות in its various editions and
arrangements (Zedner, 379), and the נגיד ומצוה by R. Jacob ben
Chayim Zemach (Zedner, 299).

129. See *Shabbath*, 10a.

130. See above, note 128, to which has to be added the פע״ח by
Vital.

131. See Shlomel, 141b. הסגר seems to mean a block of buildings
with a synagogue attached to it. According to the Ch. Y., 34c, it
means a College or a Yeshibah. See also Vital, 16 a.

132. See Graetz, *Geschichte*, XI:587 seq., and references given there.
See also כונות (ed. Jessnitz, 1723), 1a.

133. See כונות, 2d; cf. Kahana, p. 203, note 5.

134. See כונות, 11c.

135. See כונות, 1b.

136. See נגיד ומצוה, 45b.

137. See כונות 6c. Cf. אורחות צדיקים, 67a.

138. See Azkari, p. 48. See also the statement of the traveller
Samson Bak, *Jerusalem*, II, p. 145.

139. See כונות, 3a.

140. See ש״ע האר״י הלכות צדקה.

141. See כונות, 1a.

142. See Ch. Y., IV, 53a and b.

143. See כונות, 3b seq., 24b seq. Bacharach, 11d.

144. See Shlomel, 39c, Bacharach, 11a, and Cl. Y., I, 37b.

145. See Shlomel, 39, and Bacharach, ibid.

146. See גלגולים (Przemysl, 1875), 86a and b.

147. See Azulai, *s. n.* and Kaydanower, ch. 93. Cf. *Pesikta Rabbathi,*
131b seq., and II Esdras 10, *r. v.*

148. See Azulai, *s. n.*

149. See Shlomel, 39a, Bacharach, 10d. Cf. Graetz, *Geschichte,* IX:588. See also ג"ל, 50 seq.; 61 seq.; 87d seq., about various contemporaries of Loria. Cf. also Steinschneider, Catalogue Munich, 2d ed., Berlin, 1895, pp. 250–1.

150. See Shlomel, 35b.

151. See כונות, 1b, and Ch. Y., I, 48b, 51b, and 59b.

152. See Preface to the עה"ח.

153. The date of Loria's death is given by most bibliographers as the year 1572. Against this we have, however, the evidence of Conforte, 41a, who fixes it in the year 1573, for which he is attacked by Azulai and others. Sambari, p. 151, fixes it in the year 1574, which is also confirmed by the traveller Samson Bak. See *Jerusalem,* II, p. 146, text and notes.

154. See the statement of R. Moses Galanti, the Younger, in the preface to the book מגן דוד, by R. David Abi Zimra (Amsterdam, 1679).

155. Horwitz is the one who dwells more on the mystical exposition of the ideal man than any of the authors of ספרי מוסר who became popular with the large masses, and a careful reading of the first seventy pages of his של"ה (ed. Warsaw, 8°) will show that it is chiefly the קדושת הגוף and the hope consequent upon it which he is aiming at. Cf. especially page 19b; 20a seq.; 28a seq.; 30b seq.; 33a seq.; 47a seq.; 59a seq.

156. See *Jerusalem,* II, p. 143, and Frumkin, 117.

157. See Azulai under these names. Cf. also Shlomel, 36a and 41d. See also the Responsa of R. Joseph Trani, I, 82. Cf. also Sambari, 161, with regard to the Loria Synagogue.

13.

The Shulḥan 'Aruk: Enduring Code
of Jewish Law *

by Isadore Twersky

Shulḥan 'Aruk, a term taken over from early rabbinic exegesis in the Midrash [1] and applied to one of the most influential,
truly epochal literary creations of Jewish history, has a double
or even triple meaning, and its use therefore necessitates precise definition or description. *Shulḥan 'Aruk* is the title given
by R. Joseph Karo (1488–1575) to a brief, four-part code of
Jewish law which was published in 1565–66, just over four
hundred years ago. *Shulḥan 'Aruk* also designates a composite,
collaborative work, combining this original text of R. Joseph
Karo, a Spanish emigré from Toledo (1492) who lived and
studied in Turkey and finally settled in Palestine in a period
of turbulence and instability and apocalyptic stirrings, with
the detailed glosses—both strictures and supplements—of R.
Moses Isserles (c. 1525–1572), a well-to-do Polish scholar,
proud of his Germanic background, who studied in Lublin
and became de facto chief rabbi of Cracow in a period of
relative stability and tranquillity. This unpremeditated literary
symbiosis then generated a spate of commentaries and super-
commentaries, brief or expansive, defensive or dissenting, from
the *Sefer Me'irat 'Enayim* of R. Joshua Falk and the *Sefer
Siftei Kohen* of R. Shabbetai ha-Kohen to the *Mishnah Beru-
rah* of R. Israel Meir ha-Kohen; and the term *Shulḥan 'Aruk*
continued to be applied to this multi-dimensional, multi-gen-
erational, ever-expanding folio volume—a fact which attests
the resiliency and buoyancy of the Halachic tradition in
Judaism. A person must, therefore, define his frame of

* From *Judaism*, vol. XVI, no. 2, Spring, 1967.

reference when he purports to glorify or vilify, to acclaim or condemn—or, if he is able to avoid value judgments, to describe historically.[2] The genuinely modest purpose of the following remarks is, first, to chronicle the emergence of the *Shulḥan 'Aruk,* especially in its first and second meanings, and then to describe a few of its salient literary and substantive characteristics. "The rest is commentary," which we should go and study.

i

In the year 1522,[3] R. Joseph Karo, a young, struggling, volatile and ascetic scholar, having settled temporarily and discontentedly in Adrianople, Turkey, launched a massive literary project that would preoccupy him, sometimes at a frenetic pace, for over thirty years—twenty years in the composition and about twelve years in editorial revision and refinement.[4] The stimulus was provided by the worrisome decline in scholarship—"and the wisdom of their wise men shall perish" [5]—coming in the wake of the rigors and vicissitudes of exile, the endless turbulence of history, and the increasing human imperfection.[6] The need was great for a comprehensive as well as authoritative guide, which would stem the undesirable and almost uncontrollable proliferation of texts and provide a measure of religious uniformity in this period of great turmoil and dislocation. This would be accomplished, however, not by producing another compact, sinewy manual— a small volume such as the *Agur,* which R. Karo treats pejoratively [7]—but by reviewing the practical Halachah in its totality. The oracular type of code, containing curt, staccato directives and pronouncements, was neither adequate nor reliable. It did not provide for intellectual stimulus and expansion of the mind, nor did it offer correct guidance in religious practice.

R. Joseph Karo's ambitious undertaking in the field of rabbinic literature, entitled the *Bet Yosef* (*House of Joseph*),[8] was thus motivated by the need to review "all the practical laws of Judaism, explaining their roots and origins in the Talmud" and all the conflicting interpretations concerning them. No extant work answered to this need. In order to avoid duplication or reduce it to a bare minimum, he decided to build his own work around an existing code that was popular and authoritative. He selected the *Turim* of R. Jacob b. Asher (c. 1280–1340) rather than the more famous and widespread *Mishneh Torah* of R. Moses b. Maimon, because the latter was too concise and monolithic, presenting, on the whole, unilateral, undocumented decisions, while the former was expansive and more interpretive, citing alternate views and divergent explanations. At this stage, then, the text of the *Turim* was only a pretext for his own work.[9] His method was to explain every single law in the text, note its original source, and indicate whether the formulation found in the *Turim* was the result of consensus or was subject to dispute. He would, furthermore, explain the alternate interpretations and formulations which the *Turim* referred to but rejected. In addition, he would introduce and elucidate those views which the *Turim* had totally omitted from consideration. As a purely theoretical increment, he promised to examine and explain those views of predecessors—especially Maimonides—which were problematic or remained obscure despite the availability of such commentaries as the *Maggid Mishneh*.[10] He would, incidentally, correct the text of the *Turim,* which suffered many scribal corruptions. That he intended his encyclopedic review of Halachah to be used as a study-guide is indicated by his promise always to give exact bibliographical references in order to enable his readers to consult original texts or check quotations in their original contexts. However, having completed this panoramic presentation and almost detached, academic analysis of a law, he would regularly indicate the normative conclusion, for the "goal is that we should have one Torah and one law." The function of this massive work is thus twofold: to flesh out the bare-bones codifications which are too brief and uninformative, but preserve their sinewiness and pragmatic advantage by unequivocally stating the *pesak,* the binding regulation, in each case.[11] Certitude and finality are among the top-priority items that will be guaranteed.[12]

In connection with this, the author lays bare his juridical methodology, a methodology that was to be vigorously contested, as we shall see. The judicial process was complex. A Talmudist could arrive at the normative conclusion by critically reviewing and appraising all arguments and demonstrations marshalled by his predecessors and then selecting the most cogent, persuasive view. His guide would be examination of underlying texts, relying, in the final analysis, upon his autonomous judgment and not on appeal to authority.[13] This independent, assertive approach is unqualifiedly repudiated by

R. Joseph Karo for two reasons: 1) it would be presumptuous to scrutinize the judgment of such giants as R. Moses b. Naḥman, R. Solomon b. Adret, R. Nissim, and the Tosafists and then pass judgment on them—we are not qualified or competent; 2) even if the task were not beyond our powers and capacities, the process would be too long and arduous. Forcefully underscoring his subservience and *apparently* forfeiting his judicial prerogatives, he chose to arrive at the normative conclusion in each case by following the consensus or at least the majority rule of the greatest medieval codifiers—R. Isaac Alfasi (d. 1103), Maimonides (d. 1204), and R. Asher ben Yeḥiel (d. 1328).[14] Contemporary legislation, innovation, and native usage are given no role whatsoever—almost as if the law were all logic and no experience. In other words, in the realm of commentary R. Joseph Karo was bold and resourceful, while in the realm of adjudication he was laconic, almost self-effacing.

At about the same time, in entirely different circumstances and with a totally different motivation, R. Moses Isserles, born into comfort and affluence,[15] son of a prominent communal leader who was also a gentleman scholar and (for a while) son-in-law of the greatest Talmudic teacher in Poland (R. Shalom Shakna), also began to compile an exhaustive commentary on the *Turim*. He reveals the immediate stimulus which led to his project: having been persuaded by friends to assume rabbinic duties in Cracow—his youth, immaturity, and unripe scholarship notwithstanding—he found himself deciding many Halachic problems and issuing numerous judicial opinions. It was his practice to turn directly to the Talmud and consult its authoritative expositors, among whom he mentions R. Isaac Alfasi, R. Moses b. Naḥman, and R. Asher b. Yeḥiel. He found, however, that he was repeatedly subjected to criticism for having ignored the rulings of the most recent scholars (e.g., R. Jacob Weil, R. Israel Isserlein, R. Israel Bruna) who were really the progenitors of contemporary Polish Jewry and gave it its creative and directive vital force. They introduced, *inter alia*, many preventive ordinances and stringent practices which tended to nullify earlier decisions, and as a result no picture of Halachah could be true to life which did not reflect these resources, motifs and developments. This put R. Moses Isserles in a bad light, and he and his colleagues were, therefore, subjected to much severe criticism, the validity of which he fully appreciated and accepted, as we shall see.

Impromptu, *ad hoc* review—and judicious, instantaneous

application—of all this material, this panoply of interpretations and traditions, would be cumbersome, if not impossible. It therefore occurred to R. Moses Isserles that the way out was to prepare a digest and anthology of all opinions and record them alongside of a standard code. The best book was the *Turim,* for its arrangement was very attractive and useful, and it was easily intelligible to all. He set out, with great determination and commensurate perseverance, to implement this literary plan (he vividly describes his frenetic, indefatigable activity, without ease and without quiet). At a rather advanced stage of his work, he was electrified by the news that "the light of Israel, head of the exile" R. Joseph Karo had composed a comparable commentary on the *Turim,* the *Bet Yosef,* the exellence of which was immediately evident. R. Moses Isserles' anxiety was indescribable; just as he neared the hour of consummation, it appeared that his efforts and privations would turn out to be a wearying exercise in futility. He acknowledges —with what seems to be a blend of modesty and realism— that he could not hold a candle to R. Joseph Karo. However, shock did not lead to paralysis. His peace of mind and momentum were restored when, reassessing the situation, he realized that the field had not been completely preempted and that he was still in a position to make a substantive contribution.

There were three areas in which he could realign his material and operate creatively and meaningfully:

1) He would compress the material, almost encyclopedic in its present proportions, and present a more precise formulation of the law. Length, as Maimonides notes, is one of the deterrents of study.[16] Nevertheless, R. Moses Isserles is somewhat apologetic at this point, because he was fully aware of the pitfalls of excessive brevity; indeed, it had been the codificatory syndrome—the rigidities and inadequacies of delphic manuals—that initially impelled him to disavow the methodology of existing codes. As a compromise, he determined to cite—not to reproduce or summarize—all sources, so that the inquisitive or dissatisfied but learned reader will be able to pursue matters further, while the less sophisticated and less talented reader will still benefit and not be able to argue that the material is too lengthy and complicated.

2) The *Bet Yosef* was too "classical," somewhat remote, for Germanic-Polish Jewry: it failed to represent equally the more recent codifiers and commentators. His work, the *Darke*

Mosheh, would do justice to them by incorporating their positions. It would reflect the historical consciousness of R. Moses Isserles and his colleagues who looked upon themselves as heirs and continuators of the Ashkenazi tradition. On one hand, therefore, the *Darke Mosheh* would be an abridgement of the *Bet Yosef,* and, on the other, it would expand its scope. Clearly, R. Moses Isserles had taken the words of his earlier critics to heart.

3) Perhaps the most radical divergence between the two works appeared in the methodology of *pesak,* formulating the normative conclusion and obligatory pattern of behavior. Unlike R. Joseph Karo, who cautiously claimed to follow the *communis opinio,* or majority rule, of early codifiers, and unlike those who would freely exercise independent judgment in arriving at practical conclusions, R. Moses Isserles adopted a third stance: to follow most recent authorities—*halakah ke-batra'e.*[17] This method would preserve established precedent and respect local custom. It is reflected stylistically in R. Moses Isserles' habit of underwriting the most valid view by adding "and this is customary" and then identifying the source or by noting candidly "and so it appears to me." [18] He is thus more independent and resourceful than R. Joseph Karo, though less so than R. Solomon Luria.[19] In short, as R. Moses Isserles puts it in a rhetorical flourish, "And Moses took the bones of Joseph" [20]—he adapted and transformed the essence of the *Bet Yosef* and abandoned the rest.

This ends the first chapter of our story in which R. Joseph Karo made it to the press before R. Moses Isserles and forced the latter to revise his initial prospectus in light of a changed literary reality. What is, of course, striking is the remarkable parallelism and similarity of attitudes between these two Talmudists, both seeking to push back the frontiers of Halachic literature, both convinced of the need to review individual laws in their totality and not rely upon delphic manuals, and both selecting the same code (*Turim*) as their springboard.

ii

Ten years later, in the course of which the *Bet Yosef* spread far and wide and his authority was increasingly respected, R. Joseph Karo came full cycle in his own attitude towards the oracular-type code. Having previously and persuasively argued against the utility and wisdom of the apodictic compendium, he now conceded its need and efficacy. He himself abridged the voluminous *Bet Yosef*—"gathered the lilies, the sapphires"— and called his new work the *Shulḥan 'Aruk,* "because in it the reader will find all kinds of delicacies" fastidiously arranged and systematized and clarified. He was persuaded that the *Shulḥan 'Aruk* would serve the needs of a diffuse and hetero- geneous audience. Scholars will use it as a handy reference book, so that every matter of law will be perfectly clear and the answer to questions concerning Halachic practice will be immediate and decisive. Young, untutored students will also benefit by committing the *Shulḥan 'Aruk* to memory, for even rote knowledge is not to be underestimated.[21]

When the *Shulḥan 'Aruk* appeared, it elicited praise and provoked criticism; the former could be exuberant, and the latter, abrasive. Some contemporaries needed only to resusci- tate R. Joseph Karo's initial stance and refurbish his arguments against such works as the *Agur.* R. Moses Isserles' reaction moved along the same lines which had determined his reaction to the *Bet Yosef.*[22] He could not—like R. Solomon Luria or R. Yom Tob Lipman Heller—take unqualified exception to the codificatory aim and form,[23] for he had already, in his revised *Darke Mosheh,* aligned himself in principle with this tendency and had eloquently defended it. He could, however, press his substantive and methodological attack on Karo: the latter had neglected Ashkenazic traditions and had failed to abide by the most recent rulings, thereby ignoring custom which was such an important ingredient of the normative law.[24] Moreover, just as R. Joseph Karo drew upon his *Bet Yosef,* so R. Moses Isserles drew upon his *Darke Mosheh;* [25] both, coming full cycle, moved from lively judicial symposium to soulless legis- lative soliloquy. If R. Joseph Karo produced a "set table," R. Moses Isserles spread a "tablecloth" over it.[26] It is certain that the "table" would never have been universally accepted if it had not been covered and adorned with the "tablecloth." R. Moses Isserles' glosses, both strictures and annotations, were the ultimate validation of the *Shulḥan 'Aruk.* The full dialectic has here played itself out, radical opposition to codes giving way to radical codification, almost with a vengeance; for the *Shulḥan 'Aruk* is the leanest of all codes in Jewish history— from the *Bet Yosef* to the *Shulḥan 'Aruk,* from the baroque to the bare.

It is not this dialectical movement *per se* which is novel or noteworthy, for this characterizes much of the history of post-Talmudic rabbinic literature. Attempts to compress the Halachah by formal codification alternate with counter-attempts to preserve the fulness and richness of both the method and substance of the Halachah by engaging in interpretation, analogy, logical inference, and only then formulating the resultant normative conclusion. Any student who follows the course of rabbinic literature from the Geonic works of the eighth century through the *Mishneh Torah* and *Turim* and on down to the *Shulḥan 'Aruk* cannot ignore this see-saw tendency. The tension is ever present and usually catalytic. No sooner is the need for codification met than a wave of non-codificatory work rises. A code could provide guidance and certitude for a while but not finality.[27] *'Arvak 'arva zarik—* "your bondsman requires a bondsman." A code, even in the eyes of its admirers, required vigilant explanation and judicious application. The heartbeat had constantly to be checked and the pulse had to be counted. It became part of a life organism that was never complete or static. What is striking, therefore, in the case of the *Shulḥan 'Aruk* is that the dialectical movement plays itself out in the attitudes and achievements of the same person—"surfing" on the "sea of the Talmud," rising and falling on the crests of analysis and thoughts of argumentation, and then trying to "gather the water into one area," to construct a dike that would produce a slow, smooth flow of its waters. The *Shulḥan 'Aruk* thus offers an instructive example of the dialectical movement in rabbinic literature as a whole.

This whole story is important, I believe, because it expands the historical background against which the *Shulḥan 'Aruk* is to be seen and cautions against excessive preoccupation with purely sociological data, with contemporary stimuli and contingencies. It makes the *Shulḥan 'Aruk* understandable in terms of the general history of Halachic literature and its major trends. It provides an obvious vertical perspective—i.e. literary categories seen as part of an ongoing Halachic enterprise—to be used alongside of an, at best, implicit horizontal perspective—i.e. historical pressures and eschatological hopes—for an explanation of the emergence of the *Shulḥan 'Aruk*.[28] This is strengthened by the striking parallelism between the literary careers of R. Moses Isserles and R. Joseph Karo; their historical situations, environmental influences, social contexts (in a phrase of contemporary jargon, their *sitz-im-leben*) are so different, but their aspirations and attainments are so similar.

iii

When we come to gauge and appraise the impact of the *Shulḥan 'Aruk*, it is idle to speculate whether R. Joseph Karo intended the *Shulḥan 'Aruk* to circulate and be used independently, as a literary unit sufficient to itself, or to be used only as a companion volume together with the *Bet Yosef*. His intention has been disputed and variously construed. Some condemned those who studied the *Shulḥan 'Aruk in vacuo*, thereby acquiring superficial acquaintance with Halachah, claiming that this contravened the author's intention. Others treated the *Shulḥan 'Aruk* in a manner reminiscent of R. Joseph Karo's original attitude as found in the preface to the *Bet Yosef*. In this case, however, the original intention of the author is eclipsed by the historical fact, abetted or perhaps made possible by R. Moses Isserles' glosses,[29] that the *Shulḥan 'Aruk* and not the *Bet Yosef* became R. Joseph Karo's main claim to fame, and its existence was completely separate from and independent of the *Bet Yosef*. Commentators such as R. Abraham Gumbiner in the *Magen Abraham* effectively and irreparably cut the umbilical cord which may have linked the *Shulḥan 'Aruk* with the *Bet Yosef*. What some literary critics have said about poetry may then be applied here: "The design of intention of the author is neither available nor desirable as a standard for judging the success of a work of literary art." [30] In our case, consequently, we should simply see what are some of the characteristics of the *Shulḥan 'Aruk* and some of the repercussions of its great historical success.

Perhaps the single most important feature of the *Shulḥan 'Aruk* is its unswerving concentration on prescribed patterns of behavior to the exclusion of any significant amount of theoretical data. The *Shulḥan 'Aruk* is a manual for practical guidance, not academic study. This practical orientation is discernible in many areas and on different levels.

First of all, by initially adopting the classification of the *Turim*, R. Joseph Karo capitulated unconditionally to the practical orientation. The import of this becomes more vivid when we contrast the two major codes on this point. The *Mishneh Torah* is all-inclusive in scope, obliterating all distinctions between practice and theory, and devoting sustained attention to those laws and concepts momentarily devoid of practical value or temporarily in abeyance because of historical and geographical contingencies. Laws of prayer and of the Temple ceremonial are given equal treatment. Laws concerning the *sotah,* the unfaithful wife (abrogated by R. Johanan b. Zakkai in the first century), are codified in the same detail as the ever practical marriage laws. The present time during which part of the law was in abeyance was, in Maimonides' opinion, an historical anomaly, a fleeting moment in the pattern of eternity. The real historical dimensions were those in which the Torah and its precepts were fully realized, that is, the time after the restoration of the Davidic dynasty, when "all the ancient laws will be reinstituted . . . sacrifices will again be offered, the Sabbatical and Jubilee years will again be observed in accordance with the commandments set forth in the Law." [31] The Oral Law was, therefore, to be codified and studied exhaustively. The *Turim,* on the other hand, addresses itself only to those laws that are relevant, to those concrete problems and issues whose validity and applicability are not confined either temporally or geographically. For while both Maimonides and R. Jacob b. Asher were of one mind in abandoning the sequence of the Talmudic treatises and seeking an independent classification of Halachah, they differed in their goals: Maimonides sought to create a topical-conceptual arrangement that would provide a new interpretive mold for study and would also be educationally sound, while R. Jacob b. Asher was guided only by functionality and as a result was less rigorous conceptually. It involved a lesser degree of logical analysis and abstraction, and did not hesitate to group disparate items together. A code, according to this conception should facilitate the understanding of the operative laws and guide people in translating concepts into rules of conduct.

The *Shulḥan 'Aruk* adds a further rigorism to the practicality of the *Turim.* The *Turim'*s practicality expresses itself in the rigid selection of material, in the circumscribed scope, but not in the method of presentation, which is rich, varied, and suggestive, containing as it does much textual interpretation and brief discussion of divergent views, while the functionality of the *Shulḥan 'Aruk* is so radical that it brooks no expansiveness whatsoever. The judicial *process* is of no concern to the codifier; exegesis, interpretation, derivation, awareness of controversy—all these matters are totally dispensable, even undesirable, for the codifier.[32] In this respect, the *Shulḥan 'Aruk* has greater affinities with the *Mishneh Torah*, which also purports to eliminate conflicting interpretations and rambling discussions and to present *ex cathedra* legislative, unilateral views, without sources and without explanations. The fact is that the *Shulḥan 'Aruk* is much closer to this codificatory ideal than the *Mishneh Torah*, which, after all, is as much commentary as it is code. One has only to compare, at random, parallel sections of the *Turim* and *Shulḥan 'Aruk* to realize fully and directly, almost palpably, the extent to which the *Shulḥan 'Aruk* pruned the *Turim*, relentlessly excising midrashic embellishments, ethical perceptions, and theoretical amplifications. It promised to give the "fixed, final law, without speech and without words." It left little to discretion or imagination.

There is yet another area in which this austere functionality comes to the surface—in the virtually complete elimination of ideology, theology, and teleology. The *Shulḥan 'Aruk*, unlike the *Mishneh Torah* or the *Sefer ha-Rokeaḥ*, has no philosophical or Kabbalistic prolegomenon or peroration. The *Shulḥan 'Aruk*, unlike the *Mishneh Torah* or the *Turim*, does not abound in extra-Halachic comments, guiding tenets and ideological directives.[33] While, as I have tried to prove elsewhere, the *Mishneh Torah* does reveal the full intellectualistic posture of Maimonides,[34] the *Shulḥan 'Aruk* does not even afford an oblique glimpse of the Kabbalistic posture of R. Joseph Karo, who appears here in the guise of the civil lawyer for whom "nothing was more pointless, nothing more inept than a law with a preamble." [35] He was concerned exclusively with what Max Weber called the "methodology of sanctification" which produces a "continuous personality pattern," not with its charismatic goals or stimuli, the ethical underpinning or theological vision which suffuse the Halachah with significance, guarantee its radical, ineradicable spirituality and thereby nurture the religious consciousness. The *Shulḥan 'Aruk* gives the concrete idea, but omits what Dilthey called *Erlebniss*, the experiential component. In the *Shulḥan 'Aruk* the Halachah manifests itself as the *regula iuris*, a rule of life characterized by stability, regularity, and fixedness, making known to people "the way they are to go and the practices they are to follow" (Exodus 18:20). The specific, visible practices are not coordinated with invisible meaning or unspecified experience. One can say, in general, that there are two major means by which apparently trans-Halachic material has been organically linked with the Halachah proper: 1) construction of an ideational framework which indicates the ultimate concerns and gives coherence, direction and vitality to the concrete actions; 2) elaboration of either a rationale of the law or a mystique of the law which suggests explanations and motives for the detailed commandments. The *Shulḥan 'Aruk*, for reasons of its own, about which we may only conjecture, attempts neither.

iv

This restrictive, almost styptic trait of the *Shulḥan 'Aruk* was noticed—and criticized—by contemporaries, foremost among whom was R. Mordecai Jaffe (1530–1612), disciple of R. Moses Isserles and R. Solomon Luria and successor of R. Judah Loewe, the famous Maharal, of Prague. It is worth re-telling the story of the composition of his major, multi-volume work, known as the *Lebush*, inasmuch as it zeroes in on the radical functionality of the *Shulḥan 'Aruk* and also briefly reviews the tense dialectic surrounding codification which we discussed above.

R. Mordecai Jaffe, a very articulate, sophisticated writer who was well acquainted with the contemporary scene, describes the enthusiastic reception accorded to the *Bet Yosef* because people imagined it would serve as a concise, spirited compendium, obviating the need for constant, wearisome recourse to dozens of rabbinic volumes in order to determine the proper Halachic course. He shared this feeling and heightened anticipation, but enthusiasm gave way to disillusionment as he realized that the *Bet Yosef* was anything but concise. Inasmuch as a comprehensive and compact compendium remained an urgent desideratum, he began a condensation of the *Bet Yosef* that would serve this purpose. External factors—an edict of expulsion by the Austrian emperor, which compelled him to flee Bohemia and settle in Italy—interrupted his work. In Italy, where so much Hebrew printing was being done, he heard that R. Joseph Karo himself had made arrangements to print an abridgement. Again he desisted, for he could not presume to improve upon the original author who would unquestionably produce the most balanced, incisive abridgement of his own work. R. Jaffe adds parenthetically—but with remarkable candor—that there was a pragmatic consideration as well: even if he persisted and completed his work, he could not hope to compete publicly with such a prestigious master as R. Joseph Karo—and to do it just for personal consumption, to satisfy his own needs, would be extravagant.

However, upon preliminary examination of the *Shulḥan 'Aruk*—in Venice—he noted two serious deficiencies. First, it was too short and astringent, having no reasons or explanations—"like a sealed book, a dream which had no interpretation or meaning." He describes it as "a table well prepared with all kinds of refreshments, but the dishes are tasteless, lacking the salt of reasoning which makes the broth boil and warms the individual"—i.e., lacking a minimum of explanatory and exhortatory material to embellish and spiritualize the bald Halachic directives. Second, it was almost exclusively Maimonidean, or Sephardic, and Ashkenazic communities could not, therefore, be guided by it—an argument that had been tellingly and uncompromisingly put forward by both his teachers (Isserles and Luria). Again he started work on a new composition which would fill the gap, and again he abandoned his plans in deference to R. Moses Isserles who was reported to have undertaken this task. When the full *Shulḥan 'Aruk* appeared—the text of R. Joseph Karo and the glosses of R. Moses Isserles—he quickly realized that only the second deficiency had been remedied, that Ashkenazic Halachah had found a worthy and zealous spokesman, but the first deficiency remained—and this was glaring. Some measure of explanation was as indispensable for law as salt was for food. So, for the third time, he turned to producing a code which would a) strive for a golden mean between inordinate length (the *Bet Yosef*) and excessive brevity (the *Shulḥan 'Aruk*); and b) would explain, motivate, and spiritualize the law, often with the help of new Kabbalistic doctrines.

In effect, R. Mordecai Jaffe—whose code was a potential but short-lived rival to the *Shulḥan 'Aruk*—addressed himself to the problem which great Halachists, ethicists, philosophers and mystics have constantly confronted: how to maintain a rigid, punctilious observance of the law and concomitantly avoid externalization and routinization. On one hand, we hear the echoes of Maimonides, R. Eleazar ha-Rokeaḥ of Worms, and R. Menaḥem b. Zerah (author of the *Zedah la-*

Derek), who attempt to combine laws with their reasons and rationale, as well as R. Baḥya ibn Pakuda, R. Jonah Gerondi, and R. Isaac Abuhab, to mention just a few of his predecessors. On the other hand, this tone continues to reverberate in the *Shulḥan ʿAruk* of R. Shneur Zalman of Ladi, as well as in the writings of R. Isaiah Hurwitz and R. Moses Ḥayyim Luzzatto, to mention just a few of his successors. The common denominator here is the concern that the Halachic enterprise always be rooted in and related to spirituality, to knowledge of God obtained through study and experience. All difficulties notwithstanding, it was generally felt that even when dealing with the corpus of practical, clearly definable law, an attempt should be made to express the—perhaps incommunicable—values and aspirations of religious experience and spiritual existence.

V

However, when all is said, it would be incorrect and insensitive to assert unqualifiedly that the *Shulḥan ʿAruk*, that embodiment of Halachah which Jewish history has proclaimed supreme, is a spiritless, formalistic, even timid work. Its opening sentence, especially as elaborated by R. Moses Isserles, acts as the nerve center of the entire Halachic system and the fountain of its strength.

A man should make himself strong and brave as a lion [36] to rise in the morning for the service of his Creator, so that he should "awake the dawn" (Psalms 57:9) [37] . . .

"I have set the Lord always before me" (Psalms 16:8). This is a cardinal principle in the Torah and in the perfect (noble) ways of the righteous who walk before God. For [38] man does not sit, move, and occupy himself when he is alone in his house, as he sits, moves, and occupies himself when he is in the presence of a great king; nor does he speak and rejoice while he is with his family and relatives as he speaks in the king's council. How much more so when man takes to heart that the Great King, the Holy One, blessed be He, whose "glory fills the whole earth" (Isaiah 6:3), is always standing by him and observing all his doings, as it is said in Scripture: "Can a man hide himself in secret places that I shall not see him?" (Jeremiah 23:24). Cognizant of this, he will immediately achieve reverence and humility, fear and shame before the Lord, blessed be He, at all times.

Law is dry and its details are burdensome only if its observance lacks vital commitment, but if all actions of a person are infused with the radical awareness that he is acting in the presence of God, then every detail becomes meaningful and relevant. Such an awareness rules out routine, mechanical actions; everything must be conscious and purposive in a God-oriented universe, where every step of man is directed towards God. Halachah, like nature, abhors a vacuum; it recognizes no twilight zone of neutrality or futility.[39] It is all-inclusive. Consequently, every action—even tying one's shoes [40]—can be and is invested with symbolic meaning. Nothing is accidental, behavioral, purely biological. Even unavoidable routine is made less perfunctory. The opening paragraph of the *Shulḥan 'Aruk* is thus a clear and resounding declaration concerning the workings and the searchings of the spirit. Its tone should reverberate throughout all the subsequent laws and regulations. It provides—as does also paragraph 231, which urges man to see to it that *all* his deeds be "for the sake of heaven"—an implicit rationale for the entire Halachah, but it is a rationale that must be kept alive by the individual. It cannot be passively taken for granted; it must be passionately pursued.

What I am saying, in other words, is that to a certain extent the *Shulḥan 'Aruk* and Halachah are coterminous and that the "problem" of the *Shulḥan 'Aruk* is precisely the "problem" of Halachah as a whole. Halachah itself is a tense, vibrant, dialectical system which regularly insists upon normativeness in action and inwardness in feeling and thought.[41] It undertook to give concrete and continuous expression to theological ideals, ethical norms, ecstatic moods, and historical concepts but never superseded or eliminated these ideals and concepts. Halachah itself is, therefore, a coincidence of opposites: prophecy and law, charisma and institution, mood and medium, image and reality, the thought of eternity and the life of temporality. Halachah itself, therefore, in its own behalf, demands the coordination of inner meaning and external observance—and it is most difficult to comply with such a demand and sustain such a delicate, highly sensitized synthesis.[42]

There can be no doubt that R. Joseph Karo, the arch mystic passionately yearning for ever greater spiritual heights, could not have intended to create a new concept of orthopraxis, of punctilious observance of the law divorced, as it were, from all spiritual tension. While this may indeed have been one of the unintended repercussions of the *Shulḥan 'Aruk*—while it may unknowingly have contributed to the notion, maintained by a strange assortment of people, that Judaism is all deed and no creed, all letter and no spirit—its author would certainly discountenance such an interpretation and dissociate himself from it. If the *Shulḥan 'Aruk* only charts a specific way of life but does not impart a specific version or vision of meta-Halachah, it is because the latter is to be supplied and experienced independently.[43] The valiant attempt of so many scholars to compress the incompressible, imponderable values of religious experience into cold words and neat formulae, alongside of generally lucid Halachic prescriptions, did not elicit the support of R. Joseph Karo. Halachah could be integrated with and invigorated by disparate, mutually exclusive systems, operating with different motives and aspirations, as long as these agreed on the means and directives. I would suggest that R. Mordecai Jaffe's parenthetical apology for his expansive-interpretive approach to Halachah—that every person spices his food differently, that every wise person will find a different reason or taste in the law, and this reason should not be codified or legislated—may well be what prompted R. Joseph Karo, generally reticent about spiritual matters, to limit his attention to the concrete particularization of Halachah. This could be presented with a good measure of certitude and finality, but its spiritual coordinates required special and separate, if complementary, treatment.[44]

As a personal postscript, or "concluding unscientific postscript," I would like to suggest that, if the Psalmist's awareness of "I have set God before me continually" (Psalms 16:8)—the motto of the *Shulḥan 'Aruk*—*is* one of the standards of saintliness,[45] then all "*Shulḥan 'Aruk* Jews," all who abide by its regulations while penetrating to its essence and its real motive powers, should be men who strive for saintliness. But strive they must, zealously, imaginatively, and with unrelenting commitment.[46]

Notes

1. *Mekilta* on Exodus 21:1, ed. J. Z. Lauterbach (Philadelphia, 1935), v. III, p. 1: " 'And these are the ordinances which thou shalt set before them.' Arrange them in proper order before them like a set table

(*shulḥan 'aruk*)." See Rashi on this verse, who adds, "like a table set before a person with everything ready for eating." Attention should be paid to the identical use of this phrase in the thirteenth century by R. Menahem ha-Me'iri to describe his Talmudic opus; see introduction to *Bet ha-Beḥirah* on *Berakot* (Jerusalem, 1960), p. 31. Also, R. Solomon ibn Adret uses this metaphor in verbal form in the introduction to his *Torat ha-Bayit*.

Leo Baeck, *This People Israel* (Philadelphia, 1965), p. 301, suggests another association: "When Joseph Karo chose his title, he almost certainly had in mind that psalm which begins, 'He Who is my shepherd; I shall not want' and continues, 'Thou preparest a table before me in the presence of mine enemies' (*Psalms* 23)."

2. Contemporaries would sometimes criticize the *Shulḥan 'Aruk*, even stridently, but it was left for modern, post-Enlightenment writers to vilify it. See, for example, the references in L. Greenwald, *R. Joseph Karo u-Zemano* (New York, 1954), pp. 174–176; B. Cohen, *Law and Tradition in Judaism* (New York, 1959), pp. 66–68; R. J. Z. Werblowsky, *Joseph Karo* (Oxford, 1962), p. 7; *Jewish Encyclopedia*, III, p. 588.

Actually, there is no need even for devotees of the *Shulḥan 'Aruk* to indulge in meta-historical panegyrics, for supernatural phenomena carry no weight in Halachic matters. The *Shulḥan 'Aruk* is not a revealed canon, nor is it a hypostasis of the Law. In the long, creative history of the Oral Law, it is one major link connecting R. Hai Gaon, Maimonides, Naḥmanides and R. Solomon ibn Adret with R. Elijah Gaon of Vilna, R. Akiba Eiger, and R. Yosef Rosen. It is a significant work which, for a variety of reasons, became a repository and stimulus, a treasure and inspiration for Halachah, both practice and study.

3. What follows is based essentially on the authors' own, often autobiographical narratives: R. Joseph Karo's introductions to the *Bet Yosef* and R. Moses Isserles' introduction to the *Darke Mosheh*, which can conveniently be found in the Jerusalem, 1958 reprint of the *Turim*. I have interpolated historical or other explanatory comments, but have not seen fit to burden the reader with cumbersome references. I wanted simply to recount their tale.

4. He came to Palestine and settled in Safed in the year 1536. See Professor Z. Dimitovsky in *Sefunot*, VII, p. 62, n. 137.

5. The verse is Isaiah 29:14 and is quoted in similar context by Maimonides, introduction to the *Mishneh Torah*. The correlation of political adversity and intellectual decline becomes a constant theme and appears almost as a stereotype justification for Halachic abridgements or codifications. Difficult times necessitate the composition of books which would facilitate the study and perpetuate the practice of Halachah. Note, for example, the introduction to the *Turim*. See my *Rabad of Posquières* (Cambridge, 1962), pp. 133–134, n. 9.

6. This reflects the widespread attitude of humility, even self-effacement, expressed in the Talmudic dictum: "If those before us were sons of angels, we are sons of men, and if those before us were sons of men, we are like asses" (*Shabbat*, 122b; *Yoma*, 9b). It is typical of the deep-rooted veneration traditionally displayed by later scholars to early masters. However, it did not, as we shall see, restrict independence of mind or stifle creative innovation. Fidelity and freedom were felicitously combined.

7. Why this small work, written by R. Jacob Landau at the end of the fifteenth century, is singled out for special criticism is not clear. The

reason may be that it was simply one of the most recent representatives of this genre. Or was R. Joseph Karo provoked by the author's declaration that he produced this compendium in order to satisfy the minimal needs of Halachic study in the most economical way so as to provide ample time for philosophic study?

8. He thus incorporated his first name into the title—again, pretty much standard literary procedure. There is, however, an added homiletical explanation: just as the house of Joseph in Egypt supplied bodily nourishment, so this book will supply spiritual nourishment.

9. Actually, the *Mishneh Torah,* with its theoretical approach, which included all laws and concepts, even those temporarily devoid of practical value, would not have been consonant with R. Joseph Karo's practical orientation, while the *Turim,* with its limited scope, did coincide with the latter goal. Another reason for selecting the *Turim* could have been the fact that the *Turim* was the most popular textbook at the time.

10. This foreshadows his later work, the *Kesef Mishneh,* in which he reveals himself as an astute, sympathetic and resourceful student of the *Mishneh Torah.*

11. Later commentators—e.g., the authors of the *Sefer Me'irat 'Enayim* and the *Bayit Ḥadash*—felt that R. Joseph Karo's ultimate codificatory aim vitiated his commentatorial one and that the former prevailed at the expense of the latter. Their own works, which were intended exclusively as faithful text commentaries, were thus urgent desiderata. Contemporaries such as R. Solomon Luria (*Yam shel Shelomoh, Ḥullin,* introduction) note the extraordinarily wide bibliographic coverage and unusual erudition of the *Bet Yosef.*

12. His striving for a powerful, central authority is unmistakable (and, incidentally, something he shared with his Sephardic teachers and colleagues—e.g., the great R. Jacob Berab). This aspiration is quite prominent also in the *Maggid Mesharim,* a revealing and intriguing diary of instructions and messages received from his angelic mentor. Analysis of this work is the main concern of Professor Werblowsky's study. Professor Dimitrovsky's article in *Sefunot,* VII provides much background information; it is important and suggestive.

13. The following passage from Benjamin Cardozo, *The Nature of the Judicial Process* (New Haven, 1921), p. 10, comes to mind:

> What is it that I do when I decide a case? To what sources of information do I appeal for guidance? In what proportions do I permit them to contribute to the result? . . . If a precedent is applicable, when do I refuse to follow it? If no precedent is applicable, how do I reach the rule that will make a precedent for the future? If I am seeking logical consistency, the symmetry of the legal structure, how far shall I seek it? At what point shall the quest be halted by some discrepant custom, by some consideration of the social welfare, by my own or the common standards of justice and morals?

The most forceful contemporary exponent of this approach was R. Solomon Luria, as exemplified in his *Yam shel Shelomoh.* He was preceded in this by R. Isaiah of Trani. See, generally, my *Rabad of Posquières,* pp. 216–219.

14. This distinguished triumvirate was already recognized as authoritative before the time of R. Joseph Karo, as he himself implies. Explicit confirmation is found in the *Responsa* of R. David b. Zimra (Radbaz), v. IV, n. 626. R. Moses Isserles (introduction to *Shulḥan 'Aruk*) and

R. Joshua Falk (introduction to *Sefer Me'irat 'Enayim*) suggest that the Sephardic view would automatically prevail inasmuch as Alfasi and Maimonides would always coalesce to determine the majority view. The truth is that R. Asher b. Yehiel was not fully representative of the Tosafistic school of France and Germany and was at a very early date accepted in Spain, to the exclusion of other Tosafists. This was noted in the introduction to the commentary *Ma'adane Yom Tob* and also in an anonymous responsum in R. Joseph Karo's *Abkat Rokel*, n. 18, which refers to R. Asher as a "Spanish rabbi." See the literary study by José Faur in the *Proceedings of the American Academy for Jewish Research*, XXIII (1965).

15. See his *Responsa*, nn. 45, 95, 109, and others.

16. The reference is probably to the *Guide for the Perplexed*, I, 34 (tr. S. Pines [Chicago, 1963], p. 73): "For man has in his nature a desire to seek the ends; and he often finds preliminaries tedious and refuses to engage in them."

17. In formulating this principle, R. Moses Isserles relies—with good effect—upon the authority of R. Isaac Alfasi. See *Darke Mosheh*, introduction, and *Yoreh De'ah*, 35:13. An anonymous contemporary, writing against R. Joseph Karo, advances the same position; *Abkat Rokel*, n. 18. Note R. Joseph Karo's important discussion in *Kesef Mishneh*, *Hilkot Mamrim*, II:1.

18. It is noteworthy that R. Hayyim b. Bezalel, a former classmate and colleague of R. Moses Isserles, took him to task for not going far enough in his vindication of local custom. The *Wikkuah Mayyim Hayyim* is built on this premise. This work is significant also in that it opts for still another possibility of juridical methodology. The author's contention is that a code should simply review all the different opinions and arrange them systematically but leave the final determination to the specific rabbinic authority that is responsible for a given decision. He protests forcefully against "levelling" books which tend to obliterate the distinctions between scholar and layman and implicitly undermine the authority of the scholar. A code should be an auxiliary manual for the judge and scholar, not an explicit, monolithic work.

19. See n. 13. R. Solomon Luria also displays an anti-Spanish, especially anti-Maimonidean, animus or polemicism, which is not found in R. Moses Isserles.

20. Exodus 13:19, with a play on the word "bones" (*'azmot*), which may be interpreted as essence (*'azmut*).

21. See *Berakot*, 38b. It is interesting that Maimonides also intended his *Mishneh Torah* to be used by "great and small," learned and simple.

22. See *Rabad of Posquières*, p. 113, and pp. 96–97.

23. A helpful review of these attitudes can be found in H. Tchernovitz, *Toledot ha-Poskim*, v. III. The rationale of this position is eloquently stated by the Maharal of Prague in *Netibot 'Olam, Netib ha-Torah*, ch. 15. I say "unqualified exception" because the fact is that R. Moses Isserles' contribution to the *Shulhan 'Aruk* is significantly more expansive than that of R. Joseph Karo.

24. See, e.g., *Orah Hayyim*, 619; *Yoreh De'ah*, 381, 386.

25. See his *Responsa*, nn. 35, 131.

26. The imagery is provided by R. Moses Isserles himself. The "table" was bare and uninviting without his "tablecloth."

27. See B. Cardozo, *The Nature of the Judicial Process*, p. 18: "Justinian's prohibition of any commentary on the product of his codifiers is remembered only for its futility."

28. This important vertical perspective is usually left out of the picture. See e.g., R. Werblowsky, *Joseph Karo,* pp. 7, 95, 167. There can be little doubt that R. Joseph Karo was preoccupied with eschatological hopes and that he saw the catastrophic nature of his period as having messianic significance. This is attested, *inter alia,* in the introduction to *Sefer Ḥaredim.*

It would indeed be strange if the mood of that generation—physically uprooted, emotionally shattered, but spiritually exuberant—did not leave an imprint on the *Shulḥan 'Aruk.* Note in this connection the author's novel emphasis upon the desirability of unflagging awareness of the state of exile, dispersion and destruction. After reproducing (*Oraḥ Ḥayyim* 1:2) the statement of the *Turim* concerning nocturnal prayer dealing with the destruction and the dispersion, R. Joseph Karo adds in a separate entry that "it is proper for every God-fearing person to grieve and worry about the destruction of the Holy Temple." This is a cardinal principle, part of one's consciousness—over and beyond any concrete expression.

29. The fact is that R. Moses Isserles' strictures are very radical, but low-keyed and disarmingly calm. They are free of the stridency and impetuosity which punctuate the glosses of R. Abraham b. David on the *Mishneh Torah,* but are nevertheless uncompromising in their criticism. While they contain explanations, amplifications and supplements, most were designed simply to supersede R. Joseph Karo's conclusions. It is only the harmonious literary form that avoided an overt struggle for Halachic hegemony such as occurred in other periods—for example, in the 13th century when Spanish students of the great Naḥmanides attempted to impose their customs and interpretations on Provence. There was no dilution of diversity in this case, either, but there was at least a formal fusion of Ashkenazi and Sephardi Halachah in one work. Sephardim continued to rely on R. Joseph Karo, pointing to the verse, "Go unto Joseph; what he saith to you, do" (Genesis 41:55); Ashkenazim continued to rely on R. Moses Isserles, adapting the verse, "For the children of Israel go out with upraised hands" (*beyad ramah*—and "Ramah" was the acrostic for R. Moses Isserles).

30. W. K. Wimsatt and M. C. Beardsley, "The Intentional Fallacy," *Sewanee Review,* LIV (1946), 468.

31. *Hilkot Melakim,* XI:1. See Rabbi J. B. Soloveitchik, "Ish ha-Halakah," *Talpiyot,* 1944, pp. 668ff.

32. This is, of course, a codificatory utopia, never achieved. First, all the author's protestations notwithstanding, the *Shulḥan 'Aruk* is not a mechanical, scissors-and-paste compilation. For all his veneration and authority and his *a priori* declaration of subservience to the three great medieval codifiers, the author writes selectively and discriminatingly. Already his contemporary, R. Ḥayyim b. Bezalel, observed (in the *Wikkuaḥ Mayyim Ḥayyim*) that Karo did not really follow the standards he outlined theoretically. Similarly, R. Moses Isserles in the introduction to the *Darke Mosheh* called attention to inconsistencies and discrepancies between the statement of intention and actual performance. There are many examples which show how subtly but steadily the author of the *Shulḥan 'Aruk* modified positions and expressed his own judgment. This is often indicated by the deletion of a phrase or addition of a word in what is otherwise a verbatim reproduction of a source. Note *Yoreh De'ah* 246:4, which is almost an exact quotation of Maimonides, *Hilkot Talmud Torah,* I:11, 12. The author has, however, expunged the sentence which makes philosophy (*pardes*) an integral, even paramount com-

ponent of the Oral Tradition, for this statement obviously caused him
more than a twinge of discomfiture. R. Moses Isserles reinserts this
reference less conspicuously and more restrainedly toward the end of
his gloss. The author's censure of the writings of Immanuel of Rome
(*Oraḥ Hayyim*, 307:16) is an example of a novel, emphatic addition.

Second, all the author's statements about certitude, finality, and unilateral formulations notwithstanding, there are many paragraphs which
cite multiple views. Sometimes reference is even made to the authorship of these divergent views. See, e.g., *Oraḥ Hayyim*, 18:1; 32:9; 422:2
and many others. This area of indecision is one of the major concerns
of the 19th-century work, *'Aruk ha-Shulḥan* by Rabbi Y. M. Epstein,
and such earlier works as *Halacha Aharonah we-Kuntros ha-Re'ayot.*

Third, there is a sparse amount of interpretive and exegetical material.
See, e.g., *Oraḥ Hayyim*, 6:1, which contains the explanation of a liturgical
text. Note also 11:15, 14:1, 14:3, 15:4, 17:1 and many others where reasons are briefly adduced or the Halachic process is traced. What is more,
even the self-sufficiency of the work is weakened when, for example, the
author says (*Oraḥ Hayyim*, 597), "this is explained well in the *Tur* in
this section."

33. One striking illustration is provided by the prologue of the *Turim*
to the *Ḥoshen Mishpat*, where the instrumental role of positive law is
expounded. The point of departure is the apparent contradiction between
two statements in the first chapter of *Pirke Abot*. One reads: "Upon
three things the world stands, upon Torah, upon divine service, and
upon acts of lovingkindness." The other reads: "By three things is the
world sustained, by justice, truth, and peace." These are means; the
others are ends. The author of the *Shulḥan 'Aruk* omits all preambles
and plunges directly into the legal-institutional details. Compare the two
also at *Oraḥ Hayyim*, 61, 125, 242 (introduction to the laws of Sabbath)
and others. At *Yoreh De'ah*, 335 (visitation of the sick), the *Turim*
starts unhurriedly with a midrashic motif used by Naḥmanides at the
beginning of his code *Torat ha-Adam*, while the *Shulḥan 'Aruk* plunges
medias in res. It has no time—or need—for adornment.

34. In my article "Some Non-Halakic Aspects of the Mishneh Torah,"
which is scheduled to appear soon in *Medieval and Renaissance Studies,*
ed. A. Altman (Cambridge, 1967).

35. J. W. Jones, *The Law and Legal Theory of the Greeks,* p. 8.
R. Moses Isserles fleshed out a good number of the lean formulations in
the *Shulḥan 'Aruk,* introducing many Kabbalistic motifs and explanations. See, for example, *Oraḥ Hayyim*, 426 (on New Moon), 583 (on
Hoshanah Rabbah), 664 (on *kapparot*), and others. See also 290, in
comparison with the *Turim*. He is thus much less reserved and less reticent than his Sephardic counterpart.

36. See *Pirke Abot,* V:23.

37. This verse, meaning that man "awakens the dawn and not that
the dawn awakens man," is elaborated in the Palestinian Talmud,
Berakot, ch. 1 and is cited by the *Turim*.

38. What follows is part quotation, part paraphrase from the *Guide
for the Perplexed,* III, 52. Maimonides refers in this context to the Talmudic saying in *Kiddushin,* 31a forbidding a person to "walk about
proudly, with erect stature," because of the verse, "the whole earth is
full of His glory." He concludes: "This purpose to which I have drawn
your attention is the purpose of all the actions prescribed by the Law."

39. See Maimonides' definition of futile action in *Guide for the Per-*

plexed III, 25: "A futile action is that action by which no end is aimed at at all, as when some people play with their hands while thinking and like the actions of the negligent and the inattentive."

40. *Oraḥ Ḥayyim,* 2:4.

41. See the brief discussion of this in my article in *Tradition,* V (1963), pp. 144–45. For a clear, almost unnoticed example of this correlation, see *Yoreh De'ah,* 335:4 where it is stated that the external action of visiting a sick person without the concomitant feeling of compassion and inward action of prayer for his recovery does not constitute the fulfillment of a *mizvah.*

42. See in this connection G. Van der Leeuw, *Religion in Essence and Manifestation* (Harper, 1963), II, p. 459ff.; Joachim Wach, *Sociology of Religion* (Chicago, 1944), p. 17ff.

43. The introduction to the *Shulḥan 'Aruk* should perhaps be re-examined at this point. After stating that this compendium will serve the needs of the veteran scholar and the uninitiated student, the author refers to the pleasures which the *maskilim,* the wise men, will derive from his work. *Maskilim* is a common epithet for Kabbalists, for mystics proficient in esoteric lore. "The wise will shine like the brightness of heaven when they shall have rest from their travail and the labor of their hands." Does this suggest that the *Shulḥan 'Aruk* will provide a compass with the help of which the *maskilim* will be able to chart their own course in the lofty spiritual realms?

It should also be noted that R. Joseph Karo is for the most part uncommunicative about his inner world, his spiritual *Anschauung,* and even about such contemporary issues in which he was deeply involved, as the attempted re-institution of ordination in Safed. I would add that even in the *Kesef Mishnah* he remains remarkably reticent (see, e.g., *Hilkot Talmud Torah,* I:11, 12), and only occasionally is a subdued comment forthcoming (e.g., *Yesode ha-Torah,* I:10; *Teshubah* III:7; X:6).

The introduction to the *Bet Yosef* has a single laconic reference to the *Zohar.* R. Moses Isserles is more expressive in this respect; see n. 33.

44. See the balanced remarks of Werblowsky, pp. 290–92; also pp. 146–47.

45. S. Schechter, *Studies in Judaism* (New York, 1958), p. 147.

46. See R. Moses Ḥayyim Luzzatto, *Mesillat Yesharim* (Philadelphia, 1948), pp. 3–4.

14.

Preface (to the English Edition of Leo Strauss, Spinoza's Critique of Religion)

by Leo Strauss

This study on Spinoza's *Theologico-political Treatise* was written during the years 1925–28 in Germany.* The author was a young Jew born and raised in Germany who found himself in the grip of the theologico-political predicament.

At that time Germany was a liberal democracy. The regime was known as the Weimar Republic. In the light of the most authoritative political document of recent Germany—Bismarck's *Thoughts and Recollections*—the option for Weimar reveals itself as an option against Bismarck. In the eyes of Bismarck Weimar stood for a leaning to the West, if not for the inner dependence of the Germans on the French and above all on the English, and a corresponding aversion to everything Russian. But Weimar was above all the residence of Goethe, the contemporary of the collapse of the Holy Roman Empire of the German Nation, and of the victory of the French Revolution and Napoleon—Goethe whose sympathetic understanding was open to both antagonists and who identified himself in his thought with neither. By linking itself to Weimar the German liberal democracy proclaimed its moderate, non-radical character: its resolve to keep a balance between dedication to the principles of 1789 and dedication to the highest German tradition.

The Weimar Republic was weak. It had a single moment of strength, if not of greatness: its strong reaction to the

* N.B. Strauss's preface here (written in 1962) is to the English translation of his own book, *Die Religionskritik Spinozas als Grundlage seiner Bibelwissenschaft* (written in 1925–28). Ed.

murder of the Jewish Minister of Foreign Affairs, Walther Rathenau, in 1922. On the whole it presented the sorry spectacle of justice without a sword or of justice unable to use the sword. The election of Field-Marshal von Hindenburg to the presidency of the German Reich in 1925 showed everyone who had eyes to see that the Weimar Republic had only a short time to live: the old Germany was stronger—stronger in will—than the new Germany. What was still lacking then for the destruction of the Weimar Republic was the opportune moment; that moment was to come within a few years. The weakness of the Weimar Republic made certain its speedy destruction. It did not make certain the victory of National Socialism. The victory of National Socialism became necessary in Germany for the same reason that the victory of Communism had become necessary in Russia: the man with the strongest will or single-mindedness, the greatest ruthlessness, daring, and power over his following, and the best judgment about the strength of the various forces in the immediately relevant political field was the leader of the revolution.[1]

Half-Marxists trace the weakness of the Weimar Republic to the power of monopoly capitalism and the economic crisis of 1929, but there were other liberal democracies which were and remained strong although they had to contend with the same difficulties. It is more reasonable to refer to the fact that the Weimar Republic had come into being through the defeat of Germany in World War I, although this answer merely leads to the further question of why Germany had not succeeded in becoming a liberal democracy under more auspicious circumstances (for instance, in 1848), i.e. why liberal democracy had always been weak in Germany. It is true that the Bismarckian regime as managed by William II had already become discredited prior to World War I and still more so through that war and its outcome; correspondingly, liberal democracy had become ever more attractive; but at the crucial moment the victorious liberal democracies discredited liberal democracy in the eyes of Germany by the betrayal of their principles through the Treaty of Versailles.

It is safer to try to understand the low in the light of the high than the high in the light of the low. In doing the latter one necessarily distorts the high, whereas in doing the former one does not deprive the low of the freedom to reveal itself fully as what it is. By its name the Weimar Republic refers one back to the greatest epoch of German thought and letters, to the epoch extending from the last third of the eighteenth century to the first third of the nineteenth. No one can say that classical Germany spoke clearly and distinctly in favor of liberal democracy. This is true despite the fact that classical Germany had been initiated by Rousseau. In the first place Rousseau was the first modern critic of the fundamental modern project (man's conquest of nature for the sake of the relief of man's estate) who thereby laid the foundation for the distinction, so fateful for German thought, between civilization and culture. Above all, the radicalization and deepening of Rousseau's thought by classical German philosophy culminated in Hegel's *Philosophy of Right,* the legitimation of that kind of constitutional monarchy which is based on the recognition of the rights of man, and in which government is in the hands of highly educated civil servants appointed by an hereditary king. It has been said, not without reason, that Hegel's rule over Germany came to an end only on the day Hitler came to power. But Rousseau prepared not only the French Revolution and classical German philosophy, but also that extreme reaction to the French Revolution which is German romanticism. To speak politically and crudely, "the romantic school in Germany . . . was nothing other than the resurrection of medieval poetry as it had manifested itself . . . in art and in life." [2] The longing for the middle ages began in Germany at the very moment when the actual middle ages— the Holy Roman Empire ruled by a German—ended, in what was then thought to be the moment of Germany's deepest humiliation. In Germany, and only there, did the end of the middle ages coincide with the beginning of the longing for the middle ages. Compared with the medieval Reich which had lasted for almost a millennium until 1806, Bismarck's Reich (to say nothing of Hegel's Prussia) revealed itself as a little Germany not only in size. All profound German longings— for those for the middle ages were not the only ones nor even the most profound—all these longings for the origins or, negatively expressed, all German dissatisfaction with modernity pointed toward a third Reich, for Germany was to be the core even of Nietzsche's Europe ruling the planet.[3]

The weakness of liberal democracy in Germany explains why the situation of the indigenous Jews was more precarious in Germany than in any other Western country. Liberal democracy had originally defined itself in theologico-political treatises as the opposite, not of the more or less enlightened despotism of the seventeenth and eighteenth centuries, but of "the kingdom of darkness," i.e. of medieval society According to liberal democracy, the bond of society is universal human morality, whereas religion (positive religion) is a private affair. In the middle ages religion—i.e. Catholic Christianity—was the bond of society. The action most characteristic of the middle ages is the Crusades; it may be said to have culminated not accidentally in the murder of whole Jewish communities. The German Jews owed their emancipation to the French Revolution or its effects. They were given full political rights for the first time by the Weimar Republic. The Weimar Republic was succeeded by the only German regime—the only regime ever anywhere—which had no other clear principle than murderous hatred of the Jews, for "Aryan" had no clear meaning other than "non-Jewish." One must keep in mind the fact that Hitler did not come from Prussia, nor even from Bismarck's Reich.

At a time when German Jews were politically in a more precarious situation than Jews in any other Western country, they originated "the science of Judaism," the historical-critical study by Jews of the Jewish heritage. The emancipation of Jews in Germany coincided with the greatest epoch of German thought and poetry, the epoch in which Germany was the foremost country in thought and poetry. One cannot help comparing the period of German Jewry with the period of Spanish Jewry. The greatest achievements of Jews during the Spanish period were rendered possible partly by the fact that Jews became receptive to the influx of Greek thought, which was understood to be Greek only accidentally. During the German period, however, the Jews opened themselves to the influx of German thought, the thought of the particular nation in the midst of which they lived—a thought which was understood to be German essentially: political dependence was also spiritual dependence. This was the core of the predicament of German Jewry.

Three quotations may serve to illustrate the precarious situation of the Jews in Germany. Goethe, the greatest among the cosmopolitan Germans, a "decided non-Christian," summarizes the results of a conversation about a new society to be founded, between his Wilhelm Meister and "the gay Friedrich," without providing his summary with quotation marks, as follows: "To this religion [the Christian] we hold, but in a particular manner; we instruct our children from their youth in the great advantages which [that religion] has brought to us; but of its author, of its course, we speak to them only at the end. Then only does the author become dear and cherished,

and all reports regarding him become sacred. Drawing a conclusion which one may perhaps call pedantic, but of which
one must at any rate admit that it follows from the premise,
we do not tolerate any Jew among us; for how could we
grant him a share in the highest culture, the origin and
tradition of which he denies?" [4] Two generations later
Nietzsche could say: "I have not yet met a German who was
favorably disposed toward the Jews." [5] One might try to trace
Nietzsche's judgment to the narrowness of his circle of acquaintances: no one would expect to find people favorably
disposed toward Jews among the German Lutheran pastors
among whom Nietzsche grew up, to say nothing of Jakob
Burckhardt in Basel. Nietzsche has chosen his words carefully;
he surely excluded himself when making the judgment, as
appears, in addition, from the context. But his remark is not
trivial. While his circle of acquaintances was limited, perhaps
unusually limited, he was of unusual perspicacity. Besides,
being favorably disposed toward this or that man or woman
of Jewish origin does not mean being favorably disposed
toward Jews. Two generations later, in 1953, Heidegger could
speak of "the inner truth and greatness of National Socialism." [6]

In the course of the nineteenth century many Western men
had come to conceive of much, if not all, sufferings as consisting of problems which as such were soluble as a matter
of course. In this manner, too, they had come to speak of the
Jewish problem. The German-Jewish problem was never
solved. It was annihilated by the annihilation of the German
Jews. Prior to Hitler's rise to power most German Jews believed that their problem had been solved in principle by
liberalism: German Jews were Germans of the Jewish faith,
i.e. they were no less German than the Germans of the
Christian faith or of no faith. They assumed that the German
state (to say nothing of German society or culture) was or
ought to be neutral to the difference between Christians and
Jews or between non-Jews and Jews. This assumption was not
accepted by the strongest part of Germany and hence by
Germany. In the words of Herzl: "Who belongs and who does
not belong, is decided by the majority; it is a question of
power." At any rate it could seem that in the absence of a
superior recognized equally by both parties the natural judge
on the German-ness of German Jews was the non-Jewish
Germans. As a consequence, a small minority of German
Jews, but a considerable minority of German-Jewish youth

studying at the universities, had turned to Zionism. Zionism was almost never wholly divorced from traditional Jewish hopes. On the other hand, Zionism never intended to bring about a restoration like the one achieved in the days of Ezra and Nehemiah: the return to the land of Israel was not seen as culminating in the building of the third temple and restoration of the sacrificial service.

The peculiarity of Zionism as a modern movement comes out most clearly in the strictly political Zionism presented first by Leon Pinsker in his *Autoemancipation* and then by Theodor Herzl in his *The Jewish State*. Pinsker and Herzl started from the failure of the liberal solution, but continued to see the problem to be solved as it had begun to be seen by liberalism, i.e. as a merely human problem. They radicalized this purely human understanding. The terrible fate of the Jews was in no sense to be understood any longer as connected with divine punishment for the sins of our fathers or with the providential mission of the chosen people and hence to be borne with the meek fortitude of martyrs. It was to be understood in merely human terms, as constituting a purely political problem which as such cannot be solved by appealing to the justice or generosity of other nations, to say nothing of a league of all nations. Accordingly, political Zionism was concerned primarily with cleansing the Jews of their millennial degradation, with the recovery of Jewish dignity, honor or pride. The failure of the liberal solution meant that Jews could not regain their honor by assimilating as individuals to the nations among which they lived or by becoming citizens like all other citizens of the liberal states: the liberal solution brought at best legal equality, but not social equality; as a demand of reason it had no effect on the feelings of non-Jews. To quote Herzl again: "We are a nation—the enemy makes us a nation whether we like it or not." In the last analysis this is nothing to be deplored, for "the enemy is necessary for the highest effort of the personality." Only through securing the honor of the Jewish nation could the individual Jew's honor be secured. The true solution of the Jewish problem requires that the Jews become "like all the nations" (1 Samuel 8), that the Jewish nation assimilate itself to the nations of the world or that it establish a modern, liberal, secular (but not necessarily democratic) state. Political Zionism, then, strictly understood was the movement of an elite on behalf of a community constituted by common descent and common degradation, for the restoration of their honor through the acquisition of statehood and therefore of a country—of any country: the land which the strictly political Zionism promised to the Jews was not necessarily the land of Israel.

This project implied a profound modification of traditional Jewish hopes, a modification arrived at through a break with these hopes. For the motto of his pamphlet Pinsker chose these words of Hillel: "If I am not for myself, who will be for me? And if not now, when?" He omitted the sentence which forms the center of Hillel's statement: "And if I am only for myself, what am I?" He saw the Jewish people as a herd without a shepherd to protect and gather it; he did not long for a shepherd, but for the transformation of the herd into a nation that could take care of itself. He regarded the Jewish situation as a natural sickness that could be cured only by natural means. What the change effected by strictly political Zionism means, one sees most clearly when, returning to the origin, one ponders this sentence of Spinoza: "If the foundations of their religion did not effeminate the minds of the Jews, I would absolutely believe that they will at some time, given the occasion (for human things are mutable), establish their state again."

Strictly political Zionism became effective only through becoming an ingredient, not to say the backbone, of Zionism at large, i.e. by making its peace with traditional Jewish thought. Through this alliance or fusion it brought about the establishment of the state of Israel and therewith that cleansing which it had primarily intended; it thus procured a blessing for all Jews everywhere regardless of whether they admit it or not.[7] It did not, however, solve the Jewish problem. It could not solve the Jewish problem because of the narrowness of its original conception, however noble. This narrowness was pointed out most effectively by cultural Zionism: strictly political Zionism, concerned only with the present emergency and resolve, lacks historical perspective: the community of descent, of the blood, must also be a community of the mind, of the national mind; the Jewish state will be an empty shell without a Jewish culture which has its roots in the Jewish heritage. One could not have taken this step unless one had previously interpreted the Jewish heritage itself as a culture, i.e. as a product of the national mind, of the national genius.[8] Yet the foundation, the authoritative layer, of the Jewish heritage presents itself, not as a product of the human mind, but as a divine gift, as divine revelation. Did one not completely distort the meaning of the heritage to which one claimed to be loyal by interpreting it as a culture like any other high culture? Cultural Zionism believed it had found a safe middle ground between politics (power politics) and divine revelation, between the sub-cultural and the supra-cultural, but it lacked the sternness of these two extremes. When cultural Zionism understands itself, it turns into religious Zionism. But when religious Zionism understands itself, it is in the first place Jewish faith and only secondarily Zionism. It must regard as blasphemous the notion of a human solution to the Jewish problem. It may go so far as to regard the establishment of the state of Israel as the most important event in Jewish history since the completion of the Talmud, but it cannot regard it as the arrival of the Messianic age, of the redemption of Israel and of all men. The establishment of the state of Israel is the most profound modification of the Galut which has occurred, but it is not the end of the Galut: in the religious sense, and perhaps not only in the religious sense, the state of Israel is a part of the Galut. Finite, relative problems can be solved; infinite, absolute problems cannot be solved. In other words, human beings will never create a society which is free of contradictions. From every point of view it looks as if the Jewish people were the chosen people in the sense, at least, that the Jewish problem is the most manifest symbol of the human problem as a social or political problem.

To realize that the Jewish problem is insoluble means ever to bear in mind the truth proclaimed by Zionism regarding the limitations of liberalism. Liberalism stands or falls by the distinction between state and society, or by the recognition of a private sphere, protected by the law but impervious to the law, with the understanding that, above all, religion as particular religion belongs to the private sphere. Just as certainly as the liberal state will not "discriminate" against its Jewish citizens, so is it constitutionally unable and even unwilling to prevent "discrimination" against Jews by individuals or groups. To recognize a private sphere in the sense indicated means to permit private "discrimination," to protect it and thus in fact to foster it. The liberal state cannot provide a solution to the Jewish problem, for such a solution would require a legal prohibition against every kind of "discrimination," i.e. the abolition of the private sphere, the denial of the difference between state and society, the destruction of the liberal state. Such a destruction would not by any means solve the Jewish problem, as is shown in our days by the anti-Jewish policy of the USSR. It is foolish to say that that policy contradicts the principles of Communism, for it contradicts the principles of Communism to separate the principles of Communism from the Communist movement. The USSR owes its survival to Stalin's decision not to wait for the revolution of the Western proletariat, i.e. for what others would do for the USSR, but to build up socialism in a single country where his word was the law, by the use of any means however bestial, and these means could include, as a matter of course, certain means successfully used previously, not to say invented, by Hitler: the large-scale murder of party members and anti-Jewish measures. This is not to say that Communism has become what National Socialism always was, the prisoner of an anti-Jewish ideology, but it makes use of anti-Jewish measures in an unprincipled manner when and where they seem to be expedient. It is merely to confirm our contention that the uneasy "solution of the Jewish problem" offered by the liberal state is superior to the Communist "solution."

There is a Jewish problem that is humanly soluble,[9] the problem of the Western Jewish individual who or whose parents severed his connection with the Jewish community in the expectation that he would thus become a normal member of a purely liberal or of a universal human society, and who is naturally perplexed when he finds no such society. The solution to his problem is return to the Jewish community, the community established by the Jewish faith and the Jewish way of life—*teshubah* (ordinarily rendered by "repentance") in the most comprehensive sense. Some of our contemporaries believe such a return to be altogether impossible because they believe that the Jewish faith has been overthrown once and for all, not by blind rebellion, but by evident refutation. While admitting that their deepest problem would be solved by that return, they assert that intellectual probity forbids them to sacrifice intellect in order to satisfy even the most vital need. Yet they can hardly deny that a vital need legitimately induces a man to probe whether what seems to be an impossibility is not in fact only a very great difficulty.

The founder of cultural Zionism could still deny that the Jewish people have a providential mission on the ground that Darwin had destroyed the most solid basis of teleology.[10] At the time and in the country in which the present study was written, it was granted by all except the most backward that the Jewish faith had not been refuted by science or by history. The storms stirred up by Darwin and to a lesser degree by

Wellhausen had been weathered; one could grant to science and history everything they seem to teach regarding the age of the world, the origin of man, the impossibility of miracles, the impossibility of the immortality of the soul and of the resurrection of the body, the Jahvist, the Elohist, the third Isaiah, and so on, without abandoning one iota of the substance of the Jewish faith. Some haggling regarding particular items, issuing sometimes in grudging concessions, was still going on in outlying districts, but the battle for the capital had been decided by the wholesale surrender to science and history of the whole sphere in which science and history claim to be or to become competent, and by the simultaneous depreciation of that whole sphere as religiously irrelevant. It had become religiously relevant, it was affirmed, only through a self-misunderstanding of religion, a self-misunderstanding which was inevitable in earlier times and which on the whole was even harmless in earlier times. That self-misunderstanding consisted in understanding revelation as a body of teachings and rules that includes such teachings and rules as could never become known as true and binding to the unassisted human mind, such as the human mind would reject as sub-rational were they not proven to be supra-rational by the certainty that they are the word of God; men who were not ear-witness of God's declaring these teachings and rules could have that certainty only through a reliable tradition that also vouches for the reliable transmission of the very words of God, and through miracles. The self-misunderstanding is removed when the content of revelation is seen to be rational, which does not necessarily mean that everything hitherto thought to be revealed is rational. The need for external credentials of revelation (tradition and miracles) disappears as its internal credentials come to abound. The truth of traditional Judaism is the religion of reason, or the religion of reason is secularized Judaism. But the same claim could be made for Christianity, and however close secularized Judaism and secularized Christianity might come to each other, they are not identical, and as purely rational they ought to be identical. Above all, if the truth of Judaism is the religion of reason, then what was formerly believed to be revelation by the transcendent God must now be understood as the work of the human imagination in which human reason was effective to some extent; what has now become a clear and distinct idea was originally a confused idea.[11] What except demonstrations of the existence of God by theoretical reason or postulations of His existence by practical reason, which were becoming ever more incredible, could prevent one from taking the last step, i.e. to assert that God Himself is a product of the human mind, at best "an idea of reason"?

These and similar denials or interpretations suddenly lost all their force by the simple observation that they contradict not merely inherited opinions but present experience. At first hearing one may be reminded of what Leibniz had said when overcoming Bayle's doubt regarding revelation: "toutes ces difficultés invincibles, ces combats prétendus de la raison contre la foi s'évanouissent.

> Hi motus animorum atque haec discrimina tanta
> Pulveris exigui jactu compressa quiescunt." [12]

God's revealing Himself to man, His addressing man, is not merely known through traditions going back to the remote past and therefore now "merely believed," but is genuinely known through present experience which every human being can have if he does not refuse himself to it. This experience is not a kind of self-experience, of the actualization of a human potentiality, of the human mind coming into its own, into what it desires or is naturally inclined to, but of something undesired, coming from the outside, going against man's grain. It is the only awareness of something absolute which cannot be relativized in any way as everything else, rational or non-rational, can; it is the experience of God as the Thou, the father and king of all men; it is the experience of an unequivocal command addressed to me here and now as distinguished from general laws or ideas which are always disputable and permitting of exceptions. Only by surrendering to God's experienced call which calls for one's loving Him with all one's heart, with all one's soul and with all one's might can one come to see the other human being as one's brother and love him as oneself. The absolute experience will not lead back to Judaism—for instance, to the details of what the Christians call the ceremonial law—if it does not recognize itself in the Bible and clarify itself through the Bible, and if it is not linked up with considerations of how traditional Judaism understands itself and with meditations about the mysterious fate of the Jewish people. The return to Judaism also requires today the overcoming of what one may call the perennial obstacle to the Jewish faith: traditional philosophy, which is of Greek, pagan origin. For the respectable, impressive or specious alternatives to the acceptance of revelation, to the surrender to God's will, have always presented themselves and still present themselves as based on what man knows by himself, by his reason. Reason has reached its perfection in Hegel's system; the essential limitations of Hegel's system show the essential limitations of reason and therewith the radical inadequacy of all rational objections to revelation. With the final collapse of rationalism the perennial battle between reason and revelation, between unbelief and belief has been decided in principle, even on the plane of human thought, in favor of revelation. Reason knows only of subjects and objects, but surely the living and loving God is infinitely more than a subject and can never be an object, something at which one can look in detachment or indifference. Philosophy as hitherto known, the old thinking, so far from starting from the experience of God, abstracted from such experience or excluded it; hence, if it was theistic, it was compelled to have recourse to demonstrations of the existence of God as a thinking or a thinking and willing being. The new thinking as unqualified empiricism speaks of God, man and the world as actually experienced, as realities irreducible to one another, whereas all traditional philosophy was reductionist. For if it did not assert that the world and man are eternal, i.e. deny the creator-God, it sought for the reality preceding world and man as it precedes world and man and as it succeeds world and man, i.e. for what cannot be experienced by man, by the whole man, but can only be inferred or thought by him. Unqualified empiricism does not recognize any such Without or Beyond as a reality, but only as unreal forms, essences, or concepts which can never be more than objects, i.e. objects of mere thought.[13]

The new thinking had been originated above all by Franz Rosenzweig, who is thought to be the greatest Jewish thinker whom German Jewry has brought forth. It was counteracted by another form of the new thinking, the form originated by Heidegger.[14] It was obvious that Heidegger's new thinking led far away from any charity as well as from any humanity. On the other hand, it could not be denied that he had a deeper understanding than Rosenzweig of what was implied in the insight or demand that the traditional philosophy, which rested on Greek foundations, must be superseded by a new thinking. He would never have said as Rosenzweig did that "we know in the most precise manner, we know with the intuitional knowledge of experience, what God taken by Himself, what man taken by himself, what the world taken by itself 'is.' " Nor did Heidegger assume, as Rosenzweig did, that we possess without further ado an adequate understanding of Greek philosophy, of the basic stratum of that old thinking which has to be overcome: with the questioning of traditional philosophy the traditional understanding of the tradition becomes questionable. For this reason alone he could not have said as Rosenzweig did that most Platonic dialogues are "boring." [15] This difference between Rosenzweig and Heidegger, about which much more could be said, was not unconnected with their difference regarding revelation. At that time Heidegger expressed his thought about revelation by silence or deed rather than by speech. Rosenzweig's friend Martin Buber quotes a much later utterance of Heidegger which gives one, I believe, an inkling of Heidegger's argument —especially if it is taken in conjunction with well-known utterances of Nietzsche whom Heidegger evidently follows in this matter.

"The 'prophets' of these religions [sc. Judaism and Christianity]," says Heidegger according to Buber, "do not begin by foretelling the word of the Holy. They announce immediately the God upon whom the certainty of salvation in a supernatural blessedness reckons." [16] Buber comments on this statement as follows: "Incidentally, I have never in our time encountered on a high philosophical plane such a far-reaching misunderstanding of the prophets of Israel. The prophets of Israel have never announced a God upon whom their hearers' striving for security reckoned. They have always aimed to shatter all security and to proclaim in the opened abyss of the final insecurity the unwished for God who demands that His human creatures become real, they become human, and confounds all who imagine that they can take refuge in the certainty that the temple of God is in their midst." Heidegger does not speak of the prophets' "hearers," but he clearly means that the prophets themselves were concerned with security.[17] This assertion is not refuted by the well-known facts which Buber points out—by the fact, in a word, that for the prophets there is no refuge and fortress except God: the security afforded by the Temple of God is nothing, but the security afforded by God is everything. As Buber says seventeen pages earlier in the same publication, "He who loves God only as a mortal ideal, can easily arrive at despairing of the guidance of a world the appearance of which contradicts, hour after hour, all principles of his moral ideality." [18] Surely the Bible teaches that in spite of all appearances to the contrary the world is guided by God or, to use the traditional term, that there is particular providence, that man is protected by God if he does not put his trust in flesh and blood but in God alone, that he is not completely exposed or forsaken, that he is not alone, that he has been created by a being which is—to use Buber's expression—a Thou. Buber's protest would be justified if the Biblical prophets were only, as Wellhausen may seem to have hoped, prophets of insecurity, not to say of an evil end,[19] and not also predictors of the Messianic future, of the ultimate victory of truth and justice, of the final salvation and security, although not necessarily of the final salvation and security of all men. In other words, the Biblical experience is not simply undesired or against man's grain: grace perfects nature, it does not destroy nature. Not every man but every noble man is concerned with justice or righteousness and therefore with any possible extra-human, supra-human support of justice, or with the security of justice. The insecurity of man and everything human is not an absolutely terrifying abyss if the highest of which a man knows is absolutely secure. Plato's Athenian Stranger does not indeed experience that support, that refuge and fortress as the Biblical prophets experienced it, but he does the second best: he tries to demonstrate its existence. But for Heidegger there is no security, no happy ending, no divine shepherd, hope is replaced by thinking, the longing for eternity or belief in anything eternal is understood as stemming from "the spirit of revenge," from the desire to escape from all passing-away into something that never passes away.[20]

The controversy can easily degenerate into a race in which he wins who offers the smallest security and the greatest terror. It would not be difficult to guess who would be the winner. But just as an assertion does not become true because it is shown to be comforting, so it does not become true because it is shown to be terrifying. The serious question concerns man's certainty or knowledge of the divine promises or covenants. They are known through what God Himself says in the Scriptures. According to Buber, whose belief in revelation is admittedly "not mixed up with any 'orthodoxy,' " what we read in the Bible is in all cases what the Biblical authors say (even when God is said to have said something, as for example and above all in the case of the Ten Commandments), and what the Biblical authors say is never more than a human expression of God's speechless call or a human response to that call or a man-made "image," a human interpretation, an experienced human interpretation to be sure, of what God "said." Such "images" constitute not only Judaism and Christianity but all religions. All such "images" are "distorting and yet correct, perishable like an image in a dream and yet verified in eternity."[21] The experience of God is surely not specifically Jewish. Besides, can one say that one experiences God as the creator of heaven and earth, i.e. that one knows from the experience of God, taken by itself, that He is the creator of heaven and earth, or that men who are not prophets experience God as a thinking, willing and speaking being? Is the absolute experience necessarily the experience of a Thou?[22] Every assertion about the absolute experience which says more than that what is experienced is the Presence or the Call, is not the experiencer, is not flesh and blood, is the wholly other, is death or nothingness, is an "image" or interpretation; that any one interpretation is the simply true interpretation is not known but "merely believed." One cannot establish that any particular interpretation of the absolute experience is the most adequate interpretation on the ground that it alone agrees with all other experiences, for instance with the experienced mystery of the Jewish fate, for the Jewish fate is a mystery only on the basis of a particular interpretation of the absolute experience, or rather the Jewish fate is the outcome of one particular interpretation of the absolute experience. The very emphasis on the absolute experience as experience compels one to demand that it be made as clear as possible what the experience by itself conveys, that it not be tampered with, that it be carefully distinguished from every interpretation of the experience, for the interpretations may be suspected of being attempts to render bearable and harmless the experienced which admittedly comes from without down upon man and is undesired; or of being attempts to cover over man's radical unprotectedness, loneliness and exposedness.[23]

Yet—Buber could well have retorted—does not precisely this objection mean that the atheistic suspicion is as much a possibility, an interpretation and hence is as much "merely believed" as the theistic one? And is not being based on belief, which is the pride of religion, a calamity for philosophy? Can the new thinking consistently reject or (what is the same thing) pass by revelation? Through judging others, Nietzsche himself had established the criterion by which his doctrine is to be judged. In attacking the "optimistic" as well as the "pessimistic" atheism of his age, he made clear that the denial of the Biblical God demands the denial of Biblical morality however secularized, which, far from being self-evident or rational, has no other support than the Biblical God; mercy, compassion, egalitarianism, brotherly love or altruism must give way to cruelty and its kin.[24] But Nietzsche did not leave things at "the blond beast." He proclaimed "the over-man," and the over-man transcends man as hitherto known at his highest. What distinguishes Nietzsche in his view from all earlier philosophers is the fact that he possesses "the historical sense," [25] i.e. the awareness that the human soul has no unchangeable essence or limits but is essentially historical. The most profound change which the human soul has hitherto undergone, the most important enlargement and deepening which it has hitherto experienced is due, according to Nietzsche, to the Bible. ". . . these Greeks have much on their conscience—falsification was their particular craft, the whole European psychology suffers from the Greek *superficialities;* and without that little bit of Judaism, etc. etc." Hence the over-man is "the Roman Caesar with Christ's soul." [26] Not only was Biblical morality as veracity or intellectual probity at work in the destruction of Biblical theology and Biblical morality; not only is it at work in the questioning of that very probity, of "*our* virtue, which alone has remained to us"; [27] Biblical morality will remain at work in the morality of the over-man. The over-man is inseparable from "the philosophy of the future." The philosophy of the future is distinguished from traditional philosophy, which pretended to be purely theoretical, by the fact that it is consciously the outcome of a will: the fundamental awareness is not purely theoretical but theoretical and practical, inseparable from an act of the will or a decision. The fundamental awareness characteristic of the new thinking is a secularized version of the Biblical faith as interpreted by Christian theology.[28] What is true of Nietzsche is no less true of the author of *Sein und Zeit.* Heidegger wishes to expel from philosophy the last relics of Christian theology like the notions of "eternal truths" and "the idealized absolute subject." But the understanding of man which he opposes to the Greek understanding of man as the rational animal is, as he emphasizes, primarily the Biblical understanding of man as created in the image of God. Accordingly, he interprets human life in the light of "being towards death," "anguish," "conscience," and "guilt"; in this most important respect he is much more Christian than Nietzsche.[29] The efforts of the new thinking to escape from

the evidence of the Biblical understanding of man, i.e. from
Biblical morality, have failed. And, as we have learned from
Nietzsche, Biblical morality demands the Biblical God.

Considerations of this kind seemed to decide the issue in
favor of Rosenzweig's understanding of the new thinking, or
in favor of the unqualified return to Biblical revelation. As
a matter of fact, Rosenzweig's return was not unqualified. The
Judaism to which he returned was not identical with the
Judaism of the age prior to Moses Mendelssohn. The old
thinking had brought about, since the days of Mendelssohn,
to say nothing of the middle ages, some more or less important modifications of native Jewish thought. While opposing
the old thinking, the new thinking was nevertheless its heir.
Whereas the classic work of what is called Jewish medieval
philosophy, the *Guide of the Perplexed,* is primarily not a
philosophic book but a Jewish book, Rosenzweig's *Star of
Redemption* is primarily not a Jewish book but "a system of
philosophy." The new thinking is "experiencing philosophy."
As such it is passionately concerned with the difference between what is experienced, or at least capable of being experienced, by the present day believer and what is merely
known by tradition; that difference was of no concern to
traditional Judaism. As experiencing philosophy it starts in
each case from the experienced, and not from the non-ex-
perienced "presuppositions" of experience. For instance, we
experience things "here" or "there," in given "places"; we do
not experience the homogeneous infinite "space" which may
be the condition of the possibility of "places." I experience a
tree; in doing so, I am not necessarily aware of my "Ego"
which is the condition of possibility of my experiencing anything. Accordingly, when speaking of the Jewish experience,
one must start from what is primary or authoritative for the
Jewish consciousness and not from what is the primary condition of possibility of the Jewish experience: one must start
from God's Law, the Torah, and not from the Jewish nation.
But in this decisive case Rosenzweig proceeds in the opposite
manner; he proceeds, as he puts it, "sociologically." He notes
that the Jewish dogmaticists of the middle ages, especially
Maimonides, proceeded in the first manner: traditional Jewish
dogmatics understood the Jewish nation in the light of the
Torah; it was silent about the "presupposition" of the Law, *viz.*
the Jewish nation and its chosenness. One begins to wonder
whether our medieval philosophy, and the old thinking of
Aristotle of which it made use, was not more "empirical,"

more in harmony with the "given," than an unqualified empiricism which came into being through opposition to modern constructionist philosophy as well as to modern scientific empiricism: if the Jewish nation did not originate the Torah but is manifestly constituted by the Torah, it is necessarily preceded by the Torah which was created prior to the world and for the sake of which the world was created. The dogma of Israel's chosenness becomes for Rosenzweig "the truly central thought of Judaism" because, as he makes clear, he approaches Judaism from the point of view of Christianity, because he looks for a Jewish analogue to the Christian doctrine of the Christ.[30] It is not necessary to emphasize that the same change would have been effected if the starting point had been mere secularist nationalism.

Rosenzweig never believed that his return to the Biblical faith could be a return to the form in which that faith had expressed or understood itself in the past. What the author of a Biblical saying or a Biblical story or the compilers of the canon meant is one thing; how the text affects the present day believer and hence what the latter truly understands, i.e. appropriates and believes, is another. The former is the concern of history as history which, if it regards itself as self-sufficient, is one of the decayed forms of the old thinking; the latter, if it is practiced with full consciousness, calls for the new thinking. Since the new thinking is the right kind of thinking, it would seem that the understanding of the Bible of which it is capable is in principle superior to all other forms. At any rate, Rosenzweig agrees with religious liberalism as to the necessity of making a selection from among the traditional beliefs and rules. Yet his principle of selection differs radically from the liberal principle. The liberals made a distinction between the essential and unessential, i.e. they made a distinction which claimed to be objective. Rosenzweig's principle is not a principle strictly speaking but "a force": the whole "reality of Jewish life," even those parts of it which never acquired formal authority (like "mere" stories and "mere" customs) must be approached as the "matter" out of which only a part can be transformed into "force"; only experience can tell which part will be so transformed; the selection cannot but be "wholly individual." [31] The sacred law, as it were the public temple, which was a reality, thus becomes a potential, a quarry or a store-house out of which each individual takes the materials for building up his private shelter. The community of the holy people is henceforth guaranteed by the common descent of its members and the common origin of the materials which they transform by selecting them. This conscious and radical historicization of the Torah—the necessary consequence of the assumed primacy of the Jewish people under the conditions of modern "individualism" [32]—is in Rosenzweig's view perfectly compatible with the fact that the Jewish people is the a-historical people.

Rosenzweig could not believe everything that his orthodox Jewish contemporaries in Germany believed. His system of philosophy supplies the reasons why he thought that in spite of their piety they were mistaken. He has discussed by themselves two points regarding which he disagreed with them and which are of utmost importance. First, he opposed their inclination to understand the Law in terms of prohibition, denial, refusal and rejection rather than in terms of command, liberation, granting and transformation, and proposed the opposite inclination. It is not immediately clear, however, whether the orthodox austerity or sternness does not rest on a deeper understanding of the power of evil in man than Rosenzweig's view, which is at first glance more attractive, and which resembles one of "the favorite topics" of Mittler in Goethe's *Elective Affinities*.[33] Second, Rosenzweig was unable simply to believe all Biblical miracles. All Biblical miracles were indeed susceptible of becoming credible to him. For instance, when the story of Balaam's speaking she-ass was read from the Torah, it was not a fairy-tale for him, whereas on all other occasions he might doubt this miracle.[34] The orthodox Jew would reproach himself for his doubts as for failings on his part, for he would not determine what he is obliged to believe by his individual and temporary capacity or incapacity to believe; he would argue, with Maimonides' *Treatise on the Resurrection of the Dead*, that if God has created the world out of nothing and hence is omnipotent, there is no reason whatever for denying at any time any miracle vouched for by the word of God.

Considerations like those sketched in the preceding paragraphs made one wonder whether an unqualified return to Jewish orthodoxy was not both possible and necessary—was not at the same time the solution to the problem of the Jew lost in the non-Jewish modern world and the only course compatible with sheer consistency or intellectual probity. Vague difficulties remained like small faraway clouds on a beautiful summer sky. They soon took the shape of Spinoza—the greatest man of Jewish origin who had openly denied the truth of Judaism and had ceased to belong to the Jewish people without becoming a Christian. It was not the "God-intoxicated" philosopher but the hard-headed, not to say hard-hearted, pupil of Machiavelli and philologic-historical critic of the Bible. Orthodoxy could be returned to only if Spinoza was wrong in every respect.

That Spinoza was wrong in the decisive respect had been asserted about a decade earlier by the most authoritative German Jew who symbolized more than anyone else the union of Jewish faith and German culture: Hermann Cohen, the founder of the Neo-Kantian school of Marburg. Cohen was a Jew of rare dedication, the faithful guide, defender and warner of German Jewry, and at the same time, to say the least, the one who by far surpassed in spiritual power all the other German professors of philosophy of his generation. It became necessary to examine Cohen's attack on Spinoza. That attack had been occasioned by a particularly striking act of celebration of Spinoza on the part of German Jews. There were two reasons why contemporary Jews were inclined to celebrate Spinoza. The first is Spinoza's assumed merit about mankind and only secondarily about the Jews; the second is his assumed merit about the Jewish people and only secondarily about mankind. Both reasons had induced contemporary Jews not only informally to rescind the excommunication which the Jewish community in Amsterdam had pronounced against Spinoza, but even, as Cohen put it, to canonize him.

The great revolt against traditional thought or the emergence of modern philosophy or natural science was completed prior to Spinoza. One may go further and say that, far from being a revolutionary thinker, Spinoza is only the heir of the modern revolt and the medieval tradition as well. At first glance he might well appear to be much more medieval than Descartes, to say nothing of Bacon and Hobbes. The modern project as understood by Bacon, Descartes and Hobbes demands that man should become the master and owner of nature; or that philosophy or science should cease to be essentially theoretical. Spinoza, however, attempts to restore the traditional conception of contemplation: one cannot think of conquering nature if nature is the same as God. Yet Spinoza restored the dignity of speculation on the basis of modern philosophy or science, of a new understanding of "nature." He thus was the first great thinker who attempted a synthesis of pre-modern (classical-medieval) and of modern philosophy. His speculation resembles Neo-Platonism; he understands all things as proceeding from, not made or created by, a single being or origin; the One is the sole ground of the Many. Yet he no longer regards this process as a descent or decay but as an ascent or unfolding: the end is higher than the origin. According to his last word on the subject, the highest form of knowledge, which he calls intuitive knowledge, is knowledge not of the one substance or God, but of individual things or events: God is fully God not qua substance or even in His eternal attributes but in His non-eternal modes understood *sub specie aeternitatis*. The knowledge of God as presented in the First Part of the *Ethics* is only universal or abstract; only the knowledge of individual things or rather events qua caused by God is concrete.[35] Spinoza thus appears to originate the kind of philosophic system which views the fundamental *processus* as a progress: God in Himself is not the *ens perfectissimum*. In this most important respect he prepares German idealism. Furthermore, just as he returned to the classical conception of *theoria*, he returned in his political philosophy to classical republicanism. The title of the crowning chapter of the *Theologico-political Treatise* is taken as literally as possible from Tacitus. But just as his theoretical philosophy is more than a restatement of classical doctrines and in fact a synthesis of classical and modern speculation, his political philosophy is more than a restatement of classical republicanism. The republic which he favors is a liberal democracy. He was the first philosopher who was both a democrat and a liberal. He was the philosopher who founded liberal democracy, a specifically modern regime. Directly and through his influence on Rousseau, who gave the decisive impulse to Kant, Spinoza became responsible for that version of modern republicanism which takes its bearings by the dignity of every man rather than by the narrowly conceived interest of every man. Spinoza's political teaching starts from a natural right of every human being as the source of all possible duties. Hence it is free from that sternness and austerity which classical political philosophy shares with ancient law—a sternness which Aristotle expressed classically by saying that what the law does not command it forbids. Hence Spinoza is free from the classical aversion to commercialism; he rejects the traditional demand for sumptuary laws. Generally speaking, his polity gives the passions much greater freedom and correspondingly counts much less on the power of reason than the polity of the classics. Whereas for the classics the life of passion is a life against nature, for Spinoza everything that is is natural. For Spinoza there are no natural ends and hence in particular there is no end natural to man. He is therefore compelled to give a novel account of man's end (the life devoted to contemplation): man's end is not natural, but rational, the result of man's figuring it out, of man's "forming an idea of man, as of a model of human nature." He thus decisively prepares the modern notion of the "ideal" as a work of the human mind or as a human project, as distinguished from an end imposed on man by nature. The formal reception of Spinoza took place in 1785 when F. H. Jacobi published his book *On the Doctrine of Spinoza, in Letters to Herr Moses Mendelssohn*. Jacobi made public the fact that in Lessing's view there was no philosophy but the philosophy of Spinoza. The philosophy of Kant's great successors was consciously a synthesis of Spinoza's and Kant's philosophies. Spinoza's characteristic contribution to this synthesis was a novel conception of God. He thus showed the way toward a new religion or religiousness which was to inspire a wholly new kind of society, a new kind of Church. He became the sole father of that new Church which was to be universal in fact and not merely in claim, like other Churches, because its foundation was no longer any positive revelation. It was a Church whose rulers were not priests or pastors but philosophers and artists and whose flock were the circles of culture and property. It was of the utmost importance to that Church that its father was not a Christian but a Jew who had informally embraced a Christianity without dogmas and sacraments. The millennial antagonism between Judaism and Christianity was about to disappear. The new Church would transform Jews and Christians into human beings—into human beings of a certain kind: cultured human beings, human beings who because they possessed Science and Art did not need religion in addition. The new society, constituted by the aspiration common to all its members toward the True, the Good, and the Beautiful, emancipated the Jews in Germany. Spinoza became the symbol of that emancipation which was to be more than emancipation but secular redemption. In Spinoza, a thinker and a saint who was both a Jew and a Christian and hence neither, all cultured families of the earth, it was hoped, will be blessed. In a word, the non-Jewish world, having been molded to a considerable extent by Spinoza, had become receptive to Jews who were willing to assimilate themselves to it.

The celebration of Spinoza had become equally necessary

on purely Jewish grounds. As we have seen, the emphasis had shifted from the Torah to the Jewish nation, and the Jewish nation could not be considered the source of the Torah if it was not understood as an organism with a soul of its own; that soul had expressed itself originally and classically in the Bible, although not in all parts of the Bible equally. From the days of the Bible, there always had been the conflict between prophet and priest, between the inspired and the uninspired, between profound subterranean Judaism and official Judaism. Official Judaism was legalistic and hence rationalistic. Its rationalism had received most powerful support from the philosophic rationalism of alien origin that had found its perfect expression in the Platonic conception of God as an artificer who makes the universe by looking up to the unchangeable, lifeless ideas. In accordance with this, official Judaism asserted that God has created the world and governs it *sub ratione boni*. Precisely because he believed in the profoundly understood divinity of the Bible, Spinoza revolted against this official assertion, in the name of the absolutely free or sovereign God of the Bible—of the God who will be what He will be, who will be gracious to whom He will be gracious and will show mercy to whom He will show mercy. Moved by the same spirit, he embraced with enthusiasm Paul's doctrine of predestination. The Biblical God has created man in His image: male and female did He create them. The male and the female, form and matter, cogitation and extension are then equally attributes of God; Spinoza rejects both Greek idealism and Christian spiritualism. The Biblical God forms light and creates darkness, makes peace and creates evil; Spinoza's God is simply beyond good and evil. God's might is His right, and therefore the power of every being is as such its right; Spinoza lifts Machiavellianism to theological heights. Good and evil differ only from a merely human point of view; theologically the distinction is meaningless. The evil passions are evil only with a view to human utility; in themselves they show forth the might and the right of God no less than other things which we admire and by the contemplation of which we are delighted. In the state of nature, i.e. independently of human convention, there is nothing just and unjust, no duty and no guilt, and the state of nature does not simply vanish when civil society is established: pangs of conscience are nothing but feelings of displeasure that arise when a plan has gone wrong. Hence there are no vestiges of divine justice to be found except where just men reign. All human acts are modes of the one God, who possesses infinitely many attributes each of which is infinite and only two of which are known to us; who is therefore a mysterious God, whose mysterious love reveals itself in eternally and necessarily bringing forth love and hatred, nobility and baseness, saintliness and depravity; and who is infinitely lovable not in spite of but because of His infinite power which is beyond good and evil.

Compared with the fantastic flights of the Spinoza enthusiasts in the two camps, of the moralists and the immoralists, Cohen's understanding of Spinoza is sobriety itself. All the more impressive is his severe indictment of Spinoza.[36] He shows first that in his *Theologico-political Treatise* Spinoza speaks from a Christian point of view and accordingly accepts the entire Christian critique of Judaism, but goes much beyond even that Christian critique in his own critique. Spinoza accepts against his better knowledge the assertion of Jesus that Judaism commands the hatred of the enemy. He opposes spiritual and universalistic Christianity to carnal and particularistic Judaism: the core of Judaism is the Mosaic law as a particularistic not to say tribal law that serves no other end than the earthly or political felicity of the Jewish nation; the Torah does not teach morality, i.e. universal morality; the Mosaic religion is merely national; Moses' God is a tribal and in addition a corporeal God. By denying that the God of Israel is the God of all mankind Spinoza has blasphemed the God of Israel. He reduces Jewish religion to a doctrine of the Jewish state. For him, the Torah is of merely human origin. Cohen shows next that the Christianity in the light of which Spinoza condemns Judaism is not historical or actual Christianity but an idealized Christianity, and hence while idealizing Christianity, he denigrates Judaism. He shows then that Spinoza admits the universalistic character of the Old Testament prophecy, thus contradicting himself grossly. This contradiction clearly proves his lack of good faith.[37] Nor is this all. While taking the side of spiritual and transpolitical Christianity against carnal and political Judaism, Spinoza contradicts this whole argument by taking the side of the State not only against all churches but against all religion as well. "He put religion altogether [i.e. not merely Judaism] outside the sphere of truth." Starting like all other sophists from the equation of right and might, he conceives of the State entirely in terms of power politics, i.e. as divorced from religion and morality, and he puts the State thus conceived above religion.

This does not mean that he deifies the State. On the contrary, he is concerned above everything else with what he calls philosophy which he assumes to be wholly inaccessible directly or indirectly to the large majority of men. He has no compunction whatever about affirming the radical and unmodifiable inequality of men without ever wondering "how can nature, how can God answer for this difference among men?" Hence his sympathy for democracy is suspect. He is compelled to erect an eternal barrier between popular education and science or philosophy, and therewith between the State and Reason. There is no place in his thought for the enlightenment of the people. He has no heart for the people, no compassion. He cannot admit a Messianic future of mankind when all men will be united in genuine knowledge of God. This is the reason why he is altogether blind to Biblical prophecy and hence to the core of Judaism.[38]

On the basis of all these facts Cohen reached the conclusion that far from deserving celebration, Spinoza fully deserved the excommunication. Far from rescinding the excommunication, Cohen confirmed it acting as a judge in the highest court of appeal. The grounds of his verdict were not the same as the grounds of the lower court. He was not concerned with Spinoza's transgression of the ceremonial law and his denial of the Mosaic authorship of the Pentateuch. He condemned Spinoza because of his infidelity in the simple human sense, of his complete lack of loyalty to his own people, of his acting like an enemy of the Jews and thus giving aid and comfort to the many enemies of the Jews, of his behaving like a base traitor. Spinoza remains up to the present day the accuser *par excellence* of Judaism before an anti-Jewish world; the disposition of his mind and heart toward Jews and Judaism was "unnatural," he committed a "humanly incomprehensible act of treason," he was possessed by "an evil demon." [39]

Our case against Spinoza is in some respects even stronger than Cohen thought. One may doubt whether Spinoza's action is humanly incomprehensible or demoniac but one must grant that it is amazingly unscrupulous. Cohen is justly perplexed by the fact that "the center of the whole [theologico-political] treatise" is the disparagement of Moses and the idealization of Jesus, although the purpose of the work is to secure the freedom of philosophizing. He explains this anomaly by Spinoza's belief that the suppression of philosophy goes back to the Mosaic law. Cohen does not assert that Moses championed the freedom of philosophy but he raises the pertinent question whether Jesus championed it.[40] Why then does Spinoza treat Judaism and Christianity differently? Why does he take the side of Christianity in the conflict between Judaism and Christianity, in a conflict of no concern to him as a philosopher? Cohen believes that Spinoza had a genuine reverence for Jesus' teachings. According to Spinoza's own statements he preferred spiritual Christianity to carnal Judaism.[41] But is Spinoza a spiritualist? Cohen says that spirit or mind, if applied to God, is no less a metaphor than hand, voice or mouth. He thus merely repeats what Spinoza himself asserts; Spinoza may be said to have denied that God has a spirit or mind. The question returns: why does Spinoza treat Christianity differently from Judaism? Cohen comes closest to the truth in saying that Spinoza's motive was fear,[42] surely a "humanly comprehensible" motive. Or, to start again from the beginning, Spinoza, attempting to achieve the liberation of philosophy in a book addressed to Christians, cannot but appeal to the Christian prejudices which include anti-Jewish prejudices; he fights Christian prejudices by appealing to Christian prejudices; appealing to the Christian prejudice again Judaism, he exhorts the Christians to free essentially spiritual Christianity from all carnal Jewish relics (e.g. the belief in the resurrection of the body). Generally speaking, he makes the Old Testament against his better knowledge the scapegoat for everything he finds objectionable in actual Christianity. In spite of all this he asserts that the prophets were as universalistic as Jesus and the apostles or, more precisely, that both Testaments teach with equal clarity everywhere the universal divine law or the universal religion of justice and charity. Why this strange reversal, this flagrant contradiction? At this point Cohen fails to follow Spinoza's thought. The purpose of the *Treatise* is to show the way toward a liberal society which is based on the recognition of the authority of the Bible, i.e. of the Old Testament taken by itself and of the two Testaments taken together. The argument culminates in the 14th chapter, in which he enumerates seven dogmas which are the indispensable fundamentals of faith, of Biblical faith, the seven "roots," as the Jewish medieval thinkers would say. They are essential to "the catholic or universal faith," to the religion which will be the established religion in the well-ordered republic; belief in these seven dogmas is the only belief necessary and sufficient for salvation. They derive equally from the Old Testament taken by itself and from the New Testament taken by itself.[43] They do not contain anything specifically Christian nor anything specifically Jewish. They are equally acceptable to Jews and to Christians. The liberal society with a view to which Spinoza has composed the *Treatise* is then a society of which Jews and Christians can be equally members, of which Jews and Christians can be equal members. For such a society he wished to provide. The establishment of such a society required in his opinion the abrogation of the Mosaic law in so far as it is a particularistic and political law, and especially of the ceremonial laws: since Moses' religion is a political law, to adhere to his religion as he proclaimed it is incompatible with being the citizen of any other state, whereas Jesus was not a legislator but only a teacher.[44] It is for this reason that Spinoza is so anxious to prove that Moses' law lost its obligatory power, and that the Jews ceased to be the chosen people with the loss of the Jewish state: the Jews cannot be at the same time the members of two nations and subject to two comprehensive legal codes. Spinoza stresses the abrogation of the ceremonial law, however, not only because that abrogation is in his opinion a necessary condition of civic equality of the Jews but also as desirable for its own sake: the ceremonial law is infinitely burdensome, nay, a curse.[45] In providing for the liberal state, Spinoza provides for a Judaism that is liberal in the extreme. The "assimilationist" "solution to the Jewish problem" which Spinoza may be said to have suggested was more important from his point of view than the "Zionist" one which he likewise suggested. The latter as he understood it could seem to require the preservation of the ceremonial law even with the abandonment of the spirit which has animated it hitherto.[46] The former suggestion and the general purpose of the *Theologico-political Treatise* are obviously connected: freedom of philosophy requires, or seems to require, a liberal state, and a liberal state is a state which is not as such either Christian or Jewish. Even Cohen sensed for a moment that Spinoza was not entirely free from sympathy with his people.[47] Spinoza may have hated Judaism; he did not hate the Jewish people. However bad a Jew he may have been in all other respects, he thought of the liberation of the Jews in the only way in which he could think of it, given his philosophy. But precisely if this is so, we must stress all the more the fact that the manner in which he sets forth his proposal—to say nothing of the proposal itself—is Machiavellian: the humanitarian end seems to justify every means; he plays a most dangerous game; [48] his procedure is as much beyond good and evil as his God.

All this does not mean however that Cohen's critique of Spinoza's *Theologico-political Treatise* is altogether convincing. His political thought claims to be inspired by Biblical prophecy and hence is Messianic. In opposition to Spinoza it starts from the radical difference between nature and morality, the Is and the Ought, egoism and pure will. The state is essentially moral, and morality cannot be actual except in and through the state. The difficulty presented by the fact that morality is universal and the state is always particular is overcome by the consideration that the state is part of a universal moral order, as is shown by the existence of international law and by the intrinsic possibility which is at the same time a moral necessity, of a universal league of states. The radical difference between nature and morality does not amount to a contradiction between nature and morality: nature does not render impossible the fulfillment of the moral demands. The morally demanded infinite progress of morality, and in particular the "eternal progress" toward "eternal peace," nay, every single step of morality requires for its "ultimate security" the infinite duration *a parte post* of the human race and hence of nature; this infinite duration or eternity is secured by the idea of God "who signifies the harmony of the knowledge of nature and of moral knowledge," who is not a person, nor living, nor existing, nor a spirit or mind but an idea, "our" idea, i.e. our *hypothesis* in what Cohen regards as the Platonic meaning of the term. This is the Cohenian equivalent of Creation and Providence. Without "the idea of God" as Cohen understands it morality as he understands it becomes baseless. That idea is the basis of his trust in infinite progress or of his belief in history, of his "optimism," of his certainty of the ultimate victory of the good: "there is no evil." But eternal progress also requires eternal tension between the actual state and the state as it ought to be: [49] immorality is coeval with morality. Here Cohen seems to join Spinoza whose political thought is based on the truth allegedly proven by experience that there will be vices as long as there will be human beings, and who takes it therefore for granted that the state is necessarily repressive or coercive. Cohen too cannot well deny that the state must use coercion but, opposing the Kantian distinction between morality and legality, he denies that coercion is the principle of law: coercion means nothing other than law and therefore need not be mentioned.

He is as uneasy about coercion as he is about power: the state is law, for the state is essentially rational, and coercion begins where reason ends. All this follows from the premise that morality is self-legislation and that it can be actual only in and through the state. A further consequence is that Cohen must understand punishment not in terms of the protection of society or other considerations which may be thought to regard the criminal not as "an end in himself" and only as a means, but in terms of the self-betterment of the criminal alone.[50] Cohen obscures the fact that while the self-betterment is necessarily a free act of the criminal, his forcible seclusion for the purpose of that self-betterment in which he may or may not engage, is not. In other words, all men are under a moral obligation to better themselves, but the specific difference of the condemned criminal is that he is put behind bars. For it goes without saying that Cohen denies the justice of capital punishment. However justly Spinoza may deserve condemnation for his Machiavelli-inspired hard-heartedness, it is to be feared that Cohen has not remained innocent of the opposite extreme. Since he attacks Spinoza in the name of Judaism, it may suffice here to quote a Jewish saying: "but for the fear of the government, men would swallow each other alive." [51]

One may doubt whether Cohen's political teaching is unqualifiedly superior to Spinoza's from the moral point of view. Cohen "rejects war." On the other hand he does not reject revolution although, as he emphasizes, Kant had "coordinated wars to revolutions." Revolutions are political but not legal acts and hence the state is not simply law; they "suspend" positive law but are justified by natural law. They do not necessarily occur without the killing of human beings; Cohen, the sworn enemy of capital punishment, reflects only on the death of "the revolutionary martyrs" who voluntarily sacrifice their lives, but not on the death of their victims. Kant had questioned the legitimacy of revolution on the ground that its maxim does not stand the test of publicity which in his view every honest maxim stands: the preparation of every revolution is necessarily conspiratorial or secret. To counter this argument Cohen observes that the moral basis of revolutions is the original contract which, "being only an idea, is always only an interior, hence secret presupposition." The same reasoning would lead to the further conclusion that the original contract, nay, Cohen's theology must never be publicly mentioned, let alone be taught. It is altogether fitting that Cohen, who was no friend of "the irrational" or of "mysticism," should be driven in his defense of the revolutionary principle to become friendly to the "irrational" and to "mysticism." [52] To say nothing of other things, he would never have been driven to this surrender of reason if he had taken seriously the law of reason or the natural law which may be said to indicate the right mean between hard-heartedness and soft-heartedness.

While admitting "the deep injustice" of Cohen's judgment on Spinoza, Rosenzweig asserts that Cohen has honestly complied in his critique of the *Theologico-political Treatise* with the duty of scholarly objectivity.[53] This assertion must be qualified. Since Cohen accuses Spinoza of having been unfair in his treatment of the universalism of the prophets, one must consider in fairness to Spinoza whether the Jewish tradition with which Spinoza was directly confronted had preserved intact that universalism. Cohen failed to make this investigation. Once one makes it, one observes that Spinoza recognized the universalism of the prophets in some respects more clearly than did some of the greatest traditional Jewish authorities. In his critique of Spinoza Cohen is silent about the fact, which he mentions elsewhere, that prophetic universalism had become obscured in later times for easily understandable reasons.[54] Cohen is particularly indignant about Spinoza's using a remark of Maimonides in order to prove that according to Judaism non-Jews cannot be saved unless they believe in the Mosaic revelation,[55] i.e. unless, as one is tempted to say, they are Christians or Muslims. More precisely, Spinoza quotes a passage from Maimonides' Code in which it is said that a Gentile is pious and has a share in the world to come if he performs the seven commandments given to Noah qua commanded by God in the Torah, but that if he performs them because of a decision of reason, he does not belong to the pious Gentiles or to the wise ones. Cohen accuses Spinoza of having used a false reading of a single passage of the Code—of a passage which expresses only Maimonides' private opinion and which in addition is contradicted by two other passages of the Code—in order to deny the universalism of post-biblical Judaism. He (or the authority to which he defers) notes that according to the most authoritative commentator on the Code, Joseph Caro, the qualification stated by Maimonides (*viz.* that piety requires recognition of the Mosaic revelation) is his private opinion, but Cohen fails to add that Caro adds that the opinion is correct. Caro would not have said this if Maimonides' opinion contradicts the consensus of Judaism. Cohen (or his authority) also notes that, according to the most authentic text of the Code, the Gentile who performs the seven Noahidic commandments because of a decision of reason does not indeed belong to the pious Gentiles but to the wise ones.[56] But Cohen does not show that Spinoza knew that reading to be the most authentic reading. The reading used by Spinoza is still the common reading which it would not be if it were in shocking contrast to the consensus of Judaism as Cohen asserts and hence would have shocked every Jewish reader.[57] In addition, the allegedly best reading does not necessarily improve the fate of the wise Gentiles unless one proves first that the fate of the wise Gentiles is as good as that of the pious Gentiles. Cohen finally asserts that the passage in question contradicts two other passages of the Code which in his opinion do not demand that the pious Gentile believe in the revealed character of the Torah. It suffices to say that the two passages are silent on what precisely constitutes the piety of the Gentiles and are therefore irrelevant to the issue.[58] Cohen also refers to a different treatment of the subject in Maimonides' commentary on the Mishna; but this merely leads to the further question whether that commentary, composed much earlier than the Code, is equal in authority to it. But, to return to the main issue, i.e. whether the ordinary reading, used by Spinoza, of the passage under consideration makes sense as a Maimonidean utterance: can Maimonides have taught, as Spinoza asserts he did, that Gentiles who perform the seven Noahidic commandments because reason decides so are not wise men? The answer is simple: Maimonides must have taught it because he denied that there are any rational commandments. Cohen might have objected to this argument on the ground that if Maimonides' denial of the rationality of any commandments or laws were his last word, he could not well have attempted to show that all or almost all commandments of the Torah have "reasons." [59] The reply is obvious: according to Maimonides all or almost all commandments of the Torah serve the purpose of eradicating idolatry, an irrational practice, and are in this sense "rational"; they are rational in the sense in which, not a healthy body but a medicine is "healthy." [60] One could say that Maimonides' denial of the rationality of any law is implied in the incriminated passage itself regardless of which of the two readings one prefers; for the term which Cohen renders by "reason" (da'at) does not necessarily mean reason in particular but may mean thought or opinion in general: [61] it makes sense both to assert and to deny that opinion justifies the seven Noahidic commandments.

These and similar considerations do not affect the main issue, namely, the fact that Cohen may well be right in asserting that Spinoza acted ignobly in basing his denial of the universalism of traditional, post-prophetic Judaism on a single Maimonidean utterance. In the words of Rosenzweig, beneath the deep injustice of Cohen's judgment lies its still much deeper justification. What Rosenzweig meant may be stated as follows. Cohen was a more profound thinker than Spinoza because unlike Spinoza he did not take for granted the philosophic detachment or freedom from the tradition of his own people; that detachment is "unnatural," not primary, but the outcome of a liberation from the primary attachment, of an alienation, a break, a betrayal. The primary is fidelity, and the sympathy and love which go with fidelity. Genuine fidelity to a tradition is not the same as literalist traditionalism and is in fact incompatible with it. It consists in preserving not simply the tradition but the continuity of the tradition. As fidelity to a living and hence changing tradition, it requires that one distinguish between the living and the dead, the flame and the ashes, the gold and the dross: the loveless Spinoza sees only the ashes, not the flame, only the letter, not the spirit. He is not excusable on the ground that Jewish thought may have declined in the centuries preceding him from its greatest height; for he "on whose extraction, whose gifts, whose learning the Jews had put the greatest hope" was under an obligation to understand contemporary Judaism, and still more Maimonides, to say nothing of Scripture itself, in the light of the highest or, if necessary, better than they understood themselves. Within a living tradition, the new is not the opposite of the old but its deepening: one does not understand the old in its depth unless one understands it in the light of such deepening; the new does not emerge through the rejection or annihilation of the old but through its metamorphosis or reshaping. "And it is a question whether such reshaping is not the best form of annihilation." [62] This is indeed the question: whether the loyal and loving reshaping or reinterpretation of the inherited, or the pitiless burning of the hitherto worshiped is the best form of annihilation of the antiquated, i.e. of the untrue or bad. On the answer to this question the ultimate judgment on Spinoza as well as on Cohen will depend: is the right interpretation "idealizing" interpretation, i.e. the interpretation of a teaching in the light of its highest possibility regardless of whether or not that highest possibility was known to the originator, or is it historical interpretation proper, which understands a teaching as meant by its originator? Is the conservatism which is generally speaking the wise maxim of practice also the sacred law of theory?

It would not be reasonable to demand from Cohen that he should give the benefit of idealizing interpretation to Spinoza who had become an ingredient of the modern tradition on which Cohen's philosophy as a philosophy of culture is based. For the kind of interpretation which Spinoza calls for is not idealizing, since his own doctrine is not idealistic. As was shown before, Cohen's political philosophy did not pay sufficient attention to the harsh political verities which Spinoza has stated so forcefully. Accordingly, he does not pay sufficient attention to the harsh necessity to which Spinoza bowed by writing in the manner in which he wrote. He did not understand Spinoza's style, which was indeed entirely different from his own. Cohen sometimes writes like a commentator on a commentary on an already highly technical text and hence like a man whose thought is derivative and traditional in the extreme, and yet he surprises time and again with strikingly expressed original and weighty thoughts. Be this as it may, he goes so far as to deny that in Spinoza's time the freest minds were compelled to withhold and to deny the truth; "Think only of Jean Bodin who in his Heptaplomeres not only directed the strongest attacks against Christianity but also celebrated Judaism most highly. It must appear strange that this writing, which was known to Leibniz and Thomasius, which was at that time widely distributed, should have remained unknown to Spinoza." He forgets here to say what he says elsewhere: "Leibniz had seen the manuscript of the Heptaplomeres and had advised against its being printed." [63] It was not printed before the nineteenth century. Once one takes into consideration the consequences of persecution, Spinoza's conduct in the *Theologico-political Treatise* ceases to be that "psychological riddle" which Cohen saw in it. He wondered whether that conduct could not be traced to the fact that the Spanish Jews' feelings of anxiety caused by the terrors of the Inquisition had eventually turned into hatred for that for the sake of which they had been so cruelly persecuted. A different explanation was suggested by Nietzsche in his verses addressed to Spinoza. After having paid homage to Spinoza's *amor dei* and to his being "blissful through intelligence," he goes on to say that beneath the love of the "One in all" there was eating a secret desire for revenge: *am Judengott frass Judenhass.* Nietzsche understood Spinoza in his own image. He traced his own revolt against the Christian God to his Christian conscience. The premise of this explanation is Hegelian dialectics: every form of the mind perishes through its antithesis which it necessarily produces. Spinoza's break with the Torah is the consequence of the *Sithrei Torah* in the double sense of the expression, the secrets of the Torah and the contradictions of the Torah. Spinoza was not swayed by Hegelian dialectics but by the Aristotelian principle of contradiction.

Cohen read Spinoza on the one hand not literally enough and on the other hand much too literally; he understood him too literally because he did not read him literally enough. Hence, he did not find his way among the contradictions in which the *Theologico-political Treatise* abounds. As he exclaims on one occasion, "no reason of reasonable men can understand, let alone overcome, these difficulties." A single example must here suffice. He wonders whether Spinoza does not contradict himself by admitting that the Mosaic law is a divine law although he understands by a divine law a law that aims only at the highest good, i.e. true knowledge of God and love of God, or intellectual love of God; and he denies that the Mosaic law aims at that highest good. The contradiction disappears once one considers the fact, which Cohen observes, that according to Spinoza a law may also be called divine with a view to its origin: the Mosaic law is human as regards its end, since it aims only at political felicity, but it is divine qua divinely revealed. Cohen quotes Spinoza's explanation: the Mosaic law "may be called the law of God or divine law since we believe that it is sanctioned by the prophetic light." He remarks: "But why do we believe this? This question is not answered by the anonymous author." But does not the community consisting of the anonymous author who speaks as a Christian and his Christian readers believe it as a matter of course, so that the question as to "why we believe it" does not have to arise? Spinoza had originally said that the divine law aims only at the highest good; immediately before saying that the Mosaic law can be called divine with a view to its origin as distinguished from its aim, he says according to Cohen that the divine law "consists chiefly in the highest good": hence, Cohen infers, Spinoza admits now a secondary content of the divine law without stating immediately what that secondary content is, namely, the sensual means which sensual men need. But Spinoza did not say that the divine law consists in the highest good; he says that it consists in the prescriptions regarding the means required for achieving the highest good: the divine law consists chiefly of the prescriptions regarding the proximate means and secondarily of the prescriptions regarding the remote means; since "sensual man" is incapable of intellectual love of God, his needs fall wholly outside of the divine law as here considered by Spinoza. It must be added that according to Spinoza even the divine law in the strictest sense is of human origin; every law is prescribed by human beings to themselves or to other human beings. Cohen throws some light on Spinoza's teaching regarding the divine law by making this remark on Spinoza's assertion that "the highest reward of the divine law is the law itself": "here he has literally taken over a sentence of the Mishna from the well-known Sayings of the Fathers, only adding the word 'highest.'" Cohen underestimates the importance of Spinoza's addition: Spinoza's egoistic morality demands for the fulfillment of the commandments rewards other than the commandments or perhaps additional commandments; it does not leave room for martyrdom.[64]

Rosenzweig finds Cohen guilty of injustice to Spinoza not because of defective objectivity but rather because of defective "subjectivity," i.e. of "insufficient reflection about the conditions and foundations of his own person. He ought to have made his attack with a clearer consciousness of the fact that, not indeed he himself, but the times which had born and raised him, Cohen himself, would not have been possible without Spinoza." The distinction between Cohen himself and his time, which is due to idealizing or apologetic interpretation, is immaterial here, for if Cohen's thought had nothing to do with the thought of his time, he would not have met Spinoza by reflecting about the presuppositions of "his own person." Cohen accuses Spinoza of blindness to Biblical prophetism, but this phenomenon as Cohen understood it was brought to light by what he calls "the historical understanding of the Bible," and this understanding is not possible without higher criticism of the Bible, i.e. without a public effort which was originated with the necessary comprehensiveness by Spinoza. Cohen blames Spinoza for disregarding the difference between mythical and historical elements of the Bible, a distinction which, as Cohen states, was alien to our traditional exegesis; and as regards the doctrinal elements of the Bible, he blames him for not distinguishing between the less and the more mature Biblical statements; he blames him for the immaturity or incompetence of his Biblical criticism, not at all for his Biblical criticism itself: for Cohen, Biblical criticism is a matter of course. Similarly, he states that Spinoza opposed rabbinical Judaism, especially its great concern with the ceremonial law, and that his sharp opposition had a certain salutary effect on the liberation of opinion; he notes without any disapproval that "modern Judaism" has freed itself from part of the ceremonial law; he fails to admit that modern Judaism is a synthesis between rabbinical Judaism and Spinoza. As for Spinoza's denial of the possibility of miracles, Cohen gives an extremely brief summary of the chapter which Spinoza devotes to the subject of miracles without saying a word in defense of miracles.[65] In brief, Cohen does not discuss at all the issue between Spinoza and Jewish orthodoxy, i.e. the only issue with which Spinoza could have been concerned, since there was no modern or liberal Judaism in his time. One may say that in his critique of Spinoza Cohen commits the typical mistake of the conservative, which consists in concealing the fact that the continuous and changing tradition which he cherishes so greatly would never have come into being through conservatism, or without discontinuities, revolutions, and sacrileges committed at the beginning of the cherished tradition and at least silently repeated in its course.

This much is certain: Cohen's critique of Spinoza does not come to grips with the fact that Spinoza's critique is directed against the whole body of authoritative teachings and rules known in Spinoza's time as Judaism and still maintained in Cohen's time by Jewish orthodoxy. Cohen took it for granted that Spinoza had refuted orthodoxy as such. Owing to the collapse of "the old thinking" it became then necessary to examine the *Theologico-political Treatise* with a view to the question of whether Spinoza had in fact refuted orthodoxy. Cohen's critique remained helpful for this purpose almost only in so far as it had destroyed the prejudice in favor of Spinoza, or the canonization of Spinoza by German or Jewish romanticism, to say nothing of the canonization by liberalism. Cohen's critique had the additional merit that it was directed chiefly against the *Theologico-political Treatise*. The seeming neglect of the *Ethics* proved to be sound, and thus to be obligatory for the re-examination of Spinoza's critique of orthodoxy, for the following reason. The *Ethics* starts from explicit premises by the granting of which one has already implicitly granted the absurdity of orthodoxy and even of Judaism as understood by Cohen or Rosenzweig; at first glance these premises seem to be arbitrary and hence to beg the whole question. They are not evident in themselves but they are thought to become evident through their alleged result: they and only they are held to make possible the clear and distinct account of everything; in the light of the clear and distinct account, the Biblical account appears to be confused. The *Ethics* thus begs the decisive question, the question as to whether the clear and distinct account is as such true and not merely a plausible hypothesis. In the *Theologico-political Treatise,* however, Spinoza starts from premises that are granted to him by the believers in revelation; he attempts to refute them on the bases of Scripture, of theologoumena formulated by traditional authorities, and of what one may call common sense. For in the *Treatise* Spinoza addresses men who are still believers and whom he intends to liberate from their "prejudices" so that they can begin to philosophize; the *Treatise* is Spinoza's introduction to philosophy.

The results of this examination of Spinoza's critique may be summarized as follows. If orthodoxy claims to know that the Bible is divinely revealed, that every word of the Bible is divinely inspired, that Moses was the writer of the Pentateuch, that the miracles recorded in the Bible have happened and similar things, Spinoza has refuted orthodoxy. But the case is entirely different if orthodoxy limits itself to asserting that it believes the aforementioned things, i.e. that they cannot claim to possess the binding power peculiar to the known. For all assertions of orthodoxy rest on the irrefutable premise that the omnipotent God whose will is unfathomable, whose ways are not our ways, who has decided to dwell in the thick darkness, may exist. Given this premise, miracles and revelations in general, and hence all Biblical miracles and revelations in particular, are possible. Spinoza has not succeeded in showing that this premise is contradicted by anything we know. For what we are said to know, for example, regarding the age of the solar system, has been established on the basis of the assumption that the solar system has come into being naturally; miraculously it could have come into being in the way described by the Bible. It is only naturally or humanly impossible that the "first" Isaiah should have known the name of the founder of the Persian empire; it was not impossible for the omnipotent God to reveal to him that name. The orthodox premise cannot be refuted by experience or by recourse to the principle of contradiction. An indirect proof of this is the fact that Spinoza and his like owed such success as they had in their fight against orthodoxy to laughter and mockery. By means of mockery they attempted to laugh orthodoxy out of its position from which it could not be dislodged by any proofs supplied by Scripture or by reason. One is tempted to say that mockery does not succeed the refutation of the orthodox tenets but is itself the refutation. The genuine refutation of orthodoxy would require the proof that the world and human life are perfectly intelligible without the assumption of a mysterious God; it would require at least the success of the philosophic system: man has to show himself theoretically and practically as the master of the world and the master of his life; the merely given world must be replaced by the world created by man theoretically and practically. Spinoza's *Ethics* attempts to be the system but it does not succeed; the clear and distinct account of everything that it presents remains fundamentally hypothetical. As a consequence, its cognitive status is not different from that of the orthodox account. Certain it is that Spinoza cannot legitimately deny the possibility of revelation. But to grant that revelation is possible means to grant that the philosophic account and the philosophic way of life are not necessarily, not evidently, the true account and the right way of life: philosophy, the quest for evident and necessary knowledge, rests itself on an unevident decision, on an act of the will, just as faith does. Hence the antagonism between Spinoza and Judaism, between unbelief and belief, is ultimately not theoretical but moral.

For the understanding of that moral antagonism the Jewish designation of the unbeliever as Epicurean seemed to be helpful, especially since from every point of view Epicureanism may be said to be the classic form of the critique of religion and the basic stratum of the tradition of the critique of religion. Epicureanism is hedonism, and traditional Judaism always suspects that all theoretical and practical revolts against the Torah are inspired by the desire to throw off the yoke of the stern and exacting duties so that one can indulge in a life of pleasure. Epicureanism can lead only to a mercenary morality whereas traditional Jewish morality is not mercenary: "The reward for [the fulfillment of] the commandment is the commandment." Epicureanism is so radically mercenary that it conceives of its theoretical doctrines as the means for liberating the mind from the terrors of religious fear, of the fear of death, and of natural necessity. Characteristically, modern unbelief is indeed no longer Epicurean. It is no longer cautious or retiring, not to say cowardly, but bold and active. Whereas Epicureanism fights the religious "delusion" because of its terrible character, modern unbelief fights it because it is a delusion: regardless of whether religion is terrible or comforting, qua delusion it makes men oblivious of the real goods, of the enjoyment of the real goods, and thus seduces them into being cheated of the real, "this-worldly" goods by their spiritual or temporal rulers who "live" from that delusion. Liberated from the religious delusion, awakened to sober awareness of his real situation, taught by bad experiences that he is threatened by a stingy, hostile nature, man recognizes as his sole salvation and duty, not so much "to cultivate his garden" as in the first place to plant a garden by making himself the master and owner of nature. But this whole enterprise requires, above all, political action, revolution, a life and death struggle: the Epicurean who wishes to live securely and retiredly must transform himself into an "idealist" who has learned to fight and to die for honor and truth. But in proportion as the systematic effort to liberate man completely from all non-human bonds seems to succeed, the doubt increases whether the goal is not fantastic—whether man has not become smaller and more miserable in proportion as the systematic civilization progresses. Eventually the belief that by pushing ever farther back the "natural limits" man will advance to ever greater freedom, that he can subjugate nature and prescribe to it his laws, begins to wither. In this stage the religious "delusion" is rejected not because it is terrible but because it is comforting: religion is not a tool which man has forged for dark reasons in order to torment himself, to make life unnecessarily difficult, but a way out chosen for obvious reasons in order to escape from the terror, the exposedness and the hopelessness of life which cannot be eradicated by any progress of civilization. A new kind of fortitude which forbids itself every flight from the horror of life into comforting delusion, which accepts the eloquent descriptions of "the misery of man without God" as an additional proof of the goodness of its cause, reveals itself eventually as the ultimate and purest ground for the rebellion against revelation. This new fortitude, being the willingness to look man's forsakenness in its face, being the courage to welcome the most terrible truth, is "probity," "intellectual probity." This final atheism with a good conscience, or with a bad conscience, is distinguished by its conscientiousness from the atheism at which the past shuddered. Compared not only with Epicureanism but with the unbelief of the age of Spinoza, it reveals itself as a descendant of Biblical morality. This atheism, the heir and the judge of the belief in revelation, of the secular struggle between belief and unbelief, and finally of the short-lived but by no means therefore inconsequential romantic longing for the lost belief, confronting orthodoxy in complex sophistication formed out of gratitude, rebellion, longing and indifference, and in simple probity, is according to its claim as capable of an original understanding of the human roots of the belief in God, as no earlier, no less complex-simple philosophy ever was. The last word and the ultimate justification of Spinoza's critique is the atheism from intellectual probity which overcomes orthodoxy radically by understanding it radically, i.e. without the polemical bitterness of the Enlightenment and the equivocal reverence of romanticism. Yet this claim however eloquently raised can not deceive one about the fact that its basis is an act of will, of belief, and, being based on belief, is fatal to any philosophy.

The victory of orthodoxy through the self-destruction of rational philosophy was not an unmitigated blessing, for it was a victory not of Jewish orthodoxy but of any orthodoxy, and Jewish orthodoxy based its claim to superiority to other religions from the beginning on its superior rationality (Deuteronomy 4:6). Apart from this, the hierarchy of moralities and wills to which the final atheism referred could not but be claimed to be intrinsically true, theoretically true: "the will to power" of the strong or of the weak may be the ground of every other doctrine; it is not the ground of the doctrine of the will to power: the will to power was said to be a fact. Other observations and experiences confirmed the suspicion that it would be unwise to say farewell to reason. I began therefore to wonder whether the self-destruction of reason was not the inevitable outcome of modern rationalism as distinguished from pre-modern rationalism, especially Jewish-medieval rationalism and its classical (Aristotelian and Platonic) foundation. The present study was based on the premise, sanctioned by powerful prejudice, that a return to pre-modern philosophy is impossible. The change of orientation compelled me to engage in a number of studies in the course of which I became ever more attentive to the manner in which heterodox thinkers of earlier ages wrote their books. As a consequence of this, I now read the *Theologico-political Treatise* differently than I read it when I was young. I understood Spinoza too literally because I did not read him literally enough.

Notes

1. Consider Leon Trotzky, *The History of the Russian Revolution*, tr. by Max Eastman, The University of Michigan Press, I, 329–31 and III, 154–55.

2. Heinrich Heine, "Die romantische Schule," *Sämtliche Werke*, ed. Elster, V, 217. Cf. the discussion of romanticism in Hegel's *Aesthetik*.

3. Consider *Jenseits von Gut und Böse*, Chapter 8.

4. *Wilhelm Meisters Wanderjahre*, Bk. 3, ch. 11.

5. *Jenseits von Gut und Böse*, no. 251; cf. *Morgenröte*, no. 205.

6. *Einführung in die Metaphysik*, Tübingen, 1953, p. 152. This book consists of a course of lectures given in 1935, but as stated in the Preface "errors have been removed." Cf. also the allusion on p. 36 to a recent "cleansing" of the German universities.

7. Cf. Gerhard Scholem, "Politik der Mystik. Zu Isaac Breuer's 'Neuem Kusari,'" *Jüdische Rundschau*, 1934, no. 57.

8. Cf. Yehezkel Kaufmann, *The Religion of Israel*, tr. and abridged by Moshe Greenberg, The University of Chicago Press, 1960, pp. 2, 233–34.

9. Maimonides, *Mishneh Torah*, H. teshubah VI, 3.

10. Ahad ha-Am in his essay "External Freedom and Internal Servitude."

11. Cf. Spinoza, *Theologico-political Treatise*, praef. (sect. 7 Bruder).

12. *Théodicée*, Discours de la Conformité de la foi avec la raison, sect. 3, and Vergil, *Georgica* IV, 86–87. The poet speaks of the battle between two rival queens for the rule of a single beehive. The philosopher seems to think of the question whether philosophy or revelation ought to be the queen.

13. Cf. Franz Rosenzweig, *Kleinere Schriften*, Berlin, 1937, pp. 354–98.

14. On the relation between Rosenzweig's and Heidegger's thought, see Karl Löwith, *Gesammelte Abhandlungen*, Stuttgart, 1960, pp. 68–92.

15. Rosenzweig, pp. 380, 387.

16. *Eclipse of God*, New York, 1952, p. 97; cf. the German original, *Gottesfinsternis*, Zürich, 1953, pp. 87–88. I have not attempted to bring the translation somewhat closer to Heidegger's German statement which, incidentally, is not quite literally quoted by Buber. Cf. Heidegger, *Nietzsche*, II, 320.

17. Hermann Cohen, *Ethik des reinen Willens*, 4th ed., p. 422: "Der Prophet hat gut reden: Himmel und Erde mögen vergehen; er denkt sie in seinem Felsen, den ihm Gott bildet, wohlgegründet."

18. *Eclipse of God*, p. 81; *Gottesfinsternis*, p. 71. I believe that the translator made a mistake in rendering "Führung einer Welt" by "conduct of the world," and I changed his translation accordingly, but I do not know whether I am right; it does not appear from the Preface that Buber has approved the translation.

19. Cf. the reasoning with which Wellhausen justifies his athetesis of Amos 9:13–15: "Roses and lavender instead of blood and iron." *Skizzen und Vorarbeiten*, Berlin, 1893, V, 94.

20. *Der Satz vom Grund*, p. 142; *Was heisst Denken?* pp. 32ff.

21. *Gottesfinsternis*, pp. 143, 159–61; *Eclipse of God*, pp. 154, 173–75.

Cf. Rosenzweig, pp. 192, 530. Cf. above all the thorough discussion of this theme by Gershom Scholem, *On the Kabbalah and its Symbolism*, Schocken, New York, 1965, chapters I and II.

22. Cf. *Gottesfinsternis*, p. 34 with pp. 96–97 and 117 or *Eclipse of God*, pp. 39–40 with pp. 106, 127.

23. Heidegger, *Sein und Zeit*, sect. 57. Cf. C. F. Meyer's *Die Versuchung des Pescara*.

24. Cf. *Fröhliche Wissenschaft*, no. 343.

25. *Jenseits*, nos. 45, 224; *Götzen-Dämmerung*, "Die 'Vernunft' in der Philosophie," nos. 1–2.

26. Letter to Overbeck of February 23, 1887. Cf. *Jenseits*, no. 60; *Genealogie der Moral*, I, no. 7, III, nos. 23, 28 beginning; Nietzsche, *Werke*, ed. Schlechta, III, 422.

27. *Fröhliche Wissenschaft*, no. 344; *Jenseits*, no. 227; *Genealogie der Moral*, III, no. 27.

28. *Jenseits*, I; *Fröhliche Wissenschaft*, nos. 347, 377. Thomas Aquinas *S. th.* 1 qu.1. a. 4. and 2 2qu.1. a. 1.

29. *Sein und Zeit*, pp. 48–49, 190 n. 1, 229–39, 249 n. 1.

30. *Kleinere Schriften*, pp. 31–32, 111, 281–82, 374, 379, 382, 391, 392.

31. *Ibid.*, pp. 108–9, 114, 116–17, 119, 155–56.

32. Nietzsche, *Also sprach Zarathustra*, "Of Thousand and One Goals."

33. Cf. also Kant, *Die Religion innerhalb der Grenzen der blossen Vernunft*, ed. Kehrbach, p. 43.

34. *Kleinere Schriften*, p. 154: *Briefe*, Berlin, 1935, p. 520.

35. *Ethics* V, prop. 25 and prop. 36 schol.; cf. *Tr. theol.-pol.* VI, sect. 23. Cf. Goethe's letter to F. H. Jacobi of May 5, 1786.

36. "Spinoza über Staat und Religion, Judentum und Christentum," *Hermann Cohens Jüdische Schriften*, ed. Bruno Strauss, III 290–372; "Ein ungedruckter Vortrag Hermann Cohens über Spinozas Verhältnis zum Judentum," eingeleitet von Franz Rosenzweig, *Festgabe zum zehnjährigen Bestehen der Akademie für die Wissenschaft des Judentums, 1919–1929*, pp. 42–68. Cf. Ernst Simon, "Zu Hermann Cohens Spinoza-Auffassung," *Monatsschrift für Geschichte und Wissenschaft des Judentums*, 1935, pp. 181–94.

37. *Jüdische Schriften*, pp. 293, 320, 325–26, 329–31, 343, 358, 360; *Festgabe*, pp. 47–50, 57, 61–64.

38. *Jüdische Schriften*, pp. 299, 306–9, 329, 360–62.

39. *Jüdische Schriften*, pp. 333, 361, 363–64, 368, 371; *Festgabe*, p. 59.

40. *Festgabe*, pp. 46, 47, 49–50; *Jüdische Schriften*, p. 344.

41. *Jüdische Schriften*, pp. 317–21, 323, 337–38.

42. *Jüdische Schriften*, p. 367; *Festgabe*, p. 56. Cf. *Tr. theol.-pol.*, I, sects. 35 and 37 with the titles of *Ethics*, I and II (cf. *Cogitata Metaphysica*, II, 12) and V, 36 cor.

43. *Tr.* xii, 19, 24, 37; xiii, 23; xiv, 6, 22–29, 34–36; xx, 22, 40; *Tr. pol.* viii, 46. Cf. especially *Tr.* xii, 3, where Spinoza takes the side of the Pharisees against the Sadducees. The contrast of *Tr.* xiv with Hobbes' *Leviathan*, ch. 43, is most revealing.

44. *Tr.* v, 7–9.

45. *Ibid.* v, 13, 15, 30–31; xvii, 95–102; xix, 13–17.

46. Cohen, *Jüdische Schriften* III, 333.

47. *Ibid.*

48. Cohen, *Kants Begründung der Ethik*, 2nd ed., p. 490, speaks of the

"gewagte Spiel" of Kant in his *Die Religion innerhalb der Grenzen der blossen Vernunft*, a work according to Cohen rich in "ambiguities and inner contradictions."

49. *Ethik*, pp. 61, 64, 94, 439–58, 468–70, 606. Cf. *Kants Begründung der Ethik*, 2nd ed. pp. 356–57.

50. Spinoza, *Tr. pol.* i, 2. Cohen, *Ethik*, pp. 64, 269, 272, 285–86, 378, 384–86; *Kants Begründung der Ethik*, pp. 394–406, 454. Cf., however, Hegel, *Rechtsphilosophie*, sect. 94ff.

51. *Pirke Abot* III, 2.

52. *Kants Begründung der Ethik*, pp. 309, 430, 431, 439, 446, 452, 511, 544–45, 554.

53. *Festgabe*, p. 44 (*Kleinere Schriften,* p. 355).

54. *Jüdische Schriften* II, 265–67. Cf. *Tr.* iii, 25, 33, 34, e.g. with Rashi on Isaiah 19:25, Jeremiah 1:5 and Malachi 1:10–11, and Kimchi on Isaiah 48:17.

55. *Festgabe*, pp. 64–67; *Jüdische Schriften* III, 345–51. Cf. *Tr.* v, 47–48.

56. Misreading his authority or Caro, Cohen erroneously asserts that Caro declares the reading "but to the wise ones" to be the correct reading.

57. Cf. also Manasse ben Israel, *Conciliator*, Frankfurt, 1633, Deut. q. 2. (p. 221).

58. In one of the passages (*Edut* XI, 10) Maimonides says that the pious idolators have a share in the world to come; but how do we know that he does not mean by a pious idolator an idolator who has forsworn idolatry (cf. *Issure Bia* XIV, 7) on the ground that idolatry is forbidden to all men by divine revelation? In the other passage (*Teshuba* III, 5) he merely says that the pious Gentiles have a share in the world to come; the sequel (III, 6ff., see especially 14) could seem to show that the pious Gentile is supposed to believe in the revealed character of the Torah.

59. *Jüdische Schriften* III, 240.

60. *Guide* III, 29 to end; Aristotle, *Metaphysics* 1003a33ff.

61. Cf. *M. T. H. Yesode ha-Torah*, I, 1.

62. Cohen, *Die Religion der Vernunft aus den Quellen des Judentums*, p. 205.

63. *Festgabe*, p. 53; *Jüdische Schriften* III, 365; cf. II, 257.

64. *Jüdische Schriften*, pp. 335–36; *Tr.* iv, 17 (cf. 9–16), 21.

65. *Jüdische Schriften* III, 351; *Festgabe*, pp. 50–54.

15.

From the Ancient Faith to a New Historical Consciousness *

by Yitzhak F. Baer

In the second half of the seventeenth century, the foundations of the old Jewish faith were already undermined from
two sides by rationalism and by the self-contradictions of the
Messiah doctrine. Nevertheless, the Judaism recognized as
legitimate continued to exist until the middle of the eighteenth
century, still unshaken in its ancient constitution and spiritual
character. Essentially, this Judaism remained as it had been
two thousand years before, or at least, if it had developed,
it had developed only in nuances. It still upheld the same
eschatological concepts of history, with the chosen people
as center—except that the framework of this concept had been
enlarged in the course of the centuries to include the historical
and philosophical materials that had gradually accumulated
around it.

Inner attitudes to history changed very slowly. Out of the
compact and somewhat pugnacious doctrine of election had
grown a naive mythology of history full of wonderful light
and an involved and metaphysical system of historical speculation, half magical in its atmosphere. A rational philosophical
trend that prepared the way for later skepticism split off from
this system. But it all still remained within an identical historical framework, secured by tradition and by the naive
faith of the people against essential changes. The most exalted
speculations, the soberest rationalism, the grayest tones of
everyday life—all remained bound to the firm realities of
people, land, and Torah, past and future greatness, and the

* From *Galut* (In Exile), Robert Warshow, trans., New York,
Schocken Books, 1947.

inexplicable sufferings of the Galut. The people are kept together by a national consciousness unique in the world. The land is the *real* land of Palestine, however veiled by religious imagination and mystery, however bereft by political circumstances of its beauty and productivity. And the much criticized talmudic dialectic still leads always back to the miracle of the Torah. The religion renews itself in every generation through a strength that comes from the people and is at the same time mythos and purest intellect. The day-to-day fate of the people is still completely comprehended—as it was in the days of the Bible—through a firm faith in the direct influence of God upon every historical event. This is no timid spinning out of old dreams, nor is it mere inertia under the burden of an incomprehensible destiny; rather, it is a system of religious concepts—complete in itself, if over-loaded—of which every representative of the tradition can give a clear account.

This old system of thought is by no means unhistorical, for it has history as its foundation; the decisive historical events of ancient and recent times retained their fixed place in Jewish thought, more than in other religious systems, becoming milestones in the story of the testing of God's people. No complex historiography could develop out of this system, for at bottom it is always a repetition of the same ideas applied to the changing materials of history. Precisely the last epochs before the emancipation yield very numerous accounts dealing with individual historical events, which are always treated as new examples for the trial, proving, and delivery of the people of God; the apocalyptic visions, which continue almost to this time, are the constantly repeated expression of an unshaken spirit that sees in history the signs of the coming end.

The greatness and unity of this religious world are not essentially disturbed by the frequently abstruse forms of its expression or the unpleasant external circumstances of social and economic life. The community life of the Jews of this time displays no weaknesses that are not to be found also in the Christian bourgeois society. The much criticized Jewish factors and agents in the courts of the German nobles did their good and their evil acts, just like the Christian courtiers of the time. The economic behavior of the Jews of the time displays the general virtues and vices of early capitalism—to the extent, at least, that the business affairs of Jews developed sufficiently to warrant the use of such a term. There never were any specific, religiously determined, Jewish economic traits. The exigencies of the Galut forced the Jews to do the best they could with the few means of livelihood that were open to them. Commerce with its drudgery and constant risk is regarded as a burden imposed by heaven, as a form of asceticism in a dismal world, but never as a value in itself, and economic success is no subject for religious contemplation. All of the above is not noted to extenuate the faults of this generation; but it must be understood that these faults were observed and criticized by the Jews themselves as abuses and signs of worldliness.

In the last decade of the seventeenth century, however, rationalism began its victorious progress through the world. In Holland and England, the principle of religious toleration was first proclaimed, and was applied, in part, to the Jews. The Jews were given no equality in terms of politics and citizenship, but they were permitted to practice their religion freely and were guaranteed a degree of human consideration that had never before been accorded to Jews anywhere in the world. This was at a time when in the Catholic countries of Southern and Eastern Europe, especially in Poland, the treatment of the Jews was determined by the blackest bigotry or the most senseless superstition, and when in Protestant Germany the Jews were hemmed in by a frustrating system of restrictions that was about to lose its religious trappings and turn into an instrument of race hatred and racist politics.

In the more favorable intellectual atmosphere of the western countries, which gradually spread also to Germany, there arose a new approach to the basic questions of Jewish life. The Jews who partook of the new rationalism were not, like da Costa and Spinoza, rebels against an established way of life; they were simply skeptics and men of pleasure, or even men who, with no thought of undermining the tradition that had been handed down to them, gave up their political ties and their responsibility to the Jewish nation as a whole, and tried to make themselves as comfortable as possible in their "homes" in the *Golah* ("Exile"). Such types had always existed, but from the end of the seventeenth century on they became steadily more numerous until they finally stood in the foreground of Jewish life.

The first clear evidence of this new attitude may be found in the book *Sefat Emet* ("Language of Truth"), by Moshe Chagis (published in Amsterdam, 1707). Chagis came to Western Europe as an envoy from Jerusalem in order to collect money for Palestine, if possible to improve the methods of collecting money, and, as was customary with the *sheluhim* ("envoys"), to preach to the Jews and turn their hearts toward the Holy Land. In passionate words taken from the tradition, he preached to the Jews of the real and religious significance of Palestine. But the lukewarm and the skeptical among the Sephardic Jews greeted him with doubt and indifference. Their arguments were old, but at this moment they had a special importance, for they represented the starting point of the theories of two centuries. The value of the Holy Land is called into question with the usual arguments about the desolation of the country and the unfortunate conditions prevailing there in respect to political affairs and within the Jewish community. The assertion is made that, until the redemption, every country is as good as Palestine; that God hears men's prayers everywhere; that indeed it is contrary to God's command to live in Palestine, for Palestine must lie waste until the end of days. This is Marrano theology in a modernized and more comfortable form.

Chagis can classify these arguments as coming from skeptics who throw off the yoke of the commandments and think only of enjoying their wealth and their new political freedom. They consider their present home their Jerusalem, and do not concern themselves with the needs of the Holy Land or the needs of the Jews in Turkey, Germany, Poland, or Africa. These frivolous persons declare that they would be delighted if the Messiah came for the poor Jews, so that they might be left in peace; but if the Messiah is going to equalize the rich and the poor, why do they need him? And they do not fail to cite authority in the support of these arguments. These comfortable Marranos were accustomed to interpret the words of Jeremiah—"And seek the peace of the city whither I have caused you to be carried away captive, and pray unto the Lord for it; for in the peace thereof shall ye have peace" (29:7)—as meaning that it is a Jew's duty to remain in the Diaspora, whereas this passage had earlier been interpreted only as prescribing the obligation to pray for the peace of the world and its rulers. These skeptics even dared to quote the words of the Talmud (Ketuvot 111a): that "love must not be awakened too soon." Earlier, these words had been advanced against the false prophets who sought to force the redemption by an exaggeration of religious exaltation. No pious Jew would ever have thought of employing the passage in any way that could weaken religious ardor or shake that Jewish faith which rested on real values.

In Sephardic circles of this period we find for the first time an optimistic consciousness of progress. They feel themselves to have had a hand in the libertarian development of Holland. From the Sephardim of England and Holland, rationalism spread to the Jewish skeptics in France and even to the Jews of Germany. Moses Mendelssohn (1729–1786) merely gathers together the thought of his time and gives it an authoritative form, raised above mere libertinism. The tendencies of modern Jewish history that were set in motion in Mendelssohn's time have been exhaustively analyzed and criticized in recent times; we can only examine here some of the consequences of these tendencies in the history of the concept and conditions of the Galut.

Recent Jewish history has carried to its conclusion a long process of disintegration. The gap between religious promises and the debased body of the Jewish people, of which Jewish rationalists had before been aware, led to a complete or partial abandonment of the nation. Loss of faith in the national future and in the folk strength of the religion led to a denationalization of the religion. The nation's specific political constitution in the Diaspora and the consciousness of Jewish unity were destroyed. At first it was believed that this was only to reorganize Judaism legally and socially on a higher, more objective, and more reasonable plane. In reality, it quickly became clear that the result of this effort was to replace the historically determined individuality of the Jew with a different individuality, no less determined by history. Such a transformation, however, proved impossible. The medieval difficulties in the way of the relations of Jews and non-Jews simply continued, though in a more humanized form; and, in addition, the tensions that first developed out of the emergence of the Marrano problem, unique in the late Middle Ages, became characteristic of the modern Jewish question. This was less a problem for the baptized Jews than for those Jews who, though they might remain in the Jewish camp, had nevertheless undergone a change of faith. For in reality what they had done was not to take over elements of European culture and incorporate them into their own religious-national organism; rather, they had given up essential elements of that organism in favor of different ways and views of life.

This change had come about through no visible external

force, but through a conscious or unconscious moral pressure. Now the historical forces that in the course of centuries had formed the Jewish character were deflected from their path— a path that might have led to the rise of full, conscious, and responsible community life. The historical forces forsook the nation. The vision of Ezekiel, as Judah ha-Levi had interpreted it, was now fulfilled. Of the living body of the nation, there were left only scattered and dry bones, and no one could foresee that these, in the words of the prophet, would unite again into a living whole. The scattered segments of the nation either entered, in the process of assimilation, into new and fruitful human and historical amalgamations, or they retained the stamp of the history of the Galut upon their inert and hardened flesh. Out of such conditions during a very brief period in Jewish history, a comprehensive historical construction was built up in the age of historical awareness that was accepted as true by both friends and enemies of the Jews and was yet, in a historical sense, more erroneous than any previous generation's view of Judaism.

The historical thought of modern Judaism still suffers from the effects of an improperly understood religious-political heritage. The old concept of history was abandoned, but it continued to have some hold on historical thinking; no one attempted a real and thorough analysis of the factors that determine Jewish history. Not only the national character of the Jews was misunderstood, but also—following medieval rationalism in this respect—the character of the Jewish faith, which flows from the people and is bound up with the destiny of the people, and can also be renewed only by the people. Attempts were made not to clarify the situation historically, but to defend it from a fixed standpoint. The Jewish apologetics of antiquity and the Middle Ages developed out of the need to defend certain conditions of which no one was in a position to know the causes and which no human effort could change. But in the modern world there is no place for apologetics; failings and difficulties are recognized and, so far as possible, traced to their origins and overcome. Only the human tendencies of Jewish apologetics remain valid. It is the privilege of the oppressed people to arouse the conscience of the victors and to draw the moral from a millennia-long history in which not human power but God was recognized as the determining historical factor.

The plan of this book now requires that I say one more word concerning the nature of the Galut in our times. All modern views of the Galut, from whatever orientation they arise, are inadequate: they are unhistorical; they confuse cause and effect; they project the patterns of the nineteenth century into the past. There really does not exist any serious and systematic effort to analyze the material of history, or any conscientious desire to understand and appreciate the ideas of earlier generations of Jews. This is true equally of the anti-semitic conception of the Galut as a symbol of political decay and general disintegration and exploitation, of the assimilationist idea that the Galut serves as an instrument for progress and the spread of culture, and of the religious theories of later Jewish theology.

Jewish theology is wrong in appealing to ancient Judaism's concept of a historical mission. The old idea of a Jewish mission was tied up with a particular conception of history and with the reality of political servitude that was to be done away with by the Messiah. The idea of the mission could be put forward only in time of suffering and need. It presented —together with the ideas of purification and atonement—only one of several interpretations of the Galut. Even for the Hellenistic Jews, the Galut did not have the particular and special significance that the early Christians ascribed to their own Diaspora. And the carrying on of a missionary task in the Galut must surely involve religious propaganda, which the Jews have given up precisely because of the pressures of the Galut, and probably for all time. In recent times, it has been often said that the old faith in the Messiah cannot be absorbed in the ideas of religious progress.

All modern interpretations of the Galut fail to do justice to the enormous tragedy of the Galut situation and to the religious power of the old ideas that centered around it. No man of the present day, of no matter what religious orientation, dare claim that he is equipped to carry the burden of the centuries as did his forefathers, or that the modern world still presents the internal and external conditions necessary to realize a Jewish destiny in the older sense.

The Galut has returned to its starting point. It remains what it always was: political servitude, which must be abolished completely. The attempt which has been considered from time to time, to return to an idea of the Galut as it existed in the days of the Second Temple—the grouping of the Diaspora around a strong center in Palestine—is today out of the question. There was a short period when the Zionist could feel himself a citizen of two countries, and indeed in a more deeply moral sense than Philo; for the Zionist was prepared to give up his life for the home in which he had his residence. Now that the Jews have been denied the right to feel at home in Europe, it is the duty of the European nations to redeem the injustice committed by their spiritual and physical ancestors by assisting the Jews in the task of reclaiming Palestine and by recognizing the right of the Jews to the land of their fathers.

Rabbi Judah Liwa ben Bezalel of Prague, a sixteenth-century writer who was completely rooted in ancient Judaism, opens his book on the messianic redemption with the statement that the nature of the redemption can only be rightly understood through its absolute opposite, the Galut. The fact of the Galut itself is for him the decisive proof of the expected redemption. For the Galut is the abolition of God's order. God gave to every nation its place, and to the Jews he gave Palestine. The Galut means that the Jews have left their natural place. But everything that leaves its natural place loses thereby its natural support until it returns. The dispersion of Israel among the nations is unnatural. Since the Jews manifest a national unity, even in a higher sense than the other nations, it is necessary that they return to a state of actual unity. Nor is it in accord with the order of nature that one nation should be enslaved by the others, for God made each nation for itself. Thus, by natural law, the Galut cannot last forever.

We may appeal to such ideas today with the consciousness that it is up to us to give the old faith a new meaning. If we seek to end the Galut, let us not attribute our desires to earlier generations; rather, we must draw from the ideas of earlier generations those consequences which follow from a changed spiritual approach to an unchanged political situation. The Jewish revival of the present day is in its essence not determined by the national movements of Europe: it harks back to the ancient national consciousness of the Jews, which existed before the history of Europe and is the original sacred model for all the national ideas of Europe. However, it is undeniable that this turning home must involve a coming to grips with the ancient Jewish consciousness of history, on whose foundation European culture constantly and repeatedly reared itself in the decisive epochs of its history, without wishing to acknowledge its debt in a serious and conclusive manner. The question is how we ourselves stand in relation to a belief whose foundations have held unshaken for more than two thousand years. For us, perhaps, the final consequence of modern causal historical thinking coincides with the final consequence of the old Jewish conception of history, which comes to us from no alien tradition but has grown out of our own essential being: "*Our* eyes saw it, and no stranger's; *our* ears heard it, and no other's." If we today can read each coming day's events in ancient and dusty chronological tables, as though history were the ceaseless unrolling of a process proclaimed once and for all in the Bible, then every Jew in every part of the Diaspora may recognize that there is a power that lifts the Jewish people out of the realm of all causal history.

Epilogue

In the ten years that have gone by since the appearance of this essay, a chapter has been written in the history of the Jews and of the world that surpasses the most terrible imaginings. It would be presumptuous to attempt in a brief epilogue to take a stand with respect to these events. But even the most modest contribution to historical understanding may be of help in coping with the tasks of today.

It is our constant duty to keep alive before us and before other peoples the greatness of our historical past, in order that we may draw strength and confidence from it, validate our claims before mankind, and find the path that leads to the further self-education of the Jewish people.

We have introduced our own special values into history. And it was not only in the first great age of our history—the age of ancient Israel—that we created these values and made them a part of the human heritage. In the second age of our history that was no less great and lasted from the days of the Maccabees to the completion of the Mishnah, we created, with the Torah and the books of the prophets in our hands, a socio-religious commonwealth of a unique character; within the limits of a historically determined attachment to ancient ritual forms and mythical thought, we created a new culture, original and pure, which spread such a light over the decadent and barren Graeco-Roman world as had not been seen since the days of sixth- and fifth-century classical Greece.

From this culture early Christianity derived a large part

of its substance and its ethical-religious strength. It created the foundations for European moral standards. It is during this period that our simple Jewish prayers originated, prayers which the nations, wresting out of their natural and authentic context, have been able to imitate but never to equal. The culture of this epoch—its beliefs, its rites, and its social order—dominates two thousand years of Jewish history, shackling them in the rigid bonds of dogma, to be sure, yet animating them with the religious strength of myth and eternal wonder.

It is during this age and on this very soil of Palestine that the first martyrs for the sake of faith arose. We taught the world the idea of martyrdom, and in the third great age of our history—the real age of the Galut—this idea was realized in the very body of the people. For two thousand years we suffered for the sake of the redemption of mankind; we were driven forth and scattered over every part of the earth because of the fateful interaction of the religious and political factors determining our history.

We went among the nations neither to exploit them nor to help them build their civilizations. All that we did on foreign soil was a betrayal of our own spirit. Nor, finally, did we go among the nations of Europe in order to convert them in the sense of that missionary ardor which animated our people in antiquity and which later animated the followers of Christianity. Once political limitations had destroyed the possibilities of conversion, our people had to content itself with testifying to its missionary vocation in the world by its mere existence.

Our place in the world is not to be measured by the measure of this world. Our history follows its own laws, maintaining its innermost tendencies in the face of the outward dangers of dispersal, disintegration, secularization, and moral and religious petrification.

Our task remains—in spite of the inevitable loosening of the bonds of dogma that held us together in the past—to seek our support in that principle which survived in us during all the distress of the past, the principle that is constantly being disclosed to us and yet whose depths will never be entirely plumbed, the principle that must surely overcome the present inner crisis of secularization, already several generations old, just as surely as the body of our people will endure and hold together despite all the dangers and difficulties.

16.

Martin Buber's
Interpretation of Hasidism

by Gershom G. Scholem

There can be no doubt that Martin Buber has made a decisive contribution to the Western world's knowledge of the Hasidic movement. Before Buber undertook to introduce and interpret Hasidism to Western readers, this movement was all but unknown to the scientific study of religion. This was true despite the fact that since its crystallization in Podolia around the middle of the eighteenth century, it constituted one of the most important factors in the life and thought of East European Jewry. As long as the ideas of the Enlightenment, beginning at the end of the eighteenth century, asserted their influence on Jewish circles, Hasidism for Western Jews seemed essentially an outbreak of extreme obscurantism, allied with all those forces in the Jewish past to which the protagonists of a modern, enlightened Judaism were most sharply opposed.

The great Jewish scholars of the nineteenth century who inaugurated the scientific study of Judaism (men like Heinrich Graetz, Abraham Geiger, and Leopold Zunz) felt the same way. They did not care for mysticism and emotionalism in religion and they repudiated the values which such movements emphatically propagated. Not until the turn of the century did certain Jewish writers and scholars, especially in Russia, attempt to regard this phenomenon without prejudice. This new view was linked to a general revaluation of Jewish history which was now treated as the history of a living people and no longer as the model for an enlightened theology, a model which most scholars measured by the abstract criteria of philosophers and theologians. The new wave of Jewish nationalism which welled up toward the end of the nineteenth century and a romantic impulse to discover the deeper forces at work in the life of the East European Jewish masses played a large role in bringing about this change. Scholars like Simon Dubnow, enthusiasts like Samuel A. Horodetzky, and great poets like Isaac Leib Peretz heralded the new era. Dubnow's pioneering study of the history of Hasidism was conducted in a remarkably cool and reserved manner; however, the discovery of the world of Hasidic legend lent great luster to the movement. This discovery, which was especially due to Peretz and Berdichevsky, possessed tremendous poetic appeal and marked a new era in Jewish literature, especially that in Hebrew, Yiddish, and German.

It is within this context that we must examine Buber's life-long fascination with the phenomenon of Hasidism and his contribution to its understanding. When in his youthful quest for a living Judaism Buber discovered Hasidism, he was overwhelmed by the message he seemed to find in it. Thereafter he devoted more than fifty years of a distinguished literary career to ever new formulations of this message's meaning. His Zionist credo, which put him on the track of Hasidism, was now interwoven with his conviction of the significance of Hasidic doctrine for the rebirth of Judaism: "No renewal of Judaism is possible which does not bear in itself the elements of Hasidism."

As an often fascinating and always vigorous and spirited writer, Buber made a significant impact with his first books, *The Tales of Rabbi Nachman* and *The Legend of the Baal-Shem.* Since that time we owe to his pen a virtually unending stream of Hasidic material and interpretative analysis which reaches its climax in *Tales of the Hasidim* and other books of a more theoretical character, like *The Message of Hasidism,* which have exercised a lasting influence, especially since the end of World War II.

Buber's influence is not hard to explain. While the enthusiasm of certain other apologists for Hasidic teaching, like Horodetzky's for example, was essentially naïve and their books were an odd mixture of charming simplicity and dullness, in Buber we have a deep and penetrating thinker who not only admires intuition in others but possesses it himself. He has that rare combination of a probing spirit and literary elegance which makes for a great writer. When an author of such stature and such subtlety set down with untiring seriousness what to him seemed the very soul of Hasidism, it was bound to make a deep impression on our age. In one sense or another we are all his disciples. In fact most of us, when we speak about Hasidism, probably think primarily in terms of the concepts that have become familiar through Buber's philosophical interpretation. Despite Buber's own frequent indications, many authors who have written about him during these years have not in the least been aware that Buber's work *is* an interpretation and that there might be a problem in relating the interpretation to the phenomenon itself. As a thoughtful reader once remarked to me, along with his interpretation of Hasidism Buber has for the first time presented the European and American reader with a canon of what Hasidism is. His interpretation was accompanied by such a wealth of seemingly irrefutable proof in the form of Hasidic legends and sayings that it was bound to silence any critic.

The more than fifty years of Buber's neo-Hasidic activity have evoked a strong response also outside the Jewish world. Competent scholars have been rather reluctant to raise basic questions as to whether this poetic, moving, and beautifully formulated interpretation can stand up to critical and sober analysis. Dubnow did express certain general doubts regarding the all too modern style of the interpretation and said of Buber's books that they were "suited to further contemplation, not research," but he supplied no evidence for this judgment. The emotional (to say nothing of the artistic) appeal of Buber's writings was of course so infinitely greater than that of Dubnow's rather arid discussion of Hasidic ideas that there could be little doubt as to whose arguments would have the greater impact. Yet, while historical research has meanwhile progressed far beyond Dubnow's achievement and has opened up many new perspectives and insights into the origins and developments of Hasidism, Buber's writings—especially those of his later years—have only recently evoked critical analysis. Such analysis now seems to me urgent and very much in order. In taking up this discussion here I will have to restrict myself to several points I consider fundamental.

A critical analysis of Buber's interpretation of Hasidism has to confront certain particular difficulties from the very start. The greatest is that Buber, to whom no one denies possession of an exact knowledge of Hasidic literature, does not write as a scholar who gives clear references to support his contentions. Buber combines facts and quotations to suit his purpose, namely, to present Hasidism as a spiritual phenomenon and not as a historical one. He has often said that he is not interested in history. In the context of our discussion this means two things of equal importance. First, Buber omits a great deal of material which he does not even consider, although it may be of great significance for the understanding of Hasidism as a historical phenomenon. To give only two examples: the magical element, which he consistently explains away or minimizes, and the social character of the Hasidic community. Secondly, the material that he does select he often associates closely with his own interpretation of its meaning. I shall have more to say about this later.

The other great difficulty facing the critical reader of Buber is connected with the circumstances of his development. Buber began as an enthusiastic admirer or even, one might say, adherent of religious mysticism. It was his discovery that there was a mystic kernel of living Judaism in the Hasidic movement which struck him with such force when he first came into contact with Hasidic literature and tradition. At that time he saw Hasidism as the flower of Jewish mysticism, the "Kabbalah become ethos." Thus his early interpretation bears a mystical hue as, for example, in that justly famous chapter "The Life of the Hasidim" with which he introduced *The Legend of the Baal-Shem* in 1908. Several years later, however, his thinking underwent a further development which brought about a deep change in his views. This change is best characterized in his philosophical writings by the distance lying between *Daniel: Dialogues on Realization* (1913) and *I and Thou* (1923). Here he renounced the world of mysticism and took a new stand which brought him into the front rank of what we would today call religious existentialism, even if Buber rather pointedly avoids using the term in his own writings. But in this new phase as well Buber continued to find in Hasidism illustrations for his views. His brief pamphlet *The Way of Man in Hasidic Teaching* is not only a gem of literature but also an extraordinary lesson in religious anthropology, presented in the language of Hasidism and inspired by a large mass of authentic Hasidic sayings. It is precisely to this problem of determining the nature of the inspiration which Buber found in the old texts and the change they underwent when he interpreted them in his own way that I must devote the major part of my discussion.

In this last, mature phase of his selective presentation of Hasidism, Buber no longer stressed the essential identity of Kabbalah and Hasidism, as he had done in his earlier works. Although he still recognizes the strong links between the two phenomena, he was concerned with establishing and maintaining an essential distinction between them. He now likes to refer to the Kabbalah as gnosis, which he no longer regards as a mark of praise. He sees two contradictory forms of religious consciousness at work in Hasidism—even if the creators of the movements may not have been aware of this split. Kabbalistic tradition determined one of them. It aimed at knowledge of divine mysteries, or at least at insight into them, and was bound to lead Hasidism into speculations of a theosophical nature. Buber was perfectly well aware that Hasidism developed within the framework of the Lurianic Kabbalah. He even explicitly adopted my own characterization of the Kabbalah of Isaac Luria as a classic example of a gnostic system within orthodox Judaism, as I set it forth in my *Major Trends in Jewish Mysticism*. But this Kabbalistic Gnosticism was not—and here I agree with Buber—a really creative element in Hasidism. Its conceptual apparatus was used by the great masters of Hasidism, but they transferred its basic meaning from the sphere of divine mysteries to the world of man and his encounter with God. According to Buber, this was the really creative aspect of Hasidism. And since in the last analysis it is the creative impulse which matters, he felt justified in almost completely ignoring the Kabbalistic or "gnostic" element in Hasidism. For him it is nothing more than a kind of umbilical cord which must be severed as soon as the new spiritual creation exists in its own right if we are to see and understand the new phenomenon in its authentic mode of being.

Buber's writings contain numerous formulations of this attitude. I would like to cite only one of them, taken from his debate with Rudolf Pannwitz:

> The Hasidic movement takes over from the Kabbalah only what it needs for the theological foundation of an enthusiastic but not over-exalted life in responsibility—the responsibility of each individual for the piece of world entrusted to him. Gnostic theologoumena that are thus taken over are transformed; their ground and their atmosphere are transformed with them. From spiritualities enthroned in the Absolute, they become the core of realizations [*Bewährungen*]. The pneuma has settled down in the blessings of a fervor that fires with enthusiasm the service of the Creator practiced in relation to the creature. Therefore, everything has become different. In place of esoterically regulated meditations has come the unprescribable endowing of each action with strength of intention, arising ever again from the moment. Not in the seclusion of the ascetics and schools of ascetics does the holy now appear, but in the joy in one another of the masters and their communities. And—what was unthinkable in the circles of the old Kabbalah—the "simple man" is held in honor, that is, the man of the original *devotio,* the man by nature at one with himself who lacks the secret knowing as well as the rabbinical knowledge, but can do without both be-

cause united he lives the united service. Where the mystical
vortex circled, now stretches the way of man.

This statement, though delivered by a voice that demands
respect, cannot convince anyone who is familiar with both the
Kabbalistic and the Hasidic literature. But in order to understand
the extraordinary mixture of truth, error, and oversimplification
which it contains, we must direct our attention to the most basic
features of Buber's attitude to the phenomenon of Hasidism,
namely, his conviction that our main source for the understanding of Hasidism is its legends. Only this conviction, together with
Buber's method of selection, can explain assertions like the one
quoted above.

Here we must point out that the extensive literature of
Hasidism ultimately falls into two categories. First, there is a very
large body of theoretical writings which consists mostly of sermons and lectures, commentaries on biblical texts, and tractates
on the prayers and on other objects of religious life. The common
conception among general readers who draw their knowledge of
Hasidism from Buber, namely that Hasidism is the pure "lay
mysticism" of unlettered groups, is conclusively refuted by this
literature. The most important of these works were written between 1770 and 1815, when Hasidism emerged from bitter polemics as a force in East European Jewry and sought to spread its
views and manner of life orally and in writing. These works contain the teachings of the great saints of Hasidism, the Zaddikim,
which, by the way, often cite as illustration epigrammatic sayings
or short anecdotes. An even more extensive literature of the same
type came into being after 1815, but for the most part it contains
only variations of the basic motifs that were set forth and developed in the older works; only here and there do we find a few new
ideas. This literature embraces well over a thousand volumes.

The second category consists of an equally extensive body of
legends, biographies, and tales concerning the miracles of the
Zaddikim and of collections of their memorable sayings. This
genre of legends developed at the end of the eighteenth century
and enjoyed an ever-increasing popularity among the Hasidic
masses. It was thought that to tell stories of the saints was just as
productive on the spiritual level as the study of divine mysteries.
The main features of the Hasidic legends crystallized during the
first half of the nineteenth century, in many instances incorporating much earlier legends of different origin, which were then
transferred to the great personalities of Hasidism. Since about
1860, several hundred volumes of this genre have appeared, and

every single leading Hasidic personality—even of the last generations—has been adorned with such a wreath of legend.

Now it is important to note that Buber's presentation and interpretation of Hasidism is based almost exclusively on this second category of Hasidic literature—on the legends, epigrams, and anecdotes of the Hasidic saints. He writes:

> Because Hasidism in the first instance is not a category of teaching, but one of life, our chief source of knowledge of Hasidism is its legends, and only after them comes its theoretical literature. The latter is the commentary, the former the text, even though a text that has been handed down in a state of extreme corruption, one that is incapable of being restored in its purity. It is foolish to protest that the legend does not convey to us the reality of Hasidic life. Naturally, the legend is no chronicle, but it is truer than the chronicle for those who know how to read it.

This consistent emphasis on the pre-eminence of the folk tradition over the theoretical literature shows that Buber employs a methodological principle which seems to me highly dubious. Buber's terminology, of course, is rather inclined to spread confusion. What is a "category of teaching" in contrast to one of "life" when it comes to analyzing a historical phenomenon whose teaching is inextricably bound up with the life which it demands, not separated from it by an abyss? Buber's metaphors about text and commentary are misleading and conceal the historical fact that the so-called commentary was the first and most authoritative presentation of the meaning of this life, long before it was enveloped by legends. The identity of legends and life, which Buber claims, is fictitious. Strictly speaking, these legends are themselves nothing more than a commentary to what, with Buber, one might call life. Life is reflected both in the legend and in the teaching, but it must be emphasized that whereas the origins of this Hasidic life were deeply influenced and shaped by ideas laid down in the theoretical literature, its beginnings were certainly not influenced by legend.

Buber's ambiguous use of the concept of "life" has made him fall into a trap. Naturally, from an aesthetic point of view, the legends possess a considerable advantage and appeal and lend themselves more easily to a subjective interpretation than the theoretical writings in which a train of thought is more carefully developed and carried through. Nonetheless, in my opinion, a discussion of the meaning of Hasidism—even if with Buber we call it "Hasidic life"—must be based essentially on these writings. Now it is very revealing that in the course of the years, as Buber developed and elaborated his existential and subjectivist "philosophy of dialogue," his references to the theoretical literature of Hasidism became ever weaker and more scanty. I would suspect that to many readers of Buber it would not occur that such literature even exists.

Apparently Buber regarded these sources as far too dependent on the older Kabbalistic literature to be regarded as genuinely Hasidic. And this dependence is indeed immediately obvious. Many of them, including some of the most famous Hasidic books, are written totally in the language of the Kabbalah, and it is a basic problem of research to determine exactly where their ideas depart from those of their Kabbalistic predecessors. The Hasidic authors obviously did not believe that they had in any way broken with the gnostic tradition of the Kabbalah and, little as Buber wants to admit it, they wrote clearly and plainly as Gnostics. When Buber claimed that the legends of Hasidism were its truly creative achievement, he put himself into an unusually paradoxical position. He had to contend that the originality of the movement genuinely manifested itself only in a genre of literature which almost entirely came into being nearly fifty years after the period in which Hasidism was in fact creative and in which it produced those theoretical writings which Buber has so decisively shoved aside. Such a position is simply not tenable.

Buber, in short, by making his choice and leaving out whatever is in conflict with its demands, asserts an authority which we cannot concede him. To describe the world of Hasidism, the way of life it propagated and the teachings of its masters exclusively on the basis of its legends is exactly like trying to present Islamic mysticism by considering only the epigrams of the great Sufis without regard for their extensive theoretical (and likewise "gnostic") literature, or to describe Catholicism by selecting and interpreting the most beautiful sayings of the saints of the Church without regard to its dogmatic theology. Such a procedure is indeed conceivable, and an analysis or even merely a compilation of the sayings of their great spirits would undoubtedly provide wonderful insights into the worlds of Sufism or Catholicism. Such words, reflecting the reaction of a significant individual to the system of thought in which he lives or the way in which he conceives it, of course possess a strong tinge of what we would today call existential meaning. I would be the last to deny that. But the profit and the illumination we would draw from a compilation or even a profound interpretation of such words or legends should by no means seduce us into thinking that they represent the real doctrines of Sufism or Catholicism whose dogmatic features would be all too easily obliterated in a presentation of this kind.

All of this applies precisely to Buber's choice of Hasidic material. These legends and sayings are certainly most impressive and they just as certainly possess a general human interest. However, if we want to know what they really meant in their original context we would still have to revert to those primary sources which Buber pushes aside as merely secondary. We shall presently see how important this original context is when we come to a discussion of the central point in Buber's interpretation of Hasidism. Although his selection entails certain ambiguities, we willingly grant Buber as a writer and even as the advocate of a message the right to choose what appeals to him. But I very much doubt that such a selection can form the basis for a real and scholarly understanding of what most attracted Buber to Hasidism.

Naturally there is some truth to Buber's idea of the relation between Hasidism and Kabbalah. Although one may say that the Hasidim never lost their enthusiasm for the teachings of the *Zohar,* the Bible of the Jewish mystics, and for the Lurianic Kabbalah, and although no page of a Hasidic book can be understood without constant reference to these traditions, it still remains true that, in elaborating the theosophical doctrines of the Kabbalah, the Hasidic writers did not prove themselves particularly creative. All students of Hasidism are agreed that its most valuable contribution lies somewhere else. The Hasidic writers use the old formulas, concepts, and ideas, only giving them a new twist. Buber is also completely right in saying that gnostic theologoumena, which are taken over by the Hasidim, are often transformed. Into what are they transformed? Into assertions about man and his way to God. Hasidic writers are fond of reinterpreting the conceptual language of the Kabbalah, which originally referred to the mysteries of the Godhead, in such a manner that it seems to concern the personal life of man and his relation to God. A great deal of emphasis is placed on this "moral" reinterpretation of the old theosophical vocabulary. In the writings of Rabbi Dov Baer of Mezritch—the student of the Baal Shem who first organized the movement (died 1772)—we find page after page in which he almost systematically takes up individual Kabbalistic concepts in order to explain their meaning as key-words for the personal life of the pious. They do not for this reason lose their original meaning, which in fact continues likewise to appear, but they gain an additional level.

To this point I would agree with Buber. But again he carries his claims too far when he juxtaposes the ideal of the Kabbalist who is initiated into the divine mysteries to that of the simple man who, though he lacks rabbinic and gnostic knowledge, has achieved "unity" in his life. This seems a false set of alternatives. The Kabbalists never excluded the possibility that a simple and unlettered man could reach the highest spiritual perfection, nor did Hasidism declare such a "simple man" its highest ideal. He may appear here and there in Hasidic legend, which in just this respect has adopted a much older pre-Hasidic Jewish tradition, but Hasidic teaching knows nothing of his representing the highest ideal which the disciple is to realize. Quite to the contrary, it tirelessly repeats the teaching of the necessary reciprocal relationship between the truly spiritual man—who always appears as a gnostic initiate—and the simple people. These two types of men can bring about the true Hasidic community, which needs both of them, only by binding themselves to their common "roots" in the spiritual world. The Hasidic legends honoring the faith of the unlettered are essentially the same as those found in all great religions; only in the rarest instances do they shed light on the specific guiding values which Hasidic literature sets up as normative and on the methods which it prescribes for achieving intimate communion with God. This latter concern, achieving *communio* with God, is the heart of Hasidism.

I agree with Buber when he says:

> What Hasidism is striving for in relation to the Kabbalah is the deschematization of the mystery. The old-new principle that it represented, restored in purified form, is that of the cosmic-metacosmic power and responsibility of man. "All worlds depend on his works, all await and long for the teaching and the good deed of man." This principle, by virtue of its pure intensity, enabled Hasidism to become a religious *meeting*. It is not a new element of teaching. . . . Only here it has become the center of a way of life and of a community.

The idea that man's action represents a meeting with God is without doubt and quite justifiably central to Buber's point of view. It takes on enormous dimensions in his Hasidic writings, but raises the question: Does his interpretation of this principle, as he claims, really penetrate to the core of Hasidism?

Hasidism does indeed teach that man meets God in the concreteness of his dealings in the world. But what did the Hasidim mean by that? The answer is clear: According to the great mythos of exile and redemption which is the Lurianic Kabbalah, "sparks" of the divine life and light were scattered in exile over the entire world, and they long through the actions of man to be "lifted up" and restored to their original place in the divine harmony of all being. This Kabbalistic mythos, whose intricate details need not be presented here—I have dealt with the subject at length in *Major Trends in Jewish Mysticism*—is probably the most important legacy of the Kabbalah to Hasidism. The many variations to which Hasidism subjected this mythos all held that since these "holy sparks" were to be found everywhere without exception, Hasidism denied in principle the existence of a purely secular sphere of life which would have no significance for the religious task of man. Even what is profane and seems irrelevant to the religious sphere, in fact contains a specific religious challenge to man. Everywhere there is an opportunity, yea a necessity, to lift up the "holy sparks," and everywhere lurks the danger of failure. Thus religion is not a beaten track in a narrowly circumscribed course. New paths open up in all directions, and God stands at the end of every path. The contemplative mind can discover the "spark" in every sphere of life and thereby transform even what is essentially profane into something that possesses immediate religious significance.

The motto for this attitude was provided by Proverbs 3:6, "In all thy ways acknowledge Him," which the Hasidim interpreted to mean: Through every single action in which you are engaged you are enabled to gain knowledge of God, you are enabled to meet Him. As a matter of fact, the Talmud already calls this verse "a short word on which all of the chief points of the Torah depend." During the Middle Ages some commentators tried to set aside this rather bold principle by seeking to interpret it as narrowly as possible; Hasidism, in its own mystical way, restored it in its full significance. The following remark is attributed to Rabbi Pinhas of Koretz: "How then is it possible to know God in *all* ways? It is, because when God gave the Torah, the whole world was filled with the Torah. Thus there is nothing which did not contain Torah, and this is the meaning of the verse. Whoever says that the Torah is one thing and the profane sphere another is a heretic." Since the beginnings of Hasidism this doctrine has always been regarded as one of its basic principles.

The Hasidic writers placed special emphasis on such "forgotten" realms of simple and insignificant action, and Hasidism's transformation of them into vehicles for the sacred was one of the most original aspects of the movement. True to their native radicalism—and it is as radicals in temperament that the Hasidim have their place in Jewish history—they were not afraid to formulate their position in paradoxes. "Small talk with one's neighbor can be the vehicle of deep meditation," said the Baal Shem. "The main point of divine worship," says another leader of Hasidism, "lies precisely in serving Him by means of profane and non-spiritual things." "Even by political gossip and conversation about the wars of the gentiles—the ultimate in idle talk and wasted time in the eyes of contemporary Jewish moralists!—may a man be able to attain an intimate connection with God," says a third. And this amazing statement is by no means a simple exaggeration—its author gives detailed advice on how to perform the feat. The Rabbi of Polnoye, a disciple of the Baal Shem, sums it up this way: "There is nothing in the world, large or small, which is isolated from God, for He is present in all things. Therefore, the perfect man can perform deep meditations and contemplative acts of 'unification' even in such earthly actions as eating, drinking, and sexual intercourse, yes, even in business transactions." The contemplative acts of mystical spiritual concentration, which in Kabbalistic terminology are called unifications (in Hebrew: *yihudim;* singular: *yihud*), need no longer be performed in solitude and retreat from the world; they can also be done in the market place and precisely in those places which seem most removed from the realm of the spirit. It is here that the true Hasid finds the perfect arena for a perfectly paradoxical achievement.

But is this achievement really paradoxical? At this point we must come to grips with the central principle of Buber's interpretation of Hasidism. The teaching which I have just discussed is a fact of intellectual history. But how is it to be understood? What kind of contact with the concrete reality of things does man, following this radically mystical theory, achieve by lifting up the holy sparks? Does he in fact arrive at an intimate acquaintance with the concrete in its actual concreteness, i.e., with "life as it is"? In using this phrase, I am quoting Buber who says with great clarity and conviction that Hasidism "kindled in its followers a joy in the world *as it is,* in life *as it is,* in every hour of life in this world as that hour is," and that it taught a "constant, undaunted, and enthusiastic joy in the here and now."

This far-reaching thesis constitutes the basis of Buber's existentialist interpretation of Hasidism as a teaching of the complete realization of the here and now. It seems to me we can gain a more precise understanding of the truly dialectical nature of the Hasidic teaching if we clarify for ourselves what makes Buber's thesis so dubious. Of course Hasidism in a certain sense knows joy and affirmation of reality—a fact that has never eluded the attention of the many writers on Hasidism. However, the Hasidic doctrine of relation of the "concrete" is more complicated and seems to me far removed from Buber's interpretation. This is quite clear in regard to the twist which Hasidic authors gave to the Kabbalistic doctrine of the uplifting of the sparks, which I should now like to explain with the utmost possible precision.

The teaching of the uplifting of the sparks through human activity does in fact mean that there is an element in reality with which man can and should establish a positive connection, but the exposure or realization of this element simultaneously *annihilates* reality, insofar as "reality" signifies, as it does for Buber, the here and now. For the "undaunted and enthusiastic joy," which, to be sure, Hasidism did demand of its adherents, is not a joy in the here and now. In joy—and we may say with Buber: in all that he does with full concentration—man does not enter into relation with the here and now (as Buber conceives it) but with what is *hidden* in the essentially irrelevant garment of the here and now. Buber's joy in life as it is and in the world as it is seems to me a rather modern idea, and I must say that the Hasidic expressions seem to me to convey a totally different mood. They do not teach us to enjoy life as it is; rather, they advise us—better: demand of us—to extract, I am tempted to say distill, from "life as it is" the perpetual life of God. But this is the salient point: the "extraction" is an act of abstraction. It is not the fleeting here and now to which joy is directed, but the eternal unity and presence of transcendence. Now of course it is just this concept of abstraction in regard to joy and to the uplifting of the sparks to which Buber's interpretation of Hasidism objects. He does away with it because it runs counter to his essential interest in Hasidism as an anti-Platonic, existentialist teaching. Buber says: "Here where we stand the hidden divine life must be made to shine forth." This formula does in fact convey authentic Hasidic teaching, but with an ambiguity of which Buber's readers cannot become aware. For precisely in that act in which we let the hidden life shine forth we destroy the here and now, instead of— as Buber would have it—realizing it in its full concreteness.

Interestingly enough, Buber's statement may be found almost word for word in Kabbalistic writers such as Moses Cordovero, and represents a gnostic thesis whose meaning Hasidic teaching did not alter in the least. When you see a beautiful woman, says Rabbi Dov Baer of Mezritch whom I have already mentioned, you should by no means think of her beauty in its concrete tangible form—i.e., as it exists in the concrete here and now—but disregard its concrete reality and direct your spirit to the divine beauty which shines forth from the concrete phenomenon. Then you will no longer behold the beautiful and seductive here and now which is this woman, but the ideal and eternal quality of beauty itself which is one of God's attributes and one of the spheres of His manifestation; from there you will progress to the contemplation of the source of all beauty in God Himself. Statements of this kind in Hasidic literature are legion. They use the concrete meeting of man with reality as a springboard to transcend reality, not to fulfill it. Their Platonic ring sounds rather different from Buber's exaltation of the here and now, and Hasidic mysticism is not half as this-worldly as Buber's readers must be inclined to suppose. The here and now is transcended and disappears when the divine element makes its appearance in contemplation, and the Hasidim were tireless in deriving this moral from their dicta. As so often in the history of mysticism, here, too, human action is laden with contemplative meaning and thus transformed into a vehicle of the mystical deed.

Moreover, the Hasidic conception of the realization of the concrete, which in the final analysis is what concerns us here, contains an essential element of destruction of which Buber's analysis, as far as I can determine, understandably fails to take notice. The Baal Shem and his followers, however, were quite clearly aware of this element, which recurs again and again in the classical literature. Let me quote only one particularly characteristic statement that is ascribed to the Baal Shem to make clear what is at issue. It was transmitted by Rabbi Wolf of Zhitomir.

The Baal Shem once asked an outstanding scholar about his relation to prayer: "What do you do and where do you direct your thoughts when you pray?" He answered: "I bind myself to everything of individual vitality which is present in all created things. For in each and every created thing there must be a vitality which it derives from the divine effluence. I unite with them when I direct my words to God in order by my prayer to penetrate the highest regions." Then the Baal Shem said to him: "If that is what you do, you destroy the world, for in extracting its vitality and raising it to a higher level, you leave the individual created things without their vitality." He said to him: "But since I bind myself to them, how could I extract their vitality from them?" The Baal Shem replied: "Your own words indicate that your prayer cannot carry much weight, for you do not believe that you have the power to lift their vitality out of them."

Here, then, we have the clear and radical thesis: The actual and final realization of such a communion has a destructive quality. And the solution the author suggests for this dilemma points up the dialectical character of these concepts of communion and lifting up. This act, in which all that is alive in individual things is raised to a higher level, belongs only to the moment and may not last. At the same instant in which the vital force is extracted from things it must flow back into them. Or, as so many Hasidic writers like to put it: It is necessary to reduce things to their nothingness in order to restore them to their true nature. Only genuine adepts are able to perform this esoteric action, as the author is well aware. Buber's opinion that Hasidism renounced esotericism is not at all supported by an analysis of the sayings of the Baal Shem. Nor does such an action, as Buber claims, result in the realization of the concrete in its concreteness. For, as is clearly indicated by the statements of the Baal Shem, it is not of the essence of this act that it is momentary and without duration. That it must be broken off is only accidental, caused by man's decision to discontinue it or his weakness and inability to sustain such a destructive penetration and communion. As such, this penetration is much more likely to empty the concrete than to fill it totally with concreteness, as Buber would have it. We might perhaps say that the dialogue which the Hasidic author reports could be understood rather well as a dialogue between the Baal Shem and Buber.

The classical literature of Hasidism—the writings of the great disciples of the Baal Shem—contradicts Buber's interpretation also in another way: It consistently treats the individual and concrete existence or phenomenon quite disdainfully. The Hebrew expressions for the concrete, totally in contradiction to what Buber would lead us to suspect, always have a disparaging nuance. Only thus can we also understand why the "stripping off of corporeality," quite in the spirit of mysticism but not at all in the spirit of Buber's interpretation, serves as a high ideal which can be achieved in prayer or meditation. The here and now does indeed present a valuable opportunity for meeting between God and man, but such meeting can occur only where man tears open another dimension in the here and now—an act which makes the "concrete" disappear. In other words, the concrete in Buber's sense does not even exist in Hasidism. The here and now of created existence is not identical with that which shines forth from it once it has become transparent. The assumption of such an identity contradicts the real Hasidic teaching which makes perceiving the divine kernel of all existence dependent precisely on emptying the concrete phenomenon of its own weight and individual significance.

Buber's formulations always blur this essential difference. On the other hand, he establishes a distinction between the Platonic lifting up of the concrete into the realm of ideas and the existential seizing of the holy sparks hidden in all things. But this distinction belongs entirely to Buber's personal interpretation and is by no means as clear-cut in the Hasidic texts. For the Hasidim, realization, the seizing of reality, was a precarious enterprise. Under the strain of such realization, as is contained in the teaching of the lifting up of the sparks, "reality" itself might break apart. For it is not the *concrete* reality of things that appears as the ideal result of the mystic's action, but something of the *Messianic* reality in which all things have been restored to their proper place in the scheme of creation and thereby been deeply transformed and transfigured. Thus, concepts like reality and concreteness mean something totally different for Buber than for the Hasidim. He sometimes uses these terms both for the realm of the here and now and for the realm of transformed existence—a circumstance which has tended to render indistinct the problem posed by his interpretation. Since, in addition, the Hasidim laid great stress on the teaching that human activity is not able to really bring about or reveal the Messianic world—a point which likewise remains unclear in Buber's writings—they were left, in their own view, only with prescribing ways and means for the individual to use the concrete as a vehicle to the abstract and thereby to the ultimate source of all being. Though couched in the language of very personal religion, this may be conventional theology and not nearly as exciting as the new interpretation which Buber has read into it; in any case, it is what Hasidism stood for.

Yet one should not underestimate the possibility that the teaching of the lifting up of the sparks was in practice understood by many Hasidim in a less dialectical fashion than originally intended. Hasidic theory, as presented by the Baal Shem himself and the most significant among the first generations of disciples, never lost its awareness of the destructive consequences which flow from this doctrine and sought to devise ways and means to avoid them. But the complaints of both friend and foe alike testify that the practice was often more primitive than the theory. For many Hasidim lifting up the sparks did in fact mean living a fuller life. They were not concerned with emptying the real by removing the sparks, but with filling it by bringing them in. Here the holy sparks no longer appear as metaphysical elements of divine being, but as subjective feelings of joy and affirmation which are projected into the relation between man and his environment. This, however, is a view that derives not from the theology of the founders of Hasidism but from the mood of some of its followers. And of course it is this popular or vulgar version, which is sometimes (by no means always!) reflected in the world of Hasidic legend, which provides the relative justification for Buber's highly simplified view. But to call this the message of Hasidism seems to me far from the truth.

I have here dealt in detail with one central point in Buber's interpretation of Hasidism. Were we to analyze other important concepts we would face the same task of testing Buber's statements by reference to the theoretical literature of Hasidism. We would then find that the curiously vague and ambiguous terms Buber uses are always almost, but never quite, Hasidic. I can hardly think of a better illustration for this than the following sentence: "In the Hasidic message the separation between 'life in God' and 'life in the world,' the primal evil of all 'religion,' is overcome in genuine, concrete unity." This sentence seems to indicate that man's responsibility is infinitely more important than the dogmatic formulations of rigid institutional religion. But it is a fact that what Buber calls "the primal evil of all religion" asserts itself at the center of Hasidic teaching. Buber's "concrete unity," when applied to Hasidism, is a fiction, for "life in the world" is no longer life in the world when its divine roots appear in contemplation and thereby transform it into "life in God." It is naturally not surprising that, contrary to Buber, the Hasidic writings maintain that fundamental separation which so embitters Buber.

This brings us to a point that is crucial for Buber's interpretation and for the difference between him and the historical phenomenon of Hasidism. To put it bluntly, Buber is a religious anarchist and his teaching is religious anarchism. By that I mean the following: Buber's philosophy demands of man that he set himself a direction and reach a decision, but it says nothing about which direction and which decision. Rather, he says explicitly that such direction and decision can be formulated only in the world of It in which the world of the living I and Thou is objectified and dies. But in the world of living relation nothing can be formulated and there are no commandments. Whether right or wrong, Hasidism could not share this essentially anarchical view since it remained obligated to Jewish tradition. And this tradition presents a teaching in which directions and decisions could be formulated, i.e., a teaching concerning *what* should be done. Only against this background can we understand in its true context the certainly emphatic interest of Hasidism in the *how* of such action. For Buber this world of the *how* is all that has remained. "No longer the established act but the consecration of all action becomes decisive." It is this concept of consecration, which often recurs in Buber's writings, that furnishes the key for his specific type of religious anarchism. This "consecration" is the moral intensity and responsibility which determine the *how* in the relation between man and his action, but not its content. With admirable consistency Buber has always refused to pin himself down on any content of such action, on any *what*. We can therefore understand why references to the Torah and the commandments, which for the Hasidim still meant everything, in Buber's presentation become extremely nebulous. To be sure, Jewish mysticism, which developed a certain conception of the meaning of revelation, greatly expanded the realm to which the Torah, as an ultimate value system, has reference. But it is still identifiable as Torah and that separation, of which Buber speaks so disparagingly, is preserved even in Hasidism. Where the separation of the realms is overcome, it occurs at the expense of "life in the world," as the saying of Rabbi Pinhas of Koretz quoted above shows clearly. Buber's interpretation of the meaning of such Hasidic concepts an "intention" and the "quality of fervor," which accompany man's actions and are supposed to permeate them, may represent a significant and humanly impressive formulation of the basic principle of religious anarchism; but in connection with his interpretation of Hasidism this interpretation isolates a moment, which has its meaning only in the context of other considerations that Buber has neglected, and dissolves it in the completely undetermined and indeterminable.

Buber's interpretation stresses the uniqueness of the task confronting every single individual. "All men have access to God, but each has a different one." This is certainly true, but it is not a new statement of personal religion introduced by Hasidism. Rather, this idea comes originally from the Lurianic Kabbalah, i.e., from that very gnosis at which Buber in his later writings looks so askance. It holds that each individual is enjoined to raise the holy sparks which belong specifically to his spiritual root in the great soul of Adam, the common soul of all mankind. For at one time every soul and soul-root had its special place in this soul of Adam. All that Hasidism did was to formulate this theory in a popular manner and thereby give it an even more personal turn. Thus the Hasidic teaching of the sparks, which in the social and personal environment of man await meeting with him and being lifted up by him, really represents "Kabbalah become ethos."

Another example of the peculiar vagueness in Buber's use of Hasidic concepts is presented by his use of the word *yihud* ('unification"), which he considers of great importance. Following Kabbalistic parlance, the Hasidim use *yihud* to mean a contemplative act by which man binds himself to the spiritual element by concentrating his mind on the holy letters of the Torah, which is also the holy book of nature. Buber, however, asserts that in Hasidism *yihud* is no longer a magic formula or procedure as it is in the Kabbalah. Rather it is "none other than the normal life of man, only concentrated and directed toward the goal of unification." There may also still have been *yihud* in the older sense, but "this magical component never touched the center of Hasidic teaching." Yet I must say that I have been unable to find in the Hasidic writings any new shade in the meaning of this concept. In the older Hebrew literature it always had two meanings, and neither has undergone any change in the Hasidic literature. The first derives from the Kabbalists and always designates some special meditation which is to accompany a specific act, a meditation in which one unites himself with a spiritual reality—be it the soul of a departed saint or its sparks, or be it a name of God or of one of his hypostatized attributes. In this usage the concept also designates the result achieved by such meditation. The second meaning of *yihud*, however, derives above all from the once very famous ethical work of Bahya ibn Pakuda. *The Duties of the Heart*, where it refers to the directing of awareness or of action toward God. In this sense the concept is always used only in the singular. Where it occurs in the plural, it can only have the Kabbalistic meaning which has to do exclusively with contemplation and not, as Buber would have it, with the concrete unity of human life achieved by the intensity of concentration. Such acts of *yihud* are achieved by contemplative communion with the inwardness of the "letters" which are imprinted in all being. In all the sayings of the Baal Shem of which I am aware, the term is used in this precise and technical sense. Thus Buber's translations of many passages on *yihud* are very modern, appealing, and suggestive, but they are not acceptable.

To sum up, the merits of Buber's presentation of Hasidic legends and sayings are indeed very great. Precisely in the mature form of the anecdote, which dominates his later writings, this presentation will in large measure stand the test of time. But the spiritual message he has read into these writings is far too closely tied to assumptions that derive from his own philosophy of religious anarchism and existentialism and have no roots in the texts themselves. Too much is left out in this description of Hasidism, and what is included is overloaded with very personal speculations. Their character may be exalted and they may appeal deeply to the modern mind. But if we would understand the real phenomenon of Hasidism, both in its grandeur and in its decay (which are in many ways connected), we shall have to start again from the beginning.

POSTSCRIPT

When the above analysis was first published, Buber wrote a short reply which appeared at the end of his *Schriften zum Chassidismus* (1963, pp. 991-98). Here he once again commented on the relation of teaching and legend to the life of the community in the history of religions. The following is my response.

i

Buber's statements—which insofar as they touch upon general issues will scarcely encounter any basic opposition—miss the main point in our discussion. The teaching of Hasidism was developed by the immediate disciples of the Baal Shem and the Maggid of Mezritch, using concepts which the first masters had employed themselves—and these were Kabbalistic concepts. At the same time these disciples wrote under the full impact of the new group life, which to a great extent they themselves had helped to create. There is no basis whatever in the Hasidic tradition for the attempt to construct a possible contradiction between the specifics of this group life and the concepts through which it unfolded. Just those writings, in which what Buber calls the epigonic element is least prominent and the original effective impulse attains undistorted expression, characteristically reproduce many maxims of the Baal Shem (quite clearly distinguishable from the styles of the disciples), but they are not legends in Buber's sense of the term. The salient point of my critique is that these writings thoroughly contradict Buber's assertions regarding the meaning of Hasidic life as he formulated them in his later writings, and that he silently passes over this contradiction in order to rely on anecdotes which are more susceptible to his own reinterpretation. To be sure, he attempts to make it plausible that these anecdotes could perhaps be as old as the theoretical writings, but this can only rarely be shown, while in many instances just the opposite is demonstrable. It is precisely the analysis of the oldest source of Hasidic legend which makes this clear. The older and more authentic the historical and social framework within which many of these oldest legends move or are enclosed, the less do they stand in real contradiction to the theoretical writings, produced in the same milieu, at the same time or considerably earlier. Naturally I do not say that the legends are worthless as evidence. What I do say is that Buber's interpretation must be false when for anyone familiar with the texts this interpretation establishes such a contradiction—and this applies to crucial points. Buber's reference to the special task which he has set himself and which has determined his selection of the material and his attitude to the sources makes no difference. Buber does not like it when the obvious subjectivity of his selection is emphasized, and in reply refers to the "reliability of the chooser in carrying out his special task." I am convinced that his selection corresponds as much as possible to the sense of his own message. I am not convinced that the sense of his message, as he formulated it, is that of Hasidism.

ii

I should like to add a word about the parallels which Buber draws in his reply between the Hasidic anecdotes and the Zen stories. I do not believe that these parallels can be drawn. The Zen stories are not legends at all, but rather—and this does not appear in Buber's statements—exercises for meditation, and thus they belong to a completely different genre. That they are clothed in the form of a tale does not make them legends. They are exclusively statements which are at first glance totally senseless or in the highest degree paradoxical. The disciples are instructed to meditate on them for weeks or months in order thereby to drive forward to illumination. They transmit a mystical reality which, since it cannot be grasped by maxims, revels in the assertion of ultimate paradoxes. But the Hasidic anecdote, precisely as it has been so masterfully canonized in Buber's new formulations, is an entirely different matter. Its sense and meaning are immediately revealed and they transmit something which can be transmitted. Thus it moves in a totally different sphere of religious experience. I cannot believe that this juxtaposition provides any greater understanding of the specific character of the Hasidic stories. The anecdotal garb of the *koan,* which mentions names and events, is more closely related to the form in which the great teachers of jurisprudence used to give their students seminar assignments than it is to religious legend.

In order to make it clear how little Buber's selection of the Hasidic material may be compared to the category of the provocative and unintelligible Zen utterances, I would like to tell a little story which deals with Buber himself. I once asked Buber why in his writings he had suppressed the significant and unfathomable words regarding the Messianic age that were transmitted in the name of Rabbi Israel of Rizhin. I shall always remember his reply. He said: because I do not understand them.

17.

Rabbi Israel Salanter *

by Louis Ginzberg

i

The following anecdote is told about Rabbi Joshua ben Korha, who flourished about the middle of the second century. A man once left a will which caused the Probate Court no little embarrassment. The will read as follows: "My son shall not receive his inheritance until he becomes foolish." The judges, after long deliberation, betook themselves to Rabbi Joshua to get his advice in the difficult case. As they approached his house, they saw him crawling on all fours with a cord in his mouth, held by his little son, who was playing horse with his father. When the judges finally were ushered into the presence of the Rabbi, they placed before him the difficult question that was the cause of their visit. Laughingly the Rabbi said: "I have given you a concrete illustration of your case; for everyone becomes foolish as soon as he has children." The testament was therefore interpreted as meaning that it was the wish of the deceased to have his son married and the father of children before he received his patrimony.[1]

We shall not tarry to consider the legal side of this narrative. This was attended to by the parties interested in the contest over the will. It will pay us better to consider the psychological aspect of the story a little more closely.

In the mechanical world as well as in the world of feeling, it is a truth that every primary force is one-sided in its action.

* Delivered in the Course of Public Lectures of the Jewish Theological Seminary of America, February 25, 1904.

From *Students, Scholars and Saints,* Philadelphia, Jewish Publication Society of America, 1928.

It persists in one direction so long as no other force appears to counteract or thwart it.[2] Thus it happens that our feelings under strong excitement carry us along with such force that we are impelled to acts which, under other circumstances, we should regard as foolish. Rabbi Joshua sank the dignity of the scholar in the pride and affection of the father that dominated him for the moment. The Rabbis teach us this truth in their peculiar way. The pity is that writers of history, and especially of Jewish history, have often ignored it in judging the heroes who have influenced the course of events.

The law is the same in the intellectual as in the mechanical and emotional world. There is no great thought that has become an impelling power in history which has not been espoused at its origin by men willing to put all their physical and spiritual powers entirely at its service. Men who produce spiritual movements are themselves primary forces, their inner natures are filled with a single thought, and with this peculiar thought they identify their personality to the exclusion of all else, indeed to the point of isolation from all else. Our culture is therefore the resultant of a number of one-sided forces, whose originators would hear nothing of compromise, but which end in a harmonious union, because no force is strong enough to hold the field alone. The history of facts embraces only the feebler part of reality. To comprehend and properly appreciate historical events, we must go back to those primary ideas which, though never completely realized, are still the only creative forces to be considered. Therefore, we must take as the starting point of history the records of those men who, regardless of actual conditions, in their enthusiasm for one particular thought viewed life through the prism of this thought and saw nothing else.

The essential thing in this world is not to serve this or that ideal indifferently, but, with all one's soul, to serve the ideal which one has chosen. If we look at history from this point of view, we shall have to admit that the average and commonplace persons do not represent the nation so well as its heroes. On the contrary, as has been well said, "The true mind of a people at any time is best ascertained by examining that of its greatest men." What is true of the general history of a people is eminently so in the history of its religion. For in the history of religion the experience which furnishes us with the needful touchstone is that of the religious life, and for this we must have recourse to those who have best lived that life, that is to say, the saints.

Furthermore it is the saint who displays in a special degree the excellencies which characterize the religious ideals of the nation. In order, then, to understand the religion of the Jew and the history of the Synagogue, we must make diligent use of the lives of the saints.

The dearth of biographical material so conspicuous in the sources of Jewish history is one of the main reasons why it is inadequately understood and judged. The most unusual movements of Judaism have generally the fewest documents and their most remarkable leaders are the least known. The great in Israel's later history whom we know best, belong to a set of men whom it is easier to describe collectively than separately, whose minds were formed by one system of discipline. Only rarely can we gratify our desire to study Jewish ideals not written upon paper but upon living souls. In modern times such religious geniuses were Rabbi Israel Baal Shem Tob, the founder of Hasidism, and his younger contemporary, the Gaon, Rabbi Elijah Wilna, the one the complete embodiment of emotion and feeling, the other the personification of religious thought.

In the words of the first father of the Synagogue, Simeon the Just, these two men realized in their lives two of the three ideals which make the essence of Judaism: *Torah* and *Abodah* or, in modern parlance, religious thought and religious emotion. The founder of Hasidism was entirely absorbed in religious emotion, the Gaon's life was devoted to the searching and explaining of the Torah.

A life wholly consecrated to the third fundamental principle of Judaism, *Gemilut Hasadim*, ethics and morality, was that of Rabbi Israel Lipkin Salanter.

The history of the short-lived but very interesting moralist movement in Lithuania is practically the biography of this man.[3] Rabbi Israel was born on the 3d of November, 1810, in the Russian border province of Samogitia, in Lithuania. His teacher in Talmud and Rabbinics was his father, Rabbi Wolf Lipkin, who was both rabbi and scholar. While still a youth, he married and settled in Salant, the birthplace of his wife. It is from this place that the name by which he is best known is derived. Influences are subtle things, even in one's own case, yet we can clearly discern the influence of two great men of this place who, however diverse they were in capacity and character and mode of life, left their ineradicable marks upon their young and impressionable disciple. The one was the rabbi of the place, Rabbi Hirsch Braude, who was one of the keenest dialecticians among the Talmudists of his generation at a time when dialectics reigned supreme in the domain of the Talmud. Salanter, as a Talmudist, was never able to deny the influence of this master, and he endeavored to transfer this system of dialectics to another sphere of thought, that of ethics.

Quite different was the influence that proceeded from his other master, Rabbi Zundel, whom one would be inclined to describe as a lay saint were it not for the fact that the Jews have no monks, and to them the contrast between the laity and the clergy does not mean the same as to other peoples.

Rabbi Zundel,[4] though a great scholar, never accepted the position of rabbi but was satisfied to eke out a living from a small shop he kept, or from any odd job that came his way. He even refused to be recognized by any external signs as belonging to the intellectual class and would therefore dress like a common man, disregarding the custom of the country, where even the poor scholar could be distinguished by his garb. This plainness of dress and simplicity of manner were often the causes of great discomfort and unpleasantness to him. Once while travelling among a rather rough lot of people, he was taken to be one of their own class, and as he was unwilling to participate in their vulgar actions and still more vulgar conversation but spent all his time in praying and in studying the Talmud by heart, they decided to punish him for giving himself airs. Surprising him while he was asleep, they attempted to mark him by singeing his beard on one side of his face, and thus disgrace him, as no good Jew would ever dare to shave his beard. Just as they were on the point of carrying out their intention, they heard him exclaiming in great ecstasy, "Only one moment more!" Observing that he was awake, they desisted, though they did not quite understand the meaning of his words by which he expressed his great joy on being able to suffer insults without resisting. His great ideal in life was to make the whole of it a continuous divine service, and the means of realizing this ideal consisted for him in the study of the Torah with its strenuous and solitary discipline of thought and action. From his master, Rabbi Hayyim of Volozhin, he not only learned boundless reverence for the Gaon, Rabbi Elijah Wilna, the master of his master, but he also attempted to live his life in accordance with the ideals set up by this austere and ascetic saint.

The simplicity, humility and saintliness of Rabbi Zundel attracted the young Salanter, who never neglected an opportunity to be near the master that he might be able to see a saintly life with his own eyes instead of studying it from books. It is told that once when Rabbi Zundel noticed the young man following him, he turned suddenly around and said to him: "If you want to lead a pious life, study *Musar*." These simple words were the decisive factor in the life of Salanter. From now on the driving power in his very active life was the conviction that the study of the Torah and the fulfilment of its commandments, important and absolutely necessary as they are for the salvation of the Jew, do not lead to the desired goal as long as one does not work seriously and steadily at the education of self. This, however, can only be gained by a thorough study of the Musar literature, i. e., the ethico-religious books. How it is to be studied we shall see later; for the present we would remark only that in the importance attached by him to the study of Musar we can see the indirect influence of the Gaon, who declared it to be the religious duty and inviolable obligation of every person to fix a certain time of the day for reflection and meditation.[5] This teaching of the Gaon was made living to the young Salanter by Rabbi Zundel, whose powerful impression on him was so enduring that even in later life the disciple remembered the master with the greatest admiration, and he described him as "a ladder set upon the earth, with its top reaching to heaven."

"To keep aloof from men and to live in retirement from the world" was the highest ideal after which Rabbi Zundel strove, in imitation of that great hermit, the Gaon. Without doubt they also thought of the salvation of their brethren who were in and of the world; but they tried to further it by example only and at most, in cases of pressing necessity, by rare and short apparition. It is therefore not surprising that for a time Salanter was in great perplexity, swaying between the relative merits and advantages of the active and the contemplative life. We thus find in him not merely noble actions, but life in the true meaning of the word, that is, development and struggle. The outcome of this struggle could not be doubtful. Preëminently religious, however, as the motive power of his inner life was, it was essentially of an ethical bent, and hence he could not but come to the conclusion "that true salvation can be gained only by the service rendered by the individual to the community." He became convinced that there is no virtue, strictly speaking, for man as a solitary individual in the world; that virtue begins with sociability. The idea of solidarity, טובת הכלל, is at the root of all our aspirations toward the good. But not only morality, religion also in its higher form, he maintained, can be achieved in social life only, and it is a false show of self-sacrifice when religious duties are performed in partial or complete isolation, as in the cloister or the Bet ha-Midrash. Salanter, therefore, came to the conclusion that it was his duty instead of avoiding the multitude to seek them out in order to enlighten, console and improve them.

While still in the very small town of Salant, Rabbi Israel, at the age of about twenty-five years, became the leader of a small group of students and business men whom he introduced into the study of *Musar*. His fame as a great Talmudist spread very rapidly, and he was scarcely thirty years old when he was appointed head of the Meilishen Academy in Wilna. It is perhaps not without interest to note the fact that his salary amounted to four rubles a week. One is almost inclined to believe that then as now salaries were often in inverse ratio to merits. One takes it for granted that the greater the scholar, the smaller his demands upon life.

In Wilna Salanter found for the first time in his life a large field to display his energies and talents. He had arrived in that "little Jerusalem of Lithuania" at a very critical moment in the history of Lithuanian and Russian Jewry. The Haskalah movement which for about half a century was struggling in vain to gain a foothold in Lithuania, received about 1842 a strong impetus through the activity of Max Lilienthal,[7] the "emissary of Haskalah" and the agent of the Russian government in its endeavor to dejudaize the Jews as a preliminary step toward their conversion to Christianity. It is true that the plain uneducated Lithuanian Jew showed more discernment in judging the "friendly" policy of a most tyrannical government than did the learned German doctor, and Lilienthal had soon to give up the hope of ever realizing his reforms. The agitation, however, caused among the different classes of Lithuanian Jewry by the Lilienthal episode, did not abate even when the educational plans of the government came to a sudden stop, and Lilienthal, their prime mover, finally recognizing whose dupe he was, emigrated to America. Large numbers among the educated classes who hitherto had known only of one form of intellectual activity, the study of Talmud and Rabbinics, began more and more to devote themselves to secular studies, preferably to *belles lettres* in Hebrew and other languages, which they found more attractive and enjoyable, as they satisfied not only the intellect but also the emotions. And, as it is natural for the lower classes to copy the example set by the higher, Jewish studies and consequently Jewish ideals lost their attraction in the eyes of the common people.

To the credit of Salanter it must be said that not only was he the only one among the representatives of strict Talmudism who saw the danger confronting it, but he was also the only one who attempted to protect it against the threatening peril. He cannot be said to have been very successful in his main activities; some will declare that he failed completely, yet surely nobody will deny the religious fervor and sincerity, the high and saintly moral standards of the man who single-handed attempted to fight a world in arms.

Salanter, who lived only two generations after the rise of the great Hasidic movement that threatened to divide the Jewry of eastern Europe into two hostile camps, had learned from the upheaval caused by a small band of religious enthusiasts two practical things. The one was that the preponderance of intellectualism in religion estranges the great masses, and the other, that those who are to lead them must possess other qualities besides those of scholarship and saintliness. A favorite saying of his was that the Hasidim as well as their opponents, the *Mitnagdim,* err—the former in believing that they have leaders, the latter in maintaining that they have no need of them. His activity was accordingly directed toward the achievement of two objects, the attraction of the masses of the people by emphasizing the emotional element of religion, and the training of men who would in the true sense of the word be spiritual leaders of the people.

Shortly after his arrival in Wilna, he established a *Hebrah Musar,* an institute that had for its object the study of ethical literature—for example, the works of Bahya, Gabirol, and Rabbi Moses Hayyim Luzzatto. Members of the organization were recruited from all classes of society—professional scholars, business men, artisans and laborers. At his instance new editions of a number of ethical works were published in 1844 and 1845 for the use of the members of the institute as well as for others who might take up the study of these works if made accessible to them. Salanter was, however, not satisfied with the establishment of a center for those desirous to devote part of their time to the study of ethics, but he served those seekers after truth as guide and leader, frequently delivering lectures before them on the subjects of their studies. In order that his work might spread all over Lithuania, and likewise continue after his death, he selected a few chosen individuals, distinguished by learning, piety and high moral standards, to be trained as the spiritual leaders of the people.

In spite of the wide sphere of activity he had created for himself in the metropolis of Lithuania and although he enjoyed the greatest respect of the entire community, his stay in Wilna was not of very long duration. There were many reasons why he left that city. It suffices here to state that he wanted to avoid an office which it was sought to impose upon him. In 1848, the Russian government opened the Rabbinical Seminary in Wilna, and pressure was brought to bear upon him to accept the professorship of Talmud. That it was his clearsightedness and not fanaticism that forbade the acceptance of this office is shown by the result or rather lack of result obtained by this class of institutions in Russia. His sound judgment warned him against becoming the instrument of a government whose politics were directed to the end of extorting money from the Jews to be spent for institutions established for the sole purpose of destroying Judaism. The opposition of Salanter and many of his party to the Haskalah and its schemes was not the result of hostility to secular knowledge, the war-cry of the *Maskilim*, but was mainly rooted in the firm conviction that a government furthering the spread of secular knowledge among the Jews and at the same time curtailing their civil and political rights, can have but one aim in its mind—the destruction of Judaism. There can now be no doubt that this was a just estimate of the policy of the Russian government at that time. With equally fair certainty it may be stated that Salanter was in principle not at all opposed to secular knowledge. Later in life he counted among his very close and intimate friends the leaders of the German orthodoxy, men of the highest type of modern education. It is therefore not at all surprising to find Maskilim cite the authority of Salanter against those who opposed secular knowledge absolutely.

In the year 1848 he left Wilna and settled in Kovno, the second largest Jewish community in Lithuania. The close commercial relations which existed between this city and Germany were not without far-reaching effects upon the life of its Jewish inhabitants. At the time of the arrival of Salanter in Kovno, it was the most modern community in Lithuania, a real hotbed of the Haskalah. When he left it two decades later, it had become the stronghold of orthodoxy and remained such for half a century longer. This change may be said to have been exclusively the work of Salanter who put his stamp upon the spiritual life of this large community.

It was in Kovno that the development of the Musar movement reached its pinnacle. Here arose the first *Musar-Stuebel* (moralist conventicle). The central figure was Salanter and around him gathered a large number of capable young Talmudists as well as many merchants and artisans who were attracted by the high enthusiasm and kindling eloquence of the master. The energy and devotion of Salanter are the more to be admired as his achievements were gained in the face of violent opposition. The opponents were not only the Maskilim but also many among the representatives of the strictest Talmudism. Chief among the latter was the Rabbi of Kovno, Rabbi Loeb Shapiro, a critical mind of the first rank and a man of very independent character.[8] He was frequently in the habit of giving a slight twist to verse 19 of Psalm 135 and applying it maliciously to the Musar-Stuebel:

O House of Israel, Bless ye the Lord!
O House of Aaron, Bless ye the Lord!
O House of Levi, Bless ye the Lord!
O ye that fear the Lord, Bless ye the Lord!

There is a house for Israel, he said, a house for Aaron, a house for Levi, but there is no mention of a separate house for those who fear the Lord, hence there is no need of establishing conventicles for them.[9] This *bon mot* shows at the same time the course of the opposition which the Musar movement provoked. It is the deep-seated opposition of the talmudic Jew to every separatist movement. Against the study of the Musar literature neither Shapiro nor his friends had anything to say; what they condemned was the forming of a society which tended to set its members apart from the rest of the community as "the moralists." The opposition to the Musar movement and its leader was carried on with great bitterness and was not entirely free from personal animosity against Salanter and his disciples. As to the latter it must be stated that their admiration for the master whom they tried to imitate and emulate was sincere and profound, but genius is not to be copied. A good deal of the criticism levelled against the Musar movement had its origin in the extravagancies of those whom the Talmud describes as "disciples who did not wait upon their masters sufficiently," they are those who attempted rather to ape the great than to mirror them.

After living in Kovno for about twelve years, Salanter was forced by a severe illness—a nervous disorder—to change his abode and settle in Germany, where he hoped to regain his health through the famous skill of its physicians. He spent the rest of his life in Memel and Koenigsberg. In these communities new problems awaited him, and, notwithstanding the weakened state of his health, he continued his various activities. These two cities, on account of their proximity to Lithuania, contained large numbers of Jews of that country, some of whom had settled there permanently and others, especially those engaged in importing Russian merchandise into Germany, were forced by their business to spend there many a month of each year. Salanter saw the danger lurking in these large masses of Jews living unorganized in a foreign country, with the Jews of which they neither could nor would form a union. He set himself therefore the task of organizing communities of Lithuanian Jews in these two cities and thanks to his untiring energy and devotion to his people, he succeeded within a short time. He was, however, not interested in organization for its own sake. What he desired was to transplant the cultural and religious life of the Lithuanian Jews to these communities, and his endeavors were not entirely in vain. The Jewish community in Memel continued up to the great war to be the only one of its kind. Its life resembled that of Kovno and Wilna much more closely than that of Berlin or Frankfurt.

A plan that engaged the fertile mind of Salanter for many years was the popularization of the Talmud, that is, first to make the Talmud accessible to the great masses of the Jews and further to introduce its study into the non-Jewish colleges and universities. Being firmly convinced that the knowledge of the Talmud is absolutely necessary for the culture and religious welfare of the Jew, he could not but look with alarm upon the gradual disappearance of talmudic learning from among the great masses of Jewry, even those of Lithuania, the classic land of talmudic study. To stem the tide of ignorance *in re talmudica,* he advised the following means: The publication of a dictionary of the Talmud in Yiddish to help the average business man or artisan among the Lithuanian or Polish Jews in his studies of the Talmud, and the replacement of Rashi's commentary on the Talmud by a more modern one that could be put into the hands of beginners. As usual, Salanter was not satisfied with formulating plans, but immediately set about to carry them out. His plan of a Yiddish dictionary of the Talmud, it is true, did not proceed far, for there were not enough Talmudists who could and would engage in such a work, but the plan of a modern commentary advanced so far that he received a promise of collaboration from a goodly number of prominent Talmudists.

The spread of the knowledge of the Talmud among the educated classes of the Gentiles, Salanter believed would benefit them as well as the Jews. He was of the opinion that the dialectics of the Talmud are the best means for developing the mind of the youth at colleges and universities, who might greatly profit by supplementing their studies in classics and mathematics by courses in Talmud. A better acquaintance with the Talmud by the educated Gentile world would at the same time remove many prejudices against the Jew and his post-biblical literature, which are mostly to be ascribed to the false notion the world has of the Talmud.

Salanter's plan was to petition the authorities of institutions for higher learning in Germany to introduce the Talmud into their regular courses of study. As he did not master the German language, he looked for a man whom he could entrust with the preparation of such a petition that would necessarily have to contain a clear and precise description of the Talmud and its educational potentialities. It seems that Salanter met with some opposition among the Rabbis, who looked with disfavor upon any attempt at secularizing the Talmud.[10]

During his long stay in Germany, he became acquainted not only with the spiritual leaders of the Orthodox but also with the many lay members of this party whom he tried to interest in his educational schemes for the Lithuanian Jews. He finally, in 1878, succeeded in finding a wealthy man in Berlin [11] who set aside a considerable sum of money for the purpose of establishing in Kovno a great Yeshibah for the training of Rabbis, known as the Central Body of the *Perushim,* כולל הפרושים. Perushim were young married men who had left home and family—*Perushim* means those who separated themselves—

to devote themselves to study. This idea was quite an original creation of Salanter as all the other Yeshibot up to that time were mainly frequented by young unmarried men.

As the bachelor Rabbi is entirely unknown in Eastern Europe, and maturity is almost a prerequisite of the spiritual leader, it often happened that men who spent their entire youth and a part of their manhood in preparation for the ministry were forced to look for other vocations to enable them to support their wives and children. It could not but result in the increase of an intellectual proletariat—the training of a rabbi does not tend to produce a successful business man—and the gradual elimination of the poorer classes from the Rabbinate, as only the sons or sons-in-law of the wealthy could afford the long preparation. To remedy these evils Salanter established the new educational Institute which enabled the poor Talmudist to continue his studies after graduating from the Yeshibah by providing him and his family with the necessary means.

The sum donated by the Berlin Maecenas for the maintenance of the Institute, though very considerable, was not sufficient to assure its permanency, and Salanter, though burdened by old age and many ailments, took upon himself the heavy task of gaining the support of larger classes for his scheme. He addressed a stirring appeal to the Jewish communities of Russia, which was not in vain.[12] The *Kolel* (Central Institute) thus firmly established by him, not only continued to exist for a long time after his death up to the recent war, but even gained in importance very considerably. For a number of years it was the most important center of the higher Jewish learning in Lithuania. The Kolel bore through all the years of its existence the stamp of Salanter by being the only institution of its kind where the study of Musar formed a part of the curriculum.

At the same time while working feverishly at this scheme, Salanter found time and strength to go to Paris to organize there a Russian-Polish community. The conditions in the French metropolis were not dissimilar to those in Koenigsberg and Memel. The lack of organization among the Jews of Eastern Europe who had settled in Paris was greater and in some ways more deplorable than that which Salanter found among his countrymen living in the two cities of Eastern Prussia. The religious life of the French Jews had already at that time reached such a low state that not much good would have been achieved by amalgamating the newcomers with the native Jews even if it had been possible.

After spending almost two years in Paris he succeeded in bringing some order into the chaotic condition of the Eastern Jews. He returned in 1882 to Germany and there took up his residence in Koenigsberg to continue the work that he had interrupted for several years. This however was not granted to him. He died there on the second of February 1883 at the age of seventy-three and a half.

ii

In order properly to estimate the essence of the moralist movement inaugurated by Salanter, it is necessary not only to understand his character and personality but also to become acquainted with the cultural and religious life of the Lithuanian Jews, among whom this movement first arose and developed. The Jewish people, as one of the oldest of the cultural races of the world, place a very high estimate upon intellectualism—indeed sometimes too high an estimate. The older and the more deeply rooted the culture of a nation, the more strongly it is impressed with the truth that "knowledge is power," not only material but also spiritual power. This intellectualism so highly praised by the Jewish people naturally varies with age and country. For Maimonides and his followers in Spain and Provence Judaism consisted essentially of philosophical intellectualism culminating in love of God and love of man. However radically different the Polish-Lithuanian Jew of the eighteenth and nineteenth centuries may be in his entire *Weltanschauung* from the Spanish Jew of the thirteenth century schooled in a scholastic Aristotelianism, both have this belief in common—that it is knowledge that makes a man a man, and a Jew a Jew. The only difference is that the Polish-Lithuanian Jew puts talmudic dialectic, in which he is unsurpassed, in place of Aristotelian philosophy. The rise of the Kabbalah in Provence in the thirteenth century was a reaction against Jewish Aristotelianism of the Middle Ages and similarly the rise of Hasidism in the middle of the eighteenth century was an attempt to aid the emotions in regaining their legitimate place in the spiritual life of the Jew. In Lithuania, the classical land of talmudic learning, the emotional doctrine of Hasidism never secured a firm foothold.

The form that Hasidism took in certain parts of Lithuania, the so-called *Habad*, is more intellectual than emotional. To attribute the failure of the Hasidic movement in that country to the violent opposition of the Gaon Rabbi Elijah, the greatest intellectual-religious genius among the Lithuanian Jews, is to take a part for the whole. His opposition did but express the attitude, the natural bent, and the acquired traits of the Lithuanian Jew who seeks first of all to satisfy his intellect. Reaction against the too great preponderance of intellectualism could, however, not fail to make its appearance even in Lithuania. About one hundred years after the rise of Hasidism in the Carpathian Mountains among uncultured and ignorant villagers, we find a parallel phenomenon among the sharp-witted Talmudists of Lithuania. Rabbi Israel Baal Shem Tob, the founder of Hasidism, was a person of "emotion and feeling" and rejected intellectualism instinctively without having intimate knowledge thereof. On the other hand, R. Israel Salanter, the father of the moralist movement, was himself one of the greatest Talmudists of his time and, therefore, although his great heart was not able to be satisfied with a one-sidedness of logic and reason, he nevertheless could not fall into the other extreme of regarding religion as a matter of feeling exclusively.

The keystone of Salanter's teaching is best given in his own words: man is created to labor and to carry on the war of the Lord—the development of the divine in man—and accordingly it is his duty to take great pains in the service of God. It is not sufficient to follow one's good impulses and to do only that which according to one's nature is not very difficult. Such a one does not serve God, he might even be described as one who "casts off the yoke of God," since he permits nature to take its course and does not work in the service of the Lord. The essence of this service consists in man's moral-religious effort to do things which his natural inclinations oppose, and to refrain from others to which he is prompted by them. The development of the moral-religious personality is therefore only possible by the education of self or, to use the favorite phrase of Salanter and other Jewish moralists, by Musar, i. e. self-discipline. One might as well, says Salanter, attempt to see without eyes or hear without ears as to expect moral development without self-education; moral intelligence is the result of education and is not acquired at will.

Man does no wrong wilfully, says Socrates, and similar is the saying of the Rabbis: man does not commit sin unless the spirit of folly has entered into him.[13] The aim of education in general as of self-education in particular is therefore, according to Salanter, to give the reason full power over one's actions, for he who does not act as he thinks, thinks incompletely. To think rightly and completely means of course for Salanter and those to whom he addressed himself to square one's actions with one's belief in God and His revealed will, the Torah. How then, he asked himself, does it happen that people of great intellectual power who are past masters in human wisdom and in the knowledge of Torah do not understand and are, from a moral-religious point of view, idiots or weak-minded? What should the self-education of a man be that would give him the necessary intelligence which makes "the truly wise man," who "sees the consequence of his action"? Salanter's answer to these perplexing questions is that only thought transmuted into emotion has effect on our life or, in his own words: our impulses are swiftly running currents which drown our intelligence if the latter is not carried over them in the boat of emotion and enthusiasm. The purely intellectual idea has no motive power, which can be acquired only by the addition of an emotional and passionate element. Though rational life is moral, life as a whole is non-moral because the emotions are not working. It is therefore not enough for us to form correct opinions; we must pass from mere comprehension to profound conviction; and this requires feeling; we must be carried away. We remain cold even in intense intellectual work. "A passion yields only to a passion," and hence in order that our correct ideas may culminate in correct action, in other words that we may not be carried away by impulses but act in accordance with reason, the mental representation of our action must kindle a desire.

We shall now be able to understand the great importance which the dogma of Reward and Punishment plays in the teaching of Salanter. The precise and detailed definition of this dogma, he remarks, is of no great consequence, what matters is that we firmly believe that there exists after this world a condition of happiness or unhappiness for every individual. The bliss of the righteous surpasses any pleasure conceivable to human imagination. On the other hand, the suffering of the wicked is such that compared with it the greatest earthly pain might be described as pleasure. Faith in the existence of God, Salanter maintains, is of small value in true religion as long as it is not supplemented by the belief in a just God who rewards good deeds and punishes evil ones. It is faith in this sense to which the Rabbis refer in their often-quoted saying: [14] The 613 commandments of the Torah were reduced by the prophet Habakkuk to one, viz.: "The righteous liveth by his faith."

We would do great injustice to Salanter if we maintained that self-interest was for him the only motive power of religion and morality. If there be any need to disprove such a faulty conception, it suffices to quote his words in the last essay published by him; he writes, "The road that leads to eternal bliss is to follow the path of the Torah and fulfil all its commandments for the sake of the Lord. The true service of God is that which is free from the motive of receiving rewards; a person who behaves in this way may be truly described as 'serving God,' while he who does what is pleasing to God with the view of receiving reward, may really be described as 'serving himself.' " [15] As a practical moralist, however, Salanter could not dispense with the dogma of Reward and Punishment. He was firmly convinced that there is but one way to correct a vice, namely to recognize the dangers it entails, and there is but one way of acquiring a virtue, and that is, to see clearly the advantages it brings. Hence he taught that the first step in self-education is the acquisition of the fear of the Lord or, as the Rabbis say, "the fear of sin." By frequent pondering and long meditation upon the consequences of our actions for which we shall be held accountable by a just God, the idea of Reward and Punishment becomes vividly impressed upon our mind. Only when the idea is transmuted into feeling does it become a motive power for our actions. These meditations must therefore be of a nature to stir our hearts and act on our emotions. Salanter accordingly attributed great importance to the mode of studying Musar which, to be effective, must be different from merely intellectual studies. In the Musar-Stuebel, by oneself or together with others, preferably at twilight when the falling darkness creates a melancholy atmosphere, one can surrender oneself entirely to one's emotions, one can weep and recite in a loud voice those soul-stirring words of the Prophets, Psalmists and later moralists on the vanity of human life, or give oneself over to reflect in silence upon death, which will bring one before the Heavenly Judge to give an account of one's life.

The sharpening of one's sense of responsibility by the means described is, however, only the first step leading to Musar, self-discipline. When a person is thoroughly permeated with the thought of responsibility in the hereafter for his actions in this world, he has acquired the means necessary for the *Kebishat Yezer ha-Ra,* the suppression of the evil inclination. There are, says Salanter, three stages of the worship of the Holy One, blessed be He. The first is to arouse one's sense of imperfection, the fear that one may not be perfect in the sight of his heavenly Father. By frequent meditation and soulful study of the sayings of our wise men and the dicta of our moralists, this sense is created and then one is in a position to conquer his *Yezer,* which finally leads to "the changing of the Yezer." The Yezer ha-Ra and its opposite, the *Yezer Tob,* are defined by him as follows: The evil Yezer is of a two-fold nature—it is (1) the sensual desire in man that often makes him mistake momentary pleasure for the true happiness which he craves, so that he does not act in accordance with the moral-religious principles which he has established in his mind, but succumbs to the pressure of his impulses of passion. The frequent yielding to his sensual desires finally produces in man (2) an impure spirit or, to use modern parlance, the decay of his spiritual energy, with the result that he becomes a slave to his evil habits, committing at the slightest incentive the most depraved actions. Similarly the good Yezer is of a two-fold nature—it is (1) moral-religious clearsightedness unimpaired by passion and evil habits which commands man to struggle against the temptation of passion and sensual desires and to be guided in his actions not by the immediate pleasures which they produce but by their remote consequences. By continually increasing his fund of moral views and strengthening his power of true reason the (2) spirit of purity or, as we might say, automatism of morality is given to him, so that without struggle and combat he always wills the good and the right.

The suppression of Yezer consists first in the incessant discipline of one's will-power, in order to strengthen and steel it so that it gains perfect control over his passions and no evil temptations have sway over him. Meditation and continuous practice in self-control are the only means of achieving victory. More difficult, and to some extent more important, is introspection and self-analysis. The suppression of the Yezer is not possible without improving "the qualities of our souls" and, as no two men are alike either in temperament or in character, every one must study himself very carefully. Every one, Salanter says, is a world in himself, the knowledge of which is the very first prerequisite for his dealings with the "outer world."

The recognition of one's errors and deficiencies is thus the beginning of salvation, as without it no moral improvement is possible. One must learn to recognize with absolute sincerity the secret springs of his acts. Sincerity is especially important in self-criticism because our judgment of good and evil is not an act of pure reason but is greatly influenced by emotion and sentiment. Accordingly without deep sincerity we should find little to criticize in ourselves; our self-love would blind our judgment. We often, remarked Salanter, meet with people who are extremely conceited and vain, though we fail to detect the slightest reason for their good opinion of themselves. The true reason is that self-love often excites in man so strong a feeling of self-importance that he is unaware of his shortcomings and deficiencies, while those of his neighbor are seen clearly by him. Salanter even goes a step further and maintains that absolute truth can be attained only in the field of material facts directly provable or in the domain of science demonstrable by the methods of logic, while in our moral judgment there is always an element of feeling. In self-criticism our main effort must be directed toward eliminating or at least reducing to a minimum this element of self-love and turning our scrutiny upon ourselves in the same way that we would exercise our criticism upon others.

Our critical abilities should be directed toward our own actions not toward the actions of our fellow men. We all have an amazingly critical keenness when it is a case of picking to pieces, not our own conduct, but that of our neighbor. We should search again and again the depths of ourselves in the midst of our restless life; we must criticize and correct our actions without pity. We must not allow ourselves to rest on the laurels that we award to ourselves or that others too easily bestow upon us, but should utilize the time rather in self-criticism.

As we devote ourselves to the cultivation of our intellectual powers, so we must pay heed to the development of our moral potentialities. Salanter established the rule among his disciples that each should associate himself intimately with one of his fellows for the purpose of observing and being observed and exchanging friendly cautions and admonitions. In this way all would attain to the self-knowledge that corrects conduct.

The discovery of our faults will not discourage us if we look to the future instead of to the past. Repentance was indeed a doctrine upon which he laid great stress, yet for him as for nearly all Jewish theologians and moralists, repentance is not remorse for the past but a serious attempt to profit in the future by the lessons of the past. When he spoke to the people he was in the habit of making them recite with religious fervor the verse from Lamentations, "Turn Thou us unto Thee, O Lord, and we shall be turned." "Return to God" is the Jewish conception of repentance, and while Salanter was hammering into the minds of the people the great need of self-criticism, that they might be able to change their lives and return to God, he was no less indefatigable in preaching courage. No ailment of the soul, he says, is worse than discouragement; man must again and again renew the idea of courage in his mind. He must not become discouraged if he fails to observe any improvement in his moral qualities after long labor of self-discipline. He should know that his work was not in vain but has left its beneficial effects which, though invisible at the moment, will become visible in time. Drops of water continually falling upon a rock will finally wear it away though the first drops seem to produce no effect at all. It is the same with self-discipline; its effects cannot fail to penetrate our hearts if we practise it continually.

Another form of discouragement against which Salanter warns us is that which has its source in the exaggerated importance attached to the influence of heredity; he writes: "One should not say what the Lord made cannot be changed; He planted in me an evil nature, how can I hope ever to unmake it?" It is not so; man is not only master over the qualities of the soul with which he is born but he is also able to change them.

We all know how great the power of man over animals has been; he has succeeded in imposing his will upon them so that not only originally wild and ferocious animals have lost their ferocity but many species have also been tamed and their natures changed. The same applies to man; he not only can suppress his passions and impulses but he can also change his nature from evil to good by constant study and practice. One must remember further that in the worst of men there is something good and the best are not without a touch of depravity. Hence self-education is the main factor in our development.

Salanter in almost every address was in the habit of quoting the verse from Proverbs: "If thou seekest (wisdom) as silver and searchest for her as for hidden treasures. . . ." The burden of all his exhortations was that the moral life of man is like the flight of a bird in the air; he is sustained only by effort and when he ceases to exert himself he falls.

Moral effort or, to use his own term, the suppression of the evil Yezer, important as it may be, is, however, only the prelude to *Tikkun ha-Middot*, the improvement of character, by which he meant the reduction of virtue to a second nature. Moral effort is the negative part of self-education, which must finally lead to the positive, viz. the entire change of our impulses and inclinations, our passions and desires. We draw nearer to the ideal by always thinking of it, by examining everything in its light. The continuous effort, however, is fatiguing, and therefore when swept by great passions, we are unable to withstand them though we thought we had gained control over our will. Accordingly our only safeguard lies in moral knowledge which must be sufficiently clear to lay hold on us and carry us away; this knowledge must become a passion with us so that we act automatically under its imperious injunction. Impressions upon our emotions such as may be produced by the realization of retribution after death, though they may tend to weaken certain passions and impulses, are not able to change them. Their change can be accomplished only by means of knowledge. We must make ourselves the object of contemplation and, dissecting the stirrings of our hearts, seek to comprehend their complicated machinery. Then and then only will virtue become instinctive in us, so that even our unconscious actions will be directed by it. We must not forget that it is our less conscious thoughts and our less conscious actions which mainly mould our lives.

There are two forms, says Salanter, of intellectual knowledge. The child, for instance, who has just learned his alphabet has great difficulty in combining the letters though he knows well their individual sounds. After exercising for some time he is able to read fluently without being in the least conscious of the single letters and their functions. The same holds good in moral knowledge. For a time we must practise increasing the power of our will over our passions until we become so accustomed to virtue that we perform it unconsciously without being aware of any effort. This will happen when our moral ideals become sentiments by reason of being impressed upon our understanding. The truth of this view Salanter attempted to prove in quite a homely way. He writes: "In our country—Lithuania—the average Jew has trained himself in the observance of the dietary laws to such an extent that without any effort he not only abstains from the use of prohibited food but even abhors it. On the other hand, dishonesty in commercial relations is a frequent occurrence. Many do not trouble themselves to find out whether their dealings with their fellow men are always honest, and not a few will even attempt to cover their dishonest actions when they are found out. Now when we ask, how does it happen that the ceremonial law is automatically observed at great sacrifice of comfort and money, while the ethical is often disregarded—a sin which according to the Rabbis neither the Day of Atonement nor death can atone [16]—we can give only this answer: The long training of the Jew, theoretically and practically, in the observance of the dietary laws has had the result that in following his own nature he feels an abhorrence for everything ritually unclean, while the ethical teachings of the Torah theoretically never formed such an important part of the body of Jewish studies as the dietary laws, and practically did not offer themselves as an exercise in virtue but as something convenient and useful. This, however, is greatly to be regretted; the ethical teachings of the Torah are a most important part thereof, and in practical life we must train ourselves so that we may no longer obey the dicta of morality reluctantly as a severe rule, but that we may follow them with the natural bent of our desires."

Great care, however, must be taken that the automatism of virtue is not turned to that obnoxious form of stoicism which makes man indifferent to the desires and needs of his fellow man. Equanimity and calmness of temper and mind, says Salanter, is a great virtue; we must never allow ourselves to be ruffled even when the greatest misfortunes befall us. "Trust in God," the religious term for this virtue, is, however, an abominable sin if applied to shift from us our obligations towards our fellow men; one must not trust in God at the expense of those who seek our help. Humility is not only a virtue but a demand of common sense, as it is absurd to be proud of a superiority that we owe to the chance of birth or the munificence of Providence; and as to vanity, Salanter could only see in it the most grotesque trait of character. Yet he admonishes us to be very careful of the susceptibilities of others and never fail to pay them our respects in the forms established by society. Withdrawing ourselves from social life is very commendable if it affects only ourselves, but it is the foremost duty of man "to go among the people" and associate closely with them for the benefit and the good of our fellow men. Consequently the positive part of self-education consists not only in acquiring virtue as an instinct, but also in studying to comprehend and understand the desires and impulses of men, so that we may be able to feel their sufferings and wants. The task of combining these two opposites is hard but not impossible.

In spite of Salanter's originality, he has not given us a new system of ethics. He lacked philosophic training and systematic ability. His importance consists mainly in this that he emphasized and sought to put into their proper light certain aspects of Judaism which previously had been heeded but little or not at all.

The keynote of his teaching is that the aim and task of the Jew is to strive to secure the ethically ideal condition of man and of the world, no matter how far off and perhaps unreachable it may be. Judaism is for him no theoretical system, teaching speculative truths or scientific knowledge concerning a certain province of thought, but it is a doctrine intended to lead man to his moral ennoblement by prescribed ways and means. So far as the moral life is concerned the concrete plays a preponderating and decisive part. On the other hand it cannot dispense with speculative or, let us rather say, religious truths. In fact, it requires some religious truths as a support and a guarantee for the binding force of the moral law. Other religious truths, again, strengthen the will, or are of spiritual value in moral development, because they fuse together practice and theory into a harmonious unity. If morality is to be not merely a theory but a real factor in the life of man, he must so train his thoughts and feelings that his moral consciousness becomes too strong to allow him to act otherwise than morally. The religious truths which are indispensable to the ethical education of man and without which he cannot develop morally, are: Belief in God, Revelation, and Reward and Punishment.

We have seen above what important rôle the doctrine of Reward and Punishment plays in his teachings, and we may add here that Revelation or, to use the rabbinical term, the Torah is of still greater consequence. In his public addresses, Salanter hardly ever touched on any other subject than ethics and the study of the Torah. The latter is to be considered from two different angles. First, as the revealed will of God, it is the only safe guide for our religious and moral life. Hence the duty incumbent upon every one, not only on the professional scholar, to occupy himself with the study of the Torah that his conduct may always be in accordance with the divine Will. The study of the Jewish civil code however, to take one instance, is a religious work not only because it enables the student to know what is right and what is wrong in a given case, but also because it refines and deepens one's conscience. Consequently, strange as it may sound, it is from the point of view of religion more important for the business man than for the Rabbi—the judge—to be thoroughly acquainted with the civil code. The former is often tempted to dishonesty, and by continuous study of the commercial law of the Torah he will be in a better position to withstand his temptations, of which the Rabbi is innocent. Besides the practical parts of the Torah, the study of any portion thereof is a remedy against the Yezer. "The spirit emanating from the Torah makes spiritual him who occupies himself with it."

It would be underrating the importance of Salanter to measure him only by the standard of his theories on ethics. Of him, as in general of all Jewish moralists, it may be said that the practical produced the theoretical, and not vice versa. The ethical system of the Greeks developed at a time when rapidly growing skepticism threatened to destroy the basis of morality and in part did actually destroy it. The ethical systems framed in those days were the dikes erected by speculative minds to hold in check the devastating flood of immorality. Compare this phenomenon with the long and eventful history of the Jews, and it will become evident that with them there was nothing certain and absolute except God, the source of moral truth. When all things round about tottered and reeled, there always remained one fixed immovable point, that God is good, holy and just, and that it is the duty of man to walk in His ways, the ways of holiness, justice and love. The Jewish moralists, therefore, considered it their chief task not to elaborate new doctrines and speculative truths, but to impress the old lessons with ever greater emphasis upon the consciousness of the people. Their aim was to find means of augmenting the effectiveness of the old truths. And as they always proceeded from the principle that the most successful pedagogic method is teaching by example, they tried to illustrate in their own conduct the truths they wished to inculcate. The Jewish moralists, so far from setting up ideal teachings for the sake of setting them up, demonstrated concretely how the ideal can be made real in the daily walks of life.

iii

It has been well said that a man of rare moral depth, warmth or delicacy may be a more important element in the advance of civilization than the newest and truest idea derived from the fundamental principles of the science of morals. The leading of souls to do what is right and humane is always more urgent than mere instruction of the intelligence as to the exact meaning of right and humanity. If therefore the saint has his place in history, Salanter is one of the outstanding figures in Jewish history of recent times. What most appeals to our imagination and sympathy in history is heroism, and saintliness is only another word for heroism in the domain of ethics and religion. The heroism of the saint is well described by the famous French critic, Sainte-Beuve, as an inner state which above all is one of love and humility, of infinite confidence in God, and of strictness toward one's self accompanied with tenderness for others. Saintliness is however at the same time preëminently subjective, mainly on account of the great diversity of the means which help to produce the state common to all saints. The glimpses we gain of the life of a saint are therefore of incalculable value to us for the understanding of the religious milieu that produced him. Salanter, for instance, was the product of rigorous Talmudism, and hence to become better acquainted with his heroic life is tantamount to coming nearer to a true understanding of talmudic Judaism. Purity, asceticism and charity are the characteristic practical consequences of the inner conditions of all saintly souls; the forms, however, in which these virtues express themselves vary essentially, and the variation is a safe indication of the culture amidst which the saint arose.

Boundless reverence for the weak and the suffering, the helpless and the needy, best describe the particular form that Salanter's love for his fellow man took. The Lord "dwells with him that is of a contrite and humble spirit," hence

Salanter felt himself in the presence of the divine whenever he saw suffering and pain that produce a meek and contrite spirit. His religious enthusiasm, that is his love of God, instead of quenching his love of man, ennobled and transformed it. Too numerous are the stories told about Salanter's kindness and goodness to be given here; a very few characteristics of the saint may, however, be mentioned.

During his sojourn in Kovno it happened on the eve of Yom Kippur, when the Synagogue was filled with devout worshippers awaiting in solemn awe and silence the Kol Nidre service, that suddenly ominous murmurs and whispers arose on all sides. Salanter, wonderful to relate, had not yet arrived. The assembly waited half-an-hour and an hour, and still no trace of the Rabbi. Messengers were sent hither and thither to search for him. All returned from their errand unsuccessful. After long waiting and watching, it was resolved to begin the prayers without Salanter, a course calculated to increase the excitement. All sorts of probable and improbable rumors were circulated about the sudden disappearance of the beloved leader. When the congregation was on the point of dispersing, Salanter appeared in the Synagogue. The joy was great, and equally great was the amazement of the good people when they learned the reason of his absence. On his way to the Synagogue, Salanter told them, he heard a little child cry bitterly. He drew near to investigate why it was whimpering and found that the baby's mother, in order to be at the Synagogue in good time on this holiest of occasions, had put it to bed earlier than her wont. The child had soon awakened from sleep at an unaccustomed hour and was crying for its mother. As none of the women in the neighborhood signified her willingness to forego attendance at divine services upon the Holy Kol Nidre night, he resolved to stay beside the baby's cradle until its mother returned. To appreciate this act of Salanter, it must be remembered what the service at the Synagogue on the eve of the Day of Atonement meant to a man like him who was in the habit of withdrawing from the world for forty days preceding Yom Kippur, and spending his time in prayer and devotion.

His great compassion and pity for the poor and helpless often was the cause of clashes between him and the official heads of the communities where he lived as a private man. He had settled in Kovno shortly after the cholera had wrought great havoc among the Jewish population of that city, especially among the poor classes. The hospitals were overfilled with sufferers, so that quite a number were not properly cared for. Salanter insisted that the great Synagogue of the community be temporarily used as a hospital and poor-house. Needless to say that his plan found ill favor in the eyes of many who looked upon it as an attempt at desecrating the house of God. Possibly they were right, as there was hardly any need of such an extreme step to be taken. Salanter, however, in face of suffering and distress could not see their point of view. Courteous and gentle as he otherwise was, he lost his temper on this occasion. Interrupting the address he was delivering in the Synagogue, he pointed his finger in righteous anger at the president of the Congregation, a man distinguished for learning and piety alike, and cried out: "You will have to answer to the Lord for the suffering of the poor. God much rather prefers His House to be used as a sleeping place by Motel the carpenter—a very disreputable person but a homeless beggar—than as a place of worship by you." Not long after this incident, Salanter betook himself to the home of the man he had offended, to ask his forgiveness, but he never changed his mind with regard to the justification of his plan to turn the Synagogue into a poor-house.[17]

A year before this he had gotten himself into the bad graces of the spiritual leaders of Wilna. In the year of the frightful cholera epidemic Salanter, after having taken counsel with a number of physicians, became convinced that in the interest of the health of the community it would be necessary to dispense with fasting on the Day of Atonement. Many a Rabbi in this large community was inclined to agree with his view, but none of them could gather courage enough to announce the dispensation publicly. During the several years of his stay in Wilna he lived strictly the life of a private man, and in his humility would not decide a question of ritual, not even if it occurred in his own house, but would refer it to one of the local Rabbis. When he saw, however, that none of them would act in this case, he thought self-assertion to be his highest duty. He affixed announcements in all Synagogues, advising the people not to fast on the coming Day of Atonement. Knowing, however, how reluctant they would be to follow his written advice he, on the morning of the Day of Atonement at one of the most solemn moments of the service, ascended the reader's desk. After addressing a few sentences to the Congregation in which he commanded them to follow his example, he produced some cake and wine, pronounced the blessing over them, ate and drank. One can hardly imagine what moral courage and religious enthusiasm this action of his required from a man like Salanter to whom obedience to the Torah was the highest duty. He found strength for his heroic action only in the thought that what he did was for the benefit of others. Many years later he used to dwell on this episode and thank with great joy his Creator for having found him worthy to be the instrument of saving many lives. He was convinced that many a person weakened by fasting would have fallen a victim to the frightful disease, and that therefore in making people eat on the great Fast he saved many lives. Others, however, did not share his conviction of the necessity of dispensing with the fast and he was severely censured by them, not only for what he did, but also for having assumed the authority belonging to the official leaders of the community. It is not unlikely that the unpleasantness created by this incident was one of the reasons for Salanter's leaving Wilna for good.[18]

Poor as he was all his life, he had little of worldly goods or, to be accurate, nothing to give others, but he did give them more than this—he gave himself, heart and soul, to those whom he knew to be suffering. The poor and the needy could always count upon his readiness to assist them. No time of the day, no season of the year, no cold winter night, and no scorching summer day could prevent him from walking for hours from house to house to solicit help for those in need. Once a poor scholar confided to him that if he were able to preach he might succeed in maintaining himself and his family by taking up the profession of an itinerant preacher, but as the theory as well as the practice of preaching were quite unknown to him, he must forever give up the hope of gaining a livelihood in this way. Salanter, however, did not despair; he composed a number of sermons, and after spending several weeks in teaching the poor scholar how to deliver them, he dismissed him well prepared for his new calling.

As in the environment of a saint there are often found many who are the very reverse of saints, Salanter's kindness and sympathy were not rarely misused. Sometimes undeserving people would succeed in obtaining from him letters of recommendation, but he would never revoke them, even if informed by reliable persons of the deception practised on him. He used to say that a letter of this sort becomes the rightful property of the person to whom it is given and it would be plain robbery to revoke it.

The fear of being the cause, even in the remotest manner, of injury to the poor, was always present before his eyes. Once when, in obedience to the rabbinical ordinance, he was washing his hands before sitting down to a meal, his disciples noticed that he was exercising great care not to use a drop of water more than the minimum required by the law. In amazement they exclaimed: "Rabbi, does not the Talmud say that he who lets water flow abundantly over his hands will be rewarded with wealth in equal abundance?" [19] "True, but I do not want to enrich myself at the expense of the labor of the water carrier," replied Salanter. He did not for a moment question the binding character of the rabbinical ordinance concerning the washing of hands before meals, but that did not prevent him from remembering and acting in accordance with his great moral principle.

At another time while walking in the outskirts of the city, he noticed the cow of a Jewish farmer straying away and trying to enter a neighboring garden belonging to a Gentile. Knowing the ill-feeling of the Gentile farmers towards their Jewish neighbors in that part of the country, he had no doubt that if the animal should be caught it would be killed or at best kept for a high ransom. He therefore attempted to lead the cow back to the Jewish farmer, but inexperienced as he was in work of this kind, he miserably failed in driving the animal back. Yet he did not give up the fight, and for several hours he held on to the cow, and in this way prevented her from entering the dangerous zone until he was released from his task by people coming along the road. To have permitted the cow to run its own way, he thought, would have been negligence in his duty towards the poor farmer.

No less cautious was he in avoiding offense to the sensibilities of the poor. He was passionately fond of snuff, but he denied himself the pleasure of taking it at sessions of the Charity Board, when the poor appeared to present their cases. He shrank from taking out his silver snuff box in their presence, lest its splendor cause them to feel their poverty more keenly.[20]

The ascetic impulse is a general phenomenon in saintliness, and the Jewish saint does not form an exception to the general rule. Yet there can be no doubt as to the correctness of the view that Judaism is not an ascetic religion. That the highest development of a non-ascetic religion should culminate in ascetic saintliness will appear to many as an inexplicable riddle. If, however, we examine more carefully the form of Jewish asceticism, we shall find the answer to this puzzling question. A religion that sanctifies even the so-called animal appetites and desires of man, elevating them into worship and religious exaltation, and instead of despairing of the flesh, highly recommends the satisfaction and joy of the body—such a religion could never produce the excesses of asceticism found among other religions to whom the body and the material world are the seat of evil. With very few exceptions, which were of a pathological nature, we hardly ever find among the Jewish saints ascetic mortification or immolation, and even asceticism as sacrifice to God is very rare among them. Jewish asceticism takes almost always the form which a famous psychologist describes as the fruit of the love of purity that is shocked by whatever savors of the sensual.

The life of Salanter offers many instances of this special kind of asceticism. Of fasting and vigils he did not have a high opinion; indeed, he often used to admonish his disciples to eat and sleep as much as they needed. There was little need to preach temperance and sobriety to the Lithuanian Jew, distinguished for extraordinary frugality. Far more stringent was the watch he kept over the things which proceeded from the mouth. He would at times refrain for days and weeks from talking. Idle talk, indulgence in what is ordinarily called conversation, was abhorrent to him, and he employed it only as a means to brighten up people in depressed spirits. The silence he cultivated had its motive neither in the desire for self-mortification nor in that of expiation, but was the direct outcome of his highly developed sense of the purity of life. To his soul whatever was unspiritual was repugnant, and any inconsistency or discord between the ideal and the real was exceedingly painful to him. The average conversation, even of the educated, with its plenitude of insincerity and multitude of pretensions, shocked his spiritual sensibility to such an extent that he preferred silence to speech.

There was also always present with him the fear of being admired by others for qualities of heart and soul above what he merited. This fear was so strong with him that he was once found weeping after delivering a brilliant discussion on a talmudic subject; he was afraid that the display of his brilliancy would make people exaggerate his intellect; and what could there be worse than deception? His scrupulousness as to veracity and sincerity knew no bounds. The first essay published by him contains the note that it was put into literary form by somebody other than the author himself, who is rather a poor stylist. He was once asked, how is one to explain the great success of "the liberals" in their fights with "the true believers," since according to a saying of the Sages, "Truth lasts, untruth perishes." The answer he gave was: "Sincerity makes an untruth seem to be a truth, while insincerity makes a truth seem to be an untruth; the liberals succeed because they are sincere; their opponents fail because they are not always sincere."

Salanter lived all his life in dire poverty, as a matter of choice, as there were many who would have considered it a privilege to provide him with comfort. He never accepted the position of Rabbi and only for a short time did he occupy a public office, that of the head of a talmudic school. He was firmly convinced that he could do his work best by being entirely independent of the public, and after a great inner struggle he decided to accept the offer of one of his disciples to support him entirely. This disciple was the only one from whom he accepted assistance, but only as much as was absolutely necessary to keep body and soul together. When Salanter's wife died he found a small sum of money among her effects which she had saved from the weekly allowance granted to her and her family by their benefactor. The money was distributed by Salanter among the poor. He argued, "The money granted to me by my disciple was for my needs, but not to enrich myself; hence I have no right to it nor have my children, the heirs of my wife, and as the original owner refuses to accept it, the poor have the next claim to it."

Though an indefatigable student all his life and in great need of books, he never possessed a single volume. When he died, his room contained, besides a threadbare suit of clothes, nothing else than his *Tallit* and *Tefillin*. It would be a great mistake, however, to believe that Salanter, like the ascetics of other religions, idealized poverty as the loftiest individual state and sang its praises. One of his disciples, trying to persuade him to accept from a rich admirer a new Tallit, said to him, "You are certainly in need of one and the decorum of the services requires that the Tallit be not threadbare. I too hope to buy one as soon as I have the money." And the master's answer was, "I also will buy one as soon as I shall have the money."

Judaism teaches that wealth is a blessing, as it gives time for ideal ends and affords exercise to ideal energies. Jewish saints, therefore, never denounced the possession of earthly goods, provided man does not turn the blessing into a curse by his greed and passion for money. The saint, however, knew also the high moral value of poverty: liberation from material possessions, freedom of soul, and manly indifference. Salanter's craving for moral consistency and purity was developed to such a degree that he could neither occupy a public office in the community nor accept comfort and luxuries from the hand of others. He for a time thought of becoming an artisan that he might be able to support himself by "the labor of his hands," but when he saw the impossibility of such a plan, he gladly submitted to a life of want and hardship.

"Love your enemies" is not a Jewish precept, and one may doubt whether there are any examples of compliance with it. The nearest approach to it is that magnanimity which "repays evil with good," and the life of Salanter is full of acts of this kind. "Imitation of God," he used to say, "is explicitly commanded in the Torah, and accordingly it is our duty not only to confer an act of kindness upon those who have done harm to us, but to do it at the very moment we are wronged. God is kind to the sinner at the time of his sin and rebellion, since without the kindness of God that gives him life and strength he would not be able to sin, and we are to imitate Him so as to be like Him. We must be kind to those who sin against us, at the time of their wrongdoing." He took scrupulous care all his life to act in accordance with this rule. No sooner did he hear of an injury done to him than he hastened to find out whether he could not confer some kindness upon the person who injured him. The continuous practice of this kind of magnanimity, he taught further, develops tolerance and indulgence towards all men.

In one of his letters to his disciples, Salanter expresses the hope that the spark coming from his soul might kindle a holy fire in their hearts. His hope was not in vain. His was one of those conductive natures which, as was well said by a famous author, are effective because the effluence of their power and feeling stirs the hearer or onlooker to a sympathetic thrill. A Jewish saying, "Words that come from the heart enter into the heart," expresses the same thought. Few people who came in personal contact with him could withstand his charm and his power. His influence over the masses as a preacher was unique in the annals of Eastern Jewry. The inner fire of his spirit shot out its lightning flashes, dazzling the inward eye with the clearness of the truth he revealed to the consciences of his hearers. He brought the people no new doctrines to arrest their thought; he was a flame enkindling the smouldering faith of his hearers; for a while he would lift them up into the clear atmosphere of heaven where their souls stood revealed to themselves and their hearts were aglow with unwonted desire of the higher life. He saw truth so clearly that he was able to make others see it.

Salanter's power was, however, in himself not in his words, and we would do injustice to the man if we judged him by his few literary remains. Yet even they reveal not only an intellect of originality but also a soul of rare purity and great nobility, a worthy link in the long chain of Saints in Israel.

Notes

1. Midrash Tehillim, 92, 412 ed. Buber.

2. Comp. Ahad Ha-Am, על פרשת דרכים I, 178 (3d edition).

3. Most of the material in this essay is based on oral communications which the author had received in his early youth from his teachers R. Isaac Blaser, R. Naphtali of Shat and R. Loeb Raschkes, three distinguished disciples of Salanter. Some episodes given here have been told to the author by his father who was well acquainted with Salanter. I add here a selected list of the more important books, essays and articles on Salanter and the moralist movement in Lithuania. Blaser, אור ישראל Wilna, 1900 (the most important source for the life and teaching of Salanter); Benjamin, *R. Israel Lipkin Salant*, 1899 (in German); Feldberg, קדוש ישראל, 1884; Finn, כנסת ישראל 1886 (pp. 697–698); Eliezer Elijah Friedman, ספר הזכרונות Tel-Abib 1926 and in התור (Jerusalem) VI, nos. 10–12; Mark, גדולים פון אונזער צייט 1927 (pp. 97–104); Obzinski, תולדות ישיבת היהודים בקורלאנד 1908 (pp. 56–63); Rosenfeld, ר' ישראל סלנטר 1910 (in Hebrew and under the same title also in Yiddish); Steinschneider, עיר ווילנא (pp. 128–133); Weinberg, רבנו ישראל וחורתו המוסרית in הלבנון ed. Elbinger, Warsaw, 1912. See also דרשות (אור ישראל 1912 (mainly a reprint of ר' ישראל סלנט).

4. On R. Zundel, comp. E. Rivlin ספר הצדיק ר' יוסף זונדל מסלאנט ורבותיו Jerusalem, 1927.

5. Comp. R. Baer b. Tanhum מעשה רב no. 61; on the influence of the Gaon on R. Zundel, comp. Rivlin, 4.

6. Blaser, 79.

7. On Lilienthal, see David Philipson, *Max Lilienthal*, New York, 1915.

8. Shapiro was a disciple of the famous scholar R. Manasseh ben Porat and like his master had great independence of mind.

9. This witty remark by Shapiro is only a variant of the Midrashic statement, Bemidbar R. 5.2.

10. Comp. Benjamin, 27–29.

11. The name of this Maecenas was Lachman, but he insisted that his name be kept a secret.

12. It was published under the title עץ פרי, Wilna, 1881.

13. Sotah 3a.

14. Makkot 24a.

15. עץ פרי 26a–26b.

16. Mishnah Yoma (end).

17. This episode was told to me by my father who was present at the visit paid by Salanter to my grandfather, R. Asher Ginzberg, the president of the Congregation, whom Salanter had publicly chided.

18. Mark, 76, gives a somewhat different version of this incident, but the one given in this essay is on the authority of the author's uncle, R. Loeb Raschkes, whose reliability cannot be questioned, as he was a pupil of Salanter.

19. This episode was told to the author by his father.

20. This story was told to the author by his teacher, R. Isaac Blaser.

18.

The Lithuanian Yeshivas

by Gedalyahu Alon *

Twice did the Lithuanian Yeshivas suffer exile. The first exile coincided with the outbreak of the First World War, or more precisely, with the German occupation of Lithuania and parts of White Russia in the summer of 1915. It was at that time that the leading Yeshivas were uprooted from their host communities (some of which were also forced to move) and were removed to the eastern borders of White Russia, to the valleys of the Ukraine, and even to the very depths of Greater Russia. This first exile, although detrimental to the [former] host communities and their districts, and to the Yeshivas themselves, benefited those communities in which they found asylum and temporary settlement. The Jewish Ukraine, seasoned as it was with Lubavitch Hasidism, and the seat of Poltava—where the Mir Yeshivah eventually made its way—and Kremenchug—where the Knesseth Yisrael Yeshivah of Slabodka temporarily resided—although blessed with a rich, plentiful, and strong folk-nationalistic existence, experienced in those days but a small measure of the light of Torah. But now that the Ukrainian Jews, on their very own territory, were exposed to a spiritual and intellectual culture which was revealed to them in concentrated form and from its very source, from the tents of Torah, they were immediately attracted to the world of the Yeshivas. From the fusion of two worlds in Israel, a blended and harmonious light shone forth, which in some measure made up for the temporary

* Translated from the Hebrew by Sid Leiman, who notes: "This essay was first published in 1943."
From *Mehkarim be-Toledot Yisrael* (Studies in the History of Israel) vol. I. Israel, Hakibutz Hameuchad Publishing House, Ltd., 1957.

uprooting of the Torah centers from Jewish Lithuania. One may compare it to the first confrontation between the German Jews and the Polish and Lithuanian Jews, when because of the war the German Jews sought refuge among their brethren in Eastern Europe. For Western Jews this was a sort of discovery, leading to a revitalization of their Jewish consciousness. How much the more so was the Jewry of Greater Russia (as for instance in Saratov, where one of the Yeshivas was to reside temporarily and where many Jews were supporters of Czar Nicholas) blessed when it was privileged to become a haven for Torah study.

After several years, the Yeshivas returned to their original communities. Most of them did not regain their original stature, with the exception of the Mir Yeshivah which had also grown and flourished during the fifteen-year period preceding the war. Some suffered a decrease in enrollment and others broke up into smaller units, such as Knesseth Yisrael Yeshivah of Slabodka—half of which emigrated to the land of Israel in 1925. This was due to the removal of Soviet Russian Jewry from Lithuania, the former "heart and head" of Russian Jewry, from the body of Jewish culture and Jewish religion in general.

The second exile was brought about by Hitler. Here, one no longer speaks of exile from one community to another; all communities alike were destroyed. There can be no compensation for the Torah centers that were destroyed, just as there can be no compensation for the communities that were destroyed. The enemy's hand struck down all the Jewish communities in Europe. (Some three hundred students in the Mir Yeshivah, and fugitives from other Yeshivas as well, found refuge in distant Shanghai. Rumor has it that Torah is studied and taught in this city with an intensity rarely experienced in its former residences—a pittance of consolation which hardly sets the mind at ease.) A culture many generations old, with numerous roots and branches, is threatened with destruction. Will it indeed be destroyed?

i

Shortly before the Volozhin Yeshivah—Lithuanian and Russian Jewry's great beacon of light for some ninety years (1793–1892)—closed its doors, the other great Lithuanian

Yeshivas came into their own: Knesseth Yisrael, Knesseth Beth Yitzhak, Mir, Radin, Telshe, Novogrudok, and after them the Lida Yeshivah, which was unique, and distinct from all other Yeshivas. (It was founded by Rabbi Isaac Jacob Reines [1839–1915] [1] in 1894; its uniqueness lay in the secular studies which were taught there in addition to the religious studies.) Sooner or later, in response to the circumstances of the time, the appearance of these Yeshivas came to differ greatly from that of the Volozhin Yeshivah. The new concepts absorbed by the Yeshivas were responsible for the changes in appearance. Despite this, the Volozhin tradition never vanished; its spirit and tradition hovered over the Lithuanian Yeshivas, sometimes overtly, sometimes covertly. Thus, the inheritance remains intact, even with additions greater than the inheritance itself.

It is almost superfluous to add that the Lithuanian Yeshivas served not only their host communities. Indeed, from those towns and villages very few students were drawn. The three or four hundred students in attendance at each of these Yeshivas were drawn from all of Poland, the Ukraine, from Russia and from the far corners of Greater Russia including the Caucasus and Siberia. Moreover, students came from beyond these boundaries, even from across the Atlantic. The students, after spending several years (and some spent many years) in the Yeshivah returned to their towns or settled elsewhere, carrying the very fragrance and spirit of their Yeshivas with them. That widespread attraction found everywhere, attraction to the love of Torah and a yearning for the spirit of ancient Israel—that very attraction which led the students to the Yeshivah in the first place—enabled young scholars returning to their birthplace to wield influence, and lay the groundwork for their Torah-inspired, community-minded efforts.

Those attracted to the Yeshivas were mostly gifted and spirited students. Some were sent by their parents, some came voluntarily out of personal longing, even against the wishes of their parents. Many of the new arrivals were already mature pupils. They had studied at Yeshivas of lesser size and renown, including such distinguished schools as Maltz and Slutzk, which were administered by leading Torah authorities and outstanding personalities. Thus the [Lithuanian] Yeshivas, from the very start, housed a large group of students gifted in intellect or in spirit. It is no wonder, then, that so many distinguished personalities were graduates of these schools. They include scientists, administrators, writers, poets, revolutionaries, and politicians; some remained faithful to Torah and Jewish practice, others abandoned them. Needless to say, many rabbis and Jewish scholars were also among the graduates of the Yeshivas.

But having been gifted to start with is less significant than a second factor [which may account for the success of the students]: the intellectual training they received in the course of their studies. It was the nourishment and vitality which they absorbed while studying in the school; the modest culture, deep and fine, which enriched their spirit and left an imprint, inward and outward, on their personality; it was the seriousness and deliberation, the yearning for good and for perfection; the inner strength and self-sacrifice surrounding them while in the Torah environment; all these factors contributed in good measure to their worldly success. This, despite the fact that some of them did not recognize the hidden light which they themselves possessed.

ii

These students, who poured into the Yeshivah from near and far, what were they seeking? And what was the Yeshivah seeking to give them? Did the students undertake to complete their course work at the Yeshivah in order to become rabbis, like graduates of rabbinical schools in the West? Doubtless, some had this motive, but they were few in number and did not shape the character of the school. This was neither the motive of the Yeshivah, nor was its educational system directed toward this end. Thus, for example, *Yoreh Deah,*[2] the study of which was a prime requisite for the rabbinate, was never taught in the Lithuanian Yeshivas, nor were any of the later halachic authorities studied for the sake of knowing the practical application of the halachah. It is evident, then, that the "rabbinic diploma in the pocket" which Bialik's *matmid* dreamt about during the last years of the Volozhin Yeshivah was not what the student of Slabodka, Radin, etc., dreamed about. If, after having spent many years of study and companionship with his friends and teachers, a Yeshivah student decided to enter the rabbinate, he would leave the Yeshivah and devote himself for several months to those "technical studies" necessary for his profession. Slabodka students used to say: If you see a student devoting himself to the study of *Yoreh Deah,* or to the chapter of the talmudic treatise *Ḥullin*, beginning with the words "These are considered *trefah*," or to *Eben Ha-Ezer*,[3] and if he prepares himself for ordination from the very start, you can be certain that he is neither gifted nor knowledgeable in Torah. Although many graduates later became rabbis, and even though the Yeshivah considered the preparation of qualified rabbis among its goals, the period spent studying in the Yeshivah was not considered the proper time and place for those disciplines dealing directly with practical halachah. If one was steeped in Torah, and sought an appointment, either because he was inclined to the rabbinate or because circumstances left him no choice, then only would he take leave and prepare himself for his vocation. The Yeshivah per se neither served as, nor was it considered, a school for the training of rabbis.

It was also not a school where one mastered all of rabbinic literature. In practice, only six or seven talmudic tractates (from the Orders of *Nashim* and *Nezikin*) were studied in the Lithuanian Yeshivas. The deans of the Yeshivas lectured on those tractates, and the students studied and reviewed them together with the standard commentators who offered novel interpretations of the texts and elucidated them. Few students, and usually the older ones, devoted themselves to the study of the Orders of *Moed*, *Kodashim*, and *Toharoth*. (The Yeshiva of Radin was unique in this respect. The Ḥafetz Ḥayyim [4] encouraged several students to study *Kodashim* because the Messiah might appear at any moment. It was necessary, therefore, to have beforehand scholars proficient in the laws pertaining to the Temple service.) Even in the tractates studied, students were never seriously tested. Once or twice a year the student visited the dean at his home and discussed aspects of the Torah with him, much like two companions debating a legal problem among themselves. This sufficed for a test.

The general intent of the Yeshivah was to open the gates of Torah to the entering scholar and induct him into its world by means of study; to train the student, in other words, to think and make the proper distinctions, to concentrate on Torah in order rightly to extract its truths and essence. No time limit was imposed upon the student either at the beginning or the end. One never completes his studies, and one is never a beginner. As soon as the student enters the Yeshivah he becomes a *ḥaber*, a Fellow, and studies by himself and is responsible for his studies only to himself. No one trains him personally; he trains himself. (Exceptions to the rule were the Yeshivas of Telshe and Lida: they established a graduate system of lectures, each lecture-level being attended for two years.) The only official restriction is that he remain within the confines of the accepted methods of study. Nevertheless, if he breaks new ground, or follows the path of a former teacher, he will not be reprimanded. It is assumed that a *ḥaber* will not falter; and even if he does, he will correct himself. The dean's method of study serves as a model for the student. He lectures once or twice a week and is prepared to lead those who so desire into the inner chambers of his approach to Torah. He will always find time for those who wish it. A second line of defense against the possibility of a student faltering is the communal approach to study, embracing all the *ḥaberim* in the Yeshivah. Thus, from the very beginning, the methods of study and investigation of each Yeshivah student are interwoven with those of his fellow students.

Such was the independence proffered to the Yeshivah student during his entire stay in the Yeshivah. Although it could have led to harm and loss, it appears that its benefits outweighed its defects. The same independence aided and impelled a student to marshal his powers, to strengthen his spirit, and educate himself by means of self-criticism. This accounts for the unique personality developed within the walls of the Yeshivah, above and beyond that developed at other schools. But in order to counteract the evils and dangers threatening the Yeshivah student, which might cause him to err or to misspend his spiritual energies, he was provided with an antidote: fellowship. He was grouped together with other students of the same age and similar capabilities. These groups, sometimes called *vaadim* [committees], were convoked by the Yeshivah students themselves. At their sessions, the students aided each other in their quest for the proper approach to a novel Torah interpretation. This provided them with an opportunity for group study, and at the same time served as a medium for self-expression and critical analysis. Such activities insured that the basic goal of the Yeshivah student would be realized: development of the man of Torah.

iii

What were the methods of study and instruction? In the Lithuanian Yeshivas, one finds a combination of the plain-sense approach to study and the *pilpul* method of study. Nor can these two strands be entirely separated from each other. Of most importance to the Torah student was the attempt on his part, from his very first days of study, to provide a novel halachic interpretation. (An exception to the rule are those few assiduous students who study Torah by covering as much ground as possible rather than by suggesting new interpretations.)

The *pilpul* heard in the Lithuanian Yeshivas was unique; it was superior to the *pilpul* heard elsewhere, and to that which was in vogue in Yeshivas until the nineteenth century. It did not abound with ad hoc pedantries invented on the spur of the moment in order to solve a problem, such as were common in Poland (cf. Maharsha's [5] frequent "it is possible to answer . . . ," and the like). At the other extreme, one does not find here those farfetched and artificial combinations of texts claimed to be related to each other under a single principle, such as one finds in the *pilpulim* usually presented at the conclusion of each tractate. The *pilpulistic* method of study commonly used in the Lithuanian Yeshivas consisted of a classification of halachic terms and an analysis of their fundamental characteristics. This was necessary to distinguish between texts which appeared to be similar but were, in fact, contradictory. It also enabled the student to analyze various details of many scattered and complex halachas, to join them together and establish general rules. The first trend—i.e., the analytic approach—was especially espoused by Hayyim Soloveichik [1853–1919] [6] of the Lithuanian city of Brisk, when he taught at Volozhin. In general, the analytic approach reigned supreme in the Lithuanian Yeshivas, and in some of them was overdone to a point where the ground was pulled out from under one's feet. In contrast, some Yeshivas developed the synthetic and structural approach, stressing thereby the importance of valid systematic thought. Thus the *pilpul* system combines both analytic and synthetic approaches. Indeed, one finds the use of fine distinctions and legitimate parallels in many novel halachic interpretations, which serve to highlight the fundamental truths and the very spirit of the halachah. It was precisely because *pilpul* is a process combining logical analysis with systematic synthesis that the Orders of *Nezikin* and *Nashim* were selected for study in the Yeshivas. They contain juridical elements of the Talmud (such as the laws pertaining to monetary payments and family law); it is well known that graduates of Lithuanian Yeshivas were especially adept in juridical and logical thought. That the Yeshivah students used straightforward thought and logical analysis is further proven by the fact that for the most part they studied the earlier commentators, and only those later commentators noted for their perspicacity, depth, and lucidity in the use of the approaches discussed above, the author [7] of *Qetzoth Ha-Ḥoshen* and *Abney Milluim,* and others such.

Nevertheless, it is still *pilpul.* Most important: the measuring rod of objective truth is lacking. So too, that most precise element of the mind—the desire to recognize the truth. It is clear, then, that even this *pilpul* flutters in the air with few controls of any significance. It lacks the ability to create anything wholesome or lasting. R. Israel of Salant [1810–1883] [8] faced this problem and was greatly perplexed. Truth and *pilpul:* was it possible to harmonize them? If not, which took precedence? He finally concluded not to reject *pilpul* but only on the condition that one had completed "the purification of his spiritual powers" so that his thoughts could not be influenced or perverted. This purification, according to R. Israel of Salant, was the equivalent of the "critical understanding" of the philosophers. It would appear that Salanter's notion did in fact contribute in some measure to the refinement of *pilpul,* and to its lasting and critical value.

iv

We now turn to different types of Musar in the Lithuanian Yeshivas. Our description of the Lithuanian Yeshivas would be inadequate if we failed to describe an element introduced into the Yeshivas during the last fifty years of their existence— the world of Torah-ethics. First it appeared in a few of them, such as Knesseth Yisrael of Slabodka, and later in others as well, such as Mir and Telshe, in the latter only in small measure, due to opposition on the part of most of the Yeshivah students. We call it Torah-ethics—though the two words by themselves do not form a well-turned phrase—because the words do stand for first, the final phase of the Musar movement in Lithuania; and second, the primary goal of those who introduced Musar into the Yeshivas. For the sake of Musar, they fought a difficult battle until they succeeded in achieving their goals. It is well known that the Musar movement in Lithuania owed its beginnings to the personality and efforts of R. Israel Salanter. This great man and unique character urged each Jew during the forties of the nineteenth century to probe deeply into his own thought and to strengthen his spirit, in order to refine his religious and ethical behavior. R. Israel of Salant realized that successive generations were growing less sensitive to religious feeling, that Jews were losing their spiritual wholesomeness. He therefore announced that it was incumbent upon all to study Musar and to educate themselves by practicing it, to bring out their religious-ethical sense, strengthen their spirit, and refine their manners and everyday behavior. The Musar of R. Israel Salanter encompassed two areas: religious (between man and God) and ethical (between man and man). He established centers for Musar in several Lithuanian communities. He gathered about him ardent pupils and taught them orally and in writing how to study, teach, and practice the Musar doctrine of striving for perfection. There is support for the theory that at least one reason for the founding of this movement was the spread of the Haskalah influence, which in those days was supported and administered by the government and its representative, Dr. Lilienthal [1815–1882].[9] R. Israel Salanter undertook to fight against the dangers of assimilation and the abandonment of the yoke of Torah and religion, all of which he saw in Haskalah. To counteract such dangers, he proposed the elixir of life: Musar. We may safely assume, however, that also the very factors which enabled the Haskalah to spread— the impoverished life and thought, the empty surroundings and the void that made up a Jew's world—caused R. Israel to realize that a renewal of the spirit, a deepening of the spiritual world of the religious Jew, was necessary. (R. Israel was in part sympathetic to enlightenment and science. He was himself about to be appointed dean of the rabbinical seminary established by the government in Vilna. But he refused the appointment and left the country for Germany, where he urged that Talmud be taught in the universities as part of and together with the other humanities.)

R. Israel Salanter's bold and persistent efforts to disseminate Musar were effective mostly among lay Jews. In his time, no one protested against the Musar movement. After his death, one of his pupils of long standing, R. Isaac Blazer— i.e., R. Itzele Peterburger [1836–1907] [10]—introduced the study of Musar into the Kollel Perushim Academy of Kovno, which had just been founded, and by so doing, showed that Musar was on a par with Talmud as a legitimate Torah discipline, which all serious students must study in depth. This act initiated a bitter dispute among the rabbis, many of whom openly denounced and condemned the Musar enthusiasts who came "to crowd the feet of the Torah": *Do you intend to assault the Queen in my presence* etc. (Esther 7:8). That stiff dispute ended with the victory of the Musar enthusiasts. But the stiffening [of the Musar enthusiasts in the face of opposition] brought about several strange phenomena which the Maskilim too, and other writers, used as an excuse to dismiss the Musar movement *in toto*. They did not distinguish between specific and general, between the essential and the unessential, between the stalk and fruit; nor did they realize that when Musar would finally enter the Yeshivas, it would be in the diluted form which finally characterized it.

The introduction of Musar into the Yeshivah underscored a bitterly contested principle: the inclusion of Musar study in the Torah curriculum. Three aspects are to be considered: A) Just as Torah represents wisdom, deep and great and without end, so too ethical reflection on refining the soul and on good deeds toward God and man represents wisdom without end.

B) Just as Torah study is regulated and public, so too Musar study. It was not intended only for private study, and at that for only a brief moment. Together, all members of the Torah community must study it, publicly and in private.

C) Just as the Torah consists of fixed halachas incumbent upon all, whose minutiæ must be carefully examined and the least important treated like the most important, so too the rules of Musar are not mere resolutions, but obligatory and fixed regulations with no differentiation between the lesser and the greater.

Let us examine, then, a sampling of the Musar form as it appeared in the Yeshivas, and some of its fundamental principles. But before doing so, we ought to make the following distinctions:

A. With regard to its nature, there are three primary forms of Musar: 1) *the Novogrudikian Musar* may be termed the Musar of abstinence, the abstinence preached by the Cynic (of antiquity). It connotes a total aloofness from the world and society, and the suspension of all rules of etiquette and manners customary among men. One factor determining the nature of this type of Musar is antisociality, or if you prefer, anticultural sentiment. It is, on the other hand, also possible to call this Musar ecstatic Musar, characterized by enthusiasm and strength; this enthusiasm and this strength enabled these remarkable Musar enthusiasts to enter Soviet Russian towns during the frightening period of Communist-military rule, at the risk of their lives. They saved thousands of Jewish children and youngsters from assimilating, instilling into their hearts a fiery spirit and a yearning to offer their lives for the sanctification of Judaism and the sanctification of His name. 2) *The rigoristic-popular Musar of fear.* This form, inherited from earlier generations and containing both rigoristic and popular elements, is found with an element of fear, in small or large measure, in all branches of the Musar movement. It appeared in a concentrated state in the Radin Yeshivah, especially with its rigoristic-popular element. The leading spokesman for this form was the author of the *Hafetz Ḥayyim,* a saint who was the model of piety and fear of God representative of folk-Judaism. 3) The third form, *Slabodkan Musar,* spread to the Mir and other Yeshivas. Here, briefly, we shall speak only of this form, for it was central and regnant in the Lithuanian Yeshivas.

B. Although Musar encompasses two distinct areas, religion and ethics, when the two are combined the ethical element is the primary force and influences the realm of religion. The penetration of ethical Musar into the relationship between man and God was a theme of the living Torah of the founder of the Musar movement, R. Israel of Salant. Many tales related about him testify to this, such as the two that follow. It happened once that R. Israel left his home shortly before Yom Kippur eve in order to attend the *Kol Nidre* service at the synagogue. On the way, he heard the cries of a child coming from one of the shuttered homes. R. Israel entered and saw a baby in its crib, and its little sister sleeping in a nearby bed. The scholar sat down beside the crib and began singing a lullaby to soothe the baby. He sat and played with the baby for a long time, until the prayers were completed and he saw the crowd leaving the synagogue. On another occasion, it happened that R. Israel was invited to a meal at a Jewish home. On his way in, he noticed an exhausted maid carrying in the pails of water necessary for the household. After he entered, the guests rose for the ritual handwashing before the meal.

They washed their hands up to their wrists, as is expected of pious Jews. R. Israel washed only his fingers [i.e., the bare minimum required by the law]. They were astounded by this righteous man who, it seemed, treated lightly the washing of the hands. They asked: Rabbi, why did you not observe this commandment in its most proper manner? He replied: I shall not observe a commandment in its most proper manner at the expense of the physical labor of others.

C. Although deep study and meditation are integral elements of Musar, and on occasion lead to reflection on weighty problems of the religious philosophy of the Middle Ages, and at other times even touch upon the secrets of the Kabbalah, the primary concern of Musar is a reflection on immediate living, on practice, and on behavior. Thus, one should not expect a fully worked out system of thought, a harmonious philosophical system with well defined principles. Indeed, there are no dogmas in the Musar system. The primary purpose of Musar was to enable man to make use of his thought processes, to gain insight into his own mind so that he could improve himself and remember the concepts necessary for a man to sustain his spiritual and everyday well-being. (Once again we note that independence which characterized the Lithuanian method of Torah instruction.) It is therefore extremely difficult to isolate the fundamentals of Musar and present them as fixed rules. One who undertakes to present such rules will fall victim to his own subjective views. At best, whatever we say regarding this topic is said with reservations and in the briefest outline form.

v

The fundamental principle of Musar and the basic rule which it injected into the religious thought of Torah is: know thyself (γνῶθι σαυτόν). If you set off for distant worlds, however great they may be, or if you set off to explore the external and transitory expanses of your life's domain, you neglect your own powerful and true world. Your soul is the source of the abundance and the eternity of your life, i.e., the life of man, and is its seat of holiness. Were we to seek support from a farfetched parallel, we might point to the famous example of Socrates: here we see what revolutionary potential (on a small scale) resides in this motto. All the rays of light which once would emanate, then separate and disappear amid the many roads of Torah meditation, of religion, and of Jewish practice, now found their great and single point of convergence, the point of depth. (This fundamental concept may very likely have been introduced, perhaps without realizing it, to counteract the Haskalah, which concerned itself with cultural and external spiritual matters.) Moreover, Torah and man are one. By recognizing his world, by recognizing the powers of his soul, together with the means of intensifying them and revealing them, man recognizes the Torah. For the Torah is part of the natural rules of life and manifests the powers of the soul of mankind.

The study of man, however, is a great and complex science. Like the Torah itself, it has no end. It begins by exposing the fundamental elements that rest in the depths of the mind. This is followed by an analysis of the different ingredients of the soul, to learn what they are, where they originate, and their characteristics. This is done in order to evaluate each ingredient and establish its goals (the good and the evil, the revealed and the hidden, all having been mixed together). Thirdly, the secret must be explored of the struggle and intermingling of the great elements of the soul: the thoughts, inclinations, desires, and overt longings. In contrast to these are the hidden desires not readily recognized, whose power succeeds in secret ways. And more: the subservience of thought to continuous perseverance—a quality in itself commendable—as well as the chaining of thought to the mechanisms which govern its world; in short, a reflection on the world of man's soul in order to attain freedom of thought. Another aspect, one more rich and extremely difficult discipline, is the ability to discern, the implantation of that ability in the mind. For thought in itself is not complete without excitement, without being stirred up by emotion. (As for these two aspects, it is not enough to recognize the general human predicament. A man must probe to understand the uniqueness of his personal world. He does this by continually reflecting on his internal and external impressions, whether significant or insignificant.) From this emerges the ultimate probe: How are we to awaken the mind, to absorb and revive the process of thought-perception? Finally, what is the perfect deed which might complement and fulfill desires expressed by the soul?—the soul's desires representing the autonomous, absolute value of the deed.

Musar is founded upon the cognizance of man's worth. There are two aspects to this cognizance. The first is subjective. Man views his personal world, and experiences its positive content. *You have made him but little lower than the angels* (Psalms 8:6). This thought serves as a protective shield against degeneration, backsliding, submission to evil inclination. "I am ashamed and blush" because of sin and stain; they desecrate man's greatness and holiness. Such notions stir up powerful longings for perfection and purity. Just so, the subjective aspect also serves the area "between man and God." The second aspect is objective. Man's greatness and dignity require that he and his world not be harmed. They further require that men love each other and long to attach themselves to each other. He of whom it was said that "the angels wished to sing praise before him" is worthy of being loved as one would, so to speak, love God. Moreover, a good deed, however small, on behalf of mankind, is equal to all the commandments of the Torah. Nor is there any distinction between one man or another, whether he be important or unimportant, righteous or wicked. Men never lose their essence, their hidden character. They bear sins or elements of decay only when their manly character is hidden, never because it is defective. This concept includes the notion of trust in man. Since man can never destroy any part of his world, it is evident that sin and slackening are nothing more than the products of the weakened sinner's imagination. Furthermore, an eternal light always flickers in men's hearts and deeds, even when they are rooted in sin and in a state of decline. The trouble lies in the fact that men are sometimes blind, especially when it comes to themselves. Thence is derived the optimism and joy which characterize the world of Musar thought; and this despite the fact that a distant onlooker sees only its sadder, serious aspects.

The approach was responsible for creation of what may conditionally be termed the humanism of Musar, and contributed to the Torah student's "cultural" attachment to society (there never was any actual attachment). Etiquette, manners, and proper behavior are important ingredients of Musar. This may account for characteristic virtues of the students of Slabodka, Mir, and similar Yeshivas: the calm patience, a refusal to engage in improprieties against opponents (while at the same time inwardly strengthening one's resolve), rejection of the rabbinical frock as an outer garment, being amenable to obey orders when necessary, and the ability to understand others.

A man's life is like a ladder with an infinite number of rungs. The gradations and plateaus which R. Moshe Ḥayyim Luzzatto [1707–1747] [11] described in his *Mesillath Yesharim* (whose approach is based on the teaching of R. Pinḥas B. Yair, quoted at the end of tractate Sotah) are but a schematic diagram, used merely as an example. In truth, the gradations can be multiplied and increased without end. We thus confront a chain bound upward, seemingly without end. Even these few rules, and the very ways of perfection, are without end. Man may discover, indeed is obligated to discover, his own courses, so long as they lead upward. The upward movement has no end. Absolute and continuous progress—this is the way of Musar. He who does not move upward, must against his will move downward. There is no standing still in this world. Even the state of being frozen, of contraction, does not exist. Nothing is merely "permitted" in this world. Either it is a duty or it is forbidden. "There is no place where He is not"—the entire expanse of life, whether in thought or deed, folds together to serve as a stage for the whole man (for every man at every moment; perfection is not a matter of the future. Always strive for the maximum).

The way of perfection develops until it culminates in thought. Thought is the first of all beginnings and the highest of all heights. The concepts men think about come from their own resources, not from divine illumination. They are neither privilege nor generous gift. "Prepare yourself in the vestibule so that you may enter the banquet hall" (Aboth IV:16) does not mean that if you become increasingly righteous, you merit reward. It means that "the future world is really this spiritual one, this very world which man has created for himself."

But the improvement of thought occurs only in the mind, and thought itself is dependent upon the mind. Thus, the source of perfect thought is "awakening." This comes about in many ways. Concentration, excitement, emotional turbulence—these are one way. In contrast to these, are the ways of attention, of absorption of the whispers of the world, and silent meditation. (This explains why one could encounter in the Yeshivah heroes, warriors, and subduers of the evil inclination; in contrast to them, one could see dreamers— usually of few words and much splendor—and thinkers who probed the depths of the world's secrets; and one could further-more see humble students, unblemished, and practicing many good deeds of friendship and love of man. All these students were united under one banner of thought and life.)

Here was a refuge from the acute tension of thought and mind. Sometimes conceptions can successfully be conjured up from the depths of silence, even from the revelations of peaceful beauty, from even the purest pleasure.

As for the commandments, one rule applies to all com-mandments and to all good deeds: "Any defect or sparing of oneself is a destruction of worlds"; "Man's every deed is eternity." Our rabbis said: There are three commandments for which a man must allow himself to be killed rather than transgress them. But the halachah states that in every aspect of our service to God and man, we must be prepared to lay down our lives. The meaning of the rabbinic injunction that a man "should bear his friend's burden along with him" is: total identification wth him. If a man did not wholly identify with his friend, he was considered among the shedders of blood. The halachah, therefore, is to be, as it were, according to Ben Petora [see Baba Metzia 62a], who ruled: Two men were traveling in a wilderness and only one had a flask of water. If both would drink, both would die; if one would drink, he could reach inhabited land. It is better that both drink and die rather than that one drink and watch his friend die. The halachah is not according to R. Akiba, who ruled that "your life takes precedence over your friend's life."

Once again, acute tension. But it is counteracted by every shadow of a good thought in the mind and by even the slightest manifestation of kindness, the central point of the creation of the world, the source of man's nourishment. Such action is meritorious and a definite commandment. The rabbis therefore listed [see Ḥullin 92b] among the three command-ments which Noaḥites observe, that, though they eat it, they do not sell carrion in the meat market, nor do they write a marriage contract for males.[12] The slightest improvement, even in the midst of the worst degeneration, creates worlds.

Of the ideas, the perplexities, and the solutions of Musar it is said that "its owners did not lay claim to them as free-for-all property, nor did they inherit them from their fathers." Every man, small or great, "from his heart he hewed them, from his rock he hollowed them out." All its notions are accompanied by strength and intense striving, and songs of might and victory, interwoven with dirges of failure. From these derive the depth and strength of the profound impression remaining in the hearts even of those Yeshivah students who left their Yeshivas, the house which gave them life. But the great tension, the powerful desires, and the need for plentiful nourishment narrow down the boundaries, and sometimes lead to a total breakdown. Some powers restrained, in their escape, will add to the life and creativity in an expanded world. Other powers recoil, are repressed and perish on the roads of desolation. But be that as it may, whether one merits paradise or whether one is struck down by the sling, that first impression formed in the Yeshivah protects forever, and permanently resides in the mind.

Notes

1. Rabbi, talmudist, and educator, he was founder of the Mizraḥi branch of the Zionist movement. Tr.

2. The second major division of Jacob Asheri's *Turim* and Joseph Karo's *Shulḥan Aruk,* the standard codes of Jewish law. Tr.

3. The third major division of Jacob Asheri's *Turim* and Joseph Karo's *Shulḥan Aruk.* Tr.

4. R. Israel Meir Ha-Kohen (1838–1933), dean of the Radin Yeshivah, and prolific author, was popularly referred to by the title of his legal-moralistic work, *Ḥafetz Ḥayyim* (cf. Psalms 34:13ff.). Tr.

5. R. Samuel Edels (1555–1631), Polish rabbi, and author of *Ḥiddushey Maharsha,* novellae on the Talmud. Tr.

6. Rabbi of Brisk and author of novellae on Maimonides' *Code,* his analytic approach to talmudic study has been adopted by most Yeshivas. Tr.

7. R. Aryeh Loeb Ha-Kohen of Styria (d. 1813). The two works, commentaries on Karo's *Shulḥan Aruk,* were especially popular in Lithuanian Yeshivas. Tr.

8. See Louis Ginzberg's essay on R. Israel Salanter in this volume. Ed.

9. German rabbi and educator, he spent five unsuccessful years in Russia, where he attempted to introduce educational reforms into Jewish schools. He emigrated to the United States, where he was active in the Reform movement. Tr.

10. Rabbi of St. Petersburg and author of numerous responsa, he was a founder of the Slabodka Yeshivah. Tr.

11. Italian kabbalist, pietist, and poet. Luzzatto's *Mesillath Yesharim* is an ethical treatise popular among Musar enthusiasts. Tr.

12. The rabbis here allude to homosexual marriage. See Suetonius, *Lives of the Caesars,* Book VI (Nero), Chapters 28 and 29. Tr.

19.

Before the Kaddish:
At the Funeral of Those Who Were Killed in the Land of Israel

by S. Y. Agnon *

When a king of flesh and blood goes forth to war against his enemies, he leads out his soldiers to slay and to be slain. It is hard to say, does he love his soldiers, doesn't he love his soldiers, do they matter to him, don't they matter to him. But even if they do matter to him, they are as good as dead, for the Angel of Death is close upon the heels of everyone who goes off to war, and accompanies him only to slay him. When the soldier is hit, by arrow or sword or saber or any of the other kinds of destructive weapons, and slain, they put another man in his place, and the king hardly knows that someone is missing—for the population of the nations of the world is big and their troops are many. If one man is slain, the king has many others to make up for him.

But our king, the King of kings of kings, the Holy One, blessed be He, is a king who delights in life, who loves peace and pursues peace, and loves His people Israel, and He chose us from among all the nations: not because we are a numerous folk did He set His love upon us, for we are the fewest of all people. But because of the love He loves us with and we are so few, each and every one of us matters as much before Him as a whole legion, for He hasn't many to put in our place. When from Israel one is missing, God forbid, a minishing takes place in the King's legions, and in His kingdom, blessed

* Translated from the Hebrew by J.G.

"Petihah le-kaddish," from *The Works of S. Y. Agnon*, vol. X, 5th edition, Tel-Aviv, Israel, Schocken Books, 1959.

be He, there is a decline of strength, as it were, for His kingdom now lacks one of its legions and His grandeur, blessed be He, has been diminished, God forbid.

That is why for each dead person in Israel we recite the prayer "Magnified and sanctified be His great Name." Magnified be the power of the Name so that before Him, blessed be He, there be no decline of strength; and sanctified be He in all the worlds which He created according to His will, and not for ourselves let us have fear but for the superlative splendor of His exalted holiness. May He establish His sovereignty so that His kingdom be perfectly revealed and visible, and may it suffer no diminishing, God forbid. In our lifetime and in your days and in the lifetime of the whole house of Israel speedily and soon—for if His sovereignty is manifest in the world, there is peace in the world and blessing in the world and song in the world and a multitude of praises in the world and great consolation in the world, and the holy ones, Israel, are beloved in the world and His grandeur continues to grow and increase and never diminishes.

If this is what we recite in prayer over any who die, how much the more over our beloved and sweet brothers and sisters, the dear children of Zion, those killed in the Land of Israel, whose blood was shed for the glory of His blessed Name and for His people and His land and His heritage. And what is more, everyone who dwells in the Land of Israel belongs to the legion of the King of kings of kings, the Holy One, blessed be He, whom the King appointed watchman of His palace. When one of His legion is slain, He has no others as it were to put in his place.

Therefore, brethren of the whole house of Israel, all you who mourn in this mourning, let us fix our hearts on our Father in heaven, Israel's king and redeemer, and let us pray for ourselves and for Him too, as it were: Magnified and sanctified be His Great Name in the world which He created as He willed. May He establish His kingdom, may He make His deliverance to sprout forth, may He bring nigh His messiah, and so to the end of the whole prayer. May we be found worthy still to be in life when with our own eyes we may behold Him who makes peace in His high places, in His compassion making peace for us and for all Israel, Amen.